Life

TEACHER'S BOOK | PRE-INTERMEDIATE

Concorde International

NATIONAL GEOGRAPHIC
LEARNING

MIKE SAYER

Australia • Brazil • Mexico • Singapore • United Kingdom • United States

NATIONAL GEOGRAPHIC LEARNING

National Geographic Learning,
a Cengage Company

Life Pre-intermediate Teacher's Book
2nd Edition
Mike Sayer
Gabrielle Lambrick
Fiona Mauchline

Vice President, Editorial Director: John McHugh
Executive Editor: Sian Mavor
Publishing Consultant: Karen Spiller
Project Managers: Sarah Ratcliff and Laura Brant
Development Editor: Shona Rodger
Editorial Manager: Claire Merchant
Head of Strategic Marketing ELT: Charlotte Ellis
Senior Content Project Manager: Nick Ventullo
Manufacturing Manager: Eyvett Davis
Senior IP Analyst: Ashley Maynard
Senior IP Project Manager: Michelle McKenna
Cover: Lisa Trager
Text Design: Vasiliki Christoforidou
Compositor: Lumina Datamatics Ltd.
Audio: Tom Dick and Debbie Productions Ltd
DVD: Tom Dick and Debbie Productions Ltd

© 2019 Cengage Learning, Inc.

ALL RIGHTS RESERVED. No part of this work covered by the copyright herein may be reproduced or distributed in any form or by any means, except as permitted by U.S. copyright law, without the prior written permission of the copyright owner.

"National Geographic", "National Geographic Society" and the Yellow Border Design are registered trademarks of the National Geographic Society
® Marcas Registradas

For permission to use material from this text or product,
submit all requests online at **cengage.com/permissions**
Further permissions questions can be emailed to
permissionrequest@cengage.com

ISBN: 978-1-337-28588-9

National Geographic Learning
Cheriton House, North Way
Andover, Hampshire, SP10 5BE
United Kingdom

Locate your local office at international.cengage.com/region

Visit National Geographic Learning online at NGL.Cengage.com/ELT
Visit our corporate website at www.cengage.com

CREDITS

Text: Test 1 (page 210) Source: "A Typical Day in the Life of Mark Zuckerberg", by Aine Cain, Independent, June 19, 2017. Test 5 (page 223) Source: "Fresno: A City Serious About Recycling", by Dan Stone, National Geographic Magazine, December 03, 2012. Test 6 (page 226) Source: "Four Ways Long-Term Travel Could Change Your Life", by Candace Rardon, National Geographic, April 05, 2016.

Cover: © Awakening/Getty Images.

Illustrations: Lumina Datamatics Ltd.

DVD Videos: Unit 2 National Geographic; Unit 3 National Geographic; Unit 4 © Temujin Doran; Unit 5 National Geographic; Unit 6 National Geographic; Unit 8 National Geographic; Unit 9 National Geographic; Unit 10 National Geographic; Unit 11 © NASA; Unit 12 National Geographic.

DVD Photos: Unit 11 © NASA/JPL-Caltech; © Science & Society Picture Library/Getty Images; © NASA/JPL; © NASA/JPL; © NASA/JPL-Caltech; © NASA/JPL; © Sebastian Kaulitzki/Getty Images; © Henrik5000/Getty Images; © Monkey Business Images/Shutterstock.com; © Radiokafka/Shutterstock.com; © Dean Pennala/Shutterstock.com; © Robert Glusic/Getty Images; © Phil MacD Photography/Shutterstock.com; © Beboy_ltd/iStockphoto; © Dr Morley Read/Shutterstock.com; © CLIPAREA l Custom media/Shutterstock.com; © Mastering_Microstock/Shutterstock.com; © Ferenc Szelepcsenyi/Shutterstock.com; © Ekaterina Starshaya/Shutterstock.com; © Ferenc Szelepcsenyi/Shutterstock.com; © xavierarnau/Getty Images; © Marco Andras/Age Fotostock.

Printed in Greece by Bakis SA
Print Number: 03   Print Year: 2018

Contents

Student's Book contents pages	4
Introduction	8
Units 1 to 12: notes and answer key	21
Photocopiable tests	209
Photocopiable tests: answer key	247
Photocopiable tests: audioscripts	251
Photocopiable communicative activities	256
Photocopiable communicative activities: teacher's notes	293
Grammar summary: answer key	308
Workbook: answer key	312
IELTS practice test: answer key and audioscript	328

Contents

Unit	Grammar	Vocabulary	Real life (functions)	Pronunciation
1 Lifestyle pages 9–20	present simple adverbs and expressions of frequency present simple and present continuous	everyday routines wordbuilding: collocations with *do*, *play* and *go* word focus: *feel* medical problems	talking about illness	/s/, /z/ or /ɪz/ one or two syllables?
VIDEO: My local park page 18 ▶ REVIEW page 20					
2 Competitions pages 21–32	verbs for rules *-ing* form	sport wordbuilding: suffixes word focus: *like*	talking about interests	/ŋ/ silent letters
VIDEO: Mongolian horse racing page 30 ▶ REVIEW page 32					
3 Transport pages 33–44	comparatives and superlatives *as … as* comparative modifiers	ways of travelling transport nouns wordbuilding: compound nouns transport adjectives transport verbs taking transport	going on a journey	*than* sentence stress intonation
VIDEO: Indian Railways page 42 ▶ REVIEW page 44					
4 Challenges pages 45–56	past simple past continuous and past simple	risks and challenges personal qualities wordbuilding: verbs and nouns	telling a story	/d/, /t/ or /ɪd/ *was/were* intonation for responding
VIDEO: A microadventure page 54 ▶ REVIEW page 56					
5 The environment pages 57–68	quantifiers articles: *a/an*, *the* or no article	materials recycling results and figures word focus: *take*	phoning about an order	/ðə/ or /ðiː/ sounding friendly
VIDEO: Recycling Cairo page 66 ▶ REVIEW page 68					
6 Stages in life pages 69–80	*to* + infinitive future forms: *going to*, *will* and present continuous	life events describing age celebrations word focus: *get* wordbuilding: synonyms	inviting, accepting and declining	/tə/ contracted forms emphasizing words
VIDEO: Steel drums page 78 ▶ REVIEW page 80					

Listening	Reading	Critical thinking	Speaking	Writing
someone talking about a national park near a city a radio interview about long life	a quiz about how well you sleep an article about centenarians an article about how nature is good for you	giving examples	finding out about lifestyle your current life making a town healthier	text type: filling in a form writing skill: information on forms
someone describing an Ironman competition three people talking about competitive sports	an article about crazy competitions an article about female wrestlers in Bolivia	reading between the lines	explaining the rules of a competition talking about your sport preferences your opinions about Olympic sports	text type: an advert or notice writing skill: checking your writing
someone describing a photo of a woman travelling by train in India two people discussing the pros and cons of types of transport a documentary about animal transport	an article about solutions to transport problems an article about the fate of the rickshaw in Kolkata	opinions for and against	talking about and comparing journeys advice on transport a presentation about a pedicab company	text type: notes and messages writing skill: writing in note form
a caver talking about his hobby an impossible decision	an article about adventurers an article about different types of challenges	looking for evidence	asking about your past events you remember telling a story	text type: a short story writing skill: structure your writing
extract from a documentary about a house of recycled materials news about environmental projects	an article about e-rubbish an article about a boat made of plastic bottles, the *Plastiki* an online order	close reading	recycling where you are general knowledge quiz changing attitudes and behaviour	a quiz text type: emails writing skill: formal words
differences between the generations a news item about Mardi Gras	an article about how a couple changed their life an article about how Mardi Gras is celebrated around the world an article about coming-of-age ceremonies	analysing the writer's view	plan the trip of a lifetime your favourite festival planning a celebration describing annual events	text type: a description writing skill: descriptive adjectives

Contents 5

Contents

Unit	Grammar	Vocabulary	Real life (functions)	Pronunciation
7 Work pages 81–92	present perfect and past simple present perfect with *for* and *since* prepositions of place and movement	language to describe jobs jobs wordbuilding: suffixes parts of a building word focus: *make* or *do* job adverts	a job interview	intrusive /w/
VIDEO: My working life page 90 ▶ REVIEW page 92					
8 Technology pages 93–104	zero and first conditional defining relative clauses	internet verbs wordbuilding: dependent prepositions instructions	finding out how something works	linking
VIDEO: Ancient languages, modern technology page 102 ▶ REVIEW page 104					
9 Holidays pages 105–116	past perfect simple subject questions	holiday collocations wordbuilding: *-ed* / *-ing* adjectives word focus: *place*	requesting and suggesting	*'d* number of syllables /dʒə/
VIDEO: Living in Venice page 114 ▶ REVIEW page 116					
10 Products pages 117–128	the passive (present and past simple) *used to*	wordbuilding: word forms describing design websites	giving your opinion	stress in different word forms /s/ or /z/
Video: Wind turbines page 126 ▶ REVIEW page 128					
11 History pages 129–140	reported speech reporting verbs (*say* and *tell*)	wordbuilding: verb + preposition communication ancient history word focus: *one*	giving a short presentation	pausing
VIDEO: The Golden Record page 138 ▶ REVIEW page 140					
12 Nature pages 141–152	second conditional *anywhere*, *everyone*, *nobody*, *something*, etc.	extreme weather nature word focus: *start*	finding a solution	*would* / *wouldn't* / *'d*
VIDEO: Cambodia animal rescue page 150 ▶ REVIEW page 152					

COMMUNICATION ACTIVITIES page 153 ▶ GRAMMAR SUMMARY page 156 ▶ AUDIOSCRIPTS page 181

Contents

Listening	Reading	Critical thinking	Speaking	Writing
a description of a job in a steel factory an interview with a scientist two people giving instructions	an article about new jobs in an area an article about modern-day cowboys	analysing comparisons in a text	describing past experiences giving directions job satisfaction a job interview	text type: a CV writing skill: missing out words in CVs
a documentary about the importance of technology a science programme about a new invention	an explorer's blog an article about biomimetics	the writer's sources	planning a trip important inventions design an invention for everyday life favourite technology	text type: a paragraph writing skills: connecting words
three people talk about their holidays an interview with a tour guide	a holiday story an article about the two sides of Paris	the author's purpose	a story about a holiday planning the holiday of a lifetime a place you know	text type: an email requesting information writing skill: formal expressions
a description of a producer and his products a programme about a product from the past	an article about some famous logos an article about having less 'stuff'	fact or opinion?	some famous products talk about things you used to do in the past using less stuff planning a new website	text type: a review writing skill: giving your opinion
a historian talking about Scott's hut at the Antarctic a message in a bottle	the history of video gaming an article about stealing history	emotion words	planning a time capsule opinions about games reporting a message a museum in your town	a message in a bottle text type: a biography writing skill: punctuation in direct speech
a description of a photo and the life of a storm chaser a documentary about a photographer	an article about a science blog an article about Jane Goodall	close reading	hopes and dreams questions with *any* interview questions	text type: an article writing skill: planning an article

Introduction

National Geographic

The National Geographic Society is a leading nonprofit organization that pushes the boundaries of exploration to further our understanding of our planet and empower us all to generate solutions for a healthier and more sustainable future. Since its beginning in 1888, the Society has funded more than 12,500 exploration and research projects. *Life Second Edition* uses *National Geographic*'s content and principles to inspire people to learn English. A portion of the proceeds of this book help to fund the Society's work.

National Geographic topics

The topics are paramount and are the starting point for the lessons. These topics have been selected for their intrinsic interest and ability to fascinate. The richness of the texts means that students are so engaged in learning about the content, and expressing their own opinions, that language learning has to take place in order for students to satisfy their curiosity and then react personally to what they have learned. This element of transfer from the topics to students' own realities and experiences converts the input into a vehicle for language practice and production which fits the recognized frameworks for language learning and can be mapped to the CEFR scales. (Full mapping documents are available separately.)

People and places

Life Second Edition takes students around the globe, investigating the origins of ancient civilizations, showing the drama of natural forces at work and exploring some of the world's most beautiful places. These uplifting tales of adventure and discovery are told through eye witness accounts and first-class reportage. For example, Unit 6 of the Pre-intermediate level looks at coming of age ceremonies around the world and Unit 7 has an article about modern-day cowboys.

Science and technology

Students learn about significant scientific discoveries and breakthroughs, both historic and current. These stories are related by journalists or told by the scientists and explorers themselves through interviews or first person accounts. Students see the impact of the discoveries on our lifestyles and cultures. Because much of the material comes from a huge archive that has been developed and designed to appeal to the millions of individuals who make up *National Geographic*'s audience, it reflects the broadest possible range of topics. For example, Unit 8 of the Pre-intermediate level looks at the positive impact that a new design of glasses and 'lifestraws' are having in the developing world.

History

History can be a dry topic, especially if it's overloaded with facts and dates. However, the *National Geographic* treatment of historical events brings them to life and there is often a human dimension and universal themes that keep the events relevant to students and to our time.

History – or the re-telling of historical events – can also be influenced by a culture or nation's perception of the events. *National Geographic*'s non-judgemental and culture-neutral accounts allow students to look behind the superficial events and gain a deeper understanding of our ancestors. For example, Unit 11 of the Pre-intermediate level looks at the work of archeologists in Abu Sir al Malaq in Egypt and their struggle to prevent historical items being stolen from tombs.

Animals

The animal kingdom is exceptionally generative in terms of interesting topics. *Life Second Edition* provides astonishing photos that give a unique insight into the hidden lives of known and lesser-known animals, offering rare glimpses of mammals, birds, bugs and reptiles in their daily struggle for survival. It also informs and surprises with accounts of animals now extinct, species still evolving and endangered species which are literally fighting for their existence. For example, Unit 3 of the Pre-intermediate level looks at different forms of transport provided by animals.

Environment

It isn't always possible to find clarity in texts on the environment and climate change, or trust that they are true and not driven by a political agenda. *National Geographic*'s objective journalism, supported by easy-to-understand visuals, presents the issues in an accessible way. The articles are written by experts in their fields. It's often true that those who have the deepest understanding of issues are also able to express the ideas in the simplest way. For example, Unit 5 of the Pre-intermediate level contrasts the 'green' credentials of a number of different countries.

National Geographic photography

We live in a world where images are used more than ever to reinforce, and at times replace, the spoken and written word. We use our visual literacy – the ability to look at and understand images – every day of our lives. In particular, photographs tend to prompt emotive memories and help us to recall information. For this reason, the use of photographs and pictures in the classroom is a highly effective learning tool. Not surprisingly then, the *Life* series makes maximum use of the great photographs which are at the core of *National Geographic* content. The photographs in *Life Second Edition* add impact and serve as an engaging starting point to each unit. Then, in each lesson, photographs form an integral part of the written and recorded content and generate meaningful language practice in thoughtful and stimulating ways.

Introduction

There are photographs which:
- tell a story by themselves
- draw the viewer in and engage them emotionally
- support understanding of a text and make it memorable
- provoke debate
- stimulate critical thinking by asking you to examine detail *or* think about what is NOT shown *or* by questioning the photographer's motives
- are accompanied by a memorable quotation or caption
- help learners to remember a lexical set
- help to teach functional language
- lend themselves to the practice of a specific grammar point

As a first exercise when handing out the new book to your students, you could ask them to flick through the book, select their favourite photograph, and then explain to the class what it is they like about it. You will find specific suggestions in the teacher's notes for using the photographs featured within each unit, but two important things to note are:

- pictures of people or animals can capture a moment, so ask students to speculate on the events that led up to this moment and those that followed it
- pictures of places aim to capture their essence, so feed students the vocabulary they need to describe the details that together convey this (the light, the colours, the landscape, the buildings)

National Geographic video

Student's visual literacy and fascination with moving images means that, in addition to the use of photographs and pictures, video is also an extremely effective tool in the classroom. Each unit of *Life Second Edition* ends with a *National Geographic* video. These videos, which can be found on the DVD at the back of the Teachers's Book, the Student's App and on the *Life* website, are connected to the topic of the unit and are designed to be used in conjunction with the video lesson pages. Typically, a video lesson is divided into three parts:

Before you watch
This section leads students into the topic of the video and engages them in a pre-watching task. It also pre-teaches key vocabulary so that students can immediately engage with the video without being distracted by unfamiliar words and the need to reference a lengthy glossary.

While you watch
These tasks assist with comprehension of the video itself, both in terms of what students see and what they hear. The exercises also exploit the language used in the video.

After you watch
There are two parts to this section. The first is an on-screen exercise called Vocabulary in context, which focuses on useful words and expressions from the video. The second allows students to respond to the video as a whole and take part in a discussion or task that leads on from the context and theme of the video.

The videos are designed to form part of your lessons. However, if there is insufficient time in class to watch them all, you can ask students to watch the videos and complete many of the exercises on the page in the Student's Book at home. This can form a useful part of their self-study. Students can also watch the videos again after seeing them in class. This is useful for review and enables students to focus on parts of the video that particularly interest them.

For further variation with the videos, here are some more ideas you can use and develop:

- Play the video with the sound down. Students predict what the narrator or people are saying. Then play with the sound up and compare.
- Play the sound only with no video. Students predict where the video takes place and what is happening on the screen. Then play the video as normal and compare.
- Show the first part of the video, pause it, and then ask students what they think happens next.
- Give students a copy of the video script and ask them to imagine they are the director. What will they need to film and show on the screen? Afterwards, they present their 'screenplay' ideas to the class, then finally watch the original.
- Write a short text on the same topic as the one in the video. However, don't include the same amount of information and leave some facts out. Students read the text and then watch the video. They make notes on any new information and rewrite the text so it includes the new details.
- With monolingual groups, choose part of the video in which someone is talking. Ask students to listen and write down what they say. Then, in groups, ask them to create subtitles in their own language for that part of the video. Each group presents their subtitles and the class compares how similar they are.

National Geographic and critical thinking

Critical thinking is the ability to develop and use an analytical and evaluative approach to learning. It's regarded as a key 21st Century skill. *Life Second Edition* integrates and develops a learner's critical thinking alongside language learning for the following reasons:

- critical thinking tasks such as problem-solving and group discussion make lessons much more motivating and engaging
- developing critical thinking skills encourages an enquiring approach to learning which enables learners to discover language and become more independent in their study skills
- language practice activities that involve critical thinking require deeper processing of the new language on the part of the learner

Introduction

In *Life Second Edition* you will see that there is a graded critical thinking syllabus that starts at Elementary level and runs through all later levels. The sections entitled 'Critical thinking' always appear in the C lessons in each unit and are associated with reading the longer texts. These lessons begin with reading comprehension activities that test students' understanding and then may ask them to apply their understanding in a controlled practice activity. Having understood the text at a basic level, the critical thinking section requires students to read the text again more deeply to find out what the author is trying to achieve and to analyse the writing approach. For example, students may have to read between the lines, differentiate between fact or opinion, evaluate the reliability of the information, assess the relevance of information, or identify the techniques used by the author to persuade the reader or weigh up evidence. Activities such as these work particularly well with the C lesson texts in *Life Second Edition* because the texts used in these lessons are authentic. These authentic texts, which have been adapted to the level where necessary, tend to retain the author's voice or perspective, so students can work to understand the real argument behind a text. Naturally, these kinds of reading skills are invaluable for students who are learning English for academic purposes or who would like to take examinations such as IELTS. In addition, life in the twenty-first century requires people to develop the ability to assess the validity of a text and the information they receive, so this critical thinking strand in *Life Second Edition* is important for all students.

As well as applying critical thinking to the reading texts, *Life Second Edition* encourages students to apply critical thinking skills in other ways. When new vocabulary or grammar is presented, students are often expected to use the target language in controlled practice activities. Then they use the language in productive speaking and writing tasks where they are given opportunities to analyse and evaluate a situation and make use of the new language both critically and creatively. In this way, students move from using 'lower-order thinking' to 'higher-order thinking'; many of the lessons in *Life Second Edition* naturally follow this flow from exercises that involve basic checking and controlled practice to those that are productive, creative, and more intellectually engaging. This learning philosophy can also be seen at work in the way in which photos and videos are used in the book. Students are encouraged to speculate and express their opinions on many of the photographs or in the 'after you watch' sections of the video pages. Finally, on the writing pages of the units, students are asked to think critically about how they organize their writing and the language they choose to use. They are also guided to think critically to establish criteria by which their writing can then be judged.

Central to the approach to critical thinking in *Life Second Edition* is the premise that students should be actively engaged in their language learning. Students are frequently invited to ask questions and to develop their own well-informed and reasoned opinions. The overall combination of text analysis (in the C lessons), a guided discovery approach to language, and the way in which the book makes use of images in the classroom effectively supports this aim.

Life Second Edition methodology

Memorization

An important role for teachers is to help learners commit new language to longer-term memory, not just their short-term or working memory. According to Gairns and Redman (*Working with Words*, Cambridge University Press, 1986), 80% of what we forget is forgotten within the first twenty-four hours of initial learning.

So, what makes learning memorable? The impact of the first encounter with new language is known to be a key factor. *Life Second Edition* scores strongly in this area because it fulfils what are called the 'SUCCESS factors' in memorization (Simplicity, Unexpectedness, Concreteness, Credibility, Emotion and Stories) by engaging learners with interesting, real-life stories and powerful images. *Life Second Edition* also aims, through motivating speaking activities that resonate with students' own experiences, to make new language relatable. What is known is that these encounters with language need to be built on thorough consolidation, recycling, repetition and testing. It is said that a new language item needs to be encountered or manipulated between five and fifteen times before it's successfully committed to longer-term memory. With this in mind, we have incorporated the following elements in *Life Second Edition*:

a) more recycling of new vocabulary and grammar through each unit and level of the series

b) activities in the Classroom Presentation Tool (CPT) that start some new lessons with revision and recycling of previous lessons

c) progress tests and online end-of-year tests

d) activities in the Review lessons at the end of each unit, marked 'Memory booster'

These 'Memory booster' activities are based on the following methodologically proven principles:

- Relatability: learning is most effective when learners apply new language to their own experience.

- A multi-sensory approach: learning is enhanced when more than one sense (hearing, seeing, etc.) is involved in perception and retention. (Language is not an isolated system in memory; it's linked to the other senses.)

- Repetition and variation: learners need to frequently retrieve items from memory and apply them to different situations or contexts.

- Guessing/Cognitive depth: making guesses at things you are trying to retrieve aids deeper learning.

- Utility: language with a strong utility value, e.g. a function such as stating preferences, is easier to remember.

- No stress: it's important that the learner does not feel anxious or pressured by the act of remembering.

- Peer teaching: this is an effective tool in memory consolidation (as in the adage, 'I hear and I forget. I see and I remember. I do and I understand. I teach and I master.')

- Individuality: we all differ in what we find easy to remember, so co-operation with others helps the process.

Introduction

You probably already use revision and recycling in your teaching. Our hope is that these exercises will stimulate ideas for other fun and varied ways you can do this, which in turn may lead students to reflect on what learning and memorization strategies work best for them as individuals.

Treatment of grammar

Target grammar is presented in the first two lessons of each unit in the context of reading or listening texts. These texts are adapted for level as necessary from authentic sources which use the target language in natural and appropriate linguistic contexts. Such texts not only aid comprehension, but present good models for the learner's own language production through a variety of 'voices' and genres. In general, reading texts have been used in the first lesson and listening texts in the second. Where a presentation is via a listening text, written examples of the grammar structures are given on the page, for example in content comprehension tasks, so that the student gets the visual support of following the target structures on the page. In both types of presentations, the primary focus is on the topic content before the learner's attention is drawn to the target grammar structures. Learners are then directed to notice target structures by various means, such as using highlighting within the text, extracting sample sentences or asking learners to locate examples themselves. Tasks which revise any related known structures are given in the Student's Book, Teacher's Book or via the CPT package.

At the start of each grammar section is a grammar summary box with examples of form and use from the presentation text, or paradigms where this is clearer (for example, in lower levels). This supports the learners and is a 'check point' for both teacher and learner alike. The grammar box summarizes the information learners arrive at through completing discovery tasks and it also acts as a focus for tasks which then analyse the form, meaning and use of the grammar structures, as appropriate. A variety of task formats have been used to do this, usually beginning with accessible check questions. This approach is highly motivational because it actively engages learners in the lesson and allows them to share and discuss their interpretation of the new language. Each grammar box gives a cross reference to two pages of detailed explanations and additional exercises per unit at the back of the Student's Book. These are suitable for use both in class and for self-study, according to the needs of the learner. They are also presented as video tutorials for extra support in the Online Workbooks.

The grammar summary box is followed by grammar practice tasks. Depending on the level, the grammar practice exercises have a differing emphasis on form and use. In all levels, however, the practice exercises in the unit favour exercises which require students to think more deeply over those involving mechanical production. Where appropriate, contrastive and comparative formats are used. The first practice exercise is usually linked to the topic of the lesson and is content rich. Subsequent exercises move into real-life contexts and particularly to those which the learner can personalize. This gives learners an invaluable opportunity to incorporate the structures in the context of their own experiences. The practice exercises are carefully designed to move from supported tasks through to more challenging activities. This anchors the new language in existing frameworks and leads to a clearer understanding of the usage of this new or revised language. Frequently, the tasks provide a real and engaging reason to use the target structure, whether by devices such as quizzes, games and so on, or by genuine exchanges of information between students.

Each lesson ends with a 'My life' speaking task. This personalized and carefully scaffolded activity enables students to create their own output using the target grammar as well as other target language in a meaningful context. Typical formats for this final task include exchanges of information or ideas, 'gap' pair work, personal narratives, discussion and task-based activities (ranking, etc.). The emphasis from the learner's perspective is on fluency within the grammatical framework of the task.

Treatment of vocabulary

Life Second Edition pays particular attention to both receptive and productive vocabulary. All of the authentic input texts have been revised to reduce above-level lexis while retaining the original 'flavour' and richness of the text and providing an achievable level of challenge.

Lexis is effectively learned via carefully devised recycling and memorization activities. Target vocabulary is recycled continually throughout each level – for example the writing and video lessons provide the ideal opportunity to incorporate and review lexis in meaningful contexts. Memorization (see page 10) is a key feature of exercises within the unit and in the Review lessons.

Life Second Edition teaches vocabulary in a range of different ways. This eclectic approach takes account of recent research and builds on tried and tested methods. There is further practice of the vocabulary input (apart from words occurring in glossaries) in the Workbook and also in the photocopiable Communicative Activities, which can be found in this Teacher's Book. There is also frequent practice of useful expressions, collocations, idioms and phrasal verbs as well as everyday lexis.

The specific sections dealing with new lexical input are:

1 Lexical sets

Some of the benefits generally associated with teaching words in lexical sets are:

- learning words in a set requires less effort
- retrieving related words from memory is easier
- seeing how knowledge can be organized can be helpful to learners
- it mirrors how such information is thought to be stored in the brain
- the meaning of words can be made clearer by comparing and contrasting them to similar words in the set

Each unit usually has two or more lexical sets. The lexical sets also cover commonly confused words. There is evidence to suggest that once students have learned one or more of the words that belong to a group of commonly

Introduction

confused words (e.g. *job* and *work*), it's useful to compare and contrast these words directly to clarify the differences (or similarities) in meaning. *Life Second Edition* focuses on these groups of words as and when they come up.

2 Wordbuilding

There are at least eight of these sections in each level. The independent wordbuilding syllabus offers students another opportunity to expand their vocabulary. The wordbuilding boxes in the units focus on areas such as prefixes, suffixes, parts of speech, compound nouns and phrasal verbs, and they highlight contextualized examples in the reading or listening texts. The box gives a brief explanation and some examples. It's followed by one or two practice activities. Each wordbuilding focus is followed up and extended in the Workbook and CPT – giving more practice and introducing more words that belong to the same morphological area.

3 Word focus

The word focus sections take high-frequency words and give examples of the different meanings they can have according to the contexts in which they appear and the different words they collocate with. At higher levels there is increased exposure to idioms and colloquial usage. The Workbook and CPT expand the range of phrases and expressions generated by these key words and provide further practice.

4 Glossaries

Occasionally, words are important to the meaning of a text but are above the level of the student. In such cases they are glossed. Students aren't expected to learn these words, but the short and simple definitions provided on the page prevent them from being a barrier to understanding.

5 Word lists

Each level has a comprehensive word list which covers all of the vocabulary either at the level, or above the level, of the student. The rich headword entries include phonetics, definition, part of speech, examples, collocations, word family and word family collocates. These are available on the Student's App and on the *Life* website as pdfs.

Learning skills

There is a comprehensive learning skills syllabus in the Workbook. This covers traditional learning skills, such as recording new vocabulary, using a dictionary, remembering new vocabulary, planning study time and assessing your own progress.

Assessment

Students and teachers can assess progress in the following ways:
- Each unit in the Student's Book finishes with a Review lesson where students do the exercises and complete a number of 'can-do' statements linked to the objectives of the unit.
- There are photocopiable progress tests in the Teacher's Book.
- There are end-of-year tests that follow the format of international exams on the *Life* website.
- There is a *Check!* section at the end of each unit in the Workbook for students to check what they have learned (general knowledge as well as language).
- There are IELTs practice tests at the end of the Workbooks. These have been graded to the level of the course, but follow the format of the test. These allow students to benchmark their progress against the course objectives, whilst becoming familiar with a global test format.

Lessons in a Student's Book unit

Opener: a one-page introduction to the unit that gets students interested in the topic

A and B: double-page lessons that teach grammar and vocabulary through reading and listening texts

C: a double-page lesson that focuses on reading comprehension and critical thinking

D: a one-page lesson that teaches functional/situational language

E: a one-page lesson that teaches a writing skill and the features of a text type

F: a double-page video lesson

Review: a one-page lesson of practice activities, memory booster activities and 'can-do' check statements

Components

- Student's Book
- Workbook + audio CD
- Teacher's Book + DVD + class audio CD
- Student's App
- Student's eBook
- Online Workbook
- Website: www.NGL.cengage.com/life
- Classroom Presentation Tool

The CPT includes additional activities. These are labelled in the teaching notes as ★ CPT extra! This additional practice covers a wide variety of activity types. This includes:

- Activities which exploit the lesson photo (e.g. extra critical thinking-type questions, background information, etc.)
- Extra listening activities
- Revision of previously taught vocabulary/grammar
- Quizzes about the lesson topic or unit photo
- Culture notes/background notes
- Links to extra resources
- Word Focus: additional practice and extension
- Wordbuilding: additional practice and extension
- Extra lead-ins and warmers
- Further development of the skills syllabus (listening and reading)
- Extension project work
- Extra Critical Thinking activities
- Writing additional practice and extension

Lesson type

Unit opener

This single page introduces the unit topic and lists the unit contents.

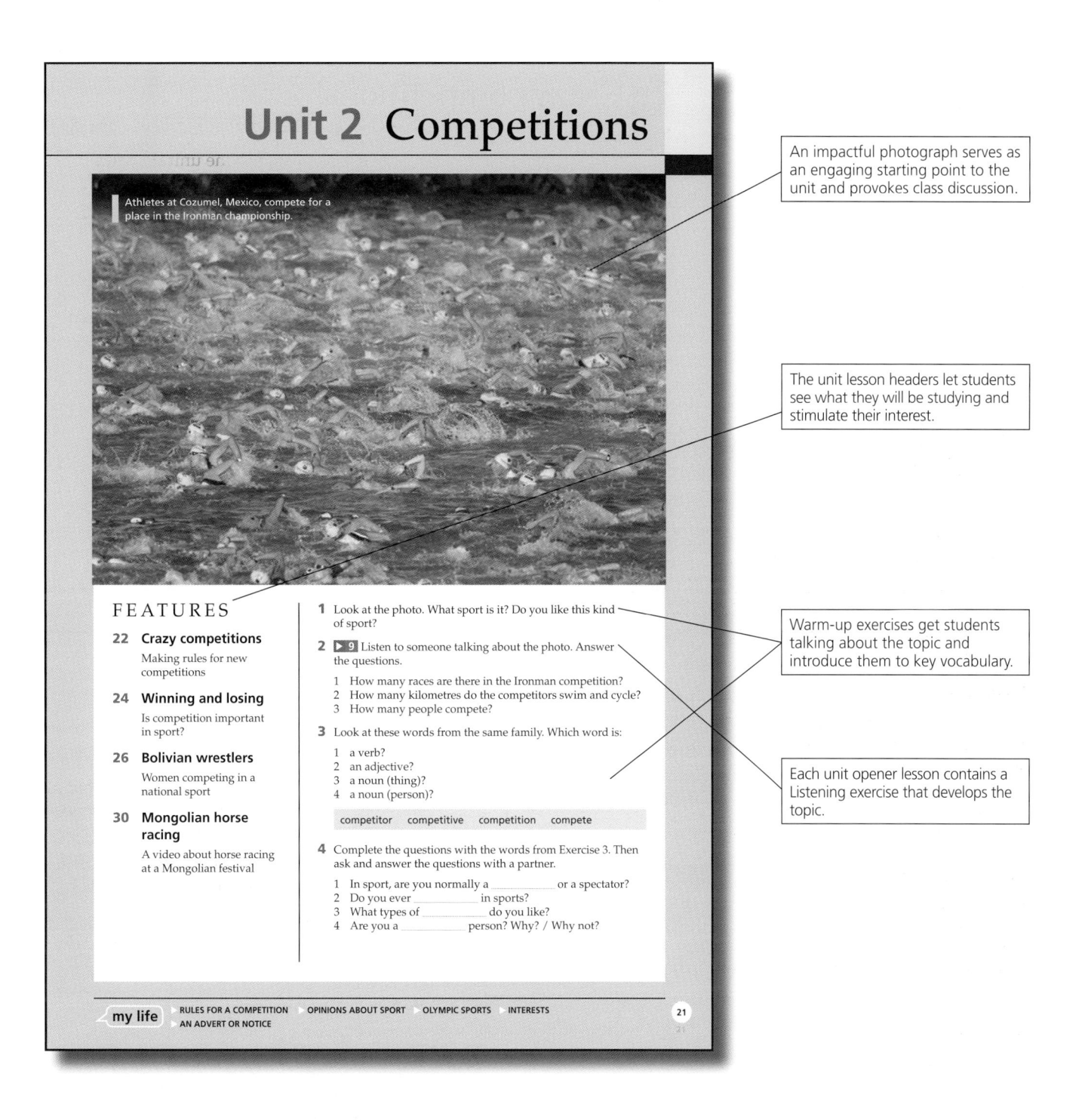

> An impactful photograph serves as an engaging starting point to the unit and provokes class discussion.

> The unit lesson headers let students see what they will be studying and stimulate their interest.

> Warm-up exercises get students talking about the topic and introduce them to key vocabulary.

> Each unit opener lesson contains a Listening exercise that develops the topic.

Unit 2 Competitions

Athletes at Cozumel, Mexico, compete for a place in the Ironman championship.

FEATURES

22 Crazy competitions
Making rules for new competitions

24 Winning and losing
Is competition important in sport?

26 Bolivian wrestlers
Women competing in a national sport

30 Mongolian horse racing
A video about horse racing at a Mongolian festival

1 Look at the photo. What sport is it? Do you like this kind of sport?

2 ▶9 Listen to someone talking about the photo. Answer the questions.
  1 How many races are there in the Ironman competition?
  2 How many kilometres do the competitors swim and cycle?
  3 How many people compete?

3 Look at these words from the same family. Which word is:
  1 a verb?
  2 an adjective?
  3 a noun (thing)?
  4 a noun (person)?

competitor   competitive   competition   compete

4 Complete the questions with the words from Exercise 3. Then ask and answer the questions with a partner.
  1 In sport, are you normally a _____ or a spectator?
  2 Do you ever _____ in sports?
  3 What types of _____ do you like?
  4 Are you a _____ person? Why? / Why not?

my life ▶ RULES FOR A COMPETITION ▶ OPINIONS ABOUT SPORT ▶ OLYMPIC SPORTS ▶ INTERESTS
         ▶ AN ADVERT OR NOTICE

Introduction   13

Lessons A and B

Grammar and vocabulary

These double-page lessons focus on grammar and vocabulary, presented through listening and reading texts.

The primary focus is on the topic content before the learner's attention is drawn to the target grammar structures.

Target grammar is presented through texts in the first two spreads of each unit. These texts are authentic reading and listening texts, adapted for level as necessary, which use the target language in natural and appropriate linguistic contexts. Such texts not only aid comprehension, but present good models for the learner's own language production through a variety of 'voices' and genres. The main input alternates between reading and listening on these first two spreads.

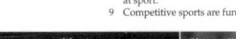

The independent wordbuilding syllabus offers students another opportunity to expand their vocabulary. The wordbuilding boxes in the units focus on areas such as prefixes, suffixes, collocations, parts of speech, compound nouns and phrasal verbs, and they highlight examples from the reading or listening texts. The box gives a brief explanation and some examples. There is an activity for further practice and a reference to an activity in the Workbook which introduces more words that belong to the same morphological area.

---

reading **crazy competitions** • vocabulary **sport** • grammar **verbs for rules** • speaking **rules for a competition**

2a Crazy competitions!

Reading

1 Look at the title of the article and the two photos. Why do you think the competitions are 'crazy'?

2 Read the article. Which competition is a race between different teams? Which is a match between two teams?

3 Read the article again and match the sentences (1–6) with the competitions (A–B). One sentence is true for both competitions.
 1 Competitors start and end at the same place. *A*
 2 The rules are the same as another real sport.
 3 The competition is once a year.
 4 You use a type of transport.
 5 It's for teams.
 6 There is a time limit.

4 Which of the two sports would you like to play or watch? Do you have any crazy competitions in your country?

Vocabulary **sport**

5 Look at the highlighted words in the article. Use the words to complete the sentences below.
 1 Runners at the Olympic Games get a gold medal when they win a _____.
 2 In football, there are eleven _____ on each side.
 3 At the beginning of the championship there are 24 _____. In the final, there can only be two.
 4 A rugby _____ lasts eighty minutes.
 5 How many _____ did you score?
 6 The ball didn't cross the _____, so it wasn't a goal.
 7 The _____ received a gold medal.

6 Work in pairs. Answer these questions.
 1 How many different kinds of race can you think of?
 2 How many players are there in your favourite team sports?
 3 What are the names of the sports teams in your town or city?
 4 In what games do you score goals and in what games do you score points?

CRAZY COMPETITIONS!
There are lots of competitions in the USA and some of them are a bit crazy!

A The Idiotarod
The Idiotarod is an annual race in twenty different US cities. Each team must have five people and a shopping cart. One person usually rides in the cart and four people pull it. Teams can decorate the shopping cart but they can't change the wheels. All the teams have to start and finish at the same place but they don't have to run on the same roads. The members of each team must cross the finish line together and they mustn't finish without the cart!

22

---

wordbuilding **suffixes** • listening **competitive sports** • grammar **-ing form** • pronunciation /ŋ/ • speaking **opinions about sport**

2b Winning and losing

Wordbuilding **suffixes**

1 Are any of the sportspeople in the photos famous in your country? Match the people with these words.

 tennis player   runner   footballer   athlete

> **WORDBUILDING suffixes**
> You can add -er to some sports to describe the sportsperson: football → footballer, golf → golfer
> You can add player to some sports:
> tennis → tennis player, squash → squash player
> Some sports don't use the suffix -er or -player:
> athletics → athlete, cycle → cyclist
> For further practice, see Workbook page 19.

2 Look at the wordbuilding box. What is the word for a person who:
 1 boxes? *boxer*   5 plays chess?
 2 motorcycles?   6 drives a racing car?
 3 plays baseball?   7 does gymnastics?
 4 swims?   8 goes surfing?

3 Who are the most famous sportspeople in your country? What type of sportspeople are they? (e.g. *a footballer, an athlete*)
Lionel Messi is very famous in my country. He's a footballer.

Listening

4 Read the quotes with the photos. Do you think winning is always important in sport? Why? / Why not?

5 ▶11 Listen to three people talking about competitive sports in schools. Match the speakers (1–3) with the opinions (a–c).
 a Speaker ____ thinks non-competitive sport is a good idea.
 b Speaker ____ thinks competitive sport is a good idea in schools.
 c Speaker ____ thinks sport in schools is a good idea but there can be a problem.

6 Look at these opinions for and against competitive sports in schools. Which are the opinions for (F) and which are the opinions against (A)?
 1 Winning and losing teaches students about life. *F*
 2 A lot of schools with good results don't have competitive sports. *A*
 3 Children get more exercise when they try to win.
 4 Winning isn't important as long as you do your best.
 5 Children learn to work well in teams when they play in matches.
 6 Students learn to work hard with competitive sports.
 7 Some parents don't like losing and get angry with their children.
 8 All children are different and some aren't good at sport.
 9 Competitive sports are fun.

'I don't like losing.' Usain Bolt

'I'm very competitive.' Jessica Ennis-Hill

'You can't win all the time.' Lionel Messi

24

---

14   Introduction

Page annotations (callouts)

Top right callout: Clear paradigms or examples of form and use are given on the page in a simple summary box. This supports the learners and is a 'check point' for both teacher and learner alike as it summarizes the information learners will have arrived at through completing the discovery tasks. A cross-reference is provided to more detailed information and additional exercises at the back of the book. These are suitable both for use in class and self-study, according to the needs of the learners.

Middle right callout: The grammar practice tasks within the unit are linked to the presentation text and topic and are thus content-rich in the same way. They move from more supported exercises through to more challenging tasks.

Lower right callout: A variety of task formats are used to lead learners to analyse the form, meaning and use of the grammar structures, as appropriate.

Bottom left callout: A final task on each spread allows the learners to create their own output and is structured so that learners have the opportunity to use the target grammar as well as other target language, for example vocabulary, in a meaningful and personalized context. This final task has a variety of formats such as discussions, personal narratives, task-based activities (ranking, etc.) and the emphasis from the learner's perspective is on content and fluency rather than grammatical accuracy.

Page content (left page)

Unit 2 **Competitions**

Grammar verbs for rules

▶ **VERBS FOR RULES**

Each team **must** have five people and a shopping cart.
They **can't** change the wheels.
All the teams **have to** start and finish at the same place.
They **don't have to** run on the same roads.
They **mustn't** finish without the cart!
Players **can** pick up the ball and run with it.

For further information and practice, see page 158.

7 Look at the sentences in the grammar box. Complete the explanations (a–d) with the verbs in bold in the grammar box.

a We use _____ or _____ when the rules say it's obligatory.
b We use _____ when it's allowed in the rules.
c We use _____ when something is not obligatory but is allowed by the rules.
d We use _____ or _____ when it isn't allowed in the rules.

8 Choose the correct option to complete the sentences about different sports.

1 In golf, you *have to* / *don't have to* hit the ball into nine or eighteen holes.
2 Competitors *can* / *mustn't* argue with the referee.
3 In football, a goalkeeper is the only player who *can* / *has to* pick up the ball.
4 Players *can't* / *must* throw the ball backwards in rugby.
5 A referee *can* / *mustn't* send a player off the pitch when he breaks the rules of the game.
6 In table tennis, the ball *has to* / *can't* hit the table.
7 In tennis, the players *must* / *don't have to* win every point to win a match.

9 Complete the description of another competition with these verbs. Use each verb once only.

must   have to   don't have to   can't   can

Every year, over three hundred competitors enter the Beard and Moustache competition in Alaska. The rules are simple. You ¹ _must_ be over eighteen years old and you ² _____ have a moustache or a beard, or both. Also, you ³ _____ put on false hair! In total, there are eighteen different categories, but competitors ⁴ _____ only enter one category. There are categories for short beards and different moustaches, so you ⁵ _____ have the longest moustache or the biggest beard to win a prize.

Speaking my life

10 Work in pairs. You are going to explain the rules for a sport or competition. Choose one of the following. Make a list of six to seven rules.

- a popular sport in your country
- a popular TV quiz show or TV competition
- an annual national or international competition

Baseball is a popular sport in my country. You have to play with two teams, a ball and a bat.

11 Work with another pair. Take turns to explain your rules. Ask questions if you don't understand.

Do I have to be over 18?
Can I enter the competition on my own or do I have to be in a team?

my life ▶ **RULES FOR A COMPETITION** ▶ OPINIONS ABOUT SPORT ▶ OLYMPIC SPORTS ▶ INTERESTS
▶ AN ADVERT OR NOTICE

Page content (right page)

Unit 2 **Competitions**

7 ▶11 Listen again. Which opinion from Exercise 6 does each speaker (1–3) give?
Speaker 1 _1_
Speaker 2 ____
Speaker 3 ____

8 Work in groups. Discuss the opinions in Exercise 6. Answer these questions.

1 Which opinions do you agree with?
2 Which do you disagree with?
3 Are there any other reasons for or against competitive sports in schools?

Grammar -ing form

▶ **-ING FORM**

1 *Learning to win and lose* is important in a child's education.
2 Competitive sports in schools are good for teaching children.
3 Some parents hate losing.

For further information and practice, see page 158.

9 Look at the grammar box. Underline the verbs in the *-ing* form. Then match them with the uses of the *-ing* form (a–c).

a It is the subject of the sentence.
b It comes after a verb, e.g. *like*, *dislike*.
c It comes after a preposition, e.g. *of*.

'I want to be number one. But being happy and healthy is the most important thing.' Venus Williams

10 Put the words in order to make quotes by famous sportspeople. Then match the *-ing* forms with the uses (a–c) in Exercise 9.

1 never / thought / losing / of / I (Muhammed Ali, boxer)
2 love / I just / winning (Ayrton Senna, racing driver)
3 A champion / afraid / losing / isn't / of (Billie Jean King, tennis-player)
4 hate / I / losing (Sachin Tendulkar, cricketer)
5 I'm / more worried about / a good person / being / than being the best football player (Lionel Messi, footballer)
6 isn't / swimming / winning is / everything, (Mark Spitz, swimmer)

11 ▶12 Choose the correct options to complete this conversation. Then listen and check.

A: What's on TV?
B: ¹ *Cycle* / *Cycling*. It's the Tour de France. I love ² *watch* / *watching* it.
A: Oh no! I ³ *think* / *thinking* it's boring.
B: I really enjoy ⁴ *see* / *seeing* them on the mountains.
A: ⁵ *Sit* / *Sitting* in front of the TV all day is not exciting. I'm bored with ⁶ *do* / *doing* nothing. Are you any good at tennis? We could ⁷ *play* / *playing* this afternoon.
B: But I want to ⁸ *watch* / *watching* this.
A: I see. Are you afraid of ⁹ *lose* / *losing*?

12 Pronunciation /ŋ/

a ▶13 Listen to six words. Tick the word you hear.

1 a thin	b think	c thing
2 a win	b wink	c wing
3 a ban	b bank	c bang
4 a sin	b sink	c sing
5 a ran	b rank	c rang
6 a pin	b pink	c ping

b ▶12 Listen again to the conversation from Exercise 11. Notice the pronunciation of the *-ing* forms.

c Work in pairs. Practise the conversation.

Speaking my life

13 Work in pairs. Ask questions to find out what sports or leisure activities your partner likes. Then complete the sentences.

A: *What sports do you love watching?*
B: *Tennis. What about you?*

1 I love watching _____ but my partner doesn't.
2 I think _____ is boring but my partner loves it!
3 We both enjoy _____ but we hate _____.
4 I'm good at _____ but my partner isn't.
5 My partner likes _____ but I prefer _____.

my life ▶ RULES FOR A COMPETITION ▶ **OPINIONS ABOUT SPORT** ▶ OLYMPIC SPORTS ▶ INTERESTS
▶ AN ADVERT OR NOTICE

25

Introduction 15

Lesson C

Reading

This is a double-page reading lesson. The reading text is always on the right-hand page, and the activities on the left.

> The mini contents section at the beginning of every lesson sets clear targets.

> The word focus sections take high frequency words and give examples of the different meanings they can have according to the contexts in which they appear and the different words they collocate with.

> Critical thinking activities require students to engage with the reading texts at a deeper level, and require them to show real understanding – not just reading comprehension. This training – in evaluating texts, assessing the validity and strength of arguments and developing an awareness of authorial techniques – is clearly a valuable skill for those students learning English for academic purposes (EAP), where reflective learning is essential. However, it is also very much part of the *National Geographic* spirit which encourages people to question assumptions, and develop their own well-informed and reasoned opinions.

---

reading **women in sport** • critical thinking **reading between the lines** • word focus *like* • speaking **Olympic sports**

2c Bolivian wrestlers

Reading

1 Discuss the questions.
1 Do many people watch boxing or wrestling in your country?
2 Why do some people dislike these types of sports?
3 What do you think about these sports?

2 Read the article about wrestling in Bolivia. Which paragraph (1–5) describes:
a the two wrestlers before the fight? 2
b the popularity of male and female wrestling in Bolivia?
c Yolanda's family life?
d the reason why a fan watches it?
e the fight between the two wrestlers?

3 Find words in the article for these definitions.
1 something people watch for pleasure
  e_ntertainment_
2 the place where two wrestlers fight
  r_____
3 a large group of people   c_____
4 the person who describes the action in a sport
  c_____
5 get very excited, shout and jump up and down
  g_____ c_____
6 people who like a sports person or famous celebrity   f_____
7 the money you earn for work   s_____

Critical thinking **reading between the lines**

4 An article doesn't always tell us about how the people feel, but we can often guess. Match the people from the article (1–3) with the sentences (a–c).
1 Yolanda
2 one of Yolanda's daughters
3 Esperanza

a 'I don't like the days when the wrestli[ng] happens.'
b 'I feel wonderful every time I go out t[here].'
c 'Life is very hard for people like me.'

5 Discuss the questions.
1 How do you feel about the women wr[estlers?]
2 Would you like to see this sport? Why[?] Why not?

Word focus *like*

6 Look at the word *like* in these sentences. Match the sentences (1–4) with the uses (a–d).
1 Most people **like** football.
2 Yolanda and Claudina **are like** famous pop stars.
3 **Would** your daughters **like** to become wrestlers one day?
4 Esperanza **likes** watching the wrestling.

a We use *like* + noun to talk about things we enjoy.
b We use *like* + *-ing* to talk about activities we enjoy doing.
c We use *be/look like* to talk about similarities between people/things/actions.
d We use *would like to* + infinitive to talk about future plans or ambitions.

7 Match these questions with *like* (1–4) with the answers (a–d).
1 What do you like doing at the weekend?
2 What kind of music do you like?
3 Are you like anyone in your family?
4 Where would you like to go on holiday next?

a I probably look like my mother.
b Spain. Or Portugal maybe.
c Anything. Rock. Classical. I don't mind.
d Going to the cinema.

8 Work in pairs. Take turns to ask the questions from Exercise 7 and give your own answers.

Speaking *my life*

9 Work in groups. Can you say ten sports in the Olympic Games?

10 These six sports are not in the Olympic Games

Unit 2 Competitions

BOLIVIAN WRESTLERS

▶ 14

In Bolivia, football is the country's national sport but the country is also famous for another sport – wrestling. Local people like watching the wrestling and it's very popular with tourists. It's an exciting mixture of sport, drama and entertainment. When modern wrestling started in Bolivia in the 1950s, the competitors were all men, but nowadays women are also competing in the ring.

10 The city of El Alto is a good place to watch the wrestling. Hundreds of spectators go to the fights in the evening. This evening, the crowd is sitting round a huge wrestling ring and they shout: 'Bring them on! Bring them on!' Suddenly, the commentator is speaking into a microphone: 'Ladies and
15 Gentlemen. It's time for Yolanda and Claudina!' The crowd is screaming with excitement as two women in colourful clothes enter the ring.

Yolanda and Claudina are like famous pop stars. They smile and wave to their fans. The music stops and the referee starts
20 the fight. Claudina jumps on Yolanda. Then Yolanda throws Claudina on the floor. As Claudina lies on the floor, Yolanda smiles and waves to the crowd. Then, Claudina gets up and pushes Yolanda onto the ground. One minute Yolanda is winning. The next minute, Claudina is winning. The spectators
25 go crazy!

Away from the ring, many wrestlers are women with families. At home Yolanda has a normal and quiet family life. She has two daughters and she makes clothes for a living. Her father was also a wrestler, so it's a family tradition. In answer to the
30 question, 'Would your daughters like to become wrestlers one day?' Yolanda says they wouldn't. She answers: 'My daughters ask me why I do this. It's dangerous and they complain that wrestling doesn't bring any money into the house.' So why does she do it?

35 Yolanda loves wrestling because of her fans, and she has lots of them. One of her fans is called Esperanza Cancina. She pays $1.50 (a large part of her salary) to sit near the ring. Esperanza likes watching the wrestling because she says: 'We laugh and we forget our problems for three or four hours.'

my life ▶ RULES FOR A COMPETITION ▶ OPINIONS ABOUT SPORT ▶ **OLYMPIC SPORTS** ▶ INTERESTS
▶ AN ADVERT OR NOTICE

16 Introduction

Lesson D

Real life

This is a one-page functional lesson focusing on real-life skills.

---

speaking **clubs and membership** • real life **talking about interests** • pronunciation **silent letters**

2d Joining a group

Speaking

1 Work as a class or in groups. Interview different people. Find someone who:
1. is a member of a team or club.
2. has to go to regular meetings (e.g. every week).
3. pays to be a member.
4. competes with their team or club.

Real life talking about interests

2 Look at the adverts. Which information (1–4) is in each advert. Underline the information.
1. when the club meets
2. the membership fee
3. reasons to join
4. how to contact the club

A
Would you like to **get fit** and **make new friends?**
Join our running groups for beginners and for more experienced runners. It's non-competitive and fun.
7 p.m. every Wednesday.
Call Mike for details on 0776 58945.

B *Join us and WIN a new camera!*
The Barton Photography Club welcomes new members. We are a busy club with regular speakers. Join before 1st March and enter our summer photography competition. First prize is a new XP8ii camera! The entry fee is 15 euros (including membership).
Visit www.bartonphotoclub.com to join.

C *Theatre group*
Have fun with a local theatre group. We are looking for actors to be in a musical comedy this summer. You must be available twice a week starting 2nd April. Enthusiasm is more important than talent!
Write to Mandy Giles on mandy76@dmail.com

3 ▶ 15 Two people are looking at the adverts in their local newspaper. Listen to their conversation and number the adverts in Exercise 2 in the order they discuss them.

4 ▶ 15 Listen again and complete the sentences.
1. You're really _____ doing that.
2. Well, _____ joining something else?
3. Are you _____ acting?
4. I _____ standing up in front of people.
5. I'm _____ good at singing.
6. Go _____ . I think you'd enjoy it.
7. I think I'd _____ join this on Wednesday evenings.
8. It _____ like fun. _____ you come too?

5 Match the sentences in Exercise 4 with the three categories in the box.

▶ **TALKING ABOUT INTERESTS**

Talking about interests and abilities
Do you like taking photos?
I'm good at acting.
I'm (not) interested in photography.

Talking about plans
I'd like/prefer to join a running club.
I wouldn't like to do it.

Recommending and encouraging
It looks interesting.
Go on.
I think you'd enjoy it.
You should do it with me.

6 Pronunciation silent letters

▶ 16 Some letters in English words are not pronounced. Listen to these words from the conversation and cross out the silent letters. Then listen again and repeat.
1. interested
2. should
3. friends
4. write
5. half
6. what

7 Work in pairs. Discuss the questions.
1. Would you like to join one of the clubs in Exercise 2? Why? / Why not?
2. What other types of clubs would you like to join? Why would you like to join them?

my life ▶ RULES FOR A COMPETITION ▶ OPINIONS ABOUT SPORT ▶ OLYMPIC SPORTS ▶ **INTERESTS** ▶ AN ADVERT OR NOTICE

- The D lessons have clear 'Real life' functional aims.
- The key expressions are made memorable through an activation activity.
- The pronunciation syllabus covers sounds and spelling, connected speech, stress and intonation.

Lesson E

Writing

This is a one-page writing lesson. All the text types that appear in international exams are covered here.

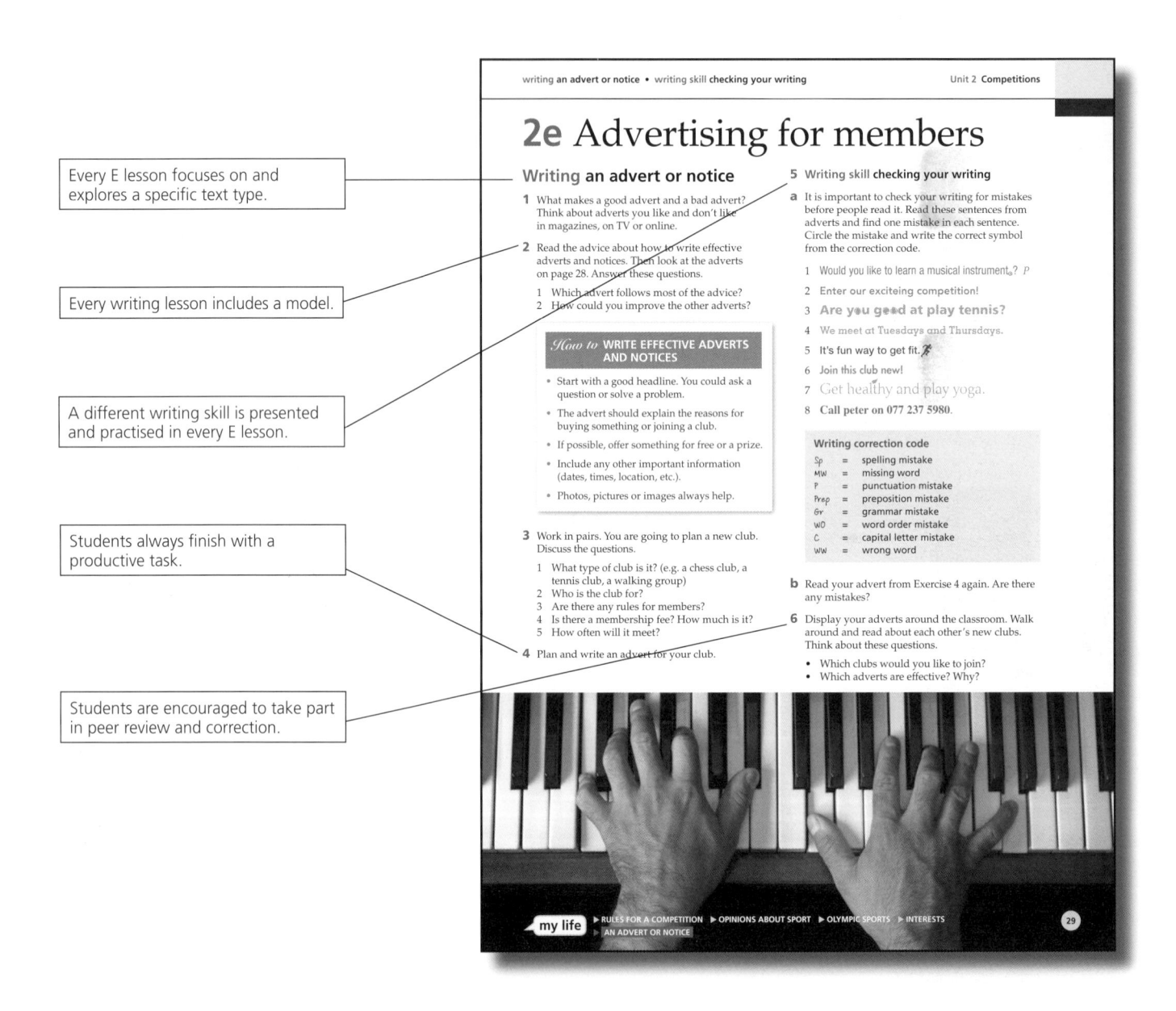

- Every E lesson focuses on and explores a specific text type.
- Every writing lesson includes a model.
- A different writing skill is presented and practised in every E lesson.
- Students always finish with a productive task.
- Students are encouraged to take part in peer review and correction.

---

writing **an advert or notice** • writing skill **checking your writing** Unit 2 Competitions

2e Advertising for members

Writing an advert or notice

1 What makes a good advert and a bad advert? Think about adverts you like and don't like in magazines, on TV or online.

2 Read the advice about how to write effective adverts and notices. Then look at the adverts on page 28. Answer these questions.
1 Which advert follows most of the advice?
2 How could you improve the other adverts?

> **How to WRITE EFFECTIVE ADVERTS AND NOTICES**
> - Start with a good headline. You could ask a question or solve a problem.
> - The advert should explain the reasons for buying something or joining a club.
> - If possible, offer something for free or a prize.
> - Include any other important information (dates, times, location, etc.).
> - Photos, pictures or images always help.

3 Work in pairs. You are going to plan a new club. Discuss the questions.
1 What type of club is it? (e.g. a chess club, a tennis club, a walking group)
2 Who is the club for?
3 Are there any rules for members?
4 Is there a membership fee? How much is it?
5 How often will it meet?

4 Plan and write an advert for your club.

5 Writing skill checking your writing

a It is important to check your writing for mistakes before people read it. Read these sentences from adverts and find one mistake in each sentence. Circle the mistake and write the correct symbol from the correction code.
1 Would you like to learn a musical instrument.? *P*
2 Enter our exciteing competition!
3 Are you good at play tennis?
4 We meet at Tuesdays and Thursdays.
5 It's fun way to get fit.
6 Join this club new!
7 Get healthy and play yoga.
8 Call peter on 077 237 5980.

Writing correction code
Sp	=	spelling mistake
MW	=	missing word
P	=	punctuation mistake
Prep	=	preposition mistake
Gr	=	grammar mistake
WO	=	word order mistake
C	=	capital letter mistake
WW	=	wrong word

b Read your advert from Exercise 4 again. Are there any mistakes?

6 Display your adverts around the classroom. Walk around and read about each other's new clubs. Think about these questions.
- Which clubs would you like to join?
- Which adverts are effective? Why?

my life ▶ RULES FOR A COMPETITION ▶ OPINIONS ABOUT SPORT ▶ OLYMPIC SPORTS ▶ INTERESTS ▶ AN ADVERT OR NOTICE

Lesson F

Video lesson

This is a double-page video lesson. A large, engaging introductory photograph is always on the left-hand page, and the activities on the right.

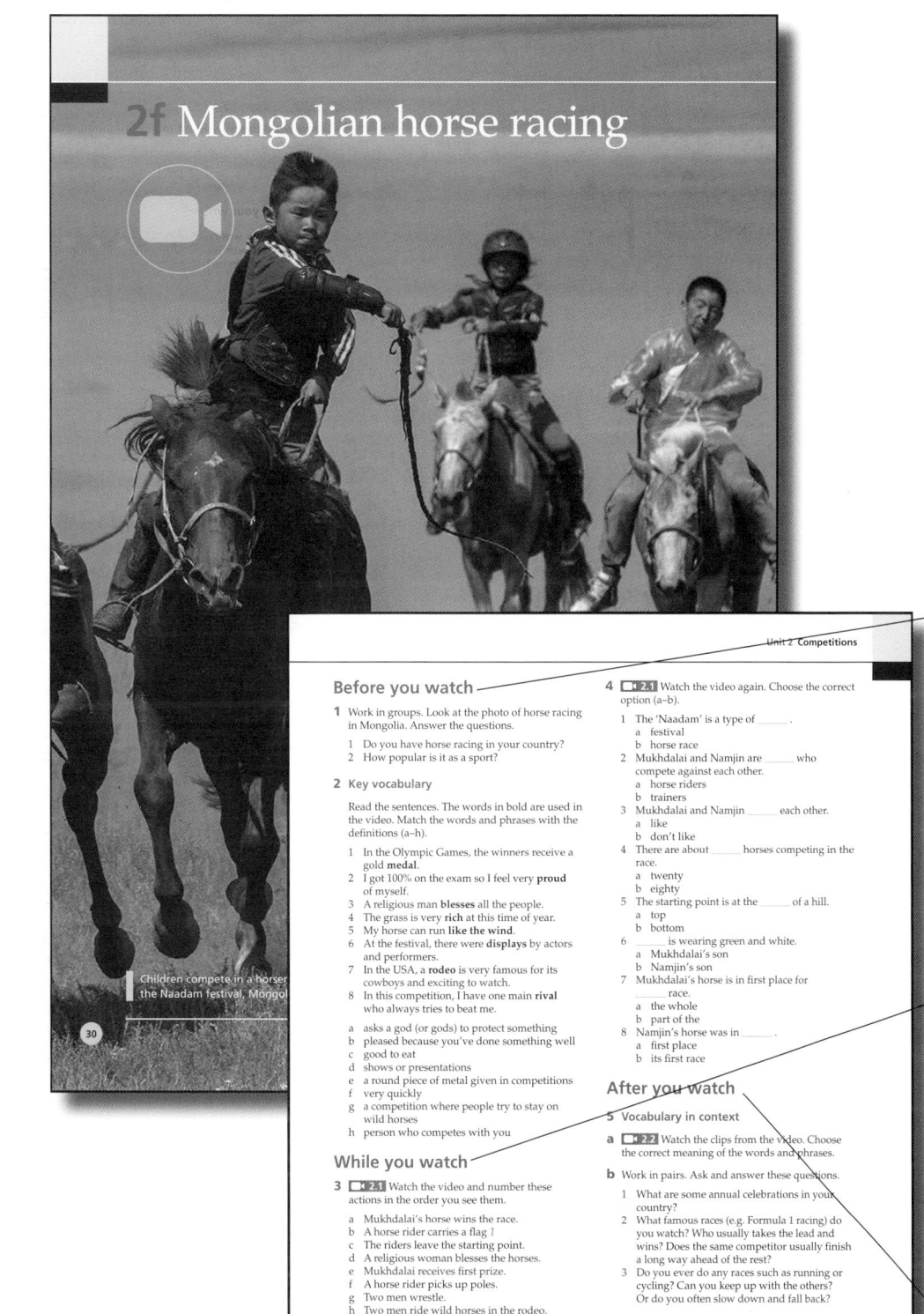

2f Mongolian horse racing

Children compete in a horse race at the Naadam festival, Mongolia

This section leads students into the topic of the video and engages them in a pre-watching task.

Before you watch

1 Work in groups. Look at the photo of horse racing in Mongolia. Answer the questions.
 1 Do you have horse racing in your country?
 2 How popular is it as a sport?

2 Key vocabulary

Read the sentences. The words in bold are used in the video. Match the words and phrases with the definitions (a–h).

 1 In the Olympic Games, the winners receive a gold **medal**.
 2 I got 100% on the exam so I feel very **proud** of myself.
 3 A religious man **blesses** all the people.
 4 The grass is very **rich** at this time of year.
 5 My horse can run **like the wind**.
 6 At the festival, there were **displays** by actors and performers.
 7 In the USA, a **rodeo** is very famous for its cowboys and exciting to watch.
 8 In this competition, I have one main **rival** who always tries to beat me.

 a asks a god (or gods) to protect something
 b pleased because you've done something well
 c good to eat
 d shows or presentations
 e a round piece of metal given in competitions
 f very quickly
 g a competition where people try to stay on wild horses
 h person who competes with you

While you watch

3 ▶ 2.1 Watch the video and number these actions in the order you see them.
 a Mukhdalai's horse wins the race.
 b A horse rider carries a flag *1*
 c The riders leave the starting point.
 d A religious woman blesses the horses.
 e Mukhdalai receives first prize.
 f A horse rider picks up poles.
 g Two men wrestle.
 h Two men ride wild horses in the rodeo.

4 ▶ 2.1 Watch the video again. Choose the correct option (a–b).
 1 The 'Naadam' is a type of ____ .
  a festival
  b horse race
 2 Mukhdalai and Namjin are ____ who compete against each other.
  a horse riders
  b trainers
 3 Mukhdalai and Namjin ____ each other.
  a like
  b don't like
 4 There are about ____ horses competing in the race.
  a twenty
  b eighty
 5 The starting point is at the ____ of a hill.
  a top
  b bottom
 6 ____ is wearing green and white.
  a Mukhdalai's son
  b Namjin's son
 7 Mukhdalai's horse is in first place for ____ race.
  a the whole
  b part of the
 8 Namjin's horse was in ____ .
  a first place
  b its first race

These exercises assist with comprehension of the video itself, both in terms of what students see and what they hear. The tasks also exploit the language used in the video.

After you watch

5 Vocabulary in context

a ▶ 2.2 Watch the clips from the video. Choose the correct meaning of the words and phrases.

b Work in pairs. Ask and answer these questions.
 1 What are some annual celebrations in your country?
 2 What famous races (e.g. Formula 1 racing) do you watch? Who usually takes the lead and wins? Does the same competitor usually finish a long way ahead of the rest?
 3 Do you ever do any races such as running or cycling? Can you keep up with the others? Or do you often slow down and fall back?

6 Work in pairs. Write five questions about the Naadam festival in the video.
 What is the Naadam festival famous for?

7 Work with a new partner. Take turns to ask and answer your questions from Exercise 6 about the Naadam.

There are two parts to this section. The first is an on-screen exercise called Vocabulary in context which focuses on useful words and expressions from the video. The second allows students to respond to the video as a whole and take part in a discussion or task that leads on from the context and theme of the video.

Introduction 19

Review lesson

This is the one-page review lesson found at the end of every unit.

- Grammar and vocabulary from the unit is clearly signposted and systematically reviewed to reinforce students' learning.

- Engaging images from the unit aid the recall of key vocabulary.

- Every review lesson concludes with a 'Real life' activity that allows students to consolidate the functional language from the unit.

- Memory Booster activities are specifically designed to enable students to recall and activate new words more easily.

- 'Can-do' statements give students the opportunity to assess their own learning.

UNIT 2 REVIEW AND MEMORY BOOSTER

Grammar

1 Choose the correct options to complete the text about an unusual competition.

The first bed race was in Knaresborough, UK, in 1966. The rules are simple. Each team [1] *can / has to* race with one bed on wheels. There are six people in a team and one passenger. The team [2] *must / doesn't have to* have either six men or six women, or you [3] *can / can't* race with a team of three men and three women. The passenger [4] *has to / doesn't have to* be an adult but he or she [5] *doesn't have to / can't* be younger than twelve years of age. The time limit for the race is thirty minutes and you [6] *mustn't / have to* take longer.

2 >> MB Work in pairs. What sports do these people play? Say two rules for each sport.

3 Complete the sentences with the *-ing* form of these verbs.

| feel | go | learn | lose | watch | win |

1 _____ to speak another language is very useful.
2 Sport is good for _____ healthy.
3 Peter hates _____ any type of game.
4 Trying is more important than _____.
5 We're bored of _____ this match.
6 I love _____ to the cinema after work.

4 >> MB Complete the sentences in your own words using *-ing* forms. Then tell your partner.

1 _____ is very good for you.
2 I'm really interested in _____.
3 I don't like _____.

I CAN
use verbs for rules (including modal verbs)
use the *-ing* form

Vocabulary

5 Write the missing vowels in these words connected with sport. Race with your partner to see who can finish first.

1 R_C_
2 G_ _LS
3 CR_WD
4 M_TCH
5 F_N_SH L_N_
6 B_S_B_LL
7 W_NN_R
8 F_NS
9 T_ _M
10 B_X_R

6 Answer these questions with four of the words from Exercise 5.

1 What do you have to cross in a race?
2 What is the opposite of *a loser*?
3 What type of competition is Formula One?
4 What are the group of people who like a sports person or team?

7 >> MB Work in pairs. Choose four more words from Exercise 5 and write four questions. Then work with another pair and ask and answer your questions.

I CAN
talk about sport and sports people

Real life

8 Complete the conversation. Write one word in each gap.

A: Are you interested [1] _____ painting? There's a new evening course at my college.
B: I'm afraid I'm not very good [2] _____ art.
A: I'm not either, but I'd like [3] _____ learn. Go [4] _____. You should do it with me.
B: Sorry. What about doing something else?
A: [5] _____ you like taking photos? There's also a course for that.
B: Actually, that looks interesting.

9 >> MB Complete these sentences in your own words. Then tell your partner.

1 I'm good at …
2 I wouldn't like to …
3 I'm also interested in …
4 I think I'd enjoy learning …

I CAN
talk about my interests

Unit 1 Lifestyle

Opener

1 ⭐ **CPT extra!** Photo activity [before Ex.1]
- Ask students to look at the photo and the caption. Ask them to work in pairs to describe the place and to discuss the question. Elicit a few ideas from the class in feedback.

> **ANSWERS**
> Students' own answers. The photo shows a man in Bukhansan National Park. The park contains forested areas, temples and granite peaks, and the man has clearly just climbed up one of the peaks. Maybe he feels relaxed or tired after a long climb.

2 💿 [1]
- Play the recording. Students listen and answer the questions. Let them compare answers in pairs before checking with the class.

> **ANSWERS**
> 1 In Seoul, South Korea
> 2 About ten million
> 3 It's a good way to relax.

Audioscript 💿 [1]

Normally, national parks are in the countryside. But Bukhansan National Park in South Korea is part of the city of Seoul. It's about forty-five minutes from the city centre by subway and about ten million people visit the park every year. People in Seoul go walking there at weekends. It's a good way to relax.

> **Background information**
> The **Bukhansan National Park** covers an area of 79.92 km² and was established on 2 April 1983. Bukhansan means 'mountains north of the Han River'. It has three main peaks and is so popular with hikers that trails are closed on a rotational basis to protect the environment.

3
- You could start by checking some of the difficult words in the box with your students. Use mime or visuals to check their meaning (see Teacher development below).
- Ask students to work in pairs to discuss the activities. In feedback, ask some students to tell the class what they found out about their partner.

> **EXAMPLE ANSWERS**
> Note that the answers here depend on the students' own experience.
> *I go jogging every morning.*
> *I don't often go clubbing.*

Extra activity

Ask students to work in pairs to decide which activities you (their teacher) often do and which you rarely or never do. Then do a live listening (see explanation below). Briefly describe the activities you often do. Find out which students predicted your answers correctly.

Note: A 'live listening' is when you talk naturally about a topic and students listen to you with a task to do. It's both fun and motivating for students at this level to listen to and follow a native or proficient speaker, and a welcome and real change from listening to recorded material.

Teacher development

Using mime or visuals to check words

At pre-intermediate level, most new words can be explained with a picture or a mime. Here are four suggestions for checking the meaning of the activities in Exercise 3:

- Find pictures for all the activities. You could choose to print off or cut out pictures to make flashcards, or you could use your classroom technology to project pictures you have found online. Start by showing the pictures and asking: *What can you see?* Alternatively, since these are activities, ask: *What are they doing?* Elicit ideas from students. At the end, ask students to look at the activities in Exercise 3 and match them with your pictures.

- Show the pictures, as suggested in 1 above, but don't try to elicit the words. Once you have shown all your pictures, ask students to work in pairs to try to remember what activities they saw. Brainstorm activities to the board in feedback. Then ask students to look at the activities in Exercise 3 and say which ones they remembered.

- Act out the activities in Exercise 3 (e.g. mime cooking, playing a violin, reading a book) and ask students to call out, write down or silently remember the activities you are miming. At the end, students match what they said, wrote or remembered with the phrases in Exercise 3.

- Ask students to look at the activities in Exercise 3. Mime six of them, telling students to tick the ones they see you act out. Let students check in pairs, then improvise their own mimes to show the meaning of the other phrases.

21

UNIT 1 Lifestyle

1a How well do you sleep?

Lesson at a glance
- vocabulary: everyday routines
- reading: the secrets of sleep
- grammar: present simple and adverbs of frequency
- pronunciation: /s/, /z/ or /ɪz/
- speaking: your habits

Vocabulary everyday routines

1 ★ **CPT extra!** Vocabulary activity [after Ex. 1]
- Ask students to work in pairs to match the expressions. Elicit answers in feedback. Check the meaning of any unusual verb + noun collocations (see Vocabulary note below).
- Ask students to describe their typical days to their partner. You could start them off by briefly describing your own routine. This provides a model of what they should say.

ANSWERS
1 g 2 f 3 h 4 a 5 d 6 e 7 c 8 b 9 j 10 i

Vocabulary note
The main thing to point out here is the specific collocation of verbs and nouns or adverbs in ways that may not directly translate into students' L1, e.g. *fall asleep* and *take a break*.

Reading

2 🔊 [2]
- Ask students to work individually to read the questionnaire and to choose their answers. Check that they understand the meaning of *take a nap* before they start (see the glossary at the bottom of the questionnaire).
- **Optional step** The reading text is recorded. You could play the recording and ask students to read and listen, selecting their answers as they go along (see Teacher development below).
- Ask students to work in pairs to compare their answers. Elicit what students found out about each other in feedback.

ANSWERS
Students' own answers

Teacher development

Reading a text while listening to a recording

Whether you choose to ask students to read with or without the recording is up to you. Here are some reasons why it's a good idea to ask students at the pre-intermediate level to listen and read:
- It gets students to read at the same speed, and as a whole class activity.
- It helps students with comprehension – the way the speaker uses stress, intonation and pauses can help students follow a text more easily.
- Students notice how words in a text are pronounced and stressed.
- It builds confidence with reading – it signals that students should read a text naturally the first time they read it, and that they should not worry about unknown words.

3
- Ask students to find the analysis of their answers on page 153. Let them compare their findings with their partner, and discuss what type of person they are. Elicit some answers in feedback, and find out what sort of sleep problems students have and what the reasons might be.

Grammar present simple and adverbs of frequency

4
- Ask students to work individually to match the sentences with the uses of the present tense.
- Let students compare answers in pairs before checking with the class.

ANSWERS
1 b 2 a

5
- Ask students to look at the grammar box. Point out the third person addition of *-s* (*sleeps*).
- Ask students to read the article quickly for general understanding first. Ask: *What is it about?* (why we sleep, why we have problems sleeping and why people sleep differently).
- Ask students to read the article again and complete it with the correct form of the verbs in brackets. Let students compare answers in pairs before checking with the class.

ANSWERS
1 do we sleep 2 spend 3 don't know 4 do we have
5 don't get 6 work 7 go 8 do we sleep
9 depends 10 need 11 don't sleep 12 take

Grammar note

Note the following form rules that often cause students problems:
- We add *-s* or *-es* in the third person. We only add *-es* after *o* (*he goes*), after *y* changes to *i* (*she flies*) and after the consonant sounds *ch, sh, x* and *ss* (*she watches, he washes, she fixes, he kisses*). Students sometimes misapply rules and change *y* to *i* when *y* comes after a vowel. Words that end with vowel + *y* don't change (e.g. *play* becomes *plays* not ~~*plaies*~~).
- We use the negative form of the auxiliary verb *do/does* + bare infinitive to form negatives (e.g. *Tom doesn't watch TV*). Students often confuse this in the third person (e.g. ~~*He don't watch/watches; He doesn't watches*~~.)
- We use the auxiliary verb *do/does* to form questions:

Q word	auxiliary	subject	main verb
Where	do	you	live?
What	does	she	do?

22 Unit 1 Lifestyle

UNIT 1 Lifestyle

Refer students to page 156 for further information and practice.

> **ANSWERS TO GRAMMAR SUMMARY EXERCISE**
> 1
> 1 doesn't live 2 drives 3 Does; speak 4 don't like
> 5 Do; see 6 are 7 don't need 8 Is 9 has

Pronunciation /s/, /z/ or /ɪz/

6a [3] ★ **CPT extra!** Pronunciation activity [before Ex. 6]
- Discuss the fact that there are three different ways to pronounce the *s/es* endings of the third person singular present simple verbs: /s/, /z/ or /ɪz/ (see Pronunciation note below).
- Play the recording and let students just listen to the words first, then play it again for them to write the correct pronunciation.
- Let students compare their answers with a partner before checking with the class.
- If necessary, play the recording again to check any disputed answers.

> **ANSWERS**
> 1 feels /z/ 2 needs /z/ 3 watches /ɪz/ 4 sleeps /s/
> 5 goes /z/ 6 dances /ɪz/ 7 does /z/ 8 works /s/

> **Pronunciation note**
>
> After a voiced sound, the third person 's' is pronounced /z/. After an unvoiced sound, it's pronounced /s/.
>
> When a verb ends in the following sibilant sounds, the third person 's' or 'es' is pronounced /ɪz/: /s/, /z/, /dʒ/, /ʃ/ or /tʃ/.
>
> Note that a voiced sound is a sound made when the voice box vibrates and an unvoiced sound is a sound made when the voice box doesn't vibrate. Say /t/ and /s/ with your hands over your ears and notice the lack of a deep vibration. Then say /d/ and /z/ and notice the different vibrating sound.
>
> A sibilant is a hissing /s/-like sound (a sound the phonemes listed above all share).

b [3]
- Play the recording again. Students listen and repeat.
- **Optional step** Write more verbs on the board and ask students to use phonemes to write the correct ending on each: *talks* /s/, *plays* /z/, *catches* /ɪz/, *reads* /z/, *gives* /z/, *washes* /ɪz/, *writes* /s/, *listens* /z/, *makes* /s/.

> **Extra activity**
>
> Students at this level often forget to add the *-s* or *-es* ending. Encourage them to use phonemes when noting new verbs in their dictionary (e.g. *watch – watches* /ɪz/, *play – plays* /z/). Many teachers keep three small flashcards with the phonemes /s/, /z/ and /ɪz/, which they show when students make mistakes. You could pin them next to the board and just point in their direction when students make the common slip of omitting this ending.

7
- Ask students to read and think about the questions for a minute.
- Then ask students to work in pairs or small groups to discuss the questions. Monitor and notice how well students are attempting the form and pronunciation of present simple questions and statements.
- **Optional step** Note any errors you hear as students speak. After feedback, write up short sentences with errors you heard and ask pairs or groups to work together to correct them.

> **ANSWERS**
> Students' own answers

8
- Look at the list with the class and ask students if they can suggest what adverbs of frequency are missing.
- Ask students to look back at the questionnaire in Exercise 2 and underline all the adverbs of frequency, then decide which are missing from the list and write them in.
- In feedback, copy the list on to the board and ask individual students to come to the front of the class to write in the missing words.

> **ANSWERS**
> 1 often 2 sometimes 3 never

9
- Ask students to read the grammar box and notice the position of the adverbs and expressions of frequency in the sentences.
- Ask students to work individually to read the rules and choose the correct options. Let them compare answers in pairs before checking with the class.

> **ANSWERS**
> 1 after the verb *to be*, before the main verb
> 2 at the beginning

Refer students to page 156 for further information and practice.

> **ANSWERS TO GRAMMAR SUMMARY EXERCISES**
> 2
> 1 I **am often** tired at work.
> 2 We eat out in a restaurant **twice a week**. / **Twice a week** we eat out in a restaurant.
> 3 correct
> 4 correct
> 5 I have a cup of coffee **two or three times a day**. / **Two or three times a day**, I have a cup of coffee.
> 6 They don't **often play** board games.
> 7 Does **she usually** take public transport?
> 3
> 1 always 2 get up 3 never 4 have 5 often 6 meet
> 7 go 8 every day 9 eat 10 two or three times a month

1a How well do you sleep? 23

UNIT 1 Lifestyle

10 ★ **CPT extra!** Grammar activity [after Ex. 10]
- Look at the example and do sentence 2 as a class. This is a good opportunity to point out that sometimes more than one answer is possible.
- Ask students to work individually to decide where to put the adverb or expression in the sentences (see Grammar note below). Let them compare answers in pairs before checking with the class.

ANSWERS
1 My brother **always** plays tennis on Saturday mornings.
2 We eat out at a restaurant **about once a month**. / **About once a month**, we eat out at a restaurant.
3 I take a bus to school **every day**. / **Every day**, I take a bus to school.
4 She is **rarely** at home in the middle of the day.
5 They go on holiday **twice a year**. / **Twice a year**, they go on holiday.
6 Are you **often** late for work?

Grammar note
Adverbs of frequency generally go between the subject and main verb (*I often sleep*), but after the verb *be* and auxiliary verbs (*He is often asleep; He doesn't often sleep*). The adverb *sometimes* is more flexible – it's often used at the start of sentences (*Sometimes we go camping in the summer*).

Expressions of frequency can be placed at the start of sentences to add emphasis, but generally they go at the end.

Speaking *my life*
11
- Ask students to work with a new partner. Look at the ideas in the box and elicit two or three possible questions and answers from the class. Then ask students to take turns to ask and answer with their partner. They should respond with answers that are true for them.
- Circulate and check correct question formation and use of the adverbs and expressions in students' answers.
- After a few minutes, say stop. Ask different individuals to tell the class what they learned about their partner.
- As students speak, note any errors with the present simple and adverbs of frequency. In feedback, write up four or five simple sentences with errors that you heard. Make sure the errors are from different students and anonymous. Ask students to work in pairs to correct the errors.

EXAMPLE ANSWERS
Here are some example questions and responses:
How often are you late for college? Never. / About once a week.
How often do you check your emails? Twice a day
How often do you go on holiday? Every summer / Twice a year.
How often are you stressed at work? Often. / Every day.

12
- Ask students to work in groups of three or four. (Make sure that there is an even number of groups.)
- Explain that they should produce a set of questions about lifestyle with three answers to choose from for each question. Elicit an example question and answer options with the class, e.g.
    How often do you go to the cinema?
    A: Every week
    B: Once a month
    C: Once a year
- If you think your students may be short of ideas when preparing, elicit a few categories or questions they could ask (e.g. sport, free time, food, work, home). Alternatively, ask different groups to prepare questions on different categories.

EXAMPLE ANSWERS
Here are some possible questions:
Sport: *Do you often do exercise / do sport / watch football live or on TV? How often do you go to the gym?*
Free time: *How often do you go to the theatre / clubbing / out?*
Food: *Do you often cook dinner? How often do you eat Indian / Chinese / Italian food?*
Work: *Are you often late for work? How often do you work in the evening / at weekends?*
Home: *Do you often do the housework? How often do you do the ironing?*

13
- Ask each group to join another group. You could ask them to sit in a circle or round a table so that they can easily ask each other their questions.
- Ask students to take turns asking and answering their questions. Tell them to note the answers and to use the information to present their findings to the class at the end.
- Elicit information from each group and discuss which group has the busiest lifestyle.

Extra activity
You could turn this into a class survey. Each student walks round the class and interviews as many students as they can in five minutes. Then they sit with their group and compare their information. They can then produce a report based on the information they share. You could ask students to write the report for homework.

UNIT 1 Lifestyle

1b The secrets of a long life

Lesson at a glance
- reading: the island of Okinawa
- wordbuilding: collocations with *do*, *play* and *go*
- listening: in search of a long life
- grammar: present simple and present continuous
- speaking: your current life

Reading
1
- Ask students to think about the answers to the questions. Students can work in groups of three or four to discuss their answers.
- Elicit some feedback as a class to see who is the oldest person anyone knows and to discuss the reasons for their long life.

2 [4] ★ **CPT extra!** Background information [before Ex. 2]
- Ask students to read the questions, then read the article to find the answers.
- **Optional step** The reading text is recorded. You could play the recording and ask students to read and listen.
- Let students compare answers in pairs before checking with the class. For the fourth question, ask students to tell the class about healthy aspects of their partner's life.

> **ANSWERS**
> 1 In Japan
> 2 It has some of the oldest people in the world.
> 3 fish, fruit, vegetables
> 4 Students' own answers

> **Background information**
> **Okinawa Island** has an area of over 1,200 square kilometres and is roughly 640 kilometres south of the rest of Japan. It's famous for thick, slimy Mozuku seaweed (shown in the photo) which is very healthy, and one reason why the islanders live so long.
> The **oldest person** who ever lived was French woman Jeanne Calment (1875–1997), who lived to the age of 122 years, 164 days. The oldest Okinawan was Kama Chinen (1895–2010) who lived to be 114 years 124 days old.

Wordbuilding collocations with *do, play* and *go*
3
- Read the information in the wordbuilding box with the class. Elicit other *do, play* and *go* collocations students already know (e.g. do crossword puzzles, play computer games, go skiing).
- Ask students to work individually to find the collocations in the article and to complete the table. Let them compare answers in pairs before checking with the class.

> **ANSWERS**
> Do: gardening, (regular) exercise
> Go: fishing, cycling, swimming
> Play: games

Refer students to Workbook page 11 for further practice.

4 ★ **CPT extra!** Wordbuilding activity [after Ex. 4]
- Ask students to work in pairs to add the activities to the table in Exercise 3. They then think of another activity for each verb (see answers in brackets below). Make sure there are dictionaries available in the classroom for students to check any collocations they aren't sure of.
- In feedback, build up a complete table on the board. You could ask students from different pairs to come up to the board to write up the activities. Ask students if they notice any pattern or rule (see Vocabulary note below).
- **Optional step** Drill the phrases for pronunciation practice. Note the English pronunciation of the following: *piano* /pɪˈænəʊ/, *yoga* /ˈjəʊɡə/, *karate* /kəˈrɑːti/.

> **ANSWERS**
> Do: homework, nothing, yoga, karate (aerobics, athletics)
> Go: hiking, running, shopping, surfing (camping, dancing)
> Play: cards, tennis, the piano, football (chess, basketball)

> **Vocabulary note**
> **Sport**
> There are basic rules with *play, do* and *go* (although there are some exceptions).
> - We use *play* with sports that involve a ball (or something similar), e.g. *play football, tennis, golf, rugby, ice hockey, badminton*.
> - We use *go* with activities that end with *-ing*, e.g. *go swimming, skiing, fishing*.
> - We use *do* with other activities when we don't say *-ing*, e.g. *do aerobics, gymnastics, athletics, martial arts*.
>
> We tend to say *do sport* (not ~~play sport~~) and *do boxing* or *wrestling* (not ~~go boxing~~).
>
> **Instruments**
> In common with many other European languages, we also use *play* with musical instruments, but we usually use *the*, e.g. *play the guitar, play the drums, play the violin*.
>
> **Uses of *do***
> We use *do* with activities with *the* when there's an idea of work, e.g. *do the shopping, do the gardening, do the housework*. We also use *do* when we don't specify the activity, e.g. *do nothing, do something fun, not do much*.

5
- Ask students to work with a new partner to talk about people they know. You could model the activity by describing people you know. As students speak, walk round and listen to how well your students are using the collocations.
- Note down some errors as you monitor. At the end, write several errors on the board and ask students to work in pairs to correct them.

1b The secrets of a long life 25

UNIT 1 Lifestyle

Listening

6 [5]
- Explain that students are going to listen to an interview.
- Ask students to read the topics, then play the recording. Students listen and tick the topics. Let students compare answers in pairs before checking with the class.
- In feedback, ask what they heard that helped them decide.

> **ANSWERS**
>
> 1 the age of men and women (*men live to the same age as women*)
> 2 family life (*the family is so important here*)
> 4 food (*Every Sunday, the whole family eats a big meal together; eating more food like chips and burgers*)
> 5 exercise (*doing less exercise*)

Audioscript [5]

P = Presenter, D = David McLain

P: No one knows exactly the reason why some people live longer than others. Why are they so healthy? Is it their diet? Do they go to the gym more than other people? Well, one man is trying to answer these questions and that man is photographer David McLain. He's currently travelling to different places around the world with large numbers of people aged a hundred and over and asking the question: Why are they so healthy? At the moment he's working on the island of Sardinia in Italy and he's speaking to us right now on the phone. David, thank you for joining us today.

D: Hello.

P: So, first of all, tell us why you decided to visit Sardinia.

D: Well, Sardinia is an interesting place because men live to the same age as women. That isn't normal for most countries. Men normally die younger.

P: And does anyone know the reason why people live longer in Sardinia?

D: There are different ideas about this. One explanation is that the family is so important here. Every Sunday, the whole family eats a big meal together. Research shows that in countries where people live longer, the family is important.

P: I see. So, do you think people live longer in traditional societies?

D: That's an interesting question. Sardinia is quite a traditional place but, even here, the younger generation are eating more food like chips and burgers. Also young people are moving to the city, so they are doing less exercise because of their lifestyle. It'll be interesting to see what happens in Sardinia in the next twenty or thirty years …

7 [5]
- Ask students to read the sentences and decide whether they are true (T) or false (F). Then play the recording again for students to check their answers.
- Let them compare answers in pairs before checking with the class.

> **ANSWERS**
>
> 1 T (*He's currently travelling to different places around the world.*)
> 2 F (*At the moment he's working on the island of Sardinia in Italy and he's speaking to us right now on the phone.*)
> 3 F (*Sardinia is an interesting place because men live to the same age as women.*)
> 4 T (*Every Sunday the whole family eats a big meal together.*)
> 5 F (*He doesn't say that.*)
> 6 T (*… the younger generation are eating more food like chips and burgers. Also young people are moving to the city, so they are doing less exercise because of their lifestyle.*)

8
- Ask students to discuss the questions briefly in pairs first before having a whole class discussion. Encourage students to talk about whether the family is important in their country, and whether the whole family eats a big meal together, and to talk about how traditional their society is, and whether it's changing, particularly for the younger generation.

> **Background information**
>
> Sardinia (/sɑːˈdɪniə/) lies to the west of the Italian mainland, south of Corsica (which belongs to France), in the Mediterranean Sea. It has a population of 1.6 million. It's noted for its wild mountainous interior, and the beauty of the sea and coasts, with clear water and silver beaches. The capital is Cagliari in the south; the other main city is Sassari in the north west. Outside of these cities, most people live a rural life in small villages.

Grammar present simple and present continuous

9 ★ **CPT extra!** Grammar activity [before Ex. 9]
- The aim here is to start by revising present simple tense uses.
- Ask students to read the sentences and do the task individually. They can then check with a partner.
- Elicit the answers from the whole class, having them recognize the present simple forms first (sentences 3 and 4) before telling you the uses.

> **ANSWERS**
>
> Sentences 3 and 4 use the present simple tense because they talk about things that are always or generally true (3) and routines and habits (4). Note the use of *Every Sunday*, which tells us this is a regular routine.

10
- Ask students to look at the sentences again and underline the present continuous forms. Ask them to discuss how to form this tense with their partner.
- Elicit the form in feedback and write it on the board. Look at the grammar box with the class and point out how to form negatives and questions also.

26 Unit 1 Lifestyle

UNIT 1 Lifestyle

> **ANSWERS**
> You form the present continuous tense with the present simple of the verb *to be* + *-ing* form (present participle) of the main verb.

Grammar note

The examples in the grammar box and the sentences in Exercise 9 illustrate some of the spelling rules for the *-ing* form. You may wish to point these out to students.
- Verbs ending in a consonant + vowel + consonant, double the last letter of the verb and add *-ing*, e.g. *travel → travelling*.

He's currently travelling to different places around the world.
- verbs ending in *-e*, delete the final *e* and add *-ing*, e.g. *move → moving*.

Young people are moving to the city.

You could also point out that we do not use continuous forms with stative verbs, e.g. *like, love, be, have*. So we would not say: *I am liking my English classes a lot at the moment*. Instead we would use an active verb such as *enjoy*, e.g. *I am enjoying my English classes at the moment*.

11

- Read the information about the uses of the present continuous with the class. Check that everyone understands (see Grammar note below).
- Ask students to work in pairs to match sentences 1, 2 and 5 from Exercise 9 with the uses a–c.
- Check answers with the class.

> **ANSWERS**
> Sentence 1: b (to talk about something happening around now, but not necessarily at this exact moment)
> Sentence 2: c (to talk about something actually in progress now)
> Sentence 5: a (to talk about a changing situation)

Grammar note

The present continuous is used to show that something is temporary, has duration and is around now. It can be shown with a timeline:

Past   Now   Future

Refer students to page 156 for further information and practice.

> **ANSWERS TO GRAMMAR SUMMARY EXERCISES**
> 4
> 1 'm waiting 2 are; going 3 isn't working
> 4 'm writing 5 's talking 6 're building 7 are becoming
> 5
> 1 'm eating; eat 2 drives; 's driving 3 's talking; talk
> 4 'm working; work 5 'm doing; do
> 6
> 1 live 2 eat 3 say 4 is 5 is changing 6 are eating

12

- Ask students to work individually to complete the sentences. Let students compare answers in pairs before checking answers with the class. Elicit the answers as complete sentences and ask students to explain why they chose the simple or continuous form each time (see Grammar note below).

> **ANSWERS**
> 1 're learning 2 spend 3 'm checking 4 do; go
> 5 'm reading 6 isn't eating 7 don't do 8 are playing

Grammar note

1 something happening around now, but not necessarily at this exact moment
2 a habit or routine
3 something in progress now
4 asking about a habit or routine
5 something happening around now, but not necessarily at this exact moment
6 something happening around now, but not necessarily at this exact moment
7 generally or always true
8 a changing situation (Students may argue that we can use the present simple in sentence 8. This is correct if you see this as a general truth as opposed to a changing situation.)

Speaking my life
13

- Read the instructions with the class and check that everyone understands what to do.
- Ask students to produce questions using the present simple and present continuous. Circulate and check correct question formation. Let students compare answers in pairs before checking with the class.

> **ANSWERS**
> 1 a How do you usually spend your free time?
>   b Are you doing much sport these days?
> 2 a Do you often read novels?
>   b Are you reading any good books at the moment?
> 3 a Where do you normally go on holiday?
>   b Where are you planning to go this year?
> 4 a Do you speak any other languages?
>   b Are you learning any new languages?

14

- Organize the class into pairs. Ask students to take turns to ask and answer their questions from Exercise 13. Monitor and notice how well students use the tenses. Note any errors which you could write on the board at the end for students to correct.
- In feedback, ask students to tell the class some facts about their partner.

1b The secrets of a long life 27

UNIT 1 Lifestyle

Extra activity

With a young class, you could turn this into a roleplay. Ask half the class, working in pairs, to prepare questions to ask somebody famous or in the news. Ask the other half to decide which person to be and to think about what they often do and what they are doing these days. Organize students into new pairs (one from each half) to carry out their interviews.

1c Nature is good for you

Lesson at a glance
- reading: nature and health
- word focus: *feel*
- critical thinking: giving examples
- speaking: making lives healthier

Reading

1
- Ask students to work in pairs to discuss the photo and the questions.
- In feedback, elicit ideas from the class, and use this opportunity to pre-teach the meaning of some key words from this section: *brain, heart rate, outdoors, nature, 3D virtual reality* (see Vocabulary note below).

ANSWERS
Students' own answers.
The woman is enjoying a virtual reality nature experience. She's standing in a studio with pictures of nature around her.

Vocabulary note

brain = the grey organ in your head that thinks

heart rate = how fast your heart beats

outdoors/outside = not inside

nature = the world not made by man, i.e. trees, lakes, mountains, seas

3D virtual reality = *3D* means three-dimensional – *virtual* and *reality* refers to the pictures and sounds made by a computer to make the user feel they are in a real place

2 [6]
- Ask students to read the article and match the topics with the paragraphs. Let students compare answers briefly in pairs before checking with the class.
- **Optional step** The reading text is recorded. You could play the recording and ask students to read and listen.

ANSWERS
a 1   b 3   c 2

3 ★ **CPT extra!** Grammar activity [after Ex. 3]
- Read the questions with the class.
- Ask students to read the article again and find the answers. Let students compare their answers in pairs before checking with the class.

28   Unit 1   Lifestyle

UNIT 1 Lifestyle

> **ANSWERS**
> 1 It's good for us.
> 2 Humans are spending more time inside and less time outside.
> 3 The number of visitors is getting lower every year.
> 4 in a 3D virtual reality room
> 5 near parks
> 6 a new shopping mall with a large garden
> 7 in forest schools
> 8 13 million

Word focus *feel*

4
- Ask students to find and underline the three phrases with *feel* in the first paragraph of the article.
- Read the uses (1-3) with the class and elicit the first answer as an example.
- Ask students to work in pairs to match the remaining two phrases with the uses. Check answers as a class and try to elicit other examples for the uses (see Vocabulary note below).

> **ANSWERS**
> 1 feel better 2 feel like going 3 feel that

Vocabulary note

1 To talk about your emotions or health: *feel better/ worse, feel tired, feel ill, feel sick, feel bored, feel under the weather*
2 To talk about wanting to do something: *I feel like going out later; I feel like singing.*
3 To talk about an opinion: *I feel (that) …*

5
- Ask students to work individually to complete the questions. Let them compare answers in pairs before checking with the class.

> **ANSWERS**
> 1 like 2 that 3 better

6
- Give students a minute or two to think about the questions in Exercise 5.
- Ask students to work in pairs to discuss the questions. Monitor and help with vocabulary as necessary.

Extra activity

Write the following sentence starters on the board. Ask students to complete them, then discuss them in pairs or small groups:
1 *I feel that the government …*
2 *I often feel tired when …*
3 *At the weekend, I usually feel … because …*
4 *… always makes me feel …*
5 *Right now, I feel like …*

Critical thinking *giving examples*

7
- Read the information with the class and elicit the answers to the questions.

> **ANSWERS**
> Sentence b has the main idea.
> Sentences a and c give examples.

8 ★ **CPT extra!** Critical thinking activity [after Ex. 8]
- Ask students to work individually to find the sentence with the main idea and the sentences with examples in paragraphs 2 and 3 of the article. Ask them to underline the words and phrases for giving examples.
- Let students compare answers in pairs before checking with the class.
- In feedback, build up a list of words and phrases on the board for giving examples and point out how they are used (see Vocabulary note below).

> **ANSWERS**
> Paragraph 2
> Main sentence:
> As a result, some doctors are studying the connection between nature and health …
> Example sentences:
> One example of this is the work of Dr Matilda van den Bosch in Sweden.
> Another good example of how nature is good for health comes from Canada.
> Paragraph 3
> Main sentence:
> Because of studies like these, some countries and cities want nature to be part of people's everyday life.
> Example sentences:
> In Dubai, for example, there are plans for a new shopping mall with a large garden …
> In some countries such as Switzerland, 'forest schools' are popular …
> And South Korea is another good example; it has new forests near its cities …

Vocabulary note

We can use *For example,* to introduce an example, or one of a number of other set phrases:
   An/One example (of this) is …
   Another / A further / A good example (of this) is …
Alternatively, we can use a phrase at the end of sentences:
   The number of visitors is going down, for example.
   The reduction in the number of visitors is an example of this.
We use *such as* + noun / noun phrase to give an example.
   In cities such as London, …

1c Nature is good for you

UNIT 1 Lifestyle

9

- Read the sentence beginnings with the class. Give students a minute or so to prepare their endings using examples from their own life. You could start them off by eliciting two or three possible ideas from the class or by providing your own, personal, model answers.
- Organize the class into new pairs or small groups. Ask students to take turns to share their sentences. Monitor and notice any errors or examples of good language.

> **EXAMPLE ANSWERS**
>
> Students' own answers. Some suggestions:
> 1 I relax in my free time in different ways. For example, I sometimes go out with friends, but sometimes I stay at home and watch TV.
> 2 My home town has some places with trees and nature, such as the park in the city centre, and the national zoo.
> 3 There are some beautiful national parks in my country. A good example is Millennium Park.

Extra activity

Write the following on the board and ask students to personalize them with examples:
> We have great beaches in my country.
> There are a lot of things to see in my city.

Speaking my life

10

- Ask students to work in groups of four. Read the instructions and the ideas with the class and check that everyone understands what to do.
- In their groups, students decide on one extra idea.
- In feedback, ask groups for their extra ideas and decide which ideas are the best.

> **EXAMPLE ANSWERS**
>
> Students' own answers. Some possibilities include: install an open-air gym in the park; build an outdoor swimming pool, provide an all-weather football pitch.

11

- Ask each group to discuss the ideas and decide on the best.
- **Optional step** Make one person in each group the 'chair'. It's their job to open the debate, make sure everybody has a chance to speak, and to summarize and choose the best idea. It's also their job to present the group's decision to the class at the end.

12

- Ask each group to present their idea to the class. Then open up the debate for a whole class discussion. You might want to end with a vote for the best idea.

Extra activity

In groups or open class, ask students to give examples of how their home city has changed to be healthier and more natural in their lifetimes. Alternatively, you could ask students to prepare and give a presentation on this topic. The preparation could be done for homework.

UNIT 1 Lifestyle

1d At the doctor's

Lesson at a glance
- vocabulary: medical problems
- pronunciation: one or two syllables?
- real life: talking about illness

Vocabulary medical problems

1 ★ **CPT extra!** Lead-in activity [before Ex. 1]

- **Optional step** With books closed, mime some of the medical problems taught in this section. Ask students to write down as many as they can (in English or L1). Then ask students to tell their partner which ones they already know or can describe in English (see Vocabulary note below).
- Ask students to work in pairs to match the people with the medical problems. Elicit the first answer with the class as an example.
- Encourage students to make guesses and use prior knowledge. When checking the answers, use mime to check the meaning.

ANSWERS

1 b   2 c   3 g   4 a   5 h   6 f   7 d   8 e

Vocabulary note

Note the fixed collocations:

a runny nose (= you can't stop 'fluid' coming out of it)

a sore throat (= it hurts when you swallow)

We use *ache* (= a pain) with various parts of the body (note also *toothache*). We always say *a headache*, but usually don't use the article with other 'aches'.

2
- Ask students to work individually to categorize the medical problems in Exercise 1. Let them compare their answers in pairs.
- There are no fixed answers so, in feedback, ask students to justify their answers.

EXAMPLE ANSWERS

1 I go to bed: headache, stomach ache, a temperature (perhaps backache)
2 I take medicine or pills: headache (paracetamol, aspirin); earache (ear drops); stomach ache; sore throat (throat sweets / lozenges); bad cough (cough syrup)
3 I go to the pharmacy or see my doctor: you might go to the pharmacy for all these – backache, earache, very bad stomach ache, and perhaps a high temperature might mean going to see the doctor.

Pronunciation one or two syllables?

3a [7]

- **Optional step** Establish what a syllable is by writing *toothache* on the board and asking students to say how many syllables there are (two) – point out that a syllable is a single sound.
- Play the recording. Students listen and underline the stressed syllables in the two syllable words.

Audioscript [7] (and answers)

ache (1 syllable)

<u>head</u>ache (2)

ear (1)

<u>ear</u>ache (2)

<u>sto</u>mach (2)

throat (1)

cough (1)

b [7]

- Play the recording again. Students listen and repeat (see Pronunciation note below).

Pronunciation note

Note the difficult pronunciation of some of these words: ache /eɪk/, ear /ɪə/, stomach /ˈstʌmək/, sore /sɔː/, throat /θrəʊt/, cough /kɒf/.

Note that the main stress is on the adjectives in the compound nouns: <u>sore</u> throat, <u>runny</u> nose, <u>bad</u> cough.

Note that the main stress is on the first syllable in compounds with *ache*: <u>head</u>ache, <u>sto</u>mach ache.

Real life talking about illness

4 [8]

- Explain that students are going to hear a conversation in a pharmacy and another one at a doctor's.
- Play the recording. Students listen and note the medical problems they hear for each conversation. Let them compare their answers in pairs before checking with the class.

ANSWERS

Conversation 1: a runny nose and a sore throat
Conversation 2: earache and temperature

Audioscript [8]

Conversation 1

P = Pharmacist, C = Customer

P: Hello, how can I help you?

C: Hello. I've got a runny nose and a sore throat. I feel terrible.

P: Have you got a temperature as well?

C: No, it's normal.

1d At the doctor's   31

UNIT 1 Lifestyle

P: Well, you should take this medicine twice a day. It's good for a sore throat.

C: Thanks.

P: And try drinking hot water with honey and lemon. That helps.

C: OK. I will.

P: Oh, and why don't you buy some cough sweets? They should help. If you still feel ill in a few days, see a doctor.

Conversation 2

D = Doctor, P = Patient

D: Good morning. So, what's the problem?

P: I've got earache in this ear. It's really painful.

D: Let me have a look. … ah … yes, it's very red in there. What about the other one?

P: It feels fine.

D: Hmm. It's a bit red as well. Do you feel sick at all?

P: No, not really.

D: Let me check your temperature. … Yes, it's higher than normal. OK, I'll give you something for your earache. You need to take one of these pills twice a day for seven days. They might make you sleepy so go to bed if you have to. And if you still feel ill, then come back and see me again.

5 [8]

- Ask students to read the advice and try to remember whether it was used in the first or second conversation.
- Play the recording again. Students listen and write the number of the conversations. Let students compare their answers in pairs before checking with the class.
- **Optional step** Ask students to work in pairs to practise the conversations in audioscript 8 on page 181 of the Student's Book.

> **ANSWERS**
> a 1 b 2 c 1 d 2 e 1

6

- Ask students to match the sentence halves from the conversations. Encourage them to use the expressions in the box for talking about illness to help them. Let students compare answers in pairs before checking with the class.
- **Optional step** Drill the sentences for pronunciation (see Pronunciation note below). Ask students to close their books. Read three or four phrases out and ask the class to repeat chorally and individually. Get students to really exaggerate the intonation – English has a very broad intonation range.

> **ANSWERS**
> 1 g 2 a 3 e 4 f 5 b 6 c 7 h 8 i 9 d

> **Pronunciation note**
> When giving strong advice, the intonation starts high, then rises, then falls: 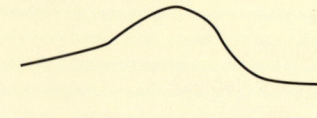
>
> *You should take this medicine.*

7

- Organize the class into new pairs. Ask students to decide who is A, and who is B. Read the instructions with the class and check that everyone understands what to do.
- It's a good idea to prepare students for this roleplay. You could ask them to write dialogues first, using expressions from the lesson. Tell them to practise reading their dialogue, then to turn over the written dialogue and try to remember and improvise it. Alternatively, ask students to choose and match expressions they could use for each dialogue. Then ask them to improvise dialogues, using the expressions they chose.
- As students speak, circulate and monitor their performance. Note down errors students make and, in feedback, write errors on the board and ask students to correct them.
- Students then change roles and have a new conversation. They could do this with a new partner.

> **Extra activity**
> Ask students to prepare and practise another dialogue between a doctor and patient using different vocabulary. You could ask pairs to record their dialogue and listen back to it critically, or ask them to perform their dialogue in front of another pair, and ask for feedback on their accuracy and pronunciation.

UNIT 1 Lifestyle

1e Personal information

Lesson at a glance
- writing: filling in a form
- writing skill: information on forms

Writing filling in a form

1
- Ask students to work in pairs to discuss the questions. In feedback, elicit ideas and write them on the board.

> **EXAMPLE ANSWERS**
> Students' own answers
> Some possible types of form: registration form at school, college or university, job application form, passport or visa application form
> Information often on forms: first name, middle name, surname, title, age, gender, date of birth, address, postcode, telephone number, email address

2
- Ask students to look at the two forms and decide what each is for. Let students compare answers in pairs before checking with the class. Explain any new vocabulary and point out the acronym *DOB* for date of birth.

> **ANSWERS**
> A medical form and a visa application form

Writing skill information on forms

3a
- Ask students to match the questions (1–7) with the headings on the forms where you write the information. Let them compare their answers in pairs before checking with the class.

> **ANSWERS**
> 1 Marital status
> 2 Current medications
> 3 No. of dependents
> 4 Country of origin
> 5 Place of birth
> 6 Contact details of person in case of emergency
> 7 Middle initial

b ★ **CPT extra!** Writing activity [after Ex. 3]
- Look at the example with the class. Ask students to work individually to answer the questions. Let them compare their answers in pairs and check answers on page 155 before discussing as a class.

4
- Ask students to work in pairs to design a form for new students at a language school. First, ask them to brainstorm all the information the form needs to ask, then to order the list in a logical order to make the form. Monitor unobtrusively and help when necessary.

> **EXAMPLE ANSWERS**
> first name, middle name, surname, title, age, gender, date of birth, address, postcode, telephone number, email address, contact details of person in case of emergency
> nationality, first language, level of English
> needs, interests, length of stay

5
- Students exchange forms with another pair. Ask pairs to check the form using the questions as a guide. Then pairs give the pair who designed the form feedback.
- In feedback, agree a 'perfect' form as a class.

> **Extra activity**
> Once the class have agreed on a 'perfect' form, ask students to write up and complete the form with personal information. They could do this for homework.

1e **Personal information** 33

UNIT 1 Lifestyle

1f My local park

Before you watch

1 ⭐ **CPT extra!** Lead-in activity [before Ex. 1]

- **Optional step** Start by asking students to describe the photo. Ask: *What can you see? Where are they? How do they feel?*
- Ask students to work in pairs or small groups to discuss the questions. Elicit a few ideas from the class in feedback.

> EXAMPLE ANSWER
>
> Students' own answers.
>
> Possible answers include: it's free, it's healthy, it's a good place to relax or do exercise, it's nature in the middle of a town or city, children can play there safely, it's a nice place for a picnic, you can feed the birds.

> **Background information**
>
> **Park Güell**, located on the northern face of Carmel Hill in Barcelona, was named after Eusebi Güell, the entrepreneur who paid for the construction of the park. It was largely designed by the famous architect Antoni Gaudí, the face of Catalan modernism, who also designed the Sagrada Família cathedral in Barcelona. The photo shows Gaudí's designs and mosaics on the steps up to the main terrace. The park was built at the start of the twentieth century. It provides great views of the city.
>
> **Barcelona** is the second largest city in Spain and the capital of the region of Catalonia.

> **Teacher development**
>
> **Using the photographs in *Life***
>
> *Life* aims to use large, interesting photographs throughout each unit. Notably, there is a half-page photo on the introductory page of each unit, large photos to go with most reading and listening texts, and a full-page photo to go with the video section. All these photographs are sourced from *National Geographic*'s vast catalogue of images taken by some of the world's greatest photographers (many of whom are referenced on the page with their photos). The aim is for the photos to be both illustrative and informative. They stimulate students' interest in the theme and topics and provide information that will be useful in their understanding of texts that they read in the lesson.
> You can often use the photo to do the following:
>
> - To get students talking and to personalize the topic, ask questions such as *What can you see?* and *What are they doing?* but also ask questions such as *How does the photo make you feel? Where did they take the photo? What are the people in the photo thinking?*
> - To get students interacting and sharing ideas and opinions, ask students to say what they expect to read or listen.
> - To introduce vocabulary, sometimes the photos will provide visual back-up to help you teach key words and phrases.
> - To preview language structures that will come up in the unit and to find out how well students can already use them, design your lead-in questions to use the tenses or grammar forms that have or will come up in the unit.

Here are some other things you can do to use *National Geographic* photos usefully:

- It isn't difficult to find the photos in the Student's Book online. Find them and project them using your classroom technology. This way you can bring this stage of the lesson off the page.
- Use other photos online to support your teaching. You don't have to use the photos in the book.
- Get students to research photographers or types of images they come across in the lessons. Ask students to describe other photos they find.

Key vocabulary

2

- Encourage students to use the context to guess the meanings of the words in bold.
- Ask students to work in pairs to discuss the words and match them with the definitions.
- **Optional step** It's a good idea to show the pronunciation of these key words – students have to hear them in continuous speech on the video. You could say the words and ask students to repeat.

> ANSWERS
>
> 1 d   2 b   3 e   4 a   5 f   6 c

> **Vocabulary note**
>
> *no matter what* = 'no matter' means 'it's not important' and can be combined with other words (*no matter who/when/where/whether*, etc)
>
> *pram* = an abbreviation of the old-fashioned word 'perambulator', a pram is used to describe the four-wheeled device used to carry babies when they are small and lying down; when babies can sit up and face forward, they are carried in a pushchair
>
> A *walkway* is used for a path that is man-made and has a specific route with a destination
>
> *blossom* = provide examples such as 'apple blossom' (*blossom* is used as a verb to mean 'grow as a person', become 'more confident')

While you watch

3 🎥 [1.1]

- Ask students to read the seven sentences carefully and check any difficult words.
- Play the video. Students watch and number the sentences in order. Let students compare their answers in pairs before checking with the class.

> ANSWERS
>
> 1 b   2 a   3 d   4 e   5 c   6 f   7 g

34 Unit 1 Lifestyle

UNIT 1 Lifestyle

4 [1.1]
- Ask students to work in pairs and decide who is A and who is B. Tell them to look at the table and see if they can remember any of the missing information.
- Play the video again. Student A completes column 1 and Student B completes column 2 of the table. Don't check answers at this stage.

Videoscript 1.1

0.00–0.31 (woman with dog) We come to the park very often, every weekend in fact, usually after lunchtime, around 2 p.m. We like coming to this park because there's a really nice walkway around the park, there are also a lot of dogs for Jasmine to play with, there are beautiful trees everywhere, so it's really nice no matter what time of year.

0.32–1.12 (cyclist) I come to the park every day. I cycle to work through the park from my home to my office, and then on some days, sunny days particularly, I like to come here and relax in my lunch break. I like this part of the park actually, it's quite high up and there's this beautiful house here, and I think that must be a great place to live because they have such a good view down onto the park.

1.12–1.48 (elderly couple) We come here when we're in the area. When our … when we were a young family and we had children we used to come and push our prams round here, and so it has happy memories. We like coming here because it's much nicer than the roadway, it's a pretty park and we like to see the different seasons.

1.49–2.13 (language student) My name is Ahmed, I am from Saudi Arabia. I am here to study English language to prepare for my academic studies. I go through the park every day, and sometimes I spend some time with my friends. I like relaxing in this park.

2.14–2.40 (jogger) I come to the park quite often. I come here about twice a week. I like to go jogging and I like to do exercise here. I like coming to the park because it's nice and quiet, there are lots of plants and trees, and it's overall a good place to do exercise.

2.41–end (woman) I try and come to the park every day. I love coming to this particular park because the trees are so beautiful. There are always wild flowers, depending on the season, and lots of blossom on the trees. It's lovely to look at.

5 [1.1]
- Ask students to share their information with their partner to complete the whole table.
- Play the video again. Students complete any missing information following their discussion, then check answers with the class.

ANSWERS

Student A:
  1 often 2 weekend 3 2 4 every day 5 break
  6 children 7 happy 8 every day 9 sometimes
  10 quite often 11 twice 12 every day

Student B:
  1 dogs 2 trees 3 high 4 house 5 road 6 pretty
  7 seasons 8 relaxing 9 go 10 exercise 11 plants
  12 flowers 13 look at

After you watch

6
- You could ask students to work with a new partner. Read the instructions with the class and check that everyone understands what to do.
- Students cover the notes for the people, leaving only their faces showing. Student A then chooses to be one of the people from the video and answers Student B's questions. As students speak, monitor and notice any errors or examples of good language use you hear.

7 ★ **CPT extra!** Video activity [after Ex. 7]
- Students repeat the activity in Exercise 6 with Student B choosing to be one of the people and answering Student A's questions.
- At the end, provide feedback by writing four or five sentences students said with errors in them on the board, and asking students to correct them with their partner.

1f My local park 35

UNIT 1 Lifestyle

UNIT 1 Review and memory booster ★ CPT extra! Language games

Memory Booster activities

Exercises 3, 6 and 8 are Memory Booster activities. For more information about these activities and how they benefit students, see page 10.

I can … tick boxes

As an alternative to students simply ticking the *I can …* boxes, you could ask them to give themselves a score from 1 to 4 (1 = not very confident; 4 = very confident) for each language area. If students score 1 or 2 for a language area, refer them to additional practice activities in the Workbook and Grammar summary exercises.

Grammar

1

- Ask students to work individually to complete the article by choosing the correct verb forms. Let students compare answers in pairs before checking with the class.

ANSWERS

1 works 2 he's taking 3 They're swimming 4 like
5 doesn't seem 6 it feels

2

- Ask students to work individually to write the sentences with the expression in the correct place. Point out that there is more than one correct answer for three of the sentences.

ANSWER

1 I **rarely** play computer and video games.
2 We're studying Spanish **at the moment**. / **At the moment**, we're studying Spanish.
3 My family does sport **every weekend**. / **Every weekend**, my family does sport.
4 All my friends are working **these days**. / **These days** all my friends are working.

3 >> MB

- Ask students to rewrite the sentences in Exercise 2 so that they're true for them. Monitor and help with vocabulary as necessary.

Vocabulary

4

- Ask students to work individually to complete the sentences.

ANSWERS

1 fall asleep 2 take a break 3 work long hours
4 get up late 5 TV; watch

5

- Ask students to cross out the word that doesn't belong in each group.

ANSWERS

1 relaxing 2 asleep 3 swimming 4 ache

6 >> MB

- Ask students to work in pairs and write five sentences using the verbs in Exercises 4 and 5. Monitor and help with vocabulary as necessary.
- Ask pairs to work with another pair. They take turns to read out their sentences, but missing out the verb. The other pair guesses the missing verb.

ANSWERS

Students' own answers

Real life

7

- Ask students to work individually to choose the correct option.

ANSWERS

1 How do 2 well 3 sore 4 Have you got
5 Try 6 should

8 >> MB

- Ask students to work in pairs. Ask them to look at the pictures and answer the questions.

ANSWERS

1 She's got backache. He's got a headache. She's got stomach ache.
2 Student's own answers. Some possibilities include: She should see a doctor. He should take an aspirin. She should go to bed.

36 Unit 1 Lifestyle

Unit 2 Competitions

Opener

1
- Ask students to look at the photo and the caption. Ask them to work in pairs to discuss the questions. Elicit a few ideas from the class in feedback.
- **Optional step** Ask students if they've ever taken part in a competition like the one in the photo. Ask any students with experiences to share them with the class.

> **ANSWERS**
> Students' own ideas. The photo shows a large group of swimmers swimming in open water (one of the three disciplines of the Ironman triathlon).

2 [9]
- Ask students to read the questions, then play the recording. Students listen and answer the questions.
- Let them compare answers in pairs before checking with the class. Check that students know the distance for a marathon (42 kilometres / 26 miles).

> **ANSWERS**
> 1 three
> 2 they swim 3.86 kilometres and cycle 180 kilometres
> 3 around one thousand, nine hundred people compete

Audioscript [9]

An Ironman competition has three different races. In the swimming race, the competitors swim for 3.86 kilometres. Then they cycle for 180 kilometres, and finally they run a marathon at the end. The world final of the Ironman Championship is in Hawaii and it's very competitive. Every year, around one thousand, nine hundred people compete against each other in front of thousands of spectators.

> **Background information**
> The **Ironman** is the longest and toughest of triathlons. By contrast, the Olympic triathlon is much shorter (swim: 1,500 m; bike: 40 km; run: 10 km).
> The World Triathlon Corporation organizes over twenty Ironman Triathlon competitions throughout the year. They take place all over the world and lead to qualification for the Ironman World Championship on Big Island, Hawaii. This Ironman event was first held in 1978.

3 ★ **CPT extra!** Listening activity [after Ex. 3]
- Ask students to work in pairs to match the words with the parts of speech. In feedback, ask students to tell the class what they notice about the endings on the words (see Vocabulary note below).
- **Optional step** Drill the words, pointing out the stress (see Teacher development below): comp<u>e</u>te, comp<u>e</u>titive, compet<u>i</u>tion, comp<u>e</u>titor.

> **ANSWERS**
> 1 a verb: compete
> 2 an adjective: competitive
> 3 a noun (thing): competition
> 4 a noun (person): competitor

> **Vocabulary note**
> The suffixes used in wordbuilding often reveal the part of speech:
> - *-ive* is a common adjective suffix
> - *-tion* is a common suffix used with nouns
> - *-er* or *-or* are often used with people.

4
- Ask students to complete the questions with the words from Exercise 3.
- Then ask students to take turns to ask and answer with their partner. They should respond with answers that are true for them.

> **ANSWERS**
> 1 competitor 2 compete 3 competition 4 competitive

> **Extra activity**
> Ask students to say what the nouns, verbs or adjectives of other words on this opener page are, e.g.
> sport (noun): sporty (adjective)
> swim (verb): swimming (noun – activity), swimmer (noun – person)
> cycle (verb): cycling (noun – activity), cyclist (noun – person)

> **Teacher development**
> **Drilling words for pronunciation**
> At this level, students need practice in hearing and repeating new words, while paying attention to stress and pronunciation. Here are some suggestions:
> - Ask students to listen and say words after your spoken model. For example, in the lesson above, ask students to close their books. Say *compete*, and ask students to repeat. Then say *competitive*, and ask them to repeat that word, and so on. Speak naturally but clearly. Make sure students aren't reading the words as they repeat.
> - Move from choral to individual repetition when drilling. Say *compete* and ask the class to repeat by using a sweeping gesture of your open arms. Then direct an open hand to individual students in the class at random, so that students have a chance to say the word. Be strict and correct any poor or inaccurate pronunciations.
> - Use visual techniques to support students when drilling. For example, to show the stress is on the second syllable of *compete*, beat the air as you say the second syllable. To show there are four syllables in *competitive*, and that the stress is on the second syllable, hold up four fingers of your left hand, and count them with the index finger of your right, making sure that you indicate the strong stress by tapping the second finger of the left hand harder than the others.

37

UNIT 2 Competitions

2a Crazy competitions!

Lesson at a glance
- reading: crazy competitions
- vocabulary: sport
- grammar: verbs for rules
- speaking: rules for a competition

Reading

1 ★ **CPT extra!** Lead-in activity [before Ex. 1]
- Ask students to work in pairs to predict from the title and photographs why the competitions are crazy. Elicit ideas in feedback. Use the opportunity to pre-teach key words using the photographs: *shopping cart, wheels, mud*.

> **EXAMPLE ANSWERS**
>
> Students' own answers. They may suggest that running with a shopping cart, and playing a game in a field of mud are 'crazy'.

2 🎧 [10]
- Ask students to read the article and find the answers to the questions. Let them compare answers in pairs before checking with the class.
- **Optional step** The reading text is recorded. You could play the recording and ask students to read and listen.

> **ANSWERS**
>
> a race between different teams: the Idiotarod
> a match between two teams: the Mud Bowl Championship

3
- Ask students to read the six sentences and match them with the two competitions in the article (A for the Idiotarod and B for the Mud Bowl Championship). Then tell them to read the article again more carefully to confirm their answers.
- Let students compare answers in pairs before checking with the class.

> **ANSWERS**
>
> 1 A 2 B 3 A 4 A 5 both 6 B

> **Background information**
>
> The **Idiotarod** is a humorous take on the more serious Iditarod, a long distance sled race that takes place annually in Alaska. The first Idiotarod was in San Francisco in 1994. Note the use of the word 'Idiot' in the name.
> **Mud Bowl** is a take on Super Bowl – the name of the final match of the American Pro Football season.

4
- Ask students to discuss the questions in pairs or small groups. In feedback, ask students to describe any crazy competitions they can think of in their country.

> **EXAMPLE ANSWERS**
>
> Students' own ideas. Crazy competitions are not the sole preserve of Americans. You might want to mention the annual Cheese Rolling event in England (people chase a large cheese down a hill), or the wife carrying race in Finland.

Vocabulary sport

5 ★ **CPT extra!** Vocabulary activity [after Ex. 5]
- Start by eliciting the first answer from the class as an example.
- Ask students to work individually to complete the sentences using the highlighted words in the article.
- Let them compare answers in pairs before checking with the class.

> **ANSWERS**
>
> 1 race 2 players 3 teams 4 match 5 goals
> 6 line 7 winner

> **Vocabulary note**
>
> Note the common collocations: *score a goal, cross the (finishing) line, win a race/match*.

6
- Ask students to work with a new partner to discuss the questions.
- In feedback, build up a list of words and phrases on the board.

> **EXAMPLE ANSWERS**
>
> 1 Long-distance running races (e.g. marathon; 10,000 metres), sprints (100 metres), cycle races (*Tour de France*), swimming races (100 m freestyle), car races (*F1 Grand Prix*), horse races (derby)
> 2 football (11), basketball (5), rugby union (15), ice hockey (6), volleyball (6)
> 3 Students' own answers
> 4 You score goals in football, rugby (but only by kicking the ball through the posts), hockey, handball, water polo. You score points in basketball (two points for a basket), rugby union (five points for a try, three points for a penalty or drop goal, two points for a conversion), badminton, tennis, volleyball, American football (six points for a touchdown, three points for a field goal, one point for a touchdown conversion).

38 Unit 2 Competitions

UNIT 2 Competitions

Grammar verbs for rules

7

- Ask students to look at the sentences in the grammar box. Note that all the sentences are from the *Crazy competitions* article.
- Ask students to complete the explanations with the bold verbs from the grammar box. Monitor students and notice any problems they have.
- Let students compare answers in pairs before checking with the class.

> **ANSWERS**
> 1 must, have to 2 can 3 don't have to 4 mustn't, can't

Refer students to page 158 for further information and practice.

> **ANSWERS TO GRAMMAR SUMMARY EXERCISES**
> **1**
> 1 a 2 b 3 a 4 c 5 b 6 c
> **2**
> 1 mustn't 2 don't have to 3 must 4 must
> 5 must / have to 6 don't have to
> **3**
> 1 have to / must 2 can't 3 mustn't 4 can't
> 5 don't have to 6 have to

8

- Ask students to choose the correct options. Elicit the first answer to get students started. Let students compare their answers in pairs before checking with the class.
- In feedback, ask students to justify their answers by referring to the explanations in Exercise 7.
- **Optional step** Ask students to listen and repeat some of the sentences. This practises the pronunciation of the modal verbs (see Pronunciation note below).

> **ANSWERS**
> 1 have to 2 mustn't 3 can 4 must 5 can
> 6 has to 7 don't have to

> **Grammar note**
>
> **Form**
>
> Verbs used for rules are modal auxiliary verbs (*can, must, can't, mustn't*) or semi-modals (*have to, don't have to*).
>
> Modal auxiliaries are followed by the infinitive without *to*, and function as auxiliary verbs (e.g. *I can …, Can I …?, I can't …*). *Have to* uses *do/don't* as an auxiliary (e.g. *I have to …, Do I have to …?*).
>
> Students at this level may misapply the form rules of regular verbs to modals: ~~They don't can to change the wheels~~.

> **Meaning and use**
>
> Many students will avoid using modals if they are not common in their language. Spanish speakers, for example, may prefer to say: *It's necessary to …, It's not permitted to …*, etc. Encourage students to avoid these over-formal ways of saying things.
>
> Modal verbs are confusing.
> - *Must* and *have to* mean more or less the same, but the negative forms *mustn't* and *don't have to* have opposite meanings.
> - *Can* and *must* have very different meanings, but *can't* and *mustn't* have similar meanings.
>
> Encourage students to see *can, can't, must* and *mustn't* as four very different verbs, each with their own range of uses depending on the context.
>
> Be aware of problems that arise from your students' own L1, too. In German, for example, *mustn't* looks similar to the German way of expressing *don't have to*. In a monolingual class, explore how English differs from the way students would express permission and obligation in their L1.

> **Pronunciation note**
>
> Note that *can't* is stressed (/kɑːnt/ /) but *can* (/kən/) is unstressed in these sentences.
>
> Note the weak /ə/ sound at the end of *have to* and *has to*, and the way the 've' at the end of *have* changes to a /f/ sound: /ˈhæftə/.
>
> The /t/ sound in the middle of *mustn't* is silent (ˈmʌsənt/) and the /t/ sound at the end of *must* and *mustn't* (and *can't*) is not pronounced in natural speech when these words are followed by a verb that starts with a consonant sound.

9 ★ **CPT extra!** Grammar activity [after Ex. 9]

- **Optional step** Ask students to predict the competition from the photo.
- Ask students to read the text quickly and to say what type of competition is described. Make sure students know the words *beard* /bɪə(r)d/ (= hair on the chin), and *moustache* /məˈstɑːʃ/ (= hair on the top lip above the mouth).
- Ask students to complete the description. Let them compare with a partner before checking answers with the class (see Grammar note below).

> **ANSWERS**
> 1 must 2 have to 3 can't 4 can 5 don't have to

> **Grammar note**
>
> 1 and 2: the rules say this is obligatory
> 3: it isn't allowed in the rules
> 4: it's allowed in the rules
> 5: not obligatory, but is allowed by the rules

2a Crazy competitions! 39

UNIT 2 Competitions

Speaking my life

10
- Organize the class into new pairs. Read the instructions with the class and check that everyone understands what to do.
- Start by eliciting sports or competitions students could choose. Then ask each pair to decide on one.
- Ask students to work together to produce a set of rules for their sport or competition. Monitor and help with ideas and vocabulary, and make sure students are using verbs for rules accurately.

11
- Organize the class into groups of four by putting pairs together. Ask students to take turns to explain their rules.
- In feedback, ask students to share any interesting or unusual rules they heard. Use the opportunity to write any errors you heard on the board. Ask students to work in pairs to correct them.

Extra activity

Organize the class into pairs. Ask Student A in each pair to sit facing the board. Ask Student B to face away from the board. Write ten sports in a column on the board (e.g. basketball, tennis, golf, boxing). Student A must describe the rules of each sport. Student B must guess each sport. Find out which pair can describe and guess each sport first.

2b Winning and losing

Lesson at a glance
- wordbuilding: suffixes
- listening: competitive sports
- grammar: -ing form
- pronunciation: /ŋ/
- speaking: opinions about sport

Wordbuilding suffixes

1 ★ CPT extra! Background information [after Ex. 1]
- Ask students to look at the photos. Note that they don't need to read the captions at this stage.
- Ask them to work in pairs to match the people in the photos with the words in the box.
- In feedback, ask students to give you an example of another famous tennis player, runner, footballer and athlete.

ANSWERS
Usain Bolt: runner/athlete (sprinter)
Jessica Ennis-Hill: athlete (heptathlete – she competed in the heptathlon in which competitors do seven athletics events)
Lionel Messi: footballer
Venus Williams: tennis player

Background information

Jamaican **Usain Bolt** (b. 1986) is the world's greatest sprinter. He won gold in the 100 metres and 200 metres in the Olympic Games of 2008, 2012 and 2016.

Briton **Jessica Ennis-Hill** (b. 1986) won gold in the heptathlon at the 2012 Olympics and silver in 2016. She retired in 2016.

Argentinian **Lionel Messi** (b. 1987) is regularly considered to be the world's greatest footballer. He plays for Barcelona.

American **Venus Williams** (b. 1980) has won seven Grand Slam singles titles and four Olympic gold medals in tennis. Her younger sister Serena is even more successful – she has over twenty Grand Slam singles titles.

A **heptathlon** consists of the following events: 100 metres hurdles, high jump, shot put, 200 metres, long jump, javelin throw and 800 metres.

2
- Read the information in the wordbuilding box as a class.
- Ask students to work in pairs to add the correct suffixes (see Vocabulary note below).
- **Optional step** Drill some of the words for pronunciation. Point out the strong stress in the following: <u>foot</u>baller, <u>gym</u>nast, <u>ath</u>lete, <u>base</u>ball <u>play</u>er.

UNIT 2 Competitions

> **ANSWERS**
> 1 boxer 2 motorcyclist 3 baseball player 4 swimmer
> 5 chess player 6 racing driver 7 gymnast 8 surfer

Refer students to Workbook page 19 for further practice.

> **Vocabulary note**
> Some words can add either -er or player: *footballer / football player, cricketer / cricket player, basketballer / basketball player.*

> **Extra activity**
> Ask students to work in pairs to make as long a list as they can of sportspeople that end with -er (e.g. *rider, jogger, sprinter, boxer, wrestler, fencer, javelin thrower, cricketer, basketballer*).

3 ★ **CPT extra!** Wordbuilding activity [after Ex. 3]
- Ask students to work in pairs or small groups to describe famous sportspeople from their country.

Listening
4
- Ask students to work in pairs to read the quotes with the photos and discuss the questions.
- In feedback, ask: *Which quote shows your opinion?*

> **ANSWERS**
> Students' own ideas.
> Some may argue that winning is important because sport is about competition, trying to win gives you an aim and focus to train hard and get better, and being a winner gives you confidence and a feeling of success.
> Some may argue that winning is not important because sport is about taking part, having fun, being with friends, improving yourself and getting fit.

5 🔊 [11]
- Read the three sentences with the class. Make sure students understand *non-competitive sport* (= a sport where nobody wins or loses).
- Play the recording. Students listen and complete the sentences with the number of the speaker.
- Let students compare answers in pairs before checking with the class. In feedback, ask what they heard that helped them decide. Ask students to say which speaker they agree with and why.

> **ANSWERS**
> a Speaker 2 thinks non-competitive sport is a good idea.
> b Speaker 1 thinks competitive sport is a good idea in schools.
> c Speaker 3 thinks sport in schools is a good idea but there can be a problem.

Audioscript 🔊 [11]

1 Learning to win and lose is important in a child's education because it teaches you about life. So I think competitive sports in schools are good for teaching children. They're also good for their physical health, because when children try to win, they work harder and get more exercise. The other good thing about competitive sports is that you learn to work well in teams when you play in matches. Competitions are a great lesson in teamwork.

2 Some children aren't good at sport, so when school sports are competitive, they always lose. That's really bad for the child. The fact is that not all children are the same and some children don't like doing sport. I think schools in my country should be more like the schools in Finland. They get good results but they aren't competitive and they don't have competitive sports either. So when a child can't do a sport very well, that's OK as long as they do their best and try hard at everything they do.

3 We have a sports day at my school and the children love it. Yes, winning is nice for a child, but the whole day is also a lot of fun. So, overall, I don't think there's a problem with having competitive sports in school – the problem is with some of the mothers and fathers. Some parents hate losing and they get very competitive. When there's a race or a match, some of them shout at their kids. They think it's the Olympic Games or something!

6
- Look at the first two sentences with the class and check that everyone understands what to do.
- Ask students to read the remaining sentences and decide whether they are opinions for (F) or against (A) competitive sports in schools. Let students compare answers in pairs before checking with the class.

> **ANSWERS**
> 1 F 2 A 3 F 4 A 5 F 6 F 7 A 8 A 9 F

7 🔊 [11]
- Play the recording again. Students listen and note which speaker expresses which opinion from Exercise 6. Point out that the speakers don't use exactly the same words as the opinions in the previous exercise. Students will have to listen for paraphrases of the same ideas.
- Let students compare answers in pairs before checking answers with the class.

> **ANSWERS**
> Person 1: 1, 3, 5, 6
> Person 2: 2, 4, 8
> Person 3: 7, 9

2b Winning and losing 41

UNIT 2 Competitions

8

- Ask students to work in groups of four or five to discuss the opinions in Exercise 6 and answer the questions. Monitor as students speak and note interesting comments or good examples of language use which you could highlight in feedback.

> **EXAMPLE ANSWERS**
>
> Other reasons for competitive sports in schools: it's the only way to produce winning athletes of the future; it develops skills needed in a competitive workplace; other subjects such as maths or English are competitive because they are tested in exams – so why shouldn't sport be competitive?
>
> Other reasons against competitive sports in schools: it can lead to low self-esteem in non-athletic students; it makes children too competitive; it can create bad feeling between students or between schools.

> **Extra activity**
>
> Have a class debate. Ask students to divide into groups according to whether they are for or against competitive sports in schools. Ask each group to prepare, then present three key arguments in favour of their opinion. At the end, have a class vote and decide whether the class supports competitive sports in school or not.

Grammar *-ing* form

9

- Read the sentences in the grammar box as a class. Then ask students to work individually to underline the verbs in the *-ing* form and match them to the uses (a–c).
- Let students compare answers in pairs before checking answers with the class.

> **ANSWERS**
>
> 1 <u>Learning</u> to win and lose is important in a child's education. – a
> 2 Competitive sports in schools are good for <u>teaching</u> children. – c
> 3 Some parents hate <u>losing</u>. – b

> **Grammar note**
>
> The *-ing* form (also called the gerund) may be hard for some students to remember, especially if their L1 uses infinitives rather than *-ing* forms.
>
> *-ing* forms are commonly used with verbs connected with *like*, e.g. *like, hate, can't stand, enjoy* + *-ing*.

Refer students to page 158 for further information and practice.

> **ANSWERS TO GRAMMAR SUMMARY EXERCISES**
>
> 4
> 1 playing 2 watching 3 Doing 4 waking up
> 5 failing 6 Reading 7 helping
> 5
> 1 cleaning 2 do 3 Staying 4 going 5 running
> 6 going 7 take 8 eating 9 make

10

- Ask students to work individually to order the words in the quotes. Let them compare answers in pairs before checking with the class.
- In feedback, ask students to explain why *-ing* is used each time (see Grammar note below).

> **ANSWERS**
>
> 1 I never thought of losing.
> 2 I just love winning.
> 3 A champion isn't afraid of losing.
> 4 I hate losing.
> 5 I'm more worried about being a good person than being the best football player.
> 6 Swimming isn't everything, winning is.

> **Grammar note**
>
> 1, 3 and 5: after a preposition
> 2 and 4: after verbs *love* and *hate*
> 6: subject of the sentence

> **Background information**
>
> American **Muhammad Ali** (1942–2016) was the world's greatest heavyweight boxer, as much for his iconic status and personality as his boxing.
> Brazilian **Ayrton Senna** (1960–1994) was an F1 world champion racing driver who died in a crash.
> American **Billie Jean King** (b. 1943) won a number of Grand Slam tennis titles and was a campaigner for women's rights in sport.
> Indian **Sachin Tendulkar** (b. 1973) is considered by many to be the greatest cricketer of modern times. He holds the record for the most runs by a batsman and is a superstar in India.
> Argentinian **Lionel Messi** (b. 1987) is regularly considered to be the world's greatest footballer. He plays for Barcelona.
> American swimmer **Mark Spitz** (b. 1950) won seven gold medals at the 1972 Summer Olympics in Munich.

11 [12]

- Ask students to read the conversation quickly and say what it's about. Explain that the Tour de France is the world's most important bike race and takes place in France every year.

42 Unit 2 Competitions

UNIT 2 Competitions

- Ask students to work individually to choose the correct options.
- Play the recording. Students listen and check. In feedback, ask students to say why they chose each option (see Grammar note below).

> **ANSWERS**
> 1 Cycling 2 watching 3 think 4 seeing 5 Sitting
> 6 doing 7 play 8 watch 9 losing

> **Grammar note**
> 1 and 5: we use *-ing* because they are the subjects of sentences
> 2 and 4: we use *-ing* because it follows the verbs *love* and *enjoy*
> 3: *think* is a state verb in the present simple first person
> 6 and 9: we use *-ing* because it follows a preposition
> 7: we use infinitive without *to* after a modal verb
> 8: we use the infinitive with *to* after the verb *want*

Pronunciation /ŋ/

12a [13] ★ **CPT extra!** Pronunciation activity [after Ex. 12a]

- Ask students to look at the groups of words.
- Play the recording. Students listen and tick the word they hear.
- **Optional step** Ask students to practise saying the words, focussing on the /ŋ/ sound (see Pronunciation note below).

Audioscript [13] (and answers)

1 thing	4 sing
2 win	5 ran
3 bank	6 pink

> **Pronunciation note**
> The /ŋ/ sound is called the velar nasal. To make the sound, you curl your tongue up against the back of your mouth and the air comes out of your nose. 'ng' is the most common spelling with the /ŋ/ sound.

b [12]
- Play the recording from Exercise 11 again. Students listen and notice the /ŋ/ sound when pronouncing *-ing*.

c
- Ask students to work in pairs to practise the conversation in Exercise 11. Monitor and notice how well students pronounce the /ŋ/ sound.

> **Extra activity**
> Ask students to adapt and personalize the conversation. Tell students to think of another major sporting event they enjoy watching and to work with their partner to prepare then practise a similar conversation. Students could act out their conversations to the class.

Speaking my life
13

- Organize the class into new pairs. Look at the gapped sentences and the example question for the first sentence with the class. Check that everyone understands what to do.
- Ask students to work together to think of questions to ask. Then ask them to take turns to ask and answer.
- Ask students to complete the sentences individually before comparing and confirming with their partner.
- In feedback, ask students to share their information with the class.

> **EXAMPLE ANSWERS**
> Students' own answers.
> Here are some questions to ask:
> *What sports do you love watching/playing?*
> *Do you enjoy playing/watching golf?*
> *What sports are you good at?*
> *What sports do you not enjoy?*

2b Winning and losing 43

UNIT 2 Competitions

2c Bolivian wrestlers

Lesson at a glance
- reading: women in sport
- critical thinking: reading between the lines
- word focus: *like*
- speaking: Olympic sports

Reading

1 ⭐ **CPT extra!** Lead-in activity [before Ex. 1]
- Ask students to work in pairs to discuss the questions. Elicit ideas in feedback. Use the opportunity to teach some key words: *wrestling* (ˈrɛs(ə)lɪŋ) (= fighting another person by holding them down or throwing them), *wrestler* (= a person who does wrestling) and *fight* (= here, a competition between two wrestlers).

> **ANSWERS**
> 1 Students' own answers
> 2 Possible answers: Some people dislike boxing and wrestling because they are dangerous (injuries are common, and head injuries are a concern), sometimes corrupt (fighters sometimes lose on purpose) and violent.
> 3 Students' own answers

> **Background information**
> In **wrestling**, the aim is for one competitor to throw his/her opponent to the floor and to hold or pin them down. Modern wrestling differs from traditional or Olympic wrestling in that it's full of showmanship to attract audiences. Wearing masks and colourful clothes, and having nicknames and acting up to particular personas are all part of the show.

2 💿 [14]
- Ask students to look at the questions, then read the article to find the answers. Let students compare answers in pairs before checking with the class.
- **Optional step** The reading text is recorded. You could play the recording and ask students to read and listen.

> **ANSWERS**
> a 2 (*two women in colourful clothes enter the ring*)
> b 1 (*Local people like watching the wrestling and it's very popular with tourists.*)
> c 4 (*At home Yolanda has a normal and quiet family life. She has two daughters …*)
> d 5 ('*We laugh and we forget our problems for three or four hours.*')
> e 3 (*Claudina jumps on Yolanda. Then Yolanda throws Claudina on the floor …*)

3
- Look at the first two definitions with the class, and elicit the answer for the second one.
- Ask students to read the article again and find the words. Point out that the order of the definitions matches the order of the words in the article. Let students compare answers in pairs before checking with the class.

> **ANSWERS**
> 1 entertainment 2 ring 3 crowd 4 commentator
> 5 go crazy 6 fans 7 salary

> **Extra activity 1**
>
> Ask students to use a dictionary to find out the difference between these words:
> 1 *scream* and *shout* (*scream* is a loud noise in the throat showing excitement or fear; *shout* is saying words loudly)
> 2 *audience* and *spectators* (*audience* is used for people at the theatre, cinema or a concert; *spectators* are people watching a sporting event)
> 3 *turn* and *spin* (*turn* is moving round in general; *spin* is continually moving round very fast)

> **Extra activity 2**
>
> You could ask students to choose five words from the article which are new for them. Get them to write five sentences of their own using one new word in each. They can exchange these with a partner to check that they have used them correctly.

Critical thinking reading between the lines

4
- Read the information with the class and make sure that everyone understands.
- Ask students to work individually to match the people from the article (1–3) with the sentences (a–c).
- Let students compare answers in pairs before checking with the class.

> **ANSWERS**
> 1 b 2 a 3 c

5
- Ask students to work in pairs to discuss the questions. Then have an open class discussion and find out how the class feel about the topic.

44 Unit 2 Competitions

UNIT 2 Competitions

Word focus *like*

6 ★ **CPT extra!** Word focus activity [after Ex. 6]
- Ask students to work in pairs to match the sentences from the article (1–4) with the uses (a–d) before discussing as a class.

> **ANSWERS**
> 1 a   2 c   3 d   4 b

> **Vocabulary note**
>
> *Like* can be both a verb and a preposition.
> Note the following:
> - *like* + noun/*-ing*
> - *would like to* + infinitive
> - *to be like* + noun (somebody) = here, *like* is a preposition meaning 'similar to'.

7
- Ask students to work individually to match the questions with the answers. Let students compare their answers in pairs before checking with the class.

> **ANSWERS**
> 1 d   2 c   3 a   4 b

8
- Give students time to prepare their own answers to the questions in Exercise 7.
- Ask students to work in pairs to ask and answer the questions.
- In feedback, ask students to tell the class anything interesting that they found out about their partner.

> **Extra activity**
>
> It's often fun for students to find out about the teacher. Ask your class to ask you the questions in Exercise 7, and provide appropriate answers. A fun task is to tell the class that you will tell them one lie during the interview. Once students have asked the questions, and you have answered them, put students in pairs to talk together and work out which of the answers you gave was probably false.

Speaking *my life*

9
- Ask students to work in groups of four to think of ten sports in the Olympic Games. Set a time limit of three minutes. In feedback, write up interesting suggestions on the board.

> **EXAMPLE ANSWERS**
>
> Possibilities include: athletics, gymnastics, swimming, triathlon, modern pentathlon, horse jumping, tennis, golf, football, rugby 7s, basketball, volleyball, beach volleyball, badminton, table tennis, sailing, canoeing, rowing, boxing, wrestling, fencing, cycling, archery, diving, water polo, weightlifting, handball, judo, taekwondo, shooting, weightlifting, hockey.

10
- Ask each group to discuss the questions about the sports and decide which ones to include in the Olympics.
- Ask each group to present their ideas. Then open up the debate for whole class discussion (see Vocabulary note below). You might want to end with a vote on which two sports to include.
- **Optional step** One good idea here is to make one person in each group the 'chair'. It's their job to open the debate, make sure everybody has a chance to speak, and to summarize and choose the best idea. It's also their job to present the group's decision to the class at the end.

> **Vocabulary note**
>
> Here are some useful phrases you could write on the board for students to use when debating:
> > In my opinion, …
> > I (completely) agree / disagree.
> > I (don't) think / believe that …
> > I take your point but …

> **Background information**
>
> Baseball was once an Olympic sport – in Beijing in 2008.
>
> Chess is recognized as a sport by the International Olympic Committee and applied unsuccessfully for inclusion in the 2020 Olympic Games in Tokyo.
>
> Currently (2016), karate, skateboarding, sports climbing, surfing and baseball/softball are under consideration for inclusion in the 2020 Olympics.

2c   Bolivian wrestlers   45

UNIT 2 Competitions

2d Joining a group

Lesson at a glance
- speaking: clubs and membership
- real life: talking about interests
- pronunciation: silent letters

Speaking

1 ★ **CPT extra!** Lead-in activity [before Ex. 1]
- Ask students to prepare questions to find out the information (e.g. *Are you a member of a team?*).
- When students are prepared, organize them into groups of five or six to ask their questions (if you have a big class). If your class is not too large, ask students to stand up, walk round, and talk to everybody.
- Ask students to find a different person for each answer. Encourage them to ask follow-up questions to find extra information. When students have found an answer to each question, tell them to sit down. At the end, ask students to tell the class what they found out.

Background information

Clubs and societies are very popular in Britain, and each town will have many of them, e.g. a natural history society, an art club, a local history association, a book circle, the musical appreciation society, and so on. One very popular club is the local drama group or theatre group. In these clubs, groups of people who enjoy acting and putting on plays work together on the production of a play for public performance. The actors and others will make the costumes, the scenery, do the lighting and sound. Some clubs are very specific, performing, for example, only Shakespeare, or only Gilbert and Sullivan operettas, while others will put on a range of plays in different styles.

Real life talking about interests

2
- Start by asking students to read the four pieces of information (1–4). Check the meaning of *membership fee* (= the money you pay to join a club).
- Ask students to read the three adverts and underline the information in each one. Point out that they won't find all of the information in each advert. Let students compare their answers in pairs before checking with the class.

ANSWERS

1 When the club meets
   A 7 p.m. every Wednesday
   B not given
   C twice a week
2 The membership fee
   A not given
   B 15 euros
   C not given
3 Reasons to join
   A get fit / make new friends / fun
   B win a new camera
   C have fun
4 How to contact the club
   A call Mike for details on 0776 58945
   B visit www.bartonphotoclub.com
   C write to Mandy Giles on mandy76@dmail.com

Vocabulary note

Point out some of the interesting verb–noun collocations in the adverts: *join a club/group; enter a competition; pay a membership/entry fee; make friends.*

3 [15]
- Explain that two friends are discussing the adverts in Exercise 2.
- Play the recording. Students listen and number the adverts in order. Let them compare their answers in pairs before checking with the class.

ANSWERS
1 photography club   2 theatre group   3 running group

Audioscript [15]

A: Hey! Have you seen this?
B: What?
A: This advert. You're really good at doing that.
B: Yes, but I have so much work at the moment, I don't have time.
A: So, this is a good way to relax.
B: I can take a good picture of friends and family, but I'm not very creative with it.
A: Alright. Well, what about joining something else? Er, this one! Are you interested in acting?
B: You're joking! I hate standing up in front of people. You're more of a performer than me.
A: Yes, but it's a musical. I'm not very good at singing.
B: Let's have a look at that. But it says here enthusiasm is more important than talent. Go on. I think you'd enjoy it.
A: Mm, well maybe, but I think I'd like to join this on Wednesday evenings.
B: What? You? Do exercise?
A: What do you mean? Anyway, it looks like fun. Why don't you come too?
B: But I can't run!
A: No, but that's the point. There's a beginner's group. You should do it with me.

UNIT 2 Competitions

4 [15]

- Ask students to read the sentences and try to remember and complete as many as they can.
- Play the recording again. Students listen and write the missing words. Let students compare their answers in pairs before checking with the class.
- **Optional step** Ask students to work in pairs to practise the conversation in audioscript 15 on page 182 of the Student's Book.

ANSWERS
1 good at   2 what about   3 interested in   4 hate
5 not very   6 on   7 like to   8 looks; Why don't

Teacher development

Top down and bottom up listening

Top down listening refers to the use of background knowledge in understanding the meaning of the message. In real life, when someone tells us an anecdote, for example, we don't listen to every word but rely on our understanding of context to follow the story. In Exercise 3 above, students need top down listening skills to do this task appropriately. Here are suggestions for helping develop those skills:

- Make sure students are clear about the context – two people talking about adverts, in this case.
- Make sure students have as much information as they need about what will be discussed – spending time on Exercise 2 introduces key language and key information they need.
- Get students to predict what people might say – in real life, in L1, we sub-consciously predict what our friends are saying or about to say – students need to apply this skill to listening in English.
- Keep the task open and general – in Exercise 3, there are plenty of clues to help students order the adverts – students don't have to hear one word or phrase.

Bottom up listening refers to having to separate the stream of speech into individual words or phrases and to decode their meaning. In real life, when someone gives directions, we have to hear individual words (street names and house numbers, for example) and we focus very carefully on what people are saying to do this. In Exercise 4 above, students need bottom up listening skills to do this task appropriately. Here are suggestions for activities to develop those skills:

- As part of your lead in, select five or six short phrases from the listening and analyse them so students see how they are pronounced, for example, point out linking or unstressed syllables. When students listen to the recording, tell them to tick the phrases when they hear them.
- Select phrases with words missing (as in Exercise 4 above). See if students can hear the missing words in the stream of speech as they listen to the recording.
- Ask students to listen and write down any strongly stressed word they hear. Then, after listening, ask them to share words they have written with a partner and see how much of the meaning or message of the recording they can recall from the words they wrote.

5

- Ask students to put the sentences in the correct categories. Elicit the first answer to get them started. Let students compare answers in pairs before checking with the class.

ANSWERS

Talking about interests and abilities:
3 Are you interested in acting?
4 I hate standing up in front of people.
5 I'm not very good at singing.

Talking about plans:
2 Well, what about joining something else?
7 I think I'd like to join this on Wednesday evenings.

Recommending and encouraging:
1 You're really good at doing that.
6 Go on. I think you'd enjoy it.
8 It looks like fun. Why don't you come too?

Pronunciation silent letters

6 [16]

- Read the instructions with the class and ask students to think which letters might be silent before they listen. Tell them to discuss their ideas with a partner.
- Play the recording. Students listen and cross out the silent letters. If students are unsure, play and pause, and ask students to repeat the words.

ANSWERS
1 interested   2 should   3 friends   4 write
5 half   6 what

Extra activity

Ask students to work in pairs or small groups to think of other words they know with silent letters. Elicit ideas and write them on the board, crossing out the silent letter, e.g. comfortable, would, where, Wednesday.

Pronunciation note

Notice how the silent letters change the number of syllables in a word, for example, interested has three syllables, and evenings has two. Get students to say the words and count the syllables.

2d Joining a group

UNIT 2 Competitions

Background information

English spelling, unlike other European languages, is regularly non-phonetic, and students face many problems understanding why the spelling of a word does not necessarily reflect its pronunciation. There are historical reasons for this. The eleventh century invasion of what is now England by French-speaking Normans resulted in the emergence of English as a fusion of French and Germanic dialects. Germanic words like *know* and *write* changed in pronunciation, and the once-pronounced *k* and *w* became redundant. The great vowel shift of the fourteenth and fifteenth centuries also changed the pronunciation, but not the spelling, of many words. For example, in southern England, six hundred years ago, the words *meet* and *meat* had different vowel sounds (/eː/ and /ɛː/, respectively). Today, they have different spellings, but the same vowel sound /iː/.

7
- Organize the class into new pairs. Ask students to discuss the questions.
- In feedback, ask a few students to tell the class what they found out about their partner.

Extra activity

Before doing Exercise 7, ask students to choose three phrases for talking about interests and write them on three separate pieces of paper. As they discuss whether they would like to join one of the clubs, students must try to use their three phrases. When they say them to their partner, they turn them over and 'play' them. Find out which students managed to say all their phrases.

2e Advertising for members

Lesson at a glance
- writing: an advert or notice
- writing skill: checking your writing

Writing an advert or notice

1
- Ask students to work in pairs to discuss the questions. Elicit ideas in a brief feedback.

EXAMPLE ANSWERS

Students' own ideas.

Good adverts: they stand out, use humour, use exciting graphics and visuals, use a powerful headline, make the thing being advertised seem important or urgent, are easy to read, give complete contact information

Bad adverts: the opposite of the above!

2
- Ask students to read the advice. Check *effective* (= it works well). Then ask them to work in pairs to discuss the adverts on page 28. Elicit ideas in a brief feedback.

ANSWERS

1 Advert B follows most of the advice.
2 Advert A needs a picture or image. Advert C doesn't have an interesting headline. It needs more details about times, etc.

3
- Organize the class into new pairs. Read the instructions with the class and check that everyone understands what to do.
- Ask pairs to decide on a type of club and to discuss the questions.
- **Optional step** Make sure students have the language they need to discuss and plan their club. Revise the following phrases, and if necessary write them on the board for students to use while discussing their plans:

Suggestion language:
We could + verb
How about + noun or *-ing* verb?
Why don't we + verb?
Why not + verb?
Responding to suggestions:
That's a good idea.
I'm not sure that's a good idea because … (Point out that if you reject somebody's suggestion, it's polite to give an explanation why.)

- Have a brief feedback and find out what ideas students have before they begin the planning stage.

48 Unit 2 Competitions

UNIT 2 Competitions

4 ★ **CPT extra!** Writing activity [before Ex. 4]
- Ask students to plan and write an advert. Tell them to make notes first – based on what they discussed in Exercise 3. Then tell them to write. Monitor and help with ideas and vocabulary.

Writing skill checking your writing
5a
- Read the information with the class and make sure students are clear about the correction code.
- Ask students to circle and correct mistakes. Let them compare their answers in pairs before checking with the class.

> **ANSWERS**
> 1 Would you like to learn a musical instrument?
> 2 Enter our exciting competition! Sp
> 3 Are you good at playing tennis? Gr
> 4 We meet on Tuesdays and Thursdays. Prep
> 5 It's a fun way to get fit. MW
> 6 Join this new club! WO
> 7 Get healthy and do yoga. WW
> 8 Call Peter on 077 237 5980. C

b
- Ask students to work in their pairs to check their adverts for these kinds of errors. Monitor to help if students have problems.

6
- Ask students to display their adverts on the classroom wall or on tables around the classroom. Give students time to walk round and read the adverts.
- In feedback, ask students to say which clubs they would join and which adverts were effective, explaining their reasons why.

2f Mongolian horse racing

Before you watch
1 ★ **CPT extra!** Photo activity [before Ex. 1]
- **Optional step** Start by asking students to describe the photo. Ask: *What can you see? Where are they? How do the children feel? Why do you think they do this sport?*
- Ask students to work in pairs or small groups to discuss the questions. Elicit a few ideas from the class in feedback.

> **ANSWERS**
> Students' own answers

> **Background information**
> **Mongolia** /mɒŋˈɡəʊliə/ is a large, flat, landlocked country in Asia, sandwiched between China to the south and Russia to the north. Throughout its history, it has relied on the horse, an animal that evolved on the plains of Central Asia, and which was domesticated in that region over 3,000 years ago. Today, Mongol horses are of a stocky build, with relatively short but strong legs and a large head. Most of them roam free.

Key vocabulary
2
- Encourage students to use the context to guess the meanings of the words in bold.
- Start by asking students to look at *medal* and ask: *Is it a verb or a noun?* (noun) *Which word goes with it?* (gold) *Where do you win it?* (the Olympics)
- Ask students to work in pairs to discuss the other words and match them with the definitions.
- **Optional step** It's a good idea to show the pronunciation of these key words – students have to hear them in continuous speech on the video. You could say the words and ask students to repeat (see Vocabulary and pronunciation note below).

> **ANSWERS**
> 1 e 2 b 3 a 4 c 5 f 6 d 7 g 8 h

> **Vocabulary and pronunciation note**
> *medal* /ˈmed(ə)l/ = at the Olympics, the winner gets a gold medal, silver for second, bronze for third
> *proud* /praʊd/ = from the noun *pride* – a positive feeling that comes from feeling you did something well or you achieved something difficult
> *blesses* /ˈblɛsɪs/ = a religious person might bless crops (so they grow), athletes (so they perform well), or soldiers (so they stay safe)
> *rich* /rɪtʃ/ = here, we say rich grass, rich vegetation, rich crops, to say that it has grown well and is healthy and there is a lot

2f Mongolian horse racing 49

UNIT 2 Competitions

> *like the wind* = we use *like* (meaning *similar to*) in many poetic expressions of this sort (*like a child*, *like a lion*, etc.)
> *display* /dɪˈspleɪ/ = a type of show which is very visual
> *rodeo* /ˈrəʊdɪˌəʊ/ = a competitive sport that arose out of the working practices of cattle herding – cowboys ride wild horses and cattle
> *rival* /ˈraɪv(ə)l/ = often used emotively (unlike *opponent*, which is the neutral term for someone you play at sport) – a rival really wants to beat you, and is someone you have competed against for a long time or on big occasions

While you watch

3 🎥 [2.1]
- Ask students to read the actions carefully. Check *flag* (= here, a piece of cloth on a stick) and remind students of the meaning of *wrestle*.
- Ask students to watch the video and number the actions in the order they see them. Let students compare their answers in pairs before checking with the class. Write the order on the board.

> **ANSWERS**
> 1 b   2 d   3 h   4 f   5 g   6 c   7 a   8 e

Videoscript 🎥 2.1

N = Narrator, **D** = Dr Wade Davis

0.00–0.58   N   The Mongolian summer festival is called the Naadam. It's famous for its horse races.

D   The Naadam is a race and a celebration. It's all about competition but it's also about community and …

N   This is Doctor Wade Davis. He is studying the festival of the Naadam. He is interested in what happens in the competition and why the horse race is so important to the local people.

D   … to endure whatever life brings them.

0.59–1.20   N   The Naadam festival is about to begin. This is 'Mukhdalai'. He's preparing his horse for the race.

1.21–1.33   This is another trainer called 'Namjin'. He's Mukhdalai's biggest rival in the competition, but also one of his oldest friends.

1.34–1.55   The day of the horse race arrives and this Buddhist woman blesses each horse for luck. There are about 20 horses competing this year. Some competitors have travelled 80 kilometres to get here.

1.56–2.27   But the Naadam is not just a horse race. It's a chance for everyone to come together and enjoy displays of traditional skills.

There's a rodeo with wild horses.

Picking up poles at high speeds needs great ability on a horse. Wrestling is also a popular national sport in Mongolia.

2.28–2.55   But the main event is the horse race over 25 kilometres. The riders take their horses to the starting point at the bottom of the valley. The horses will go up the hills and then down to the next valley and the finishing line.

2.56–3.27   When the race begins, the horses will reach speeds of 50 kilometres an hour. Early on in the race, Namjin's son in green and white is doing well but Mukhdalai's horse falls back. But eventually the power of Mukhdalai's horse takes over.

3.28–3.41   At the halfway mark the horse takes the lead and Mukhdalai's son shouts at the horse to run like the wind.

3.42–3.48   Namjin's horse can only keep up for a while, then he starts to slow down.

3.49–4.00   At the finishing line, Mukhdalai's son and horse win the race – a long way ahead.

4.01–4.10   Namjin's son is fifth.

4.11–end   Mukhdalai receives first prize with a medal, a cheque and a Mongolian fiddle. Namjin also receives a medal for fifth place. This was the first race for his horse so it's a good result. At the end of the day, everyone feels proud.

4 🎥 [2.1]
- Ask students to read the sentences and check any difficult words (e.g. *whole race* = all the race). Then play the video again and ask students to choose the correct option to complete the sentences.
- After watching, let students compare answers in pairs before checking with the class.

> **ANSWERS**
> 1 a   2 b   3 a   4 a   5 b   6 b   7 b   8 b

After you watch

Vocabulary in context

5a 🎥 [2.2]
- Explain that students are going to watch some clips from the video which contain some new words and phrases. They need to choose the correct meaning of the words.
- Play the clips. When each multiple-choice question appears, pause the clip so that students can choose the correct definition. You could let students compare answers in pairs before discussing as a class.

> **ANSWERS**
> 1 b   2 c   3 a   4 a   5 c   6 a

Videoscript 🎥 2.2

1 The Naadam is a race and a **celebration**.
   a special competition with lots of competitors
   b special event with lots of people
   c special day with horses

2 Mukhdalai's horse **falls back**.
   a goes at the same speed as others
   b goes faster than others
   c goes slower than others

3 At the halfway mark the horse **takes the lead**.
   a moves in front of all the other competitors
   b moves in front of another competitor
   c stands in front of another horse

4 Namjin's horse can only **keep up** for a while.
   a go at the same speed as another
   b go faster than another
   c go slower than another

50   Unit 2   Competitions

UNIT 2 Competitions

5 He starts to **slow down**.
   a go slower and stop
   b go behind another horse
   c go slower

6 Mukhdalai's son and horse win the race – **a long way ahead**.
   a with a lot of distance between them and the rest of the competitors
   b with a lot of competitors between them and the finishing line
   c with a short distance between them and the rest of the competitors

b
- Organize the class into pairs to ask and answer the questions. In feedback, find out what information different students found out about their partner.

6
- Ask students to work in pairs to prepare questions about the video. Monitor and help with ideas and vocabulary.

> EXAMPLE ANSWERS
> What is the Naadam festival famous for?
> When does the Naadam take place?
> What sort of displays are there at the Naadam?
> What is the main event?
> How fast do the horses go?
> What is the first prize for the horse race?

7 ★ CPT extra! Video activity [after Ex. 7]
- Organize the class into new pairs. Students take turns to ask and answer their questions.
- As students speak, monitor and notice any errors or examples of good language use you hear. In feedback, at the end, write four or five sentences students said with errors in them on the board, and ask students to correct them with their partner.

UNIT 2 Review and memory booster ★ CPT extra! Language games

Memory Booster activities
Exercises 2, 4, 7 and 9 are Memory Booster activities. For more information about these activities and how they benefit students, see page 10.

I can … tick boxes
As an alternative to students simply ticking the *I can* … boxes, you could ask them to give themselves a score from 1 to 4 (1 = not very confident; 4 = very confident) for each language area. If students score 1 or 2 for a language area, refer them to additional practice activities in the Workbook and Grammar summary exercises.

Grammar
1
- Ask students to work individually to complete the text by choosing the correct options. Let students compare answers in pairs before checking with the class.

> ANSWERS
> 1 has to 2 must 3 can 4 doesn't have to 5 can't
> 6 mustn't

2 >> MB
- Ask students to work in pairs to name the sports and say two rules for each one.

> ANSWERS
> Football (Possible rules: You mustn't touch the ball with your hands. The referee can send a player off the pitch when he/she breaks the rules of the game.)
> Tennis (Possible rules: You have to hit the ball over the net. You don't have to win every point to win the match.)

3
- Ask students to work individually to complete the sentences with the *-ing* form of the verbs.

> ANSWERS
> 1 Learning 2 feeling 3 losing 4 winning 5 watching
> 6 going

4 >> MB
- Ask students to work individually to complete the sentences in their own words with the *-ing* form of verbs. Then ask students to compare sentences with a partner.

UNIT 2 Review and memory booster 51

UNIT 2 Competitions

Vocabulary

5
- Ask students to write the missing letters to complete the sport words.

> **ANSWERS**
> 1 race 2 goals 3 crowd 4 match 5 finish line
> 6 baseball 7 winner 8 fans 9 team 10 boxer

6
- Ask students to work individually to answer the questions with words from Exercise 5.

> **ANSWERS**
> 1 finish line 2 winner 3 race 4 fans

7 >> MB
- Ask students to work in pairs to choose four more words from Exercise 5 and write questions similar to those in Exercise 6. Monitor and help with vocabulary as necessary.
- When students are ready, ask pairs to work with another pair. They take turns to ask their questions for the other pair to say the word.

Real life

8
- Ask students to work individually to complete the conversation with one word in each gap.

> **ANSWERS**
> 1 in 2 at 3 to 4 on 5 Do

9 >> MB
- Ask students to work individually to complete the sentences in their own words. Then ask students to compare sentences with a partner.

Unit 3 Transport

Opener

1 ⭐ **CPT extra!** Lead-in activity [before Ex. 1]
- Ask students to look at the photo and the caption. Ask them to work in pairs to discuss the questions (see also the Teacher development note below). Elicit a few ideas from the class in feedback.

> **ANSWERS**
> Students' own answers. As well as the answer given in the audioscript, students may suggest other ideas such as: she's too poor to buy a ticket; she's running away; she's hiding from the ticket inspector.

2 💿 [17]
- Play the recording. Students listen and answer the question. Let them compare answers in pairs before checking with the class.

> **ANSWERS**
> The woman is sitting between the carriages because tickets for the train have sold out, because it's Ramadan, and because there isn't space on top of the train.

Audioscript 💿 [17]

This photo is on a train in Bangladesh. It was the end of Ramadan and lots of people travel home at that time of year. Train tickets sell out quickly, so you often see people riding on top of the trains and the carriages. In this picture, the woman is sitting between the carriages because there isn't space on top of the train. It looks a bit dangerous but she doesn't look very worried.

> **Background information**
> **Bangladesh** is a developing Asian country with borders with India and Burma. It's low-lying, fertile and subject to flooding, and has a population of 165 million people. Most people are Muslim and speak Bengali.
> **Ramadan** is the ninth month of the Islamic calendar. It's a time of fasting. Typically, Muslims fast from dawn to dusk, and eat a simple meal (called *Iftar*) in the evening. At the end of Ramadan, there is a public holiday called *Eid al-Fitr*.

3
- You could start by checking some of the difficult words in the box with your students, e.g. *ferry* (= a boat that goes across a sea or river with passengers) and *lorry* (= a large vehicle that carries products – called a *truck* in US English).
- Ask students in pairs to discuss and match the ways of travelling with the activities (1–10). Encourage them to say *I'd prefer to …* and *because …* as in the example.
- In feedback, elicit ideas and ask students to give reasons why.

> **EXAMPLE ANSWERS**
> Note that the answers here depend on the students' own experience. For example, they may visit relatives on foot if they live nearby, or on a plane if they live in a different country. The answers below are just the most likely.
> 1 by train, on foot, by bus, in my car
> 2 by lorry (actually, a furniture van is the most common means); on a ship (if moving abroad)
> 3 in a taxi, in my car, by bus, by train (students may also suggest by underground if they live in a large city)
> 4 in my car, on a motorbike, by train, by plane (by bus is also possible, but note that we usually say on a coach if it's used for an excursion or long distance travel)
> 5 on a ferry, on a ship, by plane
> 6 in a taxi, in my car, by bus, on foot, by bicycle
> 7 in a taxi, in my car, by bus, on foot, by bicycle
> 8 on foot, in my car, by bus
> 9 on foot, by bicycle, in my car, by bus, by train
> 10 on foot, by bicycle, in my car, by bus, by train

Vocabulary note

Note the use of *in*, *on* and *by*. We can generally use *by* with a vehicle, but not if we're walking (*on foot*). There's no article, i.e. *by bus* not ~~*by the bus*~~. It's possible to say *by car* or *by taxi*, but it's more common to use *in (a/my)*.
We use *in* with *car* and *taxi*, but *on* with larger passenger-carrying vehicles, e.g. *on a bus, on a train*.

Extra activity

Write on the board: *What's your favourite way to travel? Why?* Ask students to discuss the question in pairs or small groups.

Teacher development

Visual literacy

Learners are accustomed to living in a highly visual world. Being visually literate is an important part of our lives, and we can expect our students to have inherent visual literacy skills. They know what pictures mean and what messages pictures send.

Here are some ideas for exploiting your students' visual literacy:

- Pictures communicate meaning and demand language. Use them to generate language, ideas and opinions.
- Pictures demand questions. Ask students to think of questions they would like to ask about a picture, or questions they would like to ask a person in a picture.
- Students can think critically about pictures. Ask students: *What does the picture mean? What message is the photographer trying to send?*
- Students can be creative with pictures. Ask them to write the story behind a picture. Ask them to imagine they are looking at a picture from different positions, or viewpoints, and to describe what they see. Ask them to use their own images and make them relevant to the lesson.

53

UNIT 3 Transport

3a Transport solutions

Lesson at a glance
- reading: transport solutions
- vocabulary: transport nouns
- grammar: comparatives and superlatives
- pronunciation: *than*
- speaking: everyday journeys

Reading

1 ★ **CPT extra!** Lead-in activity [after Ex. 1]

- Ask students to work in pairs to discuss the questions. Start them off by briefly describing how you go to work or college. This provides a model of what to say.
- **Optional step** You could brainstorm common traffic problems to help students answer question 3, e.g. *traffic jam, rush hour, traffic lights, road works, accident*. (Note that some of these words are taught in Exercise 4.)

ANSWERS
Students' own answers

2 [18]

- **Optional step** Ask students to look at the photos. Ask: *What can you see?* Elicit ideas from students. (Possible answers: 1 is a type of train or tram on a raised line; 2 is a transparent pod carrying one passenger; 3 is a small type of car; 4 is a big sail used with ships). Use the opportunity to pre-teach these key words with the photos: *a pod* (= here, a small, self-contained unit), *a kite* (= a sail that flies in the wind on string) and *a tube* (= a long, hollow cylinder of metal, plastic, glass, etc.).
- Ask students to work individually to read the article and match the paragraphs with the photos. Let them compare answers in pairs before checking with the class.
- **Optional step** The reading text is recorded. You could play the recording and ask students to read and listen.

ANSWERS
A 3   B 2   C 4   D 1

3

- Start by reading the sentences (1–6) with the class and checking any unknown words, e.g. *commute* (= travel to and from work; a *commuter* is someone who travels to and from work every day).
- Ask students to look at the photos and read the article again. Tell them to match the types of transport described in the paragraphs with the sentences. Point out the example to get students started. Let them compare answers in pairs before checking with the class.

ANSWERS
1 B (*can cycle over people's heads*), D (*shown in photo*)
2 B (*new solution for commuters in traffic jams during the rush hour*), D (*travel at 1,200 kilometres per hour*)
3 B (*The passenger sits in a pod and can cycle*)
4 A (*solar energy*), C (*wind*)
5 C (*reduces the fuel costs*)
6 B (*for commuters in traffic jams*)

Vocabulary transport nouns

4 ★ **CPT extra!** Vocabulary activity [before Ex. 4]

- Read the wordbuilding box with the class. Ask students if they can think of any other noun-noun collocations (e.g. *laptop, pencil sharpener, armchair, petrol station*).
- Look at the example with the class and then ask students to work in pairs to match the remaining compound nouns from the article with the definitions. When they have finished, elicit answers and use questions to fully check understanding (see Vocabulary note below).

ANSWERS
1 speed limit   2 traffic jam   3 rush hour   4 fuel costs
5 carbon emissions   6 city centres   7 container ships

Refer students to page 27 of the Workbook for further practice.

Vocabulary note

Using concept check questions in feedback to a vocabulary task is a good way of confirming understanding. Use *yes/no* questions (e.g. *Do holidaymakers travel on container ships? – No*), one word answer questions (e.g. *Is rush hour usually at 8 a.m. or 11 a.m.? – 8 a.m.*), or personalized questions (e.g. *What's the speed limit in this country? How do you feel when you are in a traffic jam? What can you see in the city centre?*).

5

- Ask students to work with a new partner to discuss the questions. The activity aims to personalize the material, and to get students expressing their own views and opinions.
- In feedback, elicit ideas from different pairs.

EXAMPLE ANSWERS

Students' own answers. However, they may suggest, for example, using driverless cars to stop pollution in a city and to solve the problem of having inconsiderate or angry drivers in a city, or using the cycle monorail because there are no good bike lanes in their city.

Grammar comparatives and superlatives

6 [19]

- Explain that students are going to listen to two colleagues discussing types of transport. Read the questions with the class.

54   Unit 3 Transport

UNIT 3 Transport

- Play the recording. Students listen and answer the questions. Let them compare answers in pairs before checking with the class.
- In the feedback, accept students' ideas, but note that it isn't necessary to go through all the answers below at this stage.

> **ANSWERS**
>
> Types of transport: bicycle, car and bus
> *bicycle*
> advantage: faster than a car in the rush hour
> disadvantage: takes too long with long distances
> *car*
> advantage: electric cars better for the environment
> disadvantages: slow in rush hour, cost of petrol, electric cars expensive
> *bus*
> disadvantage: slow – stops everywhere

Audioscript [19]

A: Sorry I'm late. Eight thirty in the morning is the worst time for traffic.
B: I know what you mean. My bicycle is faster than your car in the rush hour!
A: I'm sure it is, but I travel further than you. It'd take me hours by bicycle.
B: There's also the cost of petrol. It's so expensive!
A: Tell me about it. In fact, last week I went to look at an electric car.
B: Good idea. They're better for the environment.
A: They're better, but they're also more expensive. In fact, a new electric car is the most expensive type of car.
B: Really? Anyway, what about public transport? Isn't there a bus stop near your house?
A: Yes, but the fastest bus takes over an hour. It stops everywhere!

7 [19] ★ **CPT extra!** Grammar activity [after Ex. 7]
- Ask students to read the sentences and choose the correct option. This activity tests their knowledge of comparative and superlative forms.
- Play the recording again. Students listen and check their answers. Let them compare answers in pairs before checking with the class.

> **ANSWERS**
>
> 1 worst   2 faster   3 further   4 better
> 5 more   6 most   7 fastest

8
- Ask students to work in pairs to read the grammar box and answer the questions. Monitor students as they speak and notice any problems they have. In feedback, discuss any problems you noticed with the class (see Grammar note below).

> **ANSWERS**
>
> 1 -er and -est
> 2 (the) most
> 3 further/furthest; better/best; worse/worst
> 4 than; the

Grammar note

Note the following form rules for comparative adjectives:
- Adjectives ending in *-e*, add *-r*: *wider, nicer*.
- Adjectives ending consonant-vowel-consonant, double the last letter to avoid changing the sound of the vowel: *bigger, hotter*.
- Adjectives with two syllables, ending in *-y*, remove the *-y* and add *-ier*: *happier, busier*.
- Other adjectives with two syllables sometimes end with *-er* and sometimes take *more*: *narrower, more common, more useful*.

In a monolingual class, it's worth comparing the formation of comparatives and superlatives in English to your students' L1. This will highlight how English differs and where students are most likely to have problems. For example, speakers of romance languages such as Spanish always use the equivalent of *more* and *most* regardless of how long the adjective is. A typical error is: ~~Susie is more fast than me~~. In contrast, German speakers always add *-er* to make comparatives. A typical error: ~~He is intelligenter than me~~.

Refer students to page 160 for further information and practice.

> **ANSWERS TO GRAMMAR SUMMARY EXERCISES**
>
> 1
> 1 nicest   2 further   3 more interesting   4 worst
> 5 more beautiful   6 busier; busiest   7 better; best
> 8 bigger; biggest
> 2
> 1 The fastest   2 longest   3 deepest   4 longer than
> 5 the busiest   6 the highest   7 higher than

Pronunciation *than*

9a [20]
- Play the recording. Students listen and notice the weak /ə/ sound in *than* /ðən/ (see Pronunciation note below).

Pronunciation note

Notice the strong stress on the nouns and adjectives in the two sentences on the recording, and the weak stress on the other words. Encourage students to very strongly stress 'Cars', 'fast' and the syllable 'bi' in bicycles, and to reduce the other sounds to very weak /ə/ sounds:

/ə/   /ə/ /ə/
Cars are **fas**ter than **bi**cycles.

b [20]
- Play the recording again. Students listen and repeat.

3a   Transport solutions

UNIT 3 Transport

c
- Ask students to work in pairs. Tell them to take turns saying the sentences. Monitor and notice how well students are attempting the pronunciation (see Pronunciation note below). Correct students by getting them to beat out the stress as they speak.

Pronunciation note

Notice the strong stress and weak stress on the two sentences provided for practice:
/ə/ /ə/
I **travel fur**ther than you.
/ə/   /ə/ /ə/
A **train** is more ex**pen**sive than a **bus**.

10
- Ask students to read the report with a gist question: *What types of transport does the survey mention?* (*bus, car, taxi, bicycle*).
- Ask students to complete the report. Let them compare their answers in pairs before checking with the class.

ANSWERS
1 most popular 2 cheaper 3 better 4 slower
5 biggest 6 more popular 7 most expensive

Speaking my life
11
- Ask students to work with a new partner. Read the instructions with the class and elicit two or three possible sentences from students. Then ask students to make sentences against the clock. Monitor and help with ideas and vocabulary if necessary.
- After three minutes, stop the activity. Ask the pair with the longest list to read out their sentences. If they make any errors, ask the rest of the class to try to help correct.

EXAMPLE ANSWERS
Cars are safer than motorbikes, but trains are the safest type of transport.
Buses are cheaper than taxis, but bicycles are the cheapest way to travel.
Trains are more expensive than buses, but planes are the most expensive type of transport.

12
- **Optional step** Start by drilling the three questions, or by asking them around the class and eliciting responses.
- Ask students to work in pairs to take turns to ask and answer the questions. Tell them to note their partner's answers.

13
- Look at the example sentences with the class. Then ask students to write similar sentences using the notes they made from their interviews in Exercise 12.

14
- Ask pairs to work with another pair. Ask the group of four to compare their information and find answers to the questions.

Extra activity

You could turn this into a class survey. Ask students to work in pairs. Each student must walk round the class and interview as many students as they can in five minutes. Then they sit with their partner and compare their information. They can then produce a report based on the information they share.

56 Unit 3 Transport

UNIT 3 Transport

3b Transport around the world

Lesson at a glance
- listening: using animals for transport
- grammar: *as ... as*
- pronunciation: sentence stress
- vocabulary: transport adjectives
- grammar: comparative modifiers
- speaking: travel advice

Listening

1 ★ CPT extra! Grammar activity [after Ex. 1]
- Ask students to look at the two photos. Ask: *What can you see?* Elicit key words from the recording: *snow, sledge, dogs (huskies), desert, camels, sand.*
- Ask them to work in pairs to discuss the questions. Elicit a few ideas from the class in feedback.

> **EXAMPLE ANSWERS**
>
> Students' own answers. There is no need to provide definitive answers here. However, here are some things students might say:
> Photo 1 is probably in the far north, in Canada, Alaska, northern Scandinavia or Siberia.
> Photo 2 is probably in the Sahara Desert in North Africa or perhaps in Saudi Arabia or one of the Gulf States.
> Advantages of huskies in the Arctic: can travel long distances at speeds, are used to the cold, are more reliable than vehicles in the cold where there are no roads.
> Advantages of using camels in the desert: can go a long time without water, can carry heavy loads, don't break down in the sand like vehicles do.

2 🔊 [21]
- Explain that students are going to listen to two parts of a documentary about animal transport.
- Play the recording. Students listen and answer the question. Let students compare answers in pairs before checking with the class. In feedback, take what answers students give you. It doesn't matter if they haven't caught all the information below.

> **ANSWERS**
>
> Camels are more reliable in the sand than vehicles and better over long distances.
> Dogs are also good over long distances when the weather is bad. It's impossible for cars in such conditions but huskies are more reliable.

Audioscript 🔊 [21]

When we talk about transport, most people think of buses, cars, bicycles, and so on. But in some parts of the world, animal transport is as popular as these modern types of transport, and sometimes more popular. Because at certain times of year, animals are the only way to travel. Take the desert for example, with its 50-degree temperatures. Yes, you can cross it in the right vehicles, but for long distances, modern vehicles are not as good as camels. A camel can travel over 40 kilometres per day and go without water for three to five days. Yes, it's slower, and maybe a camel isn't as comfortable as a car. But a camel's big feet make it more reliable in the sand – unlike a car, it doesn't get stuck. Camels are so important in the desert that there are around 160 different ways of saying the word 'camel' in Arabic.

In winter, northern Alaska can be as cold as the North Pole. Temperatures go down to minus 50 degrees. Your engine can freeze, and even if your car starts, snow and ice on the road can make driving impossible. When the weather is as bad as this, the only way to travel is by sledge with a team of between six and eight huskies. These famous dogs can pull heavy sledges for hundreds of kilometres. There is even a race for huskies in Alaska called the Iditarod, where large teams of huskies pull sledges over one thousand six hundred kilometres.

3 🔊 [21]
- Ask students to look at the numbers in pairs and try to remember what they describe.
- Play the recording again. Students listen and make notes for each number. Let them compare answers in pairs before checking with the class.
- **Optional step** Students feel frustrated if they don't get all the answers when listening – and they begin to feel they are 'bad' at listening. Play the recording a third time if students have problems, or play and pause so they have time to hear all the information. Alternatively, tell students to look at the audioscript on page 182 of the Student's Book and ask them to listen and read.

> **ANSWERS**
>
> Camels
> 50 degrees = temperature in the desert
> 40 kilometres = distance a camel can travel in a day
> 3 to 5 days = length of time a camel can go without water
> 160 words = there are 160 words for camel in Arabic
> Huskies
> –50 degrees = winter temperature in northern Alaska
> 6 and 8 huskies = number of huskies in a sledge team
> 1,600 kilometres = length of the Iditarod – a race for huskies

> **Background information**
>
> The **Iditarod Trail Sled Dog Race** is an annual long-distance sled dog race run in early March from Settler's Bay to Nome in Alaska. It takes a team of dogs between 8 and 15 days to cover the 1,600 kilometre distance. Iditarod is a Native American word meaning 'faraway place'.

3b Transport around the world 57

UNIT 3 Transport

Grammar *as … as*

4

- Read the information in the grammar box with the class. Then ask students to work in pairs to answer the questions. Look at the form with the class (see Grammar note below).

> **ANSWERS**
> a 1 and 2
> b 3 and 4

> **Grammar note**
>
> Students need to notice the form: *as* + adjective + *as*. Errors may include over-applying comparative rules (*It's as colder as …*) or translating from L1 and misusing words (*It's as cold that/like …*).
>
> Note the short answer: *The bus is slower than the train, but not as expensive.*

Refer students to page 160 for further information and practice.

> ANSWERS TO GRAMMAR SUMMARY EXERCISES
> 3
> 1 Mount Fuji isn't as high as Mount Kilimanjaro.
> 2 The USA isn't as big as Canada.
> 3 A kangaroo is as fast as a horse.
> 4 A Dreamliner isn't as heavy as a Jumbo Jet.
> 4
> 1 Travelling by motorbike isn't as safe as travelling by car.
> 2 Cycling is as dangerous as driving. / Driving is as dangerous as cycling.
> 3 Gatwick Airport isn't as convenient for us as Heathrow Airport.
> 4 Usually, the beach isn't as busy during the week.
> 5 Going by car is as quick as taking the bus. / Taking the bus is as quick as going by car.

5

- Look at the example with the class and ask questions to focus students: *Is the cost of a taxi and a train the same or different?* (different) *Do we use as … as or not as … as?* (*not as … as*).
- Ask students to work individually to complete the sentences. Let students compare answers in pairs once they have written their sentences.

> **ANSWERS**
> 1 n't as expensive as   2 n't as slow as   3 as fast as
> 4 as popular as   5 n't as busy (as Atlanta)

Pronunciation *sentence stress*

6 [22] ★ **CPT extra!** Pronunciation activity [before Ex. 6]

- Ask students to look at the sentences.
- Play the recording. Students listen and underline the stressed words. Let students compare answers in pairs, and play the recording a second time, if necessary, so students can confirm answers.
- **Optional step** Model and drill the sentences, or play the recording again, and ask students to repeat the sentences. Ask students to work in pairs and take turns practising reading out the sentences (see Pronunciation note below).

> **ANSWERS**
>
> See underlined stress in the audioscript below. The strong stress on the stressed syllable of each stressed word is marked.

Audioscript [22] (with answers)

1 **Cyc**ling is as **po**pular as **jog**ging.
2 **Trains** aren't as ex**pen**sive as **ta**xis.
3 Los **An**geles **air**port is as **bu**sy as **Lon**don **Heath**row.
4 A **car** isn't as **fast** as a **bi**cycle in a **tra**ffic **jam**.

> **Pronunciation note**
>
> English is a stress-timed language, so native speakers tend to strongly stress stressed syllables while 'eating' other words in a sentence.
>
> Encourage students to say these sentences with an exaggerated stress on the main stresses. The vowel sounds of unstressed syllables should be reduced to /ə/ sounds. Students should also link words. See the example below:
>
> /əz/   /əz/
> **Cyc**ling is as **po**pular as **jog**ging.

7

- Ask students to work with a new partner. Read the instructions with the class and elicit some questions students can ask (e.g. *How tall are you? How old are you? How often do you watch films? How many people are there in your family?*).
- Ask students to interview each other and note their partner's answers.
- Tell students to use their notes to produce sentences. In feedback, ask different pairs to report what they found out to the class. If students make errors, ask the class to help to correct them.

> **Extra activity**
>
> Students could think of other questions to ask before interviewing their partner. At the end, you could ask them to write up their findings in a short report.
>
> Other possible questions: *How old are your brothers and sisters? How much homework do you do? How big / comfortable / old is your car / bike / phone?*

UNIT 3 Transport

Vocabulary transport adjectives

8
- Start by asking students to look at the photo and the headline. Pre-teach *battle* (= fight) and *black cabs* (= London taxis). Ask students to guess what the text is about.
- Ask students to read the news article. Elicit the answer to the question in feedback.

> **ANSWERS**
> It compares using traditional black cabs in London to using private hire taxis from companies such as Uber, Karhoo or Addison Lee.

Extra activity
Personalize this activity by asking students if they have similar situations in their country, or by asking if they have visited London and used the transport options there.

Background information
Uber is an American company which operates the Uber mobile app. This allows customers with smartphones to submit a trip request which is then routed to Uber drivers who use their own cars. The service is available in over 400 cities worldwide. Karhoo and Addison Lee have similar business models.

9
- Ask students to find the words in the article and match them with the definitions. Elicit the first answer from the class as an example.
- Let students compare answers in pairs before checking with the class (see Vocabulary and pronunciation note below).

> **ANSWERS**
> 1 punctual 2 frequent 3 traditional 4 comfortable
> 5 convenient 6 reliable

Vocabulary and pronunciation note
As students need to use these words in the practice sections which follow, check the meaning carefully, and point out stress and pronunciation.

Meaning
Write the following words on the board: *bus, bed, local shop, student*. Ask students which adjectives go with these words and why (e.g. *a frequent bus – it's every ten minutes; a convenient local shop – it's near and open all day; a comfortable bed, a punctual student – she's never late*). Students may suggest other ideas – it doesn't matter so long as they explain why clearly.

Pronunciation
Drill these words or ask students to listen to you say them and mark the strong stress: con**ven**ient, **freq**uent, **com**fortable, tra**di**tional, **punc**tual, re**li**able.
Note that *comfortable* is often pronounced as three syllables: /ˈkʌmf(ə)təb(ə)l/

Grammar comparative modifiers

10
- Read the grammar box with the class. Then ask students to work in pairs to complete the rules.

> **ANSWERS**
> 1 a bit, a little   2 much, a lot

Grammar note
Form
Make sure students notice the use of 'a' here: *a bit, a little, a lot*.
Alternative expressions students may know are: *slightly, a little bit* and *far*.

Pronunciation
Modifiers are stressed when speaking.

Refer students to page 160 for further information and practice.

> **ANSWERS TO GRAMMAR SUMMARY EXERCISE**
> 5
> 1 a bit more economical
> 2 much cheaper
> 3 a bit more interesting
> 4 a lot quieter; a lot busier
> 5 much more popular
> 6 a little bigger than
> 6
> 1 The best 2 much easier 3 a bit more difficult
> 4 the most convenient 5 a little more direct
> 6 quicker 7 a lot higher than 8 a bit more expensive than
> 9 much quicker 10 more comfortable

11
- Start by focussing students on the information. Ask: *What types of transport are there? (boat, cab, bus) How frequent are buses? (every five minutes) What can you buy on a river boat? (food and drink)*.
- Look at the example with the class and elicit that 'much' is also possible.
- Ask students to work individually to write the remaining sentences. Let students compare answers in pairs once they have written their sentences.

> **EXAMPLE ANSWERS**
> 1 A London bus is a lot / much less expensive than a black cab / a river boat.
> 2 London buses are a lot / much more frequent than river boats.
> 3 The river boat is a lot / much more comfortable than (standing on) the bus.
> 4 A black cab is a bit / a little more convenient than a bus.

3b Transport around the world 59

UNIT 3 Transport

12 ★ **CPT extra!** Vocabulary activity [after Ex. 12]
- Ask students to work in pairs to prepare three more sentences using the information in Exercise 11. Elicit ideas in feedback, and ask students in the class to correct or improve any sentences that are wrong.

> **EXAMPLE ANSWERS**
>
> The river boat is a lot more expensive than a bus.
> Taxis are much more convenient / frequent than river boats.
> The river boat is a little more comfortable than a taxi.

Speaking *my life*
13
- Organize the class into new pairs or small groups. Ask students to read the questions carefully, and to discuss different options. Monitor and notice how well students use comparative structures, and note any errors.
- In feedback, compare advice as a class and decide on a class list of the top five pieces of advice.
- Write four to six errors you noted on the board at the end for students to correct.

> **Extra activity**
>
> Write the following pairs on the board: *buses / trains; walking / cycling; holidays abroad / holidays at home; cycling to work / driving to work; motorways / country roads*. Ask students in pairs to decide which in each sentence is better and to say why.

3c The end of the road

> **Lesson at a glance**
> - reading: traditional transport
> - vocabulary: transport verbs
> - critical thinking: opinions for and against
> - speaking: alternative transport

Reading

1 ★ **CPT extra!** Lead-in activity [after Ex. 1]
- Explain that students are going to read an article about India.
- Ask students to think of one fact, then elicit facts from the class.
- **Optional step** Alternatively, with books closed, write *India* on the board and ask students to work in pairs to think of a fact. Ask students to come to the board and write up their facts.

> **EXAMPLE ANSWERS**
>
> Students' own answers. Some of the more interesting facts about India are:
> It's the seventh largest country in the world.
> It has the second largest population (after China).
> New Delhi is the capital and Mumbai is the largest city.
> It became independent (from Britain) in 1947.
> The most popular sport is cricket.
> It's famous for Bollywood (India's film industry), the Taj Mahal (white mausoleum in Indian city of Agra) and Mahatma Gandhi (leader of the Indian independence movement in British-ruled India).

2 [23]
- Ask students to read the three headings. Point out that *Kolkata* is a city and use the photo on the page to explain what a *rickshaw* is.
- Ask students to read the article quickly to label the paragraphs. Set a two-minute time limit. This should encourage students to just look at the first sentence of each paragraph, and to scan the rest.
- **Optional step** The reading text is recorded. You could play the recording and ask students to read and listen.
- Let students compare answers briefly in pairs before checking with the class.

> **ANSWERS**
>
> Paragraph 1: b (modern transport in Kolkata)
> Paragraph 2: a (why people like rickshaws in Kolkata)
> Paragraph 3: c (the end of the old rickshaws in Kolkata)

UNIT 3 Transport

3
- Read the questions with the class and check students understand all the words, e.g. *pedestrians* (= people walking in the street – not in a car) and *commuters* (= people going to work).
- Ask students to read the article again and find the answers. Let students compare answers in pairs before checking with the class.

> **ANSWERS**
> 1 around 15 million
> 2 All day there are traffic jams and drivers honk their horns from morning to night.
> 3 In the old parts of the city because they have smaller streets and cars can't drive down them.
> 4 Children: to go to school
>   Commuters: to go to work – if they miss the bus to work, a hand-pulled rickshaw is much cheaper than taking a taxi
>   Housewives: to go to the local market
>   Tourists: to get a photograph sitting on a rickshaw because it's a famous symbol of Kolkata
> 5 They want more rickshaw drivers to use pedicabs or modern electric rickshaws, which are clean and fast.
> 6 around 2,000
> 7 The electric rickshaws are expensive and they want to keep their traditional way of life.

> **Background information**
> **Kolkata** was known as Calcutta in colonial times.

Vocabulary transport verbs

4
- Ask students to find the verbs (1–8) in the first two paragraphs of the article and match them with the words they collocate with (a–h). Let them compare answers in pairs before checking with the class. Check students understand all the collocations (see Vocabulary note below).

> **ANSWERS**
> 1 d 2 a 3 h 4 e 5 c 6 b 7 g 8 f

> **Vocabulary note**
> *pick up children* = this means driving somewhere (e.g. to the school) in order to meet the children and take them home. (Other examples: *I'll pick you up outside the station; I'll pick you up after work.*)
>
> *drop (somebody) off* = this is the opposite of *pick somebody up* – it means that you will stop somewhere so they can get out. (Other example: *I'll drop you off at the station on my way home.*)
>
> Point out that the verbs (1–8) can go with more than just the word they collocate with in the text, e.g. *catch/get on/miss a bus or a train, go by bus, train or taxi, take a bus, a train, a taxi or the underground.*

5 ★ **CPT extra!** Vocabulary activity [after Ex. 5]
- Ask students to work in pairs to think of ways of rewriting the sentences. Monitor and notice how well students can use the new language.

> **ANSWERS**
> 1 take a / go by   2 pick up   3 catch   4 miss
> 5 go on foot   6 drop you off

> **Vocabulary note**
> There are some other interesting collocations in the article which students might not know. Use mime to show *honk your horn, cross the road,* and *pull by hand.* Point out language recycled from earlier in the unit: *rush hour, traffic jam, go on foot.*

> **Extra activity**
> Ask some personalized questions to get students using the language: *How often do you take the bus? When did you last catch the train and why? Do you sometimes pick someone up? Who and why?* Ask students to make some questions of their own to ask their partner.

Critical thinking opinions for and against

6
- Ask students to work in pairs to research the article and find reasons for the opinions of the different groups. In feedback, discuss what the students found out with the class.

> **ANSWERS**
> 1 For
>   parents (*Early in the day, the drivers pick up children and take them to school.*)
>   shoppers (*... housewives often prefer to go by rickshaw to the local markets. The driver drops the women off with their shopping outside their house; no other type of public transport can do that!*)
>   tourists (*Visitors to the city often want to get a photograph sitting on a rickshaw because it's a famous symbol of Kolkata.*)
>   rickshaw drivers (*... they don't have any other job ... the traditional rickshaw and their way of life.*)
> 2 Against
>   politicians (*... they think it's wrong for one human to pull other humans. Instead, they want more rickshaw drivers to use pedicabs or modern electric rickshaws, which are clean and fast.*)

3c The end of the road   61

UNIT 3 Transport

7

- Discuss the question as a class and encourage students to give and explain opinions.

> **ANSWER**
>
> Students' own answers. They might argue that it's balanced because, in the last paragraph, the two points against traditional rickshaws (*it's wrong for one human to pull other humans … electric rickshaws … are clean and fast*) are balanced by the arguments for (*men from villages … don't have any other job … The new electric rickshaws are very expensive*). Alternatively, they might argue that the majority of the article favours the argument for traditional rickshaws. It talks about how the rickshaws are useful and popular.

> **Extra activity**
>
> Organize the class into groups of four. Ask two students in each group to be politicians. They must prepare arguments against rickshaws. Ask the other two to be shoppers, tourists, parents or rickshaw drivers. They must prepare arguments for rickshaws. Tell students to use the text and their own ideas in preparation. When students are ready, ask them to discuss their ideas and decide on whether to keep or ban rickshaws.

> **Teacher development**
>
> **Critical thinking skills**
>
> *Life* aims to get students to analyse and apply what they learn. This requires mental effort from students, and helps students' intellectual development.
>
> Here are some ideas:
>
> - Ask your students to do more than just comprehend meaning and lexis in a text. Ask them to read texts to find facts or opinions, or to recognize the point of view of the author or of people mentioned or quoted in a text, or to notice the way a writer develops an argument in a text.
> - A key critical thinking skill is being able to look at something from the perspective of another person. Use questions like the following to get your students to notice this: *What does X think about Y? How does X feel?*
> - Use roleplays and discussions to help develop critical skills. For example, ask students to take on the roles of people in a text and to argue their points of view (see Extra activity above).

Speaking my life

8

- Ask students to work in pairs. Tell them to read the advertisement and discuss the questions. In feedback, ask students who have pedicabs in their country to say why they are popular or ask students to think of one or two other bullet points to add to the advertisement.

9

- Ask pairs to work with another pair to make groups of four. Ask them to work together to discuss the questions and make notes. Monitor and help with ideas and vocabulary.
- You could ask questions to prompt students to think of ideas: *Does your city have a lot of tourists? How far is it from the station to the city centre? How much do tourists pay for a bus tour?*

10

- Ask each group to make a presentation. A good way to do this is to ask each group, firstly, to decide which student will make the presentation, and then work as a group for two or three minutes to prepare and order what to say. After each presentation, ask the rest of the class to think of and ask questions. At the end, ask which group had the best ideas.
- **Optional step** You could write the following phrases on the board as students prepare their presentations:

    We're going to talk about …

    Now, we'd like to say why …

    Let's turn to …

    To sum up, …

    Tell students to use the phrases to organize their presentations.

> **Extra activity**
>
> Ask each group to make a poster with bullet points to advertise their pedicab company. Display the posters on the walls. One student from each group stands by their poster while the other students walk round and look at other posters. The students who are standing with their posters talk about their posters and answer questions from visiting students.

UNIT 3 Transport

3d Getting around town

> **Lesson at a glance**
> - vocabulary: taking transport
> - real life: going on a journey
> - pronunciation: intonation

Vocabulary taking transport

1 ★ **CPT extra!** Lead-in activity [before Ex. 1]
- **Optional step** Write *train, bus* and *plane* on the board. Ask students to work in pairs. Tell pairs to choose one word and think of as many words that collocate with that mode of transport as they can (e.g. *train station, express train, slow train, train timetable, crowded train, electric train, train driver; airport bus, local bus, school bus, sightseeing bus, bus ticket, bus queue, bus journey; fly a plane, jet plane, charter plane, plane ticket*). In feedback, find out which pair has the longest or best list.
- Ask students to work in pairs to match the pairs of words with the definitions. Elicit the first answer as a class as an example. Encourage students to make guesses and use prior knowledge.
- At the end, check answers as a class and provide contextualized examples to show the meaning (see Vocabulary note below), or ask students to use dictionaries to check.

> **ANSWERS**
> 1 a rank; b stop
> 2 a fare; b price
> 3 a change; b receipt
> 4 a platform; b gate
> 5 a book; b check in

> **Vocabulary note**
> 1 We say *a bus stop* but *a taxi rank* – we also say *bus station* when it's the main place where buses start from or return to.
> 2 We say *bus fare, taxi fare* or *train fare* (e.g. *How much is the fare from the station to the centre? Prices are going up in the shops.*)
> 3 Compare these example dialogues:
>   A: *That's £4.20*
>   B: *OK. Here's £5.*
>   A: *Thanks. Here's your change – eighty pence.*
>
>   A: *That's £100. Here's your receipt. Bring it with you if you have to bring the product back.*
>   B: *OK. Thanks.*
> 4 Compare these examples:
>   *The next flight to Paris is from Gate 11.*
>   *The train to London is on Platform 3.*
> 5 Compare these examples:
>   *Can I book two tickets for the play next Saturday?*
>   *You have to check in two hours before the flight departs.*

> **Pronunciation note**
> Note the pronunciation of *fare* /fɛə/ and *receipt* /rɪˈsiːt/.

Real life going on a journey

2 🔊 [24]
- Explain that students are going to listen to five conversations involving two people, Javier and Shelley, both trying to get to the airport.
- Ask students to read the questions carefully. Point out that each question relates to one conversation.
- Play the recording. Students listen and answer the questions. Let them compare their answers in pairs before checking with the class.

> **ANSWERS**
> 1 the train station
> 2 £6.30; No, he doesn't.
> 3 the airport, north terminal; a single ticket
> 4 £14.50; platform 6
> 5 her passport; none

Audioscript 🔊 [24]

Conversation 1
J = Javier, D = Driver
J: Hello? Are you the next taxi?
D: Yes, that's right.
J: I'd like to go to the station, please.
D: Bus or train?
J: Oh sorry. The train station.
D: OK. Get in then.

Conversation 2
D = Driver, J = Javier
D: There are road works up by the entrance.
J: You can stop here. It's fine. How much is that?
D: Six pounds thirty.
J: Sorry, I only have a twenty-pound note. Do you have change?
D: Sure. So, that's thirteen pounds seventy. Do you want a receipt?
J: No, it's OK, thanks. Bye.

Conversation 3
S = Shelley, D = Driver
S: Hi. Do you stop at the airport?
D: Yeah, I do. Which terminal is it? North or south?
S: Er. I need to get to the … north terminal.
D: OK. A single or return ticket?
S: Single, please.
D: That's two pounds.

Conversation 4
J = Javier, T = Ticket office clerk
J: A return ticket to the airport, please.
T: OK. The next train goes in five minutes.
J: Right. That one, please.

3d Getting around town 63

UNIT 3 Transport

T: First or second class?
J: Second.
T: OK. That's fourteen pounds fifty.
J: Wow! I don't think I have the cash.
T: Credit card is fine.
J: Oh no … maybe I have enough left.
T: OK. Here you are.
J: Which platform is it?
T: Er, platform six.

Conversation 5
A = Attendant, S = Shelley, J = Javier

A: Hello. Can I see your passport?
S: Here you are.
A: That's OK. How many bags are you checking in?
S: None. I only have this carry-on.
A: OK. Window or aisle?
S: Er, I don't mind, but can I have a seat next to my friend?
A: Has he already checked in?
S: No, I'm waiting for him.
A: Well, I can't …
J: Shelley!
S: Where have you been?
J: It's a long story.

3 [24]

- Ask students to work in pairs to read the expressions. Tell them to discuss which ones they think were used in the conversation.
- Play the recording again. Students listen and tick the expressions used. Let students compare their answers in pairs before checking with the class.
- **Optional step** Ask students to work in pairs to practise the conversations in audioscript 24 on pages 182–183 of the Student's Book.

> **ANSWERS**
> I'd like to go to the station, please.
> You can stop here.
> How much is that?
> Do you have change?
> Do you want a receipt?
>
> Do you stop at the airport?
> A single or return ticket?
> That's two pounds.
>
> A return ticket to the airport, please.
> First or second class?
> Which platform is it?
>
> Can I see your passport?
> How many bags are you checking in?
> I only have this carry-on.
> Window or aisle?
> Can I have a seat next to my friend?

Pronunciation intonation
4a [25]

- Read the information about intonation with the class.
- Play the recording. Students listen and mark the intonation.

Audioscript [25] (with answers)

1 Single or return?
2 Window or aisle?
3 Credit card or cash?
4 Bus or train?
5 North or south?
6 First or second class?

> **Pronunciation note**
>
> In these either/or questions, the intonation rises over the first choice, and falls over the second choice. Encourage students to exaggerate the intonation in their voices as they speak. By using a sweeping hand gesture down or up, you can prompt students as they repeat or practise.

b [25]

- Play the recording again, pausing after each question, for students to listen and repeat (see Pronunciation note above).
- **Optional step** Ask students to work in pairs to practise saying the questions.

5

- Organize the class into new pairs. Ask students to decide who is A, and who B.
- Read the instructions with the class and check that everyone understands what to do. Point out the captions above the photos (a–d).
- It's a good idea to prepare students for this roleplay. You could ask them to write dialogues first, using expressions from the lesson. Tell them to practise reading their dialogue, then to turn over the written dialogue and try to remember and improvise it. Alternatively, ask students to choose and match expressions they could use for each dialogue. Then ask them to improvise dialogues, using the expressions they chose.
- As students speak, circulate and monitor their performance. Note down errors students make and, in feedback, write errors on the board and ask students to correct them.
- Students then change roles and repeat the conversations. They could do this with a new partner.

UNIT 3 Transport

3e Quick communication

Lesson at a glance
- writing: notes and messages
- writing skill: writing in note form

Writing notes and messages

1
- **Optional step** Ask students to say what the last note or message they wrote was, and who it was to.
- Ask students to work in pairs to discuss the questions. Elicit ideas in a brief feedback.

EXAMPLE ANSWERS

Students' own answers. Other possible ways: social networking sites like Facebook, leaving notes or memos on paper, leaving messages on an answerphone, by letter or postcard.

2
- Ask students to read the notes and messages (1–8) and match them with the reasons for writing (a–e). You could elicit the first match as an example to get students started. Let students compare answers in pairs before checking with the class.

ANSWERS

1 d 2 b 3 e 4 c 5 a 6 c 7 d 8 b

Writing skills writing in note form

3a
- Read the information with the class and look at the example.
- Ask students to read the notes again and find examples of where the writer has missed out words. Let them compare their answers in pairs before checking as a class.

ANSWERS

1 (Can we) Meet outside (the) airport at 2? (Is that) OK?
2 (I'm) Sorry. (The) Bus (was) late. (I) Will be 15 minutes late.
3 Javier called. (Can you) Call him back? (His number is) 0770 657 655.
4 (The) Train leaves (from) platform 6.
5 Thanks for getting (the) tickets. Here's the money.
6 (The) Plane (is) at gate 6.
7 (I) Am in (a/the) taxi. (Shall I/I'll) See you outside in 5 (minutes)?
8 (I'm) Afraid I was late so (I) missed (the) meeting. (May I offer/Please accept) My apologies.

b
- Look at the example with the class and ask students to say which words have been omitted.

- Ask students to work individually to shorten the messages. Let them compare their answers in pairs before checking with the class.

ANSWERS

1 Sorry. Stuck in traffic. See you in 30 mins.
2 Thanks for booking tickets. Pay you at station.
3 Take underground to Oxford Street. Moon café opposite station.
4 Peter wants to come in taxi. Call and tell him where to meet.
5 Flight 1 hr late. Meet arrivals at 5.

4
- Ask students to work in pairs to write messages. Monitor unobtrusively and help when necessary.
- In feedback, ask students to decide as a class on the best note for each situation.

EXAMPLE ANSWERS

1 Working late. Arrive bus station 1 hr later.
2 Take taxi outside station to centre.
3 Can't travel on underground. Will take bus. Meet check-in.

5 ★ CPT extra! Writing activity [after Ex. 5]
- Students work individually to write their messages. Organize the class so students have a new partner. Ask them to exchange messages and write replies.

Extra activity

Ask students to put their messages on the classroom walls or on their desks. Ask students to walk round the class and read the messages.

3e Quick communication 65

UNIT 3 Transport

3f Indian Railways

Before you watch

1 ★ **CPT extra!** Photo activity [after Ex. 1]

- Ask students to work in small groups. Ask them to look at the photo and caption and to discuss the question. Elicit students' ideas in feedback.

> **EXAMPLE ANSWERS**
>
> Trains may be popular in India because: it's a large country with long distances to travel; it's a mountainous country and trains may be easier than roads; there may be a very good train service; trains may be cheap; many people may not have a car; the railways may be better than the roads.

Key vocabulary

2a

- Encourage students to use the context to guess the meanings of the words in bold.
- Start by asking students to look at *track* and ask: *Is it a verb or a noun?* (noun) *Which word goes with it?* (railway) *What do we find out about it?* (It's dangerous to walk on it).
- Ask students to work in pairs to discuss the other words.

b

- Ask students to read the definitions and match them with the words.
- **Optional step** It's a good idea to show the pronunciation of these key words – students have to hear them in continuous speech on the video. You could say the words and ask students to repeat, or say the words and ask students to underline the strongly stressed syllable: *impressive, miniature, rural* /ˈrʊərəl/.

> **ANSWERS**
>
> 1 b   2 a   3 d   4 e   5 c

While you watch

3 ▶ [3.1]

- Read the six sentences with the class and explain any difficult words (draw pictures on the board to show *beard* and *sword*).
- Play the video with no sound. Students watch and number the actions in order (1–6). Let students compare answers in pairs before checking with the class. Write the order on the board.

> **ANSWERS**
>
> 1 c   2 b   3 a   4 e   5 f   6 d

Videoscript ▶ 3.1

0.00–0.08 At the Victoria Terminus in Mumbai, India, it always seems to be rush hour.

0.09–0.15 Every day, approximately two million passengers pass through this train station.

0.16–0.30 The journey to Mumbai is often very stressful. But in this country of over a billion people, the best way to travel is by train.

0.31–0.35 The British built the railways in India in the 19th century.

0.36–1.00 The first steam train in India was in 1853. Now, the Indian Railways travel along 38,000 miles of track. Many of the trains have impressive names like the Himalayan Queen and Grand Trunk Express. The Grand Trunk Express has travelled up and down the country since 1929.

1.01–1.12 Most of India Railways' four billion passengers a year live in big cities. But even rural villagers do not usually have to walk for more than a day to get to a station.

01.13–01.30 With over one and a half million people on its staff, India's railways are the world's largest employer. From the Indian Railways minister down to the key man who makes sure every inch of track is in good condition, the huge workforce keeps this enormous system running.

1.31–1.33 The railway stations are often an amazing mix of people.

1.34–1.43 There are people selling food, porters carrying bags, and sometimes performance artists.

1.44–end But the railway is more than just a way to travel. It is like a miniature India. In the second-class carriages, there are people from all over the country, from different classes and cultural backgrounds. They talk, play games and tell stories. For travellers, the Indian railways are their own adventure.

4 ▶ [3.1] ★ **CPT extra!** Video activity [after Ex. 4]

- Ask students to read the sentences and check any difficult words, e.g. *staff* (= people who work for a company).
- Play the video with the sound on. Students choose the correct words. Let students compare answers in pairs before checking as a class.

> **ANSWERS**
>
> 1 two million   2 one billion   3 nineteenth
> 4 fifty-three   5 thirty-eight thousand
> 6 nineteen twenty-nine   7 four billion
> 8 one and a half million

Vocabulary note

Two hundred thousand = 200,000
One million = 1,000,000
One billion = 1,000,000,000

Background information

The current population of **India** is approximately 1.34 billion people.

66   Unit 3   Transport

UNIT 3 Transport

After you watch
Vocabulary in context
5a [3.2]

- Explain that students are going to watch some clips from the video which contain some new words and phrases. They need to choose the correct meaning of the words.
- Play the clips. When each multiple-choice question appears, pause the clip so that students can choose the correct definition. You could let students compare answers in pairs before checking with the class.

ANSWERS
1 a   2 c   3 b   4 b   5 c

Videoscript 3.2

1 At the Victoria Terminus in Mumbai, it always seems to be **rush hour.**
   a the busiest time of the day for travel
   b the time when the trains start travelling
   c the quietest hour of the day for travel
2 The journey to Mumbai is often very **stressful**.
   a slow and boring
   b busy and noisy
   c not relaxing
3 India's railways are the world's largest **employer.**
   a a person who works for an organization
   b a person or organization who employs people
   c a person who has his own business
4 … makes sure every inch of track is in good **condition** …
   a the price of something
   b the state of something
   c the strength of something
5 … the huge workforce keeps this **enormous** system running.
   a fairly big
   b big
   c very big

b

- Organize the class into new pairs to discuss the questions. Instead of asking all the questions, you could tell pairs to choose one of the three topics and to discuss it fully. Set a short time limit and ask different pairs to say what they found out from their partner in feedback.

ANSWERS
Students' own answers

6 [3.3]

- Students will watch a one-minute clip with no sound. It contains short sections of ten to twenty seconds each on the following: the rush hour in Mumbai, on the train, the workforce, and at the railway station.
- Make sure students are ready to take notes. Then play the clip. If students demand it, play the clip a second time so they can add to their notes.

7

- Ask students to work individually to prepare a script for the new video. They should use words and phrases from the box to describe what they see in the video and any important facts and figures about the Indian railway.
- **Optional step** If you think students may find it hard, ask them to work in pairs to write a script together, but make sure each student writes. Monitor and help with ideas and vocabulary.

EXAMPLE ANSWERS
See the videoscript 3.1 on the previous page.

8

- Ask students to work in pairs. If your students prepared in a pair, split them up so they all have a new partner.
- Play the video clip twice. Students take turns to read their script to their partner.

Extra activity

Ask two or three students to read their script out to the class as they watch. Ask for feedback on the scripts from the class.

If you have the technology, think about recording students' narration so you can play it at the same time as the clip. You could give written feedback on errors and let students listen to their own recording, note their errors, and re-record with errors corrected.

UNIT 3 Transport

UNIT 3 Review and memory booster ★ CPT extra! Language games

> **Memory Booster activities**
>
> Exercises 2, 5 and 7 are Memory Booster activities. For more information about these activities and how they benefit students, see page 10.

> ***I can …* tick boxes**
>
> As an alternative to students simply ticking the *I can …* boxes, you could ask them to give themselves a score from 1 to 4 (1 = not very confident; 4 = very confident) for each language area. If students score 1 or 2 for a language area, refer them to additional practice activities in the Workbook and Grammar summary exercises.

Grammar

1

- Ask students to work individually to complete the article with the correct form of the adjectives. Let students compare answers in pairs before checking with the class.

> **ANSWERS**
>
> 1 largest   2 busiest   3 most beautiful   4 most polluted
> 5 clean   6 better   7 noisy   8 more popular

2 >> MB

- Ask students to work in pairs to write four sentences comparing their town or city (or the city they are in) with Santiago. Monitor and help with vocabulary as necessary.

> **ANSWERS**
>
> Students' own answers

Vocabulary

3

- Ask students to match words from each box to form compound nouns and to use them to complete the sentences. Let students compare answers in pairs before checking with the class.

> **ANSWERS**
>
> 1 traffic jam   2 Rush hour   3 bus stop   4 speed limit
> 5 city centre

4

- Ask students to work individually to cross out the word in each group that doesn't follow the verb.
- **Optional step** Ask students to tell you the correct verb for each of the incorrect words (1 go on foot, 2 and 3 take a taxi, 4 go on the underground).

> **ANSWERS**
>
> 1 foot   2 a taxi   3 a taxi   4 the underground

5 >> MB

- Ask students to work in pairs to look at the photos and answer the questions. Encourage them to give reasons for their answers.

> **EXAMPLE ANSWERS**
>
> 1 c and e   2 a and f   3 b and c   4 d   5 d   6 a   7 a and c

Real life

6

- Ask students to work individually to complete the conversation with the words in the box.

> **ANSWERS**
>
> 1 ticket   2 Single   3 Return   4 receipt   5 platform

7 >> MB

- Ask students to work in pairs to write a similar conversation to the one in Exercise 6 but this time between two people at an airport. Monitor and help as necessary.
- You could invite pairs to act out their conversation for the class.

Unit 4 Challenges

Opener

1
- Ask students to look at the photo and discuss the questions. You could choose to do this activity in open class or ask students to talk in pairs before eliciting a few ideas from the class in feedback (see Teacher development below).

> **ANSWERS**
> Students' own answers. The photo shows a man in a cave. He's on a wire descending underground into the cave. It looks exciting and is certainly dangerous.

> **Background information**
> **Krubera Cave** is the deepest-known cave on Earth. It's located in Abkhazia, a breakaway region of Georgia.

2 [26] ★ **CPT extra!** Background information [after Ex. 2]
- Ask students to read the three questions. Check they understand *caver* (= a person who goes into caves for a hobby) and *colleague* (= a person you work with).
- Play the recording. Students listen and answer the questions. Let them compare answers in pairs before checking with the class.

> **ANSWERS**
> 1 Because they say his hobby is dangerous.
> 2 Because every cave gives you a different challenge – you look after each other when you work as a team.
> 3 You have to use a rope and climb down a hole that's about twenty metres into the ground. At the bottom, you are on your hands and knees for nearly a kilometre.

Audioscript [26]

My name's Vic and I live in the state of Tennessee. During the week I work in a bank. I like my job but most of the time I'm sitting at a desk, so I need to get exercise after work and at the weekends. Most people go running or play sports, but I like caving. My colleagues think I'm a bit crazy because they say it's dangerous. It's true that sometimes you have to take a risk when you go caving, but I always go with other cavers and we look after each other. It's important to work as a team when you go down into a new cave because every cave gives you a different challenge. The most difficult cave was called Rumbling Falls Cave. You have to use a rope and climb down a hole that's about twenty metres into the ground. At the bottom, you are on your hands and knees for nearly a kilometre, so you need to be physically fit. Then at the end, you come into the main part of the cave. It's an incredible place, like a huge room. Getting to Rumbling Falls Cave was probably my biggest achievement as a caver.

> **Background information**
> **Tennessee** /tɛnɪˈsiː/ is a state located in the south-eastern region of the United States. It's well-known for the many cave systems that are mostly located near or under the Great Smoky Mountains. They include a cave with a one-of-a-kind underground lake called the Lost Sea.

3
- Ask students to match the words in bold with the definitions. Let students compare answers in pairs before checking with the class.
- **Optional step** Point out the strong stress in *challenge* and *achievement*.

> **ANSWERS**
> 1 a   2 c   3 b

> **Vocabulary note**
> Here are other difficult words on the recording:
> *rope* = use mime to show this word: mime climbing up a rope
> *a hole* = a space in the ground that things can go down (e.g. *a golf hole, a rabbit hole*)
> *huge* = very big

4
- Pre-teach *risky* (= dangerous – the adjective from the noun *risk*).
- Ask students to work in small groups to discuss the questions. In feedback, ask some students to tell the class what they found out about their classmates.

> **ANSWERS**
> Students' own answers

> **Teacher development**
>
> **Classroom interaction**
>
> It's important in a communicative classroom to vary the interaction between students. This means taking time to plan in advance whether you want students to do any given activity individually, in pairs, in groups, as a whole class activity, or in a mingle or mill (when students walk round the class and talk to a number of other students). The exercise instructions in *Life* Pre-Intermediate sometimes suggest that students work in pairs or groups, and sometimes don't suggest an interaction pattern (implying that the activity could be done as a whole class activity or individually). Don't feel, however, that you should always follow these instructions. Feel free to vary the patterns.
>
> Here are suggested interaction patterns for the four stages in the introductory lesson above:
>
> **1** Whole class – ask the questions and elicit answers from a variety of students in the class.
> **2** Students listen and note answers individually – students check answers in pairs – teacher elicits answers from the class.

69

UNIT 4 Challenges

3 Students match words and definitions individually – students check answers in pairs – teacher elicits answers from the class.
4 Students work in groups of four with new students they haven't worked with before.

Note, however, that you could easily vary these patterns. For example, students could discuss the photo in Exercise 1 in pairs, match the vocabulary in Exercise 3 in pairs, and do Exercise 4 as a whole class activity or as a mingle. The important thing is to plan a variety of interaction patterns in advance, vary them from lesson to lesson, and make sure students get to talk to different class members rather than always working with the same partner.

4a Adventurers of the year

Lesson at a glance
- reading: adventurers' stories
- grammar: past simple
- pronunciation: /d/, /t/ or /ɪd/
- speaking: your past

Reading

1 [27] ★ **CPT extra!** Lead-in activity [before Ex. 1]
- **Optional step** Ask students to look at the two photos. Ask: *Where are they? Where do you think they are from? What do you think they do?* Elicit ideas. Ask students to read the texts very quickly to find out if they predicted correctly.
- Ask students to read the phrases they have to categorize before they read the article. Also, check that they understand how the Venn diagram works.
- Ask students to read the article and complete the diagram. Let students compare answers in pairs. Elicit the answers in feedback. Note that the answer to 6 is not given directly – students have to assume it from what the people did.
- **Optional step** The reading text is recorded. You could play the recording and ask students to read and listen.

> **ANSWERS**
> Pasang: 1
> Marjan: 2, 5
> Both: 3, 4, 6

2
- Ask students to read the article again and find answers to the questions. Let them compare their answers in pairs before checking with the class.
- Note that the answers to these questions are not all fixed – they depend on the students' interpretation of the text. In feedback, elicit and discuss different answers.

> **ANSWERS**
> 1 Students could argue for any one of the following: growing up without parents, training to be a mountaineer, climbing Everest, or helping earthquake victims.
> 2 She's famous for her voluntary work and mountaineering.
> 3 To be a cyclist.
> 4 They competed in international competitions and encouraged women in Afghanistan to take up cycling.

UNIT 4 Challenges

Vocabulary note
(mountain) guide = somebody who shows climbers or tourists the best way to go or the things to see on a route
earthquake = a natural disaster, when the ground shakes and buildings fall down
voluntary work = work that you do without pay to help other people
(cycling) coach = somebody who teaches or trains athletes in sports to get better
ambition = something you want to do or achieve in life

Background information
Nepal is a landlocked country in Asia, north of India, most famous because the Himalayan mountain range and Mount Everest, the world's highest mountain, are in the country. At 2,860 metres Lukla is a popular place for visitors to the Himalayas near Mount Everest to arrive.
Afghanistan is also a landlocked country in Asia, to the west of Nepal and north of Pakistan.

Grammar past simple
3
- Ask students to read the grammar box and decide which verbs are regular (*lived*) or irregular (*grew up, didn't have, wasn't*).
- Ask students to underline and categorize the past verbs in the article. Let them compare their answers in pairs before checking with the class.

ANSWERS
regular (in order): The mountaineer: *lived, died, trained, worked, climbed, helped*; The cyclist: *loved, entered*
irregular (in order): The mountaineer: *was, was, didn't have* (past: *had*); The cyclist: *was (born), grew up, was, had, gave, was, saw, built, wasn't, went, had, didn't win* (past: *won*)

Refer students to page 162 for further information and practice.

ANSWERS TO GRAMMAR SUMMARY EXERCISES
1
1 wanted 2 wasn't 3 didn't have 4 didn't like
5 was 6 studied
2
1 booked 2 didn't want 3 decided 4 drove
5 didn't know 6 asked 7 was 8 could 9 were
10 took 11 had

4
- Ask students to discuss the questions. You could do this in open class or ask students to work in pairs before eliciting answers as a class.
- **Optional step** If you think your students will have problems working out the infinitive forms, write them up on the board (*grow, go, be, have, give, win, see, build*) and ask them to match them with the past forms in the article.

ANSWERS
1 We add *-ed* to regular verbs to form the past simple.
 If the verb ends in *-e* (e.g. *live, dance*), we add *-d*.
 If the verb ends in *-y*, we change *y* to *i* and add *-ed*.
2 Infinitive forms of the irregular verbs underlined in the article (in order): The mountaineer: *be, be, (not) have*; The cyclist: *be (born), grow up, be, have, give, be, see, build, (not) be, go, have, (not) win*
3 We form the negative of most past simple verbs by using *didn't* (the negative past form of the auxiliary verb *do*) and the infinitive form of the main verb (e.g. *lived* becomes *didn't live*). We form the negative of *be* by adding *not* (*wasn't/weren't*).

Grammar note
Regular verbs
Note the following further form rules for regular verbs:
1 When a verb ends in consonant-vowel-consonant, the final consonant is usually doubled (e.g. *stop – stopped, ban – banned*).
2 When a verb ends in *– y* after a consonant (e.g. *carry, tidy, hurry, study*), *–y* changes to *i* (e.g. *carried*), but when a verb ends in *y* after a vowel, *y* does not change (e.g. *play – played, stay – stayed*).

Irregular verbs
Irregular verbs in English tend to be the short, common verbs that we use most often in everybody language (e.g. *be, do, go, get, take*). There are no rules governing when and why a verb might be regular or irregular (compare *live – lived* but *give – gave*, or *bake – baked, make – made* and *take – took*). Students simply have to learn the forms by heart. From now on, get students to note both the infinitive and the past form (if irregular) of any new verbs they learn. Remind students of the irregular verb list on page 180 of the Student's Book.

Pronunciation /d/, /t/ or /ɪd/

5a [28] ★ **CPT extra!** Pronunciation activity [before Ex. 5a]
- Read the instructions with the class and point out the three different pronunciations of *-ed* in the first three words (see Pronunciation note below).
- Play the recording. Students listen, notice and write the correct sound next to the remaining irregular verbs.

ANSWERS
1 /d/ 2 /t/ 3 /ɪd/ 4 /ɪd/ 5 /ɪd/ 6 /t/ 7 /ɪd/ 8 /d/
(Note that students could argue that 4 is /d/ since the infinitive *study* already ends with a /ɪ/ sound.)

Pronunciation note
- After a voiced sound (one in which the vocal chords vibrate), *-ed* is pronounced /d/.
- After an unvoiced sound (one in which they don't vibrate), it's pronounced /t/.
- When a verb ends in /t/ or /d/, *-ed* is pronounced /ɪd/. Low level students often make the mistake of applying the /ɪd/ pronunciation to all forms (e.g. they pronounce *lived* as /lɪvɪd/ instead of /lɪvd/. Emphasize that /ɪd/ is only used after /t/ or /d/.

4a Adventurers of the year

UNIT 4 Challenges

b 🔘 [28]
- Play the recording again. Students listen and repeat.

6
- **Optional step** Ask students to look at the photo. Ask: *Where is he from? How old is he? What does he do?* Elicit answers, than ask students to read the text quickly, without worrying about the gaps, to find the answers (He's an Iranian photographer in his sixties).
- Ask students to complete the text with the past simple form of the verbs. Let students compare answers in pairs before checking with the class.

> **ANSWERS**
> 1 was 2 studied 3 didn't become 4 loved 5 got
> 6 didn't want 7 went 8 took

Vocabulary note
a*broad* = in / from a different country (to your own)
architect = a person who designs buildings
*archi*tecture = buildings or the study of how to design buildings
war = when two countries fight

7
- Ask students to read the text again and answer the questions. Let students compare answers in pairs before checking with the class.

> **ANSWERS**
> 1 in 1952
> 2 in Tehran, in Iran
> 3 photography
> 4 He got a job with a newspaper as a photographer.
> 5 No, he wanted to go abroad.
> 6 in 1978

8
- Ask students to read the grammar box and choose the correct option (a or b) to complete the rules. Let them compare their answers in pairs before checking with the class.

> **ANSWERS**
> 1 b 2 a

Grammar note
- The verb *be* is its own auxiliary verb, so it forms questions using inversion (e.g. *He was from Iran* becomes *Was he from Iran?* and *They were French* becomes *Were they French?*).
- All other verbs in English use the auxiliary verb *do* (in its past form *did*) to form questions. The verb *did* inverts with the subject and the main verb reverts to the infinitive form. Note the table below (which you could write on the board for students to copy):

Q word	auxiliary	subject	main verb (in infinitive form)
Where	did	he	study architecture?
	Did	he	want to take photos?

Refer students to page 162 for further information and practice.

> **ANSWERS TO GRAMMAR SUMMARY EXERCISE**
> 3
> 1 How was your hotel?
> 2 When did you get back?
> 3 Did they get the train home?
> 4 What was your favourite experience?
> 5 Did you call me this morning?
> 6 How much did our plane tickets cost?

9 ★ CPT extra! Grammar activity [after Ex. 9]
- Look at the example with the class and point out that students need to use *did* + subject + infinitive of the verb. Elicit the second question as a class.
- Ask students to work individually to complete the questions in the interview. Note that students will need to supply the question word also in questions 4 and 5. Let them compare answers with a partner before checking with the class.

> **ANSWERS**
> 1 did you live
> 2 did you climb
> 3 did you help
> 4 Where were
> 5 When did you have / When was
> 6 Did you win

Speaking 〈 my life 〉
10
- Ask students to work individually to prepare questions from the prompts. Start by eliciting two or three possible questions from the class so that students are clear about how to form them. Monitor and help them prepare.
- **Optional step** Ask students to work in pairs to prepare questions (instead of working individually). Write the following categories on the board: *education, holidays, work, childhood*. Tell them to choose a category from the board and to work with their partner to think of six questions in that category.

11
- Organize the class into pairs to ask and answer their questions. (If they prepared questions in pairs, reorganize students so they have a new partner). Make sure students note their partner's answers as they will need the information for the next activity.
- As students speak, monitor and note any errors you hear.
- After a few minutes, stop the activity. Ask different individuals to say what they learned about their partner. If they make any errors with the past simple, ask the rest of the class to try to help correct. At the end, write up short sentences with errors you heard during the interview stage and ask pairs or groups to work together to correct them.

72 Unit 4 Challenges

UNIT 4 Challenges

> **EXAMPLE ANSWERS**
>
> Here are some example questions formed from the prompts in the Student's Book:
> *Where were you born?*
> *Where did you grow up?*
> *When did you learn to ride a bike?*
> *When did you start studying English?*
> *Where did you go on holiday last year?*
> *Did you go abroad last year?*
> *Did you go to university?*
> *What was your first job?*

12

- Organize the class into new pairs. Each student has to remember and say what they found out about their partner in Exercise 11. You could introduce some key time phrases to help them structure their descriptions: *In 2010, After that, Last year, Later, Ten years ago*.
- As students speak, monitor and note any errors you hear (see Teacher development below). At the end, write up short sentences with errors involving past forms that you heard. Ask students to correct the errors with a partner.

Extra activity

You could turn this into 'ask the teacher'. Let students interview you in a whole class activity. Only answer questions that are formed and pronounced correctly. Ask students to write a biography of the teacher for homework, based on the notes they take.

Teacher development

Handling feedback

After a fluency speaking activity, it's important to feed back on both content and language use. Here are three steps to a successful feedback:

1 Feed back on what students talked about first. Give the class an opportunity to say what they found out about each other, to show that they completed the task. In Exercises 10, 11 and 12 above, for example, the students' task was to discover and share personal information about each other's past. So, your first step in feedback is to ask about that. Do this briefly. For example, ask a handful of students to tell you the most interesting thing they found out about their partner, or ask questions like: *Who wasn't born in this country? Who went abroad last year?*

2 Feed back on how well your class used new or revised language. In the feedback stage, you could write up on the board any interesting or useful chunks of language students used when doing the activity. You could also write up phrases they didn't use, but might have used. Try to improve your students' language production by praising and reinforcing good use and making tweaks and suggestions for better use.

3 Feed back on errors your students make. It's important at the end of an extended fluency stage to provide feedback on errors students make, particularly in the area you're focussing on (in this lesson, past forms). Ideas on how to provide error feedback on a fluency stage is in a later Teacher development box (see Teacher's Book Unit 6: at the end of the 6a section).

4a Adventurers of the year

UNIT 4 Challenges

4b An impossible decision

Lesson at a glance
- vocabulary: personal qualities
- listening: an impossible decision
- grammar: past continuous and past simple
- pronunciation: was/were
- speaking: events you remember

Vocabulary personal qualities

1
- Ask students to work in small groups of three or four to discuss the questions. In feedback, elicit ideas.

ANSWERS
1 If two people work together, they have better ideas than one. They might find better solutions to difficult problems.
2 Students' own answers
3 Possible answers:
   Advantages: different people are good at different things, so a team can do a better job using everybody's skills. Some people think better by talking with other people and exchanging ideas.
   Disadvantages: It can be easier to concentrate and get on with work on your own, you waste less time.
4 Answers will be checked in the next exercise.

2
- **Optional step** Ask students to look at the words in the box. Read them out, paying attention to the stress, and ask students to repeat. (The strong stress is on the first syllable of each word except *experienced* and *intelligent*).
- Look at the example with the class. Then ask students to work individually to match the remaining adjectives with the sentences. Let students compare answers in pairs before checking with the class.

ANSWERS
1 friendly 2 kind 3 patient 4 positive
5 hard-working 6 experienced 7 intelligent

3
- Ask students to work in pairs to discuss the qualities of the different people. Elicit a few ideas from the class in feedback.

EXAMPLE ANSWERS
a close friend – 2, 3, 4 (some people might like someone who enjoys life as a friend, others might prefer someone who is a good listener)
a language learner – 3, 5, 7 (a good language learner is patient and hard-working – there is a lot to learn)
a manager – 1, 2, 3, 5, 6, 7 (a good manager is hard-working and experienced because he or she has a lot of difficult decisions to make)
a parent – 2, 3, 5 (parents are kind and patient because they have to help their children to grow up)
a president – 5, 6, 7 (a president is intelligent because there is a lot to know and understand)
a teacher – 1, 2, 3, 5 (a good teacher is patient because the students need time to learn)

Listening

4
- Start by eliciting difficult decisions that people have to make in life. Build up a list on the board.
- Organize the class into pairs to discuss difficult decisions they have had to make. Elicit a few interesting experiences in feedback.

EXAMPLE ANSWERS
what subject to study at school or college / which university to go to / whether to leave home or stay / who to marry and when / what job to take / when to change job / what house or car to buy / whether and when to start a family

5 [29] ★ **CPT extra!** Pre-listening activity [before Ex. 5]
- **Optional step** Start by asking students to say what they see in the photo and the six pictures (a–f). Use the pictures to check key words: *mountain, tent, snow, rope, climbers, cliff, fall, knife*. You could also ask students to predict the order of the pictures.
- Play the recording of the first part of the story. Students listen and number the pictures in the correct order. Let them compare answers in pairs before checking with the class.

ANSWERS
1 b 2 e 3 c 4 d 5 a 6 f

Audioscript [29]

In May 1985, Joe Simpson and Simon Yates climbed the Siula Grande mountain in the Andes. It's a dangerous mountain, but Simpson and Yates were very experienced climbers and positive about the challenge. The sun was shining when they left their tents on the first day and everything went well. Three days later, they reached the top of the mountain, but they didn't stay there long. It was snowing and the weather was getting worse. While they were going down the mountain, Simpson fell and broke his knee. Yates tied a rope between them and slowly lowered Simpson down the mountain with the rope. Sometime later, when they were getting nearer to the bottom of the mountain, Simpson slipped and fell over a cliff. For an hour, Yates held the rope while his friend was hanging in the air. But the rope was getting too heavy and it was pulling Yates off the mountain. Simon Yates had an impossible decision. Either he could hold the rope, but then they might both die, or he could cut the rope and save himself.

74 Unit 4 Challenges

UNIT 4 Challenges

> **Background information**
>
> **Siula Grande** is a mountain in the Huayhuash mountain range in the Peruvian Andes. It's 6,344 metres high. Simpson and Yates were the first climbers to climb up the west face in 1985. Their ascent and descent was made famous by Joe Simpson's best-selling book *Touching the Void*, and the film made from the book in 2003. Joe Simpson had six surgical operations as a result of the leg injuries he sustained on Siula Grande. Today he is a writer and motivational speaker. Joe Simpson never blamed Simon Yates for cutting the rope, and said he would have done the same. However, the two climbers never climbed together again. Yates has also written books about mountaineering.

6

- Ask students to work in pairs to discuss the questions. Elicit ideas in feedback, but don't reveal the ending yet.

> **ANSWER**
>
> Yates' impossible decision: to cut the rope and let his friend fall (his friend might die) or keep holding on (and they both might fall and die).

7 [30] ★ CPT extra! Grammar activity [after Ex. 7]

- Give students time to read the questions (1–6).
- Play the recording of the whole story. Students will hear the first part again followed by the story's conclusion. Students listen and answer the questions. Let them compare answers in pairs before checking with the class.
- **Optional step** Ask students for their reaction to the decision to cut the rope. Ask: *Do you think Simon was right? What else could or should he have done?*

> **ANSWERS**
>
> 1 experienced, positive
> 2 It was snowing and the weather was getting worse.
> 3 He cut the rope.
> 4 He thought he was dead.
> 5 He heard someone shouting his name.
> 6 Someone wrote a book and then there was a film about the story.

Audioscript [30]

In May 1985, Joe Simpson and Simon Yates climbed the Siula Grande mountain in the Andes. It's a dangerous mountain, but Simpson and Yates were very experienced climbers and positive about the challenge. The sun was shining when they left their tents on the first day and everything went well. Three days later, they reached the top of the mountain, but they didn't stay there long. It was snowing and the weather was getting worse. While they were going down the mountain, Simpson fell and broke his knee. Yates tied a rope between them and slowly lowered Simpson down the mountain with the rope. Sometime later, when they were getting nearer to the bottom of the mountain, Simpson slipped and fell over a cliff. For an hour, Yates held the rope while his friend was hanging in the air. But the rope was getting too heavy and it was pulling Yates off the mountain. Simon Yates had an impossible decision. Either he could hold the rope, but then they might both die, or he could cut the rope and save himself. At the last second, Yates cut the rope. The next day, Yates looked for his friend, but couldn't find him. Sadly, he decided he was dead. But amazingly, Simpson was still alive and he started to crawl towards their camp. Three days later, Yates was sleeping in his tent and planned to go home the next morning. But at midnight he suddenly woke up. Someone was shouting his name. He ran outside and looked everywhere. Finally, he found Simpson on the ground. He wasn't moving, but he was still breathing. Yates carried him to the tent and Simpson survived. Later, their story became famous as a book and a film.

> **Vocabulary note**
>
> Here are some words from the listening that you could check:
>
> *lower down* = to carry or move something or somebody down from a high place to a low place
>
> *cliff* = a sudden edge on a mountain from which there is a wall of rock going down
>
> *hanging in the air* = here, Joe is on the end of a rope and not touching the sides or the floor
>
> *crawl* = move slowly on your hands and knees
>
> *survive* = not die (in difficult and dangerous situations)

Grammar past continuous and past simple

8

- Read the information in the grammar box with the class. Then ask students to answer the questions. You could do this in open class or ask students to work in pairs.

> **ANSWERS**
>
> 1 fell
> 2 were going, wasn't moving, was breathing
> 3 The past continuous is used for the longer, continuing activity, and the past simple is used for the shorter, finished action.
> 4 auxiliary verb *was / were* + *-ing* form of the main verb (the present participle)

> **Grammar note**
>
> The past continuous is used with active verbs in English. As with all continuous forms, it shows that something is temporary and has duration. It can be shown with a timeline:
>
> ─── a moment in the past ─────── Present
> *While they **were going** down the mountain, Simpson **fell**.*

Refer students to page 162 for further information and practice.

4b An impossible decision

UNIT 4 Challenges

ANSWERS TO GRAMMAR SUMMARY EXERCISES

4
1 were waiting 2 wasn't eating 3 Were; talking
4 were; saying 5 wasn't raining 6 was; flying

5
1 arrived; was watching 2 arrived; got
3 started; were climbing 4 wasn't playing; saw
5 Was she skiing; had 6 knew; heard

6
1 was travelling 2 was eating 3 came 4 knew
5 couldn't 6 started 7 was sitting 8 was waiting

9 [30]

- Ask students to work individually to choose the correct option. Let students compare answers in pairs, then play the recording for students to check their answers.
- In feedback, ask students to explain why they chose the past simple or continuous each time (see Grammar note below).

ANSWERS
1 was shining 2 was snowing 3 broke 4 was pulling
5 woke up 6 found

Grammar note
1 action in progress – sun started shining before they left
2 action in progress
3 broke – completed action
4 action in progress
5 woke up (suddenly) – completed action
6 found – completed action

10
- Look at the example with the class and check that everyone understands what to do. You could elicit the answers to the second sentence with the class.
- Ask students to work individually to complete the remaining sentences. Let students compare answers in pairs before checking with the class.

ANSWERS
1 was working, came
2 met, were living
3 weren't getting on, agreed
4 was, wasn't raining
5 didn't stop, was running
6 was he doing, phoned
7 did they visit, travelling
8 did you answer, were watching

Pronunciation *was/were*
11a [31]
- Read the instructions with the class, then play the recording. Students listen and note when *was, were, wasn't* and *weren't* are stressed. Let students compare answers in pairs before checking with the class.

ANSWERS
The positive forms *was* and *were* are unstressed in sentences 1, 2 and 4. The negative forms *wasn't* and *weren't* are stressed in sentences 3 and 4.

b [31]
- Play the recording again. Students listen and repeat.

Speaking *my life*
12 ★ CPT extra! Vocabulary activity [before Ex. 12]
- Read the instructions with the class and check that everyone understands what to do.
- **Optional step** Start by providing three or four true sentences from your own life experience. You could write a sentence on the board (e.g. *I had an accident in 2013*), then get students to ask you questions about it. This provides a model for the pairwork activity in Exercise 13
- Give students three or four minutes to prepare sentences. Monitor and help students with ideas and vocabulary.

13
- Organize the class into new pairs. Look at the example exchange with the class.
- Ask students to take turns to ask and answer their questions, using this exchange as a model. Monitor and notice how well students use the tenses. Note any errors which you could write on the board at the end for students to correct.

Extra activity

Write the following list of strange activities on the board (and check their meaning):
  run along the High Street
  climb up a tree
  paint your bedroom window black
  climb over the school's gate
  wear your pyjamas in the garden
  swim in the river

Tell students that you saw them doing these activities yesterday evening. Say to one student in the class: *Anna, I saw you yesterday, and you were running along the High Street. Why were you doing that?* Elicit an answer (e.g. *I was running for a bus. I was practising for a marathon. I was running away from a mugger*). Ask two or three other students the same question. Provide example answers if students aren't sure what to say. Once students have got the idea, ask them to work in pairs to ask and answer questions about what they were doing and why.

UNIT 4 Challenges

4c Challenge yourself

Lesson at a glance
- reading: challenge your brain
- critical thinking: looking for evidence
- wordbuilding: verbs and nouns
- writing and speaking: challenges in English

Reading

1 ★ **CPT extra!** Vocabulary activity [before Ex. 1]
- **Optional step** Start by checking the meaning of *puzzle, riddle, crossword* and *quiz*. You could do this by showing a puzzle page from a magazine or website and asking students to label the types of puzzle they see or by providing some examples (see Vocabulary note below).
- Ask students to work in pairs to discuss the questions. Elicit a few ideas from the class in feedback.

> **ANSWERS**
> Students' own answers
> Example: *I don't like doing crosswords, but I like doing puzzles on my phone. I spend about ten hours a week playing games on my computer or on my phone.*

> **Vocabulary note**
> *puzzle* /ˈpʌz(ə)l/ = a game, a toy or a problem that is difficult to solve or complete (e.g. a jigsaw puzzle)
> *riddle* /ˈrɪd(ə)l/ = a puzzle in words – a question, story or verse that you have to think about to find out what it means or refers to (e.g. *What flies without wings? Time*)
> *crossword* /ˈkrɒswɜː(r)d/ (or crossword puzzle) = a type of word puzzle in which you read clues and complete a grid
> *quiz* /kwɪz/ = questions that you have to use general knowledge or clever thinking to answer (e.g. *What's the capital of Australia? Canberra*)

2
- Ask students to work individually to try to answer the riddle and solve the matchstick puzzle, then do the memory challenge on page 51 of the Student's Book. Set a five-minute time limit (but extend it if students need more time).
- Tell students to compare answers briefly with a partner. Then tell them to check their answers on page 155 of the Student's Book.

3
- Discuss the question in open class or ask students to discuss it with their partner before eliciting views.

> **EXAMPLE ANSWERS**
> They are fun. They make you think. They stop you thinking about other things – work, problems, stress. When you solve them, you feel good. They pass the time, so they are useful when waiting or on train journeys. Some people think they are good for the brain.

4 [32]
- Read the questions with the class. Make sure students know what a Rubik's cube is – point to the photo in the article (and see Background information below).
- Ask students to read the second part of the article and note whether the sentences are true (T) or false (F). Let students compare answers in pairs before checking with the class.
- **Optional step** The reading text is recorded. You could play the recording and ask students to read and listen.

> **ANSWERS**
> 1 T
> 2 F (to teach them about 3D geometry)
> 3 F (it took him over a month)
> 4 T
> 5 F (a challenging video game could be good for our brains.)
> 6 F (the tests showed that the brains of adults who had played video games worked better)

> **Background information**
> Erno Rubik, inventor of the **Rubik's cube,** was born in 1944. He is a Hungarian inventor, architect and professor of architecture. The Rubik's cube reached its peak of popularity in the 1980s, but it's still played today. Since 2003 the World Cube Organization has run Rubik's cube competitions and recorded world records.

Critical thinking looking for evidence

5
- Read the information with the class. Then ask students to tell you the answers to the questions.

> **ANSWERS**
> It uses all types of evidence except for quotes.
> - facts from history: *In 1974, …; In 2008, …*
> - data (e.g. numbers and amounts): *43 quintillion (43,000,000,000,000,000,000) ways; 400 million Rubik's cubes*
> - results from a scientific study: *In one study at Illinois University, …*

6
- Ask students to work individually to read the ideas and answer the questions. Let them compare answers in pairs before checking with the class.

UNIT 4 Challenges

> **ANSWERS**
>
> 1
> a (*Over 400 million Rubik's cubes have been sold around the world and one in seven people have played with one.*)
> c (*In one study at Illinois University, the researchers studied … the video game players scored higher on the test.*) (all the results of the study are the evidence)
> 2
> b (you could point out the not very factual language: *Our brain naturally loves …*)

Wordbuilding verbs and nouns

7 ★ **CPT extra!** Wordbuilding activity [after Ex. 7]

- Read the wordbuilding box with the class (see Vocabulary note below). Then look at the table and elicit the first missing word as an example.
- Ask students to work individually to complete the table with words from the article. Let students compare their answers in pairs before checking with the class.

> **ANSWERS**
>
> 1 solve   2 answer   3 play   4 memory   5 study
> 6 a test   7 score

Refer students to Workbook page 35 for further practice.

> **Vocabulary note**
>
> Point out that *-ment* and *-tion* are often used as suffixes to make a verb become a noun, and that *-ize* (or *-ise*) is often used as a suffix to make a noun become a verb.

Writing and speaking my life

8

- Ask students to work individually to complete the questions with words from the table in Exercise 7. Let students compare their answers in pairs before checking with the class.
- Ask students to work in pairs and to take turns to ask and answer the questions. In feedback, ask different pairs to share their best ideas and suggestions with the class.
- **Optional step** You could give students preparation time to think of answers to the questions before asking them to ask and answer. Monitor and help students with ideas and vocabulary.

> **ANSWERS**
>
> 1 challenge   2 solving   3 memorize   4 test

9

- Ask students to work in pairs. Tell them to prepare a list of language learning tips. You could elicit one or two ideas to get students started. Monitor and help with ideas and vocabulary.

- Once students have a list, ask different pairs to present their lists to the class or put one pair with another to make groups of four and ask each pair to share and compare their lists.

> **EXAMPLE ANSWERS**
>
> Students' own answers
> Possibilities include:
> Memorize a few new words every day.
> Test yourself every week, or work with a friend and test one another.
> Check that you understand the correct answers to exercises you do.
> If you get a low score, make sure you understand why.
> Read and listen to as many things as you can every day.
> Be proud of your achievements.

> **Extra activity**
>
> Ask students to work in pairs or groups to solve the following riddles:
> 1 Can you name three days without using the words *Monday, Tuesday, Wednesday, Thursday, Friday, Saturday* or *Sunday*? (Yesterday, Today, and Tomorrow)
> 2 What relation is your father's sister's sister-in-law to you? (your mother – or possibly your aunt if your father has married brothers as well as sisters)
> 3 What is black when you buy it, red when you use it, and grey when you throw it away? (coal)
> 4 Which letter is not me? (U)

UNIT 4 Challenges

4d True stories

> **Lesson at a glance**
> - real life: telling a story
> - pronunciation: intonation for responding

Real life telling a story

1 ★ **CPT extra!** Lead-in activity [after Ex. 1]
- Discuss the questions as a class.

> **EXAMPLE ANSWERS**
>
> We go camping in the summer holidays because it's cheaper than staying in hotels, and it's more fun. I like living outside, you meet lots of people and it's very sociable.
>
> No, we never go camping. We stay in hotels or we rent a house. It's more comfortable than camping.

2 [33]
- Explain that students are going to listen to two friends talking about a camping trip.
- **Optional step** Pre-teach key words and predict the story by writing the following on the board and asking students to check meaning in their dictionaries and say how the words might go together in a story: *camping trip, mechanic* (= a person who repairs cars), *campsite, dark, hotel*.
- Ask students to read the questions. Play the recording. Students listen and answer the questions. Let them compare their answers in pairs before checking with the class.

> **ANSWERS**
>
> 1 It was terrible.
> 2 late
> 3 It broke down.
> 4 a mechanic
> 5 it was dark and it was raining.
> 6 to a nice hotel down the road

3 [33]
- Ask students to read the conversation, and try to remember the missing words.
- Play the recording again. Students listen and write the missing words. Let students compare their answers in pairs before checking with the class.
- **Optional step** Ask students to work in pairs to practise the conversation.

> **ANSWERS**
>
> 1 First 2 What did you do? 3 Fortunately 4 when
> 5 After 6 finally 7 what happened 8 in the end
> 9 Sounds great!

4
- Ask students to look at the headings (a–d) and the expressions in the box. Then ask them to work individually to match the expressions (1–9) from the conversation in Exercise 3 with the headings. Let students compare their answers in pairs before checking with the class.

> **ANSWERS**
>
> a Sequencing the story:
>   1 first 4 when 5 After 6 finally 8 in the end
> b Introducing good and bad news
>   3 Fortunately
> c Reacting to good and bad news
>   9 Sounds great!
> d Asking about the next part of the story
>   2 What did you do? 7 what happened

Pronunciation intonation for responding

5 [34]
- Ask students to look at the expressions for reacting to good and bad news.
- Play the recording. Students listen and notice the intonation. In feedback, ask students to say what they noticed in their own words (see Pronunciation note below).

> **ANSWERS**
>
> The more exaggerated the intonation pattern, the more interest the speaker shows. Students should notice that the intonation pattern over the questions starts high, then goes down, then up:
>
> *Really?*
>
> Students should notice that the intonation pattern over the statements goes up, then down:
>
> *Oh no!*

6
- Ask students to work in pairs to practise the conversation in Exercise 3, each taking turns to be speaker A. You may wish to organize students into new pairs at this stage so students have a new partner. Monitor pairs and prompt students to attempt a good intonation.

> **Pronunciation note**
>
> English has a wide intonation range so many students may find it odd to have to vary their intonation so much. Encourage students to try to exaggerate as much as they can. Use gestures to prompt and correct students. If you hold your hand with palm flat in front of you, you can raise it to show a rising intonation and dip it to show a falling intonation. This visual clue will help students try to get the intonation right.

4d True stories 79

UNIT 4 Challenges

7

- Organize the class into new pairs. Tell students to decide who is A and who is B. Give students two or three minutes to read A's prompts. In that time, A must prepare to tell the story, and B must think about how to respond. When students are ready, they act out their improvised conversation.
- **Optional step** If you think your students may have problems with improvisation, ask them, in pairs, to write dialogues first, using expressions from the lesson. Ask them to practise reading the dialogue. Then ask them to turn over the written dialogue and try to remember and improvise it. Alternatively, ask students to choose and match expressions they could use to each dialogue. Then ask them to improvise dialogues, using the expressions they chose.
- As students speak, monitor their performance. Note down errors students make, and, in feedback, write errors on the board and ask students to correct them.

8

- Ask students to change roles and to take two or three minutes to read B's prompts. In that time, B must prepare to tell the story, and A must think about how to respond. When students are ready, they act out their improvised conversation.

9

- This activity gets students to prepare and tell a true story of their own. You could set up the task by asking students in open class whether they have had a bad journey and, if so, when, where, why and what happened.
- Give students five minutes to prepare. Tell them to make a list of events in note form. Monitor and help with ideas and vocabulary as necessary.
- When students are ready, ask them to work in pairs and take turns to tell their stories and respond to them. Monitor their performance, paying particular attention to the intonation patterns they use.

Extra activity

Tell a true bad journey anecdote of your own. After each unfortunate or fortunate event, pause and get the class to react with an appropriate expression with a good intonation pattern.

4e A story of survival

Lesson at a glance
- writing: a short story
- writing skill: structure your writing

Writing a short story

1

- Ask students to work in pairs to discuss the questions. Elicit ideas in a brief feedback. Ask: *Were people killed, injured or did they survive?*

> **ANSWERS**
> Students' own answers

2

- **Optional step** Ask students to predict the story from the headline and the photo.
- Read the questions with the class. Then ask students to read the short story and find the answers to the questions. Let students compare answers in pairs before checking with the class.

> **ANSWERS**
> 1 The islands of Atafu in the Pacific Ocean
> 2 The sun was shining; three teenage boys were there; they were fishing.
> 3 They didn't come home in the evening, and nobody could find them.
> 4 Some fishermen found a boat with the boys in it; the fishermen were sailing in the ocean, the boys were in the boat, they were living on fish and rainwater.
> 5 Happy, the boys were alive and well.

> **Background information**
>
> The **islands of Atafu** are a group of 42 coral islets in the South Pacific Ocean. The islets encircle a lagoon, thus making Atafu an atoll (an island in the form of a ring). The group of islands is 500 kilometres north of Samoa and covers 2.5 square kilometres. About 500 people live there. Atafu is one of three atolls which together make up the country of Tokelau.

Writing skill structure your writing

3

- Ask students to work individually to read and number the five parts of a story's structure in order. Let them compare answers in pairs before checking with the class.

> **ANSWERS**
> 1 d 2 a 3 b 4 e 5 c

UNIT 5 The environment

UNIT 5 Review and memory booster ★ CPT extra! Language games

Memory Booster activities

Exercises 2, 4 and 6 are Memory Booster activities. For more information about these activities and how they benefit students, see page 10.

I can ... tick boxes

As an alternative to students simply ticking the *I can ...* boxes, you could ask them to give themselves a score from 1 to 4 (1 = not very confident; 4 = very confident) for each language area. If students score 1 or 2 for a language area, refer them to additional practice activities in the Workbook and Grammar summary exercises.

Grammar

1

- Ask students to work individually to choose the correct options. Let students compare answers in pairs before checking with the class.

> **ANSWERS**
> 1 The 2 a few 3 – 4 the 5 much 6 a lot of
> 7 a little 8 any

2 ›› MB

- Ask students to work in pairs to look at the photos and answer the questions. Check answers as a class.

> **ANSWERS**
> 1 solar panel; wall of trees
> 2 to heat water and reduce energy costs; to stop the desert growing towards the cities

Vocabulary

3

- Ask students to work individually to match the objects to the materials. Let students compare answers in pairs before checking with the class.

> **ANSWERS**
> 1 book
> 2 calculator, mobile phone, radio
> 3 bottle, jar, mobile phone
> 4 can
> 5 book, envelope, magazine
> 6 bottle, calculator, mobile phone, radio

4 ›› MB

- Ask students to work in pairs to think of more objects for each material. Elicit ideas as a class.

> **EXAMPLE ANSWERS**
> 1 box, furniture 2 tablet, digital camera
> 3 mirror, window 4 car, bicycle 5 poster, notebook
> 6 toys, food containers

5

- Ask students to work individually to match the percentages to the phrases. Let students compare answers in pairs before checking with the class.

> **ANSWERS**
> 1 about 80% 2 48% 3 40% 4 65%

6 ›› MB

- Ask students to work individually to think about the percentage of time they spend doing the activities.
- Ask students to work in pairs to compare their times. Encourage them to use phrases rather than exact percentages.

Real life

7

- Read the instructions with the class and check that everyone understands what to do. Elicit the first few lines of the conversation as a class as an example.
- Ask students to work in pairs and decide who is A and who is B. Pairs act out the conversation using the prompts. As students speak, monitor and notice any errors or examples of good language use you hear.

> **EXAMPLE ANSWERS**
> Suggested dialogue:
> A: Hello. Can I help you?
> B: Hi, I'm calling about an order for a clock. It hasn't arrived.
> A: Do you have the order number?
> B: Yes, it's AG-100234L.
> A: Sorry, can you repeat that?
> B: Yes, it's AG-100234L.
> A: Let me check. Is that A as in alpha?
> B: That's correct.
> A: Sorry, we don't have this product anymore. Would you like to change the order?
> B: No, thanks. I'd like a refund.
> A: That's fine. Would you like confirmation by email?
> B: Yes, please.
> A: Is there anything else I can help you with?
> B: No, thanks. That's everything. Goodbye.

8

- Students change roles and practise the conversation again.

Unit 6 Stages in life

Opener

1
- Ask students to look at the photo and the caption. Ask them to work in pairs to discuss the question. Elicit answers from the class in feedback.

> **ANSWERS**
>
> (from left to right in the photo): elderly, middle-aged, and young adult (or teenager of under 20)

> **Vocabulary notes**
>
> It's dependent on your age as to whether you think of yourself or others as old or young. For example, a 15-year-old may be a child to a 70-year-old, but a 15-year-old will probably see herself as a young adult.
>
> Here is a rule of thumb: *child* (under 13); *teenager* (13 to 19), *young adult* (twenties to about 35); *middle-aged* (45 to 60-something); *elderly* (this term suggests very old and fragile, so nowadays you wouldn't call yourself elderly unless you were over 75 and perhaps using a walking stick).
>
> Other words you might consider introducing to extend this vocabulary area: *baby, toddler* (a baby when it can walk), *kids* (slang for children), *grown-ups* (what children call adults), *pensioner* (an old person).

2 🎧 [44]
- Explain that students are going to listen to someone talk about the photo.
- Play the recording. Students listen and answer the question. Let them compare answers in pairs before checking with the class.

> **ANSWERS**
>
> It shows people at different stages in life communicating in different ways.

Audioscript 🎧 [44]

These three people are waiting in a train station in Winterthur in Switzerland. I like the picture because it shows three people at different stages in their life communicating in different ways. The elderly lady and the middle-aged lady are chatting and the young adult woman, maybe she's eighteen or nineteen, is probably texting her friends or using social media.

> **Background information**
>
> **Winterthur** /ˈvɪntətʊə/ lies approximately 30 kilometres to the south-west of Zurich in the German-speaking north of Switzerland.

3 ⭐ **CPT extra!** Photo activity [after Ex. 3]
- Start by checking difficult words in the box with your students, e.g. *pension* (= money you get when you are over 65 or 70), *career* (= your job or profession) and *retire* (= stop work because you are old).
- Ask students to work in pairs to discuss the questions. In feedback, elicit ideas and ask students to give reasons why.

> **EXAMPLE ANSWERS**
>
> 1 Here are general rules for the UK: get a pension (65); get your driving licence (17); go to college or university (18); get married (by law, 16; on average, 25 to 29); learn to ride a bicycle (between 3 and 8, with an average of 5); leave home (many leave at 18, but 25% of 20 to 34-year-olds continue to live with their parents), start a family (the average age is 30 and rising); start your career (no clear answer here – many start at 22 when they leave university); retire from work (on average, people in the UK retire at 63), buy your first home (a report by a bank suggested 30 as an average age – but increasingly it's harder to buy a first home in the UK).
>
> 2 Students' own answers

> **Vocabulary note**
>
> *(old age) pension* = the money people claim after they retire – this could be a *state pension* (= money from the government), a *workplace pension* (= money from having paid into a pension scheme during your working life), or a *private pension*
>
> *OAPs* (*old age pensioners*) = a term used to describe people claiming a pension

> **Extra activity**
>
> Personalize the activity. Ask students to say when they did or plan to do the life events in the box.

98

UNIT 6 Stages in life

6a Changing your life

Lesson at a glance
- vocabulary: describing age
- reading: how a couple changed their life
- grammar: *to* + infinitive
- pronunciation: /tə/
- speaking: the trip of a lifetime

Vocabulary describing age

1
- Discuss the questions in open class and elicit ideas and opinions.

> **EXAMPLE ANSWER**
> Students' own answers. It can be rude. It depends on the age of the people and how well you know them. If they are young, they probably don't mind. Older people might not want to say their age, especially if you don't know them well. It also shows a lack of respect to ask an older person a personal question.

2
- Ask students to match the ages in box A with the phrases in B. Then match the words on the opener page with the ages (see answers in brackets below). Let students compare answers in pairs before checking with the class.

> **ANSWERS**
> 14: early teens (teenager)
> 25: mid-twenties (young adult / adult)
> 39: late thirties (adult)
> 53: fifties (middle-aged)
> 83: early eighties (elderly)

> **Vocabulary note**
> *early twenties* = 20 to 23
> *mid-twenties* = 24 to 26
> *late twenties* = 27 to 29

3
- Ask students to think of famous examples of different ages. In feedback, elicit a few of your students' suggestions and ask the class if they think they have got the age right.

> **EXAMPLE ANSWERS**
> Students' own answers (answers will depend on your students' context and culture). Here are some currently correct examples from the English-speaking world:
> Queen Elizabeth II: early nineties
> Donald Trump (US President): early seventies
> George Clooney (actor): mid-fifties
> Justin Timberlake (actor/singer): late thirties
> Jennifer Lawrence (actor): mid to late twenties
> Taylor Swift (singer): late twenties

Reading

4 [45] ★ **CPT extra!** Photo activity [before Ex. 4]
- **Optional step** Ask students to predict the content of the article from the photo. Ask: *Who are they? Where are they? Do they have a job?* Check the meaning of *campervan* (= a long vehicle with a place to live, including a bed and kitchen, in the back).
- Ask students to read the article and answer the questions. Let students compare answers in pairs before checking with the class.
- **Optional step** The reading text is recorded. You could play the recording and ask students to read and listen.

> **ANSWERS**
> They were probably middle-aged, because they had successful careers.
> They left because they wanted to be free to do the things they wanted.

5 ★ **CPT extra!** Grammar activity [after Ex. 5]
- Ask students to read the article again and answer the questions. Let them compare answers in pairs before checking with the class.

> **ANSWERS**
> 1 no (*They always intended to do something fun and exciting at the weekend but, in the end, there was never time.*)
> 2 They wanted to stop working and to go travelling.
> 3 They bought a campervan to travel from the bottom of South America to Brazil.
> 4 Africa (*… they hoped to get to Africa on a container ship.*)
> 5 Colleagues at work found it difficult to understand their decision.
> 6 Their closest friends thought they were crazy to go on this kind of journey.
> 7 They started to live their dream.

Grammar *to* + infinitive

6
- Ask students to read the grammar box and match the sentences (1–3) with the forms (a–c). Let them compare answers in pairs before checking with the class.

> **ANSWERS**
> 1 a 2 c 3 b

> **Grammar note**
> We use the infinitive form of the verb after an adjective (e.g. *It's easy to do, It's good to know, They're fun to try*).
>
> We use the infinitive after certain verbs. Many verbs of thinking and feeling are followed by *to* + infinitive (e.g. *intend, decide, choose, forget, remember, plan, hope, want*).
>
> The infinitive of purpose says why you do something, e.g. *Let's buy a campervan. (Why?) To travel in.*

6a Changing your life 99

UNIT 6 Stages in life

Refer students to page 166 for further information and practice.

> **ANSWERS TO GRAMMAR SUMMARY EXERCISES**
>
> **1**
> 1 to go 2 to start 3 to study 4 to organize
> 5 to stay 6 to learn
>
> **2**
> 1 a 2 g 3 c 4 h 5 d 6 f 7 b 8 e
>
> **3**
> 1 staying 2 to learn 3 to fix 4 to visit
> 5 painting 6 to buy 7 Eating 8 to hear

7
- Ask students to read the three texts briefly and say what stage of life the speakers are at. Check any difficult words, e.g. *earn* (= get money from your job) and *afford* (= have enough money to buy).
- Ask students to work individually to read the texts again and choose the correct options. Elicit the first answer as an example. Let them compare answers in pairs before checking with the class.

> **ANSWERS**
>
> Text 1: teenager or young adult (probably taking time out between finishing school and starting university)
> Text 2: middle-aged (probably in their sixties – about to retire)
> Text 3: adult (probably in twenties or thirties)
> 1 to go (after the verb *plan*)
> 2 to earn (infinitive of purpose)
> 3 like
> 4 to retire (after an adjective)
> 5 relax
> 6 to sit (after the verb *want*)
> 7 to buy (after an adjective)
> 8 afford
> 9 to buy (infinitive of purpose)
> 10 not to feel (after an adjective)

> **Grammar notes**
>
> Remind students that after modal verbs (i.e. in 3, 5 and 8 above) we don't use *to* before the infinitive.

8
- Ask students to match the correct options which used *to* + infinitive in Exercise 7 with the rules (a–c) in Exercise 6.

> **ANSWERS**
> 1 a 2 c 4 b 6 a 7 b 9 c 10 b

9
- Ask students to work individually to match the sentence beginnings with the endings. Let them compare answers in pairs before checking with the class.

> **ANSWERS**
> 1 c 2 f 3 b 4 e 5 a 6 d

Pronunciation /tə/

10 [46] ★ **CPT extra!** Pronunciation activity [after Ex. 10]
- Ask students to underline all the instances of *to* in the sentences in Exercise 9.
- Play the recording. Students listen and notice the weak /ə/ sound or strong stressed /uː/ sound in *to*.
- Play the recording again. Students listen and repeat.

> **ANSWERS**
>
> All are pronounced /tə/ (see Pronunciation note below).

Audioscript [46]

1 One day I intend to buy my own house.
2 I want to take a year off to travel overseas.
3 I'd be happy to live in another country.
4 In the future I'd like to learn to play a musical instrument.
5 When I get older I hope to spend more time with my family.
6 These days it's difficult not to take work home.

> **Pronunciation note**
>
> After verbs and adjectives the word *to* is almost always not stressed, and therefore pronounced /tə/. The word is pronounced /tuː/ when the word *to* comes at the end of a sentence, for example, in a short answer: *Are you going to buy a house? Yes, I intend to.*

11
- Ask students to prepare their own personalized sentences using the six sentence beginnings in Exercise 9.
- Ask students to work in pairs. Tell them to take turns saying the sentences. Monitor and notice how well students are attempting the pronunciation.

> **EXAMPLE ANSWERS**
>
> 1 One day I intend to live abroad / get a new job / get married.
> 2 I want to take a year off to travel round the world / to learn a new skill.
> 3 I'd be happy to get a good job / disappointed to lose my job.
> 4 In the future I'd like to learn a new language / to play the guitar.
> 5 When I get older I hope / plan / intend to buy a house / start a family.
> 6 These days it's difficult to buy a house / to get a job / to meet interesting people.

100 Unit 6 Stages in life

UNIT 6 Stages in life

Speaking my life
12
- Ask students to work in groups of four or five. Read the information as a class, and tell students they have to agree on where to go on their trip of a lifetime. Ask students to discuss the questions and make notes. Set a time limit of ten minutes. As students prepare, monitor and help with ideas and vocabulary if necessary.
- After ten minutes, say stop. Ask groups to get ready to make a presentation – one person could speak, or students could choose to break their presentation into three or more stages so that different students get to speak.

13
- Ask groups to take turns to present their trip of a lifetime. At the end, have a class vote, and ask them to decide which group planned the most interesting trip.
- **Optional step** To help guide your students' presentations, write the following sequencing expressions on the board for them to use: *First of all, …; After that, …; Then … ; If there's time, we'll …*
- As students speak, listen and note down errors students make. Pay particular attention to any errors with *to* + infinitive. Write up these errors on the board at the end, and ask students to correct them in pairs (see Teacher development below).

Teacher development
Correcting errors after a fluency activity
When students speak in pairs, act out at the front of the class or give a presentation, it's a great opportunity to listen to students' output and to give them collective class feedback.

Here are suggestions:
- Walk round and listen in on pairs or groups. Signal that you are listening but don't interrupt the flow. Similarly, when students are giving a presentation, sit and signal that you are listening and noticing errors. Students want to know that you're noticing their errors, and are there to give them useful feedback.
- Have a piece of paper to hand on which to write any errors you hear as you monitor students. This could be an exercise book, a blank sheet of A4 on a clipboard, or a piece of paper on your desk which you keep going back to every time you hear an error.
- Have a clear aim in mind. Here (in the speaking activity above), you're mostly listening for errors with the form and use of *to* + infinitive. One idea is to write headings on the piece of paper you are using to note errors. For example, write FORM, USE and PRONUNCIATION as headings, and write errors relevant to each category.
- At the end of the speaking activity, write four or five chunks or sentences on the board with errors you noticed in them. Do this anonymously – don't say which student made the error. Ask students to work in pairs to correct the errors. Go over any rules if necessary in feedback.
- As well as writing errors on the board, write up one or two really good uses of language. Point out and praise accurate uses of English.

6b World party

Lesson at a glance
- reading and vocabulary: celebrations
- listening: preparing for a festival
- grammar: future forms
- pronunciation: contracted forms
- speaking: planning a celebration

Reading and vocabulary celebrations
1 ★ **CPT extra!** Background information [after Ex. 1]
- Discuss the questions in open class.

> **EXAMPLE ANSWERS**
> Students' own answers. Events that are commonly celebrated with a party: Christmas, New Year, Independence Day, Carnival or Mardi Gras, birthdays, name days, weddings, wedding anniversaries, graduation from school or university

2
- Ask students to read the first paragraph and find the answer to the question. Let students compare answers in pairs before checking with the class.

> **ANSWERS**
> Because it's talking about a day that's celebrated in lots of places round the world.

3 [47]
- Ask students to read and match the sentences to the places in the article. Let them compare answers in pairs before checking with the class.
- **Optional step** The reading text is recorded. You could play the recording and ask students to read and listen.

> **ANSWERS**
> 1 Rio de Janeiro
> 2 Venice
> 3 New Orleans
> 4 Port-of-Spain
> 5 New Orleans (jazz), Rio de Janeiro (samba)
> 6 Venice

Background information
Mardi Gras (/ˈmɑːrdigrɑː/) means 'Fat Tuesday' in French. It refers to events of the Carnival celebrations, beginning in January on or after the Christian feast of the Epiphany (Three Kings' Day) and culminating in March or April on the day before Ash Wednesday. The most important day of the festival – the day when the Carnival parade and celebrations take place – is the day before Ash Wednesday. Originally, this was the day when a lot of food was eaten (hence Fat Tuesday) before the Christian period of fasting began (Lent). In many Christian countries, this has developed into a big festival and party.

6b World party 101

UNIT 6 Stages in life

4 ⭐ **CPT extra!** Vocabulary activity [after Ex. 4]
- Ask students to find words in the article for the pictures (1–7). Let them compare answers in pairs before checking with the class.

> **ANSWERS**
> 1 mask 2 float 3 candles 4 (jazz) band 5 fireworks
> 6 steel drum 7 costume

> **Vocabulary notes**
> A *float* is a large vehicle (e.g. a converted lorry) with a flat surface that is decorated and used in festivals
> A *steel drum* is a large oil container that has been made into a musical instrument and is played like a drum – steel drums are a feature of festival music in Caribbean countries.

5
- Organize the class into groups of four or five. Explain that students are going to describe a festival or celebration they know well.
- It's a good idea to give students five minutes' preparation time before they start speaking. Ask students to read the questions and make notes to help them talk at length about the festival. Monitor and help with ideas and vocabulary.
- **Optional step** Tell groups to interview one person in their group. Tell them to ask the questions in the Student's Book in any order. The student 'on the spot' must answer the questions. Then put another student 'on the spot'.

Listening
6 🔊 [48]
- Explain that students are going to listen to a report about one of the celebrations in the article.
- Play the recording. Ask students to listen and identify which celebration it's about. Let them compare answers in pairs before checking with the class.

> **ANSWERS**
> New Orleans Mardi Gras

Audioscript 🔊 48

R = Reporter, L = Lorette

R: It's about six o'clock in the morning here in New Orleans and the streets are very quiet. But in about six hours the city is going to have the biggest party in the world with thousands of visitors from all over. However, Mardi Gras is really about the local communities in the city. So, I've come to the traditional Tremé neighbourhood of New Orleans, where there are already some people preparing for the big day. So, I'll try to speak to some of them … Hello? Hello?

L: Hello?

R: Hello. What's your name?

L: Lorette.

R: Hi Lorette. You're wearing a fantastic costume. Are you going to be in the parade this afternoon?

L: That's right. Everyone is meeting at the float at six fifteen and then we're going to ride through the city.

R: As I say, your dress looks amazing. Did you make it?

L: Yes, we all make our own costumes for Mardi Gras.

R: And do you have a mask?

L: Sure. Here it is. I'll put it on.

R: Wow. That's perfect. So tell me – how important is Mardi Gras for the people in Tremé?

L: It's the most important part of the year. It brings people together.

R: Well, good luck this afternoon. You're going to have a great time, I'm sure!

> **Background information**
> In the 1700s, the city of **New Orleans** was the capital of Louisiana, which was a French colony. Mardi Gras was introduced by French settlers and was originally a French Catholic festival. Tremé (/trəˈmeɪ/) is located to the west of the French Quarter (the historical heart of New Orleans), and is historically a racially mixed neighbourhood.

7 🔊 [48]
- **Optional step** Remind students of the critical thinking (close reading) section in Unit 5. Here, students have to listen very carefully (closely) to hear not just the answers but whether the answers are provided at all.
- Play the recording. Students listen and answer the questions. Let students compare answers in pairs before checking with the class.

> **ANSWERS**
> 1 Yes (*thousands of visitors*)
> 2 No (*Everyone is meeting at the float …*)
> 3 No ('*And do you have a mask?*' '*Sure. Here it is. I'll put it on.*')
> 4 Don't know (It isn't mentioned.)

> **Extra activity**
> Ask students to research one of the festivals in the lesson online and find out more about its history and traditions. You could set this for homework and ask students to present their findings in a later class.

UNIT 6 Stages in life

Grammar future forms

8 ★ **CPT extra!** Listening activity [before Ex. 8]
- Read the sentences in the grammar box with the class. Then ask students to answer the questions (a–d). As there is a lot to explain, you could do this in open class. Alternatively, let students check with a partner before checking answers with the class.

> **ANSWERS**
> a 1 *be going to* + infinitive; 2 present continuous;
>   3 *will* + infinitive
> b 1
> c 3
> d 2

> **Grammar note**
>
> Choosing which future form to use can be difficult for language learners for the following reasons:
>
> 1 The choice of tense is down to what the speaker intends. For example, *I'm going to be in the parade this afternoon* and *I'll be in the parade this afternoon* are both correct. If a speaker uses the first sentence it's because he's saying what his plan is. If a speaker uses the second sentence it's because she's making a promise or offer. It's important to make students aware that 'context' dictates which form to use. Make sure they're clear about the three rules – an arrangement, a plan made before now, a decision made now – and let them think about which of these rules best applies in different contexts.
>
> 2 The use of these tenses is not likely to translate exactly into students' L1. Speakers of other European languages may naturally use the present simple to express the future, for example, a tense which is rarely used in English. It's a good idea to get students to do a language comparison – ask them to translate sentences and say how their L1 differs.

Refer students to page 166 for further information and practice.

> **ANSWERS TO GRAMMAR SUMMARY EXERCISES**
> 4
> 1 'm going to see   5 'm not going to get
> 2 Are; going to come   6 Are; going to miss
> 3 's going to have   7 aren't going to go
> 4 's going to spend   8 going to start
> 5
> 1 I'll help   2 I'll go   3 is arriving   4 I'm going to go
> 5 I'm going to have
> 6
> 1 a   2 b   3 a   4 b   5 b

9
- Ask students to work individually to choose the correct options in the sentences. Elicit the first answer as an example. Let students compare answers in pairs before checking with the class.

- In feedback, ask students to say why they chose each form. Tell students to refer to the rules (a–d) they studied in Exercise 8.

> **ANSWERS**
> 1 I'll check (decision at the time of speaking)
> 2 You're going to (a general plan or future intention)
> 3 I'll try (decision at the time of speaking)
> 4 I'm going to visit (a general plan or future intention)
> 5 are we meeting (an arrangement for a fixed time)
> 6 are we going to give (a general plan or future intention)
> 7 are you leaving (an arrangement for a fixed time)

Pronunciation contracted forms

10 [49]
- Ask students to look at sentences 1–4 in Exercise 9.
- Play the recording. Students listen and notice the contracted forms. In feedback, ask students what they heard (see Pronunciation note below).
- Play the recording again, and ask students to repeat the sentences.

Audioscript [49]

1 **A:** Did Geoff email the times of the parade?
  B: I don't know. I'll check my inbox right away.
2 You're going to visit New Orleans! When did you decide that?
3 **A:** Hey, this costume would look great on you.
  B: Maybe. I'll try it on.
4 One day when I'm older, I'm going to visit Venice.

> **Pronunciation note**
>
> Notice that the contracted forms are pronounced as one syllable: *I'll* /aɪl/, *you're* /jɔː/, *I'm* /aɪm/.

11
- Ask students to work individually to write the verbs in brackets in a future form. Elicit the first answer as an example. Let students compare answers in pairs before checking with the class.

> **ANSWERS**
> 1 'm going to leave   2 are; meeting   3 'll take
> 4 'm going to do   5 's starting   6 'll buy

6b World party 103

UNIT 6 Stages in life

> **Extra activity**
>
> Ask students to improvise conversations based on the sentences in Exercise 11, e.g.
>
> **A:** At the end of this year I'm going to leave my job and write a book.
>
> **B:** Really? Well, I'm going to travel round the world.

Speaking my life

12

- Organize the class into small groups of four or five. Read the instructions and bulleted list with the class. Check that everyone understands what to do.
- Ask students to read the list carefully, and to discuss different options in their groups.
- **Optional task** It's a good idea to organize this activity as a meeting. Ask one student to be the 'chair' – he or she must lead the discussion and make sure everybody speaks. One student is the secretary – it's his or her job to note decisions the group makes. Set a clear time limit, e.g. ten minutes. At the end, ask a third student to present findings.
- Monitor and help students with ideas and vocabulary.

13

- Ask groups to present their final plans to the class. Notice that students should switch from using *will* to make spontaneous decisions (in Exercise 12) to using *going to* to describe plans (in the presentation).
- As students make presentations, note any errors which you could write on the board at the end for students to correct.

6c Coming of age

> **Lesson at a glance**
> - reading: celebrating change
> - critical thinking: analysing the writer's view
> - word focus: *get*
> - speaking: events in the year

Reading

1 ★ CPT extra! Lead-in activity [before Ex. 1]

- Ask students to discuss the questions. You could do this in open class or in small groups.
- **Optional step** If you have a class with students from different countries, take advantage of this fact. Organize groups to mix nationalities as much as you can. Ask students to find out which country has the strictest or most liberal rules.

> **ANSWERS**
>
> Students' own answers
>
> 1 In the UK, the following is true: drive a car (17); get married (16); buy cigarettes (18); leave school (16); buy fireworks (18); open a bank account (7 – to open a savings account; 11 – to open a current account).
>
> 2 Arguably, at 16 when you can get married and start work, or at 18 when you are fully treated as an adult by the law.
>
> 3 In the UK, there is no formal 'coming of age' rite – people often celebrate their 18th and 21st birthdays as special occasions with a big party, and it's traditional to give a person a key (nowadays, usually, a large plastic key) to symbolize having the key to adulthood.

2

- Ask students what they think the lesson title *Coming of age* means (= it refers to the time when people reach maturity – you are no longer a child but an adult).
- Ask students to describe the photos and say how they connect to the title.
- Ask students to read the introduction in the website and check their ideas. Let students compare answers in pairs before checking with the class.

> **ANSWERS**
>
> According to the introductory paragraph, coming of age means different things in different cultures – ranging from getting married or getting a job to celebrations to symbolize coming of age.

3 🔊 [50]

- Ask students to read the sentences carefully. Check any unknown words, e.g. *bridegroom* (= a man on his wedding day), *legal rights* (= what you are allowed to do by the law) and *attitudes* (= the way people think).
- Ask students to read the article and note whether the sentences are true (T) or false (F). Let students compare answers in pairs before checking with the class.

104 Unit 6 Stages in life

UNIT 6 Stages in life

- In feedback, ask students to justify answers by referring to the text (see Teacher development below).
- Point out the words in the glossary at the foot of the text.
- **Optional step** The reading text is recorded. You could play the recording and ask students to read and listen.

> **ANSWERS**
> 1 T (*parts of the Caribbean, Central America and South America*)
> 2 F (*the Inca, Maya and the Aztecs probably had their own coming-of-age ceremonies already*)
> 3 F (*they have to pay the bride's family about thirty goats and twenty cows – not money*)
> 4 F (*she then gets financial control over the husband's younger brothers' money*)
> 5 T (*Twenty is an important age in Japanese society because you get several adult legal rights, such as voting in elections*)
> 6 T (*in recent years, the number of young people celebrating Seijin-no-Hi has decreased*)

Teacher development
Justifying answers
Encourage students to expand on and discuss answers to reading and listening texts, rather than just saying yes or no, or true or false. This creates interaction between students and generates oral production in class. It also helps lead students to a deeper understanding of texts and develops the important skill of reading closely.
- When doing Exercise 3 of this reading task, ask students to underline words that reveal the answer. Give students time to compare and discuss their answers in pairs or small groups.
- Often the way an answer is worded in the text is different from the way it's worded in the question. In feedback to Exercise 3, ask students to explain ways that words in the text justify their choice of answers. For example, in Exercise 3, the statement reads '*The celebration of Quinceañera is common in many different countries*'. This is shown to be *True* in the text by the sentence: '*In Latin-American cultures, Quinceañera is a well-known celebration*'. If it's *well-known*, it must be *common*.

4
- Look at the example with the class. Then ask students to match the remaining pairs of words with the definitions.
- Let students compare their answers in pairs before checking with the class (see Vocabulary note below). If students aren't sure, tell them to find the words in the text and work out meanings from the context.

> **ANSWERS**
> 1 a culture   b country
> 2 a celebration   b ceremony
> 3 a groom   b bride
> 4 a legal rights   b social traditions

Vocabulary note
1 France and Spain are countries; the way French or Spanish people cook, eat or celebrate events is part of their culture.
2 Ceremonies are public events, and often serious, e.g. an awards ceremony, a ceremony to honour the dead, a funeral ceremony; Celebrations can be private as well as public and are often a party and a happy occasion, e.g. an anniversary celebration, a celebration of the safe return of the explorers.
3 We can say groom or bridegroom (note also bridesmaids – who help the bride – and the best man – who helps the groom).
4 If you are 18, you have a legal right to vote, to get married, to buy a house; In the UK, important social traditions include shaking hands when you first meet someone, saying thank you when someone gives you something, and being on time for meetings.

Background information
Quinceañera (pronounced /kinseaˈɲeɾa/ in Spanish) literally means fifteen-year-old female. It marks the transition from childhood to young womanhood in Latin American countries. Historically, many girls were married off at fifteen in these cultures.

The **Inca**, **Maya** and **Aztecs** are Native American peoples who were present in Mexico and South America at the time Europeans first arrived.

Emperor Maximilian I was an Austrian archduke who was imposed on Mexico as its emperor by France in 1861 after the French had invaded Mexico. Maximilian was executed by Mexican republicans in 1867. His wife Carlota was a Belgian princess.

The **Hamar** people live in south-western Ethiopia in the Omo River valley. They are largely pastoralists, so their culture places a high value on cattle.

Seijin-no-Hi ceremonies are generally held in the morning at local city offices throughout Japan. Government officials give speeches, and small presents are handed out to the newly recognized adults.

Critical thinking analysing the writer's view
5
- Read the three ways of looking at a topic (a–c) with the class.
- Ask students to read the web page posts again and match them with the three ways. Tell students to underline words and phrases in the posts that helped them reach their answers. Don't check answers at this stage.

6
- Ask students to compare their answers from Exercise 5 with a partner. Elicit answers in feedback.

UNIT 6 Stages in life

> **ANSWERS**
> a Historical view: Quinceañera (*the celebration started when the Spanish first came to …; ancient tribes … probably had their own coming-of-age ceremonies already; the Quinceañera waltz, which was introduced in the 19th century*)
> b Social view: Seijin-no-Hi (*the number of young people celebrating Seijin-no-Hi has decreased …; … partly because of Japan's low birth rate; it's too expensive and … modern twenty-year-olds are less interested in these kinds of social traditions*)
> c Economic view: cattle jumping (*they have to pay the bride's family about thirty goats and twenty cows; the man will have to pay the family back over his whole life; Because of the costs involved, Hamar men are usually in their mid-thirties … when they marry; his wife … gets financial control over the husband's younger brothers' money*)

Word focus *get*

7

- Ask students to read the web page again and underline all the examples of *get*. Then ask them to match their underlined examples with the meanings in the box. Let students compare answers in pairs before checking with the class.

> **ANSWERS**
> get married (line 3) – become
> get a job (line 5) – start
> gets financial control (line 32) – receive
> get legal rights (line 40) – receive

> **Vocabulary note**
>
> *Get* is a very common verb and used in many situations. It forms part of many fixed collocations (e.g. *get married*) and idiomatic expressions (e.g. *I can't get over you*).
>
> One way of thinking about its use is that it describes a change:
> - It describes a change of possession (e.g. *get a letter, get a degree, get a present, get a prize* – receive, obtain, win).
> - It describes a change of state (e.g. *I'm getting old, I got tired, I got married* – become, start to be).
> - It describes a change of position (e.g. *get a plane, get in a car, get off a bus, get to work, get up* – move, catch, go on).
> - While it always describes some sort of change, it's used instead of many other verbs (e.g. earn: *I get £100 a week*; understand: *I don't get it*; answer: *I'll get the phone*; reach: *Get that box from the top shelf*; buy: *We got the shopping*, etc.).

8 ★ **CPT extra!** Word focus activity [after Ex. 8]

- **Optional step** Ask students to read the text for general comprehension first. Ask: *Is this wedding day similar to or different from a wedding day in your country?*
- Ask students to read the description and match the uses of *get* (1–7) with the meanings (a–g). Encourage them to use the context to work out meanings. Let students compare answers in pairs before checking with the class.

> **ANSWERS**
> 1 a 2 d 3 g 4 c 5 e 6 b 7 f

> **Extra activity**
>
> Organize the class into pairs. Ask students to find five other common uses of *get* in a learner's dictionary and to write personalized sentences showing their meaning. Ask pairs to share sentences with another pair. Pairs say what *get* means in each sentence.

Speaking my life

9

- Start by checking that students know all the events in the box (see Background information below). You could elicit or add other events that you think your students will know a lot about.
- Organize the class into pairs. Tell students to prepare notes on their chosen event individually. Set a four or five minute time limit and monitor to help with ideas and vocabulary. Encourage and suggest ways of using *get* in their descriptions.
- When students are ready, they take turns to describe their event. In feedback, ask students what interesting information they heard, and ask them how well their partner used *get*.

> **EXAMPLE ANSWER**
>
> There are no fixed answers as this depends on your students' experiences. However, here are some useful phrases you could use to prompt students: *get up early, get a present, get a card, get flowers, get to a restaurant/ party, get dinner, get a kiss*.

> **Background information**
>
> **New Year's Day** = January 1st
> **Valentine's Day** = February 14th – a day on which love and romance is celebrated in many countries.

> **Extra activity**
>
> Write the following on the board and ask students to discuss how old they have to be in their country to do the things (or, if they are studying in an English-speaking country, how old they have to be in that country to do the things). Adapt depending on the culture of your students. Answers for the UK are in brackets:
>
> buy alcohol (18); go into pubs (14); ride a moped (16); vote in a general election (18); join the army (18); get married without your parents' consent (18); get a part-time job (13); get a full-time job (16); be tried in a criminal court (10); buy a gun (17).

UNIT 6 Stages in life

6d An invitation

Lesson at a glance
- speaking: formal and informal events
- real life: inviting, accepting and declining
- pronunciation: emphasizing words

Speaking

1 ★ **CPT extra!** Lead-in activity [after Ex. 1]

- **Optional step** Start by checking key words in the box, e.g. *engagement* (= when two people say they are going to get married), *barbecue* (= an outdoor party at which people cook on an open grill called a barbecue), *leaving party* (= a party to say goodbye to someone who leaves their job), *colleague* (= a friend at work), *client* (= a person who does business with you or your company).
- Ask students to order the events from least formal to most formal. You could do this in open class or ask students to work in pairs. At the end, give feedback on the answers and build up a list on the board.

EXAMPLE ANSWER

From least formal to most formal:
a barbecue with family and friends
your grandfather's ninetieth birthday party
an end-of-course party
a leaving party for a work colleague
an engagement party
going out for dinner with a work client
(Note that this is a suggested order – there is no reason why, for example, a leaving party might be more formal than a birthday party.)

Extra activity

Ask students to make a list of five formal and informal events they have attended in the last month. Tell them to share with a partner and say, in feedback, who has had the busiest diary and who has been to the most formal events.

Real life inviting, accepting and declining

2 🔊 [51]

- **Optional step** Use concept check questions to check the section heading here. Ask: *Which word means asking someone to go somewhere?* (inviting) *Which word means saying no?* (declining) *Which word means saying yes?* (accepting).
- Ask students to read the questions carefully. Check *convince* (= persuade, make somebody accept your view). Point out that there are two conversations, and one is more formal than the other.
- Play the recording. Students listen and answer the questions. Let them compare their answers in pairs before checking with the class.

ANSWERS

1 a barbecue at his house
2 Because he has things to do, and he thinks it's a family affair.
3 He tells him he's inviting others from their class.
4 No, he doesn't.
5 on Saturday
6 to dinner at her favourite restaurant
7 Yes, she does.
8 more formal, because the speakers don't know each other very well

Audioscript 🔊 [51]

Conversation 1

I = Ian, A = Abdullah

I: Hi Abdullah. How's it going?
A: Good. I finished all my courses today so I can relax.
I: Great. Maybe you'll have time for some travelling and sightseeing now.
A: Maybe. But I think I'll take it easy this weekend.
I: Oh! Well, why don't you come to my house? My family is coming over. We're having a barbecue in the back garden. It'll be fun.
A: Thanks, but I have a few things to do at home and it's with your family so you probably don't want other people there …
I: No, really. Don't worry because I'm inviting a few people from our class as well. So you'll know people. I'd really like you to come.
A: OK. Thanks, that would be great. Is it a special occasion?
I: Well, my oldest sister has a new baby girl so it's a bit of a celebration for that.
A: Oh! So I should bring something.
I: No, please don't. It isn't like that. There's no need …

Conversation 2

J = Joanna, S = Sally

J: Hello Sally. How are you?
S: Fine, thanks. It's been a busy week.
J: Yes, I imagine. When do you finish?
S: Tomorrow.
J: Oh, really. I didn't realize it was so soon.
S: Well actually, my flight home is on Saturday.
J: But you're staying for another week?
S: No.
J: Oh. Well, what are you doing tonight?
S: Nothing at the moment. I'll be at my hotel.
J: Well, would you like to come out for dinner? Let's go somewhere this evening.
S: Really? I'd love to.

6d An invitation 107

UNIT 6 Stages in life

J: Of course. I'd like to take you to my favourite restaurant.
S: That would be wonderful. I'd like that very much.
J: Great. Let's go straight after work. I'll meet you downstairs in reception.
S: OK. What time?
J: I finish at six. Is that OK for you?
S: Sure. I'll see you then. Bye.

3 [51]
- Ask students to read the expressions. Then ask students to work in pairs and to discuss which ones they think were used in the conversation.
- Play the recording again. Students listen and tick the expressions used. Let students compare their answers in pairs before checking with the class.
- **Optional step** Ask students to work in pairs to practise the conversations in audioscript 51 on page 185 of the Student's Book.

> **ANSWERS**
> Would you like to come …?
> I'd like to take you to …
> Why don't you …?
> I'd like that very much.
> Thanks, that would be great.
> That would be wonderful.
> OK.
> I'd love to.
> Thanks, but …

> **Grammar note**
> Note the use of *would* and *'d* (the abbreviated form of *would*) in the more formal phrases. Using the hypothetical *would* distances the speaker from what is being said, which in turn makes it more tentative and polite.

Pronunciation emphasizing words
4a [52]
- Play the recording. Students listen and underline the main stress.

Audioscript [52] (and answers, with main stress shown)

1 I'd <u>love</u> to.
2 That would be <u>won</u>derful.
3 It's <u>very</u> nice of you to ask.
4 I'd like to, but I'm a<u>fraid</u> I'm busy.

b [52]
- Play the recording again for students to listen and repeat.
- **Optional step** Ask students to work in pairs to practise saying the sentences. You could also ask students to practise saying other expressions from Exercise 3 with the correct stress (e.g. *How about <u>going</u> out? I'd like to in<u>vite</u> you out. I'd like that <u>very</u> much. Sorry, I <u>can't</u>.*).

5
- Organize the class into pairs. Explain that students are going to take turns to invite each other to different formal and informal events. Look at the flow chart with the class and check that everyone understands what to do.
- It's a good idea to prepare students to do this. Start by referring students back to the events mentioned in Exercise 1, or by eliciting a few events to the board, or by asking students to make a list of five events they would like to invite someone to (e.g. my brother's birthday, a meal out with the rest of the class, my cousin's wedding, a trip to the seaside). Ask students to choose expressions to use in each situation before trying to improvise dialogues.
- Tell students to use the flow chart to help them structure their dialogues. They can choose to accept or decline – encourage then to practise doing both in different dialogues.
- As students speak, monitor their performance. Note down errors students make. In feedback, write errors on the board and ask students to correct them.

> **Extra activity**
> Once students have practised one or two dialogues in pairs, ask them to stand up, walk round, and improvise dialogues with three or four different people. This activity lends itself well to a mingle, and mingles are good because they get students to vary interaction and talk to people in the class they might not always get to talk to much.

UNIT 6 Stages in life

6e A wedding in Madagascar

Lesson at a glance
- writing: a description
- writing skill: descriptive adjectives

Writing a description

1
- **Optional step** Write *Madagascar* on the board. Ask students what they know about it. Elicit ideas (see Background information below).
- Ask students to read the travel blog and tick the things in the box that the writer mentions. Let students compare answers in pairs. Elicit a few ideas from the class in feedback.

> **ANSWERS**
> food and meals, clothes, people, festivals and ceremonies

> **Background information**
> **Madagascar** is an island country off the south-east coast of Africa. It's the fourth largest island in the world. It's most famous for its unique wildlife, which evolved independently from wildlife in Africa or Asia. Lemurs live in Madagascar.
>
> The photo on the page shows a **zebu** /ˈziːbuː/. This type of cow has a fatty hump on its shoulders and is popular in tropical countries.

Writing skill descriptive adjectives

2a
- Ask students to look at the highlighted adjectives in the travel blog. Tell them to match them with the adjectives (1–4). Let students compare their answers in pairs before checking with the class.

> **ANSWERS**
> 1 enormous, massive
> 2 miserable
> 3 beautiful, colourful, smart, delicious
> 4 dull

> **Vocabulary note**
> *Enormous* and *massive* mean very big and are synonyms. We tend to use *enormous* to emphasize that something is extremely big (e.g. *The house was so enormous we got lost in it!*) and *massive* to emphasize that something is very big and solid (e.g. *The prison had massive walls*).
>
> People who are sad and feel down are *miserable* – we also use the adjective with the weather (e.g. *a miserable day – it rained a lot*), and depressing experiences (e.g. *We had a miserable time*).
>
> We use *smart* with clothes and appearance (e.g. *a smart suit* = it's clean, pressed and well-made) and *delicious* with food (e.g. *a delicious meal*).

> *Dull* can mean grey in appearance (e.g. *dull weather, a dull building*) or boring (e.g. *a dull lecture, a dull teacher, a dull day out*).
>
> Note that some of these adjectives are gradable (*miserable, beautiful, colourful, smart, dull*) so you can grade them (*very smart, quite colourful*, etc.) but others are ungradable (*enormous, massive, delicious*) so you can't grade them (you can say *absolutely enormous* but not *very enormous*).

b
- Read the information about synonyms with the class.
- Ask students to work in pairs to improve the sentences (1–8). You could point out the example and elicit possible changes to the second sentence to get students started. In feedback, elicit ideas. You could ask different pairs to come to the board to write up sentences.

> **EXAMPLE ANSWERS**
> 1 Venice is a *beautiful* city with lots of *ancient* buildings.
> 2 In the USA, you can buy *enormous / huge / giant / gigantic / colossal* burgers.
> 3 The parade was a bit *dull / tedious* after a while.
> 4 The crowd was *delighted* because the *exciting / colourful* fireworks started.
> 5 All the costumes were *beautiful / gorgeous / lovely*.
> 6 I was *miserable / upset* to leave Paris.
> 7 I tried sushi for the first time and it was *delicious / really tasty*.
> 8 The view of the mountains was *beautiful / stunning / wonderful*.

Refer students to Workbook page 51 for further practice.

c ★ CPT extra! Writing activity [after Ex. 2c]
- Ask students to work in pairs to think of interesting adjectives for the topics in Exercise 1.
- Put pairs together to make groups of four. Ask students to share their ideas. Have a brief feedback and elicit some of the more interesting adjectives pairs have thought of.

> **EXAMPLE ANSWERS**
> food and meals: lovely, delicious, tasty
> clothes: pretty, smart, attractive, (un)fashionable, expensive
> festivals and ceremonies: interesting, exciting, amusing, enjoyable
> nature and geographic features: beautiful, attractive, dramatic, interesting
> people: happy, sad, (un)friendly, kind, annoying
> towns, cities, buildings: large, busy, attractive, ancient, historic
> transport: efficient, cheap, expensive, clean, dirty, fast, slow, old, modern

3
- Ask students to choose a topic from the bulleted list and to prepare brief notes. You could support students in their preparation by writing some prompt questions on the board (e.g. *Where? Why? Who with? When? What?*).

UNIT 6 Stages in life

- Ask students to use them as prompts for questions they could answer in the descriptions. Alternatively, you could ask students to share their ideas with a partner before they write their paragraphs (see Teacher development below).
- Once students have good notes, tell them to write. Set a time limit of ten minutes and be available to help with ideas and vocabulary.

4
- Organize the class into pairs. Ask students to exchange descriptions. Encourage students to comment on the use of adjectives in their partner's work.

Extra activity
Ask students to put their descriptions on the classroom walls or on their desks. Give students time to walk round the class and read the descriptions. At the end, ask students to say which descriptions they liked and why.

Teacher development
Writing in class
Many teachers set creative writing tasks for homework. Students can write at their own speed. Students can take time to look up words or check their own work carefully. There's a written end product which teachers can read and mark. Class time can be used for activities students can't do away from the classroom. However, it can be beneficial to allow class time for free writing. Here are two ways of making creative writing a useful class exercise:

- Involve students fully in each other's work. This means having a brainstorming stage at the start in pairs or groups in which students share ideas, an editing stage after students have written a first draft in which students feed back on and comment on each other's work, and a final stage in which students read and enjoy each other's work. You could put written work on the classroom walls and ask students to circulate and read each other's work. You could ask students to post written work on a class website and ask students to read it there. It's important to be aware, however, that asking students to comment on other people's work can sometimes be discouraging. Set very clear tasks for students when they are being asked to comment or edit. For example, in the task on this page, students are asked only to focus on noticing and commenting on the adjectives used.
- Create a positive environment for writing. Make sure students are sitting comfortably and ready to write. This could mean moving chairs and tables so that students are sitting around tables (as if in a library) rather than in rows or a semi-circle. Play background music quietly to help students relax and concentrate. Provide writing support – this might mean visuals to prompt students' imagination, dictionaries at hand to help them with vocabulary, or teacher support. Monitor and be ready to provide help with the right word or phrase to use.

6f Steel drums

Before you watch
1 ★ **CPT extra!** Lead-in activity [after Ex. 1]
- Ask students to describe the photo and answer the questions. You could do this activity in open class or ask students to work in pairs. Use the feedback to elicit ideas.

ANSWERS
1 She's playing steel drums.
2 Students' own answers
3 Students' own answers

Background information
Steel drums (or pans as they are sometimes called) are a musical instrument originating from Trinidad and Tobago in the Caribbean. They are made from steel oil drums. Steel pan musicians are called pannists. Steel drums are used to play Calypso music.

Key vocabulary
2
- Ask students to match the bold words with the definitions. Encourage students to use the context to guess the meanings.
- **Optional step** It's a good idea to show the pronunciation of these key words – students have to hear them in continuous speech on the video. You could say the words and ask students to repeat, or say the words and ask students to underline the strongly stressed syllable: *influenced*, *native*.

ANSWERS
1 e 2 b 3 c 4 d 5 a

Vocabulary note
tune = if you tune a guitar, you move the metal keys that hold the strings until the correct note is produced by each string

influenced = people can be influenced in good or bad ways by what they read online, by the actions of their favourite celebrities, by teachers and other role models

oil drums = oil drums are very large, and round so they can be rolled on and off lorries or container ships

banned = not permitted, not allowed, prohibited

to be native to (a place) = originally come from (often used with plants, e.g. *The tea plant is native to China or India.*)

110 Unit 6 Stages in life

UNIT 6 Stages in life

While you watch

3 🎬 [6.1]

- Ask students to read the actions carefully.
- Ask students to watch the video and number the actions in the order they see them. Let students compare their answers in pairs before checking with the class. Write the order on the board.

> **ANSWERS**
> 1 c 2 e 3 b 4 d 5 a

Videoscript 🎬 6.1

W = woman in market, **P** = Tony Poyer, **B** = Beverley, **D** = Dove

0.00–0.48 The islands of the Caribbean region are famous for their relaxing beaches and lively music. But the music of the instrument known as 'steelband', or 'pan', is native to only one island nation … Trinidad and Tobago … home of the steelband. Steelband music is a popular part of life here. From the small fishing villages to the hills, the whole population knows and loves the national instrument.

0.49–0.53 **W** Whoo, yeah, you got that, ha ha.

0.54–1.17 **P** Pan is most important to Trinidad and Tobago. It's part of our culture. It was invented in Trinidad and Tobago. It is the only musical instrument that was invented in the 20th century.

1.18–1.31 The special sound brings happiness to children and to adults, and to musicians from many different places and backgrounds. Through the islands' streets and markets, you can't escape the music.

1.32–2.06 Where does steelband music come from? Trinidad is an oil-producing nation. During World War II, the island's old oil drums became useful for something else – as musical instruments. The drums produced sounds that have heavily influenced the music of the region, and you can now hear in everything from island calypso to classical music. In fact, the music goes back several centuries to early Africans who were not allowed to use their own drums.

2.07–2.12 **P** They were banned from beating the Congo drums because people thought they were communicating.

2.13–2.35 At first, people played these African rhythms by hitting old tin cans. Later, people played on the tops of the steel drums, and over time that's how the steelband sound was formed. Steel drum musicians usually play by ear. Most players don't use music written on paper.

2.36–2.49 **P** In fact, in the early days, they knew nothing about music. They played by sound, they even tuned the pan by sound… tonk, tonk, tonk, and they listened until they got it right.

2.50–3.33 The steelband sound starts with the man who tunes the drums – the tuner. This tuner is called Honey Boy. He's been tuning pans for many years. It takes a long time to tune the drums. But these instruments are used by some of the region's top performers. But the steelband is more than just music to Trinidad. It's part of the local culture, and shows the world the creativity of the island's people. Every night, places called 'panyards' are full of musicians who come to learn the instrument. People like Beverley and Dove.

3.34–3.39 **B** Well, it's the music of my country, so I should learn it, you know. I should know a little bit about it.

3.40–3.50 **D** Pan is to Trinidad part of our main culture. This is ours. We made it, we created it.

3.51–end Dove says that steelband belongs to the people of Trinidad and Tobago. But it is something which they are happy to share with audiences and musicians around the world.

4 🎬 [6.1]

- Ask students to watch the video again and note answers to the questions. Let students compare their answers in pairs before checking with the class.

> **ANSWERS**
> 1 relaxing beaches and lively music
> 2 in the 20th century
> 3 It's an oil-producing nation.
> 4 the rhythms came from the early Africans centuries ago
> 5 No, most musicians play by ear.
> 6 a tuner
> 7 musicians who play steelband

Background information

The **Republic of Trinidad and Tobago** is made up of two islands. It's in the Caribbean Sea and only eleven kilometres from the South American coast (Venezuela). It was a British colony throughout the nineteenth century and achieved independence in 1962.

After you watch

Vocabulary in context

5a 🎬 [6.2]

- Explain that students are going to watch some clips from the video which contain some new words and phrases. They need to choose the correct meaning of the words.
- Play the clips. When each multiple-choice question appears, pause the clip so that students can choose the correct definition. You could let students compare answers in pairs before discussing as a class.

> **ANSWERS**
> 1 b 2 a 3 c 4 c 5 c

Vocabulary note

If you play something by ear, you listen to it and pick up how to play it from listening. This is different to being able to read and play music.

6f Steel drums 111

UNIT 6 Stages in life

Videoscript 6.2

1 … musicians from many different places and **background**s.
 a what is behind you
 b your family and experience of living, education, etc.
 c your skills and abilities

2 … you can't **escape the music**.
 a go somewhere so you can't hear
 b go somewhere to hear
 c go somewhere to record

3 … the music **goes back** several centuries to early Africans …
 a repeats parts of the music
 b is different to a time in the past
 c exists since a time in the past

4 Steel drum musicians usually **play by ear.**
 a learn to play by reading music
 b play with their ears, not their hands
 c learn to play by listening to music

5 … these instruments are used by some of the region's top **performers**.
 a people who make the instruments for other people to play
 b people who listen to other people playing the instruments
 c people who play the instruments for other people to listen to

b

- **Optional step** Ask students to look at the photo and describe the instrument in their own words. (It makes a loud, deep, bass note.)
- Ask students to read the text and complete the information. Let students compare answers in pairs before checking with the class.

> ANSWERS
>
> 1 goes back   2 backgrounds   3 play   4 escape
> 5 performers

6 ★ **CPT extra!** Research project [after Ex. 6]

- Ask students to work in pairs to discuss the first question. You could start by eliciting one or two examples. Set a four or five minute time limit. Have a brief feedback and elicit ideas students have.
- Once students have thought of national and cultural symbols, ask them to choose three or four symbols to describe. Encourage them to make notes. Tell them to use the questions provided to guide them. Set a five to ten minute time limit and monitor to help with ideas and vocabulary.

- Ask different pairs to present their ideas to the class. As students speak, listen and notice any errors or examples of good language use you hear. In feedback, at the end, write four or five incorrect sentences on the board, and ask students to correct them with their partner.

> EXAMPLE ANSWERS
>
> 1 flag, national anthem, iconic building (e.g. Big Ben in London, Eiffel Tower in Paris), a type of food or drink (e.g. whisky in Scotland), a sport (e.g. cricket in Australia), a car (e.g. a Ferrari in Italy), a type of building

Extra activity

If you have the technology in your classroom, ask pairs to make the video about their national symbols.

UNIT 6 Stages in life

UNIT 6 Review and memory booster ★ CPT extra! Language games

Memory Booster activities

Exercises 1, 3 and 5 are Memory Booster activities. For more information about these activities and how they benefit students, see page 10.

I can ... tick boxes

As an alternative to students simply ticking the *I can ...* boxes, you could ask them to give themselves a score from 1 to 4 (1 = not very confident; 4 = very confident) for each language area. If students score 1 or 2 for a language area, refer them to additional practice activities in the Workbook and Grammar summary exercises.

Grammar

1 >> MB

- Ask students to work in pairs to look at the sentences and explain the difference in meaning between the verb forms.
- Elicit answers from the class in feedback. If necessary, refer students to the grammar summary on page 166.

> **ANSWERS**
> 1 this is a plan or intention
> 2 this is a decision you have just made
> 3 this is an arrangement
> 4 this is a plan

2

- Ask students to work individually to choose the correct options. Let students compare answers in pairs before checking with the class.

> **ANSWERS**
> 1 hope to   2 'll help   3 to win   4 are you going to
> 5 is having

3 >> MB

- Ask students to work in pairs to tell each other about their plans for the weekend and their future career intentions.
- Monitor, checking students are using the correct future forms.
- Ask students to tell the class anything interesting from their conversations with their partner.

Vocabulary

4

- Ask students to work individually to match the words and phrases to make life events. Let students compare answers in pairs before checking with the class.

> **ANSWERS**
> get your first job
> go to school
> buy your own clothes
> learn to drive
> start a family

5 >> MB

- Ask students to work in pairs to discuss the questions. As students speak, monitor and note any errors you hear. At the end, write up short sentences with errors that you heard. Ask students to correct the errors with a partner.

> **ANSWERS**
> Students' own answers

Real life

6

- Ask students to work individually to complete the text with the words in the box. Let them compare answers in pairs before checking with the class.

> **ANSWERS**
> 1 parades   2 decorations   3 costumes   4 floats   5 drums

7

- Ask students to work individually to replace the words in bold with the phrases. Let students compare answers in pairs before checking with the class.

> **ANSWERS**
> 1 Would you like   2 I'd like you to   3 I'd like to
> 4 That sounds

8

- Ask students to work in pairs to practise inviting each other to do something this week. Monitor and encourage them to use as many expressions for inviting, accepting and declining as they can. If necessary, refer them to the useful expressions box on page 76.

Unit 7 Work

Opener

1 ★ **CPT extra!** Photo activity [before Ex. 1]
- **Optional step** Start by reading the words in the box with the class. Point out the strong stress in each word (it's on the first syllable of each word) and check any difficult words, e.g. *hard* (= difficult), *challenging* (= difficult but rewarding), *skilled* (= used to describe a job when you have to learn a particular ability).
- Ask students to look at the photo and describe the woman's job. You could choose to do this activity in open class or ask students to work in pairs before eliciting a few ideas from the class in feedback.

> **ANSWERS**
>
> Students' own answers. Most should say: dangerous, physical, hard, tiring. It also looks like a skilled job.

Background information

Pennsylvania /ˌpɛnsəlˈveɪnjə/ is a state in the north-eastern region of the United States. It's historically an industrial state and steel production, logging and coal mining are major industries, although much in decline since the latter part of the twentieth century.

2 🔘 [53]
- Start by reading the sentences with the class and checking the meaning of the words in the options (see Vocabulary notes below).
- Play the recording. Students listen and choose the correct options. Let them compare answers in pairs before checking with the class.

> **ANSWERS**
>
> 1 part-time 2 manual 3 low-paid 4 hard; long
> 5 in a team

Audioscript 🔘 [53]

When I left school at eighteen, I didn't have a proper job at first. I worked part-time in a restaurant and I also did some manual work for a construction company. In the end, I applied for a job as a steel worker at our local steel mill. Pennsylvania has a large steel industry, though it doesn't employ as many people nowadays. Anyway, I've been here for about five years now. At first, it was all low-paid work, but I did a lot of training and learned new skills so now my salary is better.

There are eight people in my team: six men and two women, and we all get on really well. It's hard work and the hours are long. You're inside most of the day and you're working with steel at temperatures which can reach three thousand degrees, so it gets pretty hot round here! Sometimes people are surprised when I tell them where I work. I don't think they expect women to work in a place like this, but there are quite a few other women working in this kind of industry. In fact, my supervisor is also a woman.

Vocabulary note

full-time = the number of hours that people normally work in a complete week, e.g. from 9 to 5 Monday to Friday
part-time = for only part of the working week or day, e.g. working only in the mornings or three days a week
office work = working in an office doing a job indoors, at a desk
manual work = doing a physical job
well-paid = a good salary
low-paid = a bad salary (salary is the money you earn when working)
steel mill = steel factory
supervisor = your manager at work – the person who tells you what to do

3
- Ask students to match the words in A and B to make words for jobs. Let students compare answers in pairs before checking with the class.
- **Optional step** Point out the strong stress and drill the words students make (see Vocabulary and pronunciation note below). You may also need to check the meaning of the words.

> **ANSWERS**
>
> hotel receptionist, sales representative, police officer, fashion designer, shop assistant
>
> (Note that there are other possible but less common job titles you could make, e.g. hotel/shop designer, sales assistant, police receptionist, fashion representative)

Vocabulary and pronunciation note

ho*tel* re*cep*tionist = the person who answers the phone and greets guests (at the reception desk)
sales repre*sen*tative = a person who visits clients and tries to sell a company's products
po*lice officer* = a person who works for the police
*fashion de*signer = a person who thinks of and creates new clothes
*shop as*sistant = a person who sells things in a shop (often called a sales assistant in big shops like department stores)

4
Ask students to work in pairs to describe the jobs. Encourage them to use the adjectives from Exercise 1. In feedback, ask some students to tell the class which jobs they would or wouldn't enjoy and why.

> **EXAMPLE ANSWERS**
>
> Note that the answers here depend on the students' own experience, so they all could be boring or interesting, or tiring.
>
> Students may suggest that being a police officer is hard, skilled and challenging, and perhaps dangerous, and sometimes physical. Being a fashion designer is skilled and challenging.

UNIT 7 Work

7a Changes in Pennsylvania

Lesson at a glance
- vocabulary: jobs
- reading: changes in working life
- grammar: present perfect and past simple
- grammar: present perfect with *for* and *since*

Vocabulary jobs

1 ★ **CPT extra!** Vocabulary activity [before Ex. 1]

- **Optional step** Start by reading the words in the box. Point out the strong stress in each word (see Pronunciation note below) and check any difficult words (see Vocabulary note below).
- Ask students to work in pairs to discuss which jobs are difficult to fill before eliciting possible answers from the class in feedback.
- Ask students to check their answers on page 155 of the Student's Book.

ANSWERS

computer programmer, nurse, engineer, accountant, marketing manager

Vocabulary and pronunciation note

ac<u>coun</u>tant = a person who manages the money of individuals or companies

chef /ʃɛf/ = a person who cooks in a hotel or restaurant

com<u>pu</u>ter <u>pro</u>grammer = a person who designs new programs for computers

elec<u>tri</u>cian /ɪlek'trɪʃ(ə)n/ = a person who puts in and repairs things which work with electricity (e.g. lights)

engi<u>neer</u> /ˌɛndʒɪ'nɪə(r)/ = a person who designs or builds things such as bridges or machines

<u>jour</u>nalist /'dʒɜːnəlɪst/ = a newspaper / news website writer or reporter

<u>mar</u>keting <u>ma</u>nager = a person who designs ways of promoting and selling a product

nurse /nɜː(r)s/ = a person who works in hospitals looking after ill people

<u>shop</u> a<u>ssi</u>stant = a person who sells in shops

<u>tea</u>cher = a person who educates students in a school

<u>wai</u>ter = a person who serves people in a restaurant

2

- Read the wordbuilding box with your class. Ask students to underline the suffixes in Exercise 1. Let students compare answers in pairs before checking with the class (see Vocabulary note below).

ANSWERS

account<u>ant</u>, computer programm<u>er</u>, electric<u>ian</u>, engine<u>er</u>, journal<u>ist</u>, marketing manag<u>er</u>, shop assist<u>ant</u>, teach<u>er</u>, wait<u>er</u>

Refer students to Workbook page 59 for further practice.

Vocabulary note

Jobs are often formed with a suffix: *-er, -ant, -ian* or *-ist*. We use *-ian* after a word root ending in *c*, e.g. *electrician, politician, beautician, optician*. Otherwise, there are no useful rules to say when each is used – students must just learn them. Note that sometimes *-or* is used: *actor, supervisor*.

3 ★ **CPT extra!** Speaking activity [after Ex. 3]

- Ask students to make jobs by adding suffixes. Elicit the first answer as an example. Let students compare answers in pairs before checking with the class.

ANSWERS

farmer, economist, scientist, driver, politician, builder, trainer

Extra activity

Ask students to discuss these questions (adapt them depending on the age of your class): *Do you have a job at the moment? What is it? What jobs have you done in the past? What's your dream job? What job are you studying or training for? What are your parents' jobs? Can you say your job in English? Can you describe what you do in your job?*

Reading

4 🎧 [54]

- **Optional step** Ask students to look at the title and photos. Ask them to predict what the article is about.
- Ask students to read the article and match the jobs with the people in the article. Let students compare answers in pairs before checking with the class.
- **Optional step** The reading text is recorded. You could play the recording and ask students to read and listen.

ANSWERS

1 Paul Battista 2 Lee 3 Donald Roessler

5

- Ask students to read the article again and answer the questions. Let students compare answers in pairs before checking with the class.

ANSWERS

1 2004
2 a regular monthly income
3 a job as a driver
4 she's learning to drive trucks
5 he sells construction equipment
6 his profits have increased

Vocabulary note

income = money you get paid from working

truck = a big road vehicle that carries heavy things

looking good = in a good and positive situation

7a Changes in Pennsylvania 115

UNIT 7 Work

Grammar present perfect and past simple

6
- Ask students to read the grammar box and underline past simple verbs and circle present perfect verbs. They then complete the rules (a–c). Let students compare answers in pairs before checking with the class (see Grammar note below).

> **ANSWERS**
> Past simple: discovered
> Present perfect: have changed, has lived, hasn't made
> a past simple   b present perfect   c present perfect

> **Grammar note**
> We can use timelines and concept check questions to show the difference between the present perfect and past simple. Timelines show the connection between past and present when using the present perfect:
>
> Past ——————————×—————————— Now
>   2004
>   They **discovered** gas in 2004.
>   *Do we know when? Yes.*
>
> Past ——————×—×—×—————————— Now
>   Many lives **have changed**.
>   *Do we know when? No.*
>   *Is when important? No.*
>   *Is the fact that their lives are changed now important? Yes.*
>
> Past ———— born ——————————— Now
>   He **has lived** here all his life.
>   *Did he start living here in the past? Yes.*
>   *Does he live here now? Yes.*

Refer students to page 168 for further information and practice.

> **ANSWERS TO GRAMMAR SUMMARY EXERCISES**
> **1**
> 1 I've seen that film five times.
> 2 Have you ever been to Australia?
> 3 They've always lived in the countryside.
> 4 Has she ever visited you?
> 5 I haven't finished my work.
> 6 Why have you applied for this job?
> **2**
> 1 I started   2 Have you ever been   3 They've always loved
> 4 Jill spoke   5 I worked   6 I've never been
> **3**
> 1 Have; finished   2 got   3 Did; have
> 4 Have; heard   5 have; sent   6 told
> 7 Have; been   8 stayed   9 Did; have

7
- Ask students to underline the present perfect verbs in the article and categorize them. Let students compare answers in pairs before checking with the class.

> **ANSWERS**
> Regular past participles: changed, lived, employed, increased
> Irregular past participles: made, had, run

8
- **Optional step** Ask students to read the text for comprehension first. Ask: *Why does the engineer plan to stay in Pennsylvania?* (the natural gas industry has created new jobs).
- Ask students to choose the correct options. Let them compare their answers in pairs before checking with the class.
- **Optional step** In feedback, ask students to justify their answers by referring back to the rules in Exercise 6 (see answers in brackets below).

> **ANSWERS**
> 1 I went (we say when)
> 2 I qualified (we say when)
> 3 haven't lived (started in the past and continues now)
> 4 I've worked (we don't know or don't say when)
> 5 I spent (we say when)
> 6 It's been (started in the past and continues now)
> 7 weren't (we say when – *at first*)
> 8 has created (we don't know or don't say when)
> 9 has improved (started in the past and continues now)

9
- Explain that students are going to listen to an interview with a scientist for a natural gas company.
- Ask students to make the questions. You could support students by pointing out the form of a present perfect and past simple question first. Do this by looking at the example in question 1 and elicit the question for 2 (see Grammar note below).
- Let students compare the questions they have formed with a partner, but don't check answers at this stage.

> **ANSWERS**
> 1 How long have you worked for your company?
> 2 When did you go to college?
> 3 Have you always lived in Pennsylvania?
> 4 When did you move back here?
> 5 Have you ever worked overseas?
> 6 Has it been easy living here?

UNIT 7 Work

> **Grammar note**
>
> Notice the inversion of the auxiliary verb and subject noun or pronoun in questions:
>
> | Q word | auxiliary verb | subject | main verb |
> |---|---|---|---|
> | How long | have | you | worked …? |
> | When | did | you | move back …? |

10 [55]

- Play the recording. Students listen and check they formed the questions correctly, and answer the questions. You could play the recording twice if necessary to give students a chance to catch all the answers. Let students compare answers in pairs before checking with the class.

> **ANSWERS**
> 1 For five years.
> 2 When I was nineteen.
> 3 No, I haven't.
> 4 In 2015.
> 5 Yes, I have.
> 6 Yes, it has.

Audioscript [55]

I = Interviewer, S = Scientist

I: How long have you worked for your company?
S: For five years. Since I left college.
I: When did you go to college?
S: I started when I was nineteen and I qualified with my degree about four years later.
I: And have you always lived in Pennsylvania?
S: No, I haven't. I grew up here but then I went to university in Boston and I've lived in one or two other places.
I: So, when did you move back here?
S: In 2015.
I: Have you ever worked overseas?
S: Yes, I have. I worked in Dubai, in the Middle East, two years ago.
I: And how does Pennsylvania compare with other places? Has it been easy living here?
S: Yes, it has, overall.

Grammar present perfect with *for* and *since*

11

- Ask students to look at the grammar box. Ask them to complete the rule with *for* and *since*. Let students compare answers in pairs before checking with the class.

> **ANSWERS**
> 1 since   2 for

Refer students to page 168 for further information and practice.

> **ANSWERS TO GRAMMAR SUMMARY EXERCISE**
> 4
> 1 for   2 for   3 since   4 since   5 for   6 for
> 7 since   8 for

12 ★ CPT extra! Grammar activity [after Ex. 12]

- Ask students to work individually to complete the phrases. Let students compare answers in pairs before checking with the class.

> **ANSWERS**
> 1 since   2 for   3 for   4 since   5 since   6 since
> 7 for   8 since

> **Grammar note**
>
> Students sometimes find the difference between *for* and *since* difficult. In some languages the same word is used to cover the meanings of *for* and *since*. If students have problems, use symbols to show a point in time and a period of time and ask students to categorize more phrases. Here are examples:
>
> X (a point in time): Monday, Christmas, this morning, I got up, I last saw you
>
> – (a period of time): five seconds, half an hour, ages, ever, days and days

Speaking my life
13

- Ask students to work in pairs to practise asking and answering questions about the topics. Encourage students to follow the model in the example dialogue provided – they ask general present perfect questions first, then find out about specific dates and details by using the past simple.

- It's a good idea to give students some preparation time first (see Teacher development below). Tell them to read the topics and spend five minutes individually thinking of questions to ask their partner. When students are ready, ask them to take turns to ask and answer the questions.

- As students speak, listen carefully and note errors that you could write up on the board at the end. Ask students to work in pairs to correct the sentences you write up.

- **Optional step** You could do the ask and answer practice as a mingle. Ask students to stand up, walk round, and ask three different people their questions.

7a Changes in Pennsylvania   117

UNIT 7 Work

EXAMPLE ANSWERS

Possible questions:
How long have you had your current job?
When did you start your job?
When did you move into your current home?
How long have you lived there?
Have you been to different countries?
Which countries have you been to?
Where did you go last year?
Have you learned any foreign languages?
How long have you studied English?
How long have you known your best friend?
Where did you meet?
What are your interests?
How long have you done that?

Extra activity

Write the following three sentence beginnings on the board and ask students to complete them in two ways, once using *for* and once using *since* (example answers in brackets).

1 I've lived in my current house … (for five years / since 2012).
2 I've studied English … (for ages / since I was 10).
3 I've known my best friend …. (for ten years / since I started school).

Teacher development

Preparation time

When doing a spoken fluency activity, it's a good idea to give students preparation time. Here are some suggestions:

- Ask students to prepare ideas, opinions or questions with a partner (rather than individually). Then change partners to do the task.
- Think about how you want students to prepare. For example, you could ask them to prepare and write whole dialogues. Students then practise first by reading the dialogue before covering the dialogue and trying to recall or improvise what they wrote. Alternatively, you could ask them to just prepare parts of the task – questions to ask, notes to use, prompts to help them in the activity.

7b X-ray photographer

Lesson at a glance
- vocabulary: parts of a building
- listening: phone calls in an office
- grammar: prepositions of place and movement
- pronunciation: intrusive /w/
- speaking: giving directions

Vocabulary parts of a building

1 ★ **CPT extra!** Photo activity [after Ex. 1]
- Ask students to look at the photo and read about the photographer Nick Veasey. Ask the questions in feedback and elicit answers from the class.

ANSWERS

1 It's X-ray photography.
2 He took a series of X-ray photographs and put them together in one picture.
3 Students' own answers

Background information

Nick Veasey was born in the UK in 1962. His work has featured in many international advertising campaigns and adorned products and packaging worldwide.

2

- **Optional step** Ask students to look at the photo and brainstorm as many words as you can (e.g. *lift, office, desk, chair, plant, picture, computer, lamp, sofa* – words that are useful for the later listening include: *drawers, photocopier*).
- Ask students to complete the sentences with the words in the box. Let students compare answers in pairs before checking with the class.
- **Optional step** Drill the words in the box paying attention to the strong stress (see Vocabulary note below).

ANSWERS

1 office 2 entrance 3 reception 4 ground floor; corridor
5 lift; stairs 6 emergency exit 7 canteen 8 basement

Vocabulary note

canteen = a restaurant for workers in an office building or factory

corridor = the long, narrow hallway in an office building off which there are offices and other rooms (note that we only use this word in large, public buildings – in a house it's called a hall).

emergency exit = the way out when there is a fire or accident

lift = the machine that goes up and down, carrying people to different floors (US English: elevator)

UNIT 7 Work

reception = reception or the reception area is the open area at the front of an office building where visitors and clients wait

The different levels of a building are called floors. In British English, the *ground floor* is at street level, the *basement* under street level, and then, above the ground floor, there is the first, second, third floor, and, finally, the top floor. In US English, the ground floor is often called the first floor.

Note the strong stress on these words: <u>base</u>ment, ca<u>nteen</u>, <u>corri</u>dor, e<u>mer</u>gency <u>exit</u>, <u>entr</u>ance, <u>off</u>ice, re<u>cep</u>tion

3

- Ask students to work in pairs to say which parts of a building are in their school or college. In feedback, elicit ideas from different pairs.
- **Optional step** Support students by writing up these simple sentence starters on the board:

  On the ground floor, there is/are …

  On the first/second floor, there is/are …

> **EXAMPLE ANSWERS**
>
> If your students are in a typical school or college, it's likely to have all of these parts of a building.

4

- Ask students to work in pairs to describe the photo. Point out the example and elicit one or two other sentences from your class to get them started. In feedback, elicit a few sentences from different pairs.

> **EXAMPLE ANSWERS**
>
> Someone is using / going up in the lift.
> On the first floor, someone is sitting/working at a desk / someone is walking up the stairs.
> On the second floor, two people are meeting in an office.
> On the third floor, someone is using the photocopier / someone is sitting/working at a desk.
> On the top floor, people are relaxing / someone is reading a newspaper.

Listening

5 [56]

- **Optional step** Use the photo to pre-teach key words from the listening: *drawers, photocopier, desk, folder*.
- Read the questions with the class and point out that there are two telephone conversations to listen to.
- Play the recording. Students listen and answer the questions. Let students compare answers in pairs before checking with the class.

> **ANSWERS**
>
> 1 home
> 2 on the first floor, where the person is sitting on the photo
> 3 in the top drawer on the left, behind Kristina
> 4 to mend the photocopier
> 5 on the 3rd floor next to the photocopying room

Audioscript [56]

Conversation 1

A: Hello? Kristina speaking.

B: Hi Kristina. It's Geoff.

A: Hi Geoff. Where are you calling from?

B: I'm at home, but I'm about to leave for a meeting. Can you help me? I've left a list of prices in the office and I need it for the meeting.

A: Sure. Is it on your desk?

B: I think it's next to my computer.

A: I can't see anything.

B: Oh. Well, maybe I left it in one of the drawers behind you.

A: OK. Which one?

B: Try the top drawer on the left.

A: Let me look. Yes, there's a folder called 'price lists'?

B: That's the one! Can you email me a copy of the list with prices for next year?

A: Sure, I'll do that now …

Conversation 2

C: Hello, Richard Roberts speaking.

D: Hi. I'm here to fix your photocopier, but I don't know which office. I'm standing at the entrance to the building.

C: OK. Great. So, you need to come into the entrance and go up to the third floor. Go through the door on your right and the photocopying room is there. My office is next to it so I'll meet you.

D: OK. See you in a minute.

6 [56]

- **Optional step** Give students time to read the sentences carefully and remember or guess which prepositions are missing.
- Play the recording again. Students listen and write in the prepositions. Let them compare answers in pairs before checking with the class.

> **ANSWERS**
>
> 1 at 2 on 3 next to 4 in; behind 5 on 6 at
> 7 into 8 up to 9 through 10 next to

Grammar prepositions of place and movement

7 ★ CPT extra! Grammar activity [before Ex. 7]

- Read the grammar box with the class. Then ask students to categorize the prepositions in the sentences in Exercise 6. You could do this in open class or ask students to work in pairs.

> **ANSWERS**
>
> Prepositions of place: 1, 2, 3, 4, 5, 6, 10
> Prepositions of movement: 7, 8, 9

7b X-ray photographer

UNIT 7 Work

Grammar note

It's a good idea to show these prepositions with diagrams – see the diagrams in the grammar reference on page 168 of the Student's Book and use diagrams in your teaching to show the meaning of the words on this page.

Prepositions of place

- *At* tells us that something is located at a specific point or location (e.g. *I'm at home, It's at the top, I'm at the entrance / at reception*).
- *In* tells us something is in an enclosed space – it's surrounded or closed off on all sides (e.g. *It's in the box, They're in a drawer*).
- *On* tells us that something is located on a surface (e.g. *It's on the desk*).
- Note that phrases such as *on the left, on the right, in the middle* and *at the top* don't really follow the rules above, and are best learned as fixed expressions.
- Students often confuse *in front of* (= the opposite of *behind*) with *opposite* (= face to face).

Prepositions of movement

It's a good idea to show meaning through pictures, mime or through opposites – get students to pair the following:
up / down, into / out of, towards / away from

Refer students to page 168 for further information and practice.

ANSWERS TO GRAMMAR SUMMARY EXERCISES

5
1 in   2 on   3 below   4 opposite   5 between   6 near

6
1 out of   2 across   3 along   4 past   5 through
6 up   7 outside

8

- Ask students to work individually to choose the correct option. Let them compare answers in pairs before checking with the class.

ANSWERS

1 on   2 down   3 outside   4 at   5 past   6 opposite
7 along; on   8 across

9

- Ask students to work individually to complete the messages with the prepositions in the box. Elicit the first answer as an example. Let students compare answers in pairs before checking with the class.

ANSWERS

1 in   2 at   3 on   4 next to   5 through   6 up
7 into   8 down

Grammar note

in the coffee area = it's possible to say 'at' here, but 'in' is more common because we are talking about a space in which we are surrounded – often we can choose *in* or *at* depending on what we want to say (e.g. *I'm at the coffee shop* = I'm at this specific place – maybe inside or at the door, but *I'm in the coffee shop* = I'm actually inside the place)

through the reception area = from one side or end (of a place) to another

into the lift = from outside to inside (a place)

Pronunciation intrusive /w/

10 [57] ★ **CPT extra!** Pronunciation activity [after Ex. 10]

- Read the explanation with the class (see Pronunciation note below). Then play the recording. Students listen and repeat the examples.
- **Optional step** Ask students to work in pairs to practise making sentences using *Let's* or *Why don't we* and the examples with *go* (e.g. *Let's go out, Why don't we go up to the canteen?*).

Pronunciation note

We add an intrusive consonant sound between vowel sounds at the end of one word and the start of the next because it's very difficult to say the sounds without an intrusive consonant.

We use intrusive /w/ after words that end with high back vowels: /uː/, /əʊ/, /aʊ/. (Note that a high back vowel is one where the tongue is positioned as far back as possible in the mouth without creating a constriction that would be classified as a consonant.)

Speaking my life

11

- **Optional step** Start by modelling the activity. Give one or two examples of directions to the class and ask them to say where you have directed them to (see example answers below).
- Give students three or four minutes to prepare two or three sets of directions by themselves. Monitor and help students with ideas and vocabulary but encourage students to write notes (or nothing) rather than whole sentences.
- Once students are ready, ask them to work with a partner. Tell them to take turns giving directions. Students must listen and say where they have been directed to.
- As students speak, monitor and notice how well students use prepositions. Note any errors which you could write on the board at the end for students to correct.

EXAMPLE ANSWERS

Go down the stairs to the ground floor. Go along the corridor to the big doors. Go through the doors and you're there.

Go into the lift. Go up to the top floor. Go past the manager's office. It's opposite the meeting room.

Extra activity

Write the following questions on the board:
What can you …

1 *sail across?* (a sea, an ocean, a lake, a bay)
2 *climb up?* (a mountain, a hill, a ladder, a staircase, some stairs, a wall, a tall building, a tree, a tower)
3 *walk along?* (a path, a street, a road, the side of a river)
4 *drive through?* (a city, a desert, a forest, a valley, rain, snow)

Ask students to work in pairs to make as long a list as they can of possible answers to each question. Find out which pair has the longest list.

120 Unit 7 Work

UNIT 7 Work

7c Twenty-first century cowboys

Lesson at a glance
- reading: a traditional job
- critical thinking: analysing comparisons in a text
- word focus: *make* or *do*
- speaking: job satisfaction

Reading

1 ⭐ **CPT extra!** Lead-in activity [after Ex. 1]
- Ask students to look at the photo. Ask them to work in pairs to discuss the questions. Elicit a few ideas from the class in feedback.

> **EXAMPLE ANSWERS**
>
> Students may choose to define cowboy in a number of ways. A cowboy is a person who herds cows. Cowboys wear wide cowboy hats, carry a gun, ride horses and can lasso a horse or cow with a rope. Cowboys are the heroes in American westerns who fight 'Indians' (Native Americans).
>
> The USA is most famous for cowboys – largely because of the Hollywood movie industry that has glamourized the cowboy.

> **Background information**
>
> The word **cowboy** is a translation of *vaquero*, a Spanish word for an individual who managed cattle while mounted on horseback. The life and techniques of cowboys were actually first developed in Mexico by *vaqueros* in the nineteenth century.

2 💿 [58]
- **Optional step** Ask students to say how they think the life of a twenty-first century cowboy might be different from the life of a cowboy 150 years ago. Elicit suggestions.
- Ask students to read the article and decide which sentence summarizes the text. Let them compare their answers in pairs before checking with the class.
- **Optional step** The reading text is recorded. You could play the recording and ask students to read and listen.

> **ANSWER**
> 1

3
- Ask students to read the sentences carefully. Check *ranch* (= a cattle farm) and *salary* (= money you earn from work). Note that *ranch* is in the glossary. You could check the other words in the glossary at this stage.
- Ask students to read the article again and choose the correct option. Let them compare answers in pairs before checking with the class.

- **Optional step** In feedback, ask students to say where in the text they found the answer (see notes in brackets below).

> **ANSWERS**
>
> 1 c (*it's physical with long hours and low pay*)
> 2 a (*you are in the middle of nowhere … you feel lonely*)
> 3 a (*They are brothers and have worked with cows since they were children. Their mother had a ranch …*)
> 4 c (*he wanted job satisfaction. And for a cowboy, job satisfaction doesn't come from the money or a comfortable office …*)

Critical thinking analysing comparisons in a text

4
- Read the information and task with the class. Use the example to check that everyone understands what to do.
- Ask students to look back at the article and find words and phrases to describe each idea. You could choose to ask students to do this individually before checking with a partner. Alternatively, ask students to work in pairs to do the whole task.

> **ANSWERS**
>
> 1 a the cowboy in Hollywood films: freedom, adventure, romantic image
>   b the real life of a cowboy: hard, dangerous, physical, long hours, low pay
> The two ideas are very different.
>
> 2 a the life of a cowboy in the past: hard, dangerous, physical, long hours, low pay
>   b the life of the modern cowboy: hard, dangerous, physical, long hours, low pay
> The two ideas are similar.
>
> 3 a cowboys like Blaine and Tyrel: born into the life, rode a horse before they could walk, large moustaches, traditional clothes, hat and boots
>   b cowboys like Pat Crisswell: had an office job, made good money, wanted job satisfaction, being free to wake up under the sky and being your own boss
> The two ideas are very different.
>
> 4 a the advantages of an office job in the city: good money, all day inside
>   b the advantages of working as a cowboy: job satisfaction, being free to wake up under the sky and being your own boss
> The two ideas are very different.

Word focus *make* or *do*

5
- Ask students to read the article again and find and underline phrases with *make* or *do* in paragraphs 2 and 4.
- Tell students to use the underlined examples to help them complete the phrases (1–5). Let students compare their answers in pairs before checking with the class.

7c Twenty-first century cowboys 121

UNIT 7 Work

> **ANSWERS**
>
> 1 do 2 make 3 make 4 make 5 do

6 ★ **CPT extra!** Word focus activity [after Ex. 6]
- Ask students to complete the phrases, using a dictionary if necessary (see Vocabulary note below). Let students compare their answers in pairs before checking with the class.

> **ANSWERS**
>
> 1 do 2 make 3 make 4 do 5 do 6 make
> 7 make 8 do

> **Vocabulary note**
>
> Students often confuse *make* and *do*. This is because many languages use the same verb to cover both meanings.
> - We use *do* when there is an idea of 'work' (e.g. *do homework, do the cleaning, do a job*) or when we don't say what we do specifically (e.g. *do nothing, do something interesting*).
> - We use *make* when there is an idea of 'construction or creativity' (e.g. *make a cake, make a model out of matchsticks, make a plan*).
>
> Note, however, that there are many uses which contradict these rules (e.g. *make the bed* sounds more like work than creativity!) and the collocation between these verbs and various nouns are best learnt as fixed expressions.

7
- Organize the class into pairs. Ask students to take turns to ask and answer questions.
- **Optional step** It's a good idea to give students two or three minutes of individual preparation time first before asking questions. Tell them to look at the phrases in Exercises 5 and 6 and note down or think of questions to ask.

> **EXAMPLE ANSWERS**
>
> Here are a few questions students might ask:
> *How often do you make breakfast?*
> *How many calls do you make every day?*
> *When / How often do you do your homework?*
> *When was the last time you made a big mistake? What was it?*

> **Extra activity**
>
> Write the words below on the board and ask students to decide whether they collocate with *do* or *make*. You could make this a dictionary research task:
>
> *(make) a plan   (do) the cleaning   (do) nothing*
> *(make) a suggestion   (do) a crossword*
> *(make) an appointment   (do) a test*

Speaking — my life

8
- Read the last sentence of the article with the class: *job satisfaction doesn't come from the money or a comfortable office; it comes from being free to wake up under the sky and being your own boss.* Discuss the question in open class and elicit students' views.
- **Optional step** In feedback, you could elicit other factors that give people job satisfaction (apart from money, a good work environment and being your own boss). Build up the students' list on the board. This activity leads into the activity in Exercise 9. Alternatively, elicit a list after students have completed Exercise 9.

> **ANSWER**
>
> See the answers to Exercise 10.

9
- Start by reading the bulleted list with your class and checking any new words, e.g. *regular promotion* (= getting a higher job with more money and responsibilities at regular times – i.e. every few years) and *outdoors* (= not in an office or other building).
- Ask students to work individually or in pairs to order the items. Tell them to write down their order.

10
- Once students have an order, organize them into groups of four (see Teacher development below). If students prepared in pairs, split them up so they are in different groups. Ask students to explain their order to others in their group.
- **Optional step** If you didn't brainstorm other factors from students when doing Exercise 8, ask students in feedback to this activity to say what other job satisfaction factors they would add to the list (e.g. a good working environment, a short working day or flexi-time, being able to work from home, having a job near home so you don't have to commute, a good pension scheme or health care scheme, having a job that is creative or challenging or different every day, having a job where you help other people).

> **EXAMPLE ANSWERS**
>
> Students' own answers.
>
> A person with a 'cowboy' mentality might order *learning new skills, making your own decisions, working outdoors* and perhaps *opportunities to travel to different places* above the others.
>
> An ambitious 'business person' might order *getting regular promotion, a good salary* and *making your own decisions* at the top of the list.

UNIT 7 Work

Teacher development
Organizing group speaking activities

Here are two creative ways of organizing a speaking activity to maximize interaction and create a meaningful task (they are written with Exercise 9 and 10 above in mind, but can be used in many activities in which students have to order, prioritize or categorize):

- A pyramid discussion: ask students to order the job satisfaction factors individually first. Then put students in pairs. Ask students to talk with a partner and write a new order that they both agree on – students will have to negotiate and compromise. Then tell each pair to get together with another pair in the class – the task is to negotiate and agree on a group order. Finally, ask students from each group to present their order with reasons. The final task is to write up on the board an order agreed by the whole class.

- Speaking corners: choose five of the items in the list in Exercise 9 (e.g. learning new skills, a good salary, making your own decisions, opportunities to travel, long holidays). Write these phrases on cards. Hold one up and ask the class if anybody thinks it's the most important item. When a hand goes up, give that card to that person. Once all five cards have been handed out, ask the five people with cards (the card holders) each to sit in a different part of the class (a different corner). Tell the rest of the class to stand up and visit the people with the cards. It's the job of the person with the card to persuade as many 'visitors' as possible that their factor is the most important. Once students have visited some or all of the card holders in the speaking corners, they decide who they think has the most important factor, and must then sit with that person. The winner is the card holder who has persuaded most people to join him or her.

7d A job interview

Lesson at a glance
- vocabulary: job adverts
- real life: a job interview

Vocabulary job adverts
1
- Ask students to look at the job advert and answer the questions. You could do this in open class or ask students to work in pairs or small groups to discuss the questions. Elicit a few ideas from the class in feedback.

ANSWERS
1 The restaurant needs people today.
2 Reasons for applying include flexible working times, training provided and the fact that you don't need any experience. Students may also suggest that it might be fun, you work with a team and meet people, and it's great if you like pizza.
Reasons for not applying depend on the students' point of view – the job can be tiring, stressful, long hours in the evening and at weekends, and not well paid.

2
- Ask students to work individually to find words in the advert to match with the definitions (1–7). Let students compare answers in pairs before checking with the class.
- **Optional step** Drill the words as necessary, pointing out the strong stress (see Pronunciation note below).

ANSWERS
1 staff 2 positions 3 essential 4 provide 5 apply (for)
6 CV 7 (contact) details

Vocabulary and pronunciation note

staff = a singular, uncountable noun (you can't say *staffs*) used to describe the collective group of people working for any company or institution (e.g. *teaching staff, medical staff*) – it's usually followed by a plural noun (*Our staff are happy here*).

*po*_si_*tion* = only used formally with this meaning (e.g. *We offer a new position* but not *Hey guys! I've got a new position!*)

*es*_sen_*tial* = very necessary or very important

*pro*_vide_ = give or offer

To *ap*_ply_ (for a job), people generally write a *covering letter or email*, and/or *fill in an application form*, and/or *enclose or attach a CV* (*curriculum* _vi_*tae*), which is a form or document that includes contact details (name, address, email) plus information about qualifications, work experience and personality (in the US, this is called a *resumé*).

7d A job interview 123

UNIT 7 Work

Real life a job interview

3 [59]
- **Optional step** Ask students to read the sentences and predict what sort of questions the manager may have asked Hania (e.g. *Do you have a job now? What did you like about your last job? Do you have any questions?*).
- Play the recording. Students listen and note whether the sentences are true (T) or false (F). Let students compare answers in pairs before checking with the class.
- **Optional step** In feedback, ask students to say what they heard which helped them reach their answer (see answers in brackets below).

> **ANSWERS**
> 1 T (*I've looked at your CV*)
> 2 F (*worked here last year … came back to study fashion this year*)
> 3 F (*I have some spare time in the evenings*)
> 4 T (*helping the customers*)
> 5 F (*Yes, it says in the advert you provide training. Can you give me more information about that?*)
> 6 T (*lots of experience so you probably won't need very much*)

Audioscript [59]

M = Manager, H = Hania

M: Right. Have a seat, Hania.
H: Thanks.
M: I've looked at your CV and see that you're from Poland. How long have you been in England?
H: I worked here last year to improve my English and then I came back to study fashion this year.
M: I see. So, why do you want this job?
H: I have some spare time in the evenings after college and I'd like to earn some extra money.
M: OK. And last year you worked in another restaurant. What did you like about your last job?
H: Helping the customers and trying to give good service.
M: How did you deal with any difficult situations?
H: At the weekends we were very busy in the evenings so sometimes customers had to wait for their food. But I found that most customers are OK if you are friendly and polite. Also you need to apologize when the food is late.
M: Good. Well, I think that's everything. Do you have any questions for me?
H: Yes, it says in the advert you provide training. Can you give me more information about that?
M: Well, you have lots of experience so you probably won't need very much. But on your first day, you work with another waiter and learn about the menu and the different kinds of pizza.

4
- Discuss the questions in open class or ask students to work in pairs to discuss the questions. Elicit answers from the class in feedback.

> **EXAMPLE ANSWERS**
> Students' own answers
> Reasons why she's good are: she's got experience of working in an English restaurant, she answers the questions well, she asks a good follow-up question, she doesn't need much training.
> Reasons against: she's at college and is only free in the evenings

5 [59] ★ **CPT extra!** Real life activity [after Ex. 5]
- Ask students to read the questions first, and try to recall, guess or work out the missing words.
- Play the recording again. Students listen and write the missing words. Let students compare their answers in pairs before checking with the class.
- Once students have completed the questions, ask them to match five of the questions with the correct category in the box. Tell them to read the box to find similar questions. Let students compare answers in pairs.
- **Optional step** You could ask students to look at audioscript 59 on page 186 of the Student's Book to check their answers.

> **ANSWERS**
> 1 How 2 Why 3 What 4 How 5 Do 6 Can
> Your current life and job: *How long have you been in England?*
> Reasons for applying: *Why do you want this job?*
> Past experience and qualifications: *What did you like about your last job? How did you deal with any difficult situations?*
> Questions for the interviewer: *Can you give me more information about that?*
> Note that question 5 does not match any of the categories.

6
- Ask students to work in pairs to prepare and practise the interview. You may wish to mix pairs at this stage so students have a new partner. Tell students to decide who is A, and who is B, and to read the advert carefully. Set a five-minute time limit for students to prepare questions or answers and monitor to help with ideas and vocabulary. Refer students to the job interview expressions in the box for help with thinking of and forming questions.
- When students are ready, ask them to act out the interview. It's a good idea to create a mock interview situation here. Tell students to move chairs so that they are sitting face to face (as in an interview). Tell interviewers to begin by saying *Please come in and sit down*. The more students are encouraged to act out the situation, the more likely it is to be successful.

UNIT 7 Work

- As students speak, monitor closely and note down errors or examples of good language use. In feedback, ask interviewers whether they would offer the job to their interviewees or not. Then write up errors you heard on the board for students to correct in pairs.

7

- Ask students to change roles to act out the interview again. Give them more preparation time to prepare their new roles. Alternatively, you could ask interviewers to stand and move one place round the class, thus putting students with new partners for this interview.

Extra activity

A fun way of extending this activity (or an alternative way if you prefer to do this to the roleplay above) is to write unusual or funny jobs on the board and ask students to roleplay interviews for these jobs. One scenario is to say that a circus is recruiting and they want the following: *a clown, a lion tamer, a tightrope walker, a juggler, a trapeze artist*. Use pictures or mime to explain the words. Ask students to choose which job to apply for and think about what experience and personal qualities they have to do the job before roleplaying interviews.

7e Applying for a job

Lesson at a glance
- writing: a CV
- writing skill: missing out words in CVs

Writing a CV

1

- **Optional step** Read the headings in the box with the class and check their meaning by eliciting what sort of information might be on a CV under each heading (e.g. *references* – name and email of your university professor; *work experience* – name and address of the place you last worked at).
- Ask students to read the CV. Ask simple focus questions, e.g. *Whose CV is it?* (Aldo Peterson's) *What industry does he work in?* (hotel management).
- Ask students to complete the CV with the headings. Let students compare answers in pairs before checking with the class.

ANSWERS
1 Date of birth 2 Address 3 Home telephone
4 Education 5 Work experience 6 Skills
7 Interests 8 References

Background information

A **CV** (or curriculum vitae) is a document giving details of your qualifications and the jobs you have had in the past that you send when you're applying for a job. Your students may note that the British CV is typically a sparse, informative document. It's expressed in note form and avoids descriptive adjectives and subjective opinions. In US English, it's called a resumé.

Vocabulary note

MA = Master of Arts (a postgraduate degree)
BSc = Bachelor of Science (a first degree in a science subject)

2

- **Optional step** If your students are from the same country, project a copy of a typical CV from that country and ask students to compare it to the British CV in the Student's Book.
- Discuss the questions with your class. Elicit ideas.

EXAMPLE ANSWERS

Answers depend on the students' background and experience.

Other information that may be added could be: open references about the applicant; strengths and weaknesses; personal qualities, hobbies, life experiences (e.g. places you have visited).

7e Applying for a job 125

UNIT 7 Work

Writing skill missing out words in CVs

3a
- Ask students to work in pairs to compare the full sentences with the corresponding sentences from the CV.
- In feedback, elicit which words are missing and which verb forms the CV sentences have used.

> **ANSWERS**
>
> Missing words: subjects, auxiliary or modal verbs
>
> Verb forms used: present participle (*Working*), present perfect (*Have worked*), past simple (*Met*)

b
- Ask students to underline all the sentences or phrases starting with verb forms in the CV. Let students compare their answers in pairs.
- Once students have located all the verb forms, ask them to work individually to rewrite the sentences in full. Elicit the first sentence as an example. Let students compare answers in pairs before checking with the class.

> **ANSWERS**
>
> (I am) helping the general manager.
> (I am) managing staff.
> (I) checked in guests / (I had to)* check in guests.
> (I) worked in a large team.
> (I) translated hotel correspondence … / (I had to)* translate hotel correspondence …
> (I) planned activities … / (I had to)* plan activities …
> (I) organized the schedule. / (I had to)* organize the schedule.
> (I) did most winter sports.
> (I) acted in student theatre productions.
> *Note that we can use *had to* when expressing duties or responsibilities in a job.

c ★ CPT extra! Writing activity [after Ex. 3c]
- Look at the example with the class. Ask students to rewrite the other sentences. Let students compare their answers in pairs before checking with the class.

> **ANSWERS**
>
> 1 Studying mathematics at university.
> 2 Made pizzas in the student cafeteria.
> 3 Have competed in athletics competitions for my school.
> 4 Trained / Had to train new employees.
> 5 Learning to play the drums.
> 6 Have given presentations to large groups of people.

4
- **Optional step** Start by brainstorming ideas of what to write about. Ask: *What job are you doing? Where are you studying? Where have you worked / studied in the past? What duties did you have in your last job? What interesting life experiences have you had?* Elicit ideas and ask students to use these ideas when writing sentences.
- Ask students to work individually to write six sentences about their work, study or interests. Monitor and help with vocabulary, reminding students to reduce the sentences so that they start with verb forms.
- Once students have completed their sentences, tell them to share their ideas with a partner.

5
- Ask students to write a CV. Before doing so, remind students of the headings in Exercise 1 and tell them to use these headings and the model CV on the page to guide their writing. You could set this task for homework. If so, get students to exchange and compare CVs in the next lesson.

6
- Organize the class into pairs to exchange CVs and check each other's work using the bulleted list as a guide.

> **Extra activity**
>
> Ask students to sit in groups of four. Collect the CVs from one group and pass them to another group. Tell each group to look at the four CVs they have been given and evaluate them. Tell them to decide which student they will invite for interview. In feedback, ask groups to say which CV they have selected and why.

UNIT 7 Work

7f My working life

Before you watch

Background information

Romeo and Juliet is one of William Shakespeare's most well-known tragedies. It's set in the Italian city of Verona. Romeo and Juliet are lovers from rival families who meet a tragic end. The play was written in the 1590s.

Key vocabulary

1 ★ **CPT extra!** Photo activity [before Ex. 1]

- **Optional step** Start by asking students to describe the photo. Ask: *What can you see? Where are they? How do they feel?*
- Encourage students to use the context to guess the meanings of the words in bold.
- Ask students to work in pairs to discuss the words and match them with the definitions. Note that there is one extra definition.
- **Optional step** It's a good idea to show the pronunciation of these key words – students have to hear them in continuous speech on the video. You could say the words and ask students to repeat (see Vocabulary and pronunciation note below).

ANSWERS

1 b   2 a, e   3 c   4 d   5 f

Vocabulary and pronunciation note

organic food /ɔːˈɡænɪk/ must be free of certain pesticides and fertilizers often used in farming. Organic foods are also usually not processed using irradiation, industrial solvents or synthetic food additives.

A *stall* /stɔːl/ is an individual shop in an indoor or outdoor market – often it is not much more than a bench with products on it.

If advantages *outweigh* /ˌaʊtˈweɪ/ disadvantages, it means there are more advantages than disadvantages

Variety /vəˈraɪɪti/ in a job is a positive thing – it means you do different and interesting things

bring together = here, organize an event so that everyone can come

While you watch

2 🎥 [7.1]
- Ask students to work in pairs to look at the photos and captions, and predict who says the sentences (a–f).
- Don't check answers at this stage.

3 🎥 [7.1]
- Play the video for students to check their predictions from Exercise 2.

ANSWERS

a Marcus   b Katy   c Virginia   d Marcus
e Katy   f Virginia

Videoscript 🎥 7.1

0.00–0.51   **1** My name's Katie, I sell organic fruit and vegetables in lots of different places. I always have to work at the weekends. We start about 7.30 in the morning. We set up the market stall, which gets busy about 9.30. I take a break for lunch around midday, and then we pack up and go home at three o'clock.

0.52–1.06   I like my job because I get to meet lots of different people, it's good exercise, and it's good for the environment because our farmers grow organic food.

1.07–1.23   The job can be difficult because it's long hours and sometimes the weather can be bad because it rains, but overall it's really enjoyable.

1.23–1.56   **2** My name is Virginia. I am from Argentina. I am a Spanish teacher and I have taught Spanish for 14 years, since I came to England.

1.57–2.24   When I teach at pupils' houses, I normally start at four o'clock and that can involve maybe, going to two different houses, or I also teach in the evening to a group of adults, and those lessons are from 6.30 to 8.30, in the evening.

2.25–2.46   I like teaching Spanish for many reasons. One of them is because I like sharing my culture with other people, and I feel it's a way of bringing people together through languages.

2.47–3.13   I do find the job difficult sometimes. Sometimes the work involves a lot of paperwork or marking, and after a few hours of doing that it can be a bit boring. And when I teach at different people's houses, that involves travelling from home to home and that can be tiring …

3.14–3.30   Overall the positives outweigh the negatives and it's … it's a fun job and I enjoy it very much.

3.31–4.23   **3** My name's Marcus and I'm an actor. I've been an actor for six years. At the moment, I'm in a play called *Romeo and Juliet* by William Shakespeare. I've always wanted to be an actor, so I feel very lucky to be able to do it now. There are a few reasons why I enjoy doing it. I really like the variety – no two days are the same. I enjoy working with other people and working as a team, and I really like the sense of achievement that I get from creating something.

4.24–end   There can be some difficulties being an actor. I often have to work very long hours. I could start first thing in the morning and not finish till midnight. There's a lot of travel involved as well, which can be quite difficult. I sometimes have to go up and down the country just to get to work. The pay isn't that great either. Unless you're famous, then you don't really often earn that much as an actor, but it's a really fun lifestyle and I still really enjoy it, so it's great really.

7f   My working life

UNIT 7 Work

4 [7.1]
- Ask students to work in pairs. Tell them to look at the notes in the table and see if they can remember any of the missing information.
- Play the video again. Students complete the notes. Don't check answers at this stage.

5 [7.1] ★ **CPT extra!** Speaking activity [after Ex. 5]
- Ask students to work in small groups of four or five. Let students compare their notes before checking the answers with the class.

ANSWERS
1 start / set up the stall
2 pack up and go home
3 exercise
4 hours
5 adult lessons
6 people
7 travelling (from home to home)
8 variety
9 team
10 pay

After you watch
Vocabulary in context

6 [7.2]
- Explain that students are going to watch some clips from the video which contain some new words and phrases. They need to choose the correct meaning of the words.
- Play the clips. When each multiple-choice question appears, pause the clip so that students can choose the correct definition. You could let students compare answers in pairs before discussing as a class.

ANSWERS
1 b   2 a   3 b   4 a   5 b

Videoscript 7.2

1 … sometimes the weather can be bad because it rains, but **overall** it's really enjoyable.
   a in fact
   b in general

2 … the **work involves** a lot of paperwork or marking …
   a it's part of the job
   b it's not necessary

3 … I feel very **lucky** to be able to do it now.
   a when bad things happen to you
   b when good things happen to you

4 I really like the **sense of achievement** that I get from creating something.
   a a feeling of success
   b a feeling of failure

5 I sometimes have to go up and down the country just to **get to** work.
   a find
   b travel to

7
- Ask students to work individually to complete the sentences. Monitor and help with vocabulary as necessary. (For school-age students, you could suggest they describe a parent's job.)
- Ask students to work in pairs and take turns to tell each other about their jobs.

8
- Discuss the question in open class. Encourage students to explain the reasons for their choice.
- Ask for a show of hands to find out the most popular of the three jobs.

UNIT 7 Work

Unit 7 Review and memory booster ★ CPT extra! Language games

Memory Booster activities

Exercises 2, 3, 5 and 9 are Memory Booster activities. For more information about these activities and how they benefit students, see page 10.

I can … tick boxes

As an alternative to students simply ticking the *I can …* boxes, you could ask them to give themselves a score from 1 to 4 (1 = not very confident; 4 = very confident) for each language area. If students score 1 or 2 for a language area, refer them to additional practice activities in the Workbook and Grammar summary exercises.

Grammar

1
- Ask students to work individually to complete the interview with the correct tense of the verbs. Let students compare answers in pairs before checking with the class.

> **ANSWERS**
> 1 have, worked 2 joined 3 have, wanted 4 was
> 5 did, study 6 Have, lived 7 spent

2 >> MB
- Ask students to work in pairs to explain their choice of verb forms in Exercise 1. Elicit their answers in feedback.

> **ANSWERS**
> 1 started in past and continues now
> 2 we know when
> 3 to ask about something in general
> 4 we know when
> 5 we know when
> 6 to ask about an experience
> 7 we know when

3 >> MB
- Ask students to work individually to write their questions. Monitor and help as necessary.
- Students take turns to ask their partner the questions. As students speak, monitor and notice any errors with students' use of *for* and *since*.

4
- Ask students to work individually to complete the sentences. Let students compare answers in pairs before checking with the class.

> **ANSWERS**
> 1 across 2 on 3 in 4 through 5 at 6 opposite

Vocabulary

5 >> MB
- Ask students to work individually to complete the compound nouns.

> **ANSWERS**
> 1 representative 2 designer 3 assistant 4 area
> 5 computer 6 emergency 7 manager 8 floor 9 details

6
- Ask students to work individually to complete the text with the correct form of *make* or *do*.

> **ANSWERS**
> 1 does 2 makes 3 make 4 does

7
- Ask students to work in pairs to look at the photo and discuss the questions. Elicit students' answers in feedback.

> **ANSWERS**
> Students' own answers

Real life

8
- Ask students to work individually to match the questions to the responses.

> **ANSWERS**
> 1 c 2 e 3 b 4 a 5 d

9 >> MB
- Give students a few minutes to prepare their answers to the questions in Exercise 8.
- Ask students to take turns to ask and answer the questions with their partner. As students speak, monitor and note any errors you hear. At the end, write up short sentences with errors involving past forms that you heard. Ask students to correct the errors with a partner.

Unit 7 Review and memory booster 129

Unit 8 Technology

Opener

1

- Ask students to look at the photo and caption, and discuss the questions. You could choose to do this activity in open class or ask students to work in pairs. Elicit a few ideas from the class in feedback.

> **ANSWERS**
>
> Students' own answers.
>
> Some ways robots already work with humans: on assembly lines in manufacturing; in surgery where robots are used by surgeons to perform operations; around the home where robots do things such as controlling temperature or vacuum cleaning; in films – CGI animation is done with the help of robots; in helping disabled people – robotic limbs; in cars – driverless cars, GPS; bomb disposal; automation in agriculture; robots work in big warehouses selecting items for delivery.

> **Background information**
>
> **NASA** (North American Space Agency) with the help of various companies has developed a prototype humanoid robot called Robonaut (shown in the photo). It's currently on the International Space Station (this is revealed in the listening in Exercise 2). It can use tools and drive machines.
>
> Based on the research into Robonaut, NASA has also developed a robotic exoskeleton called X1. It's a robot that a human wears over his or her body to assist or inhibit movement in leg joints. It can be used as an in-space exercise machine to supply resistance against leg movement. It's also being developed as a way of helping people on earth who have mobility problems to walk.

2 [60] ★ **CPT extra!** Listening activity [after Ex. 1]

- Explain that students are going to listen to someone talk about the importance of technology in our lives.
- Ask students to read the questions. Play the recording. Students listen and answer the questions. Let them compare answers in pairs before checking with the class.

> **ANSWERS**
>
> 1 solves mathematical problems, sends messages to friends, cooks dinner for us
> 2 because a human has given the wrong instructions
> 3 on the International Space Station, it does all the simple or repetitive jobs.

Audioscript [60]

It's difficult to remember what life was like before the types of modern technology we have today. Technology solves mathematical problems for us. It sends messages to friends in a second. It even cooks dinner for us. When technology makes a mistake, it's only because a human has given the wrong instructions. So, what's the next big step in technology? Robots are common in industries such as car manufacturing, and recently NASA sent the first humanoid robot into space, where it works on the International Space Station. It's called Robonaut 2 or R2 and it does all the simple or repetitive jobs so the astronauts can spend more time doing experiments. Perhaps in a few years' time every home will have their own robot to do all the boring work around the house.

3

- Ask students to look at the list of actions and check any unknown words, e.g. *solve problems* (= find the answer to a problem).
- Ask students which action robots can do. You could choose to do this activity in open class or ask students to work in pairs before eliciting a few ideas from the class in feedback.

> **ANSWERS**
>
> Students' own answers. Most would agree with the following: solve problems, speak a language, understand instructions.
>
> It can be argued that advanced robots can nowadays do the following: have new ideas, make decisions.
>
> Robots can't make mistakes (the listening says that they don't make mistakes – any mistakes are down to human error).
>
> The other actions are only human.

4

- Ask students to work in pairs or small groups to come up with a list of things they do which robots could do in the future. Elicit a few ideas to get students started. In feedback, ask some pairs or groups to tell the class what ideas they had.

> **EXAMPLE ANSWERS**
>
> Note that the answers here depend on the students' own experience.
>
> At work: photocopying, filing, making tea or coffee, answering routine calls, organizing junk emails from important ones, carrying or moving any heavy objects
>
> At school: photocopying, doing the register, marking tests
>
> At home: cleaning, ironing, tidying up, making the bed, ordering the shopping, taking the dog for a walk

UNIT 8 Technology

8a Mobile technology

Lesson at a glance
- vocabulary: internet verbs
- reading: an explorer's blog
- grammar: zero and first conditional
- speaking: planning a trip

Vocabulary internet verbs

1
- Ask students to work individually to make a list about their internet use. Use the opportunity to see how familiar your students already are with internet verbs. Set a time limit of three or four minutes.
- When students are ready, ask them to compare their lists with a partner, and say why they used the internet. In feedback, find out which students used the internet most.

> **EXAMPLE ANSWERS**
>
> Some possible reasons are: to find out information on train times; to check my email; to get directions; to contact friends on social messaging sites; to find out information to help with my homework; to check the weather forecast; to read the news headlines; to follow my favourite celebrity on Twitter; to send a tweet; to make a Skype call; to download music, a film or some photos.

2 ★ **CPT extra!** Vocabulary activity [before Ex. 2]
- Look at the example with the class and elicit the answer to number 2. Ask students to work individually to complete the remaining sentences before checking answers with a partner.
- In feedback, check the meaning of any words students are unsure of and point out the strong stress in longer words (see Vocabulary and pronunciation note below).

> **ANSWERS**
>
> 1 set up 2 download 3 write 4 play 5 search
> 6 subscribe 7 upload 8 log in 9 connect

> **Vocabulary and pronunciation note**
>
> *set up* = a phrasal verb used to say that you start or open something new
>
> *connect* (to the internet) = when you go online
>
> *download* (music, films, photos, etc.) = to find them online and take them on to your computer; *upload* = the opposite – you put them on the internet so other people can see or read them
>
> *log in* = when you use personal information in order to enter a site that is protected
>
> *write a blog* = a blog is a diary page on the internet
>
> *subscribe* (to) a *podcast* = if you subscribe to something, you join a mailing list or pay a fee so that you can regularly get material from the website – a *podcast* is an audio file similar to a radio broadcast, which can be downloaded and listened to

3
- Ask students to read the sentences in Exercise 2 and change the information to make the sentences personal. Once students have ideas, ask them to share with the class or with a partner.

> **EXAMPLE ANSWERS**
>
> I don't download music, but I often download photos.
> I love playing online games.
> I subscribe to a news website.
> I upload funny videos to my own webpage.

Reading

4 [61]
- **Optional step** Ask students to look at the photo and heading and predict who wrote the blog and what it is about.
- Ask students to read the blog and answer the questions. Let students compare answers in pairs before checking answers with the class.
- **Optional step** The reading text is recorded. You could play the recording and ask students to read and listen.

> **EXAMPLE ANSWERS**
>
> The blog was written by someone travelling and/or working in Kamchatka – perhaps a backpacker but probably a person on an expedition – he or she is in a group and working in a forest.
> The blog is a personal diary of the trip. It may be aimed at friends or family who want to know what the person is doing. It might be aimed at other travellers who like to hear about people's adventures

> **Vocabulary note**
>
> *time zones* = a typical time zone averages 15° of longitude in width and observes a clock time one hour earlier than the zone immediately to the east (e.g. Paris is in a different time zone to London – when it's 3 p.m. in Paris, it's 2 p.m. in London)
>
> *signal* = if you have a signal, your phone is connected – in distant places it can be hard to get a signal
>
> *painful* = it hurts a lot

> **Background information**
>
> **Kamchatka** is a peninsula in the far east of Russia. It lies between the Pacific Ocean to the east and the Sea of Okhotsk to the west. It's famous for its volcanoes.

5
- Ask students to read the blog again and choose the correct words. Let them compare their answers in pairs before checking with the class.
- **Optional step** Ask students to justify answers with reference to the text (see extracts in brackets below).

8a Mobile technology 131

UNIT 8 Technology

> **ANSWERS**
> 1 hard (*here at last*)
> 2 good (*sunny*)
> 3 very different (*in the past, explorers couldn't share their news until months after the trip*)
> 4 useful (*great if you have a problem*)
> 5 Someone else (*someone in our group*)
> 6 didn't know (*someone who knows this region well*)

Grammar zero and first conditional

6

- Ask students to look at the grammar box. Read the example sentences with your class.
- Ask students to choose the correct option to complete the sentences (1–5). Let students compare answers in pairs before checking with the class.

> **ANSWERS**
> 1 zero 2 first 3 zero 4 first 5 use

Grammar note

Form

A common error students make when manipulating the first conditional is to use *will* or *won't* in both clauses (e.g. *I'll call if I'll get lost*). Make sure students notice that the present simple is used in the *If* clause.

Use

Here's a shorthand way of thinking of the use of these forms:
- If this general situation happens → this always or generally happens (e.g. *If I feel ill, I take aspirin*).
- If this specific situation happens → this is the result (e.g. *If I feel ill during the trip, I'll take aspirin*).

Note that *if* in zero conditional sentences can often be replaced by *when* or *whenever* because it's being used to talk about general situations.

Refer students to page 170 for further information and practice.

> **ANSWERS TO GRAMMAR SUMMARY EXERCISES**
> **1**
> 1 f 2 e 3 c 4 a 5 g 6 b 7 d
> **2**
> 1 finish, 'll go out   5 go, 'll buy
> 2 'll miss, don't leave   6 doesn't do, will be
> 3 is, 'll drive   7 don't answer, 'm
> 4 won't come, feels
> **3**
> Zero conditional: 1 d; 's; prefer   2 a; don't sleep; have
> 3 b; die; don't give   4 c; likes; wakes
> First conditional: 1 c; 's; 'll invite   2 a; don't eat; 'll feel
> 3 d; won't get up; don't have to   4 b; 'll travel; can

7

- Ask students to match the beginnings of the sentences with the endings. You may need to check *satnav* (= a GPS system in cars that guides drivers to their destinations) and *virus* (= a harmful computer program).
- Ask students to compare their answers in pairs and decide if each sentence is a zero conditional or a first conditional.

> **ANSWERS**
> 1 d 2 b 3 c 4 a 5 f 6 e
> 1 and 5 are first conditional, the others are zero conditional.

8 [62]

- Ask students to complete the sentences with the correct form.
- Play the recording. Students listen and check their answers.

> **ANSWERS**
> 1 go 2 'll need 3 drives 4 see 5 'll buy
> 6 isn't 7 ring 8 won't pass

Speaking my life

9

- Look at the photos with the class and check the meaning of *sun cream* (= to protect your skin from getting burned by the sun), *torch* (= a light you can carry in your pocket) and *satnav* (= a GPS system for finding your way).
- Discuss the questions as a class.

10 ★ **CPT extra!** Speaking activity [before Ex. 10]

- Organize the class into groups of four or five. Read the information about the two-day trip with the class and ask questions to check that students understand what to do (see Teacher development below): *How long are you going for?* (two days) *Are you staying in hotels?* (No – camping) *How many items can you carry with you?* (five).
- Ask students to talk in their groups and agree on the five most useful items. Encourage students to use conditional forms, as in the examples, when making choices and giving reasons. As students speak, monitor and note down errors students make, especially any involving conditional forms.
- In feedback, ask different groups to present their list of items to the class and to give reasons for their choices.
- At the end, write up five or six sentences with errors and ask students to correct them in pairs.

132 Unit 8 Technology

UNIT 8 Technology

> **EXAMPLE ANSWERS**
>
> Students own answers. One list would be: mobile phone, suncream, sunglasses, cooker, matches (If we take a mobile phone, we won't need a camera, laptop, torch or satnav because all those things are on the phone; We'll need matches and a cooker if we want warm food; If it's sunny, we'll need sunglasses; We won't need an umbrella because it won't rain on the first day so we can use a towel to get dry when we finish the trip).

Extra activity

This activity could easily be done as a pyramid discussion. Students make an individual list of five items, then they work with a partner to negotiate and agree on a list of five items. Then students work in groups to make a final list of five items, with each student arguing for the items they want on the list. Finally, ask your class to debate a final five (see Teacher development section in Unit 7c after the notes for Exercise 10).

Teacher development

Instructions and ICQs (instruction checking questions)

Some activities we ask students to do are quite complex. It's important to think carefully about how to instruct in such situations, especially if using English as the language of instruction. Here are some suggestions:

1 Break down instructions step by step. Give an instruction (e.g. *Put the words in order; Prepare five sentences*). Then let students carry out the instruction before giving the next instruction. Don't give a list of instructions and expect students to remember and follow them.

2 Use visual ways of instructing. If you want students to categorize words by writing them in a box, show this by eliciting a word and physically writing it in the box. If you want students to ask a partner questions, show this by acting out one or two questions with a student in the class. It's easier to understand non-verbal instructions, and gives students confidence that they know what to do and how to do it. The simple rule: act out activities or provide a model.

3 Use ICQs to check understanding. Sometimes, when an instruction is complex, you can use questions such as these to ensure students understand. For example, if you want students to ask and answer questions without looking at their partner's information, give the instruction, then ask: *Are you going to work with your partner?* (Yes) *Are you going to look at his/her information?* (No). Getting students to respond to your ICQs means they can show they understand, and you avoid the confusion that arises if they start an activity unsure of what to do.

8b Invention for the eyes

Lesson at a glance
- speaking: famous inventions
- listening: a science programme
- grammar: defining relative clauses
- speaking: a new invention

Speaking

1 ★ **CPT extra!** Grammar activity [before Ex. 1]
- Organize the class into groups of four or five. Ask them to work together to put the inventions in order of importance.

2
- Ask each group to present their lists. Have a class debate and ask students to explain why they have chosen particular items. Ask students to add inventions to the list and give reasons why.

> **EXAMPLE ANSWERS**
>
> Students' own answers
>
> Here are some reasons for choosing each item:
>
> the aeroplane: allowed people to travel round the world
>
> the bicycle: allowed people to get across towns quickly – resulted in people being able to commute to work
>
> the camera: able to capture memories, news stories and history in a way we couldn't before
>
> the engine: resulted in the invention of the car
>
> the internet: revolutionized how we communicate, how we access information and how we access news
>
> the telephone and mobile phone: allowed people to communicate without having to travel to see each other – completely changed business
>
> the washing machine: a time-saving revolution – freed women, in particular, from the home
>
> Here are other items to add: wheel, sword, gun, boat, computer, glasses.

Listening

3 [63]
- **Optional step** Start by asking students to look at the photo and diagram. Ask them to predict what the listening is about.
- Play the recording. Students listen and answer the questions. Let them compare answers in pairs before checking with the class.

> **ANSWERS**
>
> 1 The problem is that they can't get glasses.
> 2 Silver has invented glasses that don't need an optician.

Audioscript [63]

More than one billion people in the world need glasses but cannot get them, because they live in places where there aren't any opticians. But now there's a scientist who has solved the problem. Joshua Silver has invented glasses which don't need an optician.

8b Invention for the eyes 133

UNIT 8 Technology

They look like a pair of normal glasses, but there is a pump on each side which uses silicone oil. First, you turn a wheel which controls the pump. The pump pushes the silicone oil through the pipe and it moves into the lenses. As the lens fills with oil, the shape of the lens changes and you turn the wheel until you can see correctly.

Silver had the idea a few years ago and he did many experiments before he got it right. A man in Ghana was the first person who used the new glasses. The man made clothes, but he had bad eyesight and found it difficult to work. When the man put on the glasses, he could start working again. Silver says, 'I will not forget that moment.'

As a result of this successful test, Silver started an organization which is called the 'Centre for Vision in the Developing World'. The glasses are cheap to produce and over one hundred thousand people now wear them. In particular, the centre works with schools in countries where people can't get glasses easily. Being able to see well can have a big effect on their education.

> **Background information**
>
> While studying mirrors, British physicist Professor **Joshua Silver** discovered a new way to change the curvature of lenses. He has applied this to create a new form of liquid-filled corrective lens.

4 [64]

- **Optional step** Give students time to read the information on the diagram.
- Play the recording of the first half of the programme. Students listen and number the instructions in order. Let them compare answers in pairs before checking with the class.

> **ANSWERS**
>
> 4, 1, 3, 2

Audioscript [64]

More than one billion people in the world need glasses but cannot get them, because they live in places where there aren't any opticians. But now there's a scientist who has solved the problem. Joshua Silver has invented glasses which don't need an optician.

They look like a pair of normal glasses, but there is a pump on each side which uses silicone oil. First, you turn a wheel which controls the pump. The pump pushes the silicone oil through the pipe and it moves into the lenses. As the lens fills with oil, the shape of the lens changes and you turn the wheel until you can see correctly.

5 [65] ★ CPT extra! Video activity [after Ex. 5]

- **Optional step** Give students time to read the sentences.
- Play the recording of the second half of the programme. Students listen and note whether the sentences are true (T) or false (F). Let students compare answers in pairs before checking with the class.
- **Optional step** Ask students to justify answers by saying what they heard (see answers in brackets below).

> **ANSWERS**
>
> 1 T (*he did many experiments before he got it right*)
> 2 T (*A man in Ghana was the first person who used the new glasses.*)
> 3 F (*cheap to produce*)
> 4 F (*in countries where people can't get glasses easily*)

Audioscript [65]

Silver had the idea a few years ago and he did many experiments before he got it right. A man in Ghana was the first person who used the new glasses. The man made clothes, but he had bad eyesight and found it difficult to work. When the man put on the glasses, he could start working again. Silver says, 'I will not forget that moment.'

As a result of this successful test, Silver started an organization which is called the 'Centre for Vision in the Developing World'. The glasses are cheap to produce and over one hundred thousand people now wear them. In particular, the centre works with schools in countries where people can't get glasses easily. Being able to see well can have a big effect on their education.

Grammar defining relative clauses

6

- Read the information in the grammar box with the class.
- Ask students to discuss the questions. You could do this in open class or ask students to discuss in pairs.

> **ANSWERS**
>
> a who   b which   c where

> **Grammar note**
>
> **Form**
>
> Note that *who*, *which* and *where* are relative pronouns – they're replacing the subject or object of the relative clause:
>
> *There is a scientist.* **He** *has solved the problem.*
>
> *There is a scientist* **who** *has solved the problem.* (here, *who* replaces the subject)
>
> In this lesson, *who* and *which* are generally used in sentences in which they replace the subject of the relative clause.
>
> **Use**
>
> Defining relative clauses give essential information – this means that the sentences lack sense or meaning without the clauses (e.g. *There is a scientist* needs a clause to tell us about the scientist).
>
> **Problems**
>
> Typical errors at this level include misspelling *which* (*glasses wich don't need an optician*), using *who* for things (*glasses who don't need an optician*) and, because of L1 interference, trying to use *what* as a relative pronoun (*glasses what don't need an optician*).

Refer students to page 170 for further information and practice.

UNIT 8 Technology

ANSWERS TO GRAMMAR SUMMARY EXERCISES

4a
1 who 2 which 3 where 4 which 5 who
6 where 7 which

4b
2, 4 and 7

5
1 Correct
2 This is the house that I want to buy ~~it~~.
3 She bought the car **which** she saw last week.
4 Look! That's the friend **who** I was talking about yesterday.
5 Those are the students who ~~they~~ are looking for a flat.
6 Correct
7 He didn't see the person who ~~he~~ took his wallet.

6
1 who; f   2 who; b   3 that / which e   4 that / which; c
5 who / that; a   6 where; d

7
- Ask students to work individually to underline the relative clause in the sentences. Elicit the first answer as an example. Let students compare answers in pairs before checking answers with the class.

ANSWERS
1 A man in Ghana was the first person who used the new glasses.
2 Silver started an organization which is called the 'Centre for Vision in the Developing World'.
3 The centre works with schools in countries where people can't get glasses easily.

Grammar note
1 *who* – replacing the subject (a person) of the defining relative pronoun
2 *which* – replacing the subject (a thing – an organization, in this case) of the defining relative pronoun
3 *where* – replacing the idea of 'in/at this place'

8 ★ CPT extra! Speaking activity [before Ex. 8]
- Ask students to work individually to complete the sentences. Let students compare answers in pairs before checking with the class.

ANSWERS
1 who 2 where 3 which 4 where 5 which 6 who

Background information
Thomas Alva Edison (1847–1931) was America's greatest inventor. As well as the light bulb, he invented the motion picture camera and the phonograph (an early sound recording device).
The **Tesla Roadster**, the first electric sports car, was manufactured in California in 2008.
Alessandro Volta (1745–1827) was an Italian physicist and chemist. The word volt, to describe units of electric power, is derived from his name.
Maria Beasley (1847–1904) was an American inventor. She invented the life raft in 1880. Her design was used on the *Titanic*.

9
- Discuss this question in open class or ask students to work in pairs. Tell them to refer back to the grammar box to find out when *that* can be used.

ANSWERS
1, 3, 5 and 6

Grammar note
We can use *that* in place of *who* or *which* (although only informally, and usually not when writing). It cannot be used instead of *where*.

10 ★ CPT extra! Web research activity [after Ex. 10]
- **Optional step** Set a task for general comprehension of the text first. Ask students to look at the photo and read the text quickly and find the answer to this question: *What is a lifestraw?* (a way of cleaning water while you drink).
- Look at the example with the class. Then ask students to work individually to complete the rest of the text with *who, which* or *where* and the phrases in the box. Let students compare answers in pairs before checking with the class.

ANSWERS
1 which cleans water
2 where there is no safe
3 where there is a lake
4 who like hiking and camping
5 which can break
6 who invented *Lifestraw*

11
- Ask students to think of famous people, inventions or places. You could elicit a few examples to get students started (e.g. Einstein, Marie Curie, William Shakespeare, the telephone, the car, the plane, Paris, New York, the Coliseum). Refer students back to the inventions in Exercise 1 for ideas.
- Once students have thought of three different things, tell them to write defining sentences. Monitor and help with ideas as they write, and be ready to prompt and correct students making errors.
- Ask students to exchange sentences with a partner. You could ask them to take turns to read out their sentences or you could ask them to hand over and read the sentences. Partners must guess the people, inventions and places described.
- Note down any recurring errors you notice in students' sentences. Use the feedback to go over and correct any errors students are making.

8b Invention for the eyes 135

UNIT 8 Technology

> **EXAMPLE ANSWERS**
>
> He's the scientist who explained relativity. (Einstein)
>
> It's a thing which people often watch in their living rooms with their families. (TV)
>
> It's a big city where there is / you can see / you can visit the Louvre Museum and the Eiffel Tower. (Paris)

Extra activity

Refer students back to the opening page of Unit 5. On this page, students were asked to describe everyday objects. Ask students to revisit this task and to write defining relative clauses to describe the objects.

Speaking my life

12

- Organize the class into groups of three or four. Make sure each group has a large sheet of paper to draw on (hand out paper if necessary). Read the three prompt questions and elicit other possible examples for each question (e.g. *a car which drives itself – people who can't drive or don't like driving – in city centres*).
- Give students five to ten minutes to discuss ideas and draw their invention. Monitor and help students with ideas and vocabulary.

13

- Organize the class to give their presentations. You could ask each group to stand up or to come to the front of the class to show their picture and make their presentation. Alternatively, you could pair groups so that they take turns to present their invention to the other group.
- As students give their presentations, listen and notice how well students use relative clauses. Note any errors which you could write on the board at the end for students to correct.

> **EXAMPLE ANSWERS**
>
> Here is a possible example presentation:
>
> Our new invention is a machine which drives itself. It's for people who can't drive or don't like driving. You can use it in a place where the traffic isn't moving quickly – in city centres, for example.

Extra activity

Write some crazy inventions on the board, e.g.

a scooter pram: a baby's pram which is on a scooter

a flask tie: a man's tie with a flask for drinks in it

a ping pong door: a door in your house which you can open so that it's a table tennis table

a baby mop: a mop you can attach to your baby so that it cleans the floor when it moves

Ask students to choose one of the inventions and write a description of it. (Note that all the inventions above are on the internet – ask students to find a funny or crazy invention online to present to the class, ideally with a picture, in the next lesson.)

8c Designs from nature

> **Lesson at a glance**
> - reading: biomimetics
> - critical thinking: the writer's sources
> - wordbuilding: dependent prepositions
> - speaking: technology

Reading

1 ★ **CPT extra!** Speaking activity [after Ex. 1]

- **Optional step** Start by asking students to describe the photos on the page. Ask: *What do they show?* (1 = a robot, 2 = a wind turbine, 3 = Velcro, 4 = a car, 5 = paint, a = boxfish, b = leaf, c = whale, d = bur, e = gecko).
- Ask students to match the inventions with the animals and plants. Let students compare answers in pairs, but don't check answers at this stage.

2 [66]

- Ask students to read the article and check their answers from Exercise 1. In feedback, point out the words in the glossary.
- **Optional step** The reading text is recorded. You could play the recording and ask students to read and listen.

> **ANSWERS**
>
> 1 e   2 c   3 d   4 a   5 b

Vocabulary note

wind turbine = a machine that converts kinetic energy (the turbine's sails go round under the force of the wind) into electricity

velcro = fabric hook and loop fasteners (*Velcro* is a company name)

boxfish = a bony fish that lives in oceans

leaf = the leaf in the photo comes from the lotus plant – the leaves lie on the surface of the water

whale flipper = whales and dolphins have long arm-like flippers on each side of the body – they work with the tail to provide and control the movement of the animal

bur = a bur (or burr) is a seed or dry fruit that has hooks or teeth and catches on the skin or fur of animals

gecko = a lizard found in warm climates throughout the world

3

- Ask students to read the article again and choose the correct options. Let students compare answers in pairs before checking with the class.

> **ANSWERS**
>
> 1 a   2 b   3 a   4 b   5 b   6 a

136   Unit 8 Technology

UNIT 8 Technology

Pronunciation note

Note the pronunciation of the noun (describing the subject of study) *biomimetics* /ˌbaɪəʊmɪˈmɛtɪks/, the noun (describing people who study this subject) *biomimeticist* /ˌbaɪəʊmɪˈmɛtɪsɪst/, and the adjective *biomimetic* /ˌbaɪəʊmɪˈmɛtɪk/.

Background information

Stanford University is a private research university in Stanford, California, between San Jose and San Francisco.

George de Mestral (1907–1990) was an electrical engineer from Lausanne.

Wilhelm Barthlott was born in 1946, and is a German botanist and biomimetics expert.

Wordbuilding dependent prepositions

4

- **Optional step** Find out if students can remember or guess the prepositions before reading.
- Ask students to read the article and find the words and their prepositions. Let students compare answers in pairs before checking with the class.

ANSWERS
1 with   2 at   3 in   4 on   5 on   6 of   7 to   8 of

5 ★ **CPT extra!** Wordbuilding activity [after Ex. 5]

- Read the wordbuilding box with the class. Ask students to work individually to match the words in Exercise 4 with the categories. Elicit the first match as an example. Let students compare their answers in pairs before checking with the class.

ANSWERS
1 noun   2 adjective   3 adjective   4 verb   5 verb
6 verb   7 adjective   8 noun

Refer students to page 67 in the Workbook for further practice.

Vocabulary note

Note that a dependent preposition is a preposition that usually follows the verb and goes before the object of the verb. So, although we can use other prepositions after the verb *wait* (e.g. *He waited at the station*), its dependent preposition is *for* (e.g. *I'm waiting for a bus*). It's the preposition that is always or usually used.

There are no useful rules to help students learn dependent prepositions – they just have to memorize them. Get students to organize new phrases into different sets to help their learning (see Teacher development below).

Teacher development

Keeping a vocabulary notebook

Noting and learning a set of dependent prepositions is a typical area where students need to be well-organized and rigorous in their use of a vocabulary notebook in order to help their learning.

Here are some tips on how to train your students to note new language in ways that will aid their learning:

- Limit how many words or phrases students try to learn from one lesson – five to ten at most. Help students by signalling which words to note carefully to learn.
- Get students to write new entries by hand. They could use different coloured pens for verbs, adjectives and nouns. The physical act of writing helps memory retention.
- Make sure students don't just write the word and a translation – students should include the word form, a definition or explanation of their own, an original sentence, synonyms and, if possible, any collocates or word families. Here is an example: *good at* (adj + prep) *I'm not very good at swimming. I'm really good at art.* The personalized example sentence is a really useful and motivating way of recording vocabulary.
- Students need to encounter new vocabulary as often as twenty times before it enters long-term memory. Simply using a new word a few times in a lesson proves insufficient. Encourage this learning by getting students to revisit vocabulary to write sentences or paragraphs, and by setting vocabulary tests so students have to revise.

6

- Ask students to choose three words with dependent prepositions in Exercise 4 and to write three sentences. Provide a model for the task (e.g. *agree with: I don't agree with giving the vote to children under 16*). Monitor and help with ideas and vocabulary if necessary.
- Organize the class into pairs. Ask students to take turns to read their sentences, saying BEEP in place of the preposition. Their partner must recall (or guess) the missing preposition.
- **Optional step** You could make this a competitive game – students get points for the prepositions they guess correctly.

Extra activity

Play dependent prepositions noughts and crosses. Write the following noughts and crosses table on the board:

good	problem	agree
similar	think	idea
interested	depend	bad

8c Designs from nature 137

UNIT 8 Technology

Organize the class into groups of four. Tell each group to draw a blank noughts and crosses on a piece of paper and place it where everyone in the group can see it (ask students to sit together round a table, if possible). Tell each group to split into two pairs – an 'O' pair and an 'X' pair. The 'O' pair goes first. They must choose a square on the grid and create an accurate sentence with a dependent preposition to win the square (e.g. they choose bottom right and say *I'm bad at football*). If it's correct, they win the square and write 'O' in that square. Now it's the 'X' pair's go. They choose a different square and make a sentence. Like ordinary noughts and crosses, the winning team is the first to create a line of three Os or Xs – for example:

X	O	O
O	X	X
		X

Critical thinking the writer's sources

7

- Read the information with the class. Ask students to tell you which sources they think were most useful for writing the text used in the lesson.
- Ask students to read the article again and say which parts of the article used information from the sources. Let students compare answers in pairs before checking with the class.

> **ANSWERS**
>
> All are possible (although '4 questionnaires' is an unlikely source here).
> 1. photographs (*they studied a whale's flippers* – perhaps the writer looks at photos of whales to see how flippers work)
> 2. interviews with people (*in 1982, Wilhelm Barthlott, …* – perhaps the writer interviewed Barthlott)
> 3. biographies (*In 1948, the Swiss engineer George de Mestral was walking in the countryside when …* - this may have come from a biography)
> 5. books about the topic (*Bio- means 'living things' and mimetics means 'copying'* – probably comes from a book about the topic)
> 6. articles in magazines (*when the car company Mercedes-Benz wanted to think of a new design for a car, they looked at a boxfish* – perhaps from a magazine)

8

- Ask students to work in pairs to discuss the question. Elicit a few ideas from the class in feedback.

> **EXAMPLE ANSWERS**
>
> 1. questionnaires; interviews with people; internet research
> 2. biographies, books about the topic, internet research
> 3. interviews with people, articles in magazines, internet research

Speaking my life

9

- Organize the class into pairs. Tell students to prepare a research questionnaire. You could elicit one or two questions (from the prompts in the Student's Book) to get students started.
- As students prepare, monitor and help with ideas and vocabulary. Set a five-minute time limit. Tell students to write the questions. (If you want to split the pairs for the next stage, make sure both students in each pair write questions down).

10

- Once students have prepared their questions, ask each pair to get together with a different pair to ask and answer questions. Alternatively, split pairs, ask everybody to stand up, and ask students to walk round the class and interview three different people.
- As students speak, monitor and note down any errors that you hear. In feedback, at the end, write up errors on the board and ask students to correct them.

> **EXAMPLE ANSWERS**
>
> Students' own answers
> Here are some possible questions:
> *What's your favourite technology?*
> *How often do you use it?*
> *What's it used for?*
> *What colour / shape / size is it?*
> *Who made / manufactured it?*
> *When / Where was it made?*
> *What is it made of?*

Extra activity

Ask students to use their questions to ask different people. Then ask them to write up their findings in an article. You could set this for homework.

UNIT 8 Technology

8d Gadgets

Lesson at a glance
- vocabulary: instructions
- pronunciation: linking
- real life: finding out how something works

Vocabulary instructions

1

- **Optional step** Pre-teach *instruction manual* (= a book which tells you how to set up or repair something) and *How to video* (= a video that explains step by step how to do something practical – e.g. make a new dress or build a model plane).
- Ask students to discuss the questions. You could do this in open class or ask students to work in pairs before eliciting answers from the class.

2

- Ask students to match the verbs (1–5) with the phrases to make instructions (a–e), and then to match the instructions with the pictures (A–E). Elicit the first match as an example to get students started. Let students compare answers in pairs before checking with the class.

> **ANSWERS**
> 1 c – turn on the remote control (Picture B)
> 2 e – pull the lever backwards (Picture E)
> 3 a – charge the battery (Picture A)
> 4 b – press the button (Picture C)
> 5 d – push the lever forwards (Picture D)

> **Vocabulary note**
> The best way to explain new words here is to use the pictures.
> *battery* = a metal thing that goes in radios, torches, etc. and supplies them with electricity
> *charge (the battery)* = connect it to electricity for a time so that it's full of power
> *lever* = a long stick that you pull or push to turn things on or off

Pronunciation linking

3a [67] ★ **CPT extra!** Vocabulary activity [before Ex. 3a]

- Read the information with the class.
- Play the recording. Students listen and notice the linking. Ask students to practise saying the instructions with linking.

b

- Ask students to work in pairs to prepare sentences. Monitor pairs and help with ideas.
- Ask students to practise saying the sentences. Monitor and prompt students to attempt linking between consonant and vowel sounds.

> **EXAMPLE ANSWERS**
> I charge‿an old laptop‿overnight.
> We turn‿our radio on‿in the morning.
> I pull‿a switch to put the lights‿on‿in the garage.

> **Pronunciation note**
> Linking occurs when a word ends in a consonant sound and the following word starts with a vowel sound. It sounds as if the consonant has left one word and joined the start of the next. For example, *turn it on* sounds like *tur ni ton*.

Real life finding out how something works

4 [68]

- **Optional step** Ask students to look at the large photo on the page. Ask: *What can you see? How does it fly?* Use the opportunity to pre-teach *drone* (= an aircraft with no pilot controlled from the ground) and *remote control* (= the machine you use to operate something when you are away from it).
- Ask students to look at the five pictures showing instructions in Exercise 2. Play the recording. Students listen and order the instructions. Let students compare answers in pairs before checking with the class.

> **ANSWERS**
> Order of pictures: A, B, D, E, C

Audioscript [68]

A: What's the problem?

B: A friend gave me this drone as a present but I don't understand the instructions.

A: Oh yes. I have one like this.

B: Can you show me how this works?

A: Sure. It looks complicated, but it's really easy to use. First of all, have you charged the battery?

B: Yes, I've done that.

A: So now, turn on the remote control.

B: How did you do that?

A: I turned it on here. It's the button on the side.

B: Oh, OK.

A: So, you have two levers. The left and the right. Let's start with the left. If you push it forwards, the propellers go faster and the drone starts to go up. If you pull it back, the propellers slow down and it comes back down.

B: And what is this other one for?

A: When your drone is in the air, you can move this right lever forwards, backwards, right or left and the drone flies in that direction.

B: OK. And what happens if I press this button?

A: It takes photos. Or if you hold it for longer, it makes a video.

B: Cool. Let's try it.

8d Gadgets 139

UNIT 8 Technology

5 [68]

- Read the list of expressions with your class. Make sure students understand the words in the expressions (see Vocabulary note below).
- Play the recording again. Students listen and tick the questions they hear. Let them compare their answers in pairs before checking with the class.

> **ANSWERS**
> Can you show me how this works?
> Have you charged the battery?
> How did you do that?
> What is this other one for?
> What happens if I press this button?

> **Vocabulary note**
> *How does it work?* = How do you operate it?
> If you *switch (something) on/off*, you press a button or switch (e.g. a light switch on a wall) to operate it. If you *turn (something) on/off*, you move a dial to the left or right (e.g. turn on the radio by turning the dial). However, often the two verbs are used interchangeably. Both are separable (e.g. *turn it on* but *turn the radio on* or *turn on the radio*).

6

- Look at the objects in the box with the class and point out pronunciation and stress (the stress is on the first syllable except for com*pu*ter, photo*co*pier, ma*chine*). Check any new words, e.g. *USB stick* (= a 'stick' with memory you attach to a computer) and *vending machine* (= a machine that has food and drink in it which you buy by putting money in the machine).
- Organize the class into pairs. Ask students to take turns to describe how the objects in the box (or in their bag) work. Encourage students to use the questions in the box in Exercise 5.
- As students speak, monitor and notice how well they use the language of instruction. Note any errors you hear and, in feedback, at the end, write some errors on the board and ask students to correct them in pairs.

> **EXAMPLE ANSWERS**
> A computer game: Press the button/icon to switch it on. If you pull the lever back, the character goes forward / shoots a gun.
> A mobile phone/tablet: Charge the battery. Press the button to switch it on. It's the button on the side.
> A photocopier/printer: Turn it on / Press the button to switch it on. Select how many copies you want. Press the button to copy. If the paper is stuck, pull the lever to open the copier.
> A USB stick: Put it in the computer. Press the button to release it.
> A vending machine: Turn it on / Press the button to select what you want. Put money in. Pull the lever to get your money back.

> **Extra activity 1**
> Note that audioscript 68 has examples of zero conditional forms. You could ask students to find examples in the audioscript on page 186 of the Student's Book before students do the speaking activity. Ask students to use some of these phrases when explaining how objects work.

> **Extra activity 2**
> Before the lesson above, ask students to bring in an interesting gadget from home which they can describe. Alternatively, bring in an unusual gadget that you have – students have to guess how it works before you explain its function. Another idea is to get students to find new or unusual gadgets online and explain how they work to the class.

UNIT 8 Technology

8e An argument for technology

Lesson at a glance
- writing: a paragraph
- writing skill: connecting words

Writing a paragraph

1
- **Optional step** Ask students to look at the photo. Elicit what LED lighting is (see Background information below). Ask students if they use LED lights.
- Ask students to read the paragraph and answer the question. Let students compare answers in pairs before checking with the class.

> **ANSWER**
> b

> **Background information**
> LED stands for light-emitting diode and is pronounced /el i: di:/. As the text says, it's more efficient and longer-lasting than other forms of lighting. LED lights are used in cars, on planes, in street lights and as the backlighting for TV and computer screens.

Writing skill connecting words

2a
- Ask students to look at the highlighted connecting words in the paragraph. Then ask them to match the words with the uses (1–6). Let students compare their answers in pairs before checking with the class.

> **ANSWERS**
> 1 Firstly 2 On the other hand, However 3 In other words
> 4 In addition 5 For example 6 As a result

> **Vocabulary note**
> Note that all these phrases generally go at the start of sentences and are followed by a comma.

b
- **Optional step** Start by asking students to read the short text for comprehension. Set a simple task: *Name two good things about the internet that are in the text* (shows videos, explains how things work).
- Ask students to complete the paragraph with the connecting words from Exercise 2a. Let students compare their answers in pairs before checking with the class.

> **ANSWERS**
> 1 Firstly 2 For example 3 In addition
> 4 On the other hand / However
> 5 However / On the other hand 6 As a result

3
- Start by asking the class to say what GPS technology is (see Background information below).
- Read the notes with your class. Explain that, like the model texts in Exercise 1 and Exercise 2b, they give the main idea and reasons.
- Ask students to write a paragraph using the notes and connecting words. As students write, monitor to help and prompt students. Encourage them to add their own ideas in addition to the notes on the Student's Book page.
- In feedback, you could ask students to exchange texts with a partner so that they can compare and correct each other's work. Alternatively, show the example answer below and ask students to compare what they wrote to the text.

> **EXAMPLE ANSWER**
> GPS is a good idea for anyone who travels a lot. **Firstly**, GPS maps are always up-to-date and correct. **In addition**, they are safer to use when driving. **On the other hand**, one disadvantage is that GPS is more expensive than a normal map. **However**, it saves time. **For example**, you will drive directly to your destination without spending time getting lost and trying to find your way. **As a result**, you will also spend less money on petrol.

> **Background information**
> GPS (Global Positioning System) is a space-based radio-navigation system owned by the United States government and operated by the United States Air Force. It's free for anyone to use and regularly used by drivers.

4
- Ask students to choose a type of technology and make notes for their paragraph. Ask them to follow the format in the notes in Exercise 3, i.e. get them to write the main idea and a series of bulleted supporting ideas.
- As students prepare, monitor and be ready to help with ideas and vocabulary. It's a good idea to ask students to compare notes with a partner so they can share advice and pick up useful ideas.

5
- Ask students to think which connecting words to use when connecting the sentences or ideas in their notes. Then ask them to write a paragraph.
- **Optional step** Ask students to write their paragraph on a separate sheet of paper (not in their notebooks) so that it's easy to pass around and share in the next activity.
- **Optional step** You could ask students to write their paragraphs for homework if you're short of class time. Students can then share their paragraphs in the next class.

UNIT 8 Technology

EXAMPLE ANSWER

Here is a model set of notes and an example text:
Mobile phones – useful in many different ways
- can use them to communicate with friends
- make calls
- send texts
- get information from the internet – dictionary and encyclopaedia
- expensive (but lots of packages to keep the price down)
- more useful than any other gadget

Mobile phones are useful in many different ways. Firstly, we can use them to communicate with friends. For example, we can make calls or send texts. In addition, they are a great way of accessing information from the internet. In other words, they're a dictionary and encyclopaedia as well as a phone. On the other hand, they can be expensive if we use them a lot. However, there are lots of packages you can buy to keep the price down. As a result, our mobile phones are probably more useful than any other gadget.

6 ★ CPT extra! Writing activity [after Ex. 6]
- Organize the class into pairs (or small groups if you prefer). Students exchange paragraphs and read them carefully. Encourage students to give feedback on the organization of paragraphs and on the use of connecting words.

8f Ancient languages, modern technology

Before you watch
1
- Ask students to look at the photo and read the caption. Point out that *ancient* means very, very old.
- Discuss the questions with your class and elicit answers.

EXAMPLE ANSWER

The photo shows a professional film camera on a tripod. The people in the photo, however, don't appear to be technologically advanced. Perhaps they are using the camera to record their traditions, customs or way of life – the title of the unit suggests they may be using it to record their ancient language.

Background information

In this *National Geographic* photo, speakers of **Aka** (an ancient language) watch playback of an Aka story told by one of the men whose name is Biga Nimasow. These people are in the village of Palizi in the East Kameng District of the Indian state of Arunachal Pradesh. It's in the far north east of India. Their language belongs to the Tibeto-Burman family. Aka is the most common of the many languages in the region – other languages include Koro and Apatani (the language featured on the video).

Key vocabulary
2
- Ask students to work individually to read the sentences. Encourage them to try to work out the meaning of the words in bold from the context before matching them with the definitions provided. Let them compare answers in pairs before checking with the class.
- **Optional step** It's a good idea to show the pronunciation of these key words – students have to hear them in continuous speech on the video. You could say the words and ask students to repeat (see Vocabulary and pronunciation note below).

ANSWERS

1 a 2 c 3 d 4 f 5 b 6 e

Vocabulary and pronunciation note

disappear = if something disappears, you can't see it any more (here, the word is used to mean stop existing)

awareness = if you are aware of something, you know about it

die out = if a type of animal dies out, it goes extinct – there are none left

survive = to stay alive despite an injury, illness, etc. (e.g. *He survived for two weeks in the desert by drinking water from plants.*)

shift = literally, a movement away from something

neglect = if you neglect something, you don't give it enough attention (e.g. *neglect a child, neglect a garden*)

UNIT 8 Technology

While you watch

3 [8.1]

- **Optional step** Point out the glossary at the bottom of page 103. Point out the pronunciation of the words.
- Ask students to read the actions carefully.
- Play the video. Students watch and number the actions in the order they see them. Let students compare their answers in pairs before checking with the class. Write the order on the board.

ANSWERS

1 c   2 a   3 d   4 b

Videoscript 8.1

C = Chris, **D** = David, **G** = Greg

0.00–0.34 David Harrison and Greg Anderson work for the Living Tongues Institute. Chris Rainier is a photographer for the *National Geographic* Society. The aim is to help save ancient languages which are disappearing by writing them down and also recording them using modern technology.

They are interviewing a man in Australia who is possibly the last speaker of a language that most people thought had died out. The team translate his words and record the interview.

0.35–0.42 Speakers that's like my father …

0.43–0.50 There are seven thousand known languages in the world, but more than half of them will probably disappear in the next 50 years.

0.51–0.57 And when a language disappears, we lose the information about the world that its speakers had.

0.58–1.17 C Every two weeks around the planet, a language disappears, completely disappears forever and ever. So what we're doing with the Enduring Voices project is really, kind of, trying to bring awareness to this whole issue of language loss around the planet.

1.18–1.27 After Australia, the team travels on. This time they travel to the northeast of India, an area near Bhutan, Myanmar and China.

1.28–1.40 It's a region where there are many different languages but many of them could die out in the next few years.

1.41–1.46 For the team, there are problems with the technology. Their equipment isn't working.

1.46–2.01 D Say something.

G Something. Something that I'm really getting annoyed at is this equipment making my life a hassle.

D Go really loud.

G HEY!

D OK, that'll work. Good enough.

2.02–2.15 Most of these local languages are not written anywhere so the researchers want to record as much of the languages as possible.

2.16–2.36 The team arrives in a large village called Hong. Many of the older people speak the local language called Apatani. But the language cannot survive if the younger people don't speak it.

2.37–2.50 D It's very easy in these communities to find young people who are speaking English and Hindi and not speaking the traditional languages. They are neglecting them. They're perhaps even abandoning them.

2.51–3.01 The team spends time trying to find some younger people who speak the language.

3.02–3.15 G We definitely want to find younger speakers because they're the ones that will be showing the shift. The older speakers of course will have the language. So it will be interesting to see if people who've been schooled in the modern times, if they've still kept it.

3.16–3.26 The team meets a young man named Vijay, who speaks English and Apatani. Vijay invites them into his home.

3.27–3.34 A local Indian called Ganesh Murmu helps the researchers while they record basic words of the local language.

3.35–3.41 (members of the family speaking)

3.42–3.45 Each member of the family says some more words.

3.46–3.48 (members of the family speaking)

3.49–4.11 As well as doing their own research, the team trains local people to use special language technology kits. These technology kits have a laptop computer, video cameras, and basic recording equipment so the local community can record the last speakers of old languages using modern technology.

4.12–4.15 (members of the family speaking)

4.16–4.28 D Not only are these languages very small, with just a few thousand speakers in some cases, but their numbers may be decreasing as people shift over to global languages.

4.29–end Finally it's time for the three men to leave this part of India but they hope that the local communities will use the technology kits and record this important part of their local culture. They hope that the people will listen to the words of the older people and try to keep the language alive and speak it themselves.

4 [8.1]

- Ask students to read the sentences and check any difficult words (see Vocabulary note below). Then play the video again and students note whether the sentences are true (T) or false (F).
- After watching, let students compare answers with a partner before checking with the class.

ANSWERS

1 T   2 T   3 F   4 T   5 F   6 T   7 F   8 T   9 T

Vocabulary note

ancient = very old

dying out = no longer spoken

half that amount = 50% of the previous number

equipment = things you use to do a job – here a camera

kit = a set of equipment

keep it alive = stop it from dying out or disappearing from the world

8f Ancient languages, modern technology   143

UNIT 8 Technology

After you watch
Vocabulary in context
5 [8.2]

- Explain that students are going to watch some clips from the video which contain some new words and phrases. They need to choose the correct meaning of the words.
- Play the clips. When each multiple-choice question appears, pause the clip so that students can choose the correct definition. You could let students compare answers in pairs before discussing as a class.

ANSWERS
1 b   2 c   3 c   4 b   5 a

Videoscript 8.2

1 There are seven thousand **known languages** in the world …
   a languages that people know
   b languages that people know about
   c languages that people have translated

2 … a language disappears, completely disappears **forever** …
   a from everyday use
   b for some of the time
   c for all time

3 Their **equipment** isn't working.
   a a special type of technology
   b a type of transportation
   c special tools for a special purpose

4 … people who've been **schooled** in the modern times …
   a sent away (to school)
   b taught
   c learned

5 … they record **basic** words of the local language.
   a simple and not complicated
   b new and different
   c old and traditional

Vocabulary note

A *known* language is one that people have heard about or recorded (compare, *a known cure, the known facts*).

We use *equipment* to describe specialized tools (e.g. climbing equipment, medical equipment).

Schooled means taught or trained. It's used to describe learning particular skills, e.g. schooled in the art of diplomacy. (Note that the phrase isn't high frequency and shouldn't be used as a synonym for *taught* by students).

6 ★ **CPT extra!** Speaking activity [before Ex. 7]

- **Optional step** Ask students to read the text for comprehension. Ask: *What do we find out about Salish?* (It's a native American language with few speakers but it's growing.)
- Ask students to complete the paragraph using words from the video. Tell them that they may have to change the form of the words. Let students compare answers in pairs before checking with the class.

ANSWERS
1 known   2 dying out   3 forever   4 equipment
5 basic   6 survived   7 schooled

7 ★ **CPT extra!** Research project activity [after Ex. 7]

- Ask students to work in groups of four or five to discuss the questions. Start them off by asking the first question in open class and eliciting answers and opinions. Tell students that they don't have to discuss all the questions – just the ones that interest them.
- **Optional step** Ask one student in each group to chair the discussion. It's that student's job to ask the questions, make sure everybody has a chance to speak and to move on the discussion.
- As students speak, monitor and note interesting things people say, and interesting or inaccurate uses of language. In feedback, at the end, ask groups to summarize their main points. Provide feedback on errors you heard.

EXAMPLE ANSWERS

Students' own answers

Technology can help save a dying language by recording it (on video and audio); by providing a video and audio resource from which people can learn it or educators can prepare ways of teaching the language to a new generation; by bringing the attention of the world or of national governments to the fact that the language is dying; by making learning a dying language 'cool' to a new generation – if they can study and learn it through technology, it becomes more attractive.

Technology is useful for learning and communicating: watching films and audio in the classroom or at home; using audio to provide listening comprehension or to practise speaking (recording yourself); using interactive white boards; studying online; using the internet as a resource (dictionary, grammar reference, user groups).

Students use technology in the classroom (video, audio, interactive whiteboards), at home (using the internet to research for homework, using an online dictionary, speaking to other language learners).

Background information

Here is information about **global languages**:
- Most speakers: Chinese (Mandarin), Spanish, English, Hindi, Arabic
- English (1.5 billion learners), French (82 million learners) and Mandarin Chinese (30 million learners) are the three most commonly studied foreign languages.

UNIT 8 Technology

UNIT 8 Review and memory booster ★ CPT extra! Language games

Memory Booster activities

Exercises 3, 5 and 8 are Memory Booster activities. For more information about these activities and how they benefit students, see page 10.

I can … tick boxes

As an alternative to students simply ticking the *I can …* boxes, you could ask them to give themselves a score from 1 to 4 (1 = not very confident; 4 = very confident) for each language area. If students score 1 or 2 for a language area, refer them to additional practice activities in the Workbook and Grammar summary exercises.

Grammar

1

- Ask students to work individually to complete the sentences with the correct form of the verbs. Ask students to say which sentences are zero and which are first conditional (answer in brackets).

ANSWERS

1 press (zero) 2 will work (first) 3 love (zero)
4 doesn't call (first) 5 won't go (first) 6 'll pass (first)

2

- Ask students to work individually to complete the sentences with the correct relative pronoun.

ANSWERS

1 which 2 who 3 where 4 which 5 who 6 which

3 >> MB

- Ask students to work individually to complete the sentences with true information.
- Ask students to explain their sentences to their partner. Encourage students to ask follow-up questions to get more details about each sentence.

Vocabulary

4

- Ask students to work individually to complete the sentences. Let students compare answers in pairs before checking with the class.

ANSWERS

1 set 2 Press 3 charge 4 technology 5 in 6 log
7 solve 8 about 9 get 10 play

5 >> MB

- Ask students to work individually to choose three more words from the unit. They write a sentence for each one, missing out the key word. Monitor, helping as necessary.

- Ask students to work in pairs and take turns to read out their sentences, saying BEEP for the missing word. Their partner guesses the missing word.

ANSWERS

Students' own answers

Real life

6

- Ask students to work individually to order the words to make questions. Let students compare answers in pairs before checking with the class.

ANSWERS

1 How do I switch it on?
2 What happens if I press this button?
3 Can you show me how this works?
4 How did you do that?
5 Have you charged the battery?
6 What does this button do?

7

- Ask students to match the questions in Exercise 6 to the responses (a–e). Make sure students realize that one response matches two of the questions.

ANSWERS

1 d 2 e 3 a 4 d 5 b 6 c

8 >> MB

- Look at the photos of two inventions with the class. Elicit what they can remember about each one.
- Ask students to work in pairs and describe the inventions, using the bullet point prompts as a guide. Monitor and help with vocabulary as necessary.

EXAMPLE ANSWERS

These are glasses which don't need an optician. There's a pump on each side which uses silicone oil. First, you turn a wheel which controls the pump. The pump pushes the silicone oil through the pipe and it moves into the lenses. As the lens fills with oil, the shape of the lens changes and you turn the wheel until you can see correctly.

This is a drone which flies in the air and takes photos or videos. It has two levers. If you push the one on the left forward, the propellers go faster and the drone starts to go up. If you pull it back, the propellers slow down and it comes back down. The lever on the right controls the direction of the drone. If you press a button, it takes photos.

Unit 9 Holidays

Opener

1

- Ask students to look at the photo and the caption. Ask them to work in pairs to discuss the question. Elicit a few ideas from the class in feedback.

> **ANSWERS**
>
> Students' own answers
>
> The photo shows a diver with a snake. He's an explorer so he travels to exciting, exotic locations in search of snakes – he probably goes on holiday to places where he can see snakes. (Note that the answer is revealed in the audio in Exercise 2.)

> **Background information**
>
> **Zoltan Takacs** is a Hungarian-born toxinologist and tropical adventurer specializing in venomous snakes. He's travelled to 133 countries, and is an aircraft pilot and a scuba diver as well as a wildlife photographer.

2 [69] ★ **CPT extra!** Vocabulary activity [after Ex. 2]

- Play the recording. Students listen and answer the question. Let them compare answers in pairs before checking with the class.
- **Optional step** You could play the recording a second time and ask students to say what is different about the people's working lives and holidays.

> **ANSWERS**
>
> 1 Zoltan's working life: travelling and studying snakes; holidays: looking for snakes
> 2 Greg's working life: has (owns) a camping and caravan site; holidays: goes camping (in southern Europe)
> 3 Moira's working life: pilot for an international airline so travels by plane; holidays: flies back to interesting cities (but stays in bed and breakfast accommodation and has more time for sightseeing).

Audioscript 69

(The words of Zoltan Takacs are spoken by an actor.)

1

My name's Zoltan and I spend a lot of time travelling and studying snakes around the world, from the rainforests to the oceans. For me, my work and my holiday is the same thing. When I travel with my family and friends, I often go diving and looking for sea snakes. I've even kept sea snakes in the hotel bath. That's what I call a holiday!

2

My name's Greg and I have a camping and caravan site in the south of England. Our busiest time is the summer so I always have my holiday later in the autumn. Because England can be cold later in the year, I put my tent in the car, drive to southern Europe and go camping and hiking in the mountains. My friends think I'm a bit crazy. They think I should do something different for my holidays, but I love camping.

3

I'm Moira and I'm a pilot for an international airline. People think my job is a good way to see the world. Sometimes I have a few hours in a city to go sightseeing, but usually I only see the airport and a hotel room. However, the good thing about my job is that I get a discount on flights, so when I have a holiday I like flying back to some of the interesting cities I've been to and spending more time there. I also prefer to stay in bed and breakfast accommodation instead of hotels because I think you meet more of the local people that way.

3 [69]

- Start by checking the meaning of the words. You could do this by finding and showing pictures of the different types of accommodation and by using mime to show the activities (see Vocabulary note below).
- Ask students to listen again and say which accommodation and activities each speaker talks about. Let students compare answers in pairs before checking with the class.

> **ANSWERS**
>
> 1 hotel, diving
> 2 caravan, camping, tent, hiking
> 3 sightseeing, hotel, bed and breakfast

> **Vocabulary and pronunciation note**
>
> *bed and breakfast* = a term used in the UK to describe a place to stay. It's often somebody's family home – they rent out rooms and provide breakfast in the morning (but not lunch or dinner)
>
> *caravan/camper van* = a caravan is a 'home on wheels' that you pull behind your car, but a camper van is a 'home on wheels' that is also a big car (or van)
>
> *camping* = staying in a tent
>
> *clubbing* = going to night clubs and dancing
>
> *hiking* = walking long distances in the countryside
>
> *sightseeing* = looking at interesting places in a city
>
> *sunbathing* = lying in the sun
>
> Note that the strong stress is on the first syllable of all the words in Exercise 3.

4

- Ask students to work in pairs to ask and answer the questions. In feedback, ask some students to tell the class what they found out about their partner.

> **ANSWERS**
>
> Students' own answers

UNIT 9 Holidays

9a Holiday stories

Lesson at a glance
- reading: a holiday problem
- vocabulary: holiday collocations
- grammar: past perfect simple
- pronunciation: 'd
- speaking: a holiday story

Reading

1
- **Optional step** Read the questions and the problems with your class. Check any unknown words (see Vocabulary note below).
- Organize the class into small groups of three or four to discuss the problems and share experiences. In feedback, ask each group to share their most interesting story with the class.

Vocabulary note

miss a plane = not get on the plane (because you arrived late or got the day wrong, etc.)

a ferry = a boat that goes from one place to another and back (e.g. from New York to Ellis Island and back)

get lost = can't find your way

2 [70] ★ **CPT extra!** Lead-in activity [before Ex. 2]
- Ask students to read the story and answer the questions. Let students compare answers in pairs before checking answers with the class.
- **Optional step** The reading text is recorded. You could play the recording and ask students to read and listen.

ANSWERS
It was small and dark, it looked over the car park, the shower didn't work. She gave a large tip to the manager and got a better room.

3 ★ **CPT extra!** Background information [before Ex. 3]
- **Optional step** Give students time to read the list of events. Check any unknown words, e.g. *a tip* (= money you give somebody in a hotel or restaurant for being helpful) and *booked* (= reserved, i.e. paid for the room before you arrived).
- Ask students to read the story again and number the events in order. Let them compare their order in pairs before checking with the class.

ANSWERS
1 e 2 b 3 i 4 f 5 g 6 c 7 d 8 a 9 h

4
- Ask students the questions and elicit answers. In a multicultural class, find out what differences there are between countries. If your students are from the same place, find out what is considered correct.

- **Optional step** You could organize this as a class survey. Organize the class into pairs. Tell students to walk round the class individually and ask four or five people about tipping. Ask students to sit with their partner, collate their information and present their findings.

Background information

Tipping culture varies from country to country. In many parts of Asia (e.g. China, South Korea and Japan), it isn't part of the culture and can be seen as insulting.

In North America, tipping is a practised social custom – failing to tip 10% or 15% of the bill in restaurants is frowned upon, and most people who provide a service (e.g. tour guides, bar workers, taxi drivers, hairdressers) expect a tip.

In Europe, a 10% tip to waiters is fairly standard, but not compulsory. In the UK, for example, people would ordinarily tip in a smart restaurant, but not in a café or pub. Increasingly, a service charge is included in the bill in many European countries.

People you might tip: waiters, hotel receptionists, porters, tour guides, taxi drivers, lift operators or bell boys, hotel maids, hairdressers, bar staff.

Vocabulary holiday collocations

5
- Ask students to complete the sentences with the verbs. Elicit the first answer as an example to get them started.
- Once students have completed the sentences, ask them to look back at the story and see how many of the collocations they can find (Note that items 1 and 2 are not in the story). Let students compare answers in pairs before checking with the class.

ANSWERS
1 go 2 book 3 stay 4 check in 5 unpack
6 call 7 give

Vocabulary note

go abroad = go to a different country

book a holiday = call or go online to reserve the holiday by paying for the dates and hotel before you go to stay

check in/check out (at reception) = when you sign your name at the front desk of the hotel, you check in; when you pay the bill and leave, you check out

pack/unpack (a bag) = put things in/take things out

give a tip = we also say *leave a tip* (= leave, for example, 10% of the bill)

Other words to check in the text:

brochure = here, a magazine describing holidays you can book

pipes = the long metal tubes that water goes down

fix = repair

furious = very angry

6
- Ask students to match the verbs with the groups of nouns. Elicit the first answer as an example to get students started. Let students compare answers in pairs before checking with the class.

9a Holiday stories 147

UNIT 9 Holidays

- **Optional step** Ask students to provide more examples of their own of collocations that could go with these verbs (e.g. *go sightseeing, go swimming, stay at school, stay overnight, book a holiday, book a hotel room, rent a bike, rent a boat, get tired, get a brochure*).

> **ANSWERS**
> 1 go 2 stay 3 book 4 rent 5 get

Extra activity
Ask students to prepare their own personalized sentences using the collocations in Exercises 5 and 6. Start students off by providing two or three examples of your own personalized sentences, e.g.

I only … clubbing on holiday. (go)

I … at home on Sunday and cook dinner for the family. (stay)

I usually … tickets for bands I like online. (book)

When we go on holiday, my parents … a car because they like to visit a lot of places. (rent)

I always … sunburned when I go to sunny countries. (get)

Organize the class into pairs. Ask students to take turns reading out their sentences, saying BEEP instead of the verb each time. Their partner must guess the missing verb.

Grammar past perfect simple

7
- Ask students to look at the example sentences in the grammar box and elicit how we form the past perfect simple.

> **ANSWERS**
> had + past participle (e.g. *been, done, gone, fixed*). *Had* is often reduced to *'d* in informal English, especially when using pronouns (e.g. *I'd, he'd, we'd*).

Refer students to page 172 for further information and practice.

> **ANSWERS TO GRAMMAR SUMMARY EXERCISES**
> **1**
> 1 h 2 f 3 d 4 c 5 g 6 a 7 e 8 b
> **2**
> 1 had; bought 2 had happened 3 had asked
> 4 had; thought 5 had; tried 6 hadn't checked
> 7 had spent
> **3**
> 1 didn't go, had … seen 2 felt, had forgotten
> 3 called, had received 4 said, had helped
> 5 had slept, felt 6 had studied, failed

8
- Ask students to answer the questions. You could do this in open class or ask students to discuss in pairs before eliciting answers as a class.

> **ANSWERS**
> a 1 main action: *wasn't sure*; happened earlier: *had been excited*
>   2 main action: *gave him money*; happened earlier: *hadn't fixed my shower*
> b 1 past simple: *wasn't*; past perfect: *had been*
>   2 past simple: *gave*; past perfect: *hadn't fixed*

Grammar note
The past perfect simple is used to refer back to something that happened before. As a result, it's commonly used when narrating because it allows the speaker to vary the sequence of events.

You could use a timeline to show the use:

Past _____ X *bought clothes*_____ X *went sightseeing*_____ Now

*I **went** sightseeing after I'**d bought** new clothes.*

The timeline is a visual way of showing that 'bought clothes' happened before 'went sightseeing' even though, in the order of the sentence, 'went sightseeing' is used first.

Problems
- Form
  You may need to revise irregular past participles (first seen in Unit 7 by students on this course. Remind students of the irregular verb table on page 180 of the Student's Book.). Students sometimes get confused by the fact that *I'd* can be *I would* as well as *I had*.
- Use
  Students sometimes think of past perfect as a distant past (e.g. ~~Many years ago, I had lived in France~~). This is incorrect. The tense is only used in contrast to another past to show an earlier event.

9 [71]
- **Optional step** Ask students to read the dialogue for comprehension first. Ask: *What two problems did the holiday-maker have?* (someone stole his bag; there was no electricity in the hotel).
- Ask students to choose the correct options. Then play the recording for students to listen and check their answers.
- **Optional step** Ask students to say why the speakers choose to use past simple or past perfect (see Grammar note below).

> **ANSWERS**
> 1 happened 2 'd run 3 reported 4 'd packed
> 5 'd bought 6 'd left 7 had 8 was

UNIT 9 Holidays

Grammar note

The key event at the start of this story is this: *Someone stole my bag and we didn't catch him*. When referring to events before this happened, the speaker uses the past perfect (e.g. *he'd run out, I'd packed my passport*). When referring to events after, the speaker uses the past simple (e.g. *The hotel reported*).

The key event in the second part of this story is this: *I went to find the manager*. When referring to events before this happened, the speaker uses the past perfect (e.g. *she'd left*). When referring to events after, the speaker uses the past simple (e.g. *had torches, was the best night*).

10

- Ask students to complete the sentences. Elicit the first answer as an example to get students started. Let students compare answers in pairs before checking with the class.

ANSWERS
1 had left 2 hadn't arrived 3 went 4 hadn't eaten
5 had lost 6 had 7 gave
8 had left (*left* also possible here)

Pronunciation *'d*

11 [72] ★ **CPT extra!** Listening activity [after Ex. 11]

- Play the recording. Students listen and notice the pronunciation of *'d* in the two sentences. In feedback, point out that *we'd* and *I'd* have only one syllable when pronounced: /wiːd/, /aɪd/.
- Play the recording again. Students listen and repeat.
- **Optional step** Ask students to practise reading out the dialogue in Exercise 9, paying attention to the pronunciation of *'d*.

Speaking my life

12

- **Optional step** Start by eliciting possible holiday stories to use from students. Ask: *Have you ever had any problems on holiday? What was the problem? What happened in the end? Have you ever lost something? Have you ever been in a bad hotel?* Elicit ideas and get various students to share brief stories. This will give students ideas about what to write about.
- Ask students to prepare their story using the prompts in the box. You could elicit or model one or two example sentences first. Point out that students should try to use past perfect forms.
- **Optional step** Ask students to work in pairs (more fun and interactive than working individually) to prepare stories. Then split the pairs so that students have new partners to tell their story to in the next activity.

13

- Organize the class into pairs to take turns to read their stories.
- As students speak, monitor and note any errors you hear.
- After a few minutes, say stop. Ask different individuals to say whether they think their partner's story is real or not.
- **Optional step** Note any errors you hear as students speak. After feedback, write up short sentences with errors you heard and ask pairs or groups to work together to correct them. Concentrate on errors with past forms.

EXAMPLE ANSWER

Here are some example sentences from a possible story:

My family and I went to Greece five years ago. When we got to the airport, we realized we had forgotten our passports. Dad drove home really fast and got the passports. The holiday was great until we decided to rent a car for the day. We'd just visited an ancient temple when we heard a loud noise. Somebody had driven into our car!

Extra activity

Write the following on the board (or project it using your classroom technology):

1 No passports

leave passports at home – get to airport – can't get on plane – go home

2 No luggage

forget to check in our bags – not get on plane – fly to Rome – not have any clothes

Ask students to prepare different ways of telling these stories using the prompts. Tell them to start in different places. (This activity prompts students to realize that we can vary the order in which we narrate events by using the past perfect).

Possible answers:

1 When we got to the airport, we realized we'd forgotten our passports. We couldn't get on the plane and had to go home. / We went home from the airport. We'd got to the airport early, but we hadn't been able to get on the plane because we had forgotten our passports.

2 We got on the plane and flew to Rome, but we didn't have any clothes to wear because we'd forgotten to check in our bags. / We didn't have any clothes on holiday. We'd got on the plane and flown to Rome but we had forgotten to check in our bags.

9a Holiday stories 149

UNIT 9 Holidays

9b A different kind of holiday

Lesson at a glance
- listening: interview with a tour guide
- wordbuilding: -ed / -ing adjectives
- pronunciation: number of syllables
- grammar: subject questions
- speaking: the holiday of a lifetime

Listening

1 ★ **CPT extra!** Grammar revision [before Ex. 1]
- Ask students to work in small groups of three or four to discuss the questions. In feedback, elicit ideas.

> **ANSWERS**
> Students' own answers

2 [73] ★ **CPT extra!** Photo activity [before Ex. 2]
- Explain that students are going to listen to an interview about a different kind of holiday (see Teacher development below). Ask students to read the questions. Check *responsible for* (= if you are responsible for something, e.g. planning a trip, then it's you who must make sure that it's done correctly).
- Play the recording. Students listen and answer the questions. Let them compare answers in pairs before checking with the class.

> **ANSWERS**
> 1 Madelaine is going to be a tour guide for a travel company.
> 2 She's responsible for taking groups of tourists on adventure holidays – she has to organize and plan different group activities for every day.

Audioscript [73]

I = Interviewer, M = Madelaine
(Note that the words in bold relate to Exercise 5.)

I: So, Madelaine. I know that you're very **excited** about your new job. What is it exactly?
M: I'm going to be a tour guide for a travel company.
I: OK. Why do you want to be a tour guide?
M: Well, I've always been **interested** in different countries and I've done a lot of independent travel – last year I spent six months travelling on my own in South America. So, I know all about visiting new places.
I: But going travelling on your own isn't the same as taking groups of tourists round famous cities or taking them from one hotel to another. Aren't you **worried** that it might be a bit **boring** for someone like you?

M: Actually, it'll be **fascinating** because the tour company specializes in adventure holidays. My first tour is very **exciting**. I'm leading a group to the Galápagos Archipelago, which is a place I've always wanted to visit.
I: That sounds **amazing**! So, who books these types of holidays?
I: They're usually people who are **bored** of traditional sightseeing and want something a bit different.
I: So, what can you do on the tours?
M: Well, for example, on day one we go walking along the coast and photographing plants and animals. Day two is kayaking. So, I have to organize and plan different group activities for every day.
I: I see. How many people go on the tour?
M: Usually eight. People often come on their own and make new friends. And if someone wants a day on their own, that's fine. I think the main thing is that they are never **bored**!
I: No, it doesn't sound like they will be! One last question. How much does it cost?
M: Er, actually I don't know the answer to that.

> **Background information**
> The **Galápagos Archipelago** is a group of islands in the Pacific Ocean off the coast of Ecuador in South America. They're famous for their unique flora and fauna. Giant tortoises live there. Charles Darwin visited the islands in the nineteenth century and the animals there inspired his theory of evolution.

3 [73]
- Give students time to read the sentences carefully.
- Play the recording again. Students listen and note whether the sentences are true (T) or false (F). Let students compare answers in pairs before checking with the class.
- **Optional step** Ask students to justify answers in feedback by saying what they heard.

> **ANSWERS**
> 1 F (*I'm going to be a tour guide*)
> 2 T (*a place I've always wanted to visit*)
> 3 T (*People often come on their own and make new friends.*)
> 4 F (*if someone wants a day on their own, that's fine*)
> 5 F (*How much does it cost? ... actually I don't know the answer to that*)

150 Unit 9 Holidays

UNIT 9 Holidays

Teacher development

Preparing to listen

Listening to speakers, and following what they say, is very challenging at this level. It's important to spend plenty of time setting up the situation and the exact task. Here are some tips:

- Make it visual. So, start with a picture of the speakers. Show where they are, what their relationship is, what they are going to talk about and what the situation is. This helps students visualize who they are listening to on a recording. Find suitable pictures to show your students before they listen.
- Establish exactly who is speaking. So, in the listening activities above, students need to be clear that there is an interviewer and a woman who is talking about her new job. The more context, the better.
- Make the task simple and clear. Don't ask students to write much – they should just put ticks and crosses or write odd words. Let students read a task carefully before listening. For example, ensure that students have read and understood all the sentences in Exercise 3 above before you play the recording.
- Allow students a sense of achievement by completing the task. So, be prepared to play the recording twice, and pause if really necessary. Use the audioscript to confirm answers.

4

- Discuss the questions in open class.

Wordbuilding -ed / -ing adjectives

5

- Read the sentences in the wordbuilding box with the class. Then ask students to discuss the questions. You could do this in open class or ask students to discuss in pairs.
- Ask students to find audioscript 73 on page 187 of the Student's Book. Tell them to read the interview and underline all the -ed and -ing adjectives. Let students compare answers in pairs.
- In feedback, elicit the words students have underlined. Check their meaning (see Vocabulary note below). Ask students to use the context of the text to try to work out the meaning of any words they aren't sure of.

ANSWERS

1 excited   2 exciting

Adjectives in audioscript (also in bold in audioscript 73 above): excited, interested, worried, boring, fascinating, exciting, amazing, bored

Refer students to page 75 of the Workbook for further practice.

Vocabulary note

ex<u>ci</u>ted = you are happy and enthusiastic and can't relax

<u>wo</u>rried = you are unhappy because you think something bad might happen

<u>bo</u>ring = not interesting at all

<u>fa</u>scinating = very, very interesting

a<u>ma</u>zing = really, really good or exciting

6

- Ask students to work individually to choose the correct adjective. Elicit the first answer as an example to get students started. Let students compare answers in pairs before checking with the class.

ANSWERS

1 amazing   2 bored   3 fascinating   4 interesting
5 frightening   6 worried   7 annoyed   8 tired

Vocabulary note

an<u>noy</u>ed = angry

an<u>noy</u>ing = something that makes you feel angry

<u>ti</u>ring = something that make you feel short of energy and ready for a rest or a sleep

Pronunciation number of syllables

7 [74]

- Play the recording. Students listen and write the number of syllables. After playing the first two pairs of words, stop the recording and check students' answers – this makes sure students are clear about the task.
- In feedback, elicit answers, and drill the words for pronunciation.
- **Optional step** If your students are permitted mobile phones in class, ask them to practise saying the words and recording (then checking) their pronunciation.

ANSWERS

1 amazed (2), amazing (3)
2 bored (1), boring (2)
3 fascinated (4), fascinating (4)
4 interested (3), interesting (3)
5 frightened (2), frightening (3)
6 worried (2), worrying (3)
7 annoyed (2), annoying (3)
8 tired (1), tiring (2)

Pronunciation note

To get the number of syllables right, students will need to listen very carefully and be aware of the following:

- *-ed* is usually pronounced /d/ – it is only /ɪd/ after the sounds /t/ or /d/ (e.g. *fascinated* = /ɪd/).
- *Interested* and *interesting* have a silent vowel – the first 'e' is not pronounced.
- *Tired* and *tiring* contain the triphthong (three vowel sounds in one syllable) /aɪə/ – /ˈtaɪəd/, /ˈtaɪərɪŋ/.

Extra activity

Ask students to make personalized sentences using other *-ed* or *-ing* words from the lesson. For example, *Psycho is a frightening film. My brother is very annoying. I'm annoyed about having homework at the weekend.*

9b   A different kind of holiday   151

UNIT 9 Holidays

8 ⭐ **CPT extra!** Grammar activity [after Ex. 8]
- Ask students to work in pairs. Tell them to talk about the topics (1–6) using -ed and -ing adjectives formed from the verbs in the box.
- **Optional step** You could support students by providing a few true sentences of your own as model sentences. It's also a good idea to give students a few minutes' individual preparation time first before they speak in pairs so that they can come up with good things to talk about.
- As students speak, monitor and notice any errors with -ed and -ing adjectives. In feedback, write up a few errors on the board and ask students to correct them.

> **EXAMPLE ANSWERS**
> Students' own answers
> 2 I'm working on a fascinating project. I'm interested in architecture and we're looking at modern buildings in Stockholm. It's exciting.
> 3 The last book I read was *War and Peace*. It's very long but it isn't boring – it's fascinating, in fact.
> 4 I met a famous novelist at a book festival. It was amazing to meet her and she was interesting.
> 5 I watched *Big Brother* last night. I'm fascinated by how people live together. But the programme was boring.
> 6 It was my birthday last week. I was excited but I only got a boring present – a shirt!

Grammar subject questions

9
- Ask students to look at the example questions in the grammar box. Ask students what they notice about subject and other questions (see Grammar note below).
- Ask students to choose the correct options to complete the rules. You could do this in open class or ask students to discuss in pairs.

> **ANSWERS**
> 1 subject questions   2 we do not use

> **Grammar note**
> A simple table can be used to illustrate the difference between subject and object questions:
>
> **Subject questions**
>
> | question word | main verb |
> |---|---|
> | Who | knows? |
> | What | happened? |
>
> In a subject question, the question word is the subject. The question words *Who* and *What* are most commonly used in subject questions.
>
> **Object questions**
>
> | question word | auxiliary verb | subject | main verb |
> |---|---|---|---|
> | Where | did | you | go? |
> | What | does | it | mean? |
>
> In an object question, the question word is the object of the sentence.

Refer students to page 172 for further information and practice.

> **ANSWERS TO GRAMMAR SUMMARY EXERCISES**
> **4**
> 1, 4, 5 and 7
> **5**
> 1 Who put this bag here?
> 2 Which computer works best?
> 3 Who broke my glasses?
> 4 Who speaks French?
> 5 How many people work here?
> 6 Who won the race?
> **6**
> 1 Where did you go last year?
> 2 Whose behaviour made you really angry?
> 3 How many people live in this building?
> 4 Why did you go outside?
> 5 Who left her coat here?
> 6 Who has spoken to Paolo today?

10
- Ask students to work individually to choose the correct option. Let students compare answers in pairs before checking with the class (see Grammar note below).

> **ANSWERS**
> 1 study   2 did you stay   3 painted   4 did you live
> 5 happened   6 should I visit   7 can help   8 did you take

> **Grammar note**
> If students have problems here, get them to think of a full sentence answer to the question, and to think whether the answer word is the subject or object of the sentence, e.g. *How many students study / do study English in your class?* could be answered *Twelve students study English in my class. Twelve students* is the subject of the sentence, so this must be a subject question – the answer is *study*.

11 🔊 [75]
- Explain that students are going to complete a conversation between four friends who are planning their next holiday together.
- Ask students to work individually to complete the questions in the conversation. Let students compare answers with a partner. Then play the recording so they can check.

> **ANSWERS**
> 1 do we want   2 wants   3 has   4 did you visit   5 agree

152 Unit 9 Holidays

UNIT 9 Holidays

Audioscript [75]

Ryan:	OK, so first of all, how much money do we want to spend this year?
Margaret:	Not much! It needs to be cheap. How about going camping?
Ryan:	Good idea. Who wants to go camping?
Adriana:	Only if we can go somewhere hot!
Margaret:	But we'll have to fly to go somewhere hot, and flying is expensive.
Peter:	Who has a car? We could drive somewhere with the tents. That's cheaper than flying.
Ryan:	I can probably borrow my brother's car. I drove to Spain last summer. It was really hot.
Adriana:	Which cities did you visit?
Ryan:	Barcelona and Madrid. I don't mind going again.
Margaret:	Great. How many people agree with going to Spain?

Extra activity

Write the following on the board before students do the speaking activity in Exercise 12:

Where do we want to …?

How much do we want to …?

Who'd like to …?

Who has …?

Who agrees with …?

Tell students to try to use these prompts to form questions as they do Exercise 12. In feedback, at the end, concentrate on giving students information about how well they used the questions.

Speaking my life
12

- Read the situation with the class. Ask some ICQs (see Teacher development on page 133) to check students understand the task: *Are you going on holiday on your own? (No – in a group) Are you going for two weeks? (No – one week) Are you going to plan where to stay and what to do? (Yes).*
- **Optional step** Give students three or four minutes to prepare questions to ask. If you give students individual preparation time, they are more likely to do the activity confidently and accurately. You can also prompt them to think of subject questions to use. Monitor and help students with ideas and vocabulary.
- Organize the class into groups of four or five students. Ask them to plan the holiday together. Emphasize that they must plan a holiday for everybody in the group, so they'll have to compromise.
- As students speak, monitor and note any errors, especially when using subject or object questions. Write errors on the board at the end for students to correct.

9c Two sides of Paris

Lesson at a glance
- reading: two sides of Paris
- critical thinking: the author's purpose
- word focus: *place*
- speaking: a place you know

Reading
1
- **Optional step** Start by asking what the title refers to. *Two sides of Paris* could mean two different parts (e.g. one in the north, one in the south), or two different aspects (e.g. rich and poor, touristy and business-like).
- Ask students to discuss the question. You could do this in open class or in pairs. Elicit ideas in feedback.

> **EXAMPLE ANSWERS**
>
> *Eiffel Tower, Arc de Triomphe, Notre Dame Cathedral, Louvre Museum, River Seine, Montmartre and its cafés, Catacombs* (see Background information below).

> **Background information**
>
> Paris is the capital of France and its biggest city. Over two million people live there.
>
> The **Paris Catacombs** (pronounced /ˈkætəˌkəʊmz/ or /ˈkætəˌkuːmz/ in English) are underground tunnels where over six million people were buried in the 19th century. The tunnels were originally dug as part of a network of mines. On guided tours, you can see the bones and skeletons. The bodies were moved here because burials in the city were banned in the late eighteenth century. (Note that this information is in the article – but you may wish to pre-teach the word *catacombs* in this lead-in stage).

2 [76]
- Ask students to read the article and answer the question. Let students compare their answers in pairs before checking with the class.
- **Optional step** The reading text is recorded. You could play the recording and ask students to read and listen.

> **ANSWER**
>
> The city above ground (cafés, museums, galleries, shopping, theatres, nightclubs) and the city underground (the catacombs).

3
- Read the notes with the class. Check *architecture* (= interesting buildings) and *tunnels* (= paths or passages underground).
- Ask students to read the first two paragraphs of the article again and complete the notes. Let students compare their answers in pairs before checking with the class.

9c Two sides of Paris 153

UNIT 9 Holidays

> **ANSWERS**
> 1 architecture   2 the Eiffel Tower
> 3 museums and art galleries   4 food in the world
> 5 shopping   6 a huge number of theatres and nightclubs
> 7 catacombs   8 bones and skeletons

> **ANSWERS**
> 1 (*That's the city that most tourists see when they visit Paris. But there is another amazing part of Paris you could visit – and it's underground. … Tourists can visit part of these tunnels called the catacombs*)
> 3 (*But there is another amazing part of Paris you could visit – and it's underground.*)
> 5 (*There are another 250 kilometres of the tunnels which are closed to the public. … Yopie says there are many other rooms like this under Paris.*)

> **Background information**
> The **Eiffel Tower** /ˈaɪfəl ˈtaʊər/ is named after its architect Gustave Eiffel. It's 324 metres high and was built in 1889.

4
- Ask students to read the questions and possible answers and try to remember any answers from their first reading.
- Ask students to read the rest of the article (the last two paragraphs) and choose the correct answers. Let students compare their answers in pairs before checking with the class (see Teacher development below).

> **ANSWERS**
> 1 b   2 c   3 c   4 c

Word focus *place*

6 ★ **CPT extra!** Word focus activity [after Ex. 6]
- Ask students to read the sentences from the article and match the phrases in bold with their use or meaning. Let them discuss their answers with a partner before checking with the class.

> **ANSWERS**
> 1 c   2 a   3 b

> **Vocabulary note**
> *Place* can cover a variety of meanings: an area, a position, a town or country, a building, an open space. Here are common uses:
> - with *to* + verb, e.g. *a place to swim, a place to work, a place to meet people*
> - with *of* + noun, e.g. *a place of work, a place of worship*
> - with *for* + noun/*-ing*, e.g. *a place for old things/keeping old things*
>
> *All over the place* can mean everywhere (e.g. *I travel all over the place*), everywhere and in large amounts (e.g. *There are insects all over the place*) or in an untidy state (e.g. *When we entered the room, her clothes were all over the place*).
>
> *Take place* = happen (often used to describe specific events: *the ceremony will take place at 9 a.m.*).

Teacher development
Checking in pairs
This Teacher's Book suggests encouraging students to check their answers in pairs after completing any task in which there's a degree of difficulty that might be resolved by peer correction or shared discussion. This might be a grammar or vocabulary exercise, or a reading or listening task. Here are some reasons why this suggestion is made:
- It allows students to confirm they've got answers right, or wrong, before having to share them with the class. This makes students more confident about giving an answer in open class.
- It allows you, the teacher, to go round and see how well students have done. You may need to offer help or redirect the task if students have problems. It's better to find this out when students are checking in pairs than in a whole class feedback when students are getting answers wrong.
- It varies interaction and helps create supportive relationships in class, and it encourages peer teaching. Try to ensure that your students don't always check with the same partner.

7
- Ask students to take turns to ask and answer the questions in pairs.
- **Optional step** You could give students some preparation time before talking to each other to think up or research possible answers to the questions.

Speaking my life
8
- Ask students to work in pairs. Tell them to read the task and the words in the list carefully before planning their presentation. Set a time limit of ten minutes.
- **Optional step** Provide support for students by eliciting examples of places and events they could include in the presentation and by introducing a set of useful phrases (written on the board) which students could use, e.g.
It's a place where …
It's a good/interesting/fantastic place to + verb.
It's no place for + -ing.
There are … all over the place.

Critical thinking *the author's purpose*

5 ★ **CPT extra!** Critical thinking activity [after Ex. 5]
- **Optional step** Start by explaining 'author's purpose' – what the writer aims to do when writing something (e.g. persuade you to think something or suggest doing something). Ask students what they think the purpose of the text is and elicit ideas.
- Ask students to tick the sentences which describe the author's purpose. Let them compare and discuss answers with a partner before checking with the class. In feedback, ask pairs to give reasons for their answers.

UNIT 9 Holidays

9
- Ask each pair to work with another pair. If possible, ask students to stand up, move round, and find space in the classroom to sit in their new group of four.
- Pairs take turns to give their presentations. As students speak, listen carefully and note any errors to focus on in feedback.

> **EXAMPLE ANSWER**
>
> It's a place where there are lots of things to do for tourists. For example, there are different museums and art galleries. A good place to eat is the Standard Café in the centre. One of the best places for sightseeing is the area near the cathedral. The cathedral is a good place to get a view of the city. In the summer, free concerts take place in the old square.

> **Extra activity**
>
> Tell students to relax and close their eyes. Then say the following: *Think of a place to relax – Where is it? Why is it relaxing?* (pause)
>
> *Think of a place to study – Where is it? What is good about it* (pause)
>
> *Think of a place that makes you happy – What sort of place is it? Why do you feel happy there?* (pause)
>
> *Think of a place you remember from your childhood – What do you remember about it? Why is it special?* (pause)
>
> Ask students to open their eyes and tell a partner about the places they thought of.

9d Tourist information

Lesson at a glance
- real life: requesting and suggesting
- pronunciation: /dʒə/
- speaking: tourist information

Real life requesting and suggesting

1 ★ **CPT extra!** Background information [before Ex. 1]
- Ask students to look at the text. Ask: *What is it?* (a tourist information brochure) *What place is it about?* (the Tarxien Temples in Malta).
- Ask students to work in pairs to discuss the question. Elicit answers in feedback.

> **EXAMPLE ANSWERS**
>
> Students' own answers. Reasons for seeing it: it's an interesting historical monument, it's not expensive.

> **Background information**
>
> The **Tarxien Temples** /ˈtarʃi.ɛn/ are an archaeological complex in the village of Tarxien on the island of Malta in the Mediterranean Sea. They date to approximately 3,150 BC.

2
- Ask students to look at the gaps in the brochure and think of questions they could ask to get the missing information. Let students check answers in pairs before checking answers with the class.

> **ANSWERS**
>
> 1 What days is it open? / Is it open today?
> 2 When / What time does it close?
> 3 How much does it cost to go in (for students)? / How much is it (for students)?
> 4 How long does the tour last?
> 5 Where do the buses go/leave from? / Where can I catch the bus?

3 🔊 [77]
- Play the recording. Students listen and complete the missing information in the brochure. Let them compare their answers in pairs before checking with the class.

> **ANSWERS**
>
> 1 Monday   2 5   3 4.50   4 two
> 5 tourist information office

9d Tourist information   155

UNIT 9 Holidays

Audioscript [77]

TI = Tourist information, T = Tourist

TI: Hello? Can I help you?

T: I'm interested in visiting the Tarxien Temples. Do you know the opening times?

TI: Sure. Let me check. Tomorrow is Monday so it might be closed. A lot of places are closed on Mondays in Malta. Oh, wait! The site is open every day.

T: Great! What time does it open?

TI: At ten and it closes at five.

T: Oh right. Could you tell me the price?

TI: It's six euros and you can book a ticket here, if you want. But are you a student?

T: Yes, I am.

TI: Then it's four euros fifty. Also, how about booking a guided tour?

T: Um, I'm not sure. How much is that?

TI: The guided tour is an extra twenty euros. It's a good tour. It lasts two hours.

T: Oh. I think I'll just buy the ticket. One other thing – is there any public transport?

TI: There's a bus every hour from outside this tourist information office. Or another option is to take a taxi. It isn't too expensive.

4 [77]

- Ask students to read the expressions. Check any unknown words (*How often does the bus go?* = here, *go* means leave or start its journey, *option* = choice or possibility).
- Play the recording again. Students listen and tick the expressions they hear. Let students compare their answers in pairs before checking with the class.

> **ANSWERS**
>
> I'm interested in visiting …
> Do you know the opening times?
> What time does it open?
> Could you tell me the price?
> Is there any public transport?
> How about … -ing?
> Another option is to …

Vocabulary note

Notice the two uses of *could* in the expressions box:
Could you tell me …? = a polite request
You could take … = a suggestion

Pronunciation /dʒə/

5a [78]

- Play the recording. Students listen and notice how the first two words of each question are pronounced. In feedback, ask students to say what they noticed in their own words.

> **ANSWERS**
>
> Spoken at normal speed, *Do you* and *Could you* are linked and assimilated – *Do you* becomes /dʒə/ and *Could you* becomes /ˈkʊdʒə/.

b [78]

- Play the recording again. Students listen and repeat.

6

- Ask students to work in pairs to prepare and practise the conversation. You may wish to mix students so that they work with classmates they don't normally sit with.
- In their pairs, students decide who is A and who is B. Tell them to find and read their information, Student A on page 155 of the Student's Book and Student B on page 154.
- Ask students to prepare questions or things to say individually first. Set a five-minute time limit and monitor to help with ideas and vocabulary.
- When students are ready, they act out their conversation at the tourist information office. When they have finished, ask them to change roles and act out again.
- **Optional step** If you think your students may have problems with improvisation, ask them in pairs to write dialogues first, using expressions from the lesson. Ask them to practise reading the dialogue. Then ask them to turn over the written dialogue and try to remember and improvise it. Alternatively, ask students to choose and match expressions they could use with each dialogue. Then ask them to improvise dialogues, using the expressions they chose.
- As students speak, monitor their performance. Note down errors students make and, in feedback, write errors on the board and ask students to correct them.

> **EXAMPLE ANSWERS**
>
> Possible questions for A/B:
> *I'm interested in visiting the Caves of Lascaux / the Catacombs of Rome. Do you know the opening times?*
> *Could you tell me the price?*
> *Is there any public transport? How often does the bus go?*
> *Is there a tour? How long does the tour last?*

Background information

The **caves of Lascaux** /læsˈkəʊ/ are a complex of caves in south-western France. Inside there are hundreds of drawings and paintings of animals and birds made by Stone Age people 17,000 years ago. The caves were discovered in 1940, opened to the public in 1948, and closed in 1963 (because the paintings were deteriorating). In 1983, an exact copy of the caves was built nearby and opened to the public.

Extra activity

Ask students to prepare and act out conversations about journeys and places in their own country that they know about.

UNIT 9 Holidays

9e Requesting information

Lesson at a glance
- writing: an email requesting information
- writing skill: formal expressions

Writing an email requesting information

1
- Ask students to answer the questions. You could do this in open class or ask students to discuss in pairs before eliciting answers as a class.

> **ANSWERS**
> Students' own answers

2
- Ask students to read the email and find the answers to the questions. Let students compare answers in pairs before checking with the class.

> **ANSWERS**
> 1 to request more information about the 'Explorer's Holidays' on their website
> 2 the exact dates of tours for next year and more details about the accommodation

Writing skill formal expressions

3
- To provide an example, start by eliciting a formal way of starting an email – an equivalent to 'Hi' in an informal email ('Dear Sir or Madam').
- Ask students to find other formal expressions in the email. Let students compare their answers in pairs before checking with the class.

> **ANSWERS**
> 1 Dear Sir or Madam
> 2 I am writing to request …
> 3 Could you provide me with …
> 4 I would be grateful if you could inform me …
> 5 as soon as they become available
> 6 I would like to receive …
> 7 Thank you in advance for providing this information.
> 8 I look forward to hearing from you.
> 9 Best regards,

> **Vocabulary note**
> A formal email is similar in style and layout to a formal letter. The major difference is that addresses and dates are omitted. However, formal conventions of an email are followed, such as completing the *Re:* section of the email heading (to say what the email is about) and *ccing* (including) interested parties.

> In a formal email, each paragraph is blocked to the left and a line space is left between paragraphs.
> Fixed expressions are used to start the email (*Dear Mr Smith* or *Dear Ms Jones* – first names aren't used; *Dear Sir or Madam* – if the person you are writing to is not known).
> Polite, impersonal fixed expressions are used at the end (*Thank you in advance; I look forward to hearing from you; Best Regards*). When starting an email with *Dear Mr Jones*, you can finish with *Yours sincerely*. If beginning with *Dear Sir or Madam*, finish with *Yours faithfully*.

4
- Ask students to look at the email and Exercise 3 and find any contracted forms. In feedback, ask why there aren't any contracted forms in the email.

> **ANSWERS**
> There are no contracted forms because we don't use contracted forms in formal emails or letters.

5 ★ **CPT extra!** Writing activity [after Ex. 5]
- Ask students to work individually to choose the more formal option. Elicit the first answer as an example to get students started. Let students compare answers in pairs before checking with the class.

> **ANSWERS**
> 1 I am writing to request
> 2 I would be grateful if you could
> 3 I would also like
> 4 Thank you; assistance
> 5 I will inform; available.
> 6 Could you confirm; I will receive
> 7 I look forward to hearing

> **Vocabulary note**
> 1 We don't contract (*I am* not *I'm*) and we use formal vocabulary (*request* not *ask for*).
> 2 We use polite, tentative, hypothetical language (*if* clauses and *could* or *would*, not *can* or *will*) when being very formal.
> 3 *I would like* is more formal than *I want*, which is direct and considered rude.
> 4 No abbreviations – so *Thank you* not *Thanks; assistance* is a more formal word than *help*
> 5 We don't contract (*I will*); *inform* and *available* are more formal words.
> 6 *Could* (= hypothetical language) and *confirm* (= formal word).
> 7 A fixed expression used at the end of formal letters – notice that we write *I look* in formal letters (but *I'm looking forward to …* when writing to a friend).

6
- **Optional step** Ask students to look at the photo. Check the meaning of *a cruise* (= a holiday on a ship) and *a cabin* (= a room on a ship). Ask students what information they would like to find out about a cruise to South America.

9e Requesting information 157

UNIT 9 Holidays

- Ask students to plan their email. Tell them to decide how to start and finish the email, who to write to and how to order their requests for information.
- Ask students to write their email. They could do this for homework (see Extra activity below).

7

- Once students have completed their emails, tell them to exchange them with a partner. Encourage students to give feedback on their partner's style, layout and use of formal expressions.

Extra activity

Ask students to write their emails and send them for real. If your students are happy to exchange email addresses they could write their emails at home and send them to a partner. Ask them to cc you in on the email. That gives you (as well as their partner) an opportunity to write back with corrections and comments.

9f Living in Venice

Before you watch

1 ★ CPT extra! Lead-in activity [before Ex. 1]

- Ask students to work in pairs to discuss the questions. Elicit a few ideas from the class in feedback. You could use the photo to teach some key words, e.g. *canals* (= man-made waterways), *gondola* (= a traditional boat).

EXAMPLE ANSWERS

1 It's popular with tourists because it's beautiful, historical and romantic. There are interesting historical buildings, bridges and monuments to see, and works of art to see in the galleries. You can visit markets, go in a gondola or *vaporetto* (water bus) and eat in nice restaurants. There's a famous carnival.
2 Living and working in the city may be great because of its beauty, history and interesting things to do; it may be difficult because of all the tourism, high prices and pollution.

Background information

Venice (pronounced /ˈvɛnɪs/ in English) is called Venezia in Italian. It is situated in north-eastern Italy and built on a group of 117 small islands, each separated by canals and linked by bridges. Famous tourist attractions include St Mark's Basilica, the Grand Canal, the Rialto Bridge, St Mark's Square and the Doge's Palace.

Key vocabulary

2 ★ CPT extra! Photo activity [after Ex. 1]

- Ask students to read the sentences carefully and try to guess the meaning from the context first. Then tell them to work individually to match the words in bold with the definitions. Let students compare their answers in pairs before checking with the class.

ANSWERS

1 d 2 e 3 a 4 c 5 b 6 g 7 f

Vocabulary note

face the challenge = a challenge is something that's difficult to do – if you face it, then you don't avoid it – you try hard to overcome the challenge

get to = here, the phrase is used to say that you were able to make the most of an opportunity (e.g. *When I was in New York, I got to see a play with famous people in it*).

gift = a synonym of *present*, but we can use it more poetically (e.g. *the gift of love, our baby boy was a gift*).

158 Unit 9 Holidays

UNIT 9 Holidays

While you watch

3 🎥 [9.1]

- Ask students to watch the video and number the things in the order they see them. Let students compare answers in pairs before checking with the class. Write the order on the board.

> **ANSWERS**
>
> 1 b   2 f   3 a   4 d   5 e   6 c

Videoscript 🎥 9.1

P = Ginao Penzo, **M** = Giovanni dal Missier

0.00–0.22   It is early morning in Venice.

Before the light of the sun fills the famous Piazza San Marco, the traders of Venice are preparing for the crowds of tourists. In a few hours, thousands of people will come to this square. But for now, the people of Venice have the city to themselves.

0.23–0.31   Market traders welcome the first visitors. 'Signori, buon giorno.' Early morning is the best time for shopping in the outdoor markets.

0.32–0.37 P   We have many, many kinds of fish.

00.38–0.49   This is the part of Venice that most people never see. This is the Venice that some people call home.

0.50–01.01   Resident Fabrizio Copano says that he lives in the most beautiful city in the world. It's a city that's clean and easy to live in, with a high quality of life.

1.02–1.07   But for some people, Venice has disadvantages, too.

1.08–1.17 P   My son, he doesn't love, uh, live in Venice. I am very sorry.

1.18–1.42   The population of Venice is getting older. Why? Fabrizio says living in Venice is not cheap. Property is particularly expensive, and house prices have increased a lot in recent years. It's especially difficult for young people who want their own place to live. Many of them must move away, which leaves Venice to the tourists.

1.43–2.01   It seems the whole world has come to the Piazza San Marco. The tourists come to experience a city that feels like it's still in the fifteenth century. And some local people say that's the problem.

2.02–2.07 M   Venice did change a lot since I was born.

2.08–2.20   Giovanni dal Missier is one of the younger people who is trying to stay in his home town. During the day, the huge crowds of visitors can make just coming home from work very difficult.

2.21–2.27 M   I get bored with the people, with the tourists. Because there are too much, too many.

2.28–2.42   Jobs are another problem. Do you want to be a gondolier or work with tourists? If you don't, it can be difficult to earn a living here. But some say that the young people who are leaving Venice will soon find that other cities are not so different.

2.43–2.51 P   Florence is very expensive, Rome is very expensive, London, Paris, Vienna.

2.52–3.07   People say that anyone who comes to Venice will fall in love … even if it's only with Venice itself. Giovanni dal Missier knows the feeling. He says that despite all the challenges here, it's difficult to think of living anywhere else.

3.08–3.21 M   I know that it's a very special gift that, for me, it's a gift to live in a city as Venice.

3.22–3.44   Only a few people get to enjoy living in Venice. These days even fewer people are ready to face the challenges of living here. But, for those who stay, it can be a wonderful experience.

3.45–end   Every day they can experience the joy of falling in love with Venice all over again.

4 🎥 [9.1]

- Give students time to read the sentences and try to remember the answers before playing the video again.
- Play the video. Ask students to check their answers. Let students compare answers in pairs before checking with the class.

> ANSWERS
>
> 1 Early morning is the best time for shopping in the outdoor markets.
> 2 the most beautiful city in the world – it's a city that's clean and easy to live in, with a high quality of life
> 3 The population of Venice is getting older.
> 4 Property is particularly expensive.
> 5 'I get bored with the people, with the tourists. Because there are too much, too many.'
> 6 They are a gondolier or work with tourists.
> 7 They are very expensive.

Background information

Piazza San Marco (St Mark's Square in English) is the main public square of Venice.

Language note

Note that a number of speakers in this video are non-native speakers. They make errors typical of Italian speakers. Here are a few:

My son, he doesn't live in Venice (you can't say the noun and the pronoun in the same sentence)

I am very sorry. (the speaker means to say *I am very sad / disappointed about this*)

Venice did change a lot since I was born. (the speaker means to say *has changed*)

there are too much, too many (tourists) (here, the correct phrase is *too many*)

it's a gift to live in a city as Venice. (The speaker means to say *such as Venice*; using the word *gift* is not wrong, but a native speaker would use another word – *privilege*)

After you watch

Vocabulary in context

5 🎥 [9.2]

- Explain that students are going to watch some clips from the video which contain some new words and phrases. They need to choose the correct meaning of the words.

9f Living in Venice

UNIT 9 Holidays

- Play the clips. When each multiple-choice question appears, pause the clip so that students can choose the correct definition. You could let students compare answers in pairs before discussing as a class.

> **ANSWERS**
>
> 1 a   2 c   3 c   4 a   5 b

Videoscript 🎥 9.2

1 Before the light of the sun **fills** the famous Piazza San Marco …
   a shines on every part of
   b shines on part of
   c doesn't shine on

2 … the people of Venice **have** the city **to themselves**.
   a enjoy without any noise
   b share with the tourists
   c don't share with anyone else

3 This is the Venice that some people **call** home.
   a wish was
   b telephone
   c describe as

4 It's a city … with **a high quality of life**.
   a a good lifestyle
   b a high cost of living
   c a large number of people living there

5 … it can be difficult to **earn a living** here.
   a get a job
   b make money from working
   c buy a home

6

- Organize the class into new pairs to discuss the questions.

> **EXAMPLE ANSWER**
>
> My home town has a great city centre near a river – there are cafés and bars and a shopping mall so the quality of life is good. Cars aren't allowed in the centre so it's clean.
>
> Apartments in the centre are expensive, but there are cheaper houses in the suburbs. There aren't enough houses for young people and rents are high.
>
> Young people are moving away because there aren't enough jobs.

7

- Ask students to work in pairs to prepare and practise the conversation. Ask students to decide who is A, and who B, and to read their information and make notes about what to say. Set a time limit of five minutes. Monitor and help with ideas and vocabulary as students prepare.
- Organize the class so that each student is sitting or standing facing their partner. Ask Students B to ask questions and Students A to respond. You could briefly model the activity with a reliable student.
- In feedback, ask some students what they found out about their partner's city.

> **EXAMPLE ANSWERS**
>
> Possible questions to ask:
> *What are the best places to see? / What should I see? / Where should I go?*
> *What are the advantages of / good things about / best things about living here?*
> *What are the disadvantages of / drawbacks of / problems with living here?*

8

- Ask students in each pair to change roles and have a new conversation. Give students preparation time before they speak. Alternatively, you could mix students at this stage so that students have to practise the conversation again with a new partner.
- As students speak, monitor and note down errors to focus on in the feedback to the activity.

160 Unit 9   Holidays

UNIT 9 Holidays

UNIT 9 Review and memory booster ★ CPT extra! Language games

> **Memory Booster activities**
>
> Exercises 2, 6 and 8 are Memory Booster activities. For more information about these activities and how they benefit students, see page 10.

> ***I can ...* tick boxes**
>
> As an alternative to students simply ticking the *I can ...* boxes, you could ask them to give themselves a score from 1 to 4 (1 = not very confident; 4 = very confident) for each language area. If students score 1 or 2 for a language area, refer them to additional practice activities in the Workbook and Grammar summary exercises.

Grammar

1
- Ask students to work individually to complete the conversation with the correct form of the verbs. Let students compare answers in pairs before checking with the class.

> **ANSWERS**
>
> 1 happened 2 arrived 3 didn't have 4 hadn't you booked
> 5 had made 6 got 7 did you do 8 had happened 9 paid

2 »MB
- Ask students to work in pairs to look at the phrases and then reconstruct the story from page 106. Students could take a phrase in turn to share re-telling the story.
- As students speak, monitor their performance. Note down errors students make (particularly with their use of the past perfect and past simple tenses) and, in feedback, write errors on the board and ask students to correct them.
- In feedback, ask individual students to tell a section of the story to build up a class version.

> **ANSWERS**
>
> Students' own answers

3
- Ask students to work individually to choose the correct option. Let students compare answers in pairs before checking with the class.

> **ANSWERS**
>
> 1 visit 2 do they photograph 3 do they usually stay
> 4 shows 5 does a tour cost
> 1 and 4 are subject questions.

Vocabulary

4
- Ask students to work individually to complete the sentences. Let students compare answers in pairs before checking with the class.

> **ANSWERS**
>
> 1 pay; give 2 call; book 3 unpack; go 4 check in; get

5
- **Optional step** Elicit the difference between *-ed* and *-ing* adjectives from the class before they start this activity (*-ed* adjectives describe how you feel, *-ing* adjectives describe a person, place or thing).
- Ask students to work individually to complete the adjectives.

> **ANSWERS**
>
> 1 bored 2 interesting 3 amazing 4 annoying
> 5 exciting 6 frightened

Real life

6 »MB
- Ask students to work in pairs. Tell them to look at the photos and discuss what they can remember about each place.
- Elicit their answers to the questions in feedback and write notes on the board. Which pair could remember the most about each place?

> **ANSWERS**
>
> (from left to right):
> The Tarxien Temples are in Malta. You can see four temples from around 5,000 years ago.
> The Caves of Lascaux are in the south-western region of Dordogne in France. You can see paintings of animals on the cave walls that are over 17,000 years old.
> The Catacombs of Rome are under the ground in Rome, Italy. You can see tunnels and bones there.

7
- Ask students to work individually to put the words in order to make questions and sentences for requesting and suggesting. Let students compare answers in pairs before checking with the class.

> **ANSWERS**
>
> 1 I'm interested in visiting the caves.
> 2 Do you know the opening times?
> 3 Another option is to take a taxi.
> 4 Could you tell me the price?
> 5 How about taking a sightseeing tour?
> 6 How often does the bus go?
> 7 You could buy a family ticket.

8 »MB
- Ask students to work in pairs and to decide who is A and who is B. Read the instructions and check that everyone understands what to do. Before students start, ask them to decide what city they are in and what museum they are going to ask about. It's also a good idea to give students a few minutes' individual preparation time first, before they speak in pairs, so that they can think of questions and suggestions they will need to make during the conversation. Monitor and help as necessary.
- You could invite pairs to act out their conversation for the class.
- **Optional step** Students can change roles and practise the conversation again.

UNIT 9 Review and memory booster

Unit 10 Products

Opener

1
- Ask students to look at the photo and discuss the questions. You could choose to do this activity in open class or ask students to talk in pairs before eliciting a few ideas from the class in feedback.

> **ANSWERS**
> Students' own answers
> The photo shows a man on a bike in Vietnam. He's selling baskets. They're used for fishing, mainly, but also for storing food.

> **Background information**
> **Hung Yen** is a province of Vietnam in south-east Asia. It's in the north near Hanoi.

2 [79] ★ **CPT extra!** Listening activity [after Ex. 2]
- Give students time to read the questions.
- Play the recording. Students listen and answer the questions. Let them compare answers in pairs before checking with the class.

> **ANSWERS**
> 1 at home / in his home, in Hung Yen in Vietnam
> 2 fishermen (for catching fish) and other people (for storing food)
> 3 in the local area

Audioscript [79]

This man and his family make these baskets in his home in Hung Yen in Vietnam. Local fishermen buy them for catching fish, but some people also use them in the home for storing food. Every morning the man puts as many baskets as he can on his bicycle and slowly cycles around the area. As he goes, people stop him to look at the baskets and discuss a price. At the end of the day, he hopes to arrive back home with none left.

3
- Discuss the questions in open class. Elicit answers from different students and find out if students have similar or different preferences. You could prompt students with further questions: *Do you go to local markets? Which shops do you go to when buying food, or clothes, or gifts?*
- **Optional step** Point out the meaning and pronunciation of *product* and *producer* (see Vocabulary and pronunciation note below). Note, however, that the wordbuilding section in Lesson 10a will look at these word forms.

> **ANSWERS**
> Students' own answers

> **Vocabulary and pronunciation note**
> *pro*duct = (countable noun) something that is made for sale
> *pro*ducer = (countable noun) a person, farm or company that grows food

4
- Ask students to work in pairs to talk about the last things they bought, answering the questions as they speak. Provide a model of what to say by describing the last thing you bought.
- In feedback, ask some students to tell the class what they found out about their classmates.

> **ANSWERS**
> Students' own answers

UNIT 10 Products

10a A lesson in logos

Lesson at a glance
- reading: a lesson in logos
- wordbuilding: word forms
- grammar: the passive
- speaking: famous products

Reading

1 [80]
- Ask students to look at the photo. Ask: *What can you see?* Elicit answers (a man on a laptop). Check the meaning of *logo* /ˈləʊgəʊ/ (= a symbol that represents a company or its products, which is often on the product and used in advertising). Ask the questions and elicit possible answers.
- Ask students to read the article briefly to find out if they predicted correctly. Let students compare answers in pairs before checking with the class.
- **Optional step** The reading text is recorded. You could play the recording and ask students to read and listen.

> **ANSWERS**
> It's the Apple logo used on Apple products. The logo on the laptop is upside down.

2
- **Optional step** Pre-teach *upside down* (if students didn't learn the word doing Exercise 1). Do this visually by turning one or two objects over.
- Ask students to read the article again and decide whether the sentences are true (T) or false (F). Let them compare answers in pairs before checking with the class.
- **Optional step** Ask students to justify their answers by quoting the relevant part of the text.

> **ANSWERS**
> 1 T (*An Apple product is recognized by people all over the world*)
> 2 F (*the customer saw the Apple logo on the top of the laptop*)
> 3 F (*when the laptop was open, the logo was upside down*)
> 4 T (*the logo was turned round so that the logo was seen correctly by other people*)
> 5 T (*when you see other people using a product, you are more likely to buy it*)

3 ★ **CPT extra!** Speaking activity [after Ex. 3]
- Discuss the questions as a class. Encourage a variety of students to speak and find out a range of opinions in your class.

> **EXAMPLE ANSWERS**
> 1 It's true. If we see a product being used a lot we remember it, and we think it must be good because it's popular. If famous or cool people use it, we buy it because we want to be like them. If we see it used in a context that is positive (e.g. a trendy café or a smart hotel) that makes us want to buy it.
> 2 Logos are important because they make us remember a product, it's a visual shorthand that helps producers easily promote their product, they're international – so they are recognized the world over.

> **Extra activity**
> Ask students to name some of the most famous logos and to say which ones work best and why. Possible list: Coca Cola (words in red), Audi (rings), Apple (bitten apple shape), Nike (swoosh), Adidas (stripes), Shell Petroleum (shell), McDonald's (M), Volkswagen (VW).

Wordbuilding word forms

4
- Ask students to match the word forms in the box with the definitions (1–5). Elicit the first match as an example to get students started. Let students compare answers in pairs before checking with the class.

> **ANSWERS**
> 1 advertise 2 advert 3 advertiser
> 4 advertisement 5 advertising

5 ★ **CPT extra!** Wordbuilding activity [after Ex. 5]
- Read the wordbuilding box with the class.
- Ask students to complete the sentences with the correct form of *produce* (see Vocabulary and pronunciation note below). Tell them to use a dictionary if necessary. Let students compare answers in pairs before checking with the class.

> **ANSWERS**
> 1 produce 2 products 3 producers
> 4 production 5 productive

Refer students to Workbook page 83 for further practice.

> **Vocabulary and pronunciation note**
> Here are variations on the word *produce* (note the strong stress underlined):
> pro<u>duce</u> = (verb) to make or grow something
> <u>prod</u>uct = (countable noun) something that is made for sale
> pro<u>duc</u>er = (countable noun) a person, farm or company that grows food
> pro<u>duc</u>tion = (noun) the process of making or growing things in large quantities
> pro<u>duc</u>tive = (adjective) a: making or growing a lot; b: working hard and achieving a lot
> Also (but not in this activity):
> <u>prod</u>uce = (uncountable noun) fruit, vegetables and other things that farmers grow

10a A lesson in logos 163

UNIT 10 Products

Pronunciation stress in different word forms

6a [81]
- Play the recording. Students listen and underline the stressed syllables. Let students compare answers in pairs before checking with the class. Write the words on the board and ask individual students to underline the stressed syllable.

> **ANSWERS**
> See Pronunciation note below and Vocabulary and pronunciation note after Exercise 5.

Pronunciation notes

Note how the stress changes on the word *advertisement*:
<u>ad</u>vert (noun), <u>ad</u>vertise (verb), <u>ad</u>vertiser (person), <u>ad</u>vertising (noun), ad<u>ver</u>tisement (noun)

See the notes after Exercise 5 for the strong stress in versions of *produce*.

In English, most two-syllable nouns and adjectives have a strong stress on the first syllable (e.g. <u>pro</u>duct), but most two-syllable verbs have a strong stress on the second syllable (e.g. to pro<u>duce</u>). Sometimes a suffix dictates the stress. For example, nouns ending with *-tion* always have strong stress on the syllable before *-tion* (e.g. pro<u>duc</u>tion) and adjectives ending with *-tive* always have strong stress on the syllable before *-tive* (e.g. pro<u>duc</u>tive).

b [81] ★ **CPT extra!** Pronunciation activity [after Ex. 6b]
- Play the recording again. Students listen and repeat.

Extra activity

Ask students to use dictionaries or the internet to find different word forms based on the following words from the *A lesson in logos* article: *successful, technology, design*

Answers (note the strong stress underlined):

suc<u>ceed</u> (verb); suc<u>cess</u> (noun); suc<u>cess</u>ful (adjective)

tech<u>no</u>logy (noun); techno<u>lo</u>gical (adjective); tech<u>no</u>logist (person)

de<u>sign</u> (verb); de<u>sign</u> (noun); de<u>sign</u>er (person)

Grammar the passive

7
- Ask students to look at the example sentences in the grammar box and answer the questions. You could do this in open class or ask students to work in pairs. Elicit answers (see Grammar note below).

> **ANSWERS**
> a the auxiliary verb *be*
> b In the active sentence, *People* is the subject. In the passive sentence, *an Apple product* is the subject.
> c Because we don't know or aren't interested in who or what does the action.
> d The word *by* introduces who does the action (the agent).

Grammar note

Form

The passive is formed with the auxiliary verb *be* in the correct form + the past participle of the main verb. The tense is dictated by the form of *be* (e.g. past passive: *was done*; present perfect passive: *has been done*).

Students have come across irregular past participles before when they studied the present perfect and the past perfect. However, you may need to revise them. Forms students need to know to do the practice exercises in the Student's Book: *make/made, sell/sold, put/put, buy/bought, build/built, write/written*. Refer students to the irregular verbs list on page 180 of the Student's Book.

Use

We use the passive when the subject is unknown or we want to give prominence to what would be the object of an active sentence (the word that 'receives' the action of the verb). Consequently, typical contexts for passives include describing a process (e.g. *the oil is filtered*), impersonal or formal language (e.g. *helmets must be worn, a CV is enclosed*), and factual or narrative texts in which the doer is not important (e.g. in a text about logos, buildings, or any other inanimate object, the passive is likely to be used a lot).

Refer students to page 174 for further information and practice.

> **ANSWERS TO GRAMMAR SUMMARY EXERCISES**
> 1
> 1 A 2 P 3 P 4 P 5 A
> 2
> 1 was designed 2 is used 3 are drunk
> 4 were produced 5 are written 6 are recognized
> 3
> 1 Amazon was created by Jeff Bezos in 2005.
> 2 The final of the World Cup was watched by over one billion viewers in 2014.
> 3 More books are bought online by readers in the USA than in shops.
> 4 The Taj Mahal in India is visited by up to four million people every year.
> 5 One thousand cars are made by workers in large car factories every day.
> 4
> 1 was normally used 2 was released 3 were sold
> 4 are sold 5 spend 6 are bought 7 found

8
- Ask students to work individually to complete the text. Elicit the first answer as an example to get them started. Let students compare answers in pairs before checking answers with the class.

> **ANSWERS**
> 1 are watched 2 are uploaded 3 was called
> 4 was made 5 was visited 6 is used 7 was sold
> 8 is owned

UNIT 10 Products

9

- *Optional step* Ask students if they know what products the company in the logo makes (*Gap* is a High Street clothes store). Ask them which logo they prefer and why. Then ask them to read the text and check their answers.
- Ask students to read the text and choose the correct options. Let students compare answers in pairs before checking with the class.
- *Optional step* Ask students to say why the passive is or isn't used each time (see Grammar note below).

> **ANSWERS**
>
> 1 are designed 2 are spent 3 are put 4 prefer
> 5 try 6 make 7 are bought 8 is recognized
> 9 decided 10 complained 11 changed 12 was loved

Grammar note

In 4, 5, 6, 9, 10 and 11 the subject of the sentences (*customers*, *companies* or *the company*) all 'do' the action of the verb.

In the other sentences, the passive is used because the subjects (*logos*, *dollars*, *Gap clothes*, *the logo*) don't 'do' the action of the verb – they receive the action of the verb. Note that they are all inanimate. Note the use of *by* + the agent in the last sentence: *its logo was loved by its customers*.

10

- Ask students to complete the sentences with their own personal information.
- *Optional step* Ask students to share their sentences with a partner. Tell students to ask follow-up questions to find out extra information about each sentence from their partner.

> **EXAMPLE ANSWERS**
>
> 1 My bag was made in Italy. (It was designed by Gucci and it cost £100.)
> 2 My favourite film was directed by Ridley Scott. (It's called *Thelma and Louise*. It stars Geena Davis.)
> 3 My home was built in 1975. (It's a city centre apartment and has three bedrooms.)
> 4 My favourite book was written by Leo Tolstoy. (It's called *Anna Karenina* and it's very long!)

Speaking my life

11

- *Optional step* Start by checking that students can form present and past passive questions. Write *It was invented in Japan* and *It is made in China* on the board and ask students to turn the sentences into questions: *Was it invented in Japan? Is it made in China?* Point out that the auxiliary verb *be* inverts with the subject of the passive sentence to form a question.

- Organize the class into pairs. Ask students to read the instructions and to prepare individually by thinking of a famous company for each product. You could help by first brainstorming some examples to get students started.
- When students are ready, tell them to take turns to ask and answer questions. Students can only ask ten questions before they have to guess the company their partner has in mind. Encourage students to ask and answer three or four times. You could mix pairs halfway through so that students get to talk to different people.
- As students speak, monitor and note any errors you hear. At the end, write up short sentences with errors you heard during the pairwork stage and ask pairs or groups to work together to correct them.

> **EXAMPLE ANSWERS**
>
> Here are some examples for each category:
> *a drink*: Coca-Cola, Pepsi, Sprite, Orangina, Starbucks
> *a car*: BMW, Mini, Ferrari, Volkswagen, Land Rover, Rolls Royce, Mercedes
> *clothes*: Gap, Zara, H&M, Marks & Spencer, Levi's, Nike
> *furniture*: IKEA
> *technology*: Apple, IBM, Samsung, Sony

Extra activity

You could turn this into 'ask the teacher'. Let students interview you in a whole class activity to find out what companies you have in mind. Only answer questions that are formed and pronounced correctly.

UNIT 10 Products

10b Product design

Lesson at a glance
- vocabulary: describing design
- listening: product design
- grammar: *used to*
- pronunciation: /s/ or /z/
- speaking: famous products

Vocabulary describing design

1 ★ **CPT extra!** Photo activity [before Ex. 1]
- Ask students to read the sentences and match the adjectives with the definitions. Let students compare answers in pairs before checking with the class.
- **Optional step** Try to get students to work out the meaning of the words from the context first before matching with the definitions.

> **ANSWERS**
> 1 c   2 e   3 a   4 f   5 g   6 d   7 b

> **Vocabulary and pronunciation note**
> As well as providing definitions, provide collocations for the adjectives in this exercise. They help show how the words can be used. Note also the strong stress (shown underlined below). You could drill the words for pronunciation.
> user-*friendly* = User-friendly software is easy to use.
> old-*fashioned* = An old-fashioned hat or dress is one that people used to wear in the past but not now.
> *basic* = If you have basic English, you have a few simple words and phrases.
> up-to-*date* = An up-to-date magazine has all the latest, most recent fashion and celebrity news.
> *fashionable* = A fashionable restaurant is one that everybody wants to go to.
> *classic* = The Mini is a classic car; the mini skirt is a classic item of clothing.
> *useful* = A useful gadget is something that does a job and that you often need (e.g. a can opener).

2
- Ask students to work in pairs to describe the objects in the different places using the words in Exercise 1. In feedback, elicit students' ideas.

> **ANSWERS**
> Students' own answers
> Sony Walkman: old-fashioned, basic, classic

> **Background information**
> The **Sony Walkman** was a portable cassette player which was invented and produced in Japan in the late 1970s. It wasn't discontinued until 2010.

Listening

3 ★ **CPT extra!** Background information [after Ex. 3]
- Ask students to discuss the question in small groups of three or four. Elicit the most popular ways in feedback.

4 [82]
- Explain that students are going to hear about the object in the photo on page 121.
- Play the recording. Students listen and answer the question.

> **ANSWER**
> cassettes

Audioscript [82]

On your way to school or work this morning, you probably listened to music on your headphones. Maybe you downloaded your favourite music onto a device which holds thousands of songs, or played your favourite songs through your phone. These days, listening to music is a personal activity that we all do on our own, but it didn't use to be so easy to get music or to listen when you were on the move. In the seventies, people used to buy music on vinyl records and play them on record players at home.

But in 1979, the Sony Walkman changed the way people listened to music. In the eighties and nineties, you used to see people everywhere with their Sony Walkman, a few cassettes and a set of headphones on. In the end Sony's product was so successful that other companies copied the idea, but Sony's original Walkman was always the most popular. By 1986 the name Walkman was included as a word in the English dictionary.

Looking back, the idea of the Walkman seems so simple, but simplicity was the reason for its success. At the time, some people thought it was a crazy idea; after all, who wanted a music player with no radio, no speakers, no way to record, and small headphones? They were wrong, of course. The Walkman did everything people wanted: it was small enough to carry, it played music, and it was personal.

5 [82]
- Give students time to read the questions and see if they can answer any from memory.
- Play the recording again. Students listen and choose the correct option. Let them compare answers in pairs before checking with the class.

> **ANSWERS**
> 1 b   2 b   3 b

Grammar *used to*

6
- Read the information in the grammar box with the class. Then ask students to say what form of the verb follows *used to*. You could do this in open class or ask students to discuss in pairs.

> **ANSWERS**
> the infinitive

166 Unit 10 Products

UNIT 10 Products

Refer students to page 174 for further information and practice.

ANSWERS TO GRAMMAR SUMMARY EXERCISES

5
1 used to take   2 ✓   3 ✓   4 didn't use to like
5 used to play   6 ✓   7 use to like   8 ✓

6
1 used to listen to music on CDs
2 didn't use to have a smartphone
3 used to buy CDs
4 didn't use to own a car
5 used to use a skateboard
6 didn't use to wear glasses
7 used to be a student
8 didn't use to wear a suit

7
1 didn't use to get up   2 used to go out   3 used to play
4 used to practise   5 didn't use to have   6 used to own
7 did; use to be

7
- Ask students to compare the past simple sentence with the sentences in the grammar box. Ask them to discuss and answer the questions. You could do this in open class or ask students to discuss in pairs.

ANSWERS

1 bought (the past simple)
2 used to buy (note, however, that it is possible to use *bought* – the past simple – with the meaning of past habit)

Grammar note

Form

used to + infinitive: Note how the verb behaves like a regular verb when conjugating: *I didn't use to …; Did you use to …?* Students often forget to remove the 'd'. Some students may feel they can use the 'present' form to talk about habits: ~~I use to get up early these days~~. This isn't possible.

Use

We can use *used to* + infinitive to talk about habits (e.g. *People used to buy music on vinyl records*) and states (e.g. *My mother used to have a Sony Walkman*) that are no longer true.

The past simple can always be used instead of *used to*. However, we can't use *used to* for a single action:

I lived in Canada when I was a boy. / I used to live in Canada when I was a boy.

Once, I went to Vancouver. / ~~*Once, I used to go to Vancouver.*~~

Here are some Concept Check Questions (CCQs) you could use to check the rules above (see Teacher development below):

People used to buy music on vinyl records.

Did they buy music on vinyl in the past? (Yes)

Do they buy music on vinyl now? (No)

Did they buy music on vinyl once or many times? (Many times)

Teacher development

Using Concept Check Questions

Using Concept Check Questions (CCQs) to check meaning is a useful skill. They can be hard to construct as they have to clarify function and meaning using simple language while not using the target language itself.

Here are some tips for making good concept questions (notice how they apply to the example CCQs in the Grammar note above):

- Start with a simply stated grammar rule and turn it into a question. *Yes/no* questions, *either/or* questions and simple *Wh-* questions are particularly effective.
- Make sure no difficult language is required to answer the question.
- Avoid using the new (target) grammar in your questions.

Thinking of good questions helps you, the teacher, understand *complexities* of form, function and meaning better, and using them in class gets you to practise grading your language.

8
- Ask students to work individually to underline the correct option. Let students compare answers in pairs before checking with the class.

ANSWERS

1 used to   2 went   3 used to play
4 didn't use to   5 didn't learn
6 didn't use to take   7 use   8 move

Grammar note

In feedback, ask students to explain why they have chosen *used to* (or not).

1, 4 and 7 test form

2, 5 and 8 have to use the past simple because they describe or refer to a single action at a specific time in the past

3 and 6 describe a past habit or state that is no longer true – note that while the context means that using *used to* + infinitive is best here, it is not wrong to use the past simple

---

Pronunciation /s/ or /z/

9a [83]
- Play the recording. Students listen and notice the pronunciation. In feedback, ask the question and elicit the pronunciation rule.

ANSWERS

In the sentences, *used to* and *didn't use to* have the sound /s/. The verb *use*, in *I use*, has the sound /z/. (See Vocabulary and pronunciation note below).

10b **Product design** 167

UNIT 10 Products

Vocabulary and pronunciation note

Used to (in *I used to buy CDs*) and *use to* (in *I didn't use to buy records*) share the same pronunciation: /juːstə/. Notice how the 'd' is not pronounced, the 's' is pronounced /s/ and the 'o' in *to* is unstressed. The verb *use* (in *I use my mobile phone*) has a different pronunciation: /juːz/. It also has a different meaning – it means take, hold or utilize something to achieve something.

b 💿 [83]

- Play the recording again. Students listen and repeat.

10

- Ask students to work individually to complete the sentences with *used to*, *didn't use to* or *did you use to* and the verb given. Elicit the first answer as an example to get students started. Let students compare answers in pairs before checking with the class.

> ANSWERS
> 1 used to spend   2 didn't use to eat
> 3 Did you use to have   4 used to play
> 5 didn't use to earn   6 Did you use to write

Extra activity

Ask students to practise saying the sentences in pairs. Tell them to pay attention to how the forms are pronounced.

Speaking *my life*
11

- **Optional step** Start by writing three sentences using *used to* about yourself on the board (e.g. *I used to have a beard; I used to live in New York; I used to live in a caravan*). Tell the class that two sentences are true and one false. Then get students to ask you *Did you use to …?* questions. Answer with a straight face and add an extra piece of information. Ask the class to guess which sentence is false – can they spot when you are lying?

- Give students three or four minutes to prepare their five sentences and write questions. Monitor and help students with ideas and vocabulary.

> EXAMPLE ANSWERS
> Here are possible sentences:
> I used to have long hair / short hair / blond hair / a beard / a moustache.
> I used to live in the country / with my parents / abroad.
> I used to play football / tennis / ice hockey.
> I used to go to dance classes / yoga classes / judo classes.

12 ★ CPT extra! Research project [after Ex. 12]

- Organize the class into pairs. Ask them to take turns to ask and answer their questions. Monitor and notice how well students use the new form. Note any errors which you could write on the board at the end for students to correct.

Extra activity

Write the following list of topics on the board:

music   sport   hobbies   travel   clothes   communication

Organize the class into pairs and ask them to choose a topic and prepare a questionnaire with five questions to ask someone twenty years or more older than they are.

Ask students to find an older person and interview them for homework. In the next lesson, ask students to present their findings. An example question for students to ask: *How did you use to listen to music? Did you buy records or CDs?*

UNIT 10 Products

10c Is stuff winning?

Lesson at a glance
- reading: is stuff winning?
- critical thinking: fact or opinion?
- speaking: using less stuff

Reading

1 ★ **CPT extra!** Lead-in activity [before Ex. 1]
- **Optional step** Start by asking what the title refers to. *Is stuff winning?* could mean many things. Encourage students to guess. Ask them what it means later in the lesson after they have read the article.
- Ask students to read the short conversation and answer the questions. Let students compare answers in pairs before checking with the class.

> **ANSWERS**
> 1 It's happening in a flat or house. The two people probably live in the same house.
> 2 It could be between flatmates, a couple or a parent and teenage or adult child. A likely scenario might be a couple – one has moved into the other's apartment and is complaining that their partner doesn't throw things away.

2
- Ask students to find *stuff* and *thing* in the conversation and to say which is countable. They can work this out from context. Check the meaning, use and pronunciation of the words in feedback (see Vocabulary note below).

> **ANSWERS**
> *Thing* is countable (e.g. two things) and *stuff* is uncountable (e.g. some stuff).

Vocabulary note

stuff /stʌf/ = used to refer to anything (e.g. matter, material, articles) in an indeterminate way. When using *stuff*, we think about what we are referring to not as individual items but as a collective, uncountable mass.

things /θɪŋz/ = used to refer to individual items – we see them as individual, countable things.

We use these words when we don't know what to call things, or don't want to use that word (perhaps because we've already used the word or because it's clear to the listener what we're referring to). In the conversation, the speakers use *stuff* and *things* interchangeably and they use them because what they're referring to is a range of lots of different things that are hard to describe specifically.

3
- **Optional step** Ask students to describe what they can see in the photo.
- Discuss the questions about the photo with the class. Find out which students are tidy. Use the opportunity to check key words, e.g. *tidy* (= organized, in good order) and *untidy* (= disorganized, not in order).

4 🔘 [84]
- Ask students to read the article and choose the best summarizing sentence. Let students compare their answers in pairs before checking with the class.
- **Optional step** The reading text is recorded. You could play the recording and ask students to read and listen.

> **ANSWER**
> c

5 ★ **CPT extra!** Vocabulary activity [after Ex. 5]
- Read the sentences with the class. Check *avoid* + *-ing* (= stop yourself from doing something), *offline* (= not online – not connected to the internet) and *minimalist* (= when you want things simple – with very few objects or possessions).
- Ask students to read the article again and decide individually where in the text the sentences go (see Teacher development below). Let students compare their answers in pairs before checking as a class.
- **Optional step** If this activity is difficult for your class or if this is the first time they have done this type of activity, see the notes below for ideas.

> **ANSWERS**
> 1 e 2 b 3 d 4 a 5 c

Teacher development

Missing sentences in a text

Trying to work out where missing sentences go in a text is a common exam technique. To do it well, students need a little training. Here are some suggestions:

- Ask students to read the first paragraph and predict what information might be in the missing sentence at the end. Then ask students to read the missing sentences provided and decide which one is closest to what they expected from a missing sentence.
- Ask students to underline key words in the first missing sentence provided. Then ask them to look at the last sentence in each paragraph. Ask if they see any similarities of lexis. For example, in the first paragraph, there is a match between 'missed three calls' and 'need to reply to a few text messages'. In the third paragraph, there is a match between 'on day three, (throw out) three objects' and 'by the end of the month, you have thrown away lots of your stuff'.
- Ask students to notice how linking words provide clues. For example, the word 'Then' is used to introduce the sentence at the end of the third paragraph, and 'By the end of the month' is used in the missing sentence. It suggests a sequence.

10c Is stuff winning? 169

UNIT 10 Products

Extra activity

There's an interesting set of phrases and phrasal verbs in this article connected to the topic. Ask students to find and underline the phrases below in the article. Then ask students to guess the meaning from context before providing definitions.

get rid of (something) = sell it, throw it away or destroy it because you don't want it

put on a pile of (something) = place it at the top (e.g. a pile of books – one on top of the other)

put away (something) = place it in the correct place (e.g. clothes in a cupboard, books on a shelf)

pick up (something) = use your hands to move it from the floor

throw out/away (something) = put it in the rubbish

give away (something) = give it to another person because you don't want it

Note that all these phrasal verbs are separable (e.g. *pick it up, give them away*). The phrase *get rid of* isn't separable.

Critical thinking fact or opinion?

6
- Ask students to read the sentences and decide whether they are facts or opinions. Let them compare and discuss answers in pairs before checking with the class.

ANSWERS

1 a 2 b 3 a 4 c 5 c 6 b

7
- Ask students to work in pairs to find and underline the words that helped them answer the questions in Exercise 6.
- In feedback, ask pairs to give reasons for their answers.

ANSWERS

1 Numbers suggest factual information: *243 unread emails; 52 visitors*
2 Point out that phrases like *We should also …* suggest a personal opinion, and phrases like *Some people think …* and *People said …* report other people's opinions. In sentence 2, adjectives like *good* and *excellent* suggest a personal point of view – these are subjective adjectives.

8
- Ask students to look at the article again and decide which of the three statements (a–c) they agree with. There is no definitive answer so let students work in pairs to discuss their view before having a whole class feedback. Ask students to argue and justify their view by referring to the text.

ANSWERS

c is the most likely answer. There's a lot of reference to factual information: numbers (*243 unread emails*), surveys (*27% of them said they were bored*). But there are also many examples of the writer's views (*I know that I want less stuff in my life*).

Speaking my life

9
- Organize the class into pairs. Ask students to read the task and the list of points to include carefully before planning their presentation.
- **Optional step** Provide support for students by breaking the task into stages. Ask students to research the article for ideas first. Then ask them to add their own opinions in note form. Ask pairs to decide what information to include under each heading before writing the presentation. Introduce a set of useful phrases (written on the board) which students could use in their presentation (see Vocabulary note below). Set a time limit of ten minutes.

Vocabulary note

Here are prompts to write on the board for students to use:

Today we'd like to talk to you about …
We're going to talk about …
The main problem with … is that …
The reason why people … is that …
One solution is to … We could also …

10
- Ask each pair to work with another pair. If possible, ask students to stand up, move round, and find space in the classroom to sit in their new group of four.
- Pairs take turns to give their presentations. As students speak, listen carefully and note any errors to focus on in feedback at the end.

Extra activity

Ask students to imagine what their bedroom is like right now. Tell them to describe it to their partner in detail, saying what's in it and where exactly those things are. At the end, ask students how tidy they think their partners are.

170 Unit 10 Products

UNIT 10 Products

10d Website design

> **Lesson at a glance**
> - vocabulary: websites
> - real life: giving your opinion

Vocabulary websites

1 ★ **CPT extra!** Web research [after Ex. 1]
- Ask students to work individually to complete the sentences with the words in the box. Elicit the first answer as an example to get them started. Let students compare answers in pairs before checking with the class.

> **ANSWERS**
> 1 home 2 links 3 contact 4 about us
> 5 adverts 6 content 7 search

> **Extra activity**
>
> Ask students to research a website and find other icons or boxes that are used to direct people to various pages on the site, e.g. *Help, Jobs, History, Product Information*. Ask students to explain what these various links are for. Choose webpages useful for your students (e.g. your school's website). Set this activity in class if your students have internet access or for homework otherwise.

2
- Ask students to discuss the questions in small groups of three or four. In feedback, elicit different suggestions.
- **Optional step** Use the opportunity to recommend websites useful for your students. For example, a good online dictionary website, a good site to research grammar, and websites connected with this course (e.g. www.ngllife.com).

> **ANSWERS**
> 1 People often use search engines such as Google to search for information. They look at online encyclopaedias such as Wikipedia.
> People use music websites such as Spotify or online radio stations.
> There are many translation websites (e.g. Google translate) and online dictionaries.
> There are many websites. People use eBay to buy almost anything, Amazon for books.
> Well-known news websites in English include CNN and Huffington Post in the US and BBC News and Mail Online in the UK.
> 2 Student's own answers
> 3 Reasons why one website might be better than another may include: it's easy to navigate around, it holds a lot of content, it's reliable, it's not biased and/or it reflects my views (news websites), it has interesting graphics, it isn't slow.

Real life giving your opinion

3 🎵 [85]
- Give students time to read the situation and topics carefully.
- **Optional step** Before playing the recording, ask students to predict what they think Sergio and Rachel should include on their record shop website.
- Play the recording. Students listen and tick the topics discussed. Let them compare their answers in pairs before checking with the class.

> **ANSWERS**
> Students should tick: 1, 2, 3, 4 and 7

Audioscript 🎵 [85]

S = Sergio, **R** = Rachel

S: So, how's it going? Did you find out about the website name?
R: Yes, I've checked it and no one else has the website name RetakeRecords.com.
S: Great. I think we should buy it today. Oh, and I also started to design the home page. Let me show you. What do you think?
R: Er, it's OK. But there's a lot of text.
S: Sure, but I think people want to know about us.
R: I see what you mean, but we can have a photo of the shop at the top, and then maybe a contact page with more information. In my opinion, it's more important that people see the records for sale as soon as they arrive on the home page. Also, it needs a search box so they can find the record they want.
S: Yes, you're right.
R: Lots of other websites have an 'About us' page. Maybe you could put the text there?
S: Good idea. Also, I think we could have a video of the shop on the page with both of us talking about who we are and what we do.
R: Yes, I agree. A video would be nice there. Customers will like it because it's personal. Maybe they can also contact us on that page.
S: I'm not sure about that. Regular customers will want to call or email us directly so I think we need a simple contact page and put information on the 'About us' page.

4 🎵 [85]
- Ask students to read the sentences from the conversation, and try to remember the missing words.
- Play the recording again. Students listen and complete the sentences. Let students compare their answers in pairs, but don't confirm answers at this stage.

> **ANSWERS**
> See Exercise 5

10d Website design 171

UNIT 10 Products

5
- Ask students to compare their completed dialogue with the expressions in the box in order to check and correct their answers.

> **ANSWERS**
> 1 should 2 think 3 mean 4 opinion
> 5 right 6 Maybe; idea 7 agree 8 sure

> **Extra activity**
> Ask students to practise the conversation in pairs. Tell them that they can find audioscript 85 on page 188 of the Student's Book.

6
- Organize the class into groups of four or five. Tell students to read the task and the prompt questions. Then brainstorm ideas for websites (e.g. selling second-hand cars, free English lessons, home-made biscuits). Encourage students to be creative and use their own idea.
- Once students have an idea, ask them to discuss the questions, and plan a presentation. Set a ten-minute time limit. Monitor and help with ideas and vocabulary. Encourage students to use expressions for discussing opinions.
- **Optional step** To prompt students to use the new expressions, choose six to eight and write them on the board. Tell students that everybody has to use at least three of the expressions as they speak. Monitor and notice who uses the expressions well. In feedback, ask students whether they managed to use at least three expressions.

7
- When groups are ready, ask them to take turns to present their new website to the class. Monitor their performance, paying particular attention to how well they use and pronounce the expressions in the box.
- **Optional step** Instead of having class presentations by each group, ask students to form new groups with one student from each of the original groups in each of the new groups. That way students can make presentations to the students in their new group.

10e A review

> **Lesson at a glance**
> - writing: a review
> - writing skill: giving your opinion

Writing a review

1
- **Optional step** Ask students to look at the layout of the text. Ask: *What type of text is it? Where do you see this?* Establish that it is an online review, perhaps from a blog.
- Ask students to read the review and answer the questions. Let students compare their answers in pairs before checking with the class.

> **ANSWERS**
> 1 It's a photo-sharing website – a place for photographers to show photos.
> 2 easy to find photographs; organized into different categories; can comment on each other's photos; professional photographer is invited to make comments; you learn a lot from this person's comments
> 3 too much advertising
> 4 useful website for anyone who loves taking photographs and communicating with other people about them

Writing skill giving your opinion

2a
- Ask students to read the review again and write down useful phrases under each category. Elicit one or two phrases as an example to get students started. Let them compare their answers in pairs before checking with the class.

> **ANSWERS**
> a give positive opinions:
> One of my favourite (websites) is …
> It's a great place for … to …
> The site has quite a few good features.
> Firstly, it's easy to …
> Another good point is that (you can) …
> b give negative opinions:
> The only problem is that (it) …
> it's annoying when …
> c sum up the writer's main opinion:
> On the whole, …

b
- Ask students to work individually to match the phrases with the uses. Let students compare their answers in pairs before checking with the class.

> **ANSWERS**
> 1 a 2 c 3 b 4 a 5 c

172 Unit 10 Products

UNIT 10 Products

Vocabulary note

Notice the way cleft sentences are used to give positive and negative opinions. They are used to emphasize the fact that the writer is introducing a positive or negative opinion. Compare these two sentences:

Too much advertising is the only problem.

The only problem is that *it has too much advertising.*

At this level, these are best learned as fixed expressions. Structurally, they all follow the same form:

One big advantage is that + clause

Another bad point is that + clause

As well as *On the whole*, *In general* and *To sum up*, we can also conclude with the expressions *To conclude* and *In conclusion*.

Note that the online review revises giving opinions language from Lesson 10d (e.g. *In my opinion*).

3

- Read the instructions with the class and check that everyone understands what to do.
- **Optional step** Brainstorm websites students often use and write a few ideas on the board. Make sure everybody can think of something to write about.
- Once students have an idea, tell them to plan their review in note form, using the questions to help.
- As students complete their notes, monitor and be prepared to help with ideas and vocabulary.

4

- Ask students to write their reviews, using their notes and the useful phrases from Exercise 2. Encourage students to write on a clean piece of paper. You could hand out blank sheets or ask students to go to an empty page in their notebook. They will have to pass on their work in the next stage.
- **Optional step** If you have the technology in the classroom, ask students to write their reviews on a computer or online.

5 ★ CPT extra! Writing activity [after Ex. 5]

- Organize the class into pairs (or small groups if you prefer). Students exchange or pass round their reviews. Encourage students to give feedback on the purpose and structure of each reader's review using the bulleted list as a guide for their feedback.
- **Optional step** Ask students to revise or rewrite their review (in class or for homework) based on the feedback of their classmates.

Extra activity

If you ask students to write and send their reviews to you online, you can place them on the class website for students to comment on.

10f Wind turbines

Before you watch

1 ★ CPT extra! Photo activity [after Ex. 1]

- Look at the photo with the class. You could ask students to work in pairs or small groups to discuss the questions. Use the photo to pre-teach interesting or key words: *wind, wind turbine, electricity*. Elicit their answers in feedback.

ANSWERS

1 Students' own answers.
2 Wind turbines operate on a simple principle: the energy in the wind turns two or three propeller-like blades around a rotor. The rotor is connected to the main shaft, which spins a generator to create electricity.

Key vocabulary

2

- **Optional step** Get students to work out the meaning of the words from context first. Look at sentence 1 as an example with the class. Elicit that *flat* is an adjective that describes *land*. Then ask students to guess the meanings of the other words in bold.
- Ask students to work individually to match the words with the definitions. Let students compare answers with a partner before checking with the class.
- **Optional step** Give students the opportunity to practise recognizing and producing these key words before they hear them in continuous speech on the video. You could say the words and ask students to repeat. Note the strongly stressed syllable: with*stand*, *national* grid, be*tween*.

ANSWERS

1 e 2 a 3 c 4 b 5 g 6 d 7 f

Vocabulary note

pay off a loan / debt / mortgage = used to say that you complete the payments on the money you borrowed

withstand = used to say that something is strong enough not to fall or fail (e.g. *The sea wall withstood the power of the sea – it didn't break*; but also, *The president withstood pressure to call an election.*)

The *National Grid* is the high-voltage electric power transmission network in Great Britain, connecting power stations and major substations and ensuring that electricity generated anywhere in England, Scotland and Wales can be used to satisfy demand elsewhere.

Anywhere between $110 and $200 literally means any price more than $110 but less than $200.

It weighs a ton = often used to describe something that's very heavy (rather than exactly one ton) – actually, a ton is about 907 kilos (a metric ton or tonne is 1,000 kilos)

UNIT 10 Products

While you watch

3 🎥 [10.1]
- Give students time to read the information (1–8).
- Play the video. Students watch and match the numbers and years with the information. Let students compare answers with a partner before checking with the class.

> **ANSWERS**
> 1 b   2 g   3 c   4 d   5 h   6 a   7 f   8 e

Videoscript 🎥 10.1

T = Jim Tirevold, **G** = Tim Grieves, **I** = Interviewer, **Gd** = Charles Goodman, **B** = Jan Bolluyt

0.00–0.27   Around the town of Spirit Lake in Iowa, the land is very flat, and the wind blows across it a lot of the time. The schools in the area have two wind turbines. These turbines help the schools save energy – and money.

0.28–0.34   T   The little turbine, since it's been paid off, has saved the district $81,530.

0.35–0.59   The first wind turbine was built in Spirit Lake in 1993. It was one of the first wind turbines in the USA to provide energy to schools. The first turbine was very effective so a second turbine was built. Together, the two turbines save the schools about $140,000 a year in energy costs. Saving this money means the schools can pay for more teachers.

1.00–1.06   G   Well, it will mean anywhere from two to three teachers, which is very important at a time right now.

1.07–1.10   On the inside, you can see how big the turbines are.

1.11–1.14   T   This turbine stands 180 feet to the hub height.

1.15–1.19   The turbines have to be very strong. They are fixed deep into the ground with metal rods so they won't fall over.

1.20–1.26   I   What type of a wind could this withstand?

T   It's rated to stand up to 130 mile an hour winds.

1.27–2.33   Spirit Lake has lots of strong winds and so energy is produced by the wind turbines when they turn. Even when there isn't much wind, the turbines can still turn. The smaller turbine sends electricity directly to the school. The larger turbine sends its power to the local electricity grid and it is used by the power company. They pay the school money for the extra energy.

The local schools aren't the only ones who make money from the wind turbines. In the countryside south of the Spirit Lake schools, there are more turbines on the local farms. In this area, 65 farmers produce and sell energy from the wind in the same way that they sell their crops. Farmer Charles Goodman thinks he'll make an extra $6,000 a year from the three turbines on his farm.

2.34–2.41   I   So when you see the wind kicking pretty good like it is, that's money in your pocket, right?

Gd   I smile all the time when the wind's blowing like this.

2.42–2.57   This part of the countryside now has 257 wind turbines. These turbines provide enough energy for a small city with about 70,000 homes!

2.58–3.07   The turbines are also good for teaching the students about how energy works.

3.08–3.17   The local physics teacher Jan Bolluyt explains why it's useful in class.

3.18–3.22   B   When I talk about force, and energy and electricity, they see that we're producing it right here.

3.23–3.32   Students at the school write down information about the wind turbines and they calculate how much energy they save and why it's good for the environment.

3.33–3.44   B   We're talking tons of carbon dioxide. We're talking tons of sulphur dioxide. We're talking hundreds of trees. So, you know, it's not just a small thing.

3.45–end   So in Spirit Lake, people are using wind power to earn money and to learn about saving the environment.

4 🎥 [10.1]
- Give students time to read the questions.
- Play the video again. Students watch and answer the questions. Let students compare answers with a partner before checking with the class.

> **ANSWERS**
> 1 Because the first turbine was so effective.
> 2 They are fixed deep into the ground with metal rods.
> 3 The smaller turbine sends electricity to the school. The larger turbine sends its power to the local electricity grid.
> 4 The farmers sell crops as well as the energy from their wind turbines.
> 5 Because he's earning money from the wind.
> 6 They're good for teaching students about how energy works.
> 7 When he's teaching his students about force, energy and electricity, they can see they are producing electricity using the wind turbines, and the students also learn about saving the environment.

After you watch

Vocabulary in context

5 🎥 [10.2] ★ **CPT extra!** Speaking activity [after Ex. 5]
- Explain that students are going to watch some clips from the video which contain some new words and phrases. They need to choose the correct word to complete the sentences.
- Play the clips. When each multiple-choice question appears, pause the clip so that students can choose the correct word. You could let students compare answers in pairs before checking with the class.

> **ANSWERS**
> 1 b   2 c   3 a   4 c   5 c

Videoscript 🎥 10.2

1 The land is very flat, and the wind ____ across it a lot of the time.
   a travels
   b blows
   c runs

UNIT 10 Products

2 Even when there isn't much wind, the turbines can still ____ .
   a make
   b switch
   c turn

3 Charles Goodman thinks he'll ____ an extra $6,000 a year from the three turbines on his farm.
   a make
   b do
   c spend

4 These turbines ____ enough energy for a small city with about 70,000 homes!
   a turn
   b take
   c provide

5 People are using wind power to ____ money and to learn about saving the environment.
   a borrow
   b spend
   c earn

6

- Ask students to work in pairs to prepare a list of reasons. You could let students look in the videoscript to help them find reasons. (http://www.ngllife.com/content/videoscripts-word).

> **EXAMPLE ANSWERS**
>
> Sample notes:
>
> They help the schools save energy – and money.
>
> The first turbine was very effective (saved the district $81,530) so a second turbine was built. Together, the two turbines save the schools about $140,000 a year in energy costs. Saving this money means the schools can pay for more teachers.
>
> 65 farmers produce and sell energy from the wind in the same way that they sell their crops.
>
> The turbines are also good for teaching the students about how energy works.
>
> In Spirit Lake, people are using wind power to earn money and to learn about saving the environment.

7

- Ask students in their pairs to use the list of reasons they prepared in Exercise 6 to put together a presentation. As students prepare, go round and help with ideas and vocabulary.
- **Optional step** Write the following useful phrases on the board which students could use to organize their presentations:
  Firstly, we'd like to explain how …
  Secondly, we're going to talk about …
  Now, we'd like to give reasons why …
  Turbines are useful because …
  The advantages of a turbine are that …
  To sum up, …

8

- Organize students into groups of four by matching each pair with another pair. Pairs take turns to give their presentations. In feedback, ask students to say whether their reasons for building wind turbines were similar or different.

10f Wind turbines 175

UNIT 10 Products

UNIT 10 Review and memory booster ★ CPT extra! Language games

> **Memory Booster activities**
>
> Exercises 2, 5 and 8 are Memory Booster activities. For more information about these activities and how they benefit students, see page 10.

> **I can ... tick boxes**
>
> As an alternative to students simply ticking the *I can ...* boxes, you could ask them to give themselves a score from 1 to 4 (1 = not very confident; 4 = very confident) for each language area. If students score 1 or 2 for a language area, refer them to additional practice activities in the Workbook and Grammar summary exercises.

Grammar
1
- Ask students to work individually to choose the correct options. Let them compare answers in pairs before checking with the class.

> **ANSWERS**
> 1 is sold   2 didn't use   3 was started   4 used to
> 5 produced   6 are made   7 was finished   8 used to buy
> 9 is built   10 used to   11 built

2 >> MB
- Ask students to look back at the text in Exercise 1 and answer the questions. Let them compare answers in pairs before checking with the class.

> **ANSWERS**
> 1 1, 3, 6, 7 and 9 are passive verb forms
> 2 The focus is on the action, not the person doing the action.

Vocabulary
3
- Ask students to work individually to complete the table with the different parts of speech.

> **ANSWERS**
> advertisement / advert (noun); advertiser (person)
> productive (adjective), produce / production (noun), producer (person)

4
- Ask students to work individually to reorder the letters to make adjectives about products.

> **ANSWERS**
> 1 user-friendly   2 basic   3 fashionable   4 classic   5 useful
> 6 old-fashioned   7 up-to-date

5 >> MB
- **Optional step** Give students a few minutes to look through the unit to find all the products and brands they looked at. Write a list on the board.
- Ask students to work in pairs to choose five of the products or brands and to match adjectives from Exercise 4 to them.
- Elicit students' answers in feedback.

> **ANSWERS**
> Students' own answers

6
- Ask students to work individually to match the parts of the website to the descriptions.

> **ANSWERS**
> 1 e   2 b   3 d   4 c   5 a

Real life
7
- Ask students to work individually to complete the missing words in the dialogue.

> **ANSWERS**
> 1 What do you think   5 Maybe (we) could
> 2 In my opinion   6 don't agree
> 3 disagree   7 you're right
> 4 see what you mean   8 Great idea

8 >> MB
- Ask students to work individually to categorize the phrases from Exercise 7.

> **ANSWERS**
> Asking for an opinion:
> What do you think ...?
>
> Giving an opinion:
> In my opinion ...
>
> Agreeing and disagreeing:
> I disagree.
> I see what you mean.
> No, I don't agree.
> Yes, you're right.
> Great idea.
>
> Making suggestions:
> Maybe we could ...?

176 Unit 10 Products

Unit 11 History

Opener

1
- Look at the photo and caption with the class. Ask students to discuss the questions. You could do this activity in open class or ask students to talk in pairs before eliciting ideas from the class in feedback.
- **Optional step** Use the opportunity to check key words from the listening, e.g. *hut* (= here, a small, temporary house), *freezing* (= very cold - below zero) and *contents* (= things that are inside something).

> **ANSWERS**
> Students' own answers
> (Note that the answers are provided in Exercise 2.)

2 [86] ★ **CPT extra!** Vocabulary activity [before Ex. 2]
- **Optional step** Start by asking students to read the questions and to predict the answers.
- Play the recording. Students listen and answer the questions. Let them compare answers in pairs before checking with the class.

> **ANSWERS**
> 1 food (butter, biscuits, tins of meat), equipment, soap, medicine bottles
> 2 It tells us a lot about Scott, but also about our own past.
> 3 A place that has not changed for a long time, with lots of things that can tell us about a time in the past.

Audioscript [86]

Just over one hundred years ago, the British explorer Captain Robert Falcon Scott died with his team of men in the snow and ice of Antarctica. He had reached the South Pole, but never returned to this hut, which was the starting point for his expedition. Now the hut is falling down under the snow, and we would like to save it – not just because of its connection to Scott, though this of course is important. Actually, we are more interested in what you find inside the hut. Because of the freezing temperatures in this part of the world, the hut has become a time capsule. There are items of food, such as butter, biscuits and tins of meat, which are one hundred years old. The ice has preserved them all. There are even some of Scott's old possessions and equipment, and things like soap and medicine bottles. When you go inside the hut, it's almost as if he has only just left it. I think we need to look after it because it tells us so much about Scott, but also about our own past.

> **Vocabulary note**
> *explorer* = person who travels to new and difficult to find places
> *expedition* = a long, organized journey to a new or dangerous place
> *preserved* = stopped from changing
> *possessions* = things you have/own
> *equipment* = things people need and use for particular purposes

> **Background information**
> **Captain Robert Falcon Scott** (1868–1912) led a party of five to the South Pole. They hoped to be the first people to reach the Pole, but they got there on 17th January 1912, four weeks after Roald Amundsen's Norwegian expedition. Scott's heroism was celebrated in the UK at the time, and his brave expedition is still remembered in the UK, even though it was unsuccessful and resulted in their deaths.

3
- **Optional step** Start by asking students if they have ever buried a time capsule. The custom of burying or hiding 'time capsules' for people to find in the future is well-established (see Background information below).
- Ask students to work in groups of four or five to decide on a time capsule of five objects, using the ideas in the box to help them. Set a time limit of five to ten minutes (depending on how long you have in your lesson) and tell students in each group that they should all agree on the list.

> **ANSWERS**
> Students' own answers

4
- Ask different groups to present their lists. You could have a class vote at the end to decide on which list is best, or you could get students to agree on a class list, drawing on the best ideas from each presentation.

> **Background information**
> Here are two famous American **time capsules**:
> - A box containing newspapers, official records, coins, a silver plate and a copper medal was buried in Boston in 1795 and opened in 2014.
> - Filled with photographs and letters from residents describing life in Detroit in 1900, the Detroit Century Box was formally opened in 2000.

| UNIT 11 | History |

11a The history of video gaming

Lesson at a glance
- reading: the history of video gaming
- wordbuilding: verb + preposition
- grammar: reported speech
- listening: reporting a conversation
- speaking: talking about games

Reading

1 ★ **CPT extra!** Lead-in activity [before Ex. 1]
- Ask students to work in pairs to look at the photo and discuss the questions. Elicit ideas in feedback, but don't confirm the answers at this stage – they are revealed in the text that follows.

ANSWERS
1 Two people (perhaps a mother and son) are playing an old-fashioned video game. You can see a TV screen and a handset device.
2 In the 1970s
3 It's black and white, two-dimensional, has simple line graphics, is connected to the handset by a lead and is used on a TV set not a computer.

Background information

The photo shows a mother and son playing **Pong**, a game that was released for computer arcades in 1972, and for use in the home in 1975. It was one of the earliest video games, and was a simple ping pong (table tennis) game. The lines on the screen are 'bats' and the dot is the ping pong ball that you hit back and forwards.

2 💿 [87]
- Ask students to read the timeline of video gaming and to answer the questions. Let students compare answers in pairs before checking answers with the class.
- **Optional step** The reading text is recorded. You could play the recording and ask students to read and listen.

ANSWERS
1 Pong, Space Invaders, Tetris, Wii
2 Students' own answers
3 Students' own answers (These games are still played today, especially by people nostalgic for old-style games.)

3
- Ask students to read the article again and choose true or false. Let them compare their answers in pairs before checking with the class.
- **Optional step** In feedback, ask students to justify answers by referring to relevant sections of the article.

ANSWERS
1 T (*People said that they had never seen anything like it before.*)
2 T (*It was one of the first home video games that you played against another person for points.*)
3 F (*everyone was talking about it at the time – people of all ages said they loved it*)
4 F (*It had lots of different games*)
5 T (*Many gamers said they played Tetris for hours and weren't able to stop!*)
6 T (*the games were active … popular with a new group of people – the over fifties*)

Background information

Japanese company **Nintendo** introduced Game Boy (in 1989) and Wii (in 2006). They both involve using handheld consoles to play different games. Microsoft's Xbox and Sony's PlayStation are rivals.

Space Invaders was a video arcade game released in 1978 and originally manufactured and sold by Taito in Japan. It involves shooting down hordes of alien icons as they march back and forth across a screen.

Tetris (released in 1974) is a tile-matching puzzle video game, designed by Russian game designer Alexey Pajitnov.

Wordbuilding verb + preposition

4 ★ **CPT extra!** Wordbuilding activity [after Ex. 4]
- Read the information in the wordbuilding box with the class and elicit any verb + preposition combinations students can think of (e.g. *ask for, help with, work with*).
- Ask students to complete the questions with the prepositions. Elicit the first answer to get students started. Let students compare answers in pairs before checking as a class.

ANSWERS
1 with   2 about   3 for   4 on   5 with   6 with

Refer students to page 91 in the Workbook for further practice

Vocabulary note

Students often confuse phrasal verbs with verb + preposition.
- In a **phrasal verb**, the particle is an adverb (i.e. it describes the verb). A phrasal verb can be transitive (i.e. it takes an object) or intransitive (i.e. it takes no object). If it is transitive, it may also be separable. Some phrasal verbs have non-literal meanings.
- In a **verb + preposition**, the preposition introduces the following noun or phrase (it doesn't describe the verb), and it doesn't change the meaning of the verb. It isn't separable.

Compare these phrasal verbs:

Joe and Jill broke up. / Dan broke the fight up.

With these verbs + prepositions:

Ben walked up the hill. / They climbed up the ladder.

Unit 11 History

UNIT 11   History

5
- Ask students to work in pairs to take turns to ask and answer the questions in Exercise 4. Model the activity first by asking the first question and nominating three or four students to answer.
- In feedback, ask students to say what they found out about their partner.

Extra activity

Ask students to choose one of the verbs in the list below and to look it up in a learner's dictionary. Tell them to find three or four prepositions it goes with and to note or make up sentences to show the meaning of these verb + preposition collocations.

A list of verbs: *work, talk, give, send*

Example answers for work: *work with (colleagues), work for (a company), work as (a police officer), work in (an office), work on (a newspaper, a project), work from (home).*

Grammar reported speech

6 ★ **CPT extra!** Grammar activity [before Ex. 6]
- Ask students to look at the sentences in the grammar box and match them with the direct speech (a–d). Elicit the first answer as an example to get students started. Let them compare answers in pairs before checking with the class.

ANSWERS
1 d   2 a   3 b   4 c

Refer students to page 176 for further information and practice.

ANSWERS TO GRAMMAR SUMMARY EXERCISES
1
1 would have   2 was playing   3 didn't like
4 had visited   5 he'd lost
2
1 the next day   2 his   3 they   4 there   5 me
6 then   7 their   8 the day before
3
1 has; left   2 'll   3 don't speak   4 was   5 am arriving
4
1 Jan said she'd lost the match.
2 She said she'd see me the next day.
3 Mehmet said my email hadn't arrived.
4 He said he didn't want to speak to me.
5 Luke said he was trying to watch the TV.

7
- Read the instructions with the class and do the first one as an example.
- **Optional step** If you think your students won't remember the names of tenses, elicit and write them up on the board before doing this activity.
- Ask students to complete the rest of the table. Let them compare answers in pairs before checking with the class (see Grammar note below).

ANSWERS
1 Past simple   2 Present continuous
3 Past perfect   4 Will

Grammar note

At this level, keep reported speech simple for students by getting them to apply and practise the one tense back rule. So, present to past, and modal verbs like *can* and *will* to *could* and *would*.

Students will also have to manipulate pronouns when reporting speech, so *I* and *you* (singular) become *he* or *she*, and *we* and *you* (plural) become *they*.

8
- Ask students to complete the sentences with reported or direct speech. Elicit the first answer as an example to get students started. Let them compare answers in pairs before checking with the class.

ANSWERS
1 loved   2 want   3 are playing   4 were planning
5 have gone   6 had bought   7 will play
8 would change

Grammar note

1 love (present) → loved (past) – note that *I* changes to *he*.
2 wanted (past) → want (present) – note that *she* changes to *I*.
3 were playing (past) → are playing (present)
4 are planning (present) → were planning (past)
5 had gone (past perfect) → have gone (present perfect)
6 bought (past) → had bought (past perfect)
7 would play → will play
8 will change → would change

9 [88]
- Explain that students are going to listen to a conversation and they have to write down exactly what Jack and Sonia say. Tell them to treat this as a dictation.
- Play the recording. You will need to play the recording two or three times or play and pause between each line so that students have time to write.
- **Optional step** Let students check their answers by looking at audioscript 88 on page 188 of the Student's Book.

11a   The history of video gaming   179

UNIT 11 History

Audioscript [88] (and answers)

JACK: I need the TV for my game.
SONIA: I'm watching a really interesting programme.
JACK: But I want to get to the next level!
SONIA: You're always using the TV. I haven't watched it for ages.
JACK: I'll play it later.

10

- Ask students to rewrite the conversation as reported speech. Let students compare answers in pairs before checking with the class.

> ANSWERS
>
> 2 was watching a really interesting programme.
> 3 wanted to get to the next level.
> 4 was always using the TV and that she hadn't watched it (the TV) for ages.
> 5 he would play it later.

Speaking my life

11

- **Optional step** Start by checking *board game* (= an indoor game, played on a board, often with pieces that are moved around it) and *card games* (= games you play with a pack of cards).
- Ask students to work with a new partner. Tell students to take turns to ask and answer the questions. Make sure students note down their partners' answers carefully.

12

- Organize the class into new pairs. Ask students to take turns to report the information their partner provided. In feedback, ask a few students to tell the class what information was reported to them.
- **Optional step** You could model this activity by asking two or three questions first in open class, then reporting back to the class what was said.
- If students make any errors with reported speech, note them down, then write up short sentences with the errors you heard on the board. Ask pairs or groups to work together to correct them.

> EXAMPLE ANSWERS
>
> Here are some possible direct answers and reported answers:
>
> 'Chess is very popular in my country. I don't play chess very often. I prefer computer games. People will play chess online in the future.'
>
> Aniko said that chess was very popular in her country. She said she didn't play chess very often because she preferred computer games. She said people would play chess online in the future.

Extra activity

Play 'whispers'. Organize the class into groups of five and ask each group to sit in a circle. Walk round the class and whisper the first sentence in the list below into the ear of one student in each group. Tell those students that they must whisper the reported version of the sentence you have whispered into the ear of the student to their right. That student must then whisper the sentence into the ear of the next student to the right, and so on.

For example, you whisper, *I have a new bike*. The student whispers, *The teacher said he/she had a new bike*. Once the sentence has been whispered into all five ears in each group, the last student says what he/she heard. Find out if it is a correct sentence. Continue the game – whisper the next sentence into the ear of a different student.

A possible list (but make up your own sentences):

I have a new bike.
I have never played cricket.
There will be a test on Tuesday.
The school is going to be closed on Friday.
I'm enjoying the lesson.

UNIT 11 History

11b Messages from the past

Lesson at a glance
- vocabulary: communication
- listening: a message in a bottle
- grammar: reporting verbs (*say* and *tell*)
- speaking: reporting a story

Vocabulary communication

1 ★ **CPT extra!** Lead-in activity [before Ex. 1]

- **Optional step** Read the words in the box with the class. Drill any words that are hard to pronounce (see Pronunciation note below).
- Ask students to work individually to put the types of communication into the categories. Let students compare answers in pairs before checking with the class.
- **Optional step** Think about how to give feedback on this task. There are some suggestions in Teacher development below.

> **ANSWERS**
> Personal (with family and friends): a letter or card, a phone conversation, a sticky note on the fridge, a text message, a WhatsApp message
> Public (with lots of people): an advert, a newspaper, a presentation, a radio programme
> Both categories: an email, a Facebook page

> **Pronunciation note**
> The strong stress is on the first syllable of all these words except for *conversation* and *presentation*. Whatsapp is pronounced: /ˈwɒtsæp/

> **Background information**
> **Facebook** is a social networking service.
> **WhatsApp Messenger** is an encrypted instant messaging application for smartphones.
> **sticky notes** = small pieces of paper with a sticky edge which people use to write messages on then stick to things like computer screens to remind themselves or others to do things.

> **Teacher development**
> **Providing feedback on categorizing tasks**
> Students are often asked to order, categorize, match or label when learning new vocabulary. Here are suggestions for varying how you provide feedback on such activities:
> - Prepare a visual representation of answers to show on the whiteboard. This saves slowly reading through the answers – students can see their answers and check in their own time.
> - Ask students to come to the board and write up the answers. If you do this after students have checked answers in pairs, they will feel confident about doing this. It creates interaction in the classroom.
> - Make the task hands-on and bring it off the page. For example, you could write the words in the box in the activity above (Exercise 1) on individual slips of paper or card. Hand out a set of cards to each pair or group and ask them to physically put the cards into categories. Students then stand up and circulate to check their answers by seeing what other pairs or groups have done.

2

- Ask students to work in pairs to discuss the types of communication used to send each message. In feedback, ask different pairs to provide examples and their reasons. Often more than one answer is possible (also answers may depend on the age or culture of your students).

> **EXAMPLE ANSWERS**
> 1 a letter or card (when formally informing people or inviting people to a wedding), a phone conversation (with close family – you would tell parents face to face or on the phone if this wasn't possible), an email or text message (but they're less personal and not formal), a Facebook page (to inform groups of friends you see less often); a newspaper (to formally announce an engagement)
> 2 a newspaper, a radio programme (this is public news for the nation)
> 3 a letter or card (if being polite and formal), an email or a phone conversation (perhaps using Skype)
> 4 a sticky note on the fridge (this is the 'traditional' way to remind family members to do this), but emails, texts or messages on social networks are possible answers
> 5 Facebook or WhatsApp or other sites that allow you to upload photos
> 6 an advert (adverts introduce new products), also a newspaper or radio programme may include an article or item about a new product

Listening

3

- Ask students to look at the newspaper headline and photo. Ask them to work in pairs to discuss the questions. Elicit a few interesting ideas in feedback.

> **ANSWERS**
> The answers are in the Listening in Exercise 4. Students may suggest any of the following: a drowning sailor to his family saying that he loves them; a person far from home to his lover back home telling her to come and join him; a survivor of a shipwreck on a desert island asking anyone to come and rescue him.

4 🔊 [89]

- Read the three parts of the story (a–c) with the class.
- Play the recording. Students listen and number the three parts in the correct order. Let them compare answers in pairs before checking with the class.

> **ANSWERS**
> 1 b 2 c 3 a

11b Messages from the past **181**

UNIT 11 History

Audioscript 🔘 [89]

Last week the captain of a Scottish fishing boat pulled an old bottle out of the sea in one of his fishing nets. He told news reporters that he had been very curious when he'd seen the message inside. However, the message was a bit disappointing. It wasn't a love letter or a message from someone lost at sea. Instead, the writer said the message needed to be returned to an address.

In fact, the bottle was part of a scientific experiment which had begun 98 years before, when scientists threw 1,900 bottles into the sea in order to find out more about the movement of the oceans. It took nearly one hundred years for someone to find this bottle. So it's the oldest message in a bottle ever found – it's a world record.

Of course, the history of messages in bottles goes back many hundreds of years. Over two thousand years ago, the ancient Greeks put bottles in the sea to find out if the Mediterranean Sea and the Atlantic Ocean were connected. And sailors in World War I sent messages home by bottles. For example, one sailor in 1915 wrote a love letter to his wife. The message said that his boat was sinking and that he loved her.

5 🔘 [89]

- Give students time to read the questions carefully. Check *curious* (= interested in finding out about something) and *experiment* (= a scientific test to find out if an idea is true). You could also check other difficult words in the listening (e.g. *sailor* = person who works on a ship; *sink* = go down in the sea).
- Play the recording again. Students listen and choose the correct option. Let them compare answers in pairs before checking with the class.

> **ANSWERS**
> 1 c 2 c 3 b 4 a 5 b

Grammar reporting verbs (*say* and *tell*)

6 ★ CPT extra! Grammar activity [before Ex. 6]

- Read the sentences in the grammar box with the class. Then ask students to discuss the questions. You could do this in open class or ask students to discuss in pairs.

> **ANSWERS**
> 1 told and said 2 told 3 said

> **Grammar note**
>
> Many students confuse *say* and *tell*. This is because in many languages the same verb is used to express *say* and *tell*. We *say something* but we *tell somebody something*. Watch out for typical errors: *He said me that he was sorry. He told that the match was cancelled. He told to me that he was tired.*

Refer students to page 176 for further information and practice.

> **ANSWERS TO GRAMMAR SUMMARY EXERCISES**
> 5
> 1 He told **me** …
> 2 Correct
> 3 She said ~~me~~ that …
> 4 Correct
> 5 Correct
> 6 Anna told **me** …
> 6
> 1 (that) he'd found something interesting.
> 2 him (that) he was holding an ancient Greek vase.
> 3 (that) it was really beautiful.
> 4 (that) it had probably been lost in the sea for thousands of years.
> 5 him (that) he'd call the museum right away.

7

- Ask students to work individually to choose the correct options. Let students compare answers in pairs before checking with the class.

> **ANSWERS**
> 1 tell 2 said 3 say 4 say 5 said 6 told

> **Grammar note**
>
> 1 and 6 are *tell* (irregular past: *told*) because they take objects.
>
> Note the use of *that* in 3 (*When did they say that would happen?*). It isn't an object. It's a demonstrative pronoun.

8

- Ask students to work in pairs to report the messages. Elicit the first answer as an example to get students started and point out the way that the pronouns change (*your – his*).
- Depending on how confident your class is with reported speech, you could either ask students to do this task orally, or write out the sentences in their notebooks.

> **ANSWERS**
> 1 She told him that his lunch was in the fridge
> 2 He said that he was lost in the middle of the city.
> 3 Maria told Joel that she had loved him for years.
> 4 They said that they were waiting for me/him/her/us at the café.
> 5 Dave told me that he would call me back later.
> 6 The message said that I needed to phone this (that) number.

Writing and speaking my life

9

- **Optional step** Start by providing an example of what you would write if you were lost at sea or on an island. For example, *I'm your teacher and I'm stuck on a desert island. I love you all, but I want you to write an essay for homework.*

182 Unit 11 History

UNIT 11 History

- Give students three or four minutes to prepare their message. For added authenticity, get them to write on a slip of paper then roll it into a scroll as you would if you were putting it in a bottle. Monitor and help students with ideas and vocabulary.

10

- Organize the class into new pairs. Ask students to exchange notes, then write a short report based on the message.

> **EXAMPLE ANSWER**
>
> Students' own answers
>
> Here is the example above (in reported form):
>
> *Today, a person found a message in a bottle. It was written 100 years ago by a teacher who was stuck on a desert island. The message said the teacher loved all his/her students but told them that he/she wanted them to write an essay for homework.*

11 ★ CPT extra! Grammar activity [after Ex. 11]

- Ask students to read their news report aloud to their partner.
- In feedback, ask some students to read out the reported messages for the class.
- As students write, and when they read out, note any errors with reported speech. Write the errors on the board at the end for students to correct.

> **Extra activity**
>
> Write the following love messages (which may or may not have been put in bottles) on the board and ask students to report them, beginning with the phrase *My lost love said that / told me that …*
>
> *I'll love you until the day after forever.*
>
> *I'm always with you.*
>
> *I'm thinking of our first day together.*
>
> *I can hear your voice across the sea.*

11c Stealing history

> **Lesson at a glance**
> - vocabulary: ancient history
> - reading: stealing history
> - critical thinking: emotion words
> - word focus: *one*
> - speaking: saving history

Vocabulary ancient history

1 ★ CPT extra! Lead-in activity [before Ex. 1]

- **Optional step** Write *Ancient Egypt* on the board. Organize the class into pairs and tell them to think of as many words and phrases as they can which are connected with the subject in two minutes. Feed back ideas to the board and check the meaning of any useful or interesting words students say or try to say (typical words might be: *pharaoh, pyramid, mummy, tomb, sand, desert, Nile, Cleopatra*).
- Ask students to match the people with the definitions and the words with the photos. Let students compare answers in pairs before checking with the class. In feedback, check the meaning and pronunciation of any difficult words (see Vocabulary note below).

> **ANSWERS**
>
> 1 d   2 b   3 c   4 a   5 h   6 f   7 g   8 e

> **Vocabulary note**
>
> archae*o*logist /ˌɑːkɪˈɒlədʒɪst/ = archaeologists are associated with an archaeological dig, when they look for old things in the ground in places where ancient people used to live
>
> *soldier* has a difficult pronunciation: /ˈsəʊldʒə/
>
> *robber, collector* = collocations help students understand these words, e.g. *a bank robber* or *grave robber*, and *an art collector* or *stamp collector*
>
> *tomb* /tuːm/ = a place where people are buried
>
> *statue* (pronounced /ˈstatjuː/ or /ˈstatʃuː/) = a figure made of wood, bronze or stone

Reading

2

- Ask students to say what they think *Stealing History* means, and predict what the article is about. You could do this in open class or in pairs. Elicit ideas in feedback, but don't confirm answers at this stage as students will find them out from doing the reading task in the next exercise.

> **EXAMPLE ANSWERS**
>
> Students' own answers
>
> *Stealing History* is an emotive title. On one level, it refers to people stealing historical objects from historical sites. On another level, it refers to the idea that these robbers are taking away a country's history, or stopping experts from finding out more about the past.
>
> The text will probably talk about the four people. Archaeologists look for ancient objects, robbers steal them and sell them to collectors for a lot of money, and soldiers try to stop the robbers.

11c Stealing history   183

UNIT 11 History

3 [90]

- Ask students to read the article and check their predictions from Exercise 2 first. Have a brief feedback (see Example answers above).
- Ask students to read the article again and answer the questions. Let students compare answers in pairs before checking with the class.
- **Optional step** The reading text is recorded. You could play the recording and ask students to read and listen.

> **ANSWERS**
> 1 Busiris
> 2 It was one of ancient Egypt's largest cities and it was famous for its architecture and buildings.
> 3 archaeologists from museums
> 4 to steal things (historical items)
> 5 to protect the area from the robbers
> 6 They throw away the rest (the less good pieces) – they destroy hundreds.
> 7 Roman armies; different countries which controlled Egypt between the 16th and mid-20th centuries.
> 8 It's big business.

> **Vocabulary note**
> Point out *robbers* (= people who steal things from places). Also, its verb *rob* and the noun describing when things are stolen from a place (*a robbery*).
> Point out the verb *steal* (= similar to *rob* but with a wider, more general meaning) and its irregular past forms, *stole* and *stolen*. *Stolen* is also an adjective: *stolen items*.
> The verb *take* (*took, taken*) can also be used in some contexts to mean *steal* or *rob*.

> **Background information**
> *Busiris* is the ancient Greek name of the lost city in Egypt. It was an important necropolis (cemetery) and a centre for the cult of the god Osiris.

Critical thinking emotion words

4

- Ask students to find the sentences in the text and underline the extra words. Let students compare answers in pairs before checking with the class.

> **ANSWERS**
> 1 hard-working 2 desperately 3 sadly

5

- Discuss the questions with the class and elicit ideas from your students.
- **Optional step** Ask students what other emotion words they could add to the three sentences in Exercise 4, e.g. *brave/courageous people; brilliant/talented team; amazing/unique history; Unfortunately/Regrettably, it …*

> **ANSWERS**
> The author uses adjectives and adverbs to show how he or she feels about things – to express an emotional viewpoint.

Word focus one

6

- Ask students to read the sentences carefully and match them with the explanations. Elicit the first answer as an example to get students started. Let students compare answers in pairs before checking with the class.

> **ANSWERS**
> 1 c 2 d 3 b 4 a 5 e

> **Vocabulary note**
> *One* can be a number (*I have one child*), a determiner (*Maybe one day*) or a pronoun (*One of Egypt's largest cities*).
> *one or two* = used when you want to emphasize that the number is imprecise but very small
> *one by one* = literally, first one, then the next, then the next, so if stones are moved one by one it suggests a very slow, careful, step-by-step process
> *one day* = when talking about the past, it refers to a particular day, but when talking about the future, it's used when being unspecific about which day (e.g. *One day we'll come back here – I don't know when*).

Speaking my life

7

- Ask students to work in small groups of three or four. Tell them to make notes under the headings for a new museum about their town. You could elicit one or two ideas to get students started. If your students are from different towns or countries, ask them to choose a place they all know or choose an interesting town that they would like to write about.
- As students make notes, monitor and help with ideas and vocabulary.
- Once students have notes, ask them to think about how to make a presentation of their reasons for opening a museum. Tell them to use emotion words to make their reasons more persuasive.

> **EXAMPLE ANSWER**
> Students' own answers
> Here are some possible reasons for opening a museum:
> *This town desperately needs a new museum for a number of reasons. Firstly, it was famous for bicycle production in the past, but there's no museum to help people remember those wonderful days. Secondly, there are many fine bicycles in private hands and we can show them in the museum. We can tell visitors about the hard-working employees of the bicycle manufacturer and of the way bicycles were once made here.*

UNIT 11 History

8 ★ **CPT extra!** Speaking activity [before Ex. 8]
- Ask each group to work with another group. Each group takes turns to present their reasons for opening a museum.
- As students speak, monitor and notice any errors students make. Note them down for the feedback stage.
- In feedback, at the end, ask groups to say whether they thought the presentations were successful. Write a few sentences with errors on the board and ask students to correct the errors in their groups.

Extra activity

Ask students to research a major world museum on the internet for homework. Tell them to prepare a presentation under these headings: *where the museum is, what you can see there, why you should visit*. In future lessons, ask students to give their presentations.

11d A journey to Machu Picchu

Lesson at a glance
- real life: giving a short presentation
- pronunciation: pausing

Real life giving a short presentation

1
- Discuss the questions with your class.

> **EXAMPLE ANSWERS**
>
> at work: in meetings (e.g. presenting sales figures); selling to a client (e.g. presenting a new product); training staff (e.g. presenting health and safety regulations; presenting company plans for the future)
>
> at school or university: in class (e.g. presenting a piece of work); in exams (e.g. making a formal presentation); at university (e.g. to present research findings, to present arguments for a debate)
>
> at the meeting of a local club or town council: people make presentations on their area of interest or expertise for pleasure (e.g. a talk on local history)
>
> at a special occasion: at a wedding people make light-hearted speeches (e.g. the speeches of the father of the bride and the best man at a wedding – telling funny stories); at a funeral people commemorate the dead person's life with stories and praise

2 🔊 [91] ★ **CPT extra!** Listening activity [after Ex. 2]
- **Optional step** Write *Machu Picchu* and *Peru* on the board and brainstorm things students know about these places. Use the opportunity to introduce and explain that Machu Picchu is an ancient city, and that Incas are native people from Peru.
- Ask students to read the topics (a–f). Explain to students that they will hear the first part of three sections of a talk, plus the final conclusion.
- Play the recording. Students listen and tick the topics mentioned. Let students compare their answers in pairs before checking with the class.

> **ANSWERS**
> b, c, e

Audioscript 🔊 [91]

Good morning and thank you all for coming. Today I'd like to talk about my holiday in Peru, and in particular, about my journey to Machu Picchu. It's also called 'The Lost City of the Incas'. Let me begin by telling you about the history of Machu Picchu. It was discovered by the explorer Hiram Bingham in 1911 …

So, that's everything I wanted to say about Hiram Bingham. Now, let's look at the history of the Incas and why they built Machu Picchu. The first Incas lived in the region of Peru around the thirteenth century …

UNIT 11 History

OK. Now, the next part of my presentation is about my own journey through Peru and up to Machu Picchu. For this, I'd like to show you some of my photos. So, this first one is a picture of me in the town of Aguas Calientes. You have to catch the bus from here to Machu Picchu …

OK. So, to sum up, Peru, and especially Machu Picchu, is a magical place and anyone who's interested in history should go there. Are there any questions?

Background information

Machu Picchu (pronounced /ˈmatʃuːˈpitʃuː/) is a 15th-century Inca citadel situated on a mountain ridge 2,430 metres above sea level. It's a very popular and spectacular tourist attraction today.

Hiram Bingham III (1875–1956) was an American academic, explorer and politician.

3 [91]

- Ask students to read the expressions, and try to remember how to complete them with the missing words.
- Play the recording again. Students listen and complete the expressions. Let students compare their answers in pairs before checking with the class.
- **Optional step** It's often hard to listen and write. So, you could ask students to listen to the whole recording again before writing answers. That way they will concentrate on the recording. You could play and pause the recording a second time to confirm answers.

ANSWERS
1 thank you 2 talk 3 begin 4 say 5 look
6 next 7 show 8 up 9 questions

Vocabulary note

Notice the use of *let* in the expressions:
Let me means *Allow me to*, and is a polite way to request permission to speak or continue to speak. In the context of a presentation, it's a polite, formal convention.
Let's (*Let us*) is used to make a suggestion or invitation. In the context of a presentation, it's used to 'invite' the audience to move with the speaker on to the next point. Again, it's a polite convention.
Similarly, *I'd like to* is used as a polite convention. The speaker is asking for permission – the convention wins over the listeners because of its polite inclusiveness.

Pronunciation pausing
4a [92]

- Read the information about pausing with the class. Tell students to read the text silently before listening, noticing and imagining the pauses marked by the slash.
- Play the recording. Students listen and read. In feedback, ask students to say where the other pauses are.

ANSWERS
Good morning / and thank you all for coming. / Today / I'd like to talk about my holiday in Peru, / and in particular, / about my journey to Machu Picchu. / It's also called / 'The Lost City of the Incas'. / Let me begin by telling you / about the history of Machu Picchu.

b

- Ask students to work in pairs to practise reading the presentation. You may wish to mix pairs at this stage so students have a new partner. Encourage students to take turns to give the presentation, and to comment on each other's performance. Monitor pairs and prompt students to attempt pausing.

Pronunciation note

Practising pausing helps students to give successful presentations for a number of reasons. Firstly, it breaks the talk into short sections, which are easier to say. Secondly, the pauses help listeners follow what is being said. Thirdly, it helps students notice linking and strong stress in each bite-size piece of speech.

5

- **Optional step** Start by giving a short presentation of your own, with pausing, as a model for students to follow. You could use the example answer below or talk about something that is true for you.
- Elicit a few places students could talk about. Then ask students to prepare presentations. Make them short. Set a five-minute time limit. Monitor and help with ideas and vocabulary.
- Organize the class into new pairs. Ask students to take turns to deliver their presentations. Alternatively, if you have a small class, you could ask students to come to the front of the class and make a presentation to the whole class.
- As students speak, note down any errors you hear. At the end, write up five or six errors on the board for students to correct in pairs or as a class. Alternatively, write errors on separate pieces of paper for each speaker and hand the errors to the individual students to correct at home (see Teacher development below).
- **Optional step** You could set the presentation preparation for homework. Ask students to write a longer presentation and be ready to present to groups or the class. They could bring in pictures or objects to illustrate their talk. Have different students speak at the start of future lessons as a warmer to your lesson.

UNIT 11   History

EXAMPLE ANSWER

Good morning / and thank you all for coming. / Today / I'd like to talk about / Windsor Castle. / It's a historic castle / in the south of England. / Let me begin / by telling you / why it's important. / It's important / because it's one of the many homes / of the Queen of the United Kingdom. / It contains / a fantastic art collection. / Now, / the next part / of my presentation / is about who lived there / in the past. / Many of the UK's / most famous kings and queens, / including King Henry the Eighth / and Queen Victoria / spent time there. / And today / many kings and queens / are buried / in the castle. / To sum up, / it's a historic / and interesting / place to visit. /

Teacher development

Providing individual feedback on errors

In a busy language classroom, it's sometimes hard to provide feedback on errors that are specific to individual students. Here are suggestions for including individual feedback on errors:

- Include spoken activities in your lessons which involve extended speaking by individuals. These may be presentations or talks, or extended interviews or roleplay in which one student speaks a lot. Such activities give you an opportunity to really listen to one student.
- As an individual student speaks, note down errors that you hear the student make on a blank A4 piece of paper. At the end of the lesson, hand this piece of paper to the student. Alternatively, you could write up and send the errors to your student after the lesson via email. Ask the student to correct the errors and to categorize them as 'slips' or 'errors I keep making'. It's important to make students aware of repeated errors that they need to work on.
- Collect and keep the piece of paper. Next time the student speaks in class at length, add other errors on the piece of paper for the student to correct at home. Comment on whether they have repeated errors or successfully dealt with them.

11e The greatest mountaineer

Lesson at a glance
- writing: a biography
- writing skill: punctuation in direct speech

Writing a biography

1

- Ask students to work in pairs to discuss what information they would find in biographies. Elicit ideas in a brief feedback but don't confirm answers at this stage.

ANSWERS
Students' own answers (Note that the answers are provided in Exercise 2.)

2

- **Optional step** Ask students to look at the photo and predict what the biography will be about. Find out if any students know anything about Reinhold Messner.
- Ask students to read the biography briefly and, in a brief feedback, say whether their ideas from Exercise 1 are mentioned.
- Ask students to read the biography again and match the topics (a–f) with the paragraphs in the biography. Let students compare answers in pairs before checking with the class.

ANSWERS

a paragraph 2 (*born in 1944 in a small village in the mountains of northern Italy*)
b paragraph 2 (*His father was a climber and took his son up a mountain when he was only five. As a teenager Messner climbed with his younger brother Günther.*)
c paragraph 1 (*one of the first men to climb Mount Everest without oxygen in 1978; first man to climb all fourteen of the world's mountains over eight thousand metres*)
d paragraph 2 (*'it's the most beautiful place in the world'*)
e paragraph 3 (*'Reinhold had so many new ideas,' says Kammerlander. 'He found new ways, new techniques.'*)
f paragraph 4 (*Nowadays Messner spends more time at home with his family and he has written over sixty books.*)

Vocabulary note

has been described as = people have said that he is

famous for + ing = we use *for* here to give the reason why someone is famous

a legend = here, a legend is used to describe a person who is so famous or so important that other people in the same field admire and respect them very much (e.g. Usain Bolt is a legend in athletics)

techniques = ways of doing something that you have to learn

11e   The greatest mountaineer   187

UNIT 11 History

Writing skill punctuation in direct speech
3a
- Ask students to read the biography again to find and underline the direct speech. Let them compare their answers in pairs before checking with the class.

> **ANSWERS**
> … he still says, 'it's the most beautiful place in the world.'
> 'Reinhold had so many new ideas,' says Kammerlander.
> 'He found new ways, new techniques.'

b
- Ask students to answer the questions. You could do this in open class or ask students to work in pairs. Elicit answers in feedback.
- **Optional step** It's a good idea to go over rules visually on the board here (see the Extra activity below).

> **ANSWERS**
> 1 Immediately before and after the quotation
> 2 only if it ends the sentence
> 3 A comma is used before or after the quotation – it separates 'he/she says/said' from the quotation.

> **Extra activity**
> In feedback to Exercise 3b, write the following on the board and ask students to tell you (or come to the board and show you) where the commas and quotation marks go (answers shown in brackets):
> It's a beautiful place he said
> ('It's a beautiful place,' he said.)
> He said It's a beautiful place
> (He said, 'It's a beautiful place.'
> It's a beautiful place he said I love it
> ('It's a beautiful place,' he said. 'I love it.')

> **Punctuation note**
> Notice how the comma goes before the quotation mark when *He says* introduces the direct speech (He says, 'It's great.'), but the comma also goes before the quotation mark when *he says* follows the direct speech ('It's great,' he says.)
> When introducing the quote, we always write *He said* or *Kammerlander said*, but when following the quote we can write either *Kammerlander said* or *said Kammerlander* (but we don't usually invert with the pronoun – *said he* is unusual).
> In American English, it is more common to use double quotation marks ("Hi!" he said.). In British English, these are only used if there is a further quote inside the original quotation.

c
- Ask students to work individually to complete the sentences with the missing punctuation. Make sure students write out full sentences carefully. Let students compare answers in pairs before checking with the class.
- In feedback, you could ask different pairs to go up to the board to write out answers.

> **ANSWERS**
> 1 My grandfather always told me, 'You should follow your dreams.'
> 2 'Yes, we can,' said Barack Obama, when he campaigned to become the US President.
> 3 Film critics said, 'She's the greatest actress of her generation.'
> 4 'Education is the most powerful weapon,' said Nelson Mandela.

> **Background information**
> **Barack Obama** was the 44th President of the United States from 2009 to 2017.
> **Nelson Mandela** was President of South Africa from 1994 to 1999.

> **Extra activity**
> Ask students to think of things that people they know have told them over the years (e.g. grandparents, teachers, coaches, friends). Ask them to write down the direct quote, then add *My grandfather / Basketball coach (etc.) said* and the correct punctuation. Students share their personal quotes in pairs or groups.

4
- **Optional step** Make sure students have a good idea for a biography before they start and ensure that they prepare fully (see the Extra activity below for ideas).
- Once students have made notes and a plan for their biography, tell them to write 100 to 140 words and to include at least two quotes. Monitor at this stage and be prepared to help with ideas and vocabulary.

> **Extra activity**
> To ensure students have something to write about, take time at the start to get students to research.
> 1 Ask the class to think of a famous person they would like to write about and share what they know with a partner first. Their partner could add or suggest extra information to use.
> 2 Tell the class to organize their biography under different headings, e.g.
>   - who they are and why they are famous
>   - when and where they were born
>   - what they did
>   - what is their importance or legacy
>   You could write these headings on the board to help. Alternatively, use the topics in Exercise 2 as headings.
> 3 If your classroom rules and technology allow, let students use the internet to research key facts for their biography in their preparation.

5 ★ **CPT extra!** Writing activity [after Ex. 5]
- **Optional step** You could ask students to write their biographies for homework if you are short of class time. Students can then read their biographies in the next class.

188 Unit 11 History

UNIT 11 History

- Organize the class into pairs (or small groups if you prefer). Students exchange and read biographies. Encourage students to give feedback on the use of punctuation and on the content and interest of the biography.

Extra activity

Ask students to sit in circles of five or six students. They pass their biography to the person on their right. That person reads the biography and makes comments about it on a sheet of paper under the headings *Structure*, *Language* and *Interest*. Each student then passes on the biography and the piece of paper. The biography and paper goes round the group until it reaches the person who wrote it. That person should have a detailed class feedback on their writing which they could use to help them revise and improve their biography for homework.

11f The golden record

Before you watch

Key vocabulary

1 ★ **CPT extra!** Photo activity [before Ex. 1]

- **Optional step** Ask students to describe the photo in detail. Find out what students already know about Voyager 1 or ask them to guess what its mission was.
- Ask students to read the sentences and work out what the words in bold mean from the context. Then ask them to match the words with the best definitions. Let students compare answers in pairs before checking with the class.
- **Optional step** It's a good idea to show the pronunciation of these key words – students have to hear them in continuous speech on the video. You could say the words and ask students to repeat, or say the words and ask students to underline the strongly stressed syllable (see Pronunciation note below).

ANSWERS

1 a launched   b spacecraft
2 a solar system   b space
3 a mission   b function
4 a classical   b jazz
5 a universe   b life forms

Pronunciation note

Note the strong stress on these words: *space*craft, *so*lar *sys*tem, inter*stel*lar, *mis*sion, *func*tion, *clas*sical, *u*niverse

Note the difficult pronunciation: *launched* /lɔːnʃt/, *solar* /ˈsəʊlə/ and *mission* /ˈmɪʃən/.

2

- Discuss the question with your class. Elicit the views of different students. You could ask students to discuss the question briefly in pairs first so that they will have more to say when they report their discussion in open class.

EXAMPLE ANSWER

Students' own answers

Reasons for exploring space include finding out more about how the universe works, developing science and technology, trying to find new life or ways that we might leave our planet and live in space.

Reasons against include the enormous cost of space exploration, and the fact that space is so big we may not find anything there.

UNIT 11 History

While you watch

3 🎥 [11.1]

- Ask students to watch the video and note answers to the questions. Let students compare answers with a partner before checking with the class.
- Note that there is a lot for students to note in answer to question 3. Don't worry if students don't catch everything – in feedback, work as a class to see how much you can collectively remember.

> **ANSWERS**
>
> 1 to fly past the planets of Jupiter and Saturn and send back photographs to help scientists understand more about the two planets and our solar system
> 2 on the side of the Voyager 1 spacecraft
> 3 116 photographs in black and white and in colour (showing Earth, human life, families, animals and different places on Earth including cities, deserts and oceans); recordings of different sounds that you find on Earth; music to represent different parts of the world; recordings of human voices from Earth

4 🎥 [11.1]

- Give students time to read the sentences and decide whether they are true (T) or false (F).
- Play the first part of the video again. Ask students to check their answers. Let students compare answers in pairs before checking with the class.

> **ANSWERS**
>
> 1 T
> 2 T
> 3 F (*information about the Earth in 1977*)
> 4 T (*nearly a year*)
> 5 F (*Voyager 1 is currently carrying it further into space*)

Videoscript 🎥 11.1

0.00–0.04 Hello from the children of planet Earth.

0.05–0.14 That child's voice is a recorded message and the spacecraft Voyager 1 is currently carrying it further into space.

0.15–0.36 The spacecraft Voyager 1 was launched on the 20th August, 1977. Its mission was to fly past the planets of Jupiter and Saturn and send back photographs to help scientists understand more about the two planets and our solar system.

0.37–0.48 Over forty years later, Voyager 1 has completed its first mission successfully but it still has an important function.

0.49–1.16 As well as sending messages back home, Voyager carries a message for other life forms in the universe. When scientists built Voyager 1, they fixed a golden record onto the side of the spacecraft. It has different information about the Earth in 1977.

1.17–1.28 It was very difficult to choose what information to put on the record and so it took a team of six people nearly a year to decide.

1.29–2.03 First of all, the team chose 116 photographs in black and white and in colour. These show pictures of Earth, pictures of human life including a human skeleton, a baby growing inside its mother and pictures of families. There are also photographs of animals and different places on Earth including cities, deserts and oceans.

2.04–2.51 Another part of the record is called 'The sounds of Earth'. The twelve minutes of recording includes the sound of wind and rain, a volcano, birds and frogs, the human heart, and a child crying.

2.52–3.22 Music was also important on the record and pieces were chosen to represent different parts of the world. There's classical music from Europe such as pieces by Bach and more modern jazz recordings by Louis Armstrong. There's also traditional music representing different cultures, from places like Azerbaijan, New Guinea, China, India and Peru.

3.23–3.29 And finally there are the recordings of human voices from Earth.

3.29–4.01 Hello from the children of planet Earth.

All the recordings are short messages with greetings in French, in Japanese, in Arabic and Mandarin Chinese.

4.02–4.08 In total, there are 55 different greetings in 55 different languages.

4.09–end So as Voyager 1 finally leaves the Earth's solar system and travels into interstellar space, it carries a message with it. And who knows? Maybe someday someone – or something – will listen to the messages and send a reply.

5 🎥 [11.1]

- Give students time to read the questions and try to recall answers before playing the video.
- Play the second part of the video again. Ask students to answer the questions. Let students compare answers in pairs before checking with the class.

> **ANSWERS**
>
> 1 116 photos (in black and white, and colour) – they show pictures of Earth, pictures of human life including a human skeleton, a baby growing inside its mother and pictures of families. There are also photos of animals and different places on Earth including cities, deserts and oceans.
> 2 1 d 2 e 3 c 4 a 5 b
> 3 a French b Japanese c Arabic d Mandarin Chinese

> **Background information**
>
> In April 2017, **Voyager 1** was over 17,000,000,000 kilometres from the Sun. That makes it the farthest spacecraft from Earth and the farthest man-made object. It's still sending data. It will probably run out of electrical power in 2025.

190 Unit 11 History

UNIT 11 History

After you watch
Vocabulary in context

6 [11.1]

- Explain that students are going to watch some clips from the video which contain some new words and phrases. They need to choose the correct meaning of the words.
- Play the clips. When each multiple-choice question appears, pause the clip so that students can choose the correct definition. You could let students compare answers in pairs before checking with the class.

> **ANSWERS**
> 1 b   2 b   3 b   4 c   5 a

Videoscript 11.2

1 That child's voice is a **recorded** message.
   a given to a lot of different people
   b put into a permanent form
   c left for someone else
2 They **fixed** a golden record **onto** the side of the spacecraft.
   a played
   b attached
   c changed
3 Music was also important on the record and pieces were chosen to **represent** different parts of the world.
   a recognize
   b symbolize
   c sound like
4 All the recordings are short messages with **greetings**.
   a words or signs of explanation
   b words or signs of description
   c words or signs of welcome
5 We hope that we will meet you **someday**.
   a at some time in the future
   b on a specific day in the future
   c in the very near future

7
- Read the instructions with the class and check that everyone understands what to do.
- Ask students to work in small groups of three to five students to plan what to put on their memory stick. Start them off by eliciting a few ideas in open class. Set a time limit of ten minutes. Monitor and help with ideas and vocabulary as students prepare.

8 ★ **CPT extra!** Web research [after Ex. 8]
- Organize the class so that each group is sitting facing another group. Ask groups to take turns to describe their plans.
- In feedback, ask groups what was similar or different about what they have included on their memory stick.
- **Optional step** Instead of pairing groups, form new groups in which each group has one representative from each of the original groups. This extends the presentation stage. Each member of the new group must now make a presentation, revealing the plans of their original group. Each group votes on whose plans were the most original or interesting.

> **EXAMPLE ANSWERS**
>
> Students' own answers
> Here is a list of what some people on blogs thought they would include on a golden record:
> - a newborn baby crying
> - a picture of the human DNA molecule
> - a video clip of a hurricane
> - people laughing at a joke
> - flags of all countries
> - speeches by Martin Luther King and Nelson Mandela
> - a picture of a human face
> - a mobile phone
> - a chocolate bar
> - some unsolved mathematical theorems
> - the song *Life on Mars* by David Bowie
> - somebody saying *Have a nice day*

> **Extra activity**
>
> Ask students to look at the list in the example answers above and choose the three best ideas (and say why).

11f   The golden record

UNIT 11 History

UNIT 11 Review and memory booster ★ CPT extra! Language games

Memory Booster activities
Exercises 3 and 7 are Memory Booster activities. For more information about these activities and how they benefit students, see page 10.

I can … tick boxes
As an alternative to students simply ticking the *I can …* boxes, you could ask them to give themselves a score from 1 to 4 (1 = not very confident; 4 = very confident) for each language area. If students score 1 or 2 for a language area, refer them to additional practice activities in the Workbook and Grammar summary exercises.

Grammar
1
- Ask students to work individually to rewrite the direct speech as reported speech. Let them compare answers in pairs before checking with the class.

> **ANSWERS**
> 1 wanted to fly in space   2 was driving home
> 3 'd visited the pyramid in Giza   4 'd gone to the museum
> 5 'd go on holiday to Rome

2
- Ask students to complete the sentences with the correct form of *say* or *tell*.

> **ANSWERS**
> 1 told   2 say   3 tell   4 said   5 say   6 said

3 ›› MB
- Ask students to work in pairs and tell each other about the three bullet points. Remind them that they read about the bottle in lesson 11b.

> **EXAMPLE ANSWER**
> A fishing captain found the one-hundred-year-old bottle in his net. It was part of an experiment. Scientists wanted to learn about the movement of water so they threw 1,900 bottles (with a message) into the sea. It's the oldest message in a bottle ever found.

Vocabulary
4
- Ask students to work individually to choose the correct option. Let them compare answers in pairs before checking with the class.

> **ANSWERS**
> 1 about   2 it   3 on   4 with   5 against

5
- Ask students to work individually to complete the text with the words in the box.

> **ANSWERS**
> 1 archaeologists   2 pots   3 paintings   4 statue   5 tomb

Real life
6
- Ask students to match the sentence beginnings and endings from a presentation.

> **ANSWERS**
> 1 c   2 e   3 a   4 f   5 g   6 b   7 d

7 ›› MB
- Ask students to work in pairs to create their own short presentation by completing sentence beginnings (1–7) in Exercise 6 with their own information.

> **ANSWERS**
> Students' own answers

Unit 12 Nature

Opener

1 ⭐ **CPT extra!** Photo activity [after Ex. 1]

- **Optional step** Start by checking the meaning of the words in the box, e.g. *storm* (= a period of black clouds and heavy rain) and *tornado* (= a strong, stormy wind that goes round and round violently). One way of doing this is to ask students to say which words go together (e.g. *sun – bright – shine*).
- Ask students to look at the photo and read the caption. You could ask them to describe the photo in open class or ask students to discuss in pairs first. Elicit opinions and answers from the class in feedback.

> **EXAMPLE ANSWERS**
>
> Students' own answers
>
> Here is a possible description: I think it's the afternoon. There's a tornado and it's moving closer. There are dark clouds in the sky. There's a bright light above the cloud. The sun is shining behind the cloud.

2 💿 [93]

- **Optional step** Give students time to read the questions and predict their answers.
- Play the recording. Students listen and answer the questions. Let them compare answers in pairs before checking with the class.

> **ANSWERS**
>
> 1 They drive in the opposite direction.
> 2 Some storm chasers are scientists, but others are just ordinary people.
> 3 The scientists want to learn about how tornadoes are formed, and the ordinary people want to get good photos.
> 4 Between 4 p.m. and 9 p.m.
> 5 They are unpredictable. They can destroy houses and trees and some storm chasers have died.

Audioscript 💿 [93]

When a tornado is coming, most people drive in the opposite direction. But storm chasers look for tornadoes and drive towards them. Some storm chasers are scientists and they try to learn more about how tornadoes are formed. Other storm chasers are just everyday people who are interested and want to get good photos. The most common time of day to see a tornado is between 4 p.m. and 9 p.m., but they can be very unpredictable. They can change direction at any moment and so they are difficult to follow. That also makes them extremely dangerous. They can destroy trees and houses in seconds and some storm chasers have died while they were following tornadoes.

> **Background notes**
>
> **Storm chasing** is popular in the USA. Chasing often involves driving thousands of miles in order to witness severe thunderstorms. The film *Twister* (1996) and the reality TV series *Storm Chasers* on the Discovery Channel have added to the popularity. In May and June, tornadoes are frequent and spectacular across the Great Plains of the USA, in the states of Oklahoma, Kansas, South Dakota, Iowa, Illinois, Missouri, New Mexico, Texas, Colorado, North Dakota, and Minnesota. This area of the USA is called Tornado Alley.

3

- Organize the class into small groups of three or four to discuss and answer the questions. Elicit students' ideas in feedback.

> **ANSWERS**
>
> Students' own answers

193

UNIT 12 Nature

12a What if …?

Lesson at a glance
- vocabulary: extreme weather
- reading: *what if …?*
- grammar: second conditional
- pronunciation: *would / wouldn't / 'd*
- speaking: hopes and dreams

Vocabulary extreme weather

1 ★ **CPT extra!** Lead-in activity [before Ex. 1]
- **Optional step** Write *the weather* on the board. Brainstorm nouns and adjectives to describe the weather and build up a list of words on the board (e.g. *rain/rainy, sun/sunny, wind/windy, snow/snowy, fog/foggy, cloud/cloudy*).
- Ask students to work individually to match the weather words with the photos. Let students compare answers in pairs before checking with the class.
- **Optional step** Drill the words for pronunciation and point out the strong stress in the words.

ANSWERS

a snowstorm   b flood   c thunder and lightning   d hail

Vocabulary and pronunciation note

flood = when water rises and covers the land after a lot of rain falls
hail = hard ice balls that fall in cold weather
*snow*storm = when snow falls very heavily
*thun*der = the loud noise before a storm
*light*ning = the electrical light in the sky before a storm
*torna*do = a strong, stormy wind that goes round and round violently

2
- Ask students to discuss the questions. You could do this in open class or ask students to talk in pairs first. Elicit answers in feedback.

EXAMPLE ANSWERS
1 Answers vary depending on your students' experience. International examples include: floods in south-east Asia (e.g. Malaysia and Bangladesh); snowstorms in Canada or Scandinavia; thunder and lightning in tropical countries; hail in central Europe; tornadoes in the American mid-west
2 & 3 Students' own answers

Extra activity

If you didn't brainstorm weather vocabulary at the start of this lesson, do so before doing Exercise 2. Ask students what other words they know to describe the weather.

Reading

3 🔘 [94]
- **Optional step** Start by writing *What if …?* on the board. Ask students to predict what a blog with that title might be about.
- Ask students to read the article and answer the question. Let students compare answers in pairs before checking as a class.
- **Optional step** The reading text is recorded. You could play the recording and ask students to read and listen.

ANSWERS
Every week, people send Randall questions about unlikely or impossible things, and Randall gives scientific answers.

4
- Ask students to read the article again and answer the questions. Let students compare answers in pairs before checking with the class.

ANSWERS
1 No (*he used to work for NASA*)
2 No (*unlikely or impossible things*)
3 Yes (*Randall gives scientific answers*)
4 Yes (*because you'd be underwater*)
5 Yes (*the electrical energy would spread outwards across the water*)
6 Yes (*if you drove fast*)

Vocabulary note

submarine = use the picture to show this underwater boat
spread outwards = move away from a central point in all directions
freezing temperatures = below zero degrees centigrade

Background information

NASA = North American Space Agency (they send rockets into space).
The **speed of sound** is about 1,200 km/hr.

Grammar second conditional

5 ★ **CPT extra!** Grammar activity [before Ex. 5]
- Ask students to read the sentences in the grammar box and choose the correct options in rules 1–4 to show their understanding of form and meaning. Let students compare answers in pairs before checking with the class.

ANSWERS
1 a   2 b   3 b   4 a

194 Unit 12 Nature

UNIT 12 Nature

Grammar note

1 *if* + present simple + *will* + verb is the first conditional – you could refer students back to Unit 8 to review its use.

Aspects of the second conditional form to focus on are:
- the fact that *would* usually shortens to *'d* and *would not* to *wouldn't*
- that we use the past form in the *if* clause. Many languages have a separate subjunctive form here, but English uses the past. Watch out for students who use *would* in both clauses.
- *if I was* can also be *if I were* – it is formally correct to use *were* with *I, he, she* and *it* in second conditional sentences – however, in spoken use, it is now common to use *was*.

2 We use the first conditional for real situations – the choice of whether a situation is real (i.e. it's possible or probable that it will happen) or unreal (i.e. it's impossible or unlikely that it will happen) depends on the circumstances or the view of the speaker (e.g. compare 'If I become prime minister, I'll cut taxes', said the leader of a political party during the election campaign, with 'If I were prime minister, I'd cut taxes', said my uncle Frank, as he looked at his tax bill). The politician sees what he's saying as possible. Uncle Frank is speaking hypothetically – it isn't going to happen.

3 Both the first and second conditional refer to present or future situations. The difference between them is about real or unreal, not present or past. The third (or past) conditional refers to hypothetical past situations (and is not covered at this level).

4 Notice that in natural speech, a native speaker pauses slightly at the comma when saying a second conditional sentence.

Refer students to page 178 for further information and practice.

ANSWERS TO GRAMMAR SUMMARY EXERCISES

1
1 will   2 would   3 became   4 would   5 won't   6 didn't

2
1 d   2 a   3 c   4 f   5 e   6 b

3
1 wasn't, 'd be able to
2 had, 'd buy
3 spoke, would understand
4 wouldn't tell, didn't think
5 'd save, were
6 Would, come, paid

6

- Ask students to work individually to order the sentences. Elicit the first sentence as an example to get students started. Let them compare answers with a partner before checking with the class.
- **Optional step** Check form by asking students to label the verbs used 'past' or 'would + infinitive'.

ANSWERS

1 If I had time, I'd help you with your homework.
2 You wouldn't need help if you listened in class.
3 Would you ask your friends for money if you didn't have any?
4 I'd visit ancient Rome if time travel was possible.
5 They wouldn't use a translator if they spoke English.
6 If you started a new business, what would you produce?

7

- **Optional step** Ask students to read the text for understanding first. Ask: *What's the Gulf Stream?* (a stream of warm water) *What would happen if there wasn't a Gulf Stream?* (places in Europe would be colder). Elicit students' answers to these questions.
- Ask students to complete the text. Elicit the first answer as an example to get students started. Let them compare answers with a partner before checking with the class.

ANSWERS

1 stopped   2 would be   3 would become
4 wouldn't last   5 wouldn't be able to   6 would go up
7 didn't have   8 would have to

Grammar note

Point out that 1 and 7 use the past form because they are part of the *if* clause (the condition). The others use *would* because they are part of the result clause.

8

- Start by reading the example and pointing out that the second conditional is used because it's describing the impossible or unlikely opposite situation to the first sentence.
- Ask students to work individually to complete the sentences. Let them compare answers with a partner before checking with the class.

ANSWERS

1 rained; wouldn't be
2 flooded, would have to (note that *flood* is used as a verb here)
3 had, would need
4 weren't, wouldn't need to
5 snowed, wouldn't be able to

Pronunciation *would / wouldn't / 'd*
9a [95]

- Play the recording. Students listen to a short conversation and note down how many times they hear *would*, *wouldn't* or *'d*. You may need to play the recording twice.

ANSWER

8 (see audioscript below)

12a   What if …?   195

UNIT 12 Nature

Audioscript [95]

A: Would you move to another country if the weather became much hotter in your country?
B: No, I'd love it if the weather became hotter.
A: I'd go and live somewhere else.
B: Would you?
A: Yes, I wouldn't want to stay. I'd find a country with a colder climate.
B: Oh, I wouldn't. I'd spend every day outside by the pool.

b ★ **CPT extra!** Listening activity [after Ex. 9b]
- Ask students to check their answers in audioscript 95 on page 189 of the Student's Book. In feedback, point out how I'd is hard to hear because it's reduced to a small sound that sometimes assimilates with the following consonant.
- Ask students to practise reading the conversation in pairs. Monitor, prompt and correct pronunciation.
- **Optional step** Practice makes perfect. Encourage your students to practise three or four times, and to try to cover up the dialogue and improvise it from memory.

Speaking my life
10
- Ask students to work in pairs to discuss the questions. Tell students that it isn't always necessary to use full conditional sentences when asking and answering questions. Answers such as *Yes, I would; I think I'd probably ask him about his family* and *I wouldn't know what to do with the money* are more natural responses than full sentences with an *If* clause.

> **EXAMPLE ANSWERS**
> 1 I'd like to live in another country if I could. / I'd never live anywhere else. / I'd move to Japan because I love the food.
> 2 It would be Justin Bieber. Definitely! I'd ask him to sing me a song. / If I could meet anyone, I'd love to meet Angela Merkel – she's brilliant. I'd ask her about the economy.
> 3 I'd stop working straightaway. / I'd keep my job. / I'd spend the money on saving whales and ending poverty.

> **Extra activity**
> Here are other questions to ask:
> *Would you like to be famous one day? Why? / Why not?*
> *What car / clothes / gadget would you buy if you could afford it?*

12b Nature in one cubic foot

Lesson at a glance
- vocabulary: nature
- listening: a documentary
- grammar: *anywhere, everyone, nobody, something*
- speaking: questions with *any*

Vocabulary nature
1
- Ask students to work in pairs to discuss the questions. Elicit ideas in feedback.
- **Optional step** If you have an interest in photography, tell students about the type of photos you take and why you take them. This will provide a model for the students' conversations.

> **ANSWERS**
> Students' own answers

2
- Discuss the questions about the photos with the class and elicit answers.

> **ANSWERS**
> A: ocean
> B: forest, mountain (possibly park)
> C: forest (possibly park)
> D: river
> field, garden and park are man-made

> **Vocabulary and pronunciation note**
> *forest* = a natural place full of trees and plants
> *mountain* = a very high hill (e.g. Mount Everest, the Himalayas, the Alps)
> *field* = a man-made stretch of grass with no trees – used for growing crops
> *river* = a stretch of water (e.g. Nile, Amazon, Rhine)
> *garden* = a man-made arrangement of trees and flowers
> *ocean* = a large sea (e.g. Atlantic, Pacific) – note that Americans use ocean instead of sea
> *park* = this has many meanings – a National Park is a protected area of natural beauty; a safari park has wild animals; a country park has trees and grass; a park in a town or city is a green space with paths, garden areas and places for children to play
> *desert* = an area with no water (e.g. Sahara, Gobi)

3 ★ **CPT extra!** Photo activity [after Ex. 3]
- Ask students to work in pairs to discuss the questions. Elicit ideas in feedback.

> **EXAMPLE ANSWERS**
> Answers depend on your students, but for typical town-dwellers the following are likely:
> See every day: garden, field, perhaps park
> On holiday: mountain, ocean
> Never see: perhaps desert

UNIT 12 Nature

Extra activity

If your students are permitted the use of phones in class, ask students (in small groups) to find and show a nature photograph they have taken. Ask students to describe the photos to their group.

Listening

4 [96]

- **Optional step** Ask students to read the definition of a cube, and point out the green cube (the green metal frame) in each of the four photographs on the page. Explain that Liitschwager takes individual photos of any living thing within the green metal frame.
- Play the recording. Students listen and answer the question. Let them compare answers in pairs before checking with the class.

ANSWER

to show us that everyone can find nature and that different species of plants and animals are always somewhere nearby / to record living things in different places around the world

Audioscript [96]

If you live in the middle of the city, maybe you think that there's nowhere to look at nature. Or if you have a local park, perhaps you don't see anything except people walking their dogs. However, David Liittschwager, the photographer, wants to show us that everyone can find nature. Different species of plants and animals are always somewhere nearby.

David spent five years recording living things in different places around the world. He used a green metal frame which measured one cubic foot and took it to different locations. Then he spent three weeks in that place and photographed everything living inside the green metal cube. That included leaves, animals, plants, fish, even living things which were smaller than one millimetre in size. Some of his photos were taken in places far away from any towns, such as the middle of a forest, the side of a mountain, the ocean or a river, but some of them were taken in parks in the middle of cities.

Background information

David Liittschwager is a contributing photographer to *National Geographic* and other magazines. He lives and works in San Francisco. *One Cubic Foot* was published as a large format book in 2012.

5 [96] ★ **CPT extra!** Video activity [after Ex. 5]

- Give students time to read the sentences carefully. Point out the meaning and pronunciation of millimetre (0.1 centimetre), centimetre (10 millimetres or 0.01 metre) and metre (100 centimetres, 1,000 millimetres).
- Play the recording again. Students listen and note whether the sentences are true (T) or false (F). Let students compare answers in pairs before checking with the class.

- **Optional step** You could ask students to look at audioscript 96 on page 189 of the Student's Book to check their answers. Ask students to underline and say which part of the text reveals the answer.

ANSWERS

1 T (*If you live in the middle of the city, maybe you think that there's nowhere to look at nature.*)
2 T (*wants to show us that everyone can find nature*)
3 T (*recording living things in different places around the world … He took it to different locations*)
4 F (*five years recording living things … around the world.*)
5 F (*photographed everything living*)

Grammar *anywhere, everyone, nobody, something,* etc.

6

- Read the examples in the grammar box with the class. Then ask students to work individually to complete the rules. Let students compare answers in pairs before checking with the class.

ANSWERS

1 -body, -one   2 -where   3 -thing

Grammar note

Form

Grammatically, words ending with -*one*, -*body* or -*thing* (e.g. *someone, everybody, nothing*) are generally pronouns whereas words ending with -*where* (e.g. *somewhere*) can be adverbs as well as pronouns (e.g. *I have to go somewhere* = to a place – describing where you go; *I have to meet someone* = a person – it is a pronoun because it replaces a noun).

Note that, uniquely, *no one* separates into two words (*nobody, nothing, nowhere*).

There is no double negative in English, so we say: *We didn't do anything* or *We did nothing*, but not *We didn't do nothing*.

Use

Somebody, anybody, nobody and *everybody* are used as singular nouns, even though *everybody* refers to more than one person and *anybody* can mean more than one person. Notice these examples:

I saw somebody in the park. (= one person)

There's nobody here. (= no people)

Everybody likes Tom. (= all people – but *likes* not *like* because it is a singular noun)

Is anyone there? (= one or more people – but *Is* not *Are*)

Note that, at this level, we tell students to use *some* in affirmative sentences and *any* in negative sentences or questions. However, it is possible to use *some* in questions, particularly requests (e.g. *Could somebody close that door?*) and it is possible to use *any* in affirmative sentences when asking about one or more (e.g. *Anything you hear is secret; Anybody can come in at any time*). At this level, it is best to avoid these more complex uses.

12b   Nature in one cubic foot

UNIT 12   Nature

Refer students to page 178 for further information and practice.

> **ANSWERS TO GRAMMAR SUMMARY EXERCISES**
>
> **4**
> 1 somewhere   2 something   3 Nowhere
> 4 anybody   5 Everyone   6 anything
>
> **5**
> 1 somewhere   2 everywhere   3 nobody
> 4 nothing   5 something   6 anything
>
> **6**
> 1 Giulia lives somewhere near here.
> 2 There was nobody on the beach so it was really quiet.
> 3 I've been everywhere in this city and the parks are my favourite.
> 4 Anywhere in the room will do.
> 5 Mike didn't have anything with him.
> 6 There's somebody waiting for you outside.

7

- Ask students to work individually to complete the sentences with *any-*, *every-*, *some-* or *no-*. Let students compare answers in pairs before checking with the class. In feedback, ask students to justify their answers by referring to the rules.

> **ANSWERS**
> 1 Every   2 No   3 some / any; any   4 Some

Grammar note

1 Everybody = all people
2 Nobody = no people
3 Here, we can use *some* or *any*: if the speaker uses *some*, they are asking 'which particular individual'; *any* is the more common answer – we generally use *any* in questions – we are asking 'any person at all'.
4 Somebody = one particular person but we don't know which

8

- **Optional step** Ask students to read the texts briefly and match the places with the photos A–D on page 144. (The photos on page 144 are of the same places described in these short texts). Explain what *a coral reef* is (= an underwater ecosystem of calcium carbonate produced by living creatures called corals – they attract tropical fish and plant life).
- Ask students to work individually to choose the correct options in the texts. Elicit the first answer as an example to get them started. Let students compare answers in pairs before checking with the class. In feedback, ask students to justify their answers by referring to the rules (see Grammar note below).

> **ANSWERS**
> C B D A

> **ANSWERS**
> 1 anywhere   2 somewhere   3 nowhere
> 4 everywhere   5 Everybody   6 Everything
> 7 something

Grammar note

1: a place (not a person)
2: one place (not no place)
3: a place (not a thing)
4: all places (here, all directions)
5: all people – it is possible grammatically to choose *somebody* (but it would be odd if only one person in Tennessee likes fishing!)
6: all things (not people)
7: affirmative sentence

Background information

Central Park is a large urban park at the heart of Manhattan in New York. It covers 341 hectares and was begun in 1857.

French Polynesia is made up of 118 islands and atolls stretching over more than 2,000 kilometres of the South Pacific Ocean. They are French overseas territories.

The **Monteverde Reserve**, on the edge of the Tilarán mountain range in the north-west of Costa Rica, has an extremely high biodiversity, consisting of over 2,500 plant species.

The **Duck River** is about 400 kilometres long, and is the longest river located entirely within the US state of Tennessee. It has 151 species of fish, making it the most biologically diverse river in North America.

9

- **Optional step** Ask students to read the four dialogues briefly and say what each situation might be (1: friends asking about the weekend; 2: work colleagues – boss and PA; 3: couple at home after a day at work; 4: work colleagues in an office or school mates in a classroom). Point out that *starving* means very hungry.
- Ask students to work individually to complete the questions and answers. Let them compare answers in pairs before checking with the class.

> **ANSWERS**
> 1 any   2 some   3 any   4 No   5 body/one   6 no
> 7 every   8 where   9 body/one   10 thing

Extra activity

Ask students to practise the dialogues in Exercise 9 in pairs. Tell them to practise two or three times and to try to cover the dialogues and remember them, or improvise and change them.

198   Unit 12   Nature

UNIT 12 Nature

Speaking my life

10 ★ **CPT extra!** Speaking activity [after Ex. 10]

- Organize the class into new pairs. Ask students to work together to complete the questions. Have a brief feedback to confirm answers.
- Ask students to take turns to ask and answer questions and to improvise answers. Monitor and note errors. At the end, ask students what they found out about their partner. Provide feedback on how accurately students used *anywhere, everyone, nobody, something*, etc. when doing this activity.
- **Optional step** Instead of asking questions in pairs, students could mingle and ask three or four different students (see Teacher development below).

> EXAMPLE ANSWERS
> 1 Are you going anywhere nice on holiday this year?
>   (Yes, I'm going somewhere hot. / No, we aren't going anywhere.)
> 2 Did you do anything interesting last weekend?
>   (Yes, I visited somewhere by the sea. / No, I did nothing.)
> 3 Have you ever met anyone/body you know while you were on holiday?
>   (I met an old school friend when I was in Paris last year. / I've never met anybody I know on holiday.)

Extra activity

Here are other questions students could ask in pairs:

Do you know anyone famous?

Have you been anywhere dangerous?

Have you done anything you are proud of?

Have you learned anything new recently?

Teacher development

Physical movement in the classroom

Think about ways of getting your students out of their chairs, and moving around, especially if your students are at the end of a long period of study. Here are four suggestions:

- Use mingles instead of pair work. In Exercise 10 above, for example, ask them to stand up, walk round, and chat briefly to three different people. Set a short time limit.
- Instead of eliciting or brainstorming words to the board and writing them up yourself, ask students to do it for you. Similarly, get students to come to the board and write up answers to tasks.
- Let students stretch and move in the class. This could be as simple as saying, before starting a new activity, 'Right, stand up and stretch!' However, you could tie it into the lesson. For example, (when starting Exercise 10), ask students who are going somewhere nice on holiday to stand up, move, and sit with someone who didn't put up their hand. This mixes pairs, and provides a bit of movement.
- Incorporate classroom management ideas that get students moving. For example, with a small class of ten, try an 'onion': five students sit in a circle, facing out, while the other five bring their chair so that they face one person in the inner circle; students do the speaking task for one minute, then students in the outer circle move one chair clockwise – thus moving, and getting a new partner to talk to. Another idea is 'speaking corners': in Exercise 10, there are three questions to discuss – ask three students to choose one of the three questions and go and sit in a corner of the classroom – the rest of the class stand up, walk round, and visit each corner, where they will be asked the question the speaking corner student has selected.

UNIT 12 Nature

12c Living with chimpanzees

Lesson at a glance
- reading: living with chimpanzees
- critical thinking: close reading
- word focus: *start*
- speaking: an interview

Reading

1 ★ **CPT extra!** Lead-in activity [after Ex. 1]
- Ask students to say what their favourite animals are and why. You could ask students to discuss this in open class or in pairs.
- **Optional step** Alternatively, write *chimpanzees* on the board and brainstorm what students can tell you about them under the headings *Facts* and *Opinions*.

ANSWERS
Students' own answers

2 🔘 [97]
- Ask students to read the article and decide which paragraphs describe each of the three summaries/headings. Let students compare answers in pairs before checking with the class.
- **Optional step** The reading text is recorded. You could play the recording and ask students to read and listen.

ANSWERS
a 1, 2   b 3   c 5

Background information
Dame Jane Goodall, born in the UK in 1934, is a UN messenger of peace as well as a leading expert on primates.
Gombe Stream National Park is in the west of Tanzania. It's only 52 km² but an excellent habitat for many primates.

3
- Read the events with the class. Check *region* (= a part of a country) and *war* (= a fight between countries or peoples).
- Ask students to read the article again and put the events in order. Tell them also to write the year or decade the event happened. Let students compare their answers in pairs before checking with the class.

ANSWERS
1 d – 1960   2 e – 1960s   3 b – 1966   4 g – 1969
5 c – 1970s   6 a – 1980s   7 h – 1989   8 f – now

4 ★ **CPT extra!** Reading activity [after Ex. 4]
- Ask students to work individually to match the words with the definitions. Elicit the first answer as an example to get students started. Let students compare their answers in pairs before checking with the class.

- **Optional step** Before matching the words with the definitions, get students to find and underline the words in the article. Students can then use the context of the article to help them work out the meaning of the words.

ANSWERS
1 a   2 c   3 e   4 d   5 b

Vocabulary note
1 tool = e.g. a stone you can use to break open a nut; we use the word to describe hammers, screwdrivers, etc.
2 natural <u>ha</u>bitat = e.g. for a tiger, it's the jungle; for a lion, it's the open plain
3 sur<u>vive</u> = continue to live, in difficult circumstances (e.g. after the plane crash, they survived for eight days in a hot desert)
4 <u>lec</u>ture = used in academic situations (e.g. a professor talking at a university; an expert talking at a conference)
5 conser<u>va</u>tion = examples include stopping people from cutting down forests, stopping people from killing animals to sell their skins

Extra activity
Drill the longer words for pronunciation. Note the strong stress (shown in the Vocabulary note above).

Critical thinking close reading

5
- **Optional step** This critical thinking task was also in Unit 5. You could refer students back to what they did then to remind them of the skill. There is a Teacher development section on close reading in that unit.
- Ask students to read the sentences and choose the correct options. Let students compare answers in pairs before discussing as a class.

ANSWERS
1 N (The information isn't in the text.)
2 T (*They didn't have very much: a tent, a few clothes and a cup*)
3 F (*Jane had always dreamed of visiting Africa and studying chimpanzees, but she didn't know much about them and she had no scientific qualifications.*)
4 T (*she made three important and new discoveries: chimpanzees ate meat …*)
5 N (The information isn't in the text.)
6 T (*there was a war in the region and Gombe became a dangerous place … As the human population increased in Gombe, more trees were cut down*)
7 N (The information isn't in the text.)
8 F (*Now in her eighties, she spends about 300 days a year giving interviews, talks and lectures, meeting with government officials about animal conservation and raising money for the Jane Goodall Institute which continues her research.*)

200 Unit 12 Nature

UNIT 12 Nature

Word focus *start*

6
- Ask students to read the sentences and recognize the different forms used before matching them with the forms provided. Let students compare answers in pairs before checking with the class.

> **ANSWERS**
> 1 c   2 a   3 d   4 b

> **Vocabulary note**
>
> *Start* can be both a noun and a verb.
> Note that there is often no difference between *start doing* and *start to do*. We can also say: *She started writing in her diary every day* and *Jane started to run towards the forest*. *Doing* emphasizes the activity and *to do* emphasizes an individual action.

7
- Ask students to match the questions with the answers. Let them compare answers in pairs before checking with the class.
- **Optional step** Ask students to work in pairs and take turns to ask the questions. Tell them to change questions as necessary (e.g. *Why did you start studying here? Why did you start to learn English?*). Students provide their own personal answers.

> **ANSWERS**
> 1 b   2 d   3 c   4 a

Speaking *my life*

8
- Ask students to work in pairs. Tell them to start by remembering (or finding in the text, if necessary) the answers to the questions. Ask students to take turns to ask and answer, or to roleplay the situation (one student is an interviewer, the other is Jane).
- As students speak, monitor and notice any errors you could give feedback on.

> **ANSWERS**
> 1 I started my new life in Africa on July 14, 1960.
> 2 I didn't have very much: a tent, a few clothes and a cup.
> 3 I saw a chimpanzee on the first day I arrived.
> 4 I discovered that chimpanzees ate meat, used tools to get food and made tools.

9
- Ask students to work in their pairs to prepare questions. You could elicit one or two possible questions to get them started. As students prepare, monitor to help with ideas and vocabulary.

> **EXAMPLE ANSWERS**
> Example questions:
> Where did you publish articles / who published your articles?
> How did you become famous?
> When was your first book published? What was it?
> Why did many people leave Gombe?
> What problems were there when the population increased?
> How did you work with local people?
> After 1989, what did you do?

10
- Ask each pair to work with another pair. They take turns to ask and answer their questions.
- As students speak, monitor and notice any errors you could give feedback on.

11
- Ask students to work individually to write down five important dates.
- **Optional step** You could start them off by writing a few dates on the board and getting students to ask you about them, e.g. *2011*.
  Students   *What happened to you in 2011?*
  You   *I got my first teaching job.*
  Students   *Who did you teach?*
  You   *I taught teenagers in a private school in Madrid.*
  This provides a model of what they could say.
- Ask students to work with their partner and take turns to ask and answer about the dates.
- In feedback, ask students to tell the class anything interesting they found out about their partner.

UNIT 12 Nature

12d Discussing issues

Lesson at a glance
- real life: finding a solution

Real life finding a solution

1
- Ask students to look at the photo and discuss the questions. You could ask the questions in open class or ask students to discuss in pairs first. Elicit opinions and answers from the class in feedback.

> **EXAMPLE ANSWERS**
> 1 The photo shows girls in a zoo looking through the glass at a tiger in an enclosure. The tiger may feel confused by the people in the glass or may be thinking of them as lunch; the girls feel excited at seeing a tiger or sorry that it's in a cage.
> 2 Possible answers: I don't like seeing animals in cages; animals in zoos look unhappy and bored. / I love looking at animals; they're amazing and beautiful; it's better to see them in real life than on the TV.

2
- Ask students to read the extract and answer the questions. Let them compare their answers in pairs before checking with the class.
- **Optional step** In feedback, check *low visitor numbers* (= not many visitors) and *lack of money* (= not enough money).

> **ANSWERS**
> 1 No – only if the city council cannot solve problems.
> 2 the problem of low visitor numbers and lack of money
> 3 The zoo would have to find them another home (in other zoos or parks).

3 [98]
- Ask students to read the five sentences carefully. Check *receive* (= get, be given) and *sponsorship* (= when people pay to 'sponsor' the zoo or an animal, e.g. companies pay money and, in return, they get positive publicity such as their name on the sign or on the souvenirs).
- Play the recording. Students listen and note whether the sentences are true (T) or false (F). Let students compare answers in pairs before checking with the class.
- **Optional step** Ask students to justify answers by saying what they heard.

> **ANSWERS**
> 1 T (*The problem is that the zoo will close without the council's help. How about giving us more money?*)
> 2 F (*It just isn't attracting enough tourists.*)
> 3 T (*It's also an important place for animal conservation.*)
> 4 F (*But if we don't have any money, we can't advertise.*)
> 5 T (*Actually, that isn't a bad idea. You might be right!*)

Audioscript [98]

Z = zoo manager, C = city council leader

Z: I'm very worried about the situation. The problem is that the zoo will close without the council's help. How about giving us more money?

C: I'm sorry, but the council doesn't have any more money for the zoo.

Z: But if we don't find a solution soon, then we'll have to close it. And the zoo is part of the city. It's a tourist attraction.

C: Yes, but that's the point. It just isn't attracting enough tourists. You're going to have to find the money from somewhere else.

Z: It's also an important place for animal conservation. If we didn't have zoos, some of these animals wouldn't survive.

C: I understand that, but we need to find a different solution. What if you advertised the zoo more? In the newspaper, on the radio or online, for example.

Z: But if we don't have any money, we can't advertise.

C: Well, why don't you try sponsorship? You know, ask a company to support the zoo.

Z: Actually, that isn't a bad idea. You might be right!

C: I have the names of some company bosses you could contact …

4 [98]
- Ask students to complete the sentences with the phrases in the box. Let students compare answers in pairs.
- **Optional step** Elicit the first answer and ask what helped them decide on *How about* (it is always followed by *-ing*). This should help students complete the task – the grammar of each sentence is a clue as to which phrase is needed.
- Play the recording again. Students listen and check their answers.
- **Optional step** Drill the sentences for pronunciation. Ask students to close their books. Read three or four phrases out and ask the class to repeat chorally and individually.

> **ANSWERS**
> 1 How about 2 I'm sorry, but 3 But if we don't
> 4 What if you 5 we can't 6 why don't you
> 7 that isn't 8 You might

5 ★ **CPT extra!** Real life activity [after Ex. 5]
- Ask students to match the sentences in Exercise 4 with the correct section of the expressions. Let students compare answers in pairs before checking with the class.
- **Optional step** Show the list of expressions on the board (or project it using your classroom technology). Students can come to the board to write up the missing phrases.

202 Unit 12 Nature

UNIT 12 Nature

> **ANSWERS**
> Stating and explaining the problem: 3
> Making suggestions: 1, 4, 6
> Responding positively: 7, 8
> Responding negatively: 2, 5

Vocabulary notes

How about + -ing, What if you/we … and *Why don't you …?* are ways of making suggestions or giving advice.

I'm sorry, but … and *We can't …* are ways of explaining why a suggestion or piece of advice won't work.

That isn't a bad idea and *You might be right* are ways of accepting a suggestion and saying it will work.

6

- Organize the class into groups of four. If your class doesn't neatly divide, have one or two groups of five, and have joint zoo managers (Students A). Ask students to decide who is A, B, C and D.

- Give students time to find their information on pages 153, 154 and 155 and prepare what to say. Tell them to think of phrases from the lesson that they could try to include in the roleplay.

- **Optional step** Here are key phrases you could try to get students using in their roleplay:
  Hello, everyone and thank you for coming. Today we are going to discuss the zoo. The problem is that the zoo will close if we don't find a solution to low visitor numbers and lack of money. Do you have any suggestions?
  Why don't you ask companies to sponsor different animals? You might put their company name on the animal's cage.
  What about starting a zoo shop?
  Actually, that isn't a bad idea.
  What if you offered special tickets with discounts?
  But we can't have lower prices. We don't make enough money.

- When students are ready, ask them to act out the roleplay (see Teacher development below). Set a ten-minute time limit. At the end, ask zoo managers to say which three suggestions were the best.

- As students speak, monitor their performance. Note down errors students make. In feedback, write errors on the board and ask students to correct them.

Teacher development

Roleplays

Roleplays are fun and motivating, and often, because there's an element of acting and pretending involved, they're a way of freeing up students to be confident and to perform unselfconsciously when using English. However, they need to be carefully managed and organized. Here are some tips:

- Make sure students have plenty of time to prepare and are clear about what they have to do. You could do this by breaking the preparation section into stages: 1 Get into groups of four; 2 Choose your role; 3 Find and read your information; 4 Prepare your role – ask the teacher for help as you prepare; 5 Act out the roleplay. Instruct each stage separately so that students know exactly what to do, and let them do that stage before moving to the next stage. Set realistic time limits at each stage. Make sure you give students some individual attention while preparing so that you know everybody is ready when the roleplay starts.

- Organize the classroom to reflect the fact that students are doing a roleplay. You might ask groups to sit in a circle or round a table to reflect the fact that they're in a meeting. If your classroom is inflexible, get students to at least turn and face each other.

- Make sure that students use the new language in the roleplay. You can achieve this in the preparation stage by prompting students to think of which phrases to use as they prepare. During the roleplay, you could prompt students to use phrases in one of these ways: 1 Write some of the phrases on the board so students can easily look over and use them as they debate; 2 Write some of the phrases on flashcards and hold different ones up as students debate – students must try to use the phrase on the card; 3 Write phrases on small cards and give a set of cards to each group – each time a student speaks they should turn over a card and try to use the phrase on the card; alternatively, groups could spread the cards on their table and turn them over when they are used in the roleplay.

UNIT 12 Nature

12e The Eden Project

Lesson at a glance
- writing: an article
- writing skill: planning an article

Writing an article

1

- **Optional step** Start by asking students to describe the photo. Use the opportunity to pre-teach *biome* (see Background information below).
- Ask students to read the article and answer the questions. Let students compare their answers in pairs before checking with the class.

> **ANSWERS**
> 1 huge plastic domes called 'biomes' – the Rainforest Biome and the Mediterranean Biome, as well as outdoor gardens, art exhibitions, theatre performances and outdoor concerts
> 2 to see the Biomes and exhibits, to learn about the natural world, and to do courses in plants and nature

> **Background Information**
> The **Eden Project** is located in a disused Kaolinite (a clay mineral) pit near the town of St Austell in Cornwall, England's most westerly county. Eden is the name of paradise in the Bible.
> In the article, **biome** /ˈbaɪ.əʊm/ refers to a huge plastic dome containing a particular ecological system. More broadly, the word biome refers to a whole ecological system (e.g. a desert is a biome, a rainforest is a biome). The Eden Project's biomes consist of hundreds of hexagonal and pentagonal, inflated, plastic cells supported by steel frames.

Writing skill planning an article

2a

- Ask students to work in pairs to think of ways of researching an article. In feedback, elicit ideas and build up a list on the board.

> **ANSWERS**
> newspapers and magazines
> interview people who work there
> find a book on the subject
> visit the place
> read websites about it (e.g. Wikipedia)

b

- **Optional step** Start by explaining how mind maps can be used to plan written work. Point out that the circle in the centre is the topic or title and that, when planning, you can draw lines off the central circle to different circles placed round that central circle. In each circle you write a different set of useful information to include. It's possible to have other lines coming off these circles to sub-divide information. Once you have made a mind map with different circles of information, you decide what to include or exclude, and what order to present the information.
- Ask students to work individually to match the questions (a–f) with the information in the mind map (1–6). Let them compare their answers in pairs before checking with the class.

> **ANSWERS**
> a 1 b 3 c 5 d 6 e 4 f 2

c

- Ask students to read the article again to find out how the writer includes the information in the mind map in each of the four paragraphs in the article. Tell students to note the information in the mind map (or just write the numbers) under each of the paragraph headings.
- Let students compare their notes in pairs before checking with the class. You could prepare the answers to show on the board.

> **ANSWERS**
> the introduction (paragraph 1): 1, 2, 3
> paragraph 2: 4
> paragraph 3: 5
> the conclusion (paragraph 4): 6

3 ★ **CPT extra!** Writing activity [after Ex. 3]

- Read the instructions with the class. Then brainstorm places for students to write about. You could ask: *Where have you visited recently? What are the most interesting places to visit in your country?* Tell students to consider historical houses, museums, galleries, etc.
- Ask students to work individually to research, prepare and plan their articles. You may want to set this research and preparation stage for homework as students will find it easier to research at home. However, if you have internet or library access at your institution, you could do the research stage in class.
- Once students have prepared mind maps, you could ask students to share ideas in pairs so that they can help each other with suggestions. If students are working at home to prepare mind maps, they could email them to you or other classmates for comments before starting to write the article.
- Students use the mind map to write their article.
- **Optional step** Students exchange articles with a partner. Encourage students to comment on and correct each other's work.

> **Extra activity**
> Collate the students' articles in a brochure or as a collection of articles online if you have a class website. Students can read each other's articles and leave comments.

UNIT 12 Nature

12f Cambodia animal rescue

Before you watch

1 ★ **CPT extra!** Background information [after Ex. 1]

- Ask students to work in pairs or small groups to look at the photo and to discuss the questions. Elicit ideas in feedback.

> **ANSWERS**
> 1 a tiger and an elephant
> 2 Possible answers: They're in a rescue centre; they're from Cambodia; something has happened to them so they needed rescuing (e.g. victims of hunters)
> 3 Possible answers: The rescue centre may give them a safe place to stay, treat their injuries, reintroduce them to the wild.

Key vocabulary

2

- Ask students to match the words with the definitions. Let students compare answers in pairs before checking with the class. Use the feedback to check key words. (Note that the video uses *re-release*, not *release – re-release* means release again).
- **Optional step** It's a good idea to show the pronunciation of these key words – students have to hear them in continuous speech on the video. You could say the words and ask students to repeat (see Vocabulary and pronunciation note below).

> **ANSWERS**
> 1 f   2 g   3 h   4 c   5 a; b   6 e   7 d

> **Vocabulary and pronunciation note**
>
> Note the strong stress in these words: pro*tec*tion, *poa*cher, *spon*sor, *rel*ease, *vic*tim, il*leg*al, *pow*der, en*dan*gered
>
> *poachers* (verb: *to poach*; topic noun: *poaching*) are people who hunt and kill animals when it is against the law – this may be people who go on to other people's land to hunt, or, as is the case here, people who hunt and kill endangered and protected animals.
>
> *sponsor* = to provide financial support for a reason (e.g. in return for advertising, or, here, in return for positive actions)
>
> If you *grind* (past: *ground*) something into *powder*, you put something in a bowl or on a hard surface and use a heavy blunt instrument to crush it until it is a powder (a soft, dry substance like dust or sand)
>
> *endangered animals* = animals that may become extinct (die out) in the future

While you watch

3 🎥 [12.1]

- **Optional step** Check the animals first. You could use mime, drawings on the board or ask students to look them up on the internet. Drill them for pronunciation – all the words start with a strong stress.
- Play the video. Students watch and number the animals in order (1–8). Let students compare answers in pairs before checking with the class. Write the order on the board.

> **ANSWERS**
> 1 c   2 h   3 e   4 a   5 d   6 b   7 f   8 g

Videoscript 🎥 12.1

Y = Matt Young, **H** = Shiree Harris

Part 1

0.00–0.59 Dara the tiger loves lying around and relaxing. She also likes to be touched and talked to. And, like many other animals, she loves to play. Unfortunately, Dara, and the other animals at the Phnom Tamao Rescue Centre, are all victims of the illegal poaching of wild animals in Cambodia.

Many animals at the centre are brought in by a special team called the 'Wilderness Protection Mobile Unit', or the 'MU'. The MU rescues animals from poachers. With the support of the government of Cambodia, they're working to stop poaching.

In many cases, rescued animals can be returned to the wild.

In others, like with these crested eagles, the animals need special care.

1.00–1.05 Matt Young works for Wild Aid, a US group that sponsors the MU and the rescue centre.

1.06–1.10 **Y** Once we're sure they're nice and healthy again, we can get them out to Kirirom and re-release them.

1.11–1.16 These wild eagles are 'hand fed', or given their food by hand, and they don't always like it!

1.17–1.18 **Y** Did you get that? Fantastic!

1.19–1.27 The crested eagles will probably be released back into the wild someday. However, many of the animals here will need human help forever.

1.28–1.41 This little gibbon lived in a birdcage at a petrol station for two years. She's now at Phnom Tamao. They're helping her to become healthy, but they probably won't be able to release her again. She'll likely be safer and happier at the centre.

1.42–1.48 Mimi was also someone's pet. A volunteer who works for 'Free the Bears', which sponsors Mimi, explains …

1.49–1.58 **H** A family bought it for their little daughter, but they only kept her for, I think they said four weeks, and then they realized she was too hard to handle, a bit nippy and everything – so they just brought her in.

1.59–2.08 Like the little gibbon, if Mimi were in the wild, she probably wouldn't have the skills to survive. The best place for her, too, is clearly the rescue centre.

12f Cambodia animal rescue   205

UNIT 12 Nature

Part 2

2.09–2.47 Unfortunately, there is one thing many of these animals have in common; poachers want them! If many of these beautiful animals were not at the rescue centre, they would be dead.

The leader of Wild Aid explains what part of the problem is for tigers. She says that poachers can make a lot of money by selling a tiger's body parts illegally. In some Asian countries, certain parts of the tiger are ground into powder. This powder is processed and sold as an expensive traditional medicine. People think that taking the product will improve their health. No one knows if this is true, but it's definitely not good for the tigers.

2.48–3.18 The Phnom Tamao Rescue Centre cares for over 800 animals of 86 different types, or species, including this friendly elephant.

Lucky was saved from poachers two years ago.

Little Sima has been at Phnom Tamao for six months.

It's hard to think that these animals may never return to their home in the wild. They can't survive without support and help from humans.

3.19–end The Phnom Tamao Rescue Centre is helping poaching victims in Cambodia. Unfortunately, the bigger problem of illegal poaching is still around. It will be as long as there's a demand for products that are made from these animals.

For now, we can only hope that the MU can help stop more wild animals from becoming endangered. Thanks to the Phnom Tamao Rescue Centre, they'll have a safe place to go.

4

- Ask students to match the sentence halves. Let students compare answers in pairs before checking with the class.

> **ANSWERS**
> 1 e 2 c 3 a 4 b 5 d

5 [12.1]

- Give students time to read the questions carefully.
- Play the video again. Students watch and answer the questions. Let them check answers in pairs before checking with the class.

> **ANSWERS**
> 1 (Wilderness Protection) Mobile Unit
> 2 The MU rescues animals from poachers.
> 3 poaching
> 4 Wild Aid sponsors the MU and the rescue centre.
> 5 in a birdcage at a petrol station
> 6 Free the Bears
> 7 She was too hard to handle – a bit nippy
> 8 Over 800 animals of 86 different types, or species

> **Vocabulary note**
> *nippy* = here, likely to bite you
> *species* = a type of animal (e.g. dogs, cats, bears)

> **Background information**
> Phnom Tamao Wildlife Rescue Centre (PTWRC) is the largest zoo in Cambodia, a country in south-east Asia. It was established in 1995, and covers an area of over 6,000 acres of protected regenerating forest. It's only 40 kilometres south of Phnom Penh, the capital city of Cambodia.

After you watch

Vocabulary in context

6a [12.2]

- Explain that students are going to watch some clips from the video which contain some new words and phrases. They need to choose the correct meaning of the words.
- Play the clips. When each multiple-choice question appears, pause the clip so that students can choose the correct definition. You could let students compare answers in pairs before discussing as a class.

> **ANSWERS**
> 1 b 2 c 3 a 4 b 5 c

Videoscript 12.2

1 With the **support** of the government of Cambodia, …
   a need
   b help
   c care

2 In many cases, **rescued** animals can be returned to the wild.
   a wild and dangerous
   b kept in cages at a zoo
   c saved from danger

3 In others, like with these crested eagles, the animals need **special care**.
   a extra help
   b medical help
   c financial help

4 … they realized she was too **hard to handle**, …
   a heavy to lift
   b difficult to deal with
   c big to keep

5 … there's a **demand** for products …
   a when people sell something
   b when people make something
   c when people want something

UNIT 12 Nature

Vocabulary note

support = Governments can provide financial support or political support or legal support

rescued = saved from danger in the wild or in people's care

special care = in different contexts, this may mean medical help or expert help (i.e. something more than ordinary care)

hard to handle = a clear example is a snake – a snake is hard to handle (i.e. difficult to pick up and control) because it is poisonous and slippery

demand = used in economics to say there is a need for the product in a particular market (note: *in demand*)

b

- Ask students to read the short summary and complete it with the missing words. Let students compare their summaries in pairs before checking with the class.

> **ANSWERS**
> 1 care   2 support   3 rescued   4 handle   5 demand

7 ★ **CPT extra!** Research project [after Ex. 7]

- Discuss the questions as a class.

> **EXAMPLE ANSWERS**
> 1 They're important because they protect animals, bring the problem to the world's attention, and provide expertise to help stop exploiting animals.
> 2 Students' own answers
> 3 Governments can make laws against poaching, increase fines or punishments for poachers, finance rescue centres and anti-poaching groups, open reserves to protect animals, stop the export of endangered animals to other countries, criminalize the use of animal products.

UNIT 12 Review and memory booster ★ CPT extra! Language games

Memory Booster activities

Exercises 4, 5 and 8 are Memory Booster activities. For more information about these activities and how they benefit students, see page 10.

I can … tick boxes

As an alternative to students simply ticking the *I can …* boxes, you could ask them to give themselves a score from 1 to 4 (1 = not very confident; 4 = very confident) for each language area. If students score 1 or 2 for a language area, refer them to additional practice activities in the Workbook and Grammar summary exercises.

Grammar

1

- Ask students to work individually to complete the second conditional sentences. Let them compare answers in pairs before checking with the class.

> **ANSWERS**
> 1 'd go   2 rained   3 lived   4 wouldn't need   5 didn't like

2

- Ask students to complete the sentences individually with information that is true for them, then compare their sentences.
- You could ask them to make questions for the statements (e.g. *If you had a million dollars, what would you do?*), then ask and answer each other in pairs.

> **ANSWERS**
> Students' own answers

3

- Ask students to complete the sentences with the pairs of words.

> **ANSWERS**
> 1 Nowhere; Everywhere   2 Someone; somewhere
> 3 anyone; anywhere   4 Everyone; anything
> 5 nobody; everybody   6 something; nothing

4 》》 **MB**

- Ask students to work in pairs to complete the sentences about the green cube. Elicit answers in feedback.

> **EXAMPLE ANSWERS**
> 1 nature   2 different places/locations   3 living inside it

UNIT 12 Nature

Vocabulary

5 >> MB

- Ask students to work in pairs to look at the photos and answer the questions. Elicit their ideas in feedback.

> **EXAMPLE ANSWERS**
>
> Photo 1: 1 early morning or late afternoon   2 very snowy / snowstorm
> Photo 2: 1 afternoon   2 flood
> Photo 3: 1 night   2 lightning

6

- Look at the example with the class and elicit a similarity and a difference for the first pair in the box to get students started, e.g. (mountain / desert) *They are both difficult to survive in for long but a mountain will likely have shelter from the sun and a river to get water from.*
- Ask students to work in pairs to write sentences for the other pairs of words. Elicit their sentences in feedback.

> **EXAMPLE ANSWERS**
>
> river / ocean: a river and an ocean both have water, but an ocean has more water and it's salty.
> park / garden: a park and a garden both have flowers and plants, but a park is much bigger.
> river / park: a river and a park both have nature and wildlife, but a river is much longer and has water.
> field / forest: a field and a forest both have a lot of nature, but a forest has trees and a field has crops or farm animals.
> ocean / desert: an ocean and a desert are both very big, but a desert is dry and an ocean is all water.

Real life

7

- Ask students to put the words in order to make phrases.
- Let them compare answers in pairs before checking with the class.

> **ANSWERS**
>
> 1 What about opening a new zoo?
> 2 Why don't we ask for help?
> 3 If we don't advertise, we won't sell any products. / We won't sell any products if we don't advertise.
> 4 The problem is that many people don't recycle plastic.
> 5 I'm sorry but that won't work.
> 6 That's a good idea.

8 >> MB

- Ask students to work in pairs to look at the problems and make suggestions. Elicit their ideas in feedback and make a list on the board.

> **ANSWERS**
>
> Students' own answers

Photocopiable tests

Name _____
Total score _____

Unit 1 Test

Vocabulary

1 Complete the text with the verbs in the box. There is one extra word you do not need. There is an example at the beginning (0).

| do | fall | feel | get | go | make | play | stay | take | ~~wake~~ | watch | work |

I usually (0) __wake__ up very early – at four o'clock. I lie in bed for a few minutes, then I (1) _____ up and start my day. I take the bus to the post office where I pick up all the letters and parcels for my area and put them in the van. I'm a postman, you see. I (2) _____ long hours and I rarely (3) _____ a break, so, at the end of the day, I (4) _____ really tired. I don't (5) _____ up late in the evening and (6) _____ TV. I usually (7) _____ to bed at eight and I (8) _____ asleep very quickly. On Sundays, I have a day off. I (9) _____ some gardening and sometimes I (10) _____ tennis but, mostly, I sleep.

___ / 10

2 Choose the correct option (A, B or C) to complete the sentences. There is an example at the beginning (0).

0 Graham _____ fishing every weekend.
  A makes   B does   Ⓒ goes

1 Janice doesn't _____ home until ten on weekdays.
  A take   B fall   C get

2 I _____ karate at the sports centre.
  A play   B do   C go

3 Rebecca's _____ her homework right now.
  A making   B doing   C going

4 I like _____ cards.
  A playing   B doing   C going

5 You'll _____ better in a few days.
  A make   B feel   C go

6 I've got a sore _____.
  A cough   B throat   C ache

7 I've got _____ ache.
  A head   B nose   C stomach

8 _____ these pills for your backache.
  A Make   B Do   C Take

9 I don't like _____ shopping.
  A making   B taking   C going

10 Can you _____ the piano?
  A play   B do   C stay

___ / 10

Grammar

3 Complete the email with the correct present simple or present continuous form of the verbs in brackets. There is an example at the beginning (0).

Hi Jenny

I (0) __am doing__ (do) a course in Spanish at the moment. My best friend Susie and I (1) _____ (stay) with a host family in Madrid. They're very friendly and talkative – Spanish people (2) _____ (talk) a lot! On the course, we (3) _____ (have) lessons every day in the morning, but we (4) _____ (not go) to lessons in the afternoon. What (5) _____ (we / do) in the afternoon? Well, we (6) _____ (usually / study), but sometimes we (7) _____ (go) shopping. Right now, Susie (8) _____ (not study) – she (9) _____ (listen) to music in her room. It's very loud!

Anyway, what's your news, Jenny? (10) _____ (you / do) anything interesting this summer? Write soon.

Alex

___ / 10

PHOTOCOPIABLE © National Geographic Learning

4 Write present simple or present continuous sentences from the prompts. Use the word in brackets. There is an example at the beginning (0).

0 Paul / stay with friends (right now) Paul *is staying with friends right now*.
1 Sarah / go swimming (often) Sarah _____.
2 Irene / start work at nine (every day) Irene _____.
3 We / eat out at the weekend (usually) We _____.
4 Simon / not feel well (at the moment) Simon _____.
5 Erica / get home early (not often) Erica _____.
6 More people / do karate (these days) More people _____.
7 Suzy / have time for breakfast (rarely) Suzy _____.
8 I / not feel worried (right now) I _____.
9 Jack / watch films on TV (sometimes) Jack _____.
10 They / visit their grandparents (twice a year) They _____.

___ / 10

Reading

A day in the life of Mark Zuckerberg

Mark Zuckerberg is a busy guy. He runs Facebook, the social media giant, so it isn't surprising that the technology wonder kid has quite a lot to do throughout the day. Despite being responsible for a company that makes over $400 billion every year, amazingly Zuckerberg still makes the time to exercise regularly, travel often, and spend time with his young family. How does he do it?

Zuckerberg tries to keep his choices in life simple. Most people spend a lot of time thinking about what to wear or what to cook, where to go and what to do, but Zuckerberg never thinks about these things. He wakes up at the same time every day, checks Facebook and WhatsApp on his phone, then he usually works out in his personal gym at home. Zuckerberg typically exercises about three times a week, and sometimes he goes jogging with his pet dog. There's nothing unusual about Zuckerberg's diet. After exercising, he eats what he feels like for breakfast, then he's ready for the day.

Zuckerberg doesn't like to waste time on small decisions. That's also why he wears the same thing almost every day: jeans, trainers and a grey t-shirt. It's not because he's lazy or hates fashion, but because he doesn't want to think about clothes. He wants to think about important things. Zuckerberg works 50 to 60 hours a week for his company, Facebook, but he thinks about the social media platform constantly. 'I spend most of my time thinking about how to connect the world and serve our community better, but a lot of that time isn't in our office or meeting with people,' he says. Most of his work is away from the office – when he's thinking of new ideas.

When he's not working, Zuckerberg spends some of his time learning new things. Currently, he's studying Mandarin Chinese. He also tries to read as many books as he can — in 2015, he read a new book every two weeks. He believes in having personal goals in life – he thinks that we feel better when we learn or do new things. Travelling or working, Zuckerberg also spends a lot of time with his wife, Dr Priscilla Chan, and his two children. Like all parents, he thinks it's important to have time with his family when they are young and growing up.

5 Read the article about Mark Zuckerberg. Choose the correct answer (A, B or C). There is an example at the beginning (0).

0 What sort of company does Mark Zuckerberg run?
   A a clothes company
   B a supermarket giant
   Ⓒ a social media company

1 How does the writer feel about Zuckerberg's lifestyle?
   A He thinks he shouldn't work a lot of hours.
   B He is surprised that he does so many things.
   C He says he doesn't have any time with his family.

2 In the writer's opinion, how is Mark Zuckerberg different from other people?
   A He does more exercise than most people.
   B He spends more time using technology than other people.
   C He spends very little time thinking about things like food or clothes.

3 How often does Mark Zuckerberg do exercise?
   A every day
   B quite often
   C not very often

4 In paragraph 2, what does 'works out' mean?
   A does a job
   B does some exercise
   C calls people

5 What does Mark Zuckerberg eat for breakfast?
   A the same things every day
   B whatever he wants to eat
   C a special diet

6 What do we find out about the clothes Mark Zuckerberg wears?
   A He never wears T-shirts.
   B He often wears old clothes.
   C He usually wears the same clothes.

7 What does the writer say about Mark Zuckerberg's work?
   A He is constantly in his office.
   B He often isn't at the company.
   C He doesn't think about the company a lot.

8 According to the writer, what is Mark Zuckerberg doing these days?
   A reading two books a week
   B learning a new language
   C travelling

9 What do we find out about his private life?
   A He isn't married yet.
   B He doesn't have any kids.
   C He is a father.

10 In paragraph 4, what does 'personal goals' mean?
   A things he wants to do in life
   B people who are important to him in life
   C characteristics that he has

___ / 10

Listening

6 [99] Listen to Mary talk about a typical day. Choose the correct answer (A, B or C). There is an example at the beginning (0).

0 Mary goes to …
   A the National College.
   (B) the International College.
   C the Inter-continental College.

1 On a typical Monday, Mary gets up at …
   A six o'clock.
   B seven o'clock.
   C eight o'clock.

2 Mary's flatmate gets up …
   A before her.
   B after her.
   C at the same time as her.

3 Mary usually has … for breakfast.
   A bread
   B cereal
   C eggs

4 Mary's flatmate …
   A doesn't have breakfast.
   B eats a different breakfast to Mary.
   C eats the same food for breakfast as Mary.

5 Mary usually …
   A takes the bus to college.
   B goes to college by car.
   C walks to college.

6 Mary tells us …
   A how far her flat is from her college.
   B how long it takes to go to her college.
   C how regularly buses go from her flat to her college.

7 In the evening, after college, Mary …
   A watches TV.
   B listens to music.
   C meets her friends.

8 At the weekend, Mary's college is …
   A open all day.
   B only open on Saturday morning.
   C not open at all.

9 On a typical day at the weekend, Mary usually …
   A goes swimming and plays tennis.
   B goes swimming and meets friends.
   C meets friends and goes to the cinema.

10 On Sundays, Mary …
   A goes cycling through the countryside.
   B goes for walks.
   C goes jogging in the mountains.

___ / 10

Writing

7 Follow the instructions below.

Write five sentences about your everyday routines. Include information about something you always do, something you sometimes do and something you never do.

___ / 10

Speaking

8 Read the task below and give your presentation in class.

Prepare to describe how you usually spend your free time. Talk about what you do in the evenings and at weekends, what sports you do and the hobbies or interests you have.

___ / 10

Unit 2 Test

Vocabulary

1 Complete the text with the correct form of the word in CAPITAL LETTERS. There is an example at the beginning (0).

The Invictus Games is a (0) _competition_ for people injured   COMPETE
in wars. All the (1) _____ are learning to live with   COMPETE
life-changing injuries. Events include (2) _____ and   CYCLE
(3) _____ as well as team sports like rugby and basketball   ATHLETE
for (4) _____ in wheelchairs. The Games are organized   PLAY
(5) _____ the Olympics – the races are shown on TV in the UK,   LIKE
and all the (6) _____ get gold medals. But, for the people   WIN
who are (7) _____, this isn't what's important. They are   COMPETE
there to make friends with other (8) _____ or swimmers   RUN
or (9) _____. The Invictus Games helps people to feel better   WRESTLE
about themselves, and to feel like champions, not (10) _____.   LOSE

___ / 10

2 Complete the sentences with the words in the box. There are two extra words you do not need. There is an example at the beginning (0).

celebrate celebration competition competitive ~~footballer~~ gymnastics like line matches race racing slow team

0 Ronaldo is a famous _footballer_ .
1 Eid is an annual _____ .
2 Ivan got tired and started to _____ down.
3 The *Tour de France* is a famous cycling _____ .
4 Olive is very _____ her sister.
5 _____ is an Olympic sport.
6 There are fifteen players in a rugby _____ .
7 Jason was first to cross the finish _____ .
8 The sport of horse _____ is popular in Ireland.
9 Jill is very _____ . She hates losing.
10 We saw two _____ at the hockey stadium.

___ / 10

Grammar

3 Complete the text with the correct form of the verbs in brackets. There is an example at the beginning (0).

(0) _Playing_ (play) rounders is a lot of fun. It's like baseball, but it isn't as difficult. You don't have to (1) _____ (wear) special clothes or caps and you can (2) _____ (use) a tennis ball when you play. The only thing you must (3) _____ (have) is a bat – rounders bats are shorter and lighter than baseball bats. Anyone can play. (4) _____ (be) good at sport isn't important. There are girls and boys, young and old, on a rounders team, and they are only interested in (5) _____ (have) fun. (6) _____ (win) isn't the main thing. Of course, some people are better at (7) _____ (play) rounders than others, but they don't want (8) _____ (score) all the points. Everybody has a go. Personally, I love (9) _____ (play) rounders because it's a game for all the family. You can (10) _____ (have) a great time together.

___ / 10

Photocopiable tests: Unit 2

4 Choose the correct option (A, B, C or D) to complete the sentences. There is an example at the beginning (0).

0 You _____ buy a ticket. The museum is free on Saturdays.
  A have to   (B) don't have to   C must   D mustn't

1 Students _____ park their cars in front of reception. Those parking places are for visitors only.
  A can   B don't have to   C can't   D have to

2 You _____ be late. If you miss the start of the play, they won't let you in.
  A can   B don't have to   C have to   D mustn't

3 You _____ buy a ticket on the door or in advance – it's your choice.
  A can   B have to   C must   D can't

4 You _____ wear a hat inside the chapel. It's not allowed.
  A must   B don't have to   C have to   D mustn't

5 Joe _____ go to the party if he doesn't want to.
  A can't   B doesn't have to   C has to   D mustn't

6 Do I _____ sign this form here?
  A have to   B can   C must   D can't

7 I'm interested in _____ this club.
  A join   B to join   C joining   D to joining

8 _____ cricket is popular in Australia.
  A Play   B Playing   C To play   D To playing

9 I can't _____ my glasses.
  A find   B finding   C to find   D to finding

10 We hate _____ all the time.
  A lose   B losing   C to lose   D to losing

___ / 10

Reading

Wimbledon

Wimbledon is the oldest tennis tournament in the world, and all the top tennis players want to win it. It's very different from most of the other international tournaments, not only because it's important and it's on grass, but because players have to follow some very old-fashioned rules. Firstly, for example, they have to wear white – white sports shoes and socks as well as white tops and white shorts or skirts. Nowadays, they can wear some colour on their clothes, but only if the colour is one centimetre wide or less. The rule is unpopular with some players because they think it is old-fashioned, and it makes people think that tennis is not a modern sport. They also want to wear what they feel like wearing, and some would like to wear advertising on their clothes, but they can't. Other players like the rule – it makes Wimbledon feel special and different. Women are allowed to wear shorts at Wimbledon, but most players prefer to wear sports dresses or skirts. Roger Federer, one of the most successful men's players, sometimes wears a smart, white evening jacket when he walks on to the court at Wimbledon! He takes it off when he starts the match!

Another tradition is also unusual in tennis. At Wimbledon, female players are called Miss or Mrs. So, the umpire will say, for example, 'Game, Set and Match to Miss Williams' at the end of the match. Again, some people like the tradition, but other players think it's too old-fashioned. Why can't they use their whole name or just their surname like they do with the men? In other ways, Wimbledon is a very modern tournament. The Centre Court at Wimbledon is a fantastic place to play and watch tennis. It has an expensive and brilliantly-designed roof, so players don't have to stop playing when it rains – something that is not uncommon in London, even in July, when the tournament takes place. Winners get over £2 million in prize money, and losing finalists get half that amount. The tournament makes a lot of money, not just from ticket sales, but also from television money, and from sales of food and souvenirs. Wimbledon is famous for selling strawberries and cream, and visitors eat an amazing 140,000 servings of strawberries every year. That's a lot of strawberries – and a great tradition!

5 Read the article about the Wimbledon tennis tournament. Are the sentences right (R) or wrong (W)? If there isn't enough information to say if the sentences are right or wrong, write doesn't say (DS). There is an example at the beginning (0).

0 There aren't any tennis tournaments older than Wimbledon.   R
1 Both men and women have to wear the same colour clothes at Wimbledon.   ___
2 Wearing a blue top is not allowed at Wimbledon.   ___
3 Most tennis players hate the rules about clothes at Wimbledon.   ___
4 A lot of people think that tennis is an old-fashioned sport.   ___
5 Players don't wear advertising on their clothes at Wimbledon.   ___
6 Men and women are called by their formal title (Mr, Mrs, etc.) at Wimbledon.   ___
7 The Centre Court at Wimbledon is old-fashioned.   ___
8 Winners and losers in the final get almost the same money.   ___
9 Wimbledon makes most of its money from TV.   ___
10 Eating strawberries is very popular at Wimbledon.   ___

___ / 10

Listening

6 [100] Listen to Penny Harris talk about her sport. Choose the correct answer (A, B or C). There is an example at the beginning (0).

0 What sport does Penny Harris do?
  A surfing
  B skiing
  Ⓒ snowboarding

1 What does she enjoy most about her sport?
  A her great friends
  B being outside in the mountains
  C it's an individual sport

2 What quality do you need the most to do Penny's sport?
  A You have to be competitive.
  B You have to be talented.
  C You have to be hard-working.

3 How do most people pay for travel and equipment when they start out?
  A They borrow money.
  B They do part-time jobs.
  C They get help from their parents.

4 What job did Penny do to help pay for her sport?
  A She was a ski tutor.
  B She didn't have a job.
  C She had a job in a café.

5 What is the problem with the sport?
  A It's expensive.
  B It's hard work.
  C It's dangerous.

6 Where does Penny live now?
  A in England
  B by the sea
  C in the mountains

7 How often does Penny train?
  A six days a week
  B every weekend
  C every day

8 What does Penny say she hates?
  A being in water
  B training every day
  C travelling to the gym

9 Where does Penny train?
  A in the gym
  B in the pool
  C at home

10 Where are Penny's next championships?
  A in Italy
  B in Austria
  C in France

___ / 10

Writing

7 Follow the instructions below.

Write five sentences about a sport you know well. Include information about how to play the sport and what you have to do to be good at the sport.

___ / 10

Speaking

8 Read the task below and give your presentation in class.

Prepare to talk about your interests and hobbies. Talk about what you like doing, and what you're good at.

___ / 10

Unit 3 Test

Vocabulary

1 Complete the text with the verbs in the box. There is an example at the beginning (0).

book drop get off get on ~~go by~~ go on miss pay pick stop take

It isn't easy to get to the volcano. You have to **(0)** ___go by___ taxi, then by train, then by bus, and, finally, you have to **(1)** _____ foot. Ask the taxi driver to come early in the morning to **(2)** _____ you up from your hotel and **(3)** _____ you off at the train station. Make sure you leave early – you don't want to **(4)** _____ the train. And make sure you **(5)** _____ your train ticket online before you go because the train is often full. **(6)** _____ the train to the end of the line, then **(7)** _____ the bus that goes up into the mountains. Make sure you have money with you because you have to **(8)** _____ the fare on the bus. Ask the bus driver to **(9)** _____ when you see the lake. Then **(10)** _____ the bus and walk up the path to the right of the lake. It's a three kilometre walk to the volcano.

___/ 10

2 Choose the correct option to complete the sentences. There is an example at the beginning (0).

0 My uncle drives a *lorry* / *train*. Every week, he drives hundreds of kilometres along motorways from Poland to Portugal.
1 It takes four days for the ship to *commute* / *cross* the ocean.
2 The roads round here are very busy during the rush *hour* / *period*.
3 The government wants to stop carbon *emissions* / *produces*.
4 Sorry I'm late. There's a traffic *limit* / *jam* in the city centre. The cars aren't moving.
5 The buses to town are *traditional* / *frequent* – they come every ten minutes.
6 Although there's only one bus a day, it's very *punctual* / *convenient* for me because it stops near my house.
7 The new trains are very *comfortable* / *traditional*. The seats are big and there's a lot of leg room.
8 The train is slow but *reliable* / *punctual*. It never breaks down – you know you will get to your destination.
9 When you're in London, *go* / *take* the underground. It's the quickest way to travel.
10 When you buy a ticket, ask for a *receipt* / *change*. It proves that you have paid.

___/ 10

Grammar

3 Choose the correct option (A, B, C or D) to complete the sentences. There is an example at the beginning (0).

0 It's one of the _____ expensive holiday resorts in the country.
   A lot   B much   **C most**   D more
1 The road isn't as long _____ some people think.
   A as   B than   C that   D for
2 The new cruise ship is _____ any built before.
   A big as   B biggest than   C bigger than   D as big
3 This is one of _____ traffic jams I can remember.
   A the badder   B as bad as   C the worst   D worse than
4 Today is _____ than yesterday.
   A sunnier   B the sunnier   C the sunniest   D sunny
5 I prefer the train because it's _____ .
   A reliable than B more reliable C as reliable as D far reliable

6 Which one is _____?
  A tastier   B more tasty   C tasty as   D tastier than
7 We want to find the _____ restaurant.
  A near   B nearly   C nearer   D nearest
8 Bikes _____ cars.
  A are slower than B are as slow C are the slowest D aren't slowly
9 This is the _____ of my life.
  A good day   B better day   C best day   D as better day as
10 We aren't all _____ as Tom.
  A clever   B the cleverest   C cleverer   D as clever

___ / 10

4 Complete the second sentence so that it has a similar meaning to the first sentence. Use two to four words including the word provided in CAPITALS. There is an example at the beginning (0).

0 No hotel in the world is more expensive than the Burj Khalifa in Dubai.
  MOST
  The Burj Khalifa in Dubai _____is the most expensive_____ hotel in the world.

1 No man is faster than Usain Bolt.
  WORLD'S
  Usain Bolt is _____ man.

2 Joe lives near the centre but Kerry's house is further away.
  CENTRE
  Kerry's house is further from _____ Joe's.

3 Jenny isn't as good at maths as her sister.
  THAN
  Jenny's sister is _____ Jenny.

4 No singer in the school is as bad as Jack.
  THE
  Jack is _____ in the school.

5 Taking the train is safer than going by car.
  ISN'T
  Going by car _____ as taking the train.

6 David is older than his brother but not by much.
  LITTLE
  David is _____ his brother.

7 Taking the bus into town is much more convenient than taking the train.
  LOT
  Taking the train into town is _____ than taking the bus.

8 In my opinion, team sports are more exciting than individual sports.
  AS
  I think individual sports _____ as team sports.

9 The Hotel Grand isn't quite as expensive as the Hotel Luxe.
  BIT
  The Hotel Luxe is _____ than the Hotel Grand.

10 The students in Class A aren't as lazy as the students in Class F.
  ARE
  The students in Class F _____ the students in Class A.

___ / 10

Reading

Taking the ferry

A
Nowadays, bridges and tunnels mean that it's easier and quicker, and often cheaper, to drive to places, or to take the train, than it is to cross rivers or seas on a ferry. The eight-kilometre-long Oresund Bridge links Sweden to Denmark, changing what was a long trip into what is now an easy commute. The Channel Tunnel between England and France means that you can leave one country and arrive in the other before you finish drinking your cappuccino. The problem is that cars and underground trains are not as romantic as ferries. It may be faster to use modern transport options but many people still prefer to take the ferry.

B
Having time to look at the scenery, to relax and breathe, and to feel you are moving along slowly and naturally are just some of the reasons why travellers and commuters often prefer ferries. Urban ferry rides, which are short and cheap, are a daily ritual for many people. In Hong Kong, for example, many commuters choose the slow ferry over the fast underground when crossing Victoria Harbour. Enjoying the sea breeze at sunset makes many feel much better than being in a crowded train. From the ferry, you can see Hong Kong's office towers in multi-coloured lights, attractive mountain tops, and the occasional historic ship sailing by. It's better to get home late, feeling relaxed, than to get home early, feeling stressed.

C
In New York City, more than 100,000 people ride ferries daily, and, every day, 80,000 people use ferries to get about Kerala in India. From the deck of the Staten Island ferry, which takes twenty-five minutes to go from New York to Staten Island, you can see amazing skyscrapers and monuments like the Statue of Liberty. From a ferry in Kerala, you can see kids riding bicycles and workers picking bananas and coconuts or laying laundry out to dry.

D
Taking a ferry is a great way to get a feel for the rhythms of a place and even to meet some fellow passengers. In south-eastern Alaska, for example, the ferry system is the water highway for Alaskans. Being on the ferry is the best way to meet the locals. People tell stories and make friends on the ferries, and look at the scenery, thinking about why they love living in Alaska. As a visitor, it is a way to fall in love with the place.

5 Read the article about travelling by ferry. Match the questions to the paragraphs (A–D). There is an example at the beginning (0).

Which paragraph …

0 describes how many people travel to and from work in Hong Kong? __B__
1 says that tourists get to know people from the area by taking this ferry? _____
2 tells you how long one of the ferry journeys lasts? _____
3 says that people like this place more after going on a ferry ride? _____
4 describes how people feel better after a ferry ride at the end of a working day? _____
5 describes the exact distance of a particular journey? _____
6 says why people don't have to take ferries anymore? _____
7 describes two countries with very different ferry experiences? _____
8 describes different ways of travelling from one country to another? _____
9 says that ferries are more expensive than other types of transport? _____
10 describes how you can see people working from this ferry? _____

___ / 10

Listening

6 [101] Listen to a customer buying a ticket at a train station. Choose the correct answer (A, B or C). There is an example at the beginning (0).

0 Where does the customer want to go?
   (A) Manchester
   B London Euston
   C London King's Cross

1 What kind of ticket does the customer want?
   A a single
   B two singles
   C a return

2 When does the customer want to leave?
   A Thursday evening
   B Tuesday morning
   C Monday afternoon

3 Why is the customer making the journey?
   A He's a tourist.
   B He's visiting relatives.
   C He's on a business trip.

4 What does the ticket salesperson say about the train route?
   A The trains are direct and leave regularly.
   B The train journey takes about twenty minutes.
   C There are two changes on the train route.

5 The first train ticket that the salesperson mentions costs over three hundred pounds. Why is it so expensive?
   A It's a first class ticket.
   B You can use it at any time of day.
   C The train is already full.

6 What sort of ticket does the customer buy in the end?
   A an at-peak
   B an on-peak
   C an off-peak

7 When does the customer decide to travel to his destination?
   A before seven
   B between seven and ten
   C after ten

8 When will the customer arrive in Manchester?
   A at eight
   B before nine
   C after ten

9 What does the customer say about the time he will arrive at his destination?
   A It's a good time to arrive.
   B He will be late for a meeting.
   C It's too early to arrive.

10 How much does the customer pay in total for his ticket?
   A £83
   B £84
   C £86

___ / 10

Writing

7 Follow the instructions below.

Write five sentences about two journeys you often take. For example, your journey to work and your journey to visit family or friends. Include information about how far you travel, how long you travel for, and how you travel. Compare the two journeys.

___ / 10

Speaking

8 Read the task below and give your presentation in class.

Prepare to describe a place you know. Talk about its appearance, what you like about it, and why people should go there.

___ / 10

Unit 4 Test

Vocabulary

1 Choose the correct option (A, B, C or D) to complete the sentences. There is an example at the beginning (0).

0 Sophie is very nice and _____ .
 A friend (B) friendly C patience D patiently

1 Some people _____ themselves difficult challenges in life.
 A give B do C take D play

2 Don't _____ risks in the mountains when the weather is bad.
 A do B make C get D take

3 Joel is very _____-working. He spends a lot of time at work.
 A strong B good C hard D long

4 After spending twenty years in my job, I think I can say I am _____ .
 A experienced B positive C kind D intelligent

5 What is the biggest _____ we have to solve today?
 A challenger B challenge C challenging D challenged

6 Did you _____ for the exam?
 A test B memory C score D study

7 We need to find a _____ to the problem.
 A solve B score C solution D achievement

8 Jill left her bag on the bus but, _____, we found it later.
 A really B fortunately C while D next

9 Thanks for buying me flowers on my birthday. That was very _____ of you.
 A positive B intelligent C kind D patient

10 On our way home, we drove _____ a tunnel.
 A across B through C on D onto

___ / 10

2 Complete the sentences with the correct form of the word in CAPITAL LETTERS. There is an example at the beginning (0).

0 Yousuf Karsh was one of the world's best-known *photographers* . PHOTOGRAPH
1 Climbing Mount Kilimanjaro was my greatest personal _____. ACHIEVE
2 Hillary and Tenzing were the first _____ to climb Everest. MOUNTAIN
3 We're trying to find a _____ to the problem. SOLVE
4 Ollie is trying to _____ the capitals of every state in the USA. MEMORY
5 It was a _____ journey across snow and ice. CHALLENGE
6 I don't know anybody as kind or as _____ as Josie. PATIENCE
7 We were lost but, _____, we found a path that took us back to the campsite. LUCK
8 Be _____ when you go down those steps. They're dangerous. CARE
9 Some people think paragliding is safe, but I think it's _____. RISK
10 Jake is an _____. He travels to dangerous places around the world. ADVENTURE

___ / 10

Grammar

3 Complete the text with the correct past simple or past continuous form of the verbs in brackets. There is an example at the beginning (0).

Ellen MacArthur **(0)** ___was___ (be) born in Derbyshire in the UK in 1976. She **(1)** _____ (grow) up far from the sea, and her parents and brothers **(2)** _____ (not be) very interested in sailing. However, she **(3)** _____ (have) an aunt who was a yachtswoman and she **(4)** _____ (learn) to sail while she **(5)** _____ (stay) with her aunt on the east coast of England. Ellen **(6)** _____ (buy) her first small boat while she **(7)** _____ (study) at school. After that, she **(8)** _____ (spend) all her free time sailing. In 2005, she **(9)** _____ (become) world famous when she **(10)** _____ (break) the world record for the fastest solo circumnavigation of the globe in a yacht.

___ / 10

4 Choose the correct option (A, B, C or D) to complete the sentences. There is an example at the beginning (0).

0 The yachtsman Sir Francis Chichester _____ in 1972.
  A die   **(B)** died   **C** is dying   **D** was dying

1 We missed the train because it _____ at the station.
  A not stop   **B** didn't stop   **C** wasn't stopping   **D** don't stop

2 We were _____ tired so we went home.
  A feel   **B** feels   **C** feeling   **D** felt

3 While she _____ through the country, she visited many interesting places.
  A was travelling   **B** were travelling   **C** travelling   **D** is travelling

4 What _____ when you saw him?
  A was Tom doing   **B** were Tom doing   **C** Tom was doing   **D** Tom were doing

5 I _____ my leg when I fell off the ladder.
  A break   **B** broke   **C** am breaking   **D** was breaking

6 _____ you see the film last Friday?
  A Do   **B** Was   **C** Did   **D** Were

7 While _____ watching the match, it started to rain.
  A we were   **B** she were   **C** were we   **D** were she

8 I was hoping to pass the exam but, in the end, I _____ it.
  A fail   **B** failed   **C** was failing   **D** am failed

9 Fiona and I _____ get on during the holidays last summer.
  A don't   **B** wasn't   **C** weren't   **D** didn't

10 I _____ breakfast when the alarm went off. I stopped eating and ran outside.
  A ate   **B** was eating   **C** eat   **D** am eating

___ / 10

Reading

5 Read the article about two adventurers. Is the following information given for Krzysztof (K), Ashima (A) or both of them (B)? There is an example at the beginning (0).

0 Their age when they started doing a new sport or skill ___B___
1 Their plans for the future _____
2 A course they did once _____
3 How people in their family help them _____
4 Why they are famous now _____
5 A place they were the first person to go to _____
6 Where they first started doing a new sport or skill _____
7 A medical problem they had _____
8 Problems they had when they first tried a new sport or skill _____
9 Two different sports or skills they can do _____
10 How they felt after trying a sport or skill for the first time _____

___ / 10

Two adventurers of the year

When Polish explorer **Krzysztof Starnawski** was eighteen years old, he went on a diving course and tried to dive, but couldn't because he had problems with pressure in his ears. A few years later, he decided to take up a new challenge: caving. From the start, he loved his new sport. In Poland, there are a number of deep caves and Krzysztof began to explore them. Every time he reached the end of a new cave, he came across deep, dark water, but he knew that he couldn't go into the water because of his ears.

Then, during a cycling trip, he met a diving instructor who taught him how to deal with the problems with his ears. As a result, he completed a diving course. He was interested in an underwater cave in the Czech Republic called Hranicka Propast. The cave was deeper than any he knew. He wondered how deep it really was and spent many hours diving into the cave to explore it. Eventually, he decided that it wasn't safe to dive any deeper so he started using an ROV, a type of robot explorer, to go down into the cave. In November 2016, the ROV hit the bottom, 404 metres below the surface. It was the deepest underwater cave in the world.

A New Yorker, **Ashima Shiraishi** discovered rock climbing when she was six years old. She was playing with friends after school in Central Park and saw some men on a climbing wall known as Rat Rock. She decided that she wanted to have a try. She started climbing in trainers and kept falling, but she loved it. She was having so much fun that she didn't mind that the men were laughing at her because she was hopeless at climbing. Eventually she got to the top. From that moment she was determined to be a champion climber.

Ashima's climbing is a family effort. Her father travels round the world with her, and her mother helps make the clothes she wears. Although only fifteen, she is a champion American rock climber, and well-known in her own country. Many people believe that she could be the best climber in the world one day. Ashima's ambition is to win an Olympic medal at the next Olympic Games. Her talent and her dreams are big.

Listening

6 [102] Listen to Dan talk about his holiday trip. Select the two activities (A–L) which Dan did on each day. There is an example at the beginning (0).

0 Sunday _E_ _H_
1 Monday ___ ___
2 Tuesday ___ ___
3 Wednesday ___ ___
4 Thursday ___ ___
5 Friday ___ ___

A went for a walk
B sat on the beach
C did some shopping
D took a lot of photographs
E arrived at the hotel
F went swimming
G went cycling
H ate on the beach
I went to a restaurant
J read a book
K went to a café
L went to museums

___ / 10

Writing

7 Follow the instructions below.

Write five sentences about a holiday you went on in the last five years. Include information about where you went, when, how long for, and where you stayed. Write about what you did and what you liked.

___ / 10

Speaking

8 Read the task below and give your presentation in class.

Prepare to tell a story about a journey you made. Talk about where you went, and what happened.

___ / 10

Unit 5 Test

Vocabulary

1 Choose the odd word out in each list. There is an example at the beginning (0).

0	A $\frac{1}{4}$	B a quarter	Ⓒ a half	D 25%
1	A about twenty	B exactly twenty	C approximately twenty	D more or less twenty
2	A scissors	B glass	C leather	D plastic
3	A paper	B cardboard	C wood	D metal
4	A carton	B jar	C plastic	D bag
5	A garbage	B bin	C trash	D rubbish
6	A under a half	B less than a half	C more than a half	D nearly a half
7	A request	B demand	C refund	D ask for
8	A can	B box	C metal	D bottle
9	A a lot	B much	C many	D a little
10	A leather	B tank	C paper	D plastic

___ / 10

2 Complete the text with the words in the box. There are two extra words you do not need. There is an example at the beginning (0).

exactly   figured out   for   glass   made of   nearly   ordered   ~~panel~~   rooftop   shower   taking   time   to

Last month, we bought a solar **(0)** _panel_ to put on our **(1)** _____ . It cost **(2)** _____ £100 – £98, in fact! Unfortunately, however, we haven't **(3)** _____ how to install it. It's **(4)** _____ metal, plastic and **(5)** _____ , and it's surprisingly light. We want to use it **(6)** _____ heating water so that we can have a bath or take a **(7)** _____ when we want to. I'm sure it'll be great once it's in place. We're really glad that we **(8)** _____ it online. It's just that it's **(9)** _____ a long time to read through and understand all the instructions. I like to take **(10)** _____ to do things properly, you see.

___ / 10

Grammar

3 Choose the correct option (A, B, C or D) to complete the sentences. There is an example at the beginning (0).

0 We didn't buy _____ boxes.
   A a   B some   Ⓒ any   D an

1 There aren't _____ places to recycle clothes.
   A some   B much   C a lot   D many

2 Only _____ people stay here during the winter.
   A any   B a few   C a little   D much

3 There are _____ different ways to save water.
   A a lot of   B much   C any   D a

4 Hurry up. We don't have _____ time.
   A some   B much   C many   D a few

5 Don't tell _____ journalists why we're here.
   A a   B much   C some   D any

6 I take _____ sugar in my coffee.
   A a lot   B a few   C a little   D any

7 We gave _____ money to charity.
   A some   B any   C many   D a few

8 How _____ people did you talk to?
   A little   B much   C any   D many

9 Sally found _____ old photographs of her grandparents.
   A a little   B much   C any   D a few

10 _____ students left early.
   A A little   B A lot   C Any   D Some

___ / 10

222 Photocopiable tests: Unit 5

4 Complete the text with *a, an, the* or – (no article). There is an example at the beginning (0).

Recently, I read **(0)** __an__ extremely interesting article about **(1)** _____ world's most amazing buildings. **(2)** _____ first building on **(3)** _____ list is **(4)** _____ Angkor Wat. In **(5)** _____ article, it's described as **(6)** _____ beautiful temple in **(7)** _____ Cambodia. Second is **(8)** _____ Pyramid of Khufu in **(9)** _____ Egypt. **(10)** _____ millions of tourists visit these amazing places every year.

___ / 10

Reading

Fresno – the recycling city

Fresno in California is a small community 200 miles north of Los Angeles, mostly known for its agriculture. **(0)** _B_ While many cities recycle 30 to 50 per cent of their waste, Fresno recycles as much as 73 per cent of its rubbish. **(1)** ___ Fresno is proud of being a city that is great at recycling.

Patrick Wiemiller, Fresno's public utilities director, showed me how the city does it. 'We provide a lot of education,' Wiemiller told me as we drove across town. 'To really get people to recycle, you have to change a family's behaviour. We find the best way of doing this is through children in the schools.' **(2)** ___ Mums and dads are more likely to listen to messages from family members than to messages from public officials. As a result, the public utilities department is now confident that recycling 90 per cent of all waste is a possible goal. **(3)** ___ That may sound impossible, but it is a great aim to have.

With so much waste to recycle, there are big challenges for private companies that have to recycle all the waste. **(4)** ___ 'When we started, it was just paper, aluminium, tin, and glass,' Mohoff said. 'Now we can do all kinds of plastics. And film too.' In total, that is nearly 7,000 tons of things that Fresnans throw out each month that end up being reused.

Why does a community like Fresno care so deeply about recycling? One Fresnan farmer explained that aside from feeling they should look after the planet, it's all about agriculture. **(5)** ___ But putting nutritious material back into soils improves crops and livestock – and ultimately, the strawberries, pistachios, or garlic that the rest of the country gets from this region.

5 Read the article about the city of Fresno, in California. Complete the gaps with the missing sentences (A–G). There is one extra sentence you do not need. There is an example at the beginning (0).

A John Mohoff of Sunset Waste Systems took me through his processing facility, a big place that sorts plastics, metals and papers.
B But, among cities with more than 100,000 people, Fresno is one of the best at recycling.
C These results are better than many people in the city predicted.
D That means that the city produces more reusable material than most other cities and is, ultimately, a healthier city than most.
E A landfill is not good for the countryside – it produces little value for farmland.
F One day, the city's government has ambitions to produce zero waste.
G Asking school kids to persuade their parents to do more recycling has been very successful.

___ / 10

Listening

6 [103] Listen to an announcement about recycling by the local council. Complete the form with one word in each gap. There is an example at the beginning (0).

Local Council Recycling Information

Recycling is cheaper and more **(0)** ___energy___ efficient.

Put waste you can recycle in the bin that is coloured **(1)** _____ .

- Use the small **(2)** _____ -coloured bin for food waste.
- Please put paper, **(3)** _____ and **(4)** _____ products in the recycling bin.
- Don't put paper products such as **(5)** _____ in the recycling bin – take them to charity shops.
- Only use **(6)** _____ plastic bags in the recycling bins.
- Jars and **(7)** _____ made of glass can be recycled.
- Don't put in any glass that is **(8)** _____ .
- Take your electrical products to the centres in Glenn Street, **(9)** _____ the sports centre in Forecourt Street, and next to the shopping centre in Barclay Street.
- Place old clothes **(10)** _____ to the recycling bin on collection day.

___ / 10

Writing

7 Follow the instructions below.

You recently bought some jeans online but they are too small. Write a formal email saying that you are returning the jeans, the reason why, and what you would like the company to do.

___ / 10

Speaking

8 Read the task below and give your presentation in class.

Prepare to talk about what you do to care for the environment. Talk about how and what you recycle and why, and what you do to save energy.

___ / 10

Unit 6 Test

Vocabulary

1 Complete the sentences with the verbs in the box. You can use the verbs more than once. There are two extra words you do not need. There is an example at the beginning (0).

ban get go leave make play ride start take

0 It's time to ___get___ ready for the party.
1 My sister can _____ the violin by ear.
2 Some of these ancient stories _____ back hundreds of years.
3 The government wants to _____ fireworks because they are dangerous. In future, they won't be allowed.
4 We should _____ together soon and have dinner.
5 Now they're married, do you think they'll _____ a family?
6 I'd like to _____ to university when I leave school.
7 I don't remember when I first learned to _____ a bicycle – when I was five or six, perhaps.
8 When did you _____ married?
9 In the UK, young people often _____ home and find their own place to live when they are eighteen or nineteen.
10 When did you _____ back from your trip to Paris?

___ / 10

2 Choose the correct option (A, B, C or D) to complete the texts. There is an example at the beginning (0).

(0) _____ , when they are fifteen or sixteen, have to be responsible for the first time in their lives. For example, they have to (1) _____ a bank account, or get a driving (2) _____ . It's a challenging time. By the time they are twenty-four or twenty-five and in their (3) _____ twenties, young adults are expected to be (4) _____ a career, earning a living and paying rent. Of course, (5) _____ people in their mid to (6) _____ fifties have challenges of their own.

The festival was wonderful. There were people in amazing (7) _____ : long gold dresses, for example, with birds' feathers all over them. Many wore (8) _____ so you couldn't see their faces. And they travelled along the streets on (9) _____ , moving platforms on lorries. Some of them were so (10) _____ that they carried twenty or thirty festival-goers, dancing and singing.

0	A Children	**B** Teenagers	C Adults	D Elderly
1	A open	B take	C make	D place
2	A allowance	B book	C pattern	D licence
3	A early	B mid	C over	D late
4	A opening	B doing	C starting	D putting
5	A mid-term	B middle-aged	C late adults	D elderly
6	A late	B far	C early	D soon
7	A costumes	B fireworks	C drums	D candles
8	A bands	B masks	C parades	D covers
9	A parties	B carriers	C ceremonies	D floats
10	A delicious	B smart	C enormous	D miserable

___ / 10

Grammar

3 Choose the correct option to complete the sentences. There is an example at the beginning (0).

0 Don't worry about your driving test! I'm sure (you'll pass) / you're passing.
1 *I won't come / I'm not coming* on Friday, sorry. I have an appointment at the dentist's.
2 Are you feeling sleepy? OK, *I'm going to / I'll* open the window.
3 Look at the traffic! *We're going to be / We're being* late for school.
4 Don't leave your laptops in the classroom! Someone *is going to steal / will steal* them.
5 Good morning and welcome to Sackville College. In this talk *I'm telling / I'm going to tell* you about …
6 I'm sorry. I forgot your drink. *I'm going to go / I'll go* and get it now.
7 *I don't think he'll / think he won't* go to the party.
8 'Are you going to the cinema tomorrow evening?' 'Yes, I *am / will*.'
9 *I'll play / I'm playing* tennis on Friday at three, so I can't come on the picnic.
10 I love Susie. *I'm marrying / I'm going to marry* her one day.

___ / 10

4 Complete the text with the correct form of the verb in brackets. There is an example at the beginning (0).

When I was in my early twenties, I had to **(0)** ___choose___ (choose) between getting married and going abroad **(1)** _____ (work). My girlfriend wanted **(2)** _____ (get) married, but I enjoyed **(3)** _____ (be) single and, in my opinion, it was important **(4)** _____ (see) the world before starting a family. 'Let's **(5)** _____ (go) away together,' I said. 'We should **(6)** _____ (make) some great memories, then we'll be ready **(7)** _____ (buy) a house.' She wasn't interested in **(8)** _____ (travel) but, in the end, she agreed **(9)** _____ (wait) for me for a year. Six months later, I was back home. It was difficult **(10)** _____ (spend) so much time away from her. Now, we're married and we have three children.

___ / 10

Reading

The lessons I learned from travelling

Lesson 1: __A__

Before I went travelling for the first time, I worried about it. I was frightened that something might go wrong. I soon learned not to worry. Here are some other lessons I learned.

Lesson 2: _____

One of the first things travel taught me is that things won't always go according to plan: buses will break down, flights will be delayed, and maps will occasionally be difficult to read. These problems made me more patient and helped me accept that I can't control most things. They also resulted in some exciting adventures – the woman in Marrakech, for example, who, when I asked her for directions, invited me into her home for coffee.

When we're travelling, our most memorable experiences are usually the result of something we didn't plan. We should continue to think like this when we get home from our travels – when things don't go to plan, we should enjoy the adventure.

Lesson 3: _____

Growing up in Virginia, I rarely met people who were very different from me. That changed when I moved to London. I soon found myself at a dinner party where every guest came from a different country. You can learn a lot from listening to people from different places.

When I began travelling beyond Europe, I experienced many different cultures. I celebrated the Hindu festival Diwali in India and families in Turkey invited me to stay in their homes. Now, in my new hometown of San Francisco, whenever I pass a mosque or a temple, I'm happy that I live in a multicultural city.

Lesson 4: _____

When I'm travelling, I have an open heart and mind. I smile at people I pass on the street and talk to people on the bus. I ask their name and learn a bit of their story. Now that I'm home, I try to be as friendly as I am when I'm travelling.

Earlier this year, a young Asian man asked me for directions. I decided to start a conversation with him. I learned his name was Chien Yu, and that he was from Taiwan. He told me stories about growing up in his grandmother's home, and taught me how to say thank you in his native language. Even at home, we can have experiences and meet people. Thinking like a traveller, when we're at home, helps us understand the world better.

5a Read the blog about lessons learned from travelling. Match the headings (A–F) to the lessons (2–4). There are two headings you don't need. There is an example at the beginning (1).

A Don't be scared of travelling
B Be ready to talk to people you don't know when you are in your home town
C Always be ready to change your itinerary during a journey
D Sometimes be careful when you are on buses, trains or planes.
E Be prepared to meet people who are different to you when you're travelling
F Never be afraid of listening to other travellers' advice.

___ / 3

5b Read the blog again. Are the sentences true (T) or false (F)? If there isn't enough information to say if the sentences are true or false, write doesn't say (DS). There is an example at the beginning (0).

0 The writer was never worried about travelling. __F__
1 Travel experiences changed the writer. _____
2 In Marrakech, the writer met a person who helped her with directions. _____
3 The people the writer met in London were not the same as people in Virginia. _____
4 The writer says that she has visited mosques in Bosnia, Turkey and the United States. _____
5 The writer is trying to change the way she behaves with people when she's in San Francisco. _____
6 Chien Yu told the writer where he was from in China. _____
7 The writer told Chien Yu things about her life. _____

___ / 7

Listening

6 [104] Listen to five people talking about their wedding plans. Listen and match the sentences to the correct speaker (A–E). There is an example at the beginning (0).

0 All the food at the wedding is Mexican. __E__
1 They're getting married in a foreign country. _____
2 A lot of people are going to their wedding. _____
3 The bride and groom come from different countries. _____
4 They aren't going on holiday after the wedding. _____
5 They aren't organizing their own wedding. _____
6 They're going to wear bright colours at the wedding. _____
7 They're going to have live music. _____
8 Somebody in their family is making the food. _____
9 They'll get married in the morning. _____
10 They're going to travel in an old vehicle. _____

___ / 10

Writing

7 Follow the instructions below.

Write five sentences about an interesting event you attended. It could be a party, a wedding, a festival, a sports event, etc. Include information about where you went, when and why, and what you saw and enjoyed.

___ / 10

Speaking

8 Read the task below and give your presentation in class.

Prepare to describe a time when you learned to do something for the first time. Talk about how you learned to do this thing, why, and how you felt about it.

___ / 10

Unit 7 Test

Vocabulary

1 Choose the correct option (A, B, C or D) to complete the sentences. There is an example at the beginning (0).

0 Sophie works Monday to Friday from 9 to 5 – it's a _____-time job.
A whole   (B) full   C half   D part

1 We're on the ground floor – the _____ is downstairs.
A basement   B first floor   C third floor   D top floor

2 Walk up the _____ on the left and you'll get to the canteen.
A lift   B stairs   C exit   D floor

3 Joe's job is boring and _____ -paid. He doesn't earn much.
A low   B high   C well   D part

4 I'm a shop _____. I serve customers in the local supermarket.
A officer   B designer   C representative   D assistant

5 I need to _____ a call. I'll be back in a minute.
A put   B do   C make   D go

6 Have you _____ your bed? I hope your room is tidy.
A done   B made   C set   D put

7 I didn't _____ very well at school. I failed most of my exams.
A show   B score   C do   D make

8 Something _____ a noise in the forest. What was it?
A gave   B made   C went   D did

9 To _____ for the job, call the manager.
A place   B apply   C provide   D make

10 There are only a few _____ staying in the hotel right now.
A clients   B customers   C applicants   D guests

___ / 10

2 Complete the sentences with the correct form of the word in CAPITAL LETTERS. There is an example at the beginning (0).

0 I have a very _interesting_ job.   INTEREST
1 We need _____ workers such as electricians and plumbers.   SKILL
2 Deep sea fishing can be a _____ profession.   DANGER
3 My uncle Tony is a sales _____ for a company that makes dishwashers.   REPRESENT
4 I'd like to be a fashion _____.   DESIGN
5 A well-known _____ has said that prices will start to rise soon.   ECONOMY
6 I always feel sorry for _____ - nobody seems to like them.   POLITICS
7 My sister is a _____ teacher. She hopes to qualify as a full-time teacher next May.   TRAIN
8 Wait for me near the _____. I'll come down in five minutes.   ENTER
9 Jerry had to make a difficult _____. He wasn't sure what to do.   DECIDE
10 Please provide two _____ on your CV.   REFER

___ / 10

Photocopiable tests: Unit 7

Grammar

3 Complete the text with the correct past simple or present perfect form of the verbs in brackets. There is an example at the beginning (0).

Jack **(0)** _has worked_ (work) in the language school for over 20 years. I **(1)** _____ (know) him since I **(2)** _____ (start) working here in 2014. Recently, he **(3)** _____ (not be) very well, and, a few days ago, he **(4)** _____ (tell) me news that I wasn't expecting: he **(5)** _____ (decide) to retire.

I think I'll miss him. For the last two years, Jack and I **(6)** _____ (plan) a number of courses together and I **(7)** _____ (learn) a lot from him. When we first **(8)** _____ (start) working together I **(9)** _____ (not know) much about teaching, to be honest. I **(10)** _____ (become) a better teacher because of him. It's going to be lonely in the school without him!

___ / 10

4 Choose the correct option (A, B, C or D) to complete the sentences. There is an example at the beginning (0).

0 How long _____ you worked in this office?
A do   B are   Ⓒ have   D did

1 We've been here _____ hours.
A in   B over   C for   D since

2 They _____ oil in this region five years ago.
A discover   B discovered   C were discovering   D have discovered

3 Have you _____ had a job abroad?
A ever   B for   C long   D last

4 What _____ when you saw him?
A do you do   B did you do   C have you done   D are you doing

5 I've known Joe _____ primary school.
A since   B for   C ever   D last

6 My office is _____ the top floor.
A in   B at   C from   D on

7 They ran _____ the building through the emergency exit.
A out of   B up   C down   D next to

8 Be careful when you walk _____ the road.
A through   B across   C opposite   D at

9 They got _____ the car and drove away.
A into   B onto   C up   D down

10 The canteen is _____ the post room.
A onto   B next to   C into   D down

___ / 10

Reading

5 Read the article about how jobs have changed. Complete the gaps with the missing sentences (A–G). There is one extra sentence you do not need. There is an example at the beginning (0).

A They had to research stories by going out and speaking to people, or by going to the library and looking at old copies of newspapers and magazines.

B It took a long time and used a lot of paper!

C One of the first companies to use this technique was Sony.

D Today, everything has changed.

E In the past, you had to go to a shop and buy what you wanted.

F Twenty years ago, they only had to write one article a day for their employer.

G For example, using a home studio to produce high quality sounds in a bedroom is now a possibility.

___ / 10

How jobs have changed

Economics, politics and new technologies have changed many industries. We've chosen three jobs to look at how they have changed.

The music industry

Musicians in the 1960s had two choices – form a band and play hundreds of concerts in local town halls for very little money, or try to persuade a record label to sign you. (0) __D__ Record companies don't sign new bands on long contracts anymore, and musicians have a lot more control over their careers. There is a lot they can do by themselves. (1) _____ And musicians can also use the internet to become popular by uploading songs and videos, and talking to fans. Often, musicians release their first album through small inexpensive distribution companies. One problem for young musicians nowadays is that there aren't as many places to play as there were in the 1960s. That's why musicians often play music in the street.

Journalism

From typewriters to Twitter, journalism has changed a lot over the past 25 years. In the past, reporters didn't have search engines like Google to find out information. (2) _____ Today, journalists use Twitter to send live updates from a court case or council meeting, and can write their stories at the same time on laptops, tablets or phones. They don't have to write notes, then return to their office to write up the story on a typewriter. Everything is quicker and easier. One problem for reporters nowadays, however, is that new technologies mean new demands. (3) _____ Now, they have to update websites, write Facebook pages and create video content as well.

Publishing

Before computers, editing a book was very different from today. Writers typed their books on paper and sent them to publishing companies by post. Then editors used different coloured pens to go through their writing and to change or correct what they wrote. (4) _____ Nowadays, digital technology means that writers and editors work on books and articles on their computers. It's good news for trees, and good news for writers and editors who can delete and replace the things they write easily. One problem for the publishing industry is that people don't always pay for their books nowadays. (5) _____ Today, you can often find illegal downloads of books on the internet.

Listening

6 [105] Listen to Ray talk about how the workplace in his country has changed since the 1960s. Choose true or false. There is an example at the beginning (0).

0	Ray is talking about the workplace in Australia.	**TRUE** / FALSE
1	There were fewer unmarried women than married women in the workplace in the 1960s.	TRUE / FALSE
2	In the 1960s, married women were unlikely to have a job with a public company.	TRUE / FALSE
3	Like today, smoking was not allowed in Australian offices in the 1960s.	TRUE / FALSE
4	In the 1960s, workers didn't have to make their own cups of tea.	TRUE / FALSE
5	Today, people get fewer paid holidays than fifty years ago.	TRUE / FALSE
6	Mothers didn't get maternity leave in the 1960s.	TRUE / FALSE
7	The number of people working in agriculture has gone down since the 1960s.	TRUE / FALSE
8	Jobs aren't as physical as they were in the 1960s.	TRUE / FALSE
9	Ray thinks jobs were better in the 1960s.	TRUE / FALSE
10	Ray thinks people are more educated nowadays.	TRUE / FALSE

___ / 10

Writing

7 Follow the instructions below.

Write five sentences about jobs you have done in your life. Include information about what the job was, how and why you got the job, what you had to do in the job, and what you liked or disliked about it.

___ / 10

Speaking

8 Read the task below and give your presentation in class.

Imagine you are at a job interview and a possible employer has asked you to say why you should get the job. Prepare to describe your work and life experience, qualifications and personal qualities.

___ / 10

Unit 8 Test

Name _____
Total score _____

Vocabulary

1 Complete the text with the missing prepositions. There is an example at the beginning (0).

One of the problems **(0)** __with__ car keys is that they get lost or stolen. That's why manufacturers are thinking **(1)** _____ getting rid of car keys altogether. In the future, car owners who are bad **(2)** _____ remembering where their keys are will be able to download a smartphone app that will lock, unlock, and start the car using Bluetooth technology. If you've got more than one car, your smartphone will work **(3)** _____ each car, so you won't need to carry lots of keys. The idea **(4)** _____ having to depend **(5)** _____ a key will be a thing of the past. Scientists are also interested **(6)** _____ using smartphone technology to lock and unlock doors and windows around our homes. The idea is similar **(7)** _____ that being developed for cars. Homeowners will be able to set **(8)** _____ and log **(9)** _____ to a computer system that controls all the security around their home. Soon you won't need to remember your keys – you will just have to be good **(10)** _____ using the technology on your phone.

___ / 10

2 Choose the correct option to complete the sentences. There is an example at the beginning (0).

0 I often *get* / *make* bored on Sundays.
1 I'm sure I've *done* / *made* a lot of mistakes already.
2 When did you first *fall* / *be* in love?
3 We're having problems trying to *log* / *connect* to the internet.
4 If you *upload* / *subscribe* your photos to this site, we'll all be able to access them.
5 *Charge* / *Push* the button to switch it on.
6 You can operate it using a remote *control* / *charger*.
7 Push the lever *forwards* / *for* to turn on the power.
8 There are about 150 *taken* / *known* Aboriginal languages in Australia.
9 They carried the heavy camera *packings* / *equipment* through the forest.
10 We hope to protect this environment *forever* / *afterwards*. We don't want to lose it.

___ / 10

Grammar

3 Choose the correct option (A, B or C) to complete the sentences. There is an example at the beginning (0).

0 If you _____ careful, you'll make a mistake.
   A aren't   **B** won't be   **C** won't

1 What will Tom do if everything _____ ?
   A goes wrong   **B** will go wrong   **C** might go wrong

2 If she leaves home, she _____ to learn how to cook.
   A will needs   **B** will need   **C** is needing

3 If we _____ hurry, we'll miss the start of the film.
   A aren't   **B** don't   **C** won't

4 What _____ if it rains?
   A will do we   **B** we will do   **C** will we do

5 You'll be late if you _____ now.
   A aren't leaving **B** don't leave   **C** won't leave

PHOTOCOPIABLE © National Geographic Learning

6 If I _____ my sandwiches, I buy something from the canteen.
  A forget   B can forget   C will forget
7 If we _____ online, we save ten per cent.
  A order   B ordered   C will order
8 Generally speaking, bikes _____ more fun if the weather's fine.
  A are being   B will be   C are
9 If you _____ for help, I'll be happy to come round.
  A ask   B asked   C will ask
10 Pets _____ kind to them.
  A are happy if people will be   B will be happy if people will be   C are happy if people are

___ / 10

4 Write one sentence using a relative pronoun to combine the two sentences provided. There is an example at the beginning (0).

0 We met a man. He was an inventor.
  We _met a man who was an inventor_ .

1 We arrived at a place. They make lifeboats there.
  We _____ .

2 Josie has a cat. It can open the doors of cupboards.
  Josie _____ .

3 Peter doesn't like beaches. They are polluted.
  Peter _____ .

4 New York is a city. There are many exciting businesses there.
  New York _____ .

5 I met some friends. I knew them from school.
  I _____ .

6 South Korea is a country. It has many important electronic companies.
  South Korea _____ .

7 My sister is a person. She gives me good advice.
  My sister _____ .

8 The local theatre is a venue. Many people in our town meet there.
  The local theatre _____ .

9 The museum is a building. I like it very much.
  The museum _____ .

10 The students are members of a club. It meets every Monday.
  The students _____ .

___ / 10

Reading

Inventions that have changed travel

A The hotel key card

Before the invention of the hotel key card, losing your metal hotel key was a big problem. Anyone who found your key could get into your hotel room, and it was expensive for hotels to replace the keys. Often guests who lost a key had to pay for a new one. That's why a Norwegian inventor called Tor Sørnes invented the key card in 1974. It was cheap and easy to use, and it solved all the problems with traditional keys. Nowadays, if you lose your card, the hotel can replace it immediately and change the lock on your hotel door so that the old, lost key card doesn't work. And if a guest leaves without returning a key, it isn't a problem for the hotel.

B Rolling luggage

Nowadays, if you go to any airport or train station in the world, you'll see hundreds of people pulling their luggage along on small wheels. It seems a simple idea. However, before 1972, there was no rolling luggage. You had to lift and carry your heavy suitcases. Bernard D Sadow, the American who had the idea for rolling luggage, wanted to make it easy for anybody to travel. At first, his idea wasn't successful. The problem wasn't with the design or quality. It was because men didn't want to buy rolling luggage. Many men liked to carry luggage – it showed they were strong. They thought that if you use rolling luggage, you must be weak! Nowadays, of course, this attitude has changed. Most luggage we buy has wheels.

C The backpack

If you go to any tourist city, all the young travellers will have a backpack. It's the best way of carrying a lot of things when you're going from place to place. That's why it's popular with campers, travellers and adventurers. The backpack has been around for centuries, but only as a way for soldiers to carry their clothes and equipment. Old military backpacks were big and heavy and didn't have any pockets. In the 1930s this changed. Gerry Cunningham, an American rock climber, invented a nylon backpack with lots of different pockets. He wanted a bag for carrying his climbing equipment without using his hands. By the 1960s, backpacks were very popular with climbers – and they were lighter than the backpack Gerry invented. However, it was only then that young people began to buy backpacks, not for climbing, but for travelling.

5 Read the three texts about inventions that changed travel.

Text A: Which of the following information is provided in text A? There is an example at the beginning (0).

0 the name of the inventor who first thought of hotel key cards ☑
1 the hotel where they first used key cards ☐
2 reasons why traditional keys were a problem for hotels ☐
3 the nationality of the person who invented key cards ☐
4 reasons why key cards cost more than traditional keys ☐
5 what hotels usually do now if you lose your key card ☐
6 how hotels find guests who leave without returning their key ☐

Text B: Which of the following information is provided in text B? There is an example at the beginning (0).

0 the type of luggage people used before the 1970s ☑
1 what sort of luggage is most popular today ☐
2 how rolling luggage was immediately a big seller ☐
3 the early problems with the design of rolling luggage ☐
4 why rolling luggage was more popular with men than women at first ☐
5 the nationality of the man who had the idea for rolling luggage ☐
6 how, compared to men in the 1970s, men today have a different opinion of rolling luggage ☐

Text C: Which of the following information is provided in text C? There is an example at the beginning (0).

0 the name of the man who invented a backpack for climbers ☑
1 a reason why people who go camping use backpacks ☐
2 the name of the person who redesigned backpacks for use by travellers in the 1960s ☐
3 the reason why people first used backpacks in the past ☐
4 ways that backpacks in the past were different from backpacks today ☐
5 reasons why climbers stopped using backpacks ☐
6 the time when backpacks became popular with young travellers ☐

___ / 10

Listening

6 [106] Listen to a woman asking about a festival. Complete the table with one word in each space. There is an example at the beginning (0).

The (0) _____July_____ Festival

Type of festival	Science and (1) _____
Runs from	Friday to (2) _____
Saturday opening time	(3) _____ a.m.
Saturday closing time	(4) _____ p.m.
Directions	Take Bus (5) _____ from town centre
Main display	Mobile phones and (6) _____
Buy tickets	online, at the (7) _____ Centre or at the (8) _____ office near the Festival entrance
Price	(9) £ _____ plus free (10) _____

___ / 10

Writing

7 Follow the instructions below.

> Here is a list of 10 inventions that have changed the world:
>
> 1 telephone 2 computer 3 television 4 automobile 5 camera 6 steam engine
> 7 sewing machine 8 light bulb 9 penicillin 10 plane

Choose one invention and write a paragraph to say why the invention is the most important and useful.

___ / 10

Speaking

8 Read the task below and give your presentation in class.

Describe a gadget that is important to you. Include information about how it works and how you use it, what you use it for, and why it is important to you.

___ / 10

Unit 9 Test

Name _____
Total score _____

Vocabulary

1 Choose the correct option (A, B or C) to complete the sentences. There is an example at the beginning (0).

0 Last summer, we _____ abroad for our holidays.
  (A) went   B had   C spent
1 You should _____ waiters a tip in the USA.
  A show   B give   C take
2 On holiday, we _____ on a campsite.
  A rented   B stayed   C spent
3 We left the cinema because the film was _____.
  A bore   B bored   C boring
4 This is no place _____ young children.
  A for   B with   C at
5 We have to _____ these challenges together.
  A head   B arm   C face
6 The festival will _____ place in August.
  A get   B take   C bring
7 We _____ from that area because of the high crime.
  A took across   B moved away   C went over
8 It isn't easy to earn a _____ in this industry.
  A live   B life   C living
9 After the concert, we _____ to meet Adele.
  A took   B gave   C got
10 We decided to _____ a hotel online.
  A book   B play   C make

___ / 10

2 Complete the sentences with the correct form of the word in CAPITAL LETTERS. There is an example at the beginning (0).

0 _Skiing_ is great fun. It's a fantastic sport. SKI
1 We drove to the south of France in a _____ van and had a great holiday. CAMP
2 As soon as I return from my holiday, I _____ my suitcase and put all my clothes in the washing machine. PACK
3 We often go _____ when we're on holiday. CLUB
4 I'm _____ by this book about Russian history. FASCINATE
5 Are you _____ of the dark? FRIGHTEN
6 We stayed in an _____ hotel at the top of the mountain. AMAZE
7 I received a _____ from my students. It was a lovely photo of the class in a photo frame. GIVE
8 We were _____ by the noise coming from the house next door. ANNOY
9 Walking all day is very _____. TIRE
10 There were a lot of _____ selling products at the market. TRADE

___ / 10

Grammar

3 Complete the story with the correct past simple or past perfect form of the verbs in brackets. There is an example at the beginning (0).

Last January, David and Emily (0) _flew_ (fly) to Australia. It was a long flight and they (1) _____ (be) really tired by the time they got there. They (2) _____ (never / be) to Australia before, and they (3) _____ (spend) months saving up for the holiday, so they (4) _____ (feel) incredibly excited to be there at last. Their friends (5) _____ (tell) them what things to do in Australia. As a result, they (6) _____ (book) trips to Uluru and to the Great Barrier Reef before leaving England. However, on their first day in the country, it (7) _____ (be) so hot that they (8) _____ (decide) not to go on any trips for a few days, but to head to the beach. Unfortunately, they (9) _____ (forget) their swimming costumes so they (10) _____ (have) to go shopping first to buy some. They couldn't believe they were in Australia at last – especially at a time of year when the weather was so awful in Europe!

___ / 10

4 Choose the correct option (A, B or C) to complete the sentences. There is an example at the beginning (0).

0 I got up early and _____ to school. I arrived at 8.30.
   (A) walked   B had walked   C was walking

1 I didn't realize I _____ my mobile phone at the club until the next morning.
   A left   B had left   C were leaving

2 The waiter chased after him because he _____ paid his bill.
   A didn't   B hadn't   C wasn't

3 Many years ago, when he _____ in the army, my father went to Singapore.
   A was   B had been   C was being

4 We didn't go to the cinema with Kate because we _____ the film before.
   A saw   B had seen   C were seeing

5 Where _____ for your holidays?
   A you went   B did you go   C went you

6 How many people _____ in this building?
   A live   B do live   C do they live

7 Which student _____ this essay?
   A has he written   B has written   C he has written

8 Why _____ like travelling so much?
   A they   B they do   C do they

9 What _____ outside?
   A is happening   B is it happening   C happening is

10 Who _____ the key to?
   A has given   B you are giving   C did you give

___ / 10

Reading

Holiday stories

A
We were really looking forward to arriving at the holiday apartment we had booked near the beach on a beautiful Greek island. However, when we arrived, we were quite annoyed to find that nobody had cleaned the place. We tried to phone the holiday company to complain but it was Sunday and nobody answered our calls. I spent two hours cleaning the place myself. Then there was a knock on the door. It was the holiday rep. She explained that we were in the wrong apartment. We had opened the wrong door – both apartments could be opened by the same key. When we packed our bags and moved next door, it was really clean!

B
A few years ago, we went to Mexico on holiday. It was our first holiday with our two young daughters, Megan and Kate. We had brought a really big bag full of clothes for them. However, when I opened the bag, I couldn't believe what I saw. There were no clothes in it – just some toys, a doll, some toilet paper and small plastic balls. I thought, for a moment, that my husband had played a joke. Then I realized that the two girls had repacked the bag. I had left it in their room. Megan had removed the clothes and put her favourite things in it instead! I wasn't annoyed. I just laughed and laughed. But we had to go and buy new clothes for the girls!

C
Two years ago, my husband and I went on a beach holiday in the Caribbean. On the last day, we decided to book a day trip on a boat. When we arrived in the harbour, we asked which boat was ours and were told to get on a big white boat. It wasn't what we had expected. There was a bar on the boat and a lot of balloons with 21 written on them. Lots of people started getting on the boat until it was really crowded. They all seemed to be in their twenties and from Brazil. Before long, the boat set off. It was then that somebody asked us if we were Luis' grandparents. It was only then that we realized we were on the wrong boat and that we were on a party boat for Luis' 21st birthday. The boat trip lasted five hours and the music was very loud, but we had a great time. I'm 67 and my husband's 74. We don't usually go to such exciting parties.

5 Read three short stories about things that went wrong on holiday.
Match the questions to the stories (A, B or C). There is an example at the beginning (0).

In which story …

0 do we know on which day of the week the event happened? __A__
1 did somebody want other people to solve the problem? _____
2 did somebody have a better time than expected? _____
3 did somebody do something they didn't need to do? _____
4 did somebody have to spend money? _____
5 did the event happen near the end of the holiday? _____
6 did somebody have to change where they were staying? _____
7 did somebody feel a bit angry? _____
8 was the storyteller in a place with people she didn't know? _____
9 did somebody do a lot of housework? _____
10 did somebody think that what happened was funny? _____

___ / 10

Listening

6 [107] Listen to three travel journalists talking about their favourite holiday destinations.
Choose the correct answer (A, B or C). There is an example at the beginning (0).

0 What is the name of the travel show?
  A On the Road   **(B)** Off Abroad
  C Overboard

1 How often is the travel show on the radio?
  A every day   B every week
  C every weekend

2 What is the best country Andrew has ever visited?
  A China   B India
  C the USA

3 When did Andrew first go to his favourite country?
  A before 2008   B in 2008
  C after 2008

4 Where did Andrew spend most of his time when he last visited his favourite country?
  A in the south   B in the capital
  C in the mountains

5 According to Andrew, what's the best reason to visit his favourite country?
  A to try the food B to meet the people
  C to see the monuments

6 Which of these countries has Susie never been to?
  A Mexico   B Brazil
  C Thailand

7 When she talks about the first of her favourite countries, which of these qualities does Susie mention?
  A its good food   B its friendly people
  C its fine weather

8 How many times has Susie been to the second of her favourite countries?
  A once   B twice
  C four times

9 How many times has Jennifer been to the USA?
  A never   B once
  C many times

10 Why does Jennifer want to go back to New York?
  A to do some shopping   B to see the shows
  C to see the monuments

___ / 10

Writing

7 Follow the instructions below.

Read the advertisement. Write an email requesting more information. Write five sentences. Ask for information about the dates, length and cost of the expedition, and what you have to do to prepare.

> **WHALE WATCHING EXPEDITION**
> See whales in their natural habitat in the North Atlantic. You will have the opportunity to see the world's largest animals up close. It's a trip of a lifetime. Write for more information.

___ / 10

Speaking

8 Read the task below and give your presentation in class.

Prepare to talk about an interesting place to visit in your home town or in a town or city you know well. Talk about what type of place it is and what it's called, when it opens and closes, how much it costs to go in, and what you can see and do there.

___ / 10

Unit 10 Test

Vocabulary

1 Complete the text with the words in the box. There is one extra word you do not need. There is an example at the beginning (0).

about us   adverts   basic   contact   content   home   link   search   up-to-date
user-friendly   website   withstand

Going online

When designing the perfect **(0)** _website_ for a business, it is important to make sure it is attractive and **(1)** _____ . You don't want people to find it difficult to find their way around your website. When they click on a **(2)** _____ they should go to the page they expect. So, if they click on **(3)** _____ , it should go to a page that provides information about your company. If they click on **(4)** _____ , it should go to a page with your number and email address. The most important page is the **(5)** _____ page because it is the first page anybody sees when they go to your website. Keep it **(6)** _____ – nobody wants to see lots of complicated graphics and images – and make sure it is free of **(7)** _____ – customers want to find out about you – they don't want to be sold things. In simple terms, make sure the **(8)** _____ you provide on the page is simple and necessary. It's a good idea to use the latest, **(9)** _____ software when designing your website as it needs to be reliable – hopefully, it will have to **(10)** _____ a lot of online traffic. You don't want it to crash all the time.

___ / 10

2 Complete the text with the correct form of the word in CAPITAL LETTERS. There is an example at the beginning (0).

0	This furniture is _old-fashioned_ . It looks like it was made in the 1980s.	FASHIONED
1	The toy company has launched a new _____ on the market.	PRODUCE
2	Karen always wears very _____ clothes. They are new and stylish.	FASHION
3	There are a lot of _____ in the magazine. Some take up the whole page.	ADVERTISE
4	The company isn't very _____. They only make thirty suitcases a week.	PRODUCE
5	Oil _____ are getting worried about the fall in the price of oil.	PRODUCE
6	The screwdriver is a very _____ invention. You can use it in many situations.	USE
7	Gemma has a job in the _____ industry.	ADVERTISE
8	Electricity is produced by the _____ grid.	NATION
9	The _____ of plastic toys at the factory has stopped because of safety concerns.	PRODUCE
10	Last year, we _____ off the loan for the car.	PAY

___ / 10

Grammar

3 Complete the text with the correct form of the verb in brackets. Use past simple active or passive or *used to* + infinitive. Use *used to* + infinitive whenever possible. There is an example at the beginning (0).

When I **(0)** _was_ (be) young in the 1970s, people **(1)** _____ (do) amazing things with colour and design in their homes. My parents **(2)** _____ (have) a very large dining room. It was so big that they often **(3)** _____ (invite) friends for dinner. Once, on their wedding anniversary, over twenty people **(4)** _____ (serve) dinner there and my parents **(5)** _____ (not have) any problems fitting them all round the table. The dining room walls were all different colours. I remember that one of them **(6)** _____ (be) blue and another orange, and a colourful painting **(7)** _____ (hang) on the wall. My parents **(8)** _____ (not worry) about having too much colour in the room! The dining room table was enormous and had a fabulous design on it. My sister **(9)** _____ (hide) under it. I don't know what **(10)** _____ (happen) to that table. I wish I had it now!

___ / 10

4 Complete the second sentence so that it has a similar meaning to the first sentence. Use two to four words including the word provided in CAPITALS. There is an example at the beginning (0).

0 The teacher tells the students the rules at the beginning of the exam.
TOLD
At the beginning of the exam, the students ___are told___ what the rules are.

1 Did we send that letter to Mrs Harris?
WAS
Do you know if _____ to Mrs Harris?

2 Experts believe that most people now have access to the internet.
IT
_____ that most people now have access to the internet.

3 The local garage repaired my car.
BY
My car _____ the local garage.

4 They built the museum between 1920 and 1929.
IN
The museum _____ the 1920s.

5 Kathy didn't write that essay.
BY
That essay _____ Kathy.

6 Tim bought both laptops in the department store.
BOUGHT
Both laptops _____ in the department store.

7 Tina didn't leave her bag on the bus.
BAG
Tina's _____ on the bus.

8 People send millions of emails every day.
ARE
Millions of emails _____ every day.

9 The duchess gave out the prizes.
BY
The prizes _____ the duchess.

10 Everybody here knows me.
I
_____ by everybody here.

___ / 10

Reading

5 Read the article about three tech companies. Match the questions to the paragraph (A, B or C) which answers the question. There is an example at the beginning (0).

0 Which company or service has a name which can't be used as a verb? __C__
1 Where is the company or service based today? _____
2 How did programmers think of a name for their company or service? _____
3 Which company or service was first developed by people who hadn't worked on any previous computer programming projects? _____
4 Which company or service was developed by people from different countries? _____
5 Which company provides significant sporting facilities for workers? _____
6 How many people use this company or service nowadays? _____
7 Which company or service has been bought by another company? _____
8 Which company or service is popular because of its cost? _____
9 Out of what type of building was the company or service first operated? _____
10 In what year did the company or service start making money? _____

___ / 10

Tech companies

A

Everybody knows Google. It's the most visited website in the world, and its name has become a verb meaning 'to search the internet'. But how long has there been a Google, and who started the company in the first place?

Google was founded in January 1996 as a research project by two students at Stanford University in California. Their names were Larry Page and Sergey Brin, and today they are two of the richest people in the world. Larry and Sergey wanted to design a different sort of search engine – one that improved the searches people made on the internet. At first, their new search engine company was based in the garage of a friend. Today, it's housed in enormous buildings in New York and California. The *Googleplex*, the company's headquarters near San Jose, is 190,000 m², and has eighteen cafeterias, two swimming pools and a number of volleyball courts to help employees relax.

B

Skype was started in 2003 by two technology entrepreneurs from Scandinavia. Niklas Zennström was born in Sweden, and Janus Friis is from Denmark, and together they had set up a number of online companies before they had the idea for Skype – an online text message and video chat service. A lot of the Skype software was created by a team of Estonian programmers named Ahti Heinla, Priit Kasesalu and Jaan Tallinn.

Skype was so successful that it was sold in 2011 for over $8 billion to Microsoft Corporation, making its founders billionaires. Skyping is particularly popular with people making international calls, partly because you can talk face to face using the video option, but mostly because call charges are so cheap. In 2014, 40% of all international calls were made on Skype.

C

In 2010, three computer programmers based in San Francisco were working on a project called Burbn when they decided to change to a different idea – their new idea was an internet-based application for sharing photos. They put together two words – instant camera and telegram – and came up with a name for their application: Instagram.

At first, when Instagram was launched in 2010, it only worked on one operating system. By 2012, however, it had been designed as an app for all the major operating systems and, as result, it was then that it became extremely popular and profitable. Instagram had 100 million users by 2013, and today has as many as 700 million users.

Listening

6 [108] Listen to the description of the life of a famous artist. Complete the notes with one word or number in each gap. There is an example at the beginning (0).

About the artist's life

Name of artist: Alberto **(0)** *Giacometti*

Year of birth: **(1)** _____

Place of birth: Borgonovo, **(2)** _____

Father's profession: **(3)** _____

Places where he studied: Geneva and **(4)** _____

About the artist's sculptures

Subject: figures of humans and **(5)** _____

Material they are made from: **(6)** _____

Appearance: strange – long, **(7)** _____ figures with flat heads

About the artist's death

Year of death: **(8)** _____

Cause of death: **(9)** _____ disease

Place where he is buried: in his home town close to his **(10)** _____

___ / 10

Writing

7 Follow the instructions below.

Write a review of a personal technological product you own (your mobile phone, laptop, computer, camera, etc). Include information about what you use the product for, why you like it, any problems you have, and whether you would recommend buying it.

___ / 10

Speaking

8 Read the task below and give your presentation in class.

Prepare to describe the design and appearance of a room in your house. Talk about its size and function, its furniture and décor, appearance, what you like about the room, and how you would change it.

___ / 10

Unit 11 Test

Vocabulary

1 Complete the text with the prepositions in the box. You can use the prepositions more than once. There is an example at the beginning (0).

about against by for in of on with

Are computer games good for you?

YES   One **(0)** ___of___ the best arguments in favour of playing computer games **(1)** _____ friends or **(2)** _____ small teams, is that it can help build social skills. Playing **(3)** _____ each other in competitive games will develop important life skills. By playing **(4)** _____ online teams in organized gaming, we will also make important friends and contacts for the future.

NO   A lot of people disagree **(5)** _____ the idea that computer games can be good. Talking **(6)** _____ computer games all the time, or taking your games console **(7)** _____ you everywhere you go is a form of anti-social behaviour. Spending all your money **(8)** _____ games or paying high prices **(9)** _____ the latest games can result in debt. In addition, games where you kill enemy soldiers one **(10)** _____ one may be 'fun', but many are concerned that this makes us insensitive to violence.

___ / 10

2 Choose the correct option (A, B or C) to complete the sentences. There is an example at the beginning (0).

0   There's a Whatsapp _____ on my screen.
  A message   **B** note   **C** letter

1   I've put some photos on my Facebook _____ .
  A book   **B** line   **C** page

2   Adam had to give a _____ to the class.
  A conversation   **B** presentation   **C** programme

3   Did you send that _____ message?
  A text   **B** sticky   **C** letter

4   The general is buried in a _____ in the cemetery.
  A statue   **B** tomb   **C** pot

5   Art _____ buy paintings at auctions.
  A selectors   **B** archaeologists   **C** collectors

6   We've got _____ very old trees in our garden.
  A one or two   **B** one by one   **C** one and two

7   The rocket was _____ into space last June.
  A started   **B** promoted   **C** launched

8   The spacecraft's _____ was to take photos of the planet.
  A plan   **B** mission   **C** function

9   I don't believe there are any life _____ on nearby planets.
  A makes   **B** shapes   **C** forms

10 The sun is at the centre of our solar _____ .
  A plan   **B** organization   **C** system

___ / 10

Grammar

3 Complete the email with the correct form of the verbs in brackets. There is an example at the beginning (0).

Hi Jerry

Hope you're well. I thought I'd write with some news.
The bad news first. Sue isn't happy at work. Last week, her boss told her she **(0)** ___wasn't___ (not be) working hard enough, and she told him she **(1)** _____ (not think) he was a good boss. And then she said she **(2)** _____ (feel) like that for a long time. So, I'm a bit worried she might lose her job. Sue told me she **(3)** _____ (not have) any trouble finding a new one, but I'm not so sure.

The good news is that we are going away next month. Do you remember that I told you we **(4)** _____ (look) at villas to buy in Portugal, and that we really **(5)** _____ (want) to buy one? Well, I didn't say that we **(6)** _____ (already / visit) a few. We've found one and decided to buy it. You said you **(7)** _____ (come) and visit if we bought a villa. Well, we have (almost)! So, you're invited.

By the way, I told Sue and Paula that you **(8)** _____ (start) doing a carpentry course and they told me they **(9)** _____ (be) very pleased. Sue said you **(10)** _____ (need) a hobby!

All the best

Write soon.

Ali x

___ / 10

4 Report the sentences. Use two to four words including the word provided in CAPITALS. There is an example at the beginning (0).

0 'We haven't been there.'
THEY
They said ___they hadn't been___ there.

1 'I'm working late.'
SAID
Sarah _____ late.

2 'Isaac won the match.'
THAT
She said _____ the match.

3 'I sometimes go to bed after midnight.'
SHE
She said _____ to bed after midnight.

4 'I'll pay for dinner.'
HE
Harry said _____ for dinner.

5 'I play tennis every week.'
US
Thomas _____ tennis every week.

6 'We love going to the cinema.'
THEY
_____ going to the cinema.

7 'I'm feeling ill.'
US
Stephanie _____ feeling ill.

8 'My parents are going to visit.'
EVERYBODY
I _____ my parents were going to visit.

9 'I like you.'
HER
Jack _____ her.

10 'I'll call your sister.'
MY
Eric said he _____ .

___ / 10

Reading

Bringing Pompeii back to life

The ancient Roman city of Pompeii in Italy was buried under volcanic rock in AD 79. **(0)** __D__ In recent years, however, many parts of the city have fallen down, and many parts have been closed to the public. The city was in danger and many experts were getting angry that the city wasn't being protected. **(1)** _____ The World Heritage site is now the scene of an ambitious restoration project. It is hoped that work being carried out now will mean that future generations will be able to visit and explore this amazing historical place.

Today, more than 200 experts and technicians are at work in Pompeii's ruins. As well as architects and archaeologists, there are painters and photographers, dentists and biologists, computer scientists and experts in art restoration. **(2)** _____ Not only that, but they are looking again at the bodies of people who died in the disaster. Although the data analysis is in the early stages, it is already opening a window on life in the Roman Empire. **(3)** _____ Indeed, one expert has said that a typical New Yorker of today would feel at home in the streets of the ancient city. Pompeii was a city of fast food restaurants, lively theatres and busy markets.

One of the most interesting of the volcano's casualties is an unusually tall man, dressed in very strange clothing. The shape of his clothes, and the shape and size of his body, were preserved in the volcanic rock that covered him. **(4)** _____ It is now believed that this man was a typical resident of first-century Pompeii, which, like today's London or New York, had a lot of ethnic diversity.

Pompeii was a rich city of Roman citizens, naturalized foreigners and freedmen (former slaves) who were working in business. Many of the people in the city had a very good diet. **(5)** _____ A surprising number of products used in the city were not from Italy. The city had a very commercial culture, with food arriving every day from many different parts of the empire. Life was good in Pompeii – but, sadly, the good life wasn't to last. When the volcano of nearby Mount Vesuvius erupted, almost everybody in the city was killed.

5 Read the article about Pompeii. Complete the gaps with the missing sentences (A–G). There is one extra sentence you do not need. There is an example at the beginning (0).

 A They ate whole grains, fruits and nuts, and used expensive spices to make their food taste good.
 B Pompeii was much larger than the experts said it would be.
 C Amazingly, life in Pompeii was similar to life now in the 21st century.
 D The disaster happened almost 2,000 years ago, but we still remember it today.
 E Over the years, people have wondered if he was a slave from the northern provinces of the empire.
 F They are all very carefully restoring and analysing all the objects and buildings in Pompeii.
 G As a result, the Italian authorities realized that they had to do something.

___ / 10

Listening

6 [109] Listen to Egyptologist Emma Simpson talk about the discovery of Tutankhamen's tomb. Choose the correct answer (A, B or C). There is an example at the beginning (0).

 0 How does the presenter describe the Valley of the Kings?
   A a city of the Nile
   (B) a city of the dead
   C a city of robbers

 1 What does Emma say about the life of the pharaoh Tutankhamen?
   A He was a teenager when he became pharaoh.
   B He was a typical teenager of his time.
   C He was a teenager when he died.

 2 What does Emma say about what the pharaoh Tutankhamen was like?
   A He was unhappy.
   B He was powerful.
   C He was often unwell.

 3 According to Emma, why was the tomb of Tutankhamen not discovered until 1922?
   A Despite looking, nobody saw the opening.
   B The tomb didn't have an entrance.
   C Nobody had tried to find it before.

 4 When did Howard Carter first go to Egypt?
   A before 1917
   B in 1917
   C after 1917

 5 Carter found Tutankhamen's tomb in 1922. Why didn't he find it much earlier?
   A He had been unlucky.
   B He hadn't had the money to search.
   C He had been interested in other tombs.

 6 What does Emma tell us about Lord Carnarvon?
   A He wasn't interested in archaeology himself.
   B He was a man who had a lot of money.
   C He joined Carter in the Valley of the Kings.

 7 What does Emma tell us about Howard Carter?
   A He wasn't sure he would find the tomb of Tutankhamen.
   B He felt sure he would be successful in his search one day.
   C He was careful with the money Carnarvon gave him.

 8 Why does Emma say that Carter was 'just in time' when he found the tomb of Tutankhamen in 1922?
   A The Egyptian government wanted him to leave the country.
   B Carnarvon didn't want to pay for the search anymore.
   C Other search teams were looking for the tomb of Tutankhamen

 9 What did Carter and his team do with the wonderful objects they found?
   A They sold them to museums and collectors.
   B They made sure they had labels on them.
   C They left them in the place they found them.

 10 How long did Carter keep his discovery of the tomb a secret?
   A He didn't keep it secret at all.
   B He never told anybody about it.
   C He told the world after removing the objects.

___ / 10

Writing

7 Follow the instructions below.

Write your autobiography. Include information about when and where you were born, your childhood and early life, and what you are doing now.

___ / 10

Speaking

8 Read the task below and give your presentation in class.

Prepare to give a presentation about an important event in your country's history. Talk about what the event was, when it happened and why. Talk about why the event is important in your country's history and why and how people remember the event.

___ / 10

Unit 12 Test

Vocabulary

1 Complete the text with the words in the box. There is an example at the beginning (0).

desert field forest garden mountain ocean park poacher river sponsor start

0 Behind the farm, there was a large, green ___*field*___ full of cows.
1 They walked through an ancient _____ in which the trees were large and old. Few people had been there before.
2 We climbed up to the top of the _____ where the air was thin but the views were amazing.
3 There is an attractive _____ in our city where children play – there is a lake, footpaths and a lot of trees.
4 We walked along the _____ to Henley, passing people who were fishing, and saying hello to people on boats who went past.
5 It used to take weeks to sail across the _____ from Europe to North America.
6 We like sitting in our _____ – it's small but it's full of beautiful flowers.
7 It was hot in the _____ . There were no plants, no water, and no sign of life.
8 A _____ has killed a chimpanzee mother and taken her baby.
9 Don't _____ trying to run a wildlife rescue centre until you know what problems you face.
10 The computer company wants to _____ the zoo to help protect animals and to get some positive publicity.

___ / 10

2 Choose the correct option to complete the weather forecast. There is an example at the beginning (0).

(0) *Extreme* / *Dark* weather will be moving in from the mountains early Saturday morning. A powerful (1) *cloud* / *storm* will bring strong winds and a lot of heavy (2) *rain* / *lightning*. It'll be so wet that there may be a chance of a (3) *shine* / *flood* in the lower part of the town. Move your valuable belongings upstairs. Watch out for loud claps of (4) *hail* / *thunder* in the sky, and dangerous, electrical (5) *lightning* / *bright*, which may cause fires. If temperatures fall, there is a chance of (6) *flood* / *hail* – if these hard balls of ice fall in your area, stay indoors. By Sunday morning, this weather front will have passed. On Sunday, the sun will (7) *storm* / *shine*, and skies will be very (8) *extreme* / *bright* and blue. There may be one white (9) *cloud* / *rain* in the sky, but no more than that. After the really (10) *dark* / *thunder* skies of Saturday, the light, sunny skies of Sunday will feel very different.

___ / 10

Grammar

3 Complete the text with the correct form of the verbs in brackets. There is an example at the beginning (0).

What (0) ___*would you do*___ (you / do) if you (1) _____ (be) alone on a desert island? Many of us dream of being lost in paradise but it (2) _____ (not be) much fun if you (3) _____ (not have) any friends with you. We asked an expert on survival what our chances of surviving on a desert island would be. He was surprisingly optimistic. 'If the island had water, you (4) _____ (survive) for a long time,' he said. 'You (5) _____ (have) to catch fish to eat, and make some sort of shelter to protect you from the sun, but if you (6) _____ (do) that, you (7) _____ (not die) … at least, not for a long time.' Being alone on a desert island has its advantages. It's warm, there are fish in the sea, and there are unlikely to be any diseases. 'Desert islands are friendlier places than most,' said the expert. 'If you (8) _____ (try) to survive in a cold climate, you would die of cold, and if you (9) _____ (get) lost in a tropical rainforest, you (10) _____ (catch) a disease.' It seems that desert islands aren't the worst places to find yourself.

___ / 10

4 Complete the sentences by adding *no*, *some*, *any* or *every* to the word in brackets. There is an example at the beginning (0).

0 I think I've got ___*something*___ in my eye. It really hurts. (thing)
1 I don't know _____ who likes doing lots of homework. (body)
2 We looked _____ but we couldn't find Lucy's phone. Perhaps it was stolen. (where)
3 I hadn't read _____ at all about the country before I visited it last summer. (thing)
4 There is _____ outside. Should we open the door and let them come in? (one)
5 _____ in my family has ever been abroad. In fact, we don't even have passports! (body)
6 Did you do _____ interesting on your holiday? (thing)
7 I invited _____ at work to the wedding, and all the people in Susie's office came, too! (body)
8 We didn't go _____ last weekend. We just stayed at home. (where)
9 There's _____ to do here. It's quite a boring place in winter. (thing)
10 _____ broke into the office at the weekend and took three of the computers. (one)

___ / 10

Reading

Today's Science Blog: tell us about the Moon

A

It's hard to imagine how life on our planet would be different if something like the Moon had never existed. If we didn't have a Moon, there would be no lunar tides, and a world where the seas didn't move would have a big effect on nature. There would also be no total solar eclipses – when the Moon moves in front of the sun – and we would notice that. More importantly, big rocks in space called asteroids which, for millions of years, have crashed into the Moon, would hit Earth instead. Everybody knows that asteroids have hit Earth and destroyed life – an asteroid killed the dinosaurs, for example. If there were more asteroids, perhaps the chance of life on Earth developing would be smaller. Perhaps there would be no us.

B

The Moon has played an important part in a lot of cultures. If it wasn't there, we would, I suppose, tell stories about different things, but it is true that many of our traditional stories are about the Moon. We talk about dreaming of the Moon, and aiming for the Moon, and we look at the Moon and think of love or mystery, of happiness or sadness. It is important to us. We have always wanted to go there. That's why there was a race to the Moon between the USA and the USSR in the 1960s, and why we have a space industry today.

C

The Moon's gravity pulls most strongly on the side of the Earth closest to the Moon and least strongly on the side of the Earth farthest from the Moon. The Earth's gravity pulls too and, as a result, material comes away from the surface of the Moon. If you lived on the Moon, you would see how strongly the pull of the Earth has an effect on the Moon's surface. Forces pull water from the Earth towards the Moon, particularly when there is a new Moon or a full Moon.

D

There are a number of theories. One is that the Earth and the Moon began life at the same time, and developed next to each other. Pieces of rock came together to make our planet, but some pieces of rock moved in the other direction and came together to make the Moon. Another idea is that the Moon was a piece of rock in space that was passing the Earth, but got caught in its gravity. There are, however, problems with both these theories. Most scientists think that a big rock hit Earth when the solar system was young and parts of our planet flew into space. These rocks then came together to make the Moon.

5 Read the science blog. Match the questions to the paragraphs (A–D) that answer each question. There is an example at the beginning (0).

0 Why are there high tides when there is a full Moon? _C_

1 What happened to the dinosaurs? ____
2 How was the Moon formed? ____
3 What would Earth be like with no Moon? ____
4 Is it possible the moon used to be part of the Earth? ____
5 How has the Moon helped our imagination? ____
6 When did people first try to go to the Moon? ____
7 How does gravity affect what happens on the Earth and on the Moon? ____
8 Do scientists agree on how the Moon started? ____
9 In what ways does the Moon protect Earth from disaster? ____
10 How does the Moon make us feel? ____

___ / 10

Listening

6 [110] Listen to an interview with Dr Holly Wilson about going to Mars. Choose the correct ending (A, B or C). There is an example at the beginning (0).

0 The presenter says that Dr Holly Wilson is an expert on
 A space.
 B science.
 C Mars.

1 In Dr Wilson's opinion, if we wanted to set up a space colony on Mars, we would
 A not have to improve technology.
 B be able to do it with 1970s technology.
 C need more advanced technology.

2 Dr Wilson says the main reason why we don't go to Mars is that
 A nobody wants to go to a place that is so dangerous.
 B governments don't have any money to spend on big projects.
 C it seems a better idea to spend money on other things.

3 Dr Wilson says that to set up a colony on Mars we need to get more support from
 A scientists.
 B politicians.
 C ordinary people.

4 According to Dr Wilson, the majority of people think that exploring space is
 A uninteresting.
 B very interesting.
 C not very interesting.

5 Dr Wilson thinks the chances of building a colony on Mars are
 A unlikely.
 B likely.
 C impossible.

6 Dr Wilson says that people might pay for a space colony on Mars if the reason was
 A political.
 B scientific.
 C economic.

7 Dr Wilson thinks that space tourism
 A would be too expensive for people to do.
 B wouldn't make enough money to support a colony.
 C would be a good reason to build a colony.

8 Dr Wilson thinks that a Mars colony might be paid for by
 A a government's military department.
 B an international tourist agency.
 C rich business people.

9 Dr Wilson says that
 A Mars only has a few minerals.
 B we don't know what minerals there are on Mars.
 C there are a lot of minerals on Mars.

10 In Dr Wilson's opinion, there needs to be
 A more major companies interested in finding Mars' minerals.
 B more scientific research into the type of minerals on Mars.
 C better technology in order to get minerals from Mars.

___ / 10

Writing

7 Follow the instructions below.

Write an article about a mountain, lake, forest or river you know well. Include information about what it's called, where it is, what it looks like, what you can do there, and why people should visit it.

___ / 10

Speaking

8 Read the task below and give your presentation in class.

Prepare to talk about what you would do in the following situations and why:

You find or win a lot of money.

You are given a year off work or college.

You get the chance to do any course you want.

___ / 10

Photocopiable tests: answer key

All tests contain a maximum of 80 marks. For a percentage mark, divide by 80 and multiply by 100 = ____ %

Unit 1 Test

Vocabulary
1

1 get 2 work 3 take 4 feel 5 stay 6 watch
7 go 8 fall 9 do 10 play

2

1 C 2 B 3 B 4 A 5 B 6 B 7 C 8 C
9 C 10 A

Grammar
3

1 are staying   6 usually study
2 talk   7 go
3 have   8 isn't studying
4 don't go   9 's listening
5 do we do   10 Are you doing

4

1 Sarah often goes swimming.
2 Irene starts work at nine every day.
3 We usually eat out at the weekend.
4 Simon isn't feeling well at the moment.
5 Erica doesn't often get home early.
6 More people are doing karate these days.
7 Suzy rarely has time for breakfast.
8 I'm not feeling worried right now.
9 Jack sometimes watches films on TV.
10 They visit their grandparents twice a year.

Reading
5

1 B 2 C 3 B 4 B 5 B 6 C 7 B 8 B
9 C 10 A

Listening
6

1 C 2 A 3 B 4 B 5 C 6 B 7 A 8 C
9 B 10 B

Unit 2 Test

Vocabulary
1

1 competitors 2 cycling 3 athletics 4 players
5 like 6 winners 7 competing 8 runners 9 wrestlers
10 losers

2

1 celebration 2 slow 3 race 4 like 5 Gymnastics
6 team 7 line 8 racing 9 competitive 10 matches

Grammar
3

1 wear 2 use 3 have 4 Being 5 having
6 Winning 7 playing 8 to score 9 playing
10 have

4

1 C 2 D 3 A 4 D 5 B 6 A 7 C 8 B
9 A 10 B

Reading
5

1 R 2 R 3 W 4 DS 5 R 6 W 7 W 8 W
9 DS 10 R

Listening
6

1 A 2 C 3 B 4 B 5 A 6 C 7 A 8 A
9 A 10 B

Unit 3 Test

Vocabulary
1

1 go on 2 pick 3 drop 4 miss 5 book 6 Take
7 get on 8 pay 9 stop 10 get off

2

1 cross 2 hour 3 emissions 4 jam 5 frequent
6 convenient 7 comfortable 8 reliable 9 take
10 receipt

Grammar
3

1 A 2 C 3 C 4 A 5 B 6 A 7 D 8 A
9 C 10 D

4

1 the world's fastest   7 a lot less convenient /
2 the centre than   a lot more inconvenient
3 better at maths than   8 aren't as exciting
4 the worst singer   9 a bit more expensive
5 isn't as safe   10 are lazier than
6 a little older than

Reading
5

1 D 2 C 3 D 4 B 5 A 6 A 7 C 8 A
9 A 10 C

Listening
6

1 C 2 B 3 C 4 A 5 B 6 C 7 A 8 B
9 A 10 C

247

Unit 4 Test
Vocabulary
1

1 A 2 D 3 C 4 A 5 B 6 D 7 C 8 B
9 C 10 B

2

1 achievement   6 patient
2 mountaineers   7 luckily
3 solution   8 careful
4 memorize   9 risky
5 challenging   10 adventurer

Grammar
3

1 grew 2 weren't 3 had 4 learned 5 was staying
6 bought 7 was studying 8 spent 9 became 10 broke

4

1 B 2 C 3 A 4 A 5 B 6 C 7 A 8 B
9 D 10 B

Reading
5

1 A 2 K 3 A 4 B 5 K 6 B 7 K 8 B
9 K 10 B

Listening
6

1 A,D 2 L,K 3 C,G 4 F,I 5 B,J

Unit 5 Test
Vocabulary
1

1 B 2 A 3 D 4 C 5 B 6 C 7 C 8 C
9 D 10 B

2

1 rooftop 2 nearly 3 figured out 4 made of 5 glass
6 for 7 shower 8 ordered 9 taking 10 time

Grammar
3

1 D 2 B 3 A 4 B 5 D 6 C 7 A 8 D
9 D 10 D

4

1 the 2 The 3 the 4 – 5 the 6 a 7 – 8 the
9 – 10 –

Reading
5

(2 marks for each item)
1 D 2 G 3 F 4 A 5 E

Listening
6

1 green 2 brown 3 plastic 4 cardboard 5 books
6 clear 7 bottles 8 broken 9 opposite 10 next

Unit 6 Test
Vocabulary
1

1 play 2 go 3 ban 4 get 5 start 6 go 7 ride
8 get 9 leave 10 get

2

1 A 2 D 3 B 4 C 5 B 6 A 7 A 8 B
9 D 10 C

Grammar
3

1 I'm not coming   6 I'll go
2 I'll   7 don't think he'll
3 We're going to be   8 am
4 will steal   9 I'm playing
5 I'm going to tell   10 I'm going to marry

4

1 to work 2 to get 3 being 4 to see 5 go 6 make
7 to buy 8 travelling 9 to wait 10 spending

Reading
5a

2 C 3 E 4 B

5b

1 T 2 DS 3 T 4 F 5 T 6 F 7 DS

Listening
6

1 A 2 B 3 B 4 D 5 E 6 C 7 D 8 D
9 C 10 E

Unit 7 Test
Vocabulary
1

1 A 2 B 3 A 4 D 5 C 6 B 7 C 8 B
9 B 10 D

2

1 skilled   6 politicians
2 dangerous   7 trainee
3 representative   8 entrance
4 designer   9 decision
5 economist   10 references

Grammar

3

1 have known	6 have planned
2 started	7 have learned
3 hasn't been	8 started
4 told	9 didn't know
5 has decided	10 have become

4

1 C   2 B   3 A   4 B   5 A   6 D   7 A   8 B
9 A   10 B

Reading

5

(2 marks for each item)
1 G   2 A   3 F   4 B   5 E

Listening

6

1 False   2 True   3 False   4 True   5 False   6 True
7 True   8 True   9 False   10 True

Unit 8 Test

Vocabulary

1

1 of   2 at   3 on   4 of   5 on   6 in   7 to   8 up
9 in   10 at

2

1 made   2 fall   3 connect   4 upload   5 Push   6 control
7 forwards   8 known   9 equipment   10 forever

Grammar

3

1 A   2 B   3 B   4 C   5 B   6 A   7 A   8 C
9 A   10 C

4

1 We arrived at a place where they make lifeboats.
2 Josie has a cat which/that can open the doors of cupboards.
3 Peter doesn't like beaches which/that are polluted.
4 New York is a city where there are many exciting businesses.
5 I met some friends (who/that) I knew from school.
6 South Korea is a country which/that has many important electronic companies.
7 My sister is a person who gives me good advice.
8 The local theatre is a venue where many people in our town meet.
9 The museum is a building (which/that) I like very much.
10 The students are members of a club which/that meets every Monday.

Reading

5

A 2, 3 and 5
B 1, 5 and 6
C 1, 3, 4 and 6

Listening

6

1 Technology	6 laptops
2 Sunday	7 Science
3 9	8 information
4 6	9 12
5 40	10 lunch

Unit 9 Test

Vocabulary

1

1 B   2 B   3 C   4 A   5 C   6 B   7 B   8 C
9 C   10 A

2

1 camper   2 unpack   3 clubbing   4 fascinated
5 frightened   6 amazing   7 gift   8 annoyed
9 tiring   10 traders

Grammar

3

1 were	6 had booked
2 had never been	7 was
3 had spent	8 decided
4 felt	9 had forgotten
5 had told	10 had

4

1 B   2 B   3 A   4 B   5 B   6 A   7 B   8 C
9 A   10 C

Reading

5

1 A   2 C   3 A   4 B   5 C   6 A   7 A   8 C
9 A   10 B

Listening

6

1 B   2 A   3 A   4 B   5 B   6 B   7 C   8 C
9 C   10 A

Unit 10 Test

Vocabulary

1

1 user-friendly	6 basic
2 link	7 adverts
3 about us	8 content
4 contact	9 up-to-date
5 home	10 withstand

Photocopiable tests: answer key   **249**

2

1 product
2 fashionable
3 advertisements
4 productive
5 producers
6 useful
7 advertising
8 national
9 production
10 paid

Grammar
3

1 used to do
2 used to have
3 used to invite
4 were served
5 didn't have
6 used to be
7 used to hang / was hung
8 didn't use to worry
9 used to hide
10 happened

4

1 that letter was sent
2 It is believed
3 was repaired by
4 was built in
5 wasn't written by
6 were bought
7 bag wasn't left
8 are sent
9 were given out by
10 I am known

Reading
5

1 A 2 C 3 A 4 B 5 A 6 C 7 B 8 B
9 A 10 C

Listening
6

1 1901
2 Switzerland
3 painter
4 Paris
5 animals
6 metal
7 thin
8 1966
9 heart
10 parents

Unit 11 Test

Vocabulary
1

1 with 2 in 3 against 4 for 5 with 6 about
7 with 8 on 9 for 10 by

2

1 C 2 B 3 A 4 B 5 C 6 A 7 C 8 B
9 C 10 C

Grammar
3

1 didn't think
2 had felt
3 wouldn't have
4 were looking
5 wanted
6 had already visited
7 would come
8 had started
9 were
10 needed

4

1 said she was working
2 that Isaac had won
3 (that) she sometimes went
4 (that) he would pay
5 told us he played
6 They said they loved
7 told us she was
8 told everybody (that)
9 told her he liked
10 would call my sister

Reading
5

(2 marks for each item)
1 G 2 F 3 C 4 E 5 A

Listening
6

1 C 2 C 3 A 4 A 5 B 6 B 7 B 8 B
9 B 10 A

Unit 12 Test

Vocabulary
1

1 forest 2 mountain 3 park 4 river
5 ocean 6 garden 7 desert 8 poacher
9 start 10 sponsor

2

1 storm 2 rain 3 flood 4 thunder 5 lightning
6 hail 7 shine 8 bright 9 cloud 10 dark

Grammar
3

1 were
2 wouldn't be
3 didn't have
4 would survive
5 would have
6 did
7 wouldn't die
8 tried
9 got
10 would catch

4

1 anybody
2 everywhere
3 anything
4 someone
5 Nobody
6 anything
7 everybody
8 anywhere
9 nothing
10 Someone

Reading
5

1 A 2 D 3 A 4 D 5 B 6 B 7 C 8 D
9 A 10 B

Listening
6

1 A 2 C 3 C 4 B 5 A 6 C 7 B 8 A
9 C 10 C

Photocopiable tests: audioscripts

Unit 1 Test [99]

W = Will; M = Mary

W: What's a typical day for you, Mary?

M: A typical day? You mean, like a Monday?

W: Sure.

M: Well, as you know, I'm at the International College. I always get up at the same time on a weekday. My flatmate gets up really early – six in the morning, sometimes. But I'm always up and out of bed at eight – always the same time. Then I have a shower and eat breakfast and I'm on my way.

W: What do you have for breakfast?

M: Oh, it depends. I always have juice, and I have cereal, not always but usually. Then some mornings I have bread and cheese, but only once or twice a week. My flatmate is very different. She eats a big breakfast with eggs, lots of bread, that sort of thing. I don't know how she eats it all.

W: How do you get to college?

M: When I started college, I took the bus, but not now. It's only forty minutes from my house so it's easy to walk, and I don't have a car or bike. My flatmate sometimes asks me if I want a lift in her car but I always say no.

W: What do you do in the evenings after college?

M: I always have coursework to do, of course, and then I'm usually tired so I sit in front of the TV all evening. I don't usually meet friends and I never listen to music. I'm not really into music.

W: And at the weekends?

M: Well, I don't go to college. It's closed at weekends. So, I get up late. I go swimming on most Saturday mornings but I hardly ever go to the gym or play tennis. I usually meet my friends in the city centre, and I sometimes go to the cinema in the evening, but not very often. I love cycling but I don't have a bike, so, on Sundays, when the weather's nice, I go for long walks. There are some beautiful mountains near here.

Unit 2 Test [100]

I = Interviewer; P = Penny

I: Hello and welcome to *Sports Tonight*. On tonight's show, we'll talk later about skiing and surfing, but our first guest in the studio is Penny Harris, the champion snowboarder. So, Penny, what do you like about your sport?

P: Well, it's in the open air – in the mountains – and you can go snowboarding when you want to – and you can do it on your own. But the thing I like the most about snowboarding is the friends you make. Up in the mountains, you meet great people, and we're always having fun together.

I: It's very competitive, too?

P: Yes, it is. But I don't think you have to be very competitive or talented to be great on a board. You have to work really hard. That's what's most important.

I: I believe a lot of people in your sport have part-time jobs in cafés and restaurants, too, to help pay for the travel and the equipment.

P: Well, yes. A lot do. Most, in fact. Especially when they're starting out. I was lucky. My parents were there for me – financially, you know. Some of my friends were ski tutors or ski guides, but I didn't work part-time.

I: OK. What are the problems with your sport? Is it dangerous?

P: No, I don't think it's dangerous, but it's not cheap. Nowadays, I live in the mountains, in Switzerland, so I don't have to travel to practise. But when I was younger, I lived in an English seaside town. It cost a lot to travel to practise back then!

I: How often do you train?

P: Usually every day. But I don't do any training on Sundays. That's my day off. A lot of snowboarders train in swimming pools, doing a lot of swimming to make them strong. But I don't. I hate the water! I often go to the gym. It's important to be strong and fit, of course, and the only way to get really fit is to work hard in the gym.

I: OK. Thanks very much, Penny. And good luck in your next championships. In Italy, aren't they?

P: Er… No, Austria. The last championships were in Italy, and they were in France the year before that.

Unit 3 Test [101]

S = Sales person; C = Customer

S: Next, please.

C: Yes, hello. I have to get to Manchester from London Euston or London King's Cross on Tuesday morning, and I'd like to know how much that costs.

S: Is that single or return?

C: Return. Or is it cheaper to buy two singles?

S: No, it's more expensive. You want return.

C: OK. I'd like to go early – but not very early – on the Tuesday and come back early evening on the Thursday of the same week. It's for business, you see. I'm not on holiday or anything.

S: I see. Er, well, the trains are very regular. They go every twenty minutes and you don't have to change. On some routes, you have to change once or twice, but not on this route. You leave from Euston station.

C: OK. Well, that's good news.

S: The cost of an anytime return leaving on Tuesday is … right, well, it's £338.

C: What? That's ridiculous. Is that a first-class ticket or super luxury or something? No, I just want a regular return.

S: That's the price of a standard return, sir.

C: There must be something cheaper.

251

S: Well, it depends on when you want to leave. Tickets are expensive at busy times. You can buy an off-peak return for £83, but you can't use that between seven and ten in the morning, I'm afraid. It depends on when you want to go.

C: OK. I see. Well, I can't afford to pay £300 or whatever, so I'll have to buy the off-peak. But going after ten will make me late for a meeting. If I take a train just before seven, when will I get there?

S: The 6.40 gets to Manchester in two hours or so. You'll be there at 8.46.

C: Well, I guess that's perfect, actually. Just a bit early to be leaving, that's all. Right. I'll buy an off-peak.

S: Yes, sir. Just remember that on your return you can't use the ticket between four and seven in the evening.

C: OK. That isn't a big problem. I wanted to head home at about six. But it's not a big problem to have to wait until seven. I'll just have to sit and buy a coffee or something.

S: There are lots of coffee shops in the station, sir. Right. That'll be £86, sir. That's £83 plus the £3 booking fee. Are you paying by card?

Unit 4 Test [102]

E = Ella; D = Dan

E: Did you enjoy your holiday, Dan?

D: Yes, I had a great time.

E: What did you do?

D: Well, we visited the island of Tenerife and stayed near the beach for a week. On Sunday, we checked in to our hotel and had a picnic on the beach.

E: That sounds like a great start to a holiday. And knowing you I guess you spent Monday sitting on the beach, too.

D: Well, on Monday morning, the weather was really good, but we wanted to do something active, so we went for a long walk near the sea. That was amazing. I carried my really good camera with me. The one I had on last year's cycling holiday. I uploaded hundreds of those photos. Did you see them?

E: Yes, I did. There was a great one of an old restaurant by the sea.

D: That's right. Anyway, on Tuesday, we wanted to go up into the mountains, but it was very rainy and windy, so we went into the city and visited some museums. They weren't as interesting as I expected. But we met some really friendly local people in a café and that was fun. We spent all afternoon there.

E: Nice!

D: On Wednesday, we went shopping in the city. I wanted to go to the beach, of course, but Annie loves malls, as you know. Anyway, we spent the morning there, and bought lots of souvenirs. In the afternoon, we rented bikes and went out of the city as far as the port.

E: That's a fun thing to do. Better than walking, I think!

D: On Thursday we visited a lake. I wanted to go water-skiing, but the water sports centre was closed. So we just had a bit of a swim in the lake. And we had lunch in a fantastic fish restaurant.

E: Really? What did you order?

D: Oh, I can't remember, but it was delicious! On Friday we were quite tired, so we went to the beach and sat and relaxed with a book. We didn't go swimming or anything. And on Saturday we came home!

E: Well, it sounds like a great holiday. But it's good to see you back, Dan.

Unit 5 Test [103]

Recycling is good. It's cheaper, more energy efficient and much better for the environment than having to make things from new materials.

That's why your local council is trying to make it as easy as possible for you to recycle as much as you can. Most of your waste can be put in your green bin for recycling. Only use your black bin for things we can't recycle. And use your small brown bin for organic waste – waste food, for example. Any paper, plastic or cardboard products can go in the green bin. That includes newspapers and magazines, but not books. We'd like you to take them to charity shops where they can be sold.

Put your recycling into your green bin loose – if you give it a quick wash with clean water, it'll keep your bin fresh and prevent bad smells. If you want to put anything into the bin in a bag, use clear plastic bags. We won't empty your green wheelie bin if the recycling is in a black or coloured bag.

We also recycle glass that you put in the green recycling bin. However, we only take bottles and jars. You must be careful. We won't take broken glass, light bulbs or anything large or dangerous – a window pane, for example.

There are still some things we can't yet recycle from in front of your house. These include electrical items. You have to take these to our waste recycling centres. There are three small recycling centres for electrical products – one is at Glenn Street car park, another is opposite the sports centre in Forecourt Street, and the third is next to the shopping centre in Barclay Street.

Many people put old clothes in the green recycling bin. Please don't do this. We are happy to collect and remove clothes, curtains and bed sheets but only if they are in a clear plastic bag placed next to the green recycling bin on collection day. Also make sure that you don't throw out clothes that are in good condition. Please take clothes that are in good condition to a charity shop.

Unit 6 Test [104]

A

We aren't planning a big wedding, but I think it'll be very romantic. My boyfriend and I are both English but we've always wanted to get married on a tropical island. That's why we're going to the Seychelles. Of course, it means that not all our friends can come. Our parents are going to fly there with us, and so is my sister and my best friend, and Tom's invited both his brothers. So, there won't be many of us there, but it'll be amazing.

252 Photocopiable tests: audioscripts

B

My girlfriend is from Germany, but we've decided to get married here in England – in the small village where I was born. Everybody I know will be there and a lot of people are coming from Germany. Fortunately, there's a lovely old church and an attractive hotel and restaurant in the village so it's the perfect place to invite guests to. As soon as the wedding is over, we're going on holiday.

C

My fiancé and I are Sikhs, and we are planning a very traditional Sikh wedding. I'm going to wear a shalwar and kameez – the Sikh blouse and trousers – and my husband will be wearing traditional clothes, too. At weddings in many countries, people wear black and white, but not at a Sikh wedding – reds and blues are common – we don't like dull colours. The wedding ceremony will be in the morning, in the temple in our home city, and after that there will be a lot to eat. There won't be a lot of people there, but they'll be very lively. We're planning to go to India on our honeymoon a few days after getting married.

D

Just about all of our guests are going to fly in especially for our wedding. That's because we have decided to get married in the small town where Don – my boyfriend – grew up. It's a long way from New York City, where most of our friends are. We haven't invited a lot of people. Don's brother is in a band, so he and his friends are going to do the music, and my sister is a professional chef, so she's planning the meal. It's great to have friends and family who can really help with the planning. It's back to New York and work the day after the wedding – we can't take too much time off.

E

We've got a wedding planner to organize our wedding. He's doing everything – from booking and decorating the venue to buying the cake. We really didn't want to do everything ourselves, so we're really happy we have somebody to do all the hard work for us. The wedding ceremony will be in the afternoon and we will travel in a 1950s car to the reception. All the food will be Mexican. It's my favourite food, you see, and I know everybody will love it, and we're going to Mexico for our honeymoon.

Unit 7 Test [105]

I = Interviewer; R = Ray

I: How has the workplace here in Australia changed since you started working, Ray?

R: It's changed a lot. Back in the 1960s, most people worked nine to five. And it was usually men in the workplace. When they got married, women stopped working to have children. Men worked to support their wives and children at home. Today, fifty years on, social changes have placed women on a more equal platform in the workplace.

I: So, did married women work at all?

R: In the public service, married women didn't work. You couldn't employ a married woman in a public company. It was illegal. Of course, private companies employed married women, but only rarely.

I: What about the office environment? How was that different in the 1960s?

R: Well, there were no computers, of course. And staff smoked at work, even in the office. Nowadays, people go and make their own tea and coffee in the staff kitchen but, when I was young, we had a tea lady – it was always a woman – and she came round and served tea and biscuits at different times of the day.

I: Were holidays the same?

R: Back then I got four weeks' paid holiday every year, and that's the same now. But today people get different types of leave from work than fifty years ago. Things like maternity or paternity leave for mums and dads with babies – well, we didn't have that in the 1960s.

I: I guess the types of jobs have changed, too?

R: Yes, absolutely. Most of the jobs in the 1960s were in production such as agriculture or manufacturing, which employed 46 per cent of workers. Now only 23 per cent work in those sectors. Many more jobs are office jobs. Because of technology, there are fewer physical jobs.

I: Do you think it was better to work in the 1960s or today?

R: Well, it's much better for women today. But I also think jobs are more interesting and challenging than in the past for men as well as women. And people are better educated than they were half a century ago so they earn more money.

Unit 8 Test [106]

M = Man; W = Woman

W: What's happening in the park this weekend?

M: There's a festival – it's called the July Festival. It's quite a big event in our town. It's really popular and lots of people go.

W: Oh, great. I love live music.

M: Ahh… It isn't a Music Festival, I'm afraid. It's a Science and Technology Festival. If you go, you'll see all the latest gadgets. You know, new inventions, and things like that.

W: Oh, OK. Well, it sounds interesting anyway. So, is it on all weekend?

M: Yes. It starts on Friday evening and it's on all day Saturday and then finishes at lunchtime on the next day. It should be fun. I went last year and I really enjoyed it.

W: OK. Well, I really like the sound of it. Are you definitely going, then? I'll go if you're going.

M: Well, I'm planning to go on Saturday. The festival starts at nine in the morning. That's when the gates open. And it ends at six in the evening. It's quite a long day.

W: Yeah. That's a bit long for me. Let's go at ten. I'll see you at the park entrance at ten. And I'll have to go before five because I'm meeting friends in the evening.

M: Sure. And I'll have to go home at four. But that's fine. Ten to four is long enough. I'll see you at the main gate at ten. If you take Bus 40 from the centre, it'll take you straight to the main entrance gate.

W: OK. I'll do that. So, what can I see at the festival?

M: Well, last year they had a display of the latest robots. This year it's different. There'll be a display of mobile phones and laptops.

W: OK. Great. I need a new phone. Oh, I forgot. Is it expensive? And how do I get a ticket?

M: Well, it won't be sold out. You can buy a ticket online or at the Science Centre in town. Or you can just buy one on the day. You can't buy tickets at the entrance gate but there is an information office in the car park near the festival entrance gate, and they sell tickets there. It'll cost £12 but that includes a free lunch.

W: Sounds good. I'll buy a ticket on the day, I think. Right, see you on Saturday.

Unit 9 Test [107]

P = Presenter; **A** = Andrew; **S** = Susie; **J** = Jennifer

P: Hello, and welcome to *Off Abroad* – the weekly travel show. On today's show, we have three travel holiday journalists, Andrew Stuart, Susie Tudor and Jennifer Hart. And we're asking them all the same question: what's the best place you've ever been to? You first, Andrew. What's your favourite destination?

A: Umm. It's a very good question. Which place is the most interesting? I think I'd go for one of the largest and most populous countries in the world.

P: You mean India?

A: India? No. I mean China. It's a wonderful place. The last time I went there was to see the Olympics in 2008. But I had been two or three times before. On my previous visits, I didn't get the chance to travel much. When I was there in 2005 and 2008, I spent most of my time in Beijing, the capital. If I go again, I'd like to go to the big cities in the south of China and I really want to see the mountains.

P: What's the best thing about the country?

A: Well, the food is amazing, and some of the historical places are really worth seeing. But it's the people that make the place. By far the main reason to go there is to get to know the locals – there are so many of them, and they are so lively and vibrant.

P: What about you, Susie? Which place makes you feel excited?

S: Oh, there are so many wonderful places to visit. And so many places I've never been to. I haven't seen India or Brazil or Peru. Of the places I have been to, I'd choose Thailand. I love the sun – it's warm and sunny all the time – and there are wonderful monuments to see there, too. The capital city, Bangkok, is very exciting and the beaches are really beautiful. Another favourite place of mine is Mexico. The best thing about that country is the food. I just love eating out there whenever I go.

P: And you've been there a lot?

S: Oh, yes. Plenty. I was there once last year, and once the year before, and twice the year before that. I can't keep away.

P: OK. Thanks, Susie. What about you, Jennifer?

J: Well, one country I've visited many times is the USA. I love New York – it's the most fantastic city in the world. So I'd love to go shopping there again. People often go there for the famous monuments and the great shows, but there's nothing I like more than going to one of the big department stores.

P: Thanks, Jennifer. And thanks to all my guests. Next week, I'm asking the question …

Unit 10 Test [108]

In this week's *World Art* magazine, we're going to look at the life and work of the famous artist Alberto Giacometti, a man who became famous during his lifetime for his sculptures.

Alberto was born in 1901, and he was brought up in Borgonovo, a small town in Switzerland. He grew up on a farm, with his three brothers and sisters, and he had a happy childhood. His father was a painter and, from an early age, Alberto and his brothers and sisters were interested in painting and sculpture. Alberto was taught art at the School of Fine Arts in Geneva. Then, in 1922, he moved away from his home country, not to London or New York, but to Paris, to study sculpture. He was influenced by other famous artists of the time including Picasso and Miró, two artists he met and admired.

Alberto Giacometti became famous for making sculptures of people and animals. However, his sculptures are very strange. Today, his work is fashionable but, at first, people didn't really understand what he was trying to do. All of his many sculptures are made of metal – he never worked with other materials such as wood or stone – and they all share a similar shape and appearance. They are very thin with long legs and bodies and big, flat heads. As he got older, his sculptures got thinner and thinner. Alberto liked to use the same person as a model many times, and his younger brother Diego was often used.

In 1962, Giacometti was awarded the grand prize for sculpture at the Venice Biennale, an important art exhibition. The award made him famous, and his works were shown in a number of large exhibitions throughout Europe. Unfortunately, however, he was already very ill and in 1966 he died of heart disease. His body was returned to his birthplace in Borgonovo, and he was buried near his parents.

Today, fifty years after his death, Giacometti's work is very fashionable and you see his influence in many products. However, experts are still unsure why he chose to make his figures so strange.

Unit 11 Test [109]

P = Presenter; E = Emma

P: The Valley of the Kings is near the River Nile in Egypt – in ancient times, it was a city of the dead, the place where Egypt's pharaohs were buried. Over the centuries, one by one, the tombs of these dead kings and queens were robbed, and the beautiful objects inside were taken away by robbers. In 1922, however, archaeologists discovered a tomb that had not been robbed – the tomb of a king which still had beautiful and amazing objects inside. Here to tell the story is Egyptologist Emma Simpson. Welcome to the programme, Emma.

E: Hello.

P: So, whose tomb was it and why was it undiscovered?

E: It was the tomb of Tutankhamen, a pharaoh who lived in Egypt over three thousand years ago. We believe he became pharaoh at the age of nine, and died ten years later. Most pharaohs were strong, but Tutankhamen was ill for most of his life, and he probably didn't have the power to be a leader or make decisions. His story is quite sad. The fact that nobody discovered the tomb before 1922 was just luck – chance. Local people had known about the treasures in the tombs for hundreds of years, so they had looked and looked. The entrance wasn't easy to find, I guess. They didn't know it was there.

P: And who discovered it?

E: An archaeologist called Howard Carter. Carter had been to Egypt when he was young, and had always been interested in finding Tutankhamen's tomb, but he didn't have the money to pay for all the hard work needed to look for the tomb. In 1917, a rich Englishman called Lord Carnarvon gave Carter money to start looking, and he went straight to the Valley of the Kings. Over the next five years, Carter organized a very careful search for the tomb. He was very confident. He really believed that one day he would find the tomb.

P: And he did find it?

E: Yes. Just in time. Carnarvon had told Carter that 1922 was the last year he would pay for anything.

P: And when they opened the tomb, it was full of objects?

E: Yes, indeed. Carter said it was full of wonderful things. They put together a team which carefully collected and labelled all the objects, and took them away to museums. It took ten years.

P: And did they do that secretly?

E: Well, not really. Today, I think, an archaeologist wouldn't tell the world about his discovery until all the research was completed. But the story of the discovery was in the London newspapers a week after Carter opened the tomb. I think he enjoyed being famous.

Unit 12 Test [110]

P = Presenter; W = Dr Holly Wilson

P: On tonight's programme, I'm talking to a world famous expert on space, Dr Holly Wilson. We're going to talk about the planet Mars. Could we visit the planet if we wanted to? Would it be possible to set up a space colony and live there? Dr Wilson, what do you think?

W: Oh, well, that's difficult. I'd say that we could if we wanted to, but it's a big 'if'.

P: Why the 'if'?

W: OK. Well, there are a lot of reasons why we might never see people on Mars in our lifetimes. It's not because we don't have the technology because we do. Our computers are more advanced than in the 1960s and 1970s. The problem is the cost – governments have the money, of course, but many people think we shouldn't spend money on this type of project.

P: I thought that lots of politicians liked the idea of space travel.

W: Oh, I agree. I think most of them do. And, of course, scientists are very enthusiastic. But ordinary people don't want to pay for space exploration. It may seem exciting, and people are always interested in talking about it but, at the moment, the cost of space flight is too high.

P: So, you're not optimistic?

W: Well, no, but I didn't say it was impossible. If there were a good economic reason for going to Mars and building a space colony, I'm sure somebody would do it.

P: Is there a reason?

W: Some people think there is. They think that space tourism would be a good reason.

P: And do you?

W: No, not really. A tourist trip to Mars would be very expensive but even if hundreds made the trip each year, it wouldn't raise enough money to pay for a colony. In my opinion, there are two good financial reasons to build a colony. First of all, governments might build a space station for military reasons – what a great place to put a missile! And major companies might want to look for minerals like oil or metal under the surface of the planet. But governments, not business people, would have to pay for the colony. That much is clear.

P: Are there a lot of minerals on Mars?

W: Scientific research shows that there are plenty of useful materials there if any company had the technology to take them out of the ground. That's what they need to develop.

P: OK. Thanks Dr Wilson. After the break, we'll be coming back with …

Photocopiable communicative activities

Unit 1 Communicative activity A (Vocabulary)

All about you

= do   = go   = play

games
cards   the piano   karate
hiking   jogging   football   sport
nothing   homework   yoga   running   for long walks   fishing   regular exercise
shopping   tennis   cycling   surfing
   gardening
clubbing   swimming

Where do you …?	Why do people usually …?	Does your family ever …?	Who do you … with?	When do you …?
Do you ever …?	How often do you …?	What do you … with?	Do you often … with friends?	Do you usually …?
How do you feel when you …?	Do you … with your family?	Do your friends often …?	How many times a week do you …?	How many hours a day do you …?

256 PHOTOCOPIABLE © National Geographic Learning

Unit 1 Communicative activity B (Grammar)

People like me

A

Do you ever _____ ?   How often do you _____ ?
What kind of _____ do you usually _____ ?
What kind of _____ are you _____ at the moment?

cook a meal   do exercise   eat out in restaurants   play games with your family   read a book

B

Do you often _____ ?   Why do you _____ ?
How many times do you _____ a day / a week?
Are you _____ too much, these days?

check your phone   feel stressed   say *I love you*   stay up after midnight   work long hours

C

When / What time do you usually _____ ?
Where do you _____ ?   Do you _____ most days?
Are you currently _____ more than usual?

cycle in the countryside   chat on social media   watch videos   do sport   check your emails   take a break

My questions	My answers	People like me
1		
2		
3		
4		
5		
6		
7		
8		
9		

Unit 1 Communicative activity C (Real life)

Take my advice …

• You need to take some medicine once a day. • Try going for a long walk. • Sleep is good for that. • Why don't you …?	• Try eating something. • You need to take a break from work. • You should have a glass of hot water. • Why don't you …?	• Why don't you buy some cough sweets? • Try not to speak today. • You should ask the pharmacist for something. • Have some …	
• Drink hot water with honey and lemon. • You should go to the pharmacy. • Why don't you rest on the sofa? • You should …	• You shouldn't go to work today. • Why don't you see a doctor? • Try doing some exercise. • Take …	• Try doing yoga. • Why don't you go to bed early? • You need some medicine. • … is good for that.	
• You need to take some medicine three times a day. • Try drinking some water. • Have a biscuit. • You need …	• Try having a cold shower. • Honey is very good for that. • You shouldn't stay up late. • You need to …	• You should take a pill twice a day. • Why don't you go swimming? • You need to rest your eyes. • If you still …, then …	
• You should drink some tea with sugar. • Why don't you go to bed for an hour? • Olive oil is good for that. • Try … (-ing).	• Go to bed. • These sweets are good for that. • Why don't you go to the hospital? • Try … (-ing) once a day.	• Try drinking some honey and lemon. • You shouldn't go to work tomorrow. • Don't go outside, you need to stay warm. • … are good for that.	

Unit 2 Communicative activity A (Grammar)
Sporty pairs

Rule cards

must have	must be	must	have to
have to run	don't have to	doesn't have to	can't play
mustn't	can	can't wear	can't
have to try to	must be good at	can try	mustn't pick up

Noun cards

tennis	professional sportspeople	spectators	professional teams
rugby players	triathletes	professional cyclists	goalkeepers
referees	marathon runners	extreme sports	mountain climbers
primary school sports teachers	wrestlers	tennis spectators	football coaches / managers

Unit 2 Communicative activity B (Vocabulary)
Sports crossword

Student A

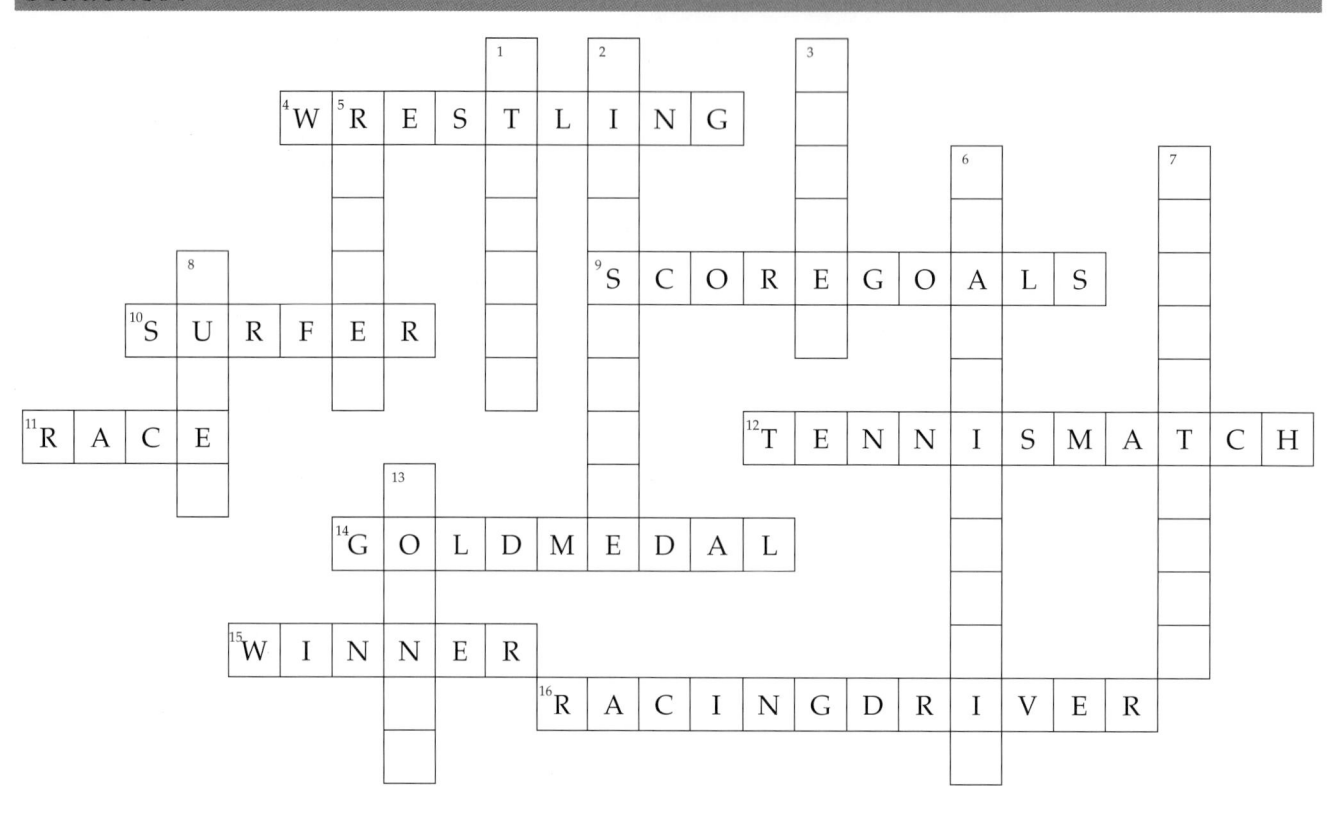

					¹		²			³					
			⁴W	⁵R	E	S	T	L	I	N	G				
												⁶		⁷	
	⁸						⁹S	C	O	R	E	G	O	A	L	S
¹⁰S	U	R	F	E	R										
¹¹R	A	C	E							¹²T	E	N	N	I	S	M	A	T	C	H
				¹³											
			¹⁴G	O	L	D	M	E	D	A	L				
		¹⁵W	I	N	N	E	R								
				¹⁶R	A	C	I	N	G	D	R	I	V	E	R

✂ -

Student B

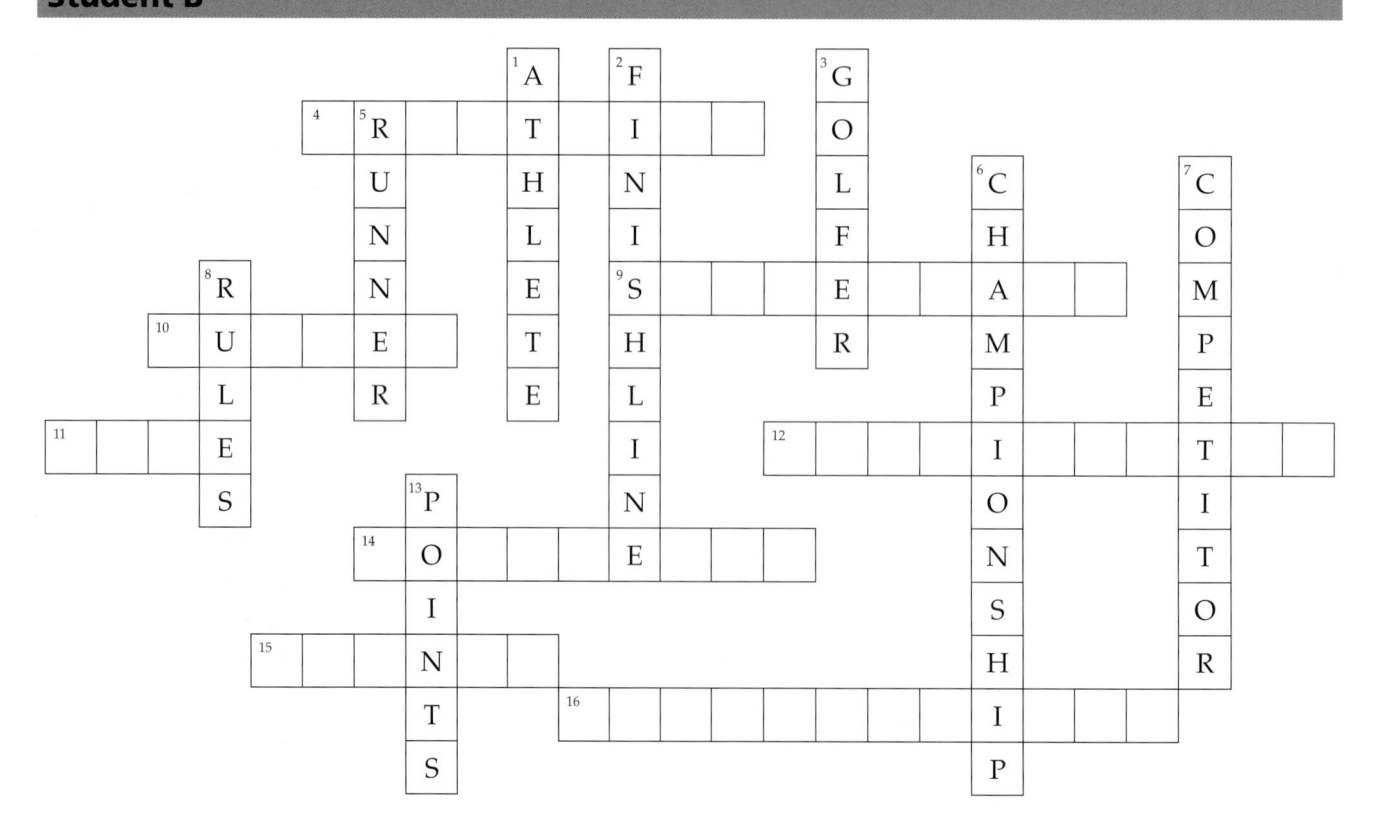

			¹A		²F		³G			
	⁴	⁵R		T		I		O		
		U		H		N		L	⁶C	⁷C
		N		L		I		F	H	O
	⁸R	N		E	⁹S		E		A	M
¹⁰	U		E		T		H		R	P
	L		R		E		L		M	E
¹¹	E						I		P	T
	S		¹³P				N		¹²	I
		¹⁴	O			E			O	T
			I						N	O
		¹⁵		N					S	R
			T		¹⁶				H	
			S						I	
									P	

260 Photocopiable communicative activities

PHOTOCOPIABLE © National Geographic Learning

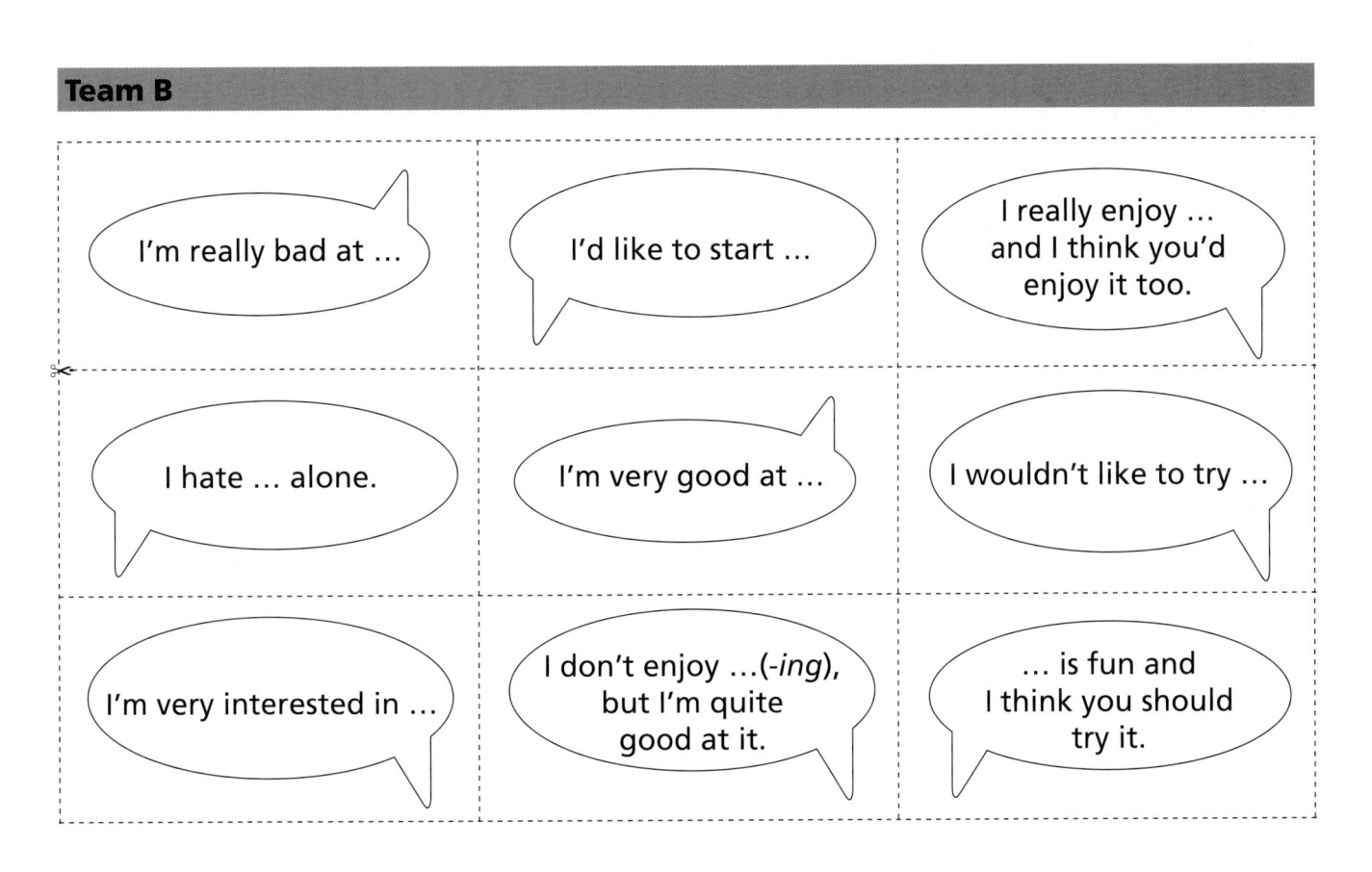

Unit 2 Communicative activity C (Real life)

The truth is …

Team A

- I'm really good at …
- I wouldn't like to …
- I love … and I think you should try it with me.
- I hate …(-ing) in public.
- I'm absolutely terrible at …
- I'd like to try …
- I'm not interested in …
- I love …(-ing), but I'm not very good at it.
- … is fun. I think you'd enjoy it.

Team B

- I'm really bad at …
- I'd like to start …
- I really enjoy … and I think you'd enjoy it too.
- I hate … alone.
- I'm very good at …
- I wouldn't like to try …
- I'm very interested in …
- I don't enjoy …(-ing), but I'm quite good at it.
- … is fun and I think you should try it.

Unit 3 Communicative activity A (Vocabulary)

Getting around town

speed limit	fuel costs	cycle path	motorbike	carbon emissions
airport	go by	rush hour	frequent	punctual
traffic jam	reliable	taxi rank	container ships	traditional
convenient	city centre	get on	pick up	drop you off

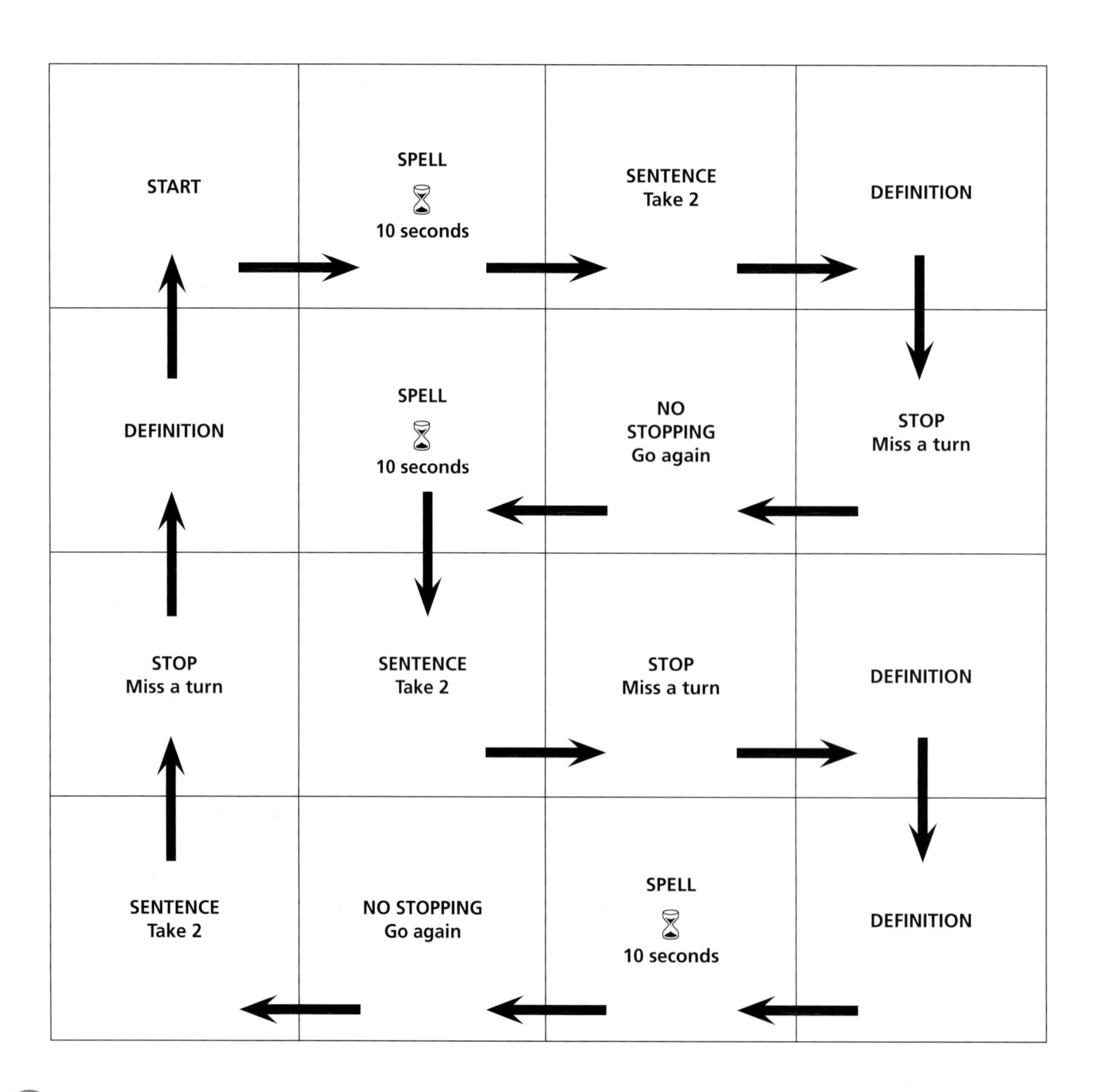

START	SPELL 10 seconds	SENTENCE Take 2	DEFINITION
DEFINITION	SPELL 10 seconds	NO STOPPING Go again	STOP Miss a turn
STOP Miss a turn	SENTENCE Take 2	STOP Miss a turn	DEFINITION
SENTENCE Take 2	NO STOPPING Go again	SPELL 10 seconds	DEFINITION

Unit 3 Communicative activity B (Grammar)
Ten transport teasers

1. The Paris Metro is _____ the New York Subway.   old   fast   busy

2. The capital city of Brazil, Brasilia, is _____ the capital city of India, New Delhi.
   big   hot   far from London

3. A passenger plane is _____ a Formula 1 racing car.   fast   expensive   easy to park

4. The bicycle is _____ the passenger train.   modern   old   practical

5. The distance from London to Paris is _____ the distance from Rome to Milan.
   short   long   same

6. In August, the ferry from England to France is _____ the ferry from Tasmania to Australia.
   slow   crowded   expensive

7. It's _____ to travel around Tenerife, in the Canary Islands, on foot _____ to take the train.   dangerous   good   hard

8. Crossing the Sahara by camel is _____ crossing by motorbike.
   dangerous   traditional   comfortable

9. The height of Mount Everest is _____ the length of New York's Fifth Avenue.
   a bit   much   as   great   small

10. In London, going from Leicester Square to Covent Garden on the underground is _____ going on foot.   a lot   a little   as   quick   direct   good for your health

Unit 3 Communicative activity C (Real life)
Travelling light

Unit 4 Communicative activity A (Vocabulary)
Team expedition

Fancy an adventure? We are looking for people to join our team on our Atlantic to Pacific Expedition. We'll start in Rio de Janeiro, Brazil, and cross South America to Antofagasta in Chile. 3,700 km of city, desert, mountain, village and fields on foot and by local transport. Interested? Contact team leader Dr Georgia Jones on info@soamcross.com by 1st August.

South America
Antofagasta • • Rio de Janeiro

Fold ....

Roles

Kitchen and kindness specialist	Communication specialist
Responsibilities: preparing and cooking meals for nine people, buying and looking after food while we travel. This person also has to help with personal or emotional problems, must be able to give advice and help solve conflict in the team.	Responsibilities: Looking after radios and phones, speaking to local people to organize transport and speak to emergency services if we have a problem. This person must speak languages, be calm and be good with people.
Maps and motivation specialist	Equipment specialist
Responsibilities: Looking after maps, finding transport options, checking weather, and helping the team leader with travel decisions. This person is also responsible for motivation when others are tired or in difficulty.	Responsibilities: Looking after equipment (technical, cooking etc.), finding solutions to technical problems and repairing things. They must prepare equipment for transport and check that everything is working.

Dr Jones' interview notes

Angie (age: 27) Dentist	Ben (age: 41) Carpenter/builder	Charlie (age: 37) Photographer
• seems friendly, very hard-working and organized • usually works alone, probably good in stressful conditions, kind and patient • speaks three languages • doesn't like cooking, seems quiet	• good at repairing things and helping people • friendly, organized and seems very positive. • loves cooking and fishing • speaks two languages • good at solving problems but not good at identifying problems	• good at making decisions, loves her job • experienced in South American travel (knows about animals, plants, weather, etc.) • plays the guitar, speaks Spanish • prefers to work alone, doesn't seem patient with others
Dev (age: 32) ICT systems expert	Emma (age: 42) Chef	Felix (age: 30) Personal trainer
• hard-working, seems very patient and friendly • experienced at using relevant map and communication apps • wants to meet new people, loves music and languages • not good at sports • doesn't seem very organized	• very positive, currently works long hours and is very experienced in her job • doesn't seem very patient with people • likes hiking, astronomy (knows a lot about the stars), nature and food	• organized, hard-working, good at motivating people. Seems practical. • experienced in working with exercise and food Also travel. • speaks three languages • not sure if very kind or patient

Unit 4 Communicative activity B (Grammar)
I remember it well

A

NEWS

Coast to coast

Author Harry Townsend finished his run from the north of Scotland to the south coast of England this evening, after ten days on the road. A group of runners and cyclists were with him when he ran across the finish line in Poole, behind Tim Hall, the tallest man and famous local runner. 'Thanks to Tim and his yellow T-shirt, it was easy to see where I was going! I'm very tired, but happy,' said Harry before he received a gold medal from politician Hugh Green. Around one hundred local people watched the event from local shops and parks.

B

New Message

To   mum <janeturner@mail.com>   Cc Bcc

Subject   Guess what?!

Mum! Harry Townsend was here and I saw him! I spoke to him! I was coming out of the supermarket and a very tall man in a yellow T-shirt was running past. There were other runners and cyclists behind him, and the second runner was Harry! There were a lot of people in the street – maybe a hundred! – and they were singing 'Come on, Harry, come on.' It was great! Harry was very tired, but he was happy and then a man with black hair gave him a medal. I've got a photo.

Send Now   Send Later   Send Later   Add Note

C

21st May
Fantastic day today. The sun was shining and I was sitting in the park when I heard a lot of people. A very tall man in a yellow T-shirt was running past the park and a group of cyclists and runners were following him, so I went to see what was happening. Harry Townsend was running behind the tall man! He was finishing his run from Scotland and Hugh Green was there too. He was waiting to give Harry a gold medal. Harry looked tired, but he was happy and I took a photo of him.

D

On Saturday, everybody in our town went to Fore Street near the supermarket to see Harry Townsend. He was here because he ran from Scotland and he was finishing his run here. He was very tall and he was wearing a red T-shirt and a very tall man in a yellow T-shirt was running behind him. Harry Townsend was very happy because it was sunny and a hundred people were there and they were singing for him. He said hello to me. He's my favourite writer.

E

Dad! I saw Harry Townsend in town!

> Really? Where was he?

In town. I was standing near the park and the supermarket and he ran past.

> Why was he running?

I don't know. Jack says he ran from Scotland but I don't know why.

> Is he there now?

No. Hugh Green was here too and gave him a medal. And Tim Hall, that very tall runner with the famous yellow T-shirt, ran with him at the end – Tim crossed the line first, then Harry – so they all took a photo and then they went way.

> Did you speak to him?

Yes I did. I was singing 'Come on, Harry' and he said hello.

Unit 4 Communicative activity C (Real life)
What's the story?

Who was she?   Where were they?   Where were they going?   What was she doing?
Why was she there?   Who was with her?   What was she looking at?
What was she thinking?   When did this happen?
How were they feeling?   What could they see?

Your questions
what   where   why   when   who   how   how many   how often

At the beginning …   Then …   Next …   While …   Luckily …   But …   Unfortunately …

Unit 5 Communicative activity A (Grammar)
Fun factoids

Student B

1 There are _____ solar power installations in Scotland.
2 You can recycle aluminium _____ times.
3 In the Arctic, you can see _____ types of penguin.

many some much a lot of a few n't any a little all

Student A

1 _____ fish have lights on their heads.
2 There is _____ litter on Mount Everest.
3 There are _____ running shoes made of recycled plastic from the sea.

many some much a lot of a few n't any a little all

Fold

1 some / a few (Some farms and houses have solar panels, but the weather and the angle of the sun in winter means a big plant isn't practical.)
2 a lot of / many (You can recycle aluminium cans hundreds of times, so they are much better for the environment than plastic bottles.)
3 can't see any (Penguins live in the Antarctic, not the Arctic.)

Fold

1 A few (Some fish live so far down that it's impossible to see, so they have lights made of bioluminescence. The lights help them see and attract other fish when they're hunting.)
2 a lot of (Over 600 people climb Everest every year and they leave litter and waste because taking it down again is too dangerous. In March 2017, climbers and Sherpas began working together to collect the waste and carry it down by helicopter.)
3 a few / some (In 2017, Adidas began to sell running shoes made from recycled sea plastic.)

Student D

1 Recycling ONE drinks can saves enough energy to watch TV for _____ hours.
2 The world's tallest tree is _____ metres taller than Big Ben in London.
3 You save _____ water if you wash your dishes in a dishwasher.

many some much a lot of a few n't any a little all

Student C

1 The oldest trees in the world are _____ centuries old.
2 There is _____ black snow from pollution in the Antarctic.
3 _____ animals can live forever.

many some much a lot of a few n't any a little all

Fold

1 a few (three hours)
2 a few (The world's tallest tree is 110 metres tall. Big Ben is 96 metres tall.)
3 a lot of (approximately 27 litres every time – that's about 9,100 litres per year. Good news if you hate washing dishes.)

Fold

1 many (They're 460 centuries old and are in the USA.)
2 a little / some (Global air pollution, mostly from burning trees, means that you can find very small areas of black snow in the Antarctic.)
3 Not many / A few (Some reptiles and amphibians can regenerate their organs, so they can live forever. Unfortunately, normally they don't, because other animals and people kill them.)

Unit 5 Communicative activity B (Vocabulary)
Tell me about it

- city life and looking after the environment
- the world's oceans and seas
- e-rubbish
- art from recycled materials
- the environment and me: what I want to do better
- **Tell me about …**
- the environment: changing attitudes and behaviour
- the world's animals
- recycling at home
- man looking after nature
- the climate
- plastic
- supermarkets and the environment

cardboard take time electronics	recycle (the) desert jar	paper take a break bottle	(juice) carton foil per cent
rubbish over a hundred metal	bag about half glass	exactly a month ago plastic cereal box	magazine over four ….. years aluminium
about a year throw away (the) ice	environmentally-friendly (a) can take a walk	nearly a quarter recycling bins take care	leather nearly a month take (a) plane(s)

Unit 5 Communicative activity C (Real life)

How can I help you?

Product cards

A	B	C	D
Men's solar watch	Solar mobile phone battery	Women's green cotton dress	Sustainable leather sandals
£50	£100	£85	£90
Order no: XG31388F	Order no: JV99054Z	Order no: PB07135K	Order no: HA99376Y
Ordered last month – not arrived	Ordered last week – not arrived	Arrived today but the wrong colour	Arrived today but only one sandal, not a pair

Role cards

Customer services assistant:
You're very friendly and positive.

Customer:
You can't hear very well and the line is bad.

Customer services assistant:
You aren't very friendly or patient.

Customer:
You're a member of the royal family, and you speak very slowly.

Customer services assistant:
You're very friendly.

Customer:
You confuse numbers. Repeat them differently at least twice.

Customer services assistant:
You can't spell any names. Ask the customer to repeat.

Customer:
You aren't very patient and you speak fast.

Dialogue flow chart

Customer services assistant
- Good *morning / afternoon*, can I help you? ......
- Ask for the customer's order number. ......
- Check the number. ......
- Check the customer's name and address. ......
- Explain the product isn't in stock. ......
- Say when. (*over three weeks / about a month, etc.*) ......
- Offer customer a *smaller / more expensive / better, etc.* product ......
- Offer customer *a refund / discount / theatre tickets, etc.* ......
- Is there anything else I can help you with? ......

Customer
- ...... Say hello. Explain the situation.
- ...... Give the order number and price.
- ...... Confirm or correct the information.
- ...... Confirm or correct the information.
- ...... Ask when the product will be back in stock.
- ...... Say this is too late and explain why. (*birthday present / need tomorrow / going on holiday, etc.*)
- ...... Say no.
- ...... Accept.
- ...... Say no. Say thank you and goodbye.

Unit 6 Communicative activity A (Grammar)
Plan B

When I have some money one day, I intend to …

For our next holiday, we're planning to …

When I get older and I have more free time, I'd really like to ….

As soon as I get home today, I'm going to …

This weekend, I hope I'm … with friends.

My … and I are going to …

Unit 6 Communicative activity B (Vocabulary)

Get a pair, say a trio

get a pension	get married (to someone)	get your driving licence	get to (Africa) / get home	get engaged
get (something) ready	get up	get together	get (presents)	get older
get (a plane)	get back	get (a mask, a campervan, etc.)	get a job	get more legal rights / financial control
be paid / receive a pension	marry (someone)	pass your driving test	reach, arrive in / at (Africa, home, etc.)	become engaged
prepare (something)	start the day, leave your bed	meet and socialize	receive (presents)	become older
catch (a plane)	return	buy (a mask, a campervan, etc.)	find (a job)	acquire, receive (more legal rights / financial control)

Unit 6 Communicative activity C (Real life)
Magic word invitations

Magic words

cake something special tomorrow	fireworks bride tonight	bottle get together always	food groom sunny
music get a present rain(s)	costumes get engaged late	masks get married taxi	candles buy no jeans
a float / floats anything else a lot of	crazy food and drink next weekend	(mid) twenties birthday convenient	afford good time traditional
fun instruments hope	present relax intend	retire special occasion plan / planning	parade celebration friends

Invitations

Fold ....

The event: _____
Where: _____
Date: _____
Time: _____
Please bring: _____

The event: _____
Where: _____
Date: _____
Time: _____
Please bring: _____

Fold ....

The event: _____
Where: _____
Date: _____
Time: _____
Please bring: _____

The event: _____
Where: _____
Date: _____
Time: _____
Please bring: _____

PHOTOCOPIABLE © National Geographic Learning

Unit 7 Communicative activity A (Vocabulary)

What do you do?

ACCOUNTANT Clue 1: .... Clue 2:	**NURSE** Clue 1: .... Clue 2: ....
CHEF Clue 1: .... Clue 2:	**FARMER** Clue 1: .... Clue 2: ....
COMPUTER PROGRAMMER Clue 1: .... Clue 2:	**ECONOMIST** Clue 1: .... Clue 2: ....
SHOP ASSISTANT Clue 1: .... Clue 2:	**SCIENTIST** Clue 1: .... Clue 2: ....
ENGINEER Clue 1: .... Clue 2:	**POLITICIAN** Clue 1: .... Clue 2: ....
ELECTRICIAN Clue 1: .... Clue 2:	**DRIVER** Clue 1: .... Clue 2: ....
WAITER Clue 1: .... Clue 2:	**DIRECTOR** Clue 1: .... Clue 2: ....
JOURNALIST Clue 1: .... Clue 2:	**TEACHER** Clue 1: .... Clue 2: ....

Photocopiable communicative activities

PHOTOCOPIABLE © National Geographic Learning

Unit 7 Communicative activity B (Grammar)
In the park

| at | in | on | past | through | along | between | opposite | next to | out of | into | up | down |

Unit 7 Communicative activity C (Real life)
A job interview

Job advert

We're looking for a computer programmer!

We are a _____ company.

Our office is in _____ and you will work in our _____ department.

We'd like you to design computer programs to help us _____

_____ .

We need someone who is _____ .

The hours are _____ .

You will receive a monthly salary of _____ .

✂--

CV

Name: _____

Education and Qualifications:

Graduated from the University of _____ with a master's degree in computer programming.

High school leaving certificates in Mathematics, English, _____ and _____ .

Work experience:

Previous jobs: _____

Achievements: _____

_____

Personality and Skills:

I am a _____ person, with good _____ skills.

I can _____

Unit 8 Communicative activity A (Vocabulary)
Internet survey

Student A

1 How often do you _____ to the internet in a café?
2 Have you ever _____ to an email newsletter that you didn't really want?
3 Have you ever forgotten your password to _____ to an important account?
4 Do you ever _____ online games with fighting and shooting?
5 Do you _____ a blog?

Student B

1 How often do you _____ to the internet on public transport?
2 Do you _____ with Google, or do you use a different search engine?
3 Do you ever _____ music from the internet?
4 How often do you _____ pictures or videos to social networking sites?
5 How often do you _____ your personal email?

Student C

1 Do you _____ to any podcasts or blogs?
2 Do you know how to _____ for pictures or videos on Google?
3 Do you know anyone who _____ their own music onto the internet?
4 Do you think you would enjoy _____ a blog?
5 When was the last time you _____ a new email account?

Student D

1 How often do you _____ to your online bank account?
2 Do you ever _____ movies from the internet?
3 How often do you _____ your email late at night?
4 Do you know anyone who has _____ their own website?
5 Do you ever _____ online word games?

Unit 8 Communicative activity B (Grammar)
Find your partner

1 People are usually very healthy.	A where I can buy a new phone charger
2 Do you know a shop?	B which I bought yesterday
3 I don't like films.	C which can drive by itself
4 I grew up in a little village.	D which are too scary
5 Children are really annoying.	E where nothing happens
6 The new shoes are too tight.	F who play a lot of sport
7 They've made a kind of car.	G which I'd like to have in the future
8 My sister knows a girl.	H who talk all the time
9 I'd like to live in a country.	I which will give you plenty of information
10 The job is an architect.	J who caught the thief
11 I'll show you a website.	K who swam in the Olympic Games
12 The policeman is going to talk to us.	L where it's always hot

Unit 8 Communicative activity C (Real life)

How does it work?

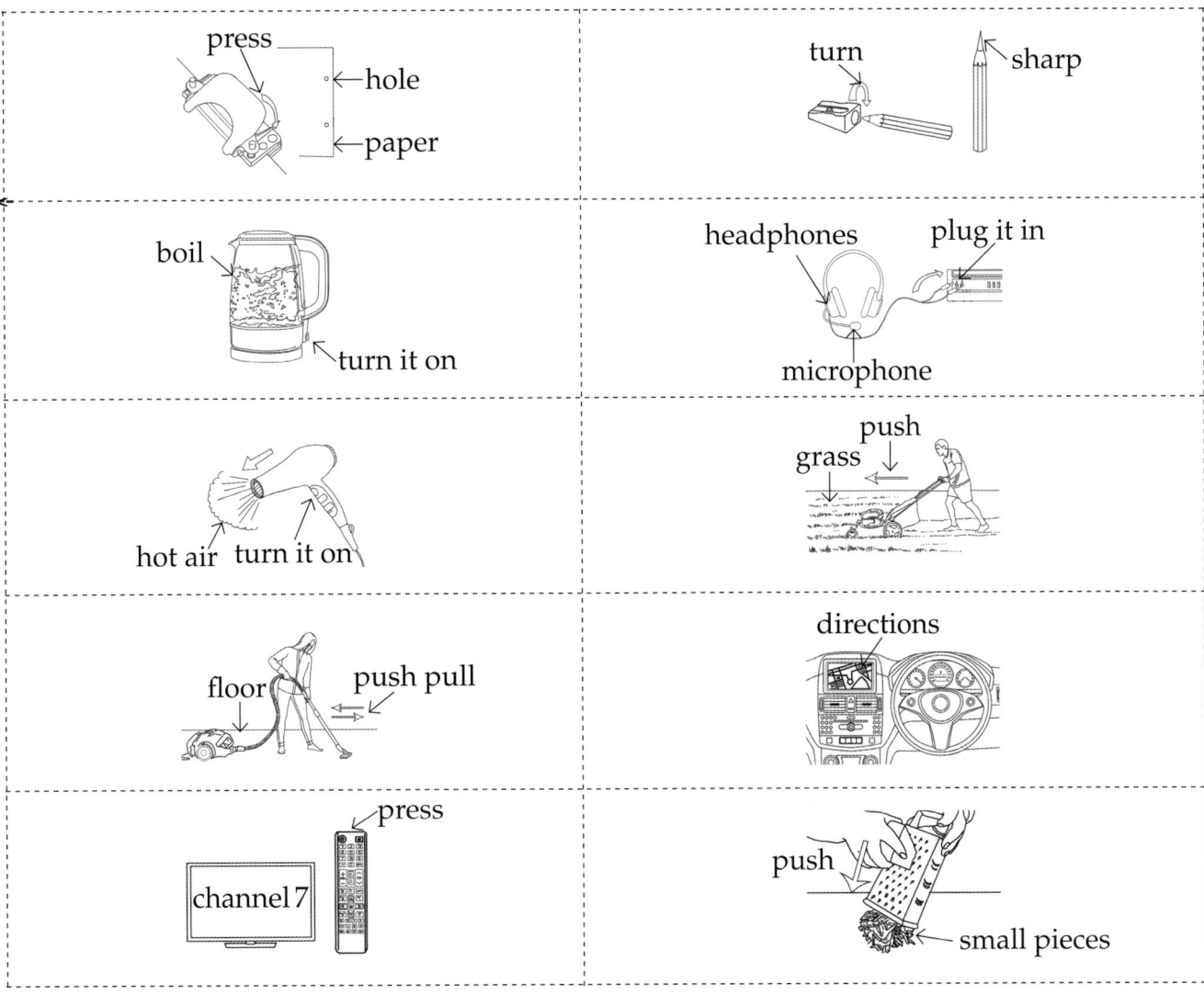

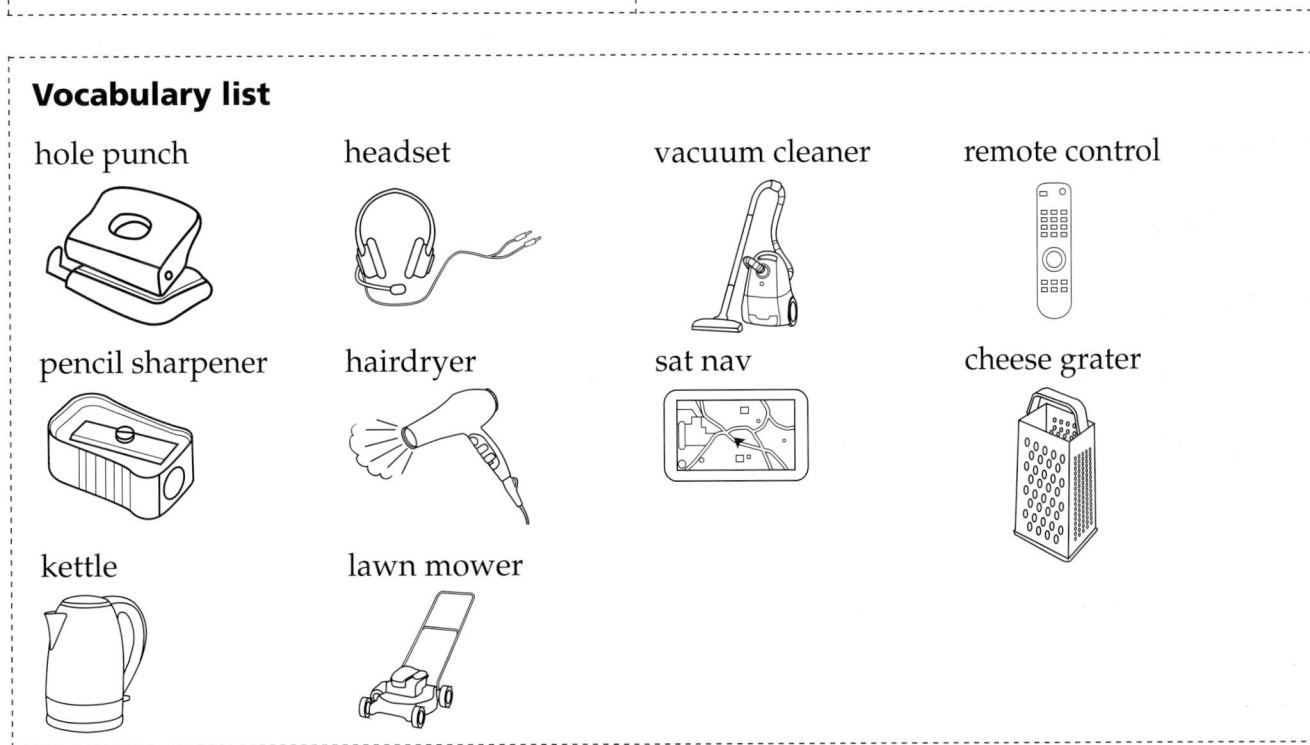

press ← hole ← paper

turn — sharp

boil — turn it on

headphones — plug it in — microphone

hot air — turn it on

push — grass

floor — push pull

directions

press — channel 7

push — small pieces

Vocabulary list

hole punch

headset

vacuum cleaner

remote control

pencil sharpener

hairdryer

sat nav

cheese grater

kettle

lawn mower

Unit 9 Communicative activity A (Grammar)
Before I arrived ...

Student A

1 Before I woke up this morning, _____.

2 Before I started learning English, _____.

3 Before I met _____, _____.

4 Before 2016, _____ (never) _____.

5 When I got home last night, I _____ (already) _____.

6 Before I was _____ years old, I _____ (learn) how to _____.

7 When I left _____, I realized that _____.

8 _____

9 _____

10 _____

Student B

1 Before I was born, my parents _____.

2 Before I started secondary school, _____.

3 When I arrived at school today, I _____ (already) _____.

4 Before I went on holiday to ...., _____.

5 Before I bought _____, _____.

6 Before I was _____ years old, I _____ (never) _____.

7 When I saw _____, I realized _____.

8 _____

9 _____

10 _____

Unit 9 Communicative activity B (Vocabulary)

That's amazing!

START

1. Talk about something exciting that's going to happen soon.
2. How many syllables are there in …?
3. Talk about a film that you thought was amazing.

amazed   *frightening*   *bored*

4. Nothing happened all day. It was very _____.

8. How many syllables are there in …?
7. What time of day do you feel tired? Why?
6. It's very _____ when someone in your family is ill.
5. What school subjects are you most interested in?

9. Do you know anyone who's really annoying?

interested   *tiring*   *worried*

10. I'm going to New York next week. I'm so _____!
11. What do you do when you feel bored?
12. My little brother is still _____ of the dark.
13. Do you often feel worried about money?

fascinated   *annoyed*   *amazing*

14. How many syllables are there in …?

18. You won first prize? That's _____!
17. Talk about a time when you felt frightened.
16. I was _____ when I missed the bus today.
15. Which sport is the most tiring? Why?

19. Talk about a fascinating place that you'd like to visit.

worrying   *tired*   *frightened*

20. How many syllables are there in …?
21. Do you feel more excited about seeing a new film, or a big sports match? Why?
22. Johanna's very _____ in politics.
23. Do you like watching frightening films? Why / Why not?

24. I was _____ when I heard that there is an insect that eats plastic.

annoying   *exciting*   *interesting*

FINISH

27. Do you think science is boring? Why / Why not?
26. How many syllables are there in …?
25. Talk about something that made you feel annoyed recently.

excited   *fascinating*   *boring*

Unit 9 Communicative activity C (Real Life)
Would you like to visit?

Description:

Name of attraction:

Picture:

Fold..

Opening times:

Getting there:

Tickets: where to buy them

Extra options:

Tickets: prices

Unit 10 Communicative activity A (Vocabulary)
Formation dominoes

-ment	describe	-tion	achieve
-ment	inform	-tion	invent
-tion	apply	-tion	produce
-ive	decide	-ion	science
-ist	compete	-ive	produce
-er	advert	-er	prepare
-tion	act	-or	invent
-ive	environment	-al	custom
-er	medicine	-al	invite
-tion	tradition	-al	advert

Unit 10 Communicative activity B (Grammar)
How much do you know?

Student A

1 The *Toy Story* films _____ (make) by Pixar for Disney.

2 The telephone _____ (invent) by Thomas Edison.
   (FALSE – by Alexander Graham Bell.)

3 Polar bears _____ (find) in the Antarctic (around the South Pole).
   (FALSE – in the Arctic)

4 Portuguese _____ (speak) by more people than Russian.

5 The country of Iceland _____ (cover) with ice.
   (FALSE – it has some ice but also a lot of rock and some fields)

6 Shakespeare's play *Romeo and Juliet* _____ (write) in the 19th century.
   (FALSE – in the 16th century)

7 The song *Hello* _____ (sing) by Adele.

8 More than 15 million people _____ (kill) in the First World War.

9 _____

10 _____

✂ -

Student B

1 Italian _____ (speak) in some parts of Switzerland.

2 The book *War and Peace* _____ (write) by Lenin.
   (FALSE – by Leo Tolstoy)

3 In the *Lord of the Rings* films, Gandalf _____ (play) by Ian McKellen.

4 Tigers _____ (find) in parts of Africa.
   (FALSE – only in Asia)

5 The magnetic compass _____ (invent) in China.

6 In the Second World War, more Russian soldiers _____ (kill) than German soldiers.

7 Most of India _____ (cover) with rainforest.
   (FALSE – only about 1%)

8 The guitarist Jimi Hendrix _____ (give) his first guitar by his father.
   (FALSE – he bought it himself)

9 _____

10 _____

Unit 10 Communicative activity C (Real life)

What are we going to do?

Situations	
1 You bought a lottery ticket as a group, and you've just won £15,000.	4 You work for a youth hostel. Your boss has just told you that next week a group of 60 schoolchildren (aged 8-9) will be staying at the hostel.
2 You're planning a party for next weekend. You're going to hire a band, and order some food from a local restaurant. What style of music and what kind of food are you going to choose?	5 You're about to go to the cinema. The films you can see today are a horror film, a documentary, or a cartoon.
3 One of your friends has invited you all to go hiking and camping in the mountains.	6 your idea

What do you think?	What's your opinion?	What about you?
I think …	In my opinion …	My personal opinion is that …
I agree.	You're right.	Good idea.
I see what you mean, but …	I don't agree.	I'm not sure about that.
Maybe we could …	I suggest we …	Why don't we …?

Unit 11 Communicative activity A (Grammar)

He said, she said …

A B Card 1

When I asked to borrow my dad's car, he said …

C D Card 1

When my dog ate my socks, the vet said …

A B Card 2

When the company was doing very well, the boss said …

C D Card 2

When the company lost a lot of money, the boss said …

A B Card 3

When only one student came to class, the teacher said …

C D Card 3

When the newspapers said that the Olympic athlete had cheated, she said …

A B Card 4

When the actor won an Oscar, he said …

C D Card 4

When we got lost in a foreign city, my friend said …

A B Card 5

When I asked my friends to come on a skiing holiday with me, they said …

C D Card 5

When the house fell down, the builder said …

A B Card 6

When I failed my driving test, my instructor said …

C D Card 6

When James asked Joanna to go out with him, she said …

A B Card 7

On my first day at school, my mum said …

C D Card 7

On my last day at school, my teachers said …

A B Card 8

On my first day in my new job, my new colleagues said …

C D Card 8

At the end of the war, the government said …

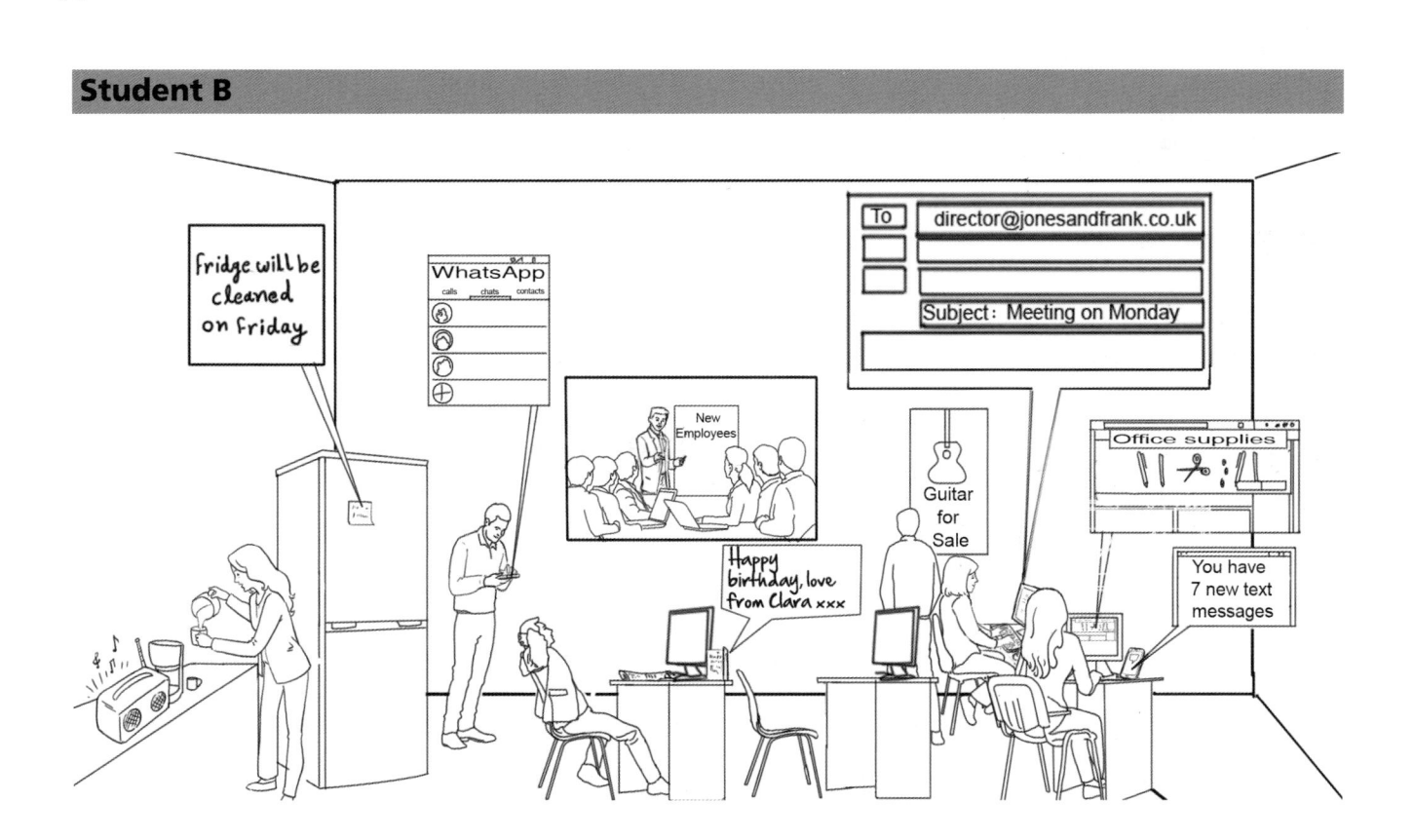

Unit 11 Communicative activity B (Vocabulary)
Office communication

Student A

Student B

Unit 11 Communicative activity C (Real life)
Ancient careers

A When he finally returned to China, he told the Emperor about the places he had seen. He said they did not have strong armies, but they made a lot of unusual products, and it would be good for China to do business with them.	**H** Other gladiators died because they were stabbed in the back. They had already lost the fight and they were lying on their stomachs on the ground.
B Because of their strong bones, some gladiators experienced several bad injuries and recovered again before they died. But head injuries were common, and many gladiators finally died this way.	**I** Zhang Qian was a Chinese explorer and diplomat in the 2nd century BC.
C Gladiators were a kind of sportspeople in ancient Rome. They fought each other while crowds watched them as entertainment.	**J** Over the next 200 years, the Silk Road gradually developed, and contact between China and Europe began.
D The Emperor Wu of Han sent Zhang Qian west, to find out if there were countries in Central Asia and Western Asia that could become trade partners with China.	**K** It seems that most gladiators were vegetarian. They ate a lot of food like bread and beans, and they were probably very fat.
E Zhang married a Xiongnu woman and they had a son. The Xiongnu people trusted him, and he left their country to continue his journey west.	**L** Zhang went to many different parts of Central Asia and he also saw the final years of the Greek empire of Alexander the Great in places like Bactria.
F Being fat meant that when they were injured, they lost a lot of blood, which made a good show for the audience, but it didn't hurt very much, and they could continue fighting.	**M** The gladiators also had drinks made from burnt wood. These drinks contained calcium, which made their bones strong.
G Before he had gone very far, Zhang Qian was caught by the Xiongnu tribes who controlled Western China.	**N** Recently, archaeologists have discovered a place where 60 gladiators were buried. It has helped them to understand more about how gladiators lived and died, including what they ate.

Unit 12 Communicative activity A (Vocabulary)

Weather forecasts

Key

cloudy (adj)

rainy (adj), wet (adj), rain (v, n)

sunny (adj), sunshine (n)

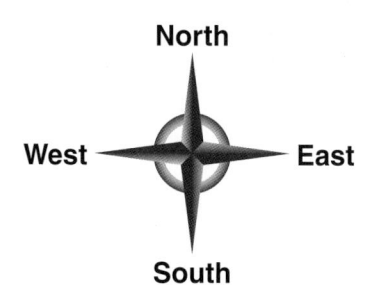

snow (v, n)

hail (v, n)

thunderstorm (n)

North, West, East, South

Student A

Argentina

Extreme weather warning: there may be tornadoes in the north of the country.

Student B

Germany

Extreme weather warning: heavy rain may cause floods in the mountains in the south of the country.

Student C

Japan

Extreme weather warning: snowstorms may continue for several days in the north and west of the country.

Student D

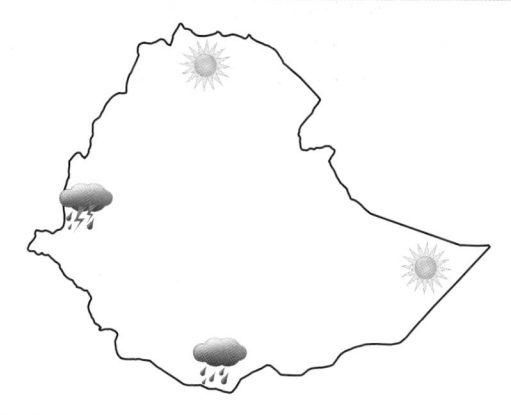

Ethiopia

Extreme weather warning: very hot weather in the north of the country: temperatures may reach 35°C.

Unit 12 Communicative activity B (Grammar)
The crossword of everything

Student A

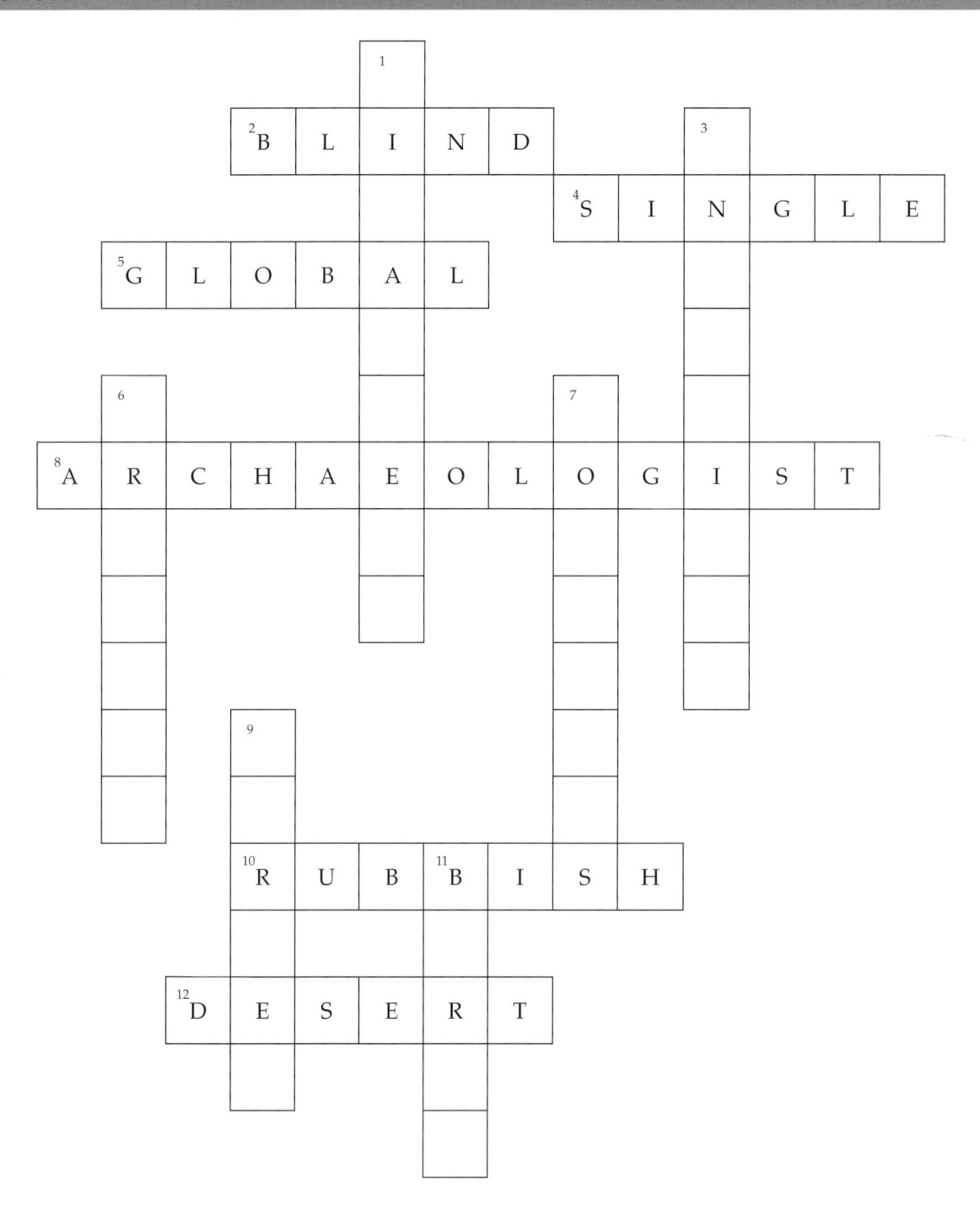

				1						
	²B	L	I	N	D		³			
						⁴S	I	N	G	L	E
	⁵G	L	O	B	A	L				
	6					7				
⁸A	R	C	H	A	E	O	L	O	G	I	S	T
				9						
			¹⁰R	U	B	¹¹B	I	S	H	
			¹²D	E	S	E	R	T		

Clues across

2 This is when a person can't see *anything / everybody / nowhere*.
4 This is when someone isn't married to *anywhere / nobody / anybody*.
5 This is when something is found *everyone / everywhere / everything* in the world.
8 This is *somebody / everything / nowhere* that studies the buildings and objects of people from the past.
10 This is *everywhere / nothing / everything* that people throw away.
12 This is *nowhere / somewhere / nobody* dry, with very little rain. There is usually sand or rocks there.

Photocopiable communicative activities **PHOTOCOPIABLE** © National Geographic Learning

Student B

[Crossword grid]

Clues down

1 This is when something goes away and you can't find it *nothing / anywhere / anyone*.
3 This is when *nowhere / no one / anywhere* can see you.
6 This is something that *everyone / nothing / somewhere* does all the time. It's when you take air into your body.
7 This is when a person has *everybody / anybody / nowhere* to live.
9 This is part of a computer or phone where you can see *anybody / everywhere / something*.
11 This is how you feel when *anybody / nothing / everywhere* is happening.

Unit 12 Communicative activity C (Real life)
What should I do?

Suggestions

a Go into a shop and ask for help.

b Buy a phone charger.

c Invite all your friends for a meal at your house.

d Don't do anything. It's not your problem.

e Get a job that pays more money.

f Stop spending all your money on going out.

g Start doing a relaxing hobby, like yoga.

h Get a taxi to your hotel.

i Don't try to do everything. Only do the most important things.

j Ask your teacher or your boss for help.

k Borrow some money from the bank.

l Try to understand what the argument was about.

Problem cards

1 Two of your friends have had an argument.	3 You're lost in a foreign city and your phone has run out of battery.
2 You're feeling really stressed because you have so much work to do for school/university/your job.	4 You want to buy a car, but you can't afford one.

Photocopiable communicative activities: teacher's notes

Unit 1A All about you

AIM: to practise using vocabulary connected to sports and activities

LANGUAGE: collocations with *do*, *play* and *go*

INTERACTION: groupwork

MATERIALS: one copy of the worksheet for each group of three or four students, with the prompts cut into cards. Groups will need two coins and a stopwatch (e.g. on a smartphone).

CLASS TIME: 30 minutes

PROCEDURE:

- See how many collocations with *do*, *play* and *go* from Unit 1 the class can remember (e.g. *do gardening, play tennis, go for long walks*).
- Organize the class into groups of three or four students and give each group one worksheet and a set of cue cards. Make sure that each group has two coins and a smartphone with a stopwatch.
- Explain that when they toss the coins, two heads means 'do', a head and a tail means 'go' and two tails means 'play'. Students shuffle the prompt cards and place them face down in a pile.
- Students take it in turns to toss the coins and take a prompt card, e.g. throw a head and a tail (*go*) and pick up the card with: *How often do you …?* The aim is to complete the question with a collocation using their verb and a word or phrase from the wordcloud, e.g. *How often do you go jogging?* They score one point if they make a collocation that hasn't been used before.
- The other students in the group should answer the player's question and must talk for at least ten seconds, for which they each score one point. After fifteen minutes, you might like to ask students to change groups and play again. At the end, find out who has the highest scores.

Unit 1B People like me

AIM: to find classmates with similar lifestyles and habits

LANGUAGE: present simple and present continuous

INTERACTION: whole class

MATERIALS: one copy of the worksheet for each student

CLASS TIME: 30 minutes

PROCEDURE:

- Explain that students are going to find out about each other's lifestyles and habits.
- Give each student one worksheet. Ask them to choose three question prompts in each section A–C. Give them ten to twelve minutes to complete their nine questions using some of the ideas in each wordpool, and write the questions in the table. Monitor as students work, making sure they are forming the questions correctly.
- Ask students to complete the column with their answers to the questions. Students can then fold or cut their worksheets as they now only need the table with the questions in it.
- Tell students to stand up and mingle to ask each other their nine questions. (With large classes, divide students into groups of twelve). Encourage them to expand on their answers and to ask each other questions to develop the conversation, where possible, e.g. *What kind of book are you reading at the moment? (A history book.) Are you enjoying it? / Is it a good book? / What is it called?*
- Teach/Remind students of the phrase *Me too*, as they might need it. Students write the name of any student with a similar lifestyle and habits in the third column of the table.
- In the feedback stage, invite individual students to report back to the whole class on their findings, e.g. *Edvard and I eat out in restaurants every weekend.*

Unit 1C Take my advice

AIM: to practise giving advice

LANGUAGE: talking about illness and giving advice

INTERACTION: groupwork

MATERIALS: one copy of the worksheet for each group of four to six students, cut into one set of picture cards and one set of solution cards

CLASS TIME: 30 minutes

PROCEDURE:

- Organize the class into groups of four to six students. Give each group a set of picture cards and a set of advice cards, placed face down in two piles on the table.
- Students take turns to be 'The Patient'. They take a picture card and mime their medical problem for the rest of the group to guess what is wrong.
- The other students in the group are 'Sympathetic Friends'. They each pick up a solution card and choose a piece of advice for 'The Patient' from the suggestions, or think of their own advice using the prompt in the last bullet point. The Patient listens to each piece of advice and chooses the best one.
- The cards are then returned to the bottom of each pile and play continues with a different student becoming 'The Patient'. Continue until each student has been the patient twice.

Unit 2A Sporty pairs

AIM: to practise expressing rules
LANGUAGE: verbs for rules
INTERACTION: groupwork
MATERIALS: one copy of the worksheet for each group of two to four students, cut into one set of rule cards and one set of noun cards
CLASS TIME: 30 minutes
PROCEDURE:

- Review verbs for rules by writing *Footballers …* on the board and eliciting ideas for how to complete the sentence, e.g. *mustn't argue with the referee, have to try to score goals, should train hard for matches, can't pick up the ball.*

- Organize the class into small groups of two to four students and give each group a set of noun cards and rules cards. Tell students to shuffle the two sets of cards separately and place them face down on the table in two piles.

- Explain that students are going to take turns to pick up the top card from each pile and try to make a grammatically correct sentence with the words on both, adding their own ideas. If they can do this, they keep the cards. If they can't make a sentence, they return the cards to the bottom of the two piles.

- When all the cards have been won, players count their cards to see who has the most.

Unit 2B Sports crossword

AIM: to practise using vocabulary connected to sports by working together to complete a crossword
LANGUAGE: suffixes and vocabulary related to sport
INTERACTION: pairwork
MATERIALS: one copy of the worksheet for each pair of students, cut in half
CLASS TIME: 30 minutes
PROCEDURE:

- Divide the class into two halves: Student As and Student Bs. Give out worksheet A to Students A and worksheet B to Students B. Explain that Students A and B have the same crossword but with different words missing. They are going to prepare to describe or define words to each other to complete their crosswords. Tell them that all the words are from Unit 2 and are related to the theme of sports.

- Give students a few minutes to check they know the meaning of the words that are already completed in their crossword, and to think about how they will define them. Working in their AA and BB pairs, give students ten to fifteen minutes to prepare their definitions.

- Organize students into AB pairs and ask them to sit facing each other, if possible. Make sure students can't see their partner's crossword.

- Check that they know how to say *across* and *down*, as well as the meaning, and that they can ask *What's 1 down, please?* etc. Students take turns to ask each other for clues to their missing words and to define or describe the word for their partner, who then writes the word in his/her crossword. Students can help each other with clues if necessary, e.g. by giving the first or last letter of the word.

- When students have finished, they compare their crosswords to make sure they have the same words and have spelt them correctly.

Unit 2C The truth is …

AIM: to practise talking about interests
LANGUAGE: expressions used for talking about interests and abilities, plans, and recommending and encouraging
INTERACTION: groups divided into two teams
MATERIALS: one copy of the worksheet for each group of six to eight students, cut into two sets of cards
CLASS TIME: 30 minutes
PROCEDURE:

- Beginning by writing *[your name] is good at surfing, but isn't very good at swimming* on the board (change the activities, if you wish). Tell the class the statement may or may not be true, and that they have to ask you questions to try to guess the truth. Elicit questions and answer them, e.g. *Do you like swimming? (No, I don't like swimming much at all.) When do you go surfing? (I go surfing every summer.)* After five questions, ask students to guess if the statement is true or not.

- Organize the class into groups of six to eight students and ask each group to get into two teams of three or four. Give each team their set of cards.

- Explain that students are going to make sentences using the prompts and the other team will have to guess if the sentence is true or not by asking questions. For each prompt, they should write one true sentence and two false sentences about their team members. Give teams ten to fifteen minutes to look through their cards, discuss ideas and write down or prepare their sentences.

- When everyone's ready, ask the members of team A each to read out their sentence made from the first prompt. Team B can then ask any of the members of team A up to three questions to help them guess which sentence is true. Team B then reads out the three sentences from their first prompts and team A asks questions. The winning team is the one who identified the most true sentences.

Photocopiable communicative activities: teacher's notes

Unit 3A Getting around town

AIM: to practise using vocabulary connected to transport while playing a board game

LANGUAGE: transport adjectives, compound nouns related to transport and transport verbs

INTERACTION: groupwork

MATERIALS: one copy of the worksheet for each group of three or four students, with the word cards cut out. Groups will need two coins, a stopwatch (e.g. on a smartphone) and a counter per player.

CLASS TIME: 30 minutes

PROCEDURE:

- Organize the class into groups of three or four students. Explain that students are going to play a board game and that they each need a counter. When they toss their coins, two heads = move one square, a head and a tail = move two squares and two tails = move three squares. You may wish to write these on the board. Hand out a board game and a set of cards to each group. Tell them to shuffle the cards and place them face down on the table.

- Explain that they start at the Start square. As they move around the board, they encounter different instructions.
  SPELL: If they land on SPELL, the player next to them takes a word card, reads the word and they have ten seconds (timed on a smartphone stopwatch) to spell it correctly. If they are correct, they score a point. If they are incorrect, they miss the next turn.
  SENTENCE: If they land on SENTENCE, they must take two word cards and make a correct sentence using both words. The other players decide if the sentence is correct. If they are correct, they score a point. If they are incorrect, they miss the next turn.
  DEFINITION: If they land on DEFINITION, they must take a word card and define the word for others to guess. They may not use any part of the word in their definition. If others guess the correct word in fewer than three attempts, the definer and the player who guesses correctly each win a point. If the player accidentally says part of a word, he/she misses a turn.

- The winner is the first player to win twenty points.

Unit 3B Ten transport teasers

AIM: to complete a quiz about transport

LANGUAGE: comparative forms, *as ... as*, comparative modifiers

INTERACTION: pairwork

MATERIALS: one copy of the worksheet for each pair of students

CLASS TIME: 30 minutes

PROCEDURE:

- Organize the class into pairs (or groups of three) and give each pair a copy of the worksheet. Explain that students are going to try to complete the statements with the correct form of the adjectives in brackets. They don't need to complete each statement in three different ways (i.e. using all the adjectives), but they will win a point for each factually correct sentence, so the more ways they can find to complete each sentence, the better.

- You may wish to do the first sentence as a class to check that everyone understands what to do. Elicit that the three factually correct ways to complete the statement: *The Paris Metro is ___ the New York Subway. (old / fast / busy)* are
  1 older than (Paris opened in 1900, and New York opened in 1904)
  2 not as fast as (average speed of Paris trains is 20 km/hr, New York is 27 km/hr)
  3 not as busy as / less busy than (Paris has 4.2 million passengers per day, New York has 5.7 million)

- Pairs then try to complete the remaining statements.

- In feedback, ask pairs to report their ideas to the class and take a vote on the correct answer before revealing the truth. Award a point for each factually correct statement. The pair with the most points is the winner.

ANSWERS:

1 older than (Paris opened in 1900, New York in 1904)
   not as fast as (Paris average speed = 20 km/hr, New York = 27km/hr)
   not as busy as / less busy than (Paris = 4.2 million passengers/day, New York = 5.7 million passengers/day)

2 bigger than (Brasilia = 5,802 km^2, New Delhi = 42.7km^2)
   not as hot as (Brasilia = 25.1–28.3°C, New Delhi = 20.5–39.5°C)
   further from London than (Brasilia = 8,787 km, New Delhi = 6,707 km)

3 faster than (passenger plane (jumbo) = over 615 km/hr, F1 = speed records around 372 km/hr)
   more expensive than (passenger plane = approx $71m, F1 = approx $9.4m)
   not as easy to park as (the weight, length and inability of a plane to go backwards make parking more difficult)

4 more modern than (first bicycle in 1840, first passenger train in 1825)
   not as old as
   as practical as (it depends on where and how far you want to go)

5 shorter than; not as long as; not the same as (London to Paris = 344km by air; 456 km by sea and road, Rome to Milan = 476 km by air; 572 km by road)

6 not as slow as (Dover to Calais = 1.5 hours, Tasmania to Australia = 10.5 hours)
   more crowded than (August is summer in the northern hemisphere and peak time)
   not as expensive as (car + 2 passengers: from Dover to Calais = £75; Tasmania to Australia £171.54 – although it's much more expensive per km or per minute)

7 less dangerous ... than; better ... than; not as hard ... as (Note: This is a trick question. There are no railways in the Canary Islands. The only trains are small sightseeing trains in various parks, which would be dangerous on the open road.)

Photocopiable communicative activities: teacher's notes

8 less dangerous than / not as dangerous as; more traditional than; as comfortable as

9 a bit smaller than the length of Fifth Avenue; not much smaller than; not as great as (Mount Everest = 8.85 km high, Fifth Avenue = 10 km long.

10 a little less quick than; a lot less direct; as good for your health as (Leicester Square and Covent Garden Market are 500 m apart, but by Tube, you have to walk to Leicester Square station (3 minutes), take the Tube to Covent Garden station (1 minute) and walk from the station to the market (3 minutes). You also have to get from the street to the platform and from the platform to the street, so you walk at least as much when you go by Tube.)

Unit 3C Travelling light

AIM: to practise language used for going on a journey

LANGUAGE: expressions used for going on a journey (in a taxi, on a bus, at a train station and at the airport)

INTERACTION: groupwork

MATERIALS: one copy of the worksheet for each group of three students, cut into six picture cards

CLASS TIME: 25 to 35 minutes

PROCEDURE:

- Organize the class into groups of three (or six if you prefer) and give each group a set of picture cards placed face down on the table. Ask students to take an equal number of cards each.

- Students describe their pictures to each other and try to put the story in the correct order without showing each other their cards. Point out that the labels A–F don't give the order of the pictures.

- When they have decided on the order, they can lay the cards on the table to check their answers.

- Students now work together to think of what goes in each speech bubble.

- Groups then act out the story and the various conversations.

SUGGESTED ANSWERS

D 1 Good morning. Where would you like to go?
  2 I'd like to go to the airport, please.

B 1 How much is that? 2 It's sixty dollars. 3 Do you want a receipt?

A 1 Do you go to the airport? 2 No, we don't. / Yes, but the bus is full.

F 1 A first class (single) ticket to the airport, please.
  2 Sorry, there aren't any trains today.

C 1 You can stop here. 2 That's two dollars, please.

E 1 How many bags are you checking in? 2 I only have this carry-on.

Unit 4A Team expedition

AIM: to practise using vocabulary connected to personal qualities by matching candidates to roles on an expedition

LANGUAGE: adjectives of personal qualities

INTERACTION: groupwork

MATERIALS: one copy of the worksheet for each group of three or four students, folded as shown

CLASS TIME: 20 to 30 minutes

PROCEDURE:

- Organize the class into groups of three or four students and give each group a copy of the worksheet, with the advertisement face up. Ask students to read the advertisement and check meaning. Ask students to discuss in their groups what kind of people they think Dr Jones will be looking for. Tell them to consider possible roles and personal qualities. After four or five minutes, ask groups to share their ideas with the class. Write their ideas on the board.

- Explain that students are going to read the profiles of four roles that Dr Jones wants to find people for, and her notes on six possible candidates. Tell them to read the profiles of the roles and the notes, and to discuss and agree on the best candidate for each role. You may wish to write the following prompts on the board:
It's important for the [name of job] to be (adjective).
The [name of job] needs to be …
I (don't) think [name] is the best person for [name of job] because …

- In feedback, ask individual groups to report to the class, and explain their choices. See if the whole class can agree on the final four team members.

Unit 4B I remember it well

AIM: to practise using the past simple and past continuous tenses to talk about an event

LANGUAGE: past simple and past continuous

INTERACTION: groupwork

MATERIALS: one copy of the worksheet for each group of five students, cut up into five reports

CLASS TIME: 30 minutes

PROCEDURE:

- Explain that students are each going to read a report of an event written by different people. Explain that one of the reports is by someone who wasn't there.

- Organize the class into groups of five and give each student a different report to read. (If there are only four students in a group, one card must go in the middle, face down.) Students read their reports and think of questions to ask group members to check facts, e.g. *What colour T-shirt was the tall man wearing?* Allow about ten minutes for this preparation stage.

- Students take turns to ask their questions. If there is a report in the middle, students should take turns to read it quickly to look for the answers.

- When they have finished asking questions, students discuss in their groups which person they think wasn't really there, and why (they should look for the greatest number of discrepancies).
- Groups report back to the class, explaining their choice.

> ANSWER
>
> Person D (the order of the runners is different).

Unit 4C What's the story?

AIM: to practise the language used for telling a story by building a story together

LANGUAGE: expressions for telling a story, sequencers, past simple and past continuous, review of question words

INTERACTION: groupwork, whole class, then pairwork

MATERIALS: one copy of the worksheet for each group of three students

CLASS TIME: 30 to 45 minutes

PROCEDURE:

- Review the language used for telling a story by writing *At the beginning …, Then …, Next …, While …, Luckily …, But …, Unfortunately …* on the board and asking the class to build a story about the previous lesson. Elicit a first sentence, e.g. *At the beginning, the board pen didn't work and Ms Turner didn't have another one.* Build the story around the class. Encourage students to ask questions for more detail, e.g. *Then what happened? What did she do?* and others to answer.
- Organize the class into groups of three and give each group a copy of the worksheet. Ask groups to look at the picture and write down at least six words they think they'll need in their story. Elicit all the words from the groups and write them on the board.
- Tell groups to build their story together by thinking of answers to the questions in the box. Ask them to add three more questions to ask other groups about the picture, using three different question words.
- When groups have their questions, as a class ask individual groups to call out their questions for others to answer using their imagination. Encourage them to enjoy this stage and to be as imaginative as possible.
- Back in their groups, students incorporate some of the class answers to questions into their stories. Tell them to prepare to tell their stories to a partner.
- Put students from different groups into pairs to tell each other their stories. Make sure they ask questions such as *What happened next?*
- Invite individual students to tell you about the picture. (Note: Although the aim is not to guess the real story, the picture shows Gladys Aylward, a British woman who was working with orphans in China in the 1930s and, during the Second World War, took over 100 children to safety by walking with them over mountains for twelve days.)

Unit 5A Fun factoids

AIM: to practise using quantifiers while doing a general knowledge quiz with an environmental slant

LANGUAGE: quantifiers

INTERACTION: pairwork, then groupwork

MATERIALS: one copy of the worksheet for each group of four students, cut into cards and folded as shown

CLASS TIME: 30 minutes

PROCEDURE:

- Organize the class into groups of four so that you have Students A, B, C and D. Then put students in pairs or small groups so that As are together, Bs are together, and so on. Give the students in each pair or group the same fact card with the gapped sentences face up. Tell them not to turn their card over yet.
- Ask students, working in their pairs, to read the three facts on their card and to discuss together which quantifier they think is missing. Point out the quantifiers printed along the bottom of their card. They should discuss quietly so other groups cannot hear them.
- After three to five minutes, allow students to turn the cards over to check their ideas and to read the information on the back. Check they understand the information, monitoring and helping as needed.
- Ask students to go back into their original groups so that each student in the group has a different card. They take turns to show the group their gapped sentences, holding their cards so that group members can see the gapped facts, but not the answers. The rest of the group discuss what they think is the correct answer. When they agree on their quantifiers for the three facts, the student holding the card tells them if they are correct or not and gives them the background information.

Unit 5B Tell me about it

AIM: to practise using vocabulary related to the environment while playing a game

LANGUAGE: vocabulary from Unit 5, including recycling (materials, containers), expressions with *take*, results and figures

INTERACTION: groupwork

MATERIALS: one copy of the worksheet for each group of four or five students, with the word cards cut out. Each group will need a stopwatch (e.g. on a smartphone).

CLASS TIME: 30 minutes

PROCEDURE:

- Explain that students are going to play a game where they have to speak for at least a minute on various subjects.

Photocopiable communicative activities: teacher's notes

- Organize the class into groups of four or five and give each group a copy of the topics and a set of word cards, placed face down on the table. Give them time to read the topics and check that they understand them all. Explain that while one group member speaks, the others will listen and try to guess what the three words or phrases on the speaker's word card are.

- Players take it in turns to take the top word card, without showing it to anyone, and to choose a topic to speak on. They will have to speak for one minute without pausing or repeating themselves. They will also have to include their three words or phrases in a way that sounds natural, so that other players can't guess which three words or phrases they have. Before they start speaking, they can take twenty seconds to think about what to say.

- When a player starts speaking, other group members start a stopwatch and make sure they speak for exactly one minute. If the speaker manages to speak for one minute without pausing too much or repeating, they win one point and the topic is crossed off so that it cannot be used again. The listening students must then try to guess which three words are on the card. They get a point for each correct guess. The speaker gets a point for each word they included that the listening students didn't guess.

- As play progresses, more and more topics are crossed off. When all the topics have been crossed off, the winner is the player with the most points.

Unit 5C How can I help you?

AIM: to practise language used for phoning about orders
LANGUAGE: expressions used for phoning about an order
INTERACTION: pairwork
MATERIALS: one copy of the worksheet for each pair of students, cut into product cards, role cards (optional) and a dialogue flow chart
CLASS TIME: 30 minutes
PROCEDURE:

- Check that students can spell in English by asking them to spell the names of things you can see around you.

- Explain that students are going to do a roleplay 'phoning' classmates about a problem with their order.

- Organize the class into pairs and give each pair a set of product cards and a set of role cards, both to be placed face down on the table. Give each student half of the dialogue flow chart. In each pair, there is one customer services assistant and one customer.

- Point out that the parts of text in the dialogue flow chart that are in *italics* are places where they can use the suggestions or their own ideas. Also explain that the dotted lines …… indicate when their partner will speak. Check that students understand all the cues on the flow chart and refer them to the language box on page 64 of the Student's Book, if necessary. Point out that there are small differences in the dialogue flow chart, so students will have to listen carefully and respond to what their partner says each time, not just deliver the next speech from their prompt.

- Tell each student to pick up a role card from the pile but not to show it to their partner. The role card gives instructions to be friendly, impatient, etc. Tell the customer in each pair to pick up a product card from the pile without showing it to the customer services assistant.

- If you wish, model a roleplay for the class with a strong student, by writing your own product card on the board and pretending to be impatient or friendly. Allow the student to refer to his/her card and help with any language. At the end, ask students to guess how you were trying to sound.

- Tell students to act out their roleplay. They take turns to be the customer and to pick up a product card, but they should change role cards when they have used both roles on it. At the end of each roleplay, they should try to guess what is on their partner's card. Monitor and listen, helping as necessary. As they repeat the roleplay, ask them to turn the dialogue flow chart face down and work from memory.

- Finally, invite individual pairs to perform roleplays for the class to guess which role cards they are working from. Encourage applause.

Unit 6A Plan B

AIM: to practise using future tenses in a milling activity
LANGUAGE: future forms, *to* + infinitive
INTERACTION: whole class
MATERIALS: one copy of the worksheet per student
CLASS TIME: 30 minutes
PROCEDURE:

- Give each student a copy of the worksheet. Ask them to think about plans and ideas for the future and to fill in the table. Remind them to take care to use the correct forms of the verbs, and encourage them to use their imagination.

- Explain that students are going to try to find as much information as possible about their classmates' plans. They will take turns to choose and explain two of their plans and ask two or three questions for more information. Tell them they should also think of a possible problem with the plan for their partner to think of a Plan B, e.g.
A *When I have some money one day, I intend to go on a cruise.*
B *Where are you going to go?*
A *We're going to go to the Greek Islands.*
B *Who are you going to go with?*
A *I'm going to take my husband.*
B *Imagine he doesn't like the sea; what will you do?*
A *Oh, I think we'll probably get off the ship and visit Athens.*

- When they have each explained and asked about two plans, students change partners and explain two more of their plans to a new partner. Students keep changing partner until they have talked about all their plans at least once and spoken to three to six different students.
- In feedback, ask students to tell the class which of the plans they listened to seemed the most interesting, exciting, original etc.

Unit 6B Get a pair, say a trio

AIM: to practise using expressions with *get* while playing a game of pelmanism
LANGUAGE: expressions with *get*
INTERACTION: groupwork
MATERIALS: one copy of the worksheet for each group of three students, cut up into cards
CLASS TIME: 30 minutes
PROCEDURE:
- Organize the class into groups of three and give each group a set of word cards. Tell them to shuffle the cards and place them on the table face down, in six rows of five.
- Explain that they are going to take turns to try to match a phrase with *get* and its meaning by turning over two cards. If the cards don't match, they turn them face down again, without moving them and pass the turn to the next student. If the cards match, they have to say three sentences using the phrase with *get*. The three sentences must be quite different and use different tenses or forms of the verb, and different ideas, e.g. *I don't like getting up in the morning in winter. I get up later than usual at the weekend. Tomorrow morning, I'm going to get up early to watch the Olympics.* (NOT *I usually get up at 7 a.m. Yesterday I got up at 7 a.m. I imagine I'll get up at 7 a.m. tomorrow.*)
- The listening students decide if the sentences are correct. If they are, the student keeps the pair and the next student turns over two cards. The remaining cards should not be moved into spaces, but left where they were.
- The winner is the player with the most cards when all the pairs have been won. Students may like to change partners and play again – tell them they get an extra point if they think of new sentences.

Unit 6C Magic word invitations

AIM: to practise inviting, accepting and declining
LANGUAGE: expressions used for inviting, accepting invitations and declining invitations, with vocabulary related to celebrations
INTERACTION: groupwork, then whole class
MATERIALS: one copy of the worksheet for each group of four students, cut into sets of magic word cards and invitation cards, folded as shown
CLASS TIME: 30 minutes

PROCEDURE:
- Organize the class into groups of four and give each group a set of invitation cards. Explain that they are going to invent a celebration to invite the class to and complete their invitation card with notes about it. On the board, write an example of your own, e.g.
The event: Grandma's 80th birthday
Where: Dickens Restaurant, High Street
Date: Saturday, April 17th
Time: 1 p.m.
Please bring: Flowers for grandma
- Give students a few minutes to complete their invitation cards.
- Review the language of invitations, eliciting phrases and responses from the class by saying: *This is informal: Why don't you come to my party? What's the formal expression?* (Would you like to …, I'd like to invite you to …).
- Working with different students, roleplay the conversation using the invitation you have written on the board as the basis and referring them to the language box on page 76 of the Student's Book, if necessary. Tell students to look on the back of their invitation to see if their event is formal (a bowtie) or informal (sunglasses).
- Give each group a set of magic word cards placed face down on the table. Tell students to take one card each and not to show it to anyone. The cards are divided into four sets of three words. Explain that they will speak to different classmates about different events and that they must choose a different set of three words each time they change partner.
- Divide the class into As and Bs. As will invite and need their invitation cards. Bs need their magic words card, and will listen for magic words and either accept or decline.
- Ask students to stand up and find a partner, forming A/B pairs. Student A holds their card up so Student B can see the picture and invites B to their event. Student B then asks two questions about the event, without using a magic word, e.g. *Is that near the park? Do I have to wear smart clothes? Can I bring a friend? What time will it finish?*
If Student A uses one of Student B's magic words when inviting, describing the event, or answering a question, B must accept the invitation. If not, B must decline. When Students A have asked at least five people, students change roles and Students B now do the inviting.
- In feedback, ask students to tell the class how many people are coming to their party!

Unit 7A What do you do?

AIM: to practise vocabulary for different jobs by doing a mingling activity
LANGUAGE: names of jobs and other words and phrases for describing jobs
INTERACTION: whole class

MATERIALS: one copy of the worksheet for classes up to 16 students, cut into job cards (make further copies for larger classes)

CLASS TIME: 25 to 35 minutes

PROCEDURE:

- Give each student a job card and tell them to keep it secret. Explain that everyone has the name of a job on their card, and the aim of the activity is to find out what everyone's job is. To do this, students will mingle and tell each other a bit about their job.
- Before the mingle starts, give the students a few minutes to write two sentences about their job in the spaces on their card. These will be clues to help other students guess what their job is, so they shouldn't make them too easy.
- Monitor and provide support as the students write their sentences. You might like to put the following ideas on the board as a guide: *Where do you work? What do you do every day? Who do you help? Do you wear a uniform? Do you earn a lot of money?*
- Once the students are ready, ask them to mingle, taking their card and a pen or pencil with them. They should ask each other *What do you do?* and then answer with clue 1. The questioner has one guess at this stage, and if they guess correctly, they score two points (they can write their score on the back of their card). If their guess is wrong, they can hear clue 2. If they guess correctly this time, they score one point. If their second guess is wrong, the other student should tell them what their job is. They score no points, and move on to speak to someone else.
- The students move around the class, speaking to as many people as possible, guessing their jobs, and keeping track of their score.
- After 15 to 20 minutes, ask students to sit down again, and discuss with their partner how many people's jobs they can remember. Then compare everyone's scores – the student with the highest score is the winner.

Unit 7B In the park

AIM: to practise prepositions of place and movement by describing a picture

LANGUAGE: prepositions of place and movement (e.g. *at, in, on, along, through, into, past*)

INTERACTION: pairwork

MATERIALS: one copy of the worksheet for each pair of students

CLASS TIME: 20 to 30 minutes

PROCEDURE:

- Organize the class into pairs and give each pair a copy of the worksheet. Before starting the main activity, you may wish to use the picture to pre-teach the following vocabulary: *bench, pond, playground, climbing frame, tunnel, path*. It might also be useful to remind students of how to describe a picture, using *There is / There are*

and the present continuous, e.g. *There is a café in the park. A boy is running along the path.* Point out the prepositions at the bottom of the worksheet and explain that this activity is an opportunity to practise using these.

- Give pairs three minutes to describe as much as they can of what is happening in the picture. At this stage they should only speak to each other, not write anything.
- Tell everyone to cover or fold the worksheet so they cannot see the picture, but they can still see the list of prepositions. Pairs work together to write down as many sentences as they can to describe the picture from memory. Encourage them to use the prepositions from the box. Set a time limit of five or six minutes for this stage (or more, if you think students will need it). Once time is up, insist that all writing stops.
- The pairs take turns to read out their sentences to the whole class. The teacher and the rest of the class decide if each sentence is acceptable and award points accordingly. The pair with the highest score wins. (Note: If your class is so large that this would take too long, you can put pairs together into groups of four to compare their lists and see which pair has the most correct sentences. Monitor and provide assistance with any sentences that they are unsure of.)

> EXAMPLE ANSWERS
>
> (These are suggestions only – the teacher and students collaborate to decide what answers are acceptable.)
>
> There is a pond between the café and the trees. There is a bench opposite the café. A dog is jumping into the pond. A boy is running along the path. Some children are waiting at the café. A bird is standing on the roof of the café, etc.

Unit 7C A job interview

AIM: to practise asking about and describing job requirements, qualifications and skills, etc. by roleplaying a job interview

LANGUAGE: questions and answers relating to job interviews

INTERACTION: pairwork

MATERIALS: one copy of the worksheet for each student, cut in half

CLASS TIME: 45 to 60 minutes

PROCEDURE:

- Write *computer programmer* in the middle of the board. Ask students to brainstorm what kinds of companies employ computer programmers and what kinds of programs they design. Elicit a wide range of ideas and add them to the board as a mind map.
- Explain that the students are going to carry out a roleplay of a job interview. The job is a computer programmer, but first the students need to complete a job advert and a CV giving details of the position and the candidate.

- Organize the class into pairs. Give the job advert to one student in each pair and the CV to the other student. While the students are completing their worksheets, circulate and check that they understand what kind of information is required in each space. Also, encourage them to be creative, using the ideas on the board.
- Once most students are ready, prepare them for the roleplay. Explain that the interviewer needs to find out about the candidate, while the candidate needs to find out about what the job involves. Elicit some ideas of what questions they might ask, and write these on the board.
- Give each student the other half of the worksheet (i.e. those who just filled in a CV now have a blank copy of the advert, and vice versa).
- Tell the students to roleplay the interview, using the questions on the board. As they go, they should fill in the details of the job advert or the CV using the details given by their partner. Monitor and support as necessary.
- Once they have finished, they can check that their worksheets match. When everyone has finished, round off the activity by asking a few of the interviewers whether they would hire the candidates. Ask a few candidates whether they thought the job description sounded attractive.

Unit 8A Internet survey

AIM: to practise using internet verbs by carrying out a class survey

LANGUAGE: collocations relating to the internet (e.g. *write a blog, upload photos, set up an account, check your email, log in to a website*)

INTERACTION: pairwork, groupwork, then whole class

MATERIALS: one copy of the worksheet for every four students in the class, cut into four sections (Note: Make sure that you have an even number of worksheets in total, so that pairs can work together on the same section.)

CLASS TIME: 30 to 40 minutes

PROCEDURE:

- Explain that students are going to conduct a class survey, asking each other questions about internet use.
- Organize the class into pairs, and give each student the same section of the worksheet so that pairs are working together on the same set of questions.
- Write on the board the verbs *connect, download, subscribe, log in, play, upload, write, check, search, set up*. Tell the students to work with their partner to complete the survey questions using some of these verbs. Monitor and provide support with this, reminding students to use the correct form of the verb each time. If they are struggling, allow them to look at page 94 of the Student Book to remind themselves of the collocations.
- Once most pairs have finished, write the answers on the board or read them out for the students to check.

- Rearrange the students into groups of four with an A, B, C and D student in each group. Each student takes turns to ask their questions and record the answers of the other group members. Encourage them to ask follow-up questions to find out extra details for at least some questions. Allow 15 to 20 minutes for this. Monitor and help with any problems.
- Ask each group to choose two or three questions and report back on them to the class, e.g. *Three people connect to the internet in a café almost every day. Two people often forget their password, but one person has never forgotten their password.* During feedback, ask other groups to comment on whether they found similar patterns.

ANSWERS
Student A: 1 connect   2 subscribed   3 log in   4 play
          5 write
Student B: 1 connect   2 search   3 download   4 upload
          5 check
Student C: 1 subscribe   2 search   3 uploads   4 writing
          5 set up
Student D: 1 log in   2 download   3 check   4 set up   5 play

Unit 8B Find your partner

AIM: to practise forming relative clauses by mingling to find a partner

LANGUAGE: defining relative clauses with *which, who,* and *where*

INTERACTION: whole class, then pairwork

MATERIALS: one copy of the worksheet for each class of up to twelve students, cut up into cards (for larger classes, make more copies, and remove the appropriate number of matching pairs so that each student has a card – see answers below). You will also need one copy of the worksheet (NOT cut up) for each pair of students

CLASS TIME: 20 to 30 minutes (for each round, including checking answers)

PROCEDURE:

- Give each student a card. Before starting the activity, tell the class that half the cards have a relative clause written on them, and the other half have the rest of the sentence (the main clause). Their aim is to find the matching clause for their card.
- Explain that students are going to stand up and mingle, reading their clauses to each other and listening to see if they match. Warn the students that they must listen and think carefully to decide if their cards match. First, they must check that they have one relative clause and one main clause (i.e. only one of them has *who, which* or *where*). Then they will need to think about where the relative clause goes in the sentence. It could go in the middle or at the end. You may wish to use the following clauses to demonstrate this on the board:

| The student won a prize. | who laugh a lot |
| I like spending time with people. | who got the best mark in the exam |

Photocopiable communicative activities: teacher's notes   301

- *The student who got the best mark in the exam won a prize.*
- *I like spending time with people who laugh a lot.*

- If their clauses don't match, they must swap cards with each other and move on to talk to someone else. If they match, they can sit down together and work as a pair to make the complete sentence.
- Once a pair has found each other, give them a fresh copy of the whole worksheet and ask them to work out all the matches.
- Once all the pairs have found each other, ask each pair to say their completed sentence. Ask the other students to listen and check that the sentence is correct both logically and grammatically. Write any problem sentences on the board and discuss them as a class.

ANSWERS
1 F 2 A 3 D 4 E 5 H 6 B 7 C 8 K 9 L 10 G 11 I 12 J

Unit 8C How does it work?

AIM: to practise describing how things work by playing a guessing game
LANGUAGE: phrases for describing how things work
INTERACTION: groupwork
MATERIALS: one copy of the worksheet for each group of three or four students, cut into a set of picture cards and the vocabulary list
CLASS TIME: 25 to 35 minutes (not including the follow-up task)
PROCEDURE:

- Organize the class into groups of three (or four, if necessary) and give each group a copy of the vocabulary list. Ask them to look at it carefully and to use their dictionaries or ask you for help if there are any items that they are unsure about.
- Give each group a set of the picture cards and ask them to shuffle them and place them face down on the table.
- Students take turns to pick up a card (without the others seeing it), e.g. hole punch, and use the words to describe how the item works, e.g. *You put a piece of paper in it. You press it down and it makes two holes in the paper.* They should not say the name of the item. You may want to demonstrate beforehand.
- The other students look at the items on the vocabulary list and try to guess which item is being described. The first student to guess correctly can keep the card.
- Play continues until all the cards have been used, and the player with the most cards wins.
- Follow-up: each student chooses one item and writes a short list of step-by-step instructions for how to use it.

Unit 9A Before I arrived ...

AIM: to practise using the past perfect by forming true and false sentences about personal experiences
LANGUAGE: past perfect
INTERACTION: pairwork
MATERIALS: one copy of the worksheet for each pair of students, cut in half
CLASS TIME: 25 to 35 minutes
PROCEDURE:

- Organize the class into pairs and give each student half the worksheet so that Student A is working with Student B.
- Explain that students are going to make true and false sentences about their lives using the past perfect. Later, their partner will listen to their sentences and guess which ones are true and which are false. Demonstrate how to complete the sentence prompts by completing two sentences from the worksheets about yourself, e.g. *Before I was six, I had learned how to swim. Before I woke up this morning, I had received five text messages.* As you do so, draw attention to how the past perfect is used, and how to include the verbs and adverbs in brackets. Then ask the students to guess if your sentences are true or false.
- Give students 10 to 15 minutes to complete their sentences. Monitor and provide support, as necessary, and remind students to write some true and some false sentences.
- Once both partners are ready, they take turns to read out their sentences. They should listen to each other's sentences and guess whether they are true or false. They get a point for each correct guess.
- Fast finishers can ask each other follow-up questions to find out more details about each other's experiences.
- Once everyone has finished, round off the activity by seeing who got the highest score in the whole class, and then asking a few students to share something interesting they learned about their partner.

Unit 9B That's amazing!

AIM: to practise -ed and -ing adjectives by playing a board game
LANGUAGE: -ed and -ing adjectives, e.g. *interested, interesting, amazed, amazing, worried, worrying*
INTERACTION: groupwork
MATERIALS: one copy of the worksheet for each group of three or four students, a stopwatch (e.g. on a smartphone), a die for each group and a counter for each student
CLASS TIME: 30 to 40 minutes
PROCEDURE:

- Organize the class into groups of three to four students, and give each group a worksheet, a die, and enough counters for each student to have one.

Photocopiable communicative activities: teacher's notes

- Explain that students are going to play a board game to practise -*ed* and -*ing* adjectives. Draw attention to the different types of squares on the board and explain the rules.
  If they land on a **white** square, they need to talk about the topic or answer the question. They must speak for one minute. If they do this successfully, they can move forward two squares. If they speak for 30 seconds, they can move forward one square. If they land on a **grey** square, they must choose one of the adjectives written around the board to complete the sentence. If they are the second player to land on a grey square, they should try to choose a different adjective if possible and explain why it could make sense.
  If they land on a **black** square, another student chooses one of the adjectives written around the board, and the playing student must say how many syllables it has.
  For grey and black squares, if they get the answer right, they stay on this square until their next turn; if they get the answer wrong, they go back one square.
- As students play the game, monitor and provide support as necessary. You may need to confirm correct answers for the grey and black squares. Listen to the students speaking when they are on white squares, and write down examples of correct and incorrect use of the target language. As most groups begin to get towards the end of the game, write these up on the board.
- When a group finishes, tell them to look at the sentences on the board and decide which are right and wrong. Ask them to correct the wrong ones.
- Once all the groups have finished, go through the sentences on the board as a class and discuss which ones are correct and how to correct the incorrect ones.

Unit 9C Would you like to visit?

AIM: to practise requesting information and making suggestions

LANGUAGE: phrases for requesting information and making suggestions, e.g. *Do you know what time it opens? Could you tell me the price? How about ..., Another option is to ...*

INTERACTION: pairwork, then whole class

MATERIALS: one copy of the worksheet for each pair of students

CLASS TIME: 30 to 40 minutes

PROCEDURE:

- Organize the class into pairs and give each pair a copy of the worksheet. Explain that students are going to design a leaflet for a tourist attraction (which can be real or imaginary) and then they are going to try to persuade their classmates to visit this attraction.
- Point out the different parts of the worksheet, and elicit what information might go in each. Check that students understand what might be suitable for the *Description* (a few sentences saying what the attraction is and why people might want to visit it), *Getting there* (means of transport – probably more than one option) and *Extra options* (guided tours, cafés, special exhibitions, children's activities, etc.) Show them how the worksheet folds and explain that their classmates will see the top half, while only they will see the bottom half.
- Give students 15 to 20 minutes to think of an attraction and complete their leaflet with information, including a sketch. Remind them to write clearly and neatly in this section so that others can read it. Encourage them to include full details in the bottom half, e.g. different opening times for different seasons/days of the week, different ticket prices for students/children, different ways of getting to the attraction and at least one extra option.
- Before doing the mingle, remind students of the language on page 112 of the Student's Book (*I'm interested in visiting ... Do you know the opening times? Could you tell me the price? Is there any public transport? How often does the bus go? Are there any ...? How about ...-ing? You can also ... Another option is to ... Or you could take ...*) You may wish to put these phrases on the board and drill them. In particular, demonstrate how the question *Are there any ...?* can be used to discover some of the extra options, which might otherwise be difficult to find out about.
- During the mingle stage, each pair should stay together. Tell pairs to work with another pair. The pairs take turns to show the other pair their folded worksheet. The other pair reads the name and description of their tourist attraction, and then asks for details such as prices and extra options. Monitor and remind the students to ask for plenty of detail, and to use the target language. Every five minutes tell the pairs to move on and work with a different pair.
- Once students have had a chance to hear about several tourist attractions, ask them to sit back down and discuss together which attraction they would choose to visit. Finish off the activity by asking each pair where they have decided to go, and why.

Unit 10A Formation dominoes

AIM: to practise using different forms of words by playing a dominoes game

LANGUAGE: word forms with different endings (e.g. advertiser – advertisement; deliver – delivery; competition – competitor)

INTERACTION: groupwork

MATERIALS: one copy of the worksheet for each group of three students, cut up into dominoes

CLASS TIME: 20 to 30 minutes

PROCEDURE:

- Organize the class into groups of three students and give each group a set of dominoes placed face down on the table. Tell each student to take four dominoes and leave the others face down in the pile.

- Tell each group to turn over the first domino from the pile. Explain that players take it in turns to add a domino to the end of the chain. The next domino must always match, i.e. the root word on the left of the gap can be modified with the ending on the right of the gap, e.g. *science* and *-ist* to form *scientist*. The player must write down the word that is formed, paying attention to correct spelling. To complete their turn, the player must make a sentence using this word, e.g. *Would you like to be a scientist in the future?*
- If a player does not have a domino that matches either end of the chain, they must take a domino from the top of the pile. If a player has a domino that matches, but they fail to spell the word correctly or make a correct sentence, they must return that domino to the bottom of the pile, and take two new dominoes from the top of the pile. They cannot immediately use the dominoes they have picked up, but must wait until their next turn.
- The winner is the first player to use up all their dominoes. However, encourage groups who finish quickly to continue to work together to incorporate all the dominoes into one chain. (Note that on the worksheet the dominoes are laid out to show how this is possible.)

Unit 10B How much do you know?

AIM: to practise using the passive (present and past simple forms) by doing a general knowledge quiz

LANGUAGE: the passive (present simple and past simple)

INTERACTION: pairwork

MATERIALS: one copy of the worksheet for each pair of students, cut in half

CLASS TIME: 25 to 30 minutes

PROCEDURE:

- Organize the class into pairs and give each student half the worksheet, so that As are working with As and Bs are working with Bs.
- Explain that the students are going to do a quiz, but first they need to prepare the questions. Tell them to read the sentences together and complete the gaps by putting the verbs into the present simple passive or past simple passive. Monitor and help with this.
- Pairs who finish quickly can write two new true/false questions – remind them to use the passive.
- Check that everyone has the correct passive forms – you can do this by writing the answers on the board, going through them orally, or circulating and looking at each pair's worksheets.
- Rearrange students into AB pairs. Students take turns to read their sentences for their partner to guess whether they are true or false. Students get a point for each correct guess. The student with the most points is the winner.

- Round off the activity with some whole-class feedback – who got the most points? Which fact was the most surprising?

> **ANSWERS**
> Student A: 1 were made   2 was invented   3 are found
> 4 is spoken   5 is covered   6 was written
> 7 is/was sung   8 were killed
> Student B: 1 is spoken   2 was written   3 is/was played
> 4 are found   5 was invented   6 were killed
> 7 is covered   8 was given

Unit 10C What are we going to do?

AIM: to practise language for giving opinions, by discussing different situations

LANGUAGE: phrases for asking for and giving opinions, agreeing, disagreeing and making suggestions

INTERACTION: groupwork

MATERIALS: one copy of the worksheet for each group of three to four students, cut into the list and one set of cards. Each group will also need six small pieces of paper with the numbers 1–6 written on them, and a hat (or other container) to hold them.

CLASS TIME: 30 to 40 minutes

PROCEDURE:

- Organize the class into groups of three to four students, and give each group a copy of the situations list. Ask them to read it and check any unknown vocabulary.
- Explain that students are going to decide, as a group, what to do in each situation. However, first they need to add one more situation to the list (number 6). Allow time for the groups to come up with an idea. Monitor and support as necessary, making sure that they choose a situation that will create a good discussion. Suggestions: Going on a group holiday – decide where to go. Working for a café – decide how to attract more customers during the summer.
- Give each group a set of cards and tell them to shuffle them and distribute them equally among the group. Explain that, during the discussion, they must try to use the phrases on their cards. Each time they do so, they can lay down the card. The aim is for all the students to use all their cards during each round of discussion.
- Each group picks a number from the hat to choose a situation to discuss. Give them three to four minutes for the discussion, and then check how many cards have been used in total by each group. Write this score on the board.
- Each group shuffles and deals the cards again before picking another number to choose a new situation. (If they get the same situation twice, they should pick a new number without replacing the one they just picked.) Again, set a limit of three to four

304 Photocopiable communicative activities: teacher's notes

minutes, and check how many cards have been used by each group at the end of this time. You can repeat this for up to six rounds, although you may be ready to stop after four or five. At the end, total the scores for each group and announce the winning group.

- After announcing the winners, ask each group to tell the class about one round of discussion, including what opinions people gave, and what agreement (if any) they reached.

Unit 11A He said, she said …

AIM: to practise reported statements by carrying out a competition to write the most interesting reported statements
LANGUAGE: reported speech
INTERACTION: groupwork, then whole class
MATERIALS: two copies of the worksheet, cut into cards (Note: Keep the A/B cards and the C/D cards separate)
CLASS TIME: 25 to 35 minutes
PROCEDURE:

- Write on the board: *When my wallet was stolen, the police said …* and elicit some suggestions of how to complete the sentence from the class (e.g. *… they would catch the thief.*) Make sure these are correctly expressed in reported speech, and write them on the board. As you do so, check that the class are happy with the rules of reported statements, introduced on page 131 of the Student's Book.
- Explain that students are going to play a game which involves completing sentences in this way. Organize the class into four groups, A, B, C and D, and explain that groups A and B are competing against each other, while groups C and D are competing against each other.
- Give each group a set of cards: A and B each have a set of the A/B cards, and C and D each have a set of the C/D cards. Explain that they need to work together to write an ending to each sentence, using reported speech. The aim is to write an interesting, clever or funny ending. Later, these endings will be judged by students in the other groups.
- Give the groups time to come up with interesting endings. Circulate, encouraging them to consider various options. Provide suggestions and help with the grammar as necessary.
- Once all the groups have completed their sentences, move on to the judging stage.
- Groups A and B read out their respective endings for Card 1. Groups C and D listen, and then vote on which ending is the best. Award one point to the group who wins the vote. Then groups C and D read out their endings for their Card 1. Groups A and B listen and vote, and a point is awarded. Repeat until all the endings have been read out. The group with the most points at the end wins.

Unit 11B Office Communication

AIM: to practise collocations for communication vocabulary by playing spot the difference
LANGUAGE: collocations to describe communication, e.g. *receive a text message, give a presentation, listen to a radio programme*
INTERACTION: pairwork
MATERIALS: one copy of the worksheet for each pair of students, cut in half
CLASS TIME: 25 to 35 minutes
PROCEDURE:

- Write the following words on the board (well spaced out): *a radio programme, a text message, a presentation, a card, a newspaper, a website*. Ask the students what verbs can go with these nouns, and add them to the nouns, e.g. *listen to / speak on a radio programme; write/send/receive/read a text message; give/listen to a presentation; write/send/receive/read a card; read a newspaper; look at/design a website*.
- Organize the class into pairs and give each student half of the worksheet.
- Explain that there are ten differences between the two pictures, and they need to find all of them, without looking at their partner's picture. To do this, they must describe what is happening in their picture for their partner to notice what is different in their picture. At this stage, they should work orally, and circle the differences they find on the pictures.
- Give the students 15 to 20 minutes to do this. Any fast finishers can look at each other's pictures to check their answers, and write sentences to describe the differences they found, e.g. *In picture A, the woman has received three text messages, but in picture B she has received seven.*
- Once everyone has finished, check as a class what the ten differences are. Encourage students to use the correct collocations to describe the communication that is taking place.

ANSWERS
1 A man/woman is writing an email.
2 A woman is looking at a Facebook page/an office supplies website.
3 The woman has received three/seven new text messages.
4 The sticky note is about not stealing milk/cleaning the fridge.
5 The woman making a cup of coffee is talking on the phone/listening to music on the radio.
6 There is a woman/man giving a presentation.
7 The presentation is about sales/new employees.
8 The man is reading/not reading a newspaper.
9 The man has received a birthday card from his mum/Clara.
10 The man is looking at an advert for a jazz concert/a guitar for sale.

Photocopiable communicative activities: teacher's notes

Unit 11C Ancient careers

AIM: to practise giving a presentation

LANGUAGE: phrases for giving a presentation, e.g. *Today, I'd like to talk about … Now, let's look at … To sum up, …*

INTERACTION: pairwork

MATERIALS: one copy of the worksheet for each pair of students, cut into cards

CLASS TIME: 30 to 40 minutes

PROCEDURE:

- Organize the class into pairs and give each pair a copy of the worksheet, cut into cards. Explain that here they have the information for two different presentations about two historical topics. Students must sort the cards into two sets and discover what the two topics are. Tell them not to worry about difficult vocabulary for the moment.
- Check that each pair has sorted the cards correctly and they have identified the topics. Write these titles on the board: *Zhang Qian* and *Gladiators*. Help students with the pronunciation of Zhang Qian /dʒɒnˈtʃiːen/.
- Pre-teach the following words and write them on the board under *Zhang Qian*: *explorer* (= a person who visits new places to find out about them), *diplomat* (= a person who works for the government of one country, talking to other countries' governments, so that different countries can work together peacefully), *army* (= a group of soldiers), *empire* (= a group of different countries that are controlled by one leader or government), *emperor* (= the ruler of an empire) and *trade* (= buying and selling products, often between different countries).
- Under *Gladiators*, pre-teach and write these words on the board: *archaeologist* (= a person who studies the past by digging up buildings and objects from the ground), *stab* (= to hurt someone by pushing a knife into them), *blood* (= the red liquid that moves around inside the body), *bones* (= the hard parts of the body which make its structure, i.e. the skeleton) and *calcium* (= a white chemical element that is an important part of bones and teeth).
- Each pair divides the presentations between them, each student choosing one of the two topics.
- Organize students into new pairs, so that they are working with someone who has chosen the same topic as them. They work together to organize the main points of their presentation into a logical order, and decide which of the phrases on page 136 of the Student's Book to use. Then they rehearse their presentations, listening to each other and giving feedback on pronunciation, pauses, body language, etc. Circulate and give guidance and support in these areas, as necessary. Encourage more confident students to write their own brief prompts, and to refer to the strips of paper as little as possible.
- Students return to their original partner and give their presentations to each other. Encourage the students who are listening to take notes and ask questions, if necessary. Round off the activity by asking a few students to give any details they remember about the presentation they listened to (not the one they gave!)

> **ANSWERS**
> Zhang Qian: I, D, G, E, L, A, J
> Gladiators: C, N, K, F, M, B, H

Unit 12A Weather forecasts

AIM: to practise language to describe the weather by exchanging weather forecast information

LANGUAGE: weather vocabulary, e.g. *rain, snow, hail, thunderstorm, floods, tornadoes*

INTERACTION: groupwork

MATERIALS: one copy of the worksheet for each group of three to four students, cut up into the key and four weather forecast cards

CLASS TIME: 25 to 30 minutes

PROCEDURE:

- Organize the class into groups of three to four and give each group a copy of the key. It's probably a good idea to review the weather vocabulary by eliciting sentences such as *It will be sunny tomorrow* or *It's going to rain on Saturday*. Draw attention to the indications of parts of speech, and remind them to use *It will be* + adj, *There will be* + noun and *It will* + verb.
- Give each student in a group a different weather forecast card. Explain that each card has the weather forecast for tomorrow in a different country, and they need to exchange this information without showing each other their cards. Give students a few minutes to prepare to describe the weather that the card shows. At this stage all students can look at the key for help.
- Draw the following table on the board and ask students to copy it into their notebooks, to help them take detailed notes while listening to each other:

Country			
North			
South			
East			
West			
Extreme weather			

- Students take turns to act out being a TV weather forecaster for their country. They describe tomorrow's weather to their group, including the symbols on the map, and the extreme weather warning. Encourage the students to look at the key as little as possible while doing this. Meanwhile the other students in the group fill in the table with details of the weather forecast in different areas of each country, and the extreme weather warning.
- After finishing, groups can compare notes to check they caught all the important information.

306 Photocopiable communicative activities: teacher's notes

Unit 12B The crossword of everything

AIM: to practise using the words *anywhere, everyone, nobody, something*, etc. by completing an interactive crossword

LANGUAGE: *anywhere, anyone, anybody, anything, everywhere, everyone, everybody, everything, somewhere, someone, somebody, something, nowhere, no one, nobody, nothing*

INTERACTION: pairwork

MATERIALS: one copy of the worksheet for each pair of students, cut in half

CLASS TIME: 20 to 30 minutes

PROCEDURE:

- Organize the class into pairs and give each student half of the worksheet.
- Explain that they have a crossword with words from previous units in the Student's Book. Only half of the words are filled in, so they will need to ask their partner for clues to complete the crossword.
- Tell students to prepare the clues first: they must choose the correct word to complete the sentence. If the students are not confident with this grammar, you could put them in a pair with someone who has the same half of the worksheet for this stage, before rearranging the pairs for the next stage.
- Check the answers to the clues. (Note: Don't read out or write up the whole clue, so as not to spoil the next stage for the students.)
- Students take turns to read a clue to their partner. When their partner guesses the word correctly, they confirm it and their partner writes it into the crossword.
- If some students are struggling, encourage their partners to help without simply giving the word away, e.g. by giving the first letter, using 'sounds like' clues or giving examples. Pairs can also help each other with the spelling.
- Once pairs have finished, they can check that their crosswords match. Ask fast finishers to choose three or four words that they want to remember from the crossword and to write example sentences for them.

Unit 12C What should I do?

AIM: to practise suggesting and discussing solutions, by considering different solutions to a range of problems

LANGUAGE: phrases for suggesting and discussing solutions, e.g. *What about …? That's a good idea … But if we don't …*

INTERACTION: groupwork

MATERIALS: one copy of the worksheet for each group of three or four students, with the four problem cards cut out

CLASS TIME: 30 to 40 minutes

PROCEDURE:

- Organize the class into groups of three or four students. Give each group a copy of the worksheet and a set of problem cards. Explain that the worksheet shows possible solutions to the problems written on the cards. The aim of the activity is to match possible solutions to each problem, and to decide which is the best. To do this, the students will act out short conversations.
- Remind students of the language they will need (from page 148 of the Student's Book) by eliciting a short dialogue about a different problem (e.g. You need to learn a foreign language very quickly, for a business trip next week). Make sure you include phrases for explaining the problem, making a suggestion, responding negatively and responding positively. Write these phrases on the board as they arise. You may wish to drill them and work on pronunciation, etc.
- Each student takes one of the four problem cards. The first student explains their problem to the group and asks for advice. The other students take turns to choose a different solution from the worksheet, and suggest it using an appropriate phrase. The first student can choose to respond positively or negatively to these suggestions, and the group should then discuss the pros and cons of each option, and finally decide on which one is best. Repeat for each of the other students' problems. As soon as a solution has been suggested, it should be crossed out on the worksheet, and it cannot be used again.
- Fast finishers could write one or two different possible solutions to each problem.
- Conduct a brief class feedback session, asking each group which solutions they thought were particularly good or bad, and why.

> **SUGGESTED ANSWERS**
> 1 c, d, l   2 g, i, j   3 a, b, h   4 e, f, k

Grammar summary: answer key

UNIT 1 (page 157)

1
1 doesn't live
2 drives
3 Does; speak
4 don't like
5 Do; see
6 are
7 don't need
8 Is
9 has

2
1 I **am often** tired at work.
2 We eat out in a restaurant **twice a week**. / **Twice a week** we eat out in a restaurant.
3 correct
4 correct
5 I have a cup of coffee **two or three times a day**. / **Two or three times a day**, I have a cup of coffee.
6 They don't **often play** board games.
7 Does **she usually** take public transport?

3
1 always
2 get up
3 never
4 have
5 often
6 meet
7 go
8 every day
9 eat
10 two or three times a month

4
1 'm waiting
2 are; going
3 isn't working
4 'm writing
5 's talking
6 're building
7 are becoming

5
1 'm eating; eat
2 drives; 's driving
3 's talking; talk
4 'm working; work
5 'm doing; do

6
1 live
2 eat
3 say
4 is
5 is changing
6 are eating

UNIT 2 (page 159)

1
1 a 2 b 3 a 4 c 5 b 6 c

2
1 mustn't
2 don't have to
3 must
4 must
5 must / have to
6 don't have to

3
1 have to / must
2 can't
3 mustn't
4 can't
5 don't have to
6 have to

4
1 playing
2 watching
3 Doing
4 waking up
5 failing
6 Reading
7 helping

5
1 cleaning
2 do
3 Staying
4 going
5 running
6 going
7 take
8 eating
9 make

UNIT 3 (page 161)

1
1 nicest
2 further
3 more interesting
4 worst
5 more beautiful
6 busier; busiest
7 better; best
8 bigger; biggest

2
1 The fastest
2 longest
3 deepest
4 longer than
5 the busiest
6 the highest
7 higher than

3
1 Mount Fuji isn't as high as Mount Kilimanjaro.
2 The USA isn't as big as Canada.
3 A kangaroo is as fast as a horse.
4 A Dreamliner isn't as heavy as a Jumbo Jet.

4
1 Travelling by motorbike isn't as safe as travelling by car.
2 Cycling is as dangerous as driving. / Driving is as dangerous as cycling.
3 Gatwick Airport isn't as convenient for us as Heathrow Airport.
4 Usually, the beach isn't as busy as this during the week.
5 Going by car is as quick as taking the bus. / Taking the bus is as quick as going by car.

5
1 a bit more economical
2 much cheaper
3 a bit more interesting
4 a lot quieter; a lot busier
5 much more popular
6 a little bigger than

6
1 The best
2 much easier
3 a bit more difficult
4 the most convenient
5 a little more direct
6 quicker
7 a lot higher than
8 a bit more expensive than
9 much quicker
10 more comfortable

308

UNIT 4 (page 163)

1
1 wanted
2 wasn't
3 didn't have
4 didn't like
5 was
6 studied

2
1 booked
2 didn't want
3 decided
4 drove
5 didn't know
6 asked
7 was
8 could
9 were
10 took
11 had

3
1 How was your hotel?
2 When did you get back?
3 Did they get the train home?
4 What was your favourite experience?
5 Did you call me this morning?
6 How much did our plane tickets cost?

4
1 were waiting
2 wasn't eating
3 Were; talking
4 were; saying
5 wasn't raining
6 was; flying

5
1 arrived; was watching
2 arrived; got
3 started; were climbing
4 wasn't playing; saw
5 Was she skiing; had
6 knew; heard

6
1 was travelling
2 was eating
3 came
4 knew
5 couldn't
6 started
7 was sitting
8 was waiting

UNIT 5 (page 165)

1
1 a much, b many
2 a a little, b a few
3 a much, b many
4 a any, b Some

2
1 a 2 b 3 b 4 c 5 a 6 b 7 c

3
1 a lot of
2 lots of
3 a few
4 many
5 a lot
6 some
7 any

4
1 the 2 – 3 an, The 4 the 5 – 6 the

5
1 an 2 – 3 the 4 the 5 the 6 – 7 the 8 a 9 the

6
1 a 2 – 3 – 4 the 5 a 6 The 7 the 8 –

UNIT 6 (page 167)

1
1 to go
2 to start
3 to study
4 to organize
5 to stay
6 to learn

2
1 a 2 g 3 c 4 h 5 d 6 f 7 b 8 e

3
1 staying
2 to learn
3 to fix
4 to visit
5 painting
6 to buy
7 Eating
8 to hear

4
1 'm going to see
2 Are; going to come
3 's going to have
4 's going to spend
5 'm not going to get
6 Are; going to miss
7 aren't going to go
8 going to start

5
1 I'll help
2 I'll go
3 is arriving
4 I'm going to go
5 I'm going to have

6
1 a 2 b 3 a 4 b 5 b

UNIT 7 (page 169)

1
1 I've seen that film five times.
2 Have you ever been to Australia?
3 They've always lived in the countryside.
4 Has she ever visited you?
5 I haven't finished my work.
6 Why have you applied for this job?

2
1 I started
2 Have you ever been
3 They've always loved
4 Jill spoke
5 I worked
6 I've never been

3
1 Have; finished
2 got
3 Did; have
4 Have; heard
5 have; sent
6 told
7 Have; been
8 stayed
9 Did; have

4
1 for
2 for
3 since
4 since
5 for
6 for
7 since
8 for

5
1 in
2 on
3 below
4 opposite
5 between
6 near

Grammar summary: answer key 309

6

1 out of
2 across
3 along
4 past
5 through
6 up
7 outside

UNIT 8 (page 171)

1

1 f 2 e 3 c 4 a 5 g 6 b 7 d

2

1 finish, 'll go out
2 'll miss, don't leave
3 is, 'll drive
4 won't come, feels
5 go, 'll buy
6 doesn't do, will be
7 don't answer, 'm

3

Zero conditional:
1 d; 's; prefer
2 a; don't sleep; have
3 b; die; don't give
4 c; likes; wakes

First conditional:
1 c; 's; 'll invite
2 a; don't eat; 'll feel
3 d; won't get up; don't have to
4 b; 'll travel; can

4a

1 who
2 which
3 where
4 which
5 who
6 where
7 which

4b

2, 4 and 7

5

1 Correct
2 This is the house that I want to buy it.
3 She bought the car **which** she saw last week.
4 Look! That's the friend **who** I was talking about yesterday.
5 Those are the students who they are looking for a flat.
6 Correct
7 He didn't see the person who he took his wallet.

6

1 who; f
2 who; b
3 that / which; e
4 that / which; c
5 who / that; a
6 where; d

UNIT 9 (page 173)

1

1 h 2 f 3 d 4 c 5 g 6 a 7 e 8 b

2

1 had; bought
2 had happened
3 had asked
4 had; thought
5 had; tried
6 hadn't checked
7 had spent

3

1 didn't go; had … seen
2 felt; had forgotten
3 called; had received
4 said; had helped
5 had slept; felt
6 had studied; failed

4

1, 4, 5 and 7

5

1 Who put this bag here?
2 Which computer works best?
3 Who broke my glasses?
4 Who speaks French?
5 How many people work here?
6 Who won the race?

6

1 Where did you go last year?
2 Whose behaviour made you really angry?
3 How many people live in this building?
4 Why did you go outside?
5 Who left her coat here?
6 Who has spoken to Paolo today?

UNIT 10 (page 175)

1

1 A 2 P 3 P 4 P 5 A

2

1 was designed
2 is used
3 are drunk
4 were produced
5 are written
6 are recognized

3

1 Amazon was created by Jeff Bezos in 2005.
2 The final of the World Cup was watched by over one billion viewers in 2014.
3 More books are bought online by readers in the USA than in shops.
4 The Taj Mahal in India is visited by up to four million people every year.
5 One thousand cars are made by workers in large car factories every day.

4

1 was normally used
2 was released
3 were sold
4 are sold
5 spend
6 are bought
7 found

5

1 used to take
2 ✓
3 ✓
4 didn't use to like
5 used to play
6 ✓
7 use to like
8 ✓

310 Grammar summary: answer key

6

1 used to listen to music on CDs
2 didn't use to have a smartphone
3 used to buy CDs
4 didn't use to own a car
5 used to use a skateboard
6 didn't use to wear glasses
7 used to be a student
8 didn't use to wear a suit

7

1 didn't use to get up
2 used to go out
3 used to play
4 used to practise
5 didn't use to have
6 used to own
7 did; use to be

UNIT 11 (page 177)

1

1 would have
2 was playing
3 didn't like
4 had visited
5 he'd lost

2

1 the next day
2 his
3 they
4 there
5 me
6 then
7 their
8 the day before

3

1 has; left
2 will/'ll
3 don't speak
4 was
5 am arriving

4

1 Jan said she'd lost the match.
2 She said she'd see me the next day.
3 Mehmet said my email hadn't arrived.
4 He said he didn't want to speak to me.
5 Luke said he was trying to watch the TV.

5

1 He told **me** …
2 Correct
3 She said ~~me~~ that …
4 Correct
5 Correct
6 Anna told **me** …

6

1 (that) he'd found something interesting.
2 him (that) he was holding an ancient Greek vase.
3 (that) it was really beautiful.
4 (that) it had probably been lost in the sea for thousands of years.
5 him (that) he'd call the museum right away.

UNIT 12 (page 179)

1

1 will
2 would
3 became
4 would
5 won't
6 didn't

2

1 d 2 a 3 c 4 f 5 e 6 b

3

1 wasn't; 'd be able to
2 had; 'd buy
3 spoke; would understand
4 wouldn't tell; didn't think
5 'd save; were
6 Would; come; pay

4

1 somewhere
2 something
3 Nowhere
4 anybody
5 Everyone
6 anything

5

1 somewhere
2 everywhere
3 nobody
4 nothing
5 something
6 anything

6

1 Giulia lives somewhere near here.
2 There was nobody on the beach so it was really quiet.
3 I've been everywhere in this city and the parks are my favourite.
4 Anywhere in the room will do.
5 Mike didn't have anything with him.
6 There's somebody waiting for you outside.

Workbook: answer key

Unit 1

1a (pages 4 and 5)

1
1 works 2 specializes 3 goes 4 studies 5 wants
6 spends 7 don't stay 8 travel 9 visit
10 don't realize 11 helps 12 don't have

2
1 starts 2 watches 3 flies 4 passes 5 lives
6 studies 7 finishes 8 relaxes

3
/s/   helps, visits, wants
/z/   has, is, spends, stays, travels
/ɪz/   realizes, specializes, studies

4
1 Where does Nathan work?
2 Where does he often go?
3 What does he find and study?
4 Where does he spend a lot of time?
5 Why do new viruses travel more easily?
6 What does he need for his work?
7 Do people have electricity in every part of the world?
8 How does Nathan communicate?

5
1 c 2 b 3 a 4 a

6
1 I always do exercise in the evening.
2 It is always colder in the winter.
3 I take this medicine twice a day.
4 They don't often go on holiday.
5 We are sometimes busy at weekends.
6 She rarely eats out during the week.
7 You are never on time for work.
8 Do you always check your emails at lunchtime?

1b (pages 6 and 7)

1
1 b 2 c 3 b 4 b 5 c 6 b 7 a

2
1 is responsible for 2 pregnant 3 patient
4 mothers-to-be 5 hospital 6 deliver
7 shortage 8 mobile 9 serious 10 local

3
Today they <u>are visiting</u> their first patient.
Sarubai <u>is checking</u> Rani …
While they <u>are checking</u> the baby …
… and the number <u>is growing</u>.

4
1 I'm driving
2 has
3 do you come
4 is flying
5 I never cycle
6 is standing
7 Do you always leave
8 it's getting
9 aren't staying
10 Are you working; are you taking

5
a 5 b 4 c 3 d 3 e 4 f 4

6
1 living 2 dropping 3 letting 4 swimming 5 having
6 lying 7 taking 8 travelling 9 getting 10 jogging

7
I usually get up at about seven o'clock and go running for half an hour. Then I feel ready for the day. I leave the house at about eight thirty and arrive at the hospital by nine. Currently, I'm seeing lots of children with flu. After work I often walk home. Sometimes friends come round for dinner, but I need eight hours of sleep a night so I'm always in bed by eleven o'clock.

1c (page 8)

1
1 happy 2 money 3 students 4 country

2
1 c 2 b 3 b 4 c 5 a 6 a

3
1 f 2 c 3 b 4 a 5 d 6 e

4
1 e 2 d 3 a 4 c 5 b

5
Possible answers:
Do you feel like a coffee?
Do you feel like doing something?
How do you feel today?
Do you feel OK?
Does it feel cold outside?
What do you feel like doing?

1d (page 9)

1
1 nose 2 ear 3 tooth 4 head 5 throat 6 back
7 mouth 8 stomach

2
1 How does your <u>sto</u>mach feel?
2 Is your throat sore or is it <u>bet</u>ter?
3 Drink this hot <u>wa</u>ter.
4 My <u>hea</u>dache is worse to<u>day</u>.
5 Can I see the <u>doc</u>tor a<u>bout</u> my ear?
6 This is good for a <u>runny</u> nose.

3
Tick the following for 1–3:
1 sore throat, cough 2 high 3 pills
4 Advice: Go to bed for two days. Drink lots of water. Come back if you still feel ill.

4
1 How do you feel
2 Let me have a
3 Do you feel
4 Have you got
5 Let me check
6 take this prescription
7 You need to
8 They are good
9 try drinking
10 If you still feel ill

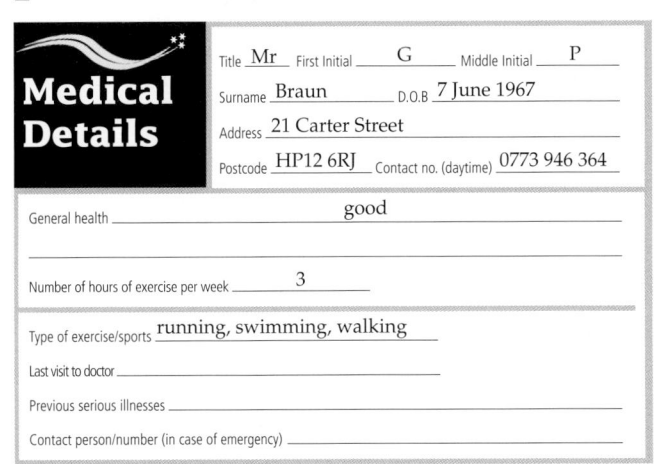

5

Model answers:
You need to take some pills.
Try taking some hot water with lemon and honey.
Go to bed for a couple of days.
You need to see a doctor.
Take this medicine. It's good for flu.

1e (page 10)

1 title
2 Middle initial
3 D.O.B.
4 Contact no (daytime)
5 General health
6 Previous serious illnesses
7 Number of hours of exercise per week
8 Contact person/number (in case of emergency)
9 Postcode
10 Surname

2

Medical Details

Title: Mr First Initial: G Middle Initial: P
Surname: Braun D.O.B: 7 June 1967
Address: 21 Carter Street
Postcode: HP12 6RJ Contact no. (daytime): 0773 946 364

General health: good
Number of hours of exercise per week: 3
Type of exercise/sports: running, swimming, walking
Last visit to doctor:
Previous serious illnesses:
Contact person/number (in case of emergency):

3

Students' own answers.

Wordbuilding / Learning skills (page 11)

1

1 run a marathon
2 go hiking
3 play the piano
4 read a book
5 do exercise
6 take public transport
7 check … emails
8 have a coffee

2, 3, 4 and 5

Students' own answers.

6

Across: 3 Sardinia 6 gardening 7 temperature
8 centenarian 10 sleepy
Down: 1 advice 2 medicine 4 rate 5 Okinawa 9 nap

Unit 2

2a (pages 12 and 13)

1

1 T 2 F 3 T 4 T 5 T 6 F 7 F 8 T

2

1 surfing 2 rowing 3 kneel 4 oars 5 waves 6 athletic

3

1 have to 2 can 3 mustn't/can't 4 have to 5 can
6 must/have to

4

1 mustn't 2 don't 3 can 4 must 5 can't

5

1 Basketball: Each team has to / must have five players on the court.
2 Football: Players can't / mustn't get a red card.
3 Rugby: The referee can stop the match.
4 Running: You don't have to use any special equipment.
5 Tennis: The ball has to / must go over the net.

6

1 championship 2 Winners 3 score 4 line 5 referee
6 team 7 rules 8 spectators

2b (pages 14 and 15)

1

1 the World Cup
2 famous teams, local teams, school teams
3 over fifty
4 It's a good way to keep fit, it can help them live longer.
5 Players have to walk with the ball and have to keep one foot on the ground.
6 It's very slow.
7 Over 800

2a

a love b really like c enjoy d don't mind
e don't like f hate, can't stand

2b

Students' own answers.

3

1 Playing 2 Competing 3 cycling 4 Learning 5 losing
6 Sitting 7 being 8 flying 9 becoming 10 watching

4a

1 watching 2 language 3 waiting 4 thinks 5 cycling
6 losing 7 winning 8 English 9 competing 10 thanks

5

1 loves skiing all over the world
2 She's good at other sports
3 doesn't like running or going to the gym
4 sports people compete in different sports
5 they don't normally do
6 the competition
7 she'd like to win

2c (page 16)

1

1 b 2 c 3 d 4 a

2

1 c 2 b 3 c 4 a 5 c

3

1 e 2 f 3 c 4 d 5 g 6 a 7 b

4

1 'd like to play tennis later / feel like playing tennis later
2 look like someone
3 'd like to play
4 'd like some ice cream
5 isn't like

Workbook: answer key 313

2d (page 17)

1
1 A 2 A 3 B 4 C 5 C 6 A 7 A

2
1 Boot Camp 2 Zumba 3 Pilates

3
1 interested in 2 not very 3 sounds good 4 we should
5 What about 6 Go on 7 I'd prefer 8 it looks

4
Model answers:
No, I wouldn't like to do it.
I hate getting up early.
I'm not very good at dancing.
Yes, I'd prefer that to Boot Camp or Zumba.

2e (page 18)

1
Possible answer:

> COME JOIN THE FUN AFTER WORK THIS WEEK!
> - **Where?** In the park
> - **What?** A barbecue with a 'fun' football match afterwards
> - **When?** Friday at six
> - **Why?** It's a great chance to meet some of your colleagues out of the office and really get to know each other.
>
> Please confirm by emailing me on r_shaw@shaw.com

2
1 capital letter 2 full stop, exclamation mark 3 comma
4 apostrophe

3
1 I (capital letter) 2 ✓ 3 gaming, cycling (comma)
4 It's (apostrophe) 5 ✓ 6 Canada (capital letter)
7 Saturday (capital letter) 8 ✓ 9 month. We (full stop) 10 win. (full stop) / win! (exclamation mark)

Wordbuilding / Learning skills (page 19)

1
1 golfer 2 cyclist 3 swimmer 4 racing driver 5 athlete
6 runner

2
1 pronunciation 2 verb 3 present participle
4 past participle 5 definition 6 noun 7 plural form
8 first meaning 9 second meaning 10 main stress
11 adjective 12 example sentence

3
1 180 2 300 3 60 4 1.50 5 4 6 5 7 2 8 42

Unit 3

3a (pages 20 and 21)

1
a

2
1 T 2 F 3 F 4 T 5 F

3
1 rush hour 2 traffic jam 3 fuel costs 4 public transport 5 speed limit

4
more interesting, better, slower, the greenest, the most rewarding, longer, much cheaper, more detailed, greener than

5
1 cheaper, cheapest 2 angrier, angriest 3 larger, largest
4 bigger, biggest 5 safer, safest 6 funnier, funniest
7 thinner, thinnest 8 lower, lowest 9 easier, easiest
10 greener, greenest 11 fitter, fittest 12 faster, fastest

6
Possible answers:
1 travelling by bus is more relaxing than travelling by car
2 cake is tastier than bread.
3 email is faster than letters.
4 teachers work harder than politicians.
5 aeroplanes are worse for the environment than trains.

7
1 tallest 2 smallest 3 fastest 4 longest 5 most dangerous
6 largest

8
1 Your car is faster than mine.
2 Bicycles are the greenest transport.
3 Walking is slower than cycling.
4 Trains are cheaper than planes.
5 Hybrid transport is the most efficient.

3b (pages 22 and 23)

1
1 Because they can walk further across deserts than any other kind of animal.
2 Carrying heavy loads, producing milk and meat.
3 No. People at the competition from countries like Oman, Saudi Arabia and Qatar think they are beautiful.
4 Ten days.
5 Around 24,000.
6 Rice, meat and the hump of the camel.

2
1 Horses are as good as modern transport in the forest.
2 The weather is always as hot as this in my country.
3 Silver isn't as expensive as gold.
4 New cars aren't as stylish as cars from the sixties.
5 Bicycles are as fast as cars in the city centre.
6 I'm not as young as I used to be.

4
1 d 2 b 3 a 4 c

5
1 as there was a traffic jam 2 You look as
3 a bicycle is as 4 as we drove home

6
1 frequent 2 punctual 3 traditional 4 convenient
5 reliable 6 comfortable

7
1 a bit 2 much 3 a little 4 a lot 5 a little 6 a bit
7 much 8 a bit

8
1 a lot / much higher 2 a lot / much more popular
3 a little / a bit lower 4 a little / a bit less popular

3c (page 24)

1
1 d   2 b   3 c   4 a

2
1 c   2 b   3 b   4 a   5 b

3
1 pick up   2 catch   3 go by   4 miss   5 go in   6 go

4
/æ/ catch, jam, plan, rank, taxi
/eɪ/ change, day, gate, plane, take, train

3d (page 25)

1
1 fare   2 rank   3 stop   4 receipt   5 gate   6 platform
7 check in   8 book

2
1 b   2 c   3 d   4 a

3
1 Outside the cinema.   2 A return ticket.   3 €20.50   4 At five fifteen.   5 Platform twelve.   6 Two bags.   7 £10   8 Yes.   9 Because it can't stop at a bus stop.   10 $13.30

4
1 Do you go   2 Can I have   3 I'd like a   4 Which platform   5 How many   6 Can I pay   7 How much   8 Have you got

5
1 Return, please.
2 Yes, this one.
3 No, with cash.
4 Yes, I do. Here you are.
5 Platform nine.

3e (page 26)

1
Message one: Get on the number 68 bus from the bus stop outside your house. Take it to the underground station. Catch the first train and get off at Oxford Road station. Then call me. I'll come and get you.

Message two: My flight is late and I'm still in Berlin. Don't wait for me at the airport. I'll catch the bus to the city centre and walk to your house. See you later.

Message three: Chris wants to meet us tonight, so please can you call him and tell him where to meet us? And send me the address of the restaurant as well. What time do you want to meet?

2
Possible answers:
Message one: Get 68 bus outside house to underground. Catch train to Oxford Road. Call. I'll get you.
Message two: Flight late. Still in Berlin. Don't wait. Will catch bus to yours.
Message three: Chris meeting us too. Tell him and me restaurant address and meeting time.

Wordbuilding / Learning skills (page 27)

1
1 credit   2 time   3 centre   4 transport   5 snow
6 driver   7 town   8 seat

2
1 alarm clock   2 bank account   3 boxing gloves   4 football pitch   5 letter box   6 mobile phone   7 tennis court   8 town centre

3 and 4
Students' own answers.

5
1 sledge   2 Kolkata   3 Iditarod   4 rank   5 luggage   6 adjective

Unit 4

4a (pages 28 and 29)

1
1 take risks   2 adventure   3 dangerous   4 my biggest achievement   5 a big challenge   6 ambition   7 crazy

2
1 visited   2 arrived   3 dried   4 stayed   5 jogged   6 lived
7 studied   8 moved

3
1 was born   2 studied   3 became   4 went   5 started
6 survived   7 grew up   8 played   9 learned   10 joined

4
1 F (Eskil was born in Norway.)
2 F (Brady studied at university.)
3 T
4 F (Eskil joined a circus.)
5 T
6 F (A python attacked Brady on his TV show.)
7 F (Eskil started performing on his own after he left the circus.)
8 T

5
1 When were you
2 did you grow up
3 did you study at university
4 did you learn
5 When did you join
6 When did you start

6a
1 bit   2 bought   3 hit   4 did   5 said   6 went
7 fought   8 brought   9 met

6b
/e/   said, went, met
/ɪ/   bit, hit, did
/ɔː/   bought, fought, brought

4b (pages 30 and 31)

1

			¹F					
			R					
²P	A	T	I	E	N	T		
			E					
			N		³P		⁴K	
⁵H	A	R	D	-	W	O	R	K	I	N	G
			L		S		N	
			Y		I		D	
					T			
⁶I	N	T	E	L	L	I	G	E	N	T
					V			
⁷E	X	P	E	R	I	E	N	C	E	D

2a
Across: 2 <u>pa</u>tient, 5 <u>hard</u>-<u>work</u>ing, 6 in<u>tell</u>igent, 7 ex<u>per</u>ienced
Down: 1 <u>friend</u>ly, 3 <u>pos</u>itive, 4 <u>kind</u>

3
1 E   2 B   3 D   4 A   5 C, E   6 B, E   7 B   8 B, E

4
was changing, was flying, were climbing, was sailing

5
1 The sun was shining and people were sunbathing on the beach.
2 The phone was ringing, but I was leaving the house so I didn't answer it.
3 We weren't studying when the teacher walked in.
4 We were walking past the building when the fire started.
5 She wasn't thinking about her exam results when the envelope arrived.
6 It wasn't raining, so we went for a picnic.

6
1 Did you see   2 were following   3 saw
4 didn't hear   5 was listening   6 Did you have
7 didn't arrive   8 Were you waiting

7
1 c   2 b   3 e   4 a   5 d

8
1 fell in love   2 fell by 3%   3 fell off   4 fell asleep

4c (page 32)

1
1 e   2 c   3 a   4 g   5 c   6 b   7 d   8 f

2
Topics 2, 3, 4, 6

3
1 He led the team. / He was the team leader.
2 To find out if the tents could survive the difficult conditions in the rainforests.
3 Humans don't really need clothes in the rain forest.
4 Food and water.
5 He lost about twenty kilos.
6 Determination.

4
1 In   2 In   3 in   4 at   5 on   6 –   7 on   8 –   9 on

4d (page 33)

1
1 e   2 a   3 c   4 d   5 f   6 b

2
1 One day   2 after a few days   3 In the end
4 For some time   5 suddenly   6 While   7 luckily
8 Then   9 amazingly   10 after three weeks   11 Sadly

3
a One day, after a few days, after three weeks, For some time
b While, Then, In the end
c suddenly, amazingly
d luckily
e Sadly

4a
Speakers 1, 3 and 5

5
Model answers:
Why?
Oh no!
That was a good idea!
That was lucky!
Wow!

4e (page 34)

1a
1 C   2 A   3 E   4 B   5 D

1b
1 b   2 e   3 f   4 g   5 h   6 c   7 d   8 a

2b
1 We walked for three hours, and **then** we sat and enjoyed the view.
2 I arrived home **just** as the sun went down.
3 The explorers tried to leave their camp **again,** but the weather was still too bad.
4 After three hours we were **still** lost.
5 We were three days from anywhere, but we **only** had food and water for one more day.
6 The jungle is hot. **Also**, there are many dangerous animals.

3
Students' own answers.

Wordbuilding / Learning skills (page 35)

1
1 achievement   2 study   3 player   4 solution   5 answer
6 test   7 memory   8 score

2
1 test   2 solve   3 score   4 remember   5 play   6 achieve

3 and 4
Students' own answers.

5
1 and 2
Lukla: Pasang lived there, her parents died, she trained as a mountaineer, then there was an earthquake.
Kabul: Marjan Sadequi grew up there, she became a cyclist.
Tehran: Reza studied architecture there.
Siula Grande: Simpson and Yates climbed this mountain, but Simpson fell and broke his knee, then he fell over a cliff. Yates had to cut the rope. Simpson survived and made it back to the camp
Atafu: three boys went fishing, they were lost in the middle of the Pacific Ocean. But they were found and survived.

Unit 5

5a (pages 36 and 37)

1
Possible answers:
jar [C] – made of glass – for storing food
newspaper [C] – made of paper – for reading
aluminium foil [U] – made of metal – for wrapping food

2
1 a   2 some   3 a   4 a   5 an   6 some   7 some (also *a coffee* as in *a cup of coffee*)   8 a carton

3
1 jars   2 buses   3 countries   4 holidays   5 women   6 cans
7 boxes   8 children   9 phones   10 classes   11 stories
12 cartridges

4

1 a some, b any 2 a much, b some 3 a many, b any
4 a a lot of, b much 5 a a few, b a little 6 a many, b a few
7 a a little, b much

5

1 some 2 any 3 few 4 many 5 lot

6

1 d 2 b 3 a 4 e 5 c

7

1 Reusing them.
2 Old cotton shirts, old socks and old towels.
3 Glass jars, yoghurt pots and plastic containers.
4 Wrapping presents, protecting fragile objects, and compost.
5 Wrap old clothing around them.
6 Carrying shopping or putting bottles of liquid in when you travel.

5b (pages 38 and 39)

1

1 just over 2 well over 3 exactly 4 nearly

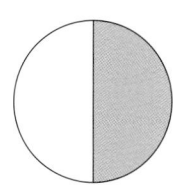

2

3

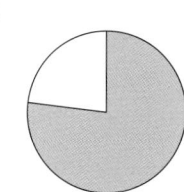

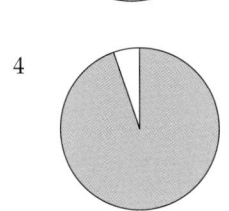

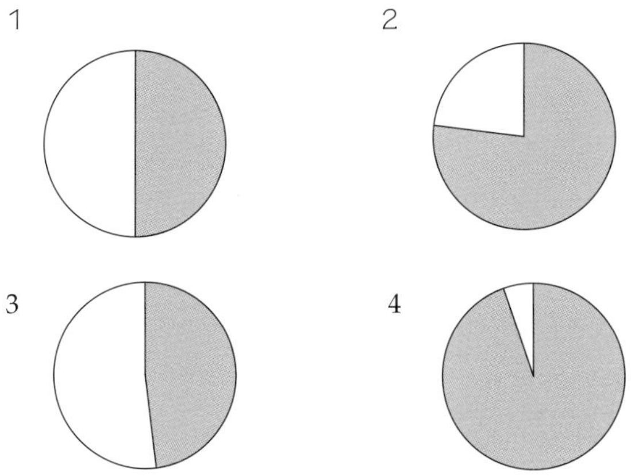

1 Australians 2 French 3 Indians
4 Chinese, Indians, Mexicans 5 Brazilians, Japanese
6 Chinese 7 Germans 8 Hungarians

4

1 B 2 C 3 A

5

1 40% 2 more people 3 cardboard 4 six hours
5 glass bottles 6 about 1905, 51,000
7 London, 10,000 plants 8 plants and trees, air quality
9 noise and heat

6

1 – 2 the 3 – 4 The 5 a 6 the 7 – 8 the 9 an
10 – 11 the 12 the

7

/ðə/   Sentences 4, 8, 11 and 12
/ði:/   Sentences 2, 6

8

Over three hundred million people live in **the** United States of America. It is **the** world's most multi-cultural country. It was part of **the** United Kingdom but it became **a** new country in 1776. Washington DC became **the** capital city and the President still lives in **the** White House today. However, it isn't **the** biggest city. New York is **a** bigger city, and it's also more popular with tourists. In particular, they come to see **the** Statue of Liberty.

5c (page 40)

1

1 go by 2 go for 3 last 4 Slow down! 5 have
6 be careful 7 drink 8 carry

2

Students' own answers.

3

1 Environmental news
2 The USA
3 mobile phones, music players, laptops, computers, digital cameras
4 Yes (It can produce gold and reduce greenhouse gases.)
5 Paper recycling

4

1 243 2 82 3 24 4 32 5 17 6 3,500 7 150, 380 8 87

5d (page 41)

1

1 7786-P 2 £22 3 Bruce 4 31 5 Visa
6 4456 8938 9604 9500 7 bob.bruce51@email.com

2

1 d 2 c 3 f 4 h 5 b 6 a 7 g 8 e 9 i

3

Model answers
Yes, I'd like to order a laptop.
It's GR897-01
[Student's name]
Mastercard, please
7558 6799 3647 1023
Yes please
[Student's own email address]

5e (page 42)

1

1 d 2 b 3 c 4 f 5 e 6 g 7 h 8 a

2

1 would like … inform 2 'd be delighted 3 receive 4 request
5 apologize 6 provide 7 refund 8 require … assistance

3

1 Could you send me information about a DVD called '…'?
2 I'd like to know the price.
3 Please send me details as soon as possible.
4 Thank you for your interest in our products.
5 The price of this DVD is $10.
6 This includes delivery.
7 Thank you for your immediate reply.
8 I would like to order the DVD.
9 Please send me information on how to pay.

Wordbuilding / Learning skills (page 43)

1

1 Please board the plane as we are ready for take-off.
2 There's some out-of-date chicken here, I'll have to throw it away.
3 A lot of people are pro-European.
4 Nearly three-quarters of the population regularly recycles glass.
5 I only use eco-friendly washing detergent.

6 Do you have an up-to-date bus timetable?
7 My birthday is on the thirty-first of January.
8 My wife's mother is my mother-in-law.
9 A marathon is a twenty-six mile run. That's forty-two kilometres.
10 All our products use state-of-the-art technology.

2

Students' own answers.

3

1 uncountable: there is a U in brackets after 'noun'.
2 *foot* and *tooth* are countable, *information*, *luggage* and *time* are uncountable. *Time* can also be countable when it means 'occasion' or 'time on the clock', e.g. *I remember the time when ..., What's the time now?*
3-5, Students' own answers.

4

1 Nearly thirty percent of the land on Earth is desert.
2 Computers use copper inside them.
3 They have the same meaning, but we use *a few* with countable nouns and *a little* with uncountable nouns.
4 They have the same meaning but 'tell' is less formal and more commonly used than the word 'inform'.
5 The Great Wall of China is a famous old wall, but the Green Wall is a wall of trees. The Chinese started planting it in 1978.
6 The Plastiki was made with plastic bottles.
7 The Pacific Ocean has an area called the Great Garbage Patch.
8 Something that is toxic is poisonous.
9 The African green wall will go from Senegal to Djibouti.
10 The Atacama desert is in Chile.

Unit 6

6a (pages 44 and 45)

1

1 go to university   2 leave home   3 buy their first home
4 get my driving licence   5 retire from work   6 start a family

2

1 B   2 D   3 A   4 C

3

1 Locally – perhaps in the nicer neighbourhoods.
2 He had visited the Palau islands many times.
3 About 7,500 kilometres west.
4 Green forests, interesting wildlife and a blue ocean full of colourful fish.
5 150
6 The head of the island.
7 $100
8 A free holiday by the beach.
9 The head of the island.

4

However, one day they decided <u>to leave</u> it all behind.

But actually, they planned <u>to find</u> a place in paradise to create their home.

For Alex, it was fairly easy <u>to choose</u> an island with everything he wanted.

He continued <u>to go</u> back there from time to time, so this seemed like a good choice.

The islands are ... difficult <u>to reach</u>.

Before Alex and Sarah could start <u>to work</u> on building the house, they had <u>to get</u> permission from the head of the island – an 83-year-old woman.

She was worried they intended <u>to develop</u> the area for other tourists, but Alex explained that they just wanted <u>to build</u> a simple house.

Alex and Sarah didn't want <u>to pay</u> for a construction company, so they taught themselves a lot about building.

A lot of their friends from Iowa came out <u>to help</u>.

5

1 d   2 b   3 f   4 a   5 e   6 c   7 h   8 g

6

1 nice to see   2 difficult to keep   3 sad to see
4 afraid to move   5 easy to make   6 great to live

7

1 to help   2 throw   3 to meet   4 playing   5 going
6 to get

9

Students' own answers.

6b (pages 46 and 47)

1

1 parades   2 floats   3 masks / costumes
4 masks / costumes   5 fireworks   6 candles   7 bands

2

1 c   2 b   3 a   4 c

3

1 Because they want to discuss a surprise leaving party for Rosemary.
2 Because it isn't a good place to have fun.
3 It's next door and it's good.
4 Pizzas and Italian food.
5 About 20.
6 Between five and six.
7 The person is working late.
8 She loves plants and is going to do lots of gardening when she retires.
9 Because Rosemary is coming back from lunch.

4

1 is everyone going to meet
2 I'm working
3 are we going to give
4 she's going to spend
5 Will the restaurant make
6 I'll ask

5

1 a   2 b   3 b   4 b   5 a

6

1 a   2 b   3 b   4 a   5 b   6 a

7

1 ✓   2 ✗   3 ✗   4 ✓   5 ✗   6 ✓   7 ✗   8 ✗

8

Tomorrow our town will be two hundred years old. We are going to have a huge celebration. We plan to have a street parade with costumes and masks. Local musicians are going to play traditional music and at midnight there are going to be fireworks!

Workbook: answer key

6c (page 48)

1
1 d 2 c 3 b 4 a 5 e

2
1 4th July 2 girls 3 four 4 sun 5 child 6 ten
7 faces 8 women

3
1 up 2 back 3 ready 4 plane 5 presents 6 pension
7 married

6d (page 49)

1
1 On holiday. 2 After work. 3 Outside Sonia's office.
4 A friend from France. 5 Go into his lesson.
6 He has an exam tomorrow. 7 They could get home early or he could study first. 8 No.

2
1 Do you want 2 Yes, OK 3 How about 4 It sounds
5 Why don't you 6 That would 7 I'd like
8 It's very nice 9 I'd love to

3
Model answers:
Invitation 1
Sorry, I can't because I'm going to a football match tonight.
OK. That'd be great.

Invitation 2
It's very nice of you to ask, but isn't it only for your friend's family and close friends?
OK. I'd like that very much. Thank you.

4a
1 Speaker 1 2 Speaker 1 3 Speaker 2 4 Speaker 2
5 Speaker 1

6e (page 50)

1a
1 tasty 2 colourful 3 dull 4 massive 5 miserable
6 exciting

1b
1 b 2 a 3 e 4 f 5 c 6 d

1c
Possible answers:
a amazing, beautiful, dull, enormous, fun, pretty, smart, uncomfortable
b amazing, delicious, dull, unhealthy, enormous
c fun, amazing, attractive, smart, dull, unhealthy, enormous, miserable, friendly, beautiful
d amazing, polluted, speedy
e fun, amazing, enormous, friendly, beautiful
f amazing, enormous, beautiful

1d
Possible answers:
a scruffy clothes b huge meals c energetic people
d busy transport and towns e international festivals
f stunning nature and geographic features

2
Model answer:
Our town festival is once a year at the end of August. It's always great fun because there are lots of different events. For example there are parades for children with colourful costumes. Then in the evening there is a big party with dancing and food. The food is always delicious. Lots of local shops sell food and you can try some of our traditional dishes. But my favourite part of the whole event is at midnight when there are lots of fireworks. They light the whole night sky up, and then it's time to go home.

3
Students' own answers.

Wordbuilding / Learning skills (page 51)

1
1 afraid 2 warm 3 awful 4 strong 5 tall 6 polite
7 hide 8 touch 9 needy 10 relaxed

2
Students' own answers.

3
A place: Port-of-Spain, Tremé
Type of dish or something you can eat: Feijoada
Something that gives light: firework, candle
Stage of life: infant, middle-aged
A group of people: Hamar, teenagers

Unit 7

7a (pages 52 and 53)

1
1 have been 2 have spent 3 has created
4 has become 5 hasn't survived 6 was 7 were
8 made 9 didn't have 10 have disappeared

2
1 have oil companies been in the area
2 have they spent in the last decade
3 has the industry created
4 was Jim Boucher a child here
5 did people make a living
6 Did the area have

3
Person 1: I've lived here for five years. I moved here to work for the oil company. I think it's been good for the area. Before, there was nothing here. Now lots of people have moved here and they've built new towns.

Person 2: I've always lived in this area. It was a beautiful place, but then the oil companies came here. In my opinion they've polluted the rivers and have changed the area forever.

4
/ɔː/   bought, brought, taught, thought
/ʌ/   come, done, run, won
/əʊ/   flown, grown
/aʊ/   found

5
1 receptionist 2 sales representative
3 shop assistant 4 fashion designer
5 computer programmer 6 police officer
7 marketing manager

6
1 dangerous 2 boring 3 skilled 4 physical 5 challenging

7
1 've taught, for
2 haven't flown, since
3 has run, for
4 have grown, since
5 haven't seen, for
6 has lived, since

8
1 have you lived
2 have you known
3 have you had
4 have you been
Students' own answers.

9
1 been   2 gone   3 been   4 gone   5 been

7b (pages 54 and 55)
1
1 landscape architect   2 environmental cartoonist
3 in the garden

2
1 When he was a child.
2 He/She designs areas outside with trees and flowers.
3 It's creative and highly-skilled.
4 He thinks about his next cartoon.
5 She helps with ideas for the dialogues.
6 When he has lots of ideas.
7 a book award

3
1 down   2 in   3 opposite   4 on   5 next   6 across
7 through   8 up

4a
1 Go /w/ up the steps.
2 no /w/
3 no /w/
4 Sue /w/ often works on the third floor.
5 You /w/ are on the fifth floor today.
6 no /w/
7 Go /w/ in the lift.
8 no /w/
9 Go /w/ out of this door.

5

		¹C						
	²B	A	S	E	M	E	N	T
		N						
		T		³G				
⁴O		⁵E	N	T	R	A	N	C	⁶E
F		E		O				X	⁷S
F		N		U		⁸L	I	F	T
I				N				T	A
⁹C	O	R	R	I	D	O	R		I
E									R
									S

7c (page 56)
1
1 promotion   2 salary   3 colleagues   4 opportunities
5 pension   6 training

2
Person 1: c   Person 2: e   Person 3: f   Person 4: a   Person 5: b

3
1 Everyone in the village   2 Computer programs
3 Upstairs in the marketing department
4 Twenty years   5 Lots of training

4
make: a call, a mistake, a noise, coffee, dinner, money, your bed
do: a job, business, housework, well, work

5
1 money, make   2 make, a noise   3 do, housework
4 do, well   5 make, coffee   6 make, your bed
7 make, call   8 do, job

7d (page 57)
1
1 staff   2 description   3 provide   4 essential   5 position
6 apply   7 contact details / CV   8 contact details / CV

2
1 Her CV and letter of application.
2 receptionist
3 She works at the front desk in a hotel.
4 Welcoming people, answering the phone and dealing
   with any problems.
5 She's more interested in the interviewer's business.
6 She helped with organizing a conference.
7 She works hard, enjoys working with other people and she
   can solve problems.
8 training

3
1 g   2 e   3 a   4 c   5 d   6 b   7 f

4a
Students' own answers.

4b
Model answers:
1 I've been there since 2008.
2 I suppose so. I like hard work and I'd like to become
   successful in my career.
3 I enjoy working in a team. I think I'm good with other people.
4 Sometimes I work too hard. I don't know when to stop.
5 Once, I was in charge of some colleagues and it was difficult
   to tell them what to do.
6 As I said before, I like working in teams and I think people
   like working with me.
7 Let me think. Well, once we had a customer. She wasn't
   happy with the service and I had to deal with the problem.

7e (page 58)
1
1 Nationality   2 Date of birth   3 Address   4 Education
5 Work experience   6 Skills   7 Interests   8 Reference

2a
1 Taught   2 Advised   3 Designed   4 Welcomed
5 Looked after   6 Managed   7 Sold   8 Translated
9 Played   10 Assisted

2b
Education
1 *studying Geography at University*
2 learning English at a language school

Hobbies and interests
3 played in two football teams
4 play the Saxophone

Work experience
5 worked in a café at weekends
6 managed a group of teenagers on a summer camp

Wordbuilding / Learning skills (page 59)

1
1 librarian   2 actor   3 musician   4 photographer
5 accountant   6 writer   7 electrician   8 receptionist
9 employee / employer   10 manager   11 student
12 painter

2
1 ✗   2 ✓   3 ✗   4 ✗   5 ✓   6 ✓   7 ✓   8 ✗   9 ✓   10 ✗
11 ✓   12 ✓

3
1 waiter / waitress   2 artist   3 bank manager
4 geologist / geology student   5 ballet dancer   6 pianist

5
1 CV   2 do   3 won   4 BSc   5 on   6 X-ray
Job: cowboy

Unit 8

8a (pages 60 and 61)

1
1 download   2 log in to   3 subscribe to   4 search
5 write   6 set up   7 connect to   8 do

2
1 The GPS
2 It has a problem getting a signal when it rains.
3 A place for the helicopter to pick them up.
4 Two days away.
5 There are too many trees.
6 The battery.

3
1 it always has a problem.
2 if you want our location,
3 Press it again
4 he won't find anywhere to land
5 If we walk all day tomorrow
6 if the weather's good
7 we'll try to leave the day after

4
If it's raining, it always has a problem.
… if you want our location, press the button with a star.
Press it again if you want a closer view.
… if he flies closer to us, he won't find anywhere to land.
If we walk all day tomorrow, we might get there by the evening.
If the weather's good. If it isn't, then we'll try to leave the day after.

5
1 rains   2 I'll be amazed   3 connect   4 we'll leave
5 He usually texts   6 don't   7 don't   8 will

6a
1 ✗   2 ✗   3 ✓   4 ✓   5 ✗   6 ✓

6b
1 If   2 If   3 when   4 unless   5 unless

7
Possible answers:
If we don't take a camera, we can't take photos.
If we don't take a satnav we can't find our location.
If we don't take an umbrella, we can't stay dry.
If we don't take a torch, we can't see in the dark.
If we don't take matches, we can't light a fire.
If we don't take a cooker, we can't make a hot meal.

8b (pages 62 and 63)

1
1 invention   2 communicate   3 experiment   4 solve
5 instruction   6 decide

2
1 in<u>vent</u> (2), in<u>ven</u>tion (3)   2 com<u>mu</u>nicate (4),
communi<u>ca</u>tion (5)   3 ex<u>per</u>iment (4), ex<u>per</u>iment (4)
4 <u>solve</u> (1), so<u>lu</u>tion (3)   5 in<u>struct</u> (2), in<u>struc</u>tion (3)
6 de<u>cide</u> (2), de<u>ci</u>sion (3)

3
1 have   2 solve   3 follow   4 do   5 find   6 invent
7 make   8 get

4
b

5
1 An inventor.   2 Over fifty years ago.
3 Volvo.   4 No, not for many years.   5 Many governments made laws that forced drivers to wear the seat belt.

6
which have changed our lives
which we don't notice and we don't know who invented them
who invented the modern-day car seatbelt
who worked for the car manufacturer Volvo
which went across the chest and across the legs and then joined at the same place
which no one had tried before
where it had the most customers
which had the invention

7
1 b   2 e   3 a   4 c   5 d

8
1 which changes with the sun
2 where the sun shines brightly
3 who works in a hot office
4 where there is less sunlight
5 who invented the windows

8c (page 64)

1
1 b   2 a   3 d   4 e   5 f   6 c   7 h   8 g

2
1 b   2 e   3 c   4 a   5 d

3
1 eyes and hair   2 ways of walking or moving   3 in security
4 if you lose your identity card, passport or credit card   5 finger print, eyes   6 expensive   7 sometimes it makes mistakes

8 cheaper and more effective, so it will become more and more important in our everyday lives.

4

1 d 2 b 3 c 4 a 5 f 6 e

5

1 check in 2 checks 3 security check 4 check out
5 check for

8d (page 65)

1

1 the button 2 backwards 3 the battery 4 red button
5 forwards

2

Conversation 1: helmetcam
Conversation 2: GPS

3

a What is this for?
b Why do you need to do that?
c How do you switch it off?
d How long does the battery last?
e How did you do that?
f How does it work?
g Where do I switch it on?
h What happens if I press this other button?

4

1 a 2 f 3 g 4 d 5 e 6 h 7 b 8 c

5

1 How does‿it work?
2 This bit goes‿on your belt.
3 You can take‿it.
4 Let me have‿a look.
5 I can press this‿as well.

6

Model answers:
1 Really? How does it work?
2 I see.
3 That's very cool.
4 Let me have a look.

8e (page 66)

1

Paragraph 1: 1 b 2 a 3 d 4 e 5 c 6 f
Paragraph 2: 1 k 2 g 3 h 4 i 5 j

2

1 Firstly 2 For 3 In addition 4 In 5 Finally 6 As

3

1 b 2 e 3 g 4 b 5 d 6 a 7 f

4

Model answer:
Firstly, you can find any kind of information using a search engine. You type in a word and it will find lots of information about it. Secondly, you can find information in only a few seconds, so it's a very fast way of doing research. In addition, we can find information we need for everyday life, such as train times or the weather for the next week. In other words, it's a valuable source of information for work and studies.

Wordbuilding / Learning skills (page 67)

1

1 f 2 a 3 g 4 c 5 b 6 h 7 d 8 e

2

1 a about   b of
2 a about   b with
3 a with   b at
4 a about   b to
5 a with   b of

3

verb + preposition: *think of, think about, talk about, talk to*
adjective + preposition: *good at, annoyed with, annoyed about, good at, good with* noun + preposition: *problem with, problem of*

4 and 5

Students' own answers.

6

1 biomimetics 2 velcro 3 LED 4 Robonaut 2 or R2
5 Joshua Silver 6 GPS

Unit 9

9a (pages 68 and 69)

1

1 It had looked great in the brochure.
2 There'd been a delay on the motorway.
3 It was full of furniture, books, pictures and objects in boxes.
4 She thought she heard someone in the house.
5 clothes
6 The clothes were back in the wardrobe.
7 the owner of the cottage
8 The owner asked them not to move his clothes because he needed to use the house from time to time.

2

Paragraph 1: in the brochure; the sea, empty beaches
Paragraph 2: a six-hour drive
Paragraph 3: I woke up once; there were clothes in her wardrobe
Paragraph 4: the clothes were back in the wardrobe; My daughter's clothes were in the box on top of the wardrobe.
Paragraph 5: In the evening, as it got darker; lived in his shed when visitors stayed.
Paragraph 5: The next day, we loaded the car and left.

3

1 e 2 b 3 d 4 f 5 c 6 a

4

1 b 2 a 3 e 4 c 5 d 6 f

5

1 book a tour
2 visit the pyramids
3 stay at comfortable hotels
4 rent a bicycle
5 go sightseeing
6 buy tickets

6

1 had been 2 had seen 3 hadn't imagined
4 had driven 5 had arrived 6 hadn't expected

7

1 Had you ever been 2 wasn't 3 had left 4 did that happen
5 He'd wanted 6 I received 7 had broken 8 gave

322 Workbook: answer key

8

2 Contractions not possible
3 The hotel **didn't** have our reservation.
4 They **hadn't** eaten since they left home in the morning.
5 **I'd** lost my wallet so I called the police.
6 **You'd** left a message on my phone but you **hadn't** said where you were.

9b (pages 70 and 71)

1

1 c 2 e 3 f 4 a 5 d

2

a 3 b 5 c 4 d 1 and 2 e 4 f 5 g 1 h 2

3

1 amazing time with
2 the middle of
3 a fascinating place
4 were all worried about
5 was tired
6 was exciting because
7 was a bit frightened on
8 was surprised

4

●   tire, tired
●●   amaze, amazed, excite, surprise, surprised
●●   frighten, frightening, frightened, worry, worried, interest, tiring
●●● amazing, exciting, excited, surprising
●●● fascinate, interesting, interested, worrying
●●●● fascinating, fascinated

5

1 Who showed
2 Where did
3 Who plays
4 What came
5 Where did
6 did they go
7 Who drove
8 Who met

6

1 d 2 g 3 e 4 h 5 b 6 a 7 f 8 c

7

1 S 2 O 3 S 4 S 5 O 6 O 7 S 8 S

9c (page 72)

1

1 b 2 a 3 c 4 a 5 c

2

The USA or Canada: 20% is normal, 10% if you don't get good service.
Central and South America: 10% is normal
Europe: 10% is normal
China or Japan: It isn't common to tip.
India and internationally: In many countries there is a service charge added so you don't need to tip.

3

1 cinema 2 museum 3 catacombs 4 gallery 5 theatre
6 tunnels

4

1 take place
2 a good place
3 all over the place
4 no place for

9d (page 73)

1

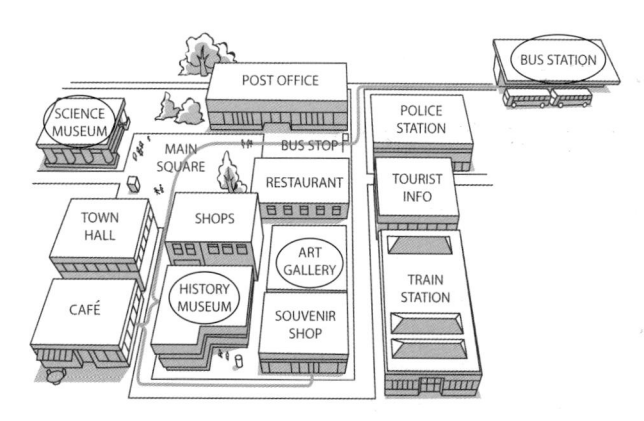

2

1 I'm interested in
2 Do you know
3 What time does
4 Could you tell
5 Are there any
6 How about
7 How much
8 You can also take
9 Is there any
10 Another option is

5

Model answers:
MA: I'm interested in visiting the city castle. Do you know the opening times?
MA: Great. Could you tell me the price?
MA: Is there a bus?
MA: How often does it leave?

9e (page 74)

1

1 a 2 c 3 g 4 d 5 f 6 h 7 i 8 e 9 j 10 b

2

1 b 2 a 3 b 4 b 5 a 6 c 7 b 8 c

Wordbuilding / Learning skills (page 75)

1

1 a amazing, b amazed
2 a fascinated, b fascinating
3 a interested, b interesting
4 a frightening, b frightened
5 a worried, b worrying
6 a tired, b tiring
7 a excited, b exciting
8 a surprising, b surprised

2

Students' own answers.

3

1 Let's stay at this hotel.
2 I'd like to book/buy two tickets for the tour.

3 I hadn't seen my friend for a long time.
4 Who lived in this house?
5 This is a good place to eat.
6 I'm interested in the museum.
7 Could you tell me the opening times?

5

1 abroad 2 tip 3 Tarxien 4 catacombs 5 gondola
6 Lascaux

Unit 10

10a (pages 76 and 77)

1

1 g 2 a 3 b 4 c 5 e 6 d 7 f

2

1 logo 2 customer 3 discount 4 marketing 5 advert
6 sales 7 poster

3

1 c 2 b 3 d 4 a

4

1 T 2 F 3 F 4 T 5 F 6 F 7 T

5

1 is made 2 are transported 3 are worn 4 is recognized
5 are sold 6 are advertised 7 are spent 8 is visited

6

1 The first bottle of Coca-Cola was made by John Pemberton in 1892.
2 The first email was sent by Ray Tomlinson in 1971.
3 The first Harry Potter book was written by JK Rowling in 1997.
4 The first plane was flown by the Wright brothers in 1903.
5 The first commercial film was shown by Louis and Auguste Lumiere in Paris in 1895.

7

1 recognize 2 are sold 3 is made 4 were called
5 changed 6 are taken 7 says 8 was chosen

8

1 was grown by the
2 was used to make boats, baskets, boxes, tables,
3 was most famous as a
4 was cut into
5 were put
6 is rarely made from papyrus
7 the plant is still used in

10b (pages 78 and 79)

1

1 a basic   b up-to-date
2 a fashionable   b old fashioned
3 a out-of-date   b classic
4 a useless   b useful

2

1 to connect with us through the internet
2 it lets humans 'talk' to their devices
3 They can text you.
4 You can switch the heating on when you are going home, or switch it off after you leave.
5 Because employers can check when workers are at their desk and when they aren't.

6 To check their health and measure their physical exercise.
7 From the data their devices collect about them.
8 When you are in and when you are out of the house.

3

1 use to 2 used to 3 used to 4 used to 5 worked
6 became 7 used to 8 used

4

1 used to love
2 Did you use to have
3 didn't use to take
4 used to ride
5 never used to work
6 Did they use to know
7 didn't use to let
8 did you used to pay

6

1 My sister didn't use to be interested in business when she was a student.
2 not possible
3 not possible
4 My family used to record music on tape cassettes.
5 Before I had a car, I used to cycle everywhere and I was / used to be much fitter!
6 not possible
7 My grandfather didn't use to pay for anything with a credit card.
8 Europeans didn't use to eat pasta before the thirteenth century.

10c (page 80)

1a

1 b 2 c 3 a

1b

1 b 2 a 3 c

1c

Stuff is uncountable, *thing* is uncountable

2

1 stuff 2 things 3 thing 4 stuff 5 thing 6 stuff

3

a 6 b 1 c 2 d 5 e 3 f 4

4

1 b 2 c 3 c 4 b 5 a 6 b

10d (page 81)

1

1	w	e	b	s	i	t	e	
2			c	o	n	t	e	n	t
3		c	o	n	t	a	c	t
4		a	d	v	e	r	t	s
5			s	e	a	r	c	h
6				l	i	n	k	s
7		h	o	m	e			
8	a	b	o	u	t			

2

1 a blog
2 because they like reading news

324 Workbook: answer key

3 news about products, interviews with customers who use their products, and photos of employees in their free time
4 That Katarina writes the first post and they see if people read it.

3
1 What do you think 2 we should 3 in my opinion
4 I agree 5 I'm not sure 6 I see what 7 Maybe
8 we could 9 You're right

10e (page 82)

1
1 c 2 a 3 e 4 f 5 b 6 d 7 h 8 g

2
1 d 2 a 3 b 4 g 5 e 6 c 7 f

3
One of my favourite apps is Starfinder. It's a great app for looking at stars at night and recognizing them.
The app has quite a few different features. Firstly, it gives you lots of information about the star when it sees one. Another good point is that it gives you links to websites with more information. The only problem with the app is that if you move your phone too quickly it can give the wrong information.
On the whole, it's a useful app for anyone who is fascinated by the stars and the planets.

Wordbuilding / Learning skills (page 83)

1
1 advert 2 advertising 3 advertise 4 productive
5 product 6 invention 7 inventor 8 sold 9 sale

2
O: sales, sell, sold
Oo: *advert*, product
oO: invent, produce
Ooo: advertise
oOo: production, productive, invention, inventor
Oooo: advertising
oOoo: advertisement

5 Example answers
1 The man in the photo makes baskets in his home in Hung Yen in Vietnam.
2 The first YouTube video was called 'Me at the zoo' and it was made by Jawed Karim.
3 On the first Apple laptops, the logo was upside down when the laptop was open.
4 Gap changed its famous blue logo in 2010, but then changed it back.
5 In 1986, *Walkman* was included as a word in the English dictionary.
6 The website called The Minimalists helps people to have less stuff, and has 2,000,000 visitors a month.

Unit 11

11a (pages 84 and 85)

1
1 B 2 C 3 F 4 A 5 E

2
1 1990; In a library; Someone was sending an email.
2 1945; (doesn't say where); There were parties and people celebrated.
3 1987; Outside a hotel; lines of people waiting, a lot of excitement, and the yellow symbol.
4 1969; At aunt and uncle's because they had a TV; Remembers the words, 'one giant leap for mankind.'
5 1989; In Germany; The speaker travelled across Europe to get a piece of the wall.

3
1 The astronaut thought, 'I hope this works.'
2 The climber shouted, 'Hello!'
3 'See me after class,' the teacher said to the student.
4 The customs officer asked, 'Can I see your passport, please?'
5 'Sorry, I've lost it,' replied the tourist.

4
1 could 2 was 3 showed 4 loved 5 would

5
2 'It's one small step for man, one giant leap for mankind.'
3 'The mission shows how the two countries can work together.'
4 'I love space!'
5 'The USA will send the first humans to Mars by 2030.'

6
1 He said that he wasn't interested in science.
2 They said that they were leaving early in the morning.
3 The girl shouted that she had found her purse.
4 My grandmother said that she had lived here when she had been a girl.
5 The scientist said that one day they would discover the solution.
6 The tourist said that he was lost.
7 The astronauts said that they had landed.

11b (pages 86 and 87)

1
1 c 2 b 3 c 4 b 5 c 6 a 7 a

2
1 b 2 a 3 d 4 e 5 c

3
1 T 2 F 3 F 4 T 5 F 6 F

4
1 say 2 tell 3 said 4 tell 5 told 6 said 7 told 8 said

5a
1 I love this video game.
2 Lizzie, I left a message on your phone.
3 We'll meet you later.
4 Peter, I'm sending you an email.
5 They've put a job advert in the newspaper.
6 Your picture is on Facebook, Sally.

5b
1 He said that he loved this video game.
2 She told Lizzie that she had left a message on her phone.
3 They said they would meet us later.
4 I told Peter I was sending him an email.
5 I told my manager that they had put a job advert in the newspaper.
6 He told Sally that her picture was on Facebook.

6
1 But you told me you had a great time!
2 But you told me you loved them!
3 No, I said I wanted to watch football.
4 But you said the tickets were cheap.
5 No, she told us that it happened in nineteen eighty-three.

11c (page 88)

1

1 statues 2 paintings 3 archaeologists 4 robbers
5 pots 6 soldiers 7 tombs 8 collectors

2

1 Rio de Janeiro is one of Brazil's largest cities but it isn't the largest.
2 Normally the shop is busy but we've only had one or two people this morning.
3 Reinhold Messner is one person who has climbed Mount Everest.
4 I'd like to talk to you one by one, not as a group.
5 We plan to visit Egypt one day.

3

71 AD   c
9th century   e
11th century   d
1980s   b
Now   a

4

1 two 2 thousands 3 good places to eat 4 history
5 walls 6 Norway, Sweden 7 statues, pots (for cooking)
8 in the north 9 buildings

11d (page 89)

1

1 the first few days
2 the job
3 her journeys through the country and experiences of the culture
4 questions

2

1 l 2 b 3 j 4 f 5 d 6 h 7 c 8 e 9 a 10 g
11 k 12 i

3

Introducing the talk and the different parts: l, b, j, f, a, d
Ending a part of the presentation: h
Introducing the next part: c, e
Announcing the conclusion and ending: g, k, i

4

Hello and thank you for coming. / Today / I would like to talk about my gap year in Vietnam. / First / I'll describe my first few days there. / Then I'll move on to my job there / and I'll show you some of my photographs. / Finally, / I'll talk about my journeys through the country / and describe my experiences of the culture. / So let's begin …/

So that's everything I wanted to say about the first few days. / Now let's move on to the kind of work I was doing. / We'll take a look at this photo. / It shows you the school I worked in / and all the children … /

OK. / So the final part of my presentation is about my journeys. / I travelled a bit at weekends / but also I took a longer journey in the last month of my gap year. / So I'd like to show you some of my photos from that period / and I'll read a few comments from my diary… /

Right. / That's the end of my talk. / As you can see, / I had an amazing few months and, / to sum up, / I'd recommend it to anyone. / We have about ten minutes left / so are there any questions?

11e (page 90)

1

Tenzing Norgay is famous because, with the climber Edmund Hillary, he was the first man to reach the summit of Mount Everest on May 29, 1953. He was born in 1914 in a village called Thami near the border with Tibet. He spent most of his life in the region and worked on many expeditions to Everest before he reached the top. Afterwards, his life completely changed and he travelled all over the world. Before he died in 1986 he said about his life, 'It has been a long road.'

2

Possible answer:
Edmund Hillary was born in 1919 in Auckland, New Zealand. He began climbing in the Alps aged 16, but he is famous because, with Tenzing Norgay, he was the first man to reach the summit of Mount Everest. After climbing Everest he spent a lot time raising money to help local people in the Everest region. Before he died in 2008 he said about climbing, 'It is not the mountain we conquer but ourselves.'

Wordbuilding / Learning skills (page 91)

1

1 work on 2 pick up 3 play against 4 talk about
5 come out 6 think of

2

1 c 2 e 3 d 4 a 5 f 6 b

3 and 4

Students' own answers.

5

Possible answer:

The life of Reinhold Messner

1944: born in northern Italy. Father also a climber.

In his twenties: climbed with younger brother called Günther – died in accident.

1980: one of the first men to climb Everest without oxygen. First man to climb 14 mountains over 8,000 feet.

2006: opened museum.

Now: spends more time at home with family. Written sixty books.

6

1 the South Pole
2 1972
3 Scottish
4 the ancient Greeks
5 Busiris
6 the city of Machu Picchu
7 Oxygen

Unit 12

12a (pages 92 and 93)

1

1 weather 2 tornado 3 flood 4 snow storm 5 sun
6 thunderstorm

2

1 b 2 b 3 c 4 b 5 c 6 a

3
1 would happen if the fault opened
2 it opened and there was an earthquake, we'd probably fall over.
3 It'd be really difficult to stand up
4 we'd probably be safer
5 we knew this, we could make a much bigger difference

4
1 won   2 didn't   3 I'd go   4 had   5 I'd set up
6 wouldn't want   7 I'd give   8 I spent

6
1 If I saw a tornado, I'd run!
2 If she was more qualified, she'd get the job.
3 If it stopped raining, we'd go out.
4 If he had a car, he wouldn't take the bus.
5 If they knew the answer, they'd tell you.

12b (pages 94 and 95)
1

Crossword:
1 across: PARK
2 down: RIVE (RIVER)
3 down: MOUNTAIN
4 down: FIELD
5 across: FOREST
6 down: OCEA (OCEAN)
7 across: DESERT
8 across: GARDEN

2
1 C   2 B   3 A   4 A   5 D   6 C   7 D   8 B   9 C   10 D

3
1 beaver   2 alligator   3 leopard   4 duck   5 turtle

4
1 anywhere   2 no one   3 somewhere   4 something
5 Everyone   6 nothing   7 Everywhere   8 anything
9 Everything   10 somebody

5
1 somewhere   2 anything   3 Everyone / Everybody
4 no one / nobody   5 everywhere   6 nothing
7 everywhere   8 Someone / Somebody

12c (page 96)
1
1 tool   2 discovery   3 habitat   4 survive   5 conservation
6 lecture

2
1 c   2 e   3 d   4 a   5 b

3
1 d   2 e   3 a   4 b   5 c

4
1 b   2 a   3 c   4 b   5 c

12d (page 97)
1
1 They are going to pull down all the old buildings and do something with the area.
2 The council doesn't have any money this year.
3 Selling the land for more housing.
4 Somewhere to relax.
5 Make it into a park.
6 Make a lake.
7 They don't have any money to pay professionals.
8 They will ask the local community for ideas and volunteers.

2
1 e   2 a   3 g   4 c   5 b   6 h   7 f   8 d

3
a 4   b 7   c 2   d 5   e 1   f 6   g 8   h 3

4
Model answers:
1 That's a good idea.
2 Sounds great!
3 I'm not sure.
4 No, that won't work.

12e (page 99)
1
1 a, d
2 b, c, g, i
3 e, f, h

2
1 1840
2 south-east London
3 for specialists who want to study and research plants
4 to educate people and to keep many species of different plants alive
5 100 attractions, including an art gallery
6 the Pagoda, which was built in 1762
7 the Treetop Walkway
8 to get children interested in trees
9 growing rare plants and flowers

Wordbuilding / Learning skills (page 99)
1

After a weekend of <u>violent storms</u>, the <u>good news</u> is that the country will return to normal. If you live in the north of the country, there will be some <u>heavy rain</u> through the night, but by morning this will disappear and you'll have a day of <u>bright sunshine</u>. You won't get any rain if you live further south, but expect some <u>strong winds</u> after midday. Other than that, you'll have a <u>beautiful day</u>.

2
1 storm   2 rain   3 wind   4 sun   5 park
6 attraction   7 climate   8 news

3
Student's own answers.

4
Possible answers:
1 snow / thunder   2 windscreen   3 anybody   4 tornado
5 If anyone else drove in that direction, they'd be mad.
6 comma   7 natural   8 Why don't we go to the cinema?

IELTS Practice test: answer key

Listening
1. A the hotel you're going to work at is actually called the Bristol.
2. C So for the first few days you will help out in the manager's office
3. 5/five Yes, but it means working five hours a day, six days a week.
4. midday/noon/12.00 And during your stay, you'll do morning, afternoon and evening shifts. That means starting at either seven in the morning, at midday or at five in the evening. For the first week, you'll be on the afternoon shift.
5. Friday(s) I've agreed that you'll be free on Fridays.
6. shared room free accommodation is included – but that's in a shared room.
7. breakfast Breakfast is provided free of charge in the hotel.
8. (hotel) shop if you buy anything in the hotel shop, you get 10% off
9. (Mrs) D R I N K S T O N E
10. report you'll be asked to write a report each week.
11. C the main university campus … can be found just next door.
12. B The majority … stay in host-family accommodation
13. A students can use the football pitch without having to pay.
14. D/E There's also a selection of English language films on DVD, which students can watch
15. E/D got a selection of magazines, which is updated weekly,
16. morning(s) fifteen-hour course … come to school in the morning only
17. 12/twelve There are twelve students in the class
18. 465 this course costs £465 per week
19. Friday with the exception of Friday
20. personal tutorial each student has a personal tutorial once a week
21. Three/3 two days a week for … three weeks
22. (shopping) centre I thought outside the shopping centre would be a good place
23. C whilst one of us counts the cars, the other one can be in the car park doing the interviews … Let's take it in turns to do both these jobs
24. C whilst one of us counts the cars, the other one can be in the car park doing the interviews … Let's take it in turns to do both these jobs
25. B Adam: … prepare the questionnaire … would you mind doing that? Becky: I'd be happy to.
26. A Becky: Then maybe you could save the data onto the laptop each day. Adam: OK, I think I could manage that.
27. A we need to ask them why they chose to travel at that time
28. C Adam: … ask them what they think about climate change … Becky: That's a good idea.
29. A Adam: I think that writing the actual report is a job that's best done by one person. Becky: I'm happy to do that if you like.
30. B Adam: It will do me good to do it actually – give me more confidence about speaking in public.
31. cities / city streets As cities became cleaner, there was less for the birds to eat
32. dirty Some people even killed them because they thought they were dirty
33. eggs it became a target for people who collected birds' eggs as a hobby
34. committee 1903 … people interested in red kite conservation formed a committee.
35. Spain the first reintroduced birds came from Spain and Sweden.
36. Ninety-three/93 a total of ninety-three birds being set free
37. Scotland in 1996 a similar one began in Scotland
38. human the birds must have disappeared due to human activity
39. habitat there must still be a habitat which is suitable for the birds in the country.
40. genetically must be similar genetically to the birds that used to live in the area

Reading
1. F kitchen corner with microwave and sink
2. D rent includes meals on a half-board basis
3. E private shower and wc
4. F free for two months in July and August
5. C space for one bicycle in the (lockable) garden shed
6. B wrongly delivered mail
7. E weight and size guide
8. C international parcels
9. E restricted and prohibited goods
10. E sending cash
11. A compare sending options
12. B redirection options
13. D buy stamps online
14. E wrapping and packaging
15. iv You are coming to the UK for a limited period
16. v You are coming to live in the UK for a longer period
17. iii You must tell the DVLA about relevant conditions or disabilities that existed before you came to the UK
18. viii You want to take a British driving test
19. ii which are exempt from the normal large vehicle driver licensing requirements
20. vii You drive a coach or lorry as your job
21. theory test You cannot normally take the practical test without first having passed the theory test.
22. computerized touch screen The first is a computerized touch screen test
23. video clips You will be shown a set of video clips of driving hazards
24. 40/forty minutes and normally lasts 40 minutes
25. vehicle safety The practical test also includes two questions on vehicle safety
26. photocard provisional licence if you have a photocard provisional licence and your personal details have not changed, you can hand it over to the examiner,
27. driving offences If during the probationary period, you are convicted of driving offences for which six or more penalty points are awarded, your driving licence will be revoked.
28. 1887 a game was played that was very similar to the one we call badminton today
29. 1893 A set of modern rules was drawn up and published in 1893
30. 1895 and the Badminton Association of England was formed in 1895
31. 1899 held in 1899 and 1900, for men and women respectively

32 1934 in 1934 an International Badminton Federation (IBF) was set up
33 1957 The first international women's championships were held in 1957.
34 1992 it was 1992 before badminton was played as a fully recognized Olympic sport
35 TRUE although they were kicked rather than being hit with a racquet in those days.
36 FALSE shuttlecocks were first used about 2,500 years ago in China
37 FALSE in England. That's where a net was first introduced in 1867
38 FALSE Badminton can be played by both men and women, although slightly different rules and scoring systems apply.
39 TRUE Olympic sport – with the mixed doubles being added in 1996.
40 NOT GIVEN It is one of the fastest racquet sports, with shuttlecocks travelling at up to 260 miles per hour

How to mark the Writing Test
Task 1

There are four criteria for marking the Part One tasks, which are equally weighted.

Task achievement

This is an assessment of how well the student has fulfilled the task.

A successful task will:
- include at least the minimum number of words
- have a text structure appropriate to a letter
- be relevant to the context established in the input material
- achieve the writer's intended purpose
- cover the functions indicated in the bullet points

Coherence and cohesion

This is an assessment of how clear and fluent the writing is.

A successful task will:
- be appropriately organized
- successfully link information and ideas
- contain logical sequencing
- make effective use of cohesive devices

Lexical resource

This is an assessment of the use of vocabulary.

A successful task will:
- include a range of relevant vocabulary
- use vocabulary accurately
- use vocabulary in an appropriate way

Grammatical resource

This is an assessment of the use of grammar.

A successful task will:
- use an appropriate range of grammatical forms at sentence level
- use grammatical forms accurately

Task 2

There are four criteria for marking the Part Two tasks, which are equally weighted.

Task response

This is an assessment of how well the student has responded to the task.

A successful task will:
- make clear the writer's position on the issues raised in a question or statement
- develop arguments to support that position
- support the arguments with evidence and examples
- include at least the minimum number of words

Coherence and cohesion

This is an assessment of how clear and fluent the writing is.

A successful task will:
- be appropriately organized
- successfully link information and ideas
- contain logical sequencing
- make effective use of cohesive devices

Lexical resource

This is an assessment of the use of vocabulary.

A successful task will:
- include a range of relevant vocabulary
- use vocabulary accurately
- use vocabulary in an appropriate way

Grammatical resource

This is an assessment of the use of grammar.

A successful task will:
- use an appropriate range of grammatical forms at sentence level
- use grammatical forms accurately

How to mark the Speaking Test

The speaking test is an assessment of how effectively students can communicate in English.
There are four criteria for marking the Speaking Test, which are equally weighted.

Fluency and coherence

This is the ability to:
- talk at a consistently normal speed
- link ideas and language together in logical sequences
- use the language features which create coherent, connected speech

Lexical resource

This is the ability to:
- use a range of relevant vocabulary
- use words appropriately to convey meaning
- use paraphrase strategies when required

Grammatical range and accuracy

This is the ability to:
- use a range of grammatical forms appropriately
- use grammatical forms accurately

Pronunciation

This is the ability to:
- use a range of phonological features to convey meaning
- produce intelligible individual sounds
- use stress, rhythm and intonation effectively

IELTS Practice test: audioscript

🔊 82

Presenter: In this test you'll hear a number of different recordings and you'll have to answer questions on what you hear. There will be time for you to read the instructions and questions, and you will have a chance to check your answers. The recording will be played once only. The test is in four sections.

Now turn to section one on page 100 of your book. You will hear a hotel manager telling an employee called Steffi about her work trip to Australia. First you have time to look at questions 1 and 2. You will see that there is also an example which has been done for you.

Presenter: Now we shall begin. You should answer the questions as you listen, because you will not hear the recording a second time. Listen carefully and answer questions 1 and 2.

Man: Hello, Steffi.
Steffi: Hello.
Man: Thanks for coming. I want to brief you about your trip to Australia.
Steffi: Great. I'm really excited about it.
Man: So, let's see. You'll work at one of the company's hotels in Australia for one month, and you're leaving in a week's time. I'm going to be away myself from tomorrow, so I wanted to make sure you were fully briefed.
Steffi: Thank you.
Man: Now although it's part of the Ambassador group, the hotel you're going to work at is actually called the Bristol. The company's other hotel in Sydney is called the Carlton, by the way – another member of staff went there last year and had a great time.
Steffi: I see.
Man: Now, I know you usually work on reception here, but in a new place that's not a good idea. So for the first few days you will help out in the manager's office – doing general duties. Then later on, you'll work in different areas, including the dining room and the conference centre.
Steffi: Sounds great.

Presenter: Before you listen to the rest of the conversation, you have some time to read questions 3 to 10. Now listen and answer questions 3 to 10.

Steffi: Can I ask about the working hours?
Man: Sure. Now, you do thirty-five hours a week here, but on this kind of work experience placement, you only have to do thirty.
Steffi: Really?
Man: Yes, but it means working five hours a day, six days a week. I hope that's OK for you.
Steffi: Oh, yes. No problem.
Man: And during your stay, you'll do morning, afternoon and evening shifts. That means starting at either seven in the morning, at midday or at five in the evening. For the first week, you'll be on the afternoon shift.
Steffi: Oh, that's good. So I get one day off?
Man: That's right. Obviously in Australia weekends are busy, so you'll work on Saturdays and Sundays, but I've agreed that you'll be free on Fridays. I hope that's alright?
Steffi: Absolutely. Thank you. And will I stay in the hotel itself?
Man: Yes, free accommodation is included – but that's in a shared room. If you want a single room, then you have to pay a little extra – but only a few dollars.
Steffi: Oh yes, I'm sure I'd prefer that.
Man: OK, I'll let them know. Breakfast is provided free of charge in the hotel, but if you want to eat lunch or dinner there, you have to pay.
Steffi: I see. Are there any staff discounts?
Man: Not in the restaurant. But, if you buy anything in the hotel shop, you get 10% off.
Steffi: Right.
Man: There may be other perks I'm not aware of, but you'll have what's called a mentor at the hotel, who can tell you more.
Steffi: Sorry .... what's that?
Man: A mentor. It's a member of staff who's available to give advice and help if you need it. I've got her name here somewhere ... umm. Ah yes, Mrs Drinkstone. That's D-R-I-N-K-S-T-O-N-E. I don't seem to have her first name – but I'll get it for you.
Steffi: Thanks. It all sounds fantastic.
Man: Oh – one last thing. We want to know how the trip goes, what's different about the two hotels from the employee's point of view, positive or negative. So you'll be asked to write a report each week. There's a template available. I'll email it to you.
Steffi: Oh great. Thanks.
Man: So I think that's all. I hope you have a wonderful time.
Steffi: Thank you.

Presenter: Now turn to Section 2 on page 101 of your book. You will hear some information about English language courses. First you have some time to look at questions 11 to 15.

Woman: Thanks for coming to this short presentation about the courses available at the Central Language School in Hanford.

First of all, let me tell you where the language school is. Most people arrive in the city by train, and the station's on the edge of the city-centre area. It's about half-an-hour on foot from there to the main university campus, and the Central Language School can be found just next door. There are frequent buses if you don't fancy the walk.

Because Hanford's a university city, there's plenty of student accommodation. Most university students rent houses which they share with friends. The majority of language school students, however, stay in host-family accommodation, where meals are provided and there's a chance to practise language skills. There are also self-catering rooms available in a student residence, but this works out more expensive, so isn't so popular.

In terms of leisure activities, the school doesn't have tennis courts or anything like that. There's a public park opposite, though, where students can use the football pitch without having to pay. In addition, the school has an arrangement with a local gym, so that students can use its facilities at a discounted price.

Some students prefer to spend their free time in the school library. It has a collection of reference books that can be used on site, but not taken away. There's also a selection of English-language films on DVD, which students can watch on site or borrow overnight. There's internet access too. Students get a password and an hour's free use each day – though there's a booking system for busy periods. The library's also got a selection of magazines, which is updated weekly, but daily newspapers are not provided.

Presenter: Before you hear the rest of the presentation, you have some time to look at questions 16 to 20.

Woman: OK – so what about the courses themselves? Basically, there are three courses available. You can study either for fifteen hours per week, for eighteen hours per week, or for twenty-one hours per week. Let me tell you about the three different courses.

Students on the fifteen-hour course study General English and come to school in the morning only, leaving the afternoons free for self-study or free-time activities. There are twelve students in the class, and there are classes at four different levels. Students do an entry test on arrival, to see which level is best for them. The price of this course is £430 per week.

The eighteen-hour course combines general English with exam preparation. This has the same programme as the 15-hour course, with the addition of special exam preparation sessions four afternoons a week; that is, each weekday with the exception of Friday. This course is suitable for those doing an exam at some time in the future. There are ten students in the class and this course costs £465 per week.

Finally, we have intensive exam preparation courses. These are more expensive at £495. There are only eight students in the class, all preparing to do the exam in the near future. As well as 21 class hours, each student has a personal tutorial once a week.

So that's our school. Before I go on, does anyone have any questions?

Presenter: Now turn to Section 3 on page 102 of your book. You will hear two students called Adam and Becky talking about a traffic survey they have to do as part of their college course. First you have some time to look at questions 21 to 26.

Adam: Hi Becky.
Becky: Hi Adam.
Adam: So we're going to be working together on the traffic survey – that'll be fun.
Becky: Yeah, I'm really looking forward to it. I guess we should start making some plans. Are you free now?
Adam: Sure. Where shall we begin? The idea is to do some research into local road traffic, isn't it?
Becky: That's right. On the worksheet it says we've got to choose one important place on the local road system, count the number of cars using it in a given period, and also try and find out why it's busier at certain times than at others.
Adam: Mmm, sounds interesting. How long have we got?
Becky: Well, we should choose two days in the week – like a weekday and a weekend day and do the survey over a number of weeks – you know, to be sure that we get data that represents an average, which is based on a sample of days and not just one day that might be unusual for some reason.
Adam: Sure. So that's two days a week for what, three weeks?
Becky: Yes, I reckon that should be enough. I'm free on Mondays if that's alright with you, and then perhaps we should do Saturdays as the contrast.
Adam: Yes, that's good for me too. But do we just set up at the roadside – don't we have to get permission or anything?
Becky: Well, the local police will tell us where is the best place to set up from a safety point of view, and they'll keep an eye on us to make sure there are no problems. But we have to tell them which road we want to do.
Adam: Great. So where should we ask for?
Becky: Well, I thought outside the shopping centre would be a good place. We could count how many cars using the road were going into the centre, and how many drove past it.
Adam: Good idea.
Becky: But we've got to do more than just count the cars, haven't we?
Adam: Yes, we've also got to interview some drivers. So whilst one of us counts the cars, the other one can be in the car park doing the interviews.
Becky: OK. Let's take it in turns to do both these jobs because just counting the cars could get boring.
Adam: I agree. And there are other jobs we could share out too. Somebody's got to prepare the questionnaire we use for the interviews. You're good at writing that sort of thing, Becky. Would you mind doing that?
Becky: I'd be happy to, though we'd need to discuss it a bit first. Then maybe you could save the data onto the laptop at the end of each day.
Adam: OK, yes. What does that involve?
Becky: Well, we're going to have an electronic counter for the cars. You press a button each time one passes, and it records it. Then you put the figures into the database on the laptop at the end of the day.
Adam: OK. I think I could manage that!
Becky: Thanks, Adam.

Presenter: Before you hear the rest of the conversation, you have some time to look at questions 27 to 30.

Adam: So, what do you think we should ask in the questionnaire?
Becky: Well, the questionnaire's meant to find out some reasons that explain the data. You know, it's no good saying how many cars use the route at a given time without having some idea of why they do that.
Adam: OK – so the main focus needs to be on why they chose to go by car rather than catch the bus, or go by bike?
Becky: Oh, I'm not sure that's it really. Isn't it more why the drivers chose that route and not another one?
Adam: Umm – well, we're only asking the ones who drive into the car park, so I guess we already know that.
Becky: You're right. OK then, I reckon we need to ask them why they chose to travel at that time.
Adam: Yes, OK – that can be the main focus of the questionnaire – various questions about that. But maybe we should ask a supplementary question, to get an idea of the type of people they are.

Becky:	What do you mean?
Adam:	Well, like if we ask them what they think about climate change – then we'd see if they were concerned about green issues or not.
Becky:	That's a good idea. That would tell us more about them than asking them what they think of the car park itself or why they use their cars instead of the bus.
Adam:	Great – let's do that then.
Becky:	Then once we've finished the survey, we've got to write a report which we then present to the class.
Adam:	I think that writing the actual report is a job that's best done by one person – it would be messy trying to join different bits together.
Becky:	I agree. And I'm happy to do that if you like. I mean, I'm sure you'd do it very well, but I'm happier writing things than I am presenting them. If you want to do a draft though, for me to work from, that would be OK. Or I could just show you mine before I write up the final version?
Adam:	Well, there's no point in having two drafts. I'll look at yours and make comments.
Becky:	OK. And you'll do the presentation?
Adam:	Sure. I mean as far as I'm concerned that's the easy part. You're a very good presenter, I know, but that's because you've had a lot more experience than me. It will do me good to do it actually – give me more confidence about speaking in public.
Becky:	Great. That's agreed then.
Presenter:	Now turn to Section 4 on page 103 of your book. You will hear part of a lecture about a type of bird called a red kite, which is found in western Europe. First you have some time to look at questions 31 to 40. Now listen carefully and answer questions 31 to 40.
Woman:	Good evening. Tonight's lecture is about a bird of prey called the red kite. This bird used to be common in the British Isles, but died out in England and Scotland during the nineteenth century. In recent years, however, the red kite has been reintroduced to these countries, and it's the story of that programme that I want to tell you about tonight. Firstly, why did the red kite disappear from most of Britain? Well, there are a number of reasons.

Many centuries ago, the red kite was a valued bird that helped keep the streets clean by eating waste food. As cities became cleaner, there was less for the birds to eat, so their numbers began to fall. Some people even killed them because they thought they were dirty. In the nineteenth century, as the kite became rarer, it became a target for people who collected birds' eggs as a hobby. The red kite became extinct in England in 1871 and in Scotland in 1879.

However, people have been trying to help the birds. As long ago as 1903, British people interested in red kite conservation formed a committee to protect the bird. By then there were only a small number of birds left in Wales. Until about 1950, the number of birds did not increase much. This is why a reintroduction programme was needed and plans for this began in the year 1986. The idea was to bring birds living in other countries to England. Red kites were still found in various Western European countries like France and Germany but, in 1989, the first reintroduced birds came from Spain and Sweden. These birds were released in sites in southern England, with a total of ninety-three birds being set free. On the whole, the programme was successful and, by 1992, the first pairs of birds had begun breeding in the wild. Indeed the programme was so successful that in 1996 a similar one began in Scotland.

The reintroduction programme was organized following strict rules. These rules say that reintroduction should only be allowed if certain criteria apply. For example, the birds must have disappeared due to human activity rather than through natural causes – that's the first of the criteria. The second one says that there must still be a habitat which is suitable for the birds in the country. If it has disappeared, then reintroduction wouldn't work. Thirdly, the birds which are introduced from another country must be similar genetically to the birds that used to live in the area where they will be released. And finally, the removal of birds from another place mustn't endanger the survival of the species there. Happily, in the case of the red kite's reintroduction to Britain, all these criteria were met.

Consequently, the red kite's future as a British breeding species is now much brighter. There are probably around 1,800 breeding pairs in Britain.